HITLER'S
DEATH
CAMPS

HITLER'S DEATH CAMPS

THE SANITY OF MADNESS

KONNILYN G. FEIG

HOLMES & MEIER PUBLISHERS
NEW YORK LONDON

First published in the United States of America 1981 by
Holmes & Meier Publishers, Inc.

Library of Congress Cataloging in Publication Data

Feig, Konnilyn G.
    Hitler's death camps.

    Bibliography: p. 464
    Includes index.
    1. Holocaust, Jewish (1939–1945)   2. Concentra-
tion camps.   I. Title.
D810.J4F36   1981   943.086   81-140
ISBN 0-8419-0675-0   AACR2
ISBN 0-8419-0676-9 (pbk.)

Book design by Dana Kasarsky Design

Photography by Lisa Wilhelm and Konnilyn Feig

Manufactured in the United States of America

To Lisa Wilhelm, research associate, editor, photographer, without whose professional help this book would not have been written.

To my family and friends whose support gave me endurance.

To so many colleagues, students, rabbis, Jewish community leaders, and survivors, whose sensitivity and sharing was vital.

To Max Holmes, my publisher, whose combination of wisdom, compassion, and commitment to quality is so rare.

To Irving Halperin, Elie Wiesel, Lucy Dawidowicz, Raul Hilberg, whose pioneering writings catalyzed my thoughts.

CONTENTS

ACKNOWLEDGMENTS

The author and publishers would like to thank the following for permission to reprint their material in this book:

Pergamon Press for excerpts from *The Death Factory* by Otto Kraus and Erich Kulka; Georges Borchardt, Inc., for excerpts from *Ravensbrück* by Germaine Tillion and *An Ordinary Camp* by Micheline Maurel; Her Majesty's Stationery Office, London, for excerpts from *International Military Tribunal;* Chaim Grade and *Midstream* for the poem "At the End of the Days," translated by Inna Hecker Grade; Black Sparrow Press for the poem from *Holocaust* by Charles Reznikoff; Mrs. Leo Schwarz for excerpts from *Root and Bough* by Leo W. Schwarz; Thomas Yoseloff and A. S. Barnes for excerpts from *The Yellow Star* by S. B. Unsdorfer; the Czechoslovakian Embassy for excerpts from *Terezin;* the Polish Embassy for maps and excerpts from *German Crimes in Poland.*

Excerpts from *Ravensbrück* by Germaine Tillion, translation copyright © 1975 by Doubleday & Company, Inc., reprinted by permission of the publisher.

"A Year in Treblinka Horror Camp," by Yankel Wiernik, from Jacob Gladstein, ed., *An Anthology of the Holocaust,* copyright © 1968 by the Jewish Publication Society of America, is used through the courtesy of the Society.

Excerpts from *Eyewitness Auschwitz*, copyright © 1979 by Filip Muller, translation copyright © 1979 by Routledge & Kegan Paul, are reprinted with the permission of Stein & Day Publishers and Routledge & Kegan Paul Ltd.

Excerpts from *Thy Brother's Blood* by Malcolm Hay, copyright © 1975 by Hart Publishing Company, Inc., reprinted by permission of Hart Publishing Co.

Excerpts from *Treblinka* by Jean-Francois Steiner, copyright © 1967 by Simon and Schuster, Inc., reprinted by permission of Simon & Schuster, a Division of Gulf and Western Corporation.

Poems from *Swastika Poems* by William Heyen, copyright © 1977 by William Heyen, reprinted by permission of Vanguard Press, Inc.

"Visitor from Buchenwald" reprinted from *Bright Winter* by Virginia Mishnun-Hardman, copyright © 1977 by Virginia Mishnun-Hardman, by permission of the author and New York University Press.

"If the prophets broke in . . ." from *O The Chimneys* by Nellie Sachs, reprinted by permission of Farrar, Straus and Giroux, Inc. Translation copyright © 1967 by Farrar, Straus and Giroux, Inc.

"T. S. Eliot at Bergen Belsen" by Leslie Mittleman is reprinted by permission of the *Reconstructionist*, published by the Jewish Reconstructionist Foundation.

CAMP NAMES AND LOCATIONS

The areas in which the camps were located changed hands over the course of the first half of this century. When these areas came under German control before and during World War II, the boundaries within Europe were once again redefined. The Germans divided the newly acquired territories into districts of the Third Reich and gave the areas and the camps they built there German names.

Often, a camp was simply given the German name for the neighboring town or village. Today, many of the camps have become commonly known by their German names (though use of either name is accepted), while the names of the areas in which they were located and the towns near which they were situated have reverted back to their original forms.

The reader may be confused by the fact that the camps are referred to by both their German names and their native language names (e.g., Polish, Czech, French). The publishers hope that this glossary will serve as a guide in clarifying any inconsistencies within the text.

Below the entry for each camp, the reader will find the nearest town or village as well as the status of that community before the war. During the war, the areas referred to were divided into several major classifications, based on the status awarded them by the Reich. Germany "liberated," annexed, incorporated, or occupied the areas; and the category dictated the kind of German rule imposed.

To clarify current alignment, the province and country under whose jurisdiction each area presently falls has been given as well.

/ = also known as
( ) = name in other language, usually native one
GDR = German Democratic Republic (East Germany)
GFR = German Federal Republic (West Germany)

Auschwitz (Polish: Oswiecim)
     near town of Oswiecim, Poland
     incorporated into district of Upper Silesia under German Reich

Auschwitz complex included:

Auschwitz I—known as the "mother camp"

Auschwitz II/Birkenau (Polish: Brzezinka)—near village of Brzezinka

Auschwitz III/Buna—assigned to I.G.-Farben-Werke chemical factories in neighboring town of Monowitz

Currently: in district of Cracow, Poland

Belzec

in town of Belzec, Poland

incorporated into district of Lublin under German occupation

Currently: in district of Linow, Poland

Bergen-Belsen

near village of Bergen, German: close to city of Hannover

in province of Hannover under German Reich

Currently: in district of Lower Saxony, state of Saxony, GFR

Birkenau

see Auschwitz

Buchenwald

outside city of Weimar, central Germany

in province of Thuringia under German Reich

Currently: in state of Thuringia, GDR

Chelmno

see Kulmhof

Dachau

at edge of town of Dachau, Germany; close to city of Munich

in province of Bavaria under German Reich

Currently: in state of Bavaria, GFR

Dora/Nordhausen

near town of Nordhausen

in province of Saxony under German Reich

Currently: in state of Thuringia, GDR

Flossenbürg

at edge of town of Flossenbürg

in province of Bavaria under German Reich

Currently: in district of Neustadt, Upper Palatinate of state of Bavaria, GFR

Gross-Rosen

near town of Stiegau (Polish: Strzegom)

incorporated into district of Lower Silesia under German Reich

Currently: in province of Silesia, Poland

Kulmhof (Polish: Chelmno)

near village of Chelmno, Poland; close to city of Lodz
incorporated into district of Warthegau under German Reich
Currently: in province of Poznan, Poland
(Original village of Chelmno no longer exists.)

Majdanek

outside city of Lublin, Poland
incorporated into district of Lublin under German occupation
Currently: in district of Lublin, Poland

Mauthausen

near town of Linz, Austria
in province of Upper Austria during German annexation
Currently: in province of Upper Austria, Austria

Natzweiler/Struthof

in mountain area of Struthof, near city of Strasbourg, in region of Alsace,
France. (Alsace-Lorraine has long been a disputed area claimed by both
Germany and France. After the Treaty of Versailles, the area came under
French rule.)
incorporated into district of Baden-Alsace under German Reich
Currently: in district of Lower Rhine, region of Alsace, France

Neuengamme

in town of Neuengamme, near city of Hamburg, Germany
in German Reich
Currently: in state of Hamburg, GFR

Nordhausen

see Dora/Nordhausen

Oranienburg

see Sachsenhausen/Oranienburg

Oswiecim

see Auschwitz

Ravensbrück

near town of Furstenberg, Germany; not far from Berlin
in province of Brandenburg under German Reich
Currently: town is in state of Mecklenburg, GDR; site of camp is in state of
Brandenburg, GDR

Sachsenhausen/Oranienburg
> in town of Oranienburg, Germany; near Berlin
> in province of Brandenburg under German Reich
> *Currently:* in state of Brandenburg, GDR

Sobibor
> edge of village of Sobibor, Poland; close to town of Chelm
> incorporated into district of Lublin under German occupation
> *Currently:* in district of Lublin, Poland (1 kilometer from Russian border)

Struthof
> see Natzweiler

Stutthof (Polish: Sztutowo)
> near city of Danzig (Polish: Gdansk), which between the two World Wars had
>   formed the Free City of Danzig
> incorporated into district of Danzig-West Prussia under German Reich
> *Currently:* near city of Gdansk, Poland

Terezin
> see Theresienstadt

Theresienstadt (Czech: Terezin)
> is now as then the town of Terezin, Czechoslovakia; in country of Litomerice;
>   not far from Prague
> in province of Bohemia, which was claimed by Germany as a protectorate, after
>   the acquisition of the Sudetenland
> *Currently:* in province of Bohemia, Czechoslovakia

Treblinka
> until German occupation a small railroad station between Siedlce and Mal-
>   kinia, Poland; not far from Warsaw
> incorporated into district of Lublin under German occupation
> *Currently:* in district of Lublin, Poland

Animus meminisse horret

"My mind shudders to remember"

Aeneas' account of the Trojan War from Virgil's Aeneid

PREFACE

An Overview

Hitler's Death Camps is a study of the Holocaust: of the Nazi concentration camps, the concentration system, and the human beings who experienced it. It is, by necessity, an interdisciplinary analysis. Attempting to understand both the unique and universal implications of the Holocaust forces the student and the writer to draw upon the insights of poetry, literature, art, music, and drama; history, political science, and geography; sociology, psychology, and anthropology; medicine and science; philosophy and religion; memoirs, interviews, and documents.

It is extremely difficult to secure reliable information on anything that happened during this period because so much was lost or destroyed, and what remains, from the Nazi side at least, is tainted. The system encouraged lying—lying in speeches, memos, reports, diaries, letters. No historian could write of this period if he insisted upon using only materials whose accuracy is unimpeachable. I, like others, have used a wide variety of sources and hope that the result approximates reality. My purpose has been to pull together the available material on the major camps in one book, one central source, leaving to future specialized studies the challenge of filling in the remaining gaps.

The book focuses on the major Nazi concentration camps as defined by Heinrich Himmler; the concentration system as it evolved; the actions, reactions, and feelings of the different groups of people involved in it; and the many phases of the process of dehumanization, destruction, and death. At the core are the nineteen official camps with their similarities and differences. Each camp exemplifies a major aspect of the system. Dachau is the creation of a model for scientific experimentation on human beings, while Ravensbrück illustrates the fate of Aryan and non-Aryan women in the Third Reich. Chelmno incarnates the crude, primitive killing phase; Treblinka, the victory of technology in achieving the efficient disposal of subhumans; and Buchenwald, the internal political system. Theresienstadt embodies the frantic measures taken by Himmler to create a positive illusion for the outside world, and also the magnificent strength of the strugglers as evidenced in the literature, music, and art created in that fortress. Majdanek demonstrates the profitable economic enterprise in the plunder, disposal, and sale of Jewish goods, hair, teeth. Sobibor portrays revolt, while Natzweiler illuminates the participation of university research teams in medical experimentation on human beings.

In Part Two each camp is treated separately in a chapter divided into two sections: the present and the past (1933–1945). In the first section I have presented a picture of the camp as it is today—an impression of the superior works of art that dominate some of the camps, and a commentary on the environment, the countryside, the community. The camp illustrations are selected from my own photographs and focus on art. They contain no piles of bodies, no grinning SS men. The second section treats the camps from a historical perspective, and allows the participants to speak for themselves—from their diaries and memoirs.

The book centers on the Nazis, the strugglers, and the surrounding populations. In the camps the Nazis imprisoned, degraded, and destroyed a wide variety of classes and individuals. But it is not unusual for an incoming political regime to incarcerate, torture, or even kill its political opponents, real or imagined. The process of imprisonment and killing that Hitler developed, however, had unusual features to it. The Nazis identified four special groups which, unlike normal authoritarian regimes, they determined to focus upon: Jehovah's Witnesses, homosexuals, Gypsies, and Jews. All four groups experienced the concentration system and deprivation, persecution, incarceration, and oftentimes death from 1933–1945. The last two groups faced unrelenting, inescapable extermination. This book concentrates on the extermination of the six to eight million Jews. No group is ignored—I mention the Witnesses, include all the available information on homosexuals and Gypsies, and detail the human devastation faced by all Europeans—but the emphasis is on the erasure of the Jewish people and their culture from the European world. This emphasis is dictated by the material available and Nazi theory and practice.

Emerging from these pages is a variety of people who talk and write about their actions, their feelings, their puzzlement, their reasoning, their sources of strength and pockets of weakness. Those who slaughtered pinpoint their priorities in their memos and recorded conversations: concern with the inadequacy of killing machinery; frustration with the slowness of the bureaucracy; excitement over the research discoveries in the freezing and high-altitude experiments; conviction that Jews were vermin, nonhuman. The indifferent—the Allied and church leaders—explain their inaction, their disinterest, the difficulties in winning the war. And the nonhumans—the strugglers—describe their twilight world, their anger, their dialogues with God and with themselves. The survivors speak of their anticipations, their joy at liberation, their horror of returning home to face scornful neighbors and new pogroms and persecution.

I have drawn upon many sources, both original and secondary, including recent research from Eastern European and Western scholars, to provide the basic ingredient missing in the vast literature on Nazi Germany and the Holocaust: a comprehensive interdisciplinary analysis of the Nazi concentration camps. Part One analyzes the Final Solution process and describes the complex system of concentration and destruction that stretched like a giant net over the whole of Europe. It links the basic elements and contradictions that produced killing centers, concentration camps, and labor/extermination complexes conceived by master builders. Part Three reformulates the major questions erupting out of the Holocaust. It poses no answers but it does suggest elements for a possible causation model.

The Sanity of Madness

Writing about such a subject (and I suspect reading as well) is painful, ponderous, and difficult. "At every page, in front of every image," agonizes Elie Wiesel, "I stop to catch my breath." It has been no better for me. As I write, I gasp and shake my head, fighting with myself: "This is horrible; I cannot read this page—correct, edit it—one more time." It does not improve with time, this "literature of decomposition."[1]

In staring at the core of the Holocaust, one must be wary of developing a "corrupt fascination." But at the center lie the "dark places," and we must not allow ourselves to ignore them, for if we avoid the hellish, we eliminate the possibilities of any serious discussion about human beings. As one Jewish survivor testified: "Everything I'm telling you now is like a grain of sand by the sea—absolutely nothing compared to what happened." Said another: "Not all of it can be described. There are things we lived through, we witnessed, that we can't begin to talk about. Such things have no equivalent in words. It remains inside us as our deepest part."[2]

The English language produces barriers. Prejudice is not raw hatred, is it? And conversely, is raw hatred prejudice? *Stereotyping* reminds one of the old assumption that all short men are insecure. Years ago I rejected any talk of deicide, as did others; and I realized that popular uses of *anti-Semitism* and *prejudice* explained nothing. Anti-Semitism as a "cluster of behaviors" has always existed alongside so many other isms. Yet, in Hitler's time, anti-Semitism seemed to transcend, or a form of it did. Transcendence. Thus I now return, full circle, to deicide and anti-Semitism, persuaded that a second careful look is critical.

I use often the terms *terrible, horrible,* and *ghastly* as I write of the camps. The Holocaust was so much more than that, but I have no other words. And the inner struggle continues. How can one continue to remember? How can one not? How can one write? How can one not? How can one believe in God? How can one not? How can one forgive; how can one continue to plod onward? How can one not? How can I return to the camps another time?

How can I not? How can I mourn for so long? How can I not? Elie Wiesel writes "in order not to go mad," or "to touch the bottom of madness." So do I. How can one deal with the theme of "ultimate inhumanity"? I think one must try, even if it seems beyond hope to contribute anything useful.[3]

Adolf Hitler has marked this century. He changed the lives of every member of this generation. Out of the Final Solution have come the code words that trigger our reactions: Buchenwald, Auschwitz, Dachau. But worse places existed—Chelmno, Belzec, Sobibor, unfamiliar names because they had no survivors. World War II was Hitler's war. National Socialism was Hitler. His death obliterated his regime. A sanity of madness was his legacy. It was also the original title of this book. "Let us tell tales," writes Elie Wiesel, "of times gone mad. Of humanity gone mad." The madness of the killers, the madness of the energetic ignorers, the madness of the strugglers, the madness of the sufferers—of all of us. Hitler's madness made logical, sane sense. Ours in the aftermath does also. "To want to survive in such an evil world is madness," a madness as a liberation of the self.[4]

In a brilliant novel by Silvano Arieti, his main character, the Parnas of Pisa, cautions a young colleague before their destruction by the Nazis:

Let hope grow in your heart, like roses in a garden; don't leave room only for the weeds of despair. If a holocaust is taking place now, I believe it is the decisive event that divides time into a period in which man did not know total evil and one in which he learned to know it. Such knowledge is like that acquired by the first couple on earth. . . . We must love one another more after what we have discovered during this war.

The Parnas concluded that "the world is not friendly," but "we have to make it *friendly*; it is up to us."[5]

A Long Journey into Darkness

Where did it all begin? Why does a Gentile with a strong Lutheran background put her mind and heart into the Holocaust for twenty long years? I don't know. For me it just happened when at age twenty-two I read in horror, but quite by accident, Eugen Kogon's *Theory and Practice of Hell.*

My first twenty years were surrounded by the ritual and intensity of High Church Lutheranism. I lived with Luther's catechism, and with his (and my) constant struggle between good and evil. But that struggle occurred in a relaxed and spacious, small Montana ranching community, where we were all cowboys and cowgirls. The small town library's most extensive holdings were collections of *The Hardy Boys, Nancy Drew, Tom Swift*, and Zane Grey. Surrounded by a raw beauty, we heard no poetry, saw no art, heard no symphonies. Those of us who left discovered that world much later. I was determined to continue my commitment to the church, so I went away to a Lutheran college. But I ran back to my Montana roots after one year, dismayed at the narrowness, prejudice, and arrogance of what I found in that religious environment.

When I read Kogon's book, for some reason I decided to do everything possible to understand man's inhumanity to man. Naïve perhaps, but I tried. I did not become a historian and discover the Holocaust. I stumbled across the Holocaust and became a historian to acquire the tools and insight to help me understand.

Hitler's Death Camps is a stopping point after twenty years of single-minded thinking and research, of considerable time spent in Western Europe, Poland, East Germany, Rumania, Bulgaria, Hungary, Yugoslavia, and Czechoslovakia. I began driving my car through Europe to the camps in 1963. I stood in all nineteen official camps between 1963 and 1979, some on several occasions; and I recorded my developing impressions and changing reactions to each country, each people. A large number of concerned people helped me, and former Nazis added to my insight. Most of the men and women I talked with over the years were candid. I cannot use the word "interview" to describe my encounters with these people, because they were two-way involvements that often gave me strength and sustenance.

I began teaching the Holocaust some seventeen years ago. I did it first under the guise of a course termed "Modern Germany," then "Nazi Germany," and finally, nine years ago, bravely, "The History and Literature of the Holocaust"—with my own text, *The Voyage of the Damned,* a long essayed bibliography of the Holocaust. There were no paperbacks available for class use in those days. Raul Hilberg's monumental study stood alone. Those few of us whose Holocaust classes stretch back at least a decade are eternally grateful to Lucy Dawidowicz and Nora Levin, who gave us critical texts for our students.[6] Still, a class on the Holocaust is a shared experience, and a profound one, in which teacher and students learn from one another. My students taught me more than anyone, and but for them, I would not have written this book. *For I wrote it singularly for them.* They asked for it.

I have taken a long time to get about this. First I wanted to know—for myself. Then I needed to share—with my students. There were times when I wanted to rush forward and write but held myself back. There were times when others pushed me and I retreated. My mind needed twenty years. (Actually, it needed forty.) But when I went back to the camps again in 1976, I knew there was no point in returning yet another time if I did nothing with what I saw.

I do not have a morose preoccupation with the camps and the SS crimes, although I possess a day-by-day commitment to the knowledge of this event. Hard as it is to answer the *how,* and particularly the *why* of the Holocaust, I believe that a refusal to try reflects a lack of courage. As a historian I bear responsibility to pose options. Unless I confront, I betray those who suffered so dreadfully. The dead and the living strugglers, it is clear, want us to try to know. So I began my study of the Holocaust with Hitler's concentration camps and end with them. The subject of the Holocaust is so vast, I can only try to light it from this one angle.

If the prophets broke in
through the doors of night
and sought an ear like a home and—

Ear of mankind
overgrown with nettles,
would you hear?
If the voice of the prophets
blew
on flutes made of murdered children's bones
and exhaled airs burnt with
martyrs' cries—
if they built a bridge of old men's dying
groans—

Ear of mankind
occupied with small sounds,
would you hear?

If the prophets
rushed in with the storm-pinions of eternity
if they broke open your acoustic duct with the words:
Which of you wants to make war against a mystery
who wants to invent the star-death?

If the prophets stood up
in the night of mankind
like lovers who seek the heart of the beloved,
night of mankind
would you have a heart to offer?

—Nellie Sachs, O The Chimneys[7]

PART
ONE

A
BEGINNING

A BEGINNING

To visit the camps is to visit Europe: especially Poland, Czechoslovakia, France, East and West Germany, Italy—the range of this study. To appreciate the full impact of the camp universe, one must add the countries of Belgium, Holland, Bulgaria, Rumania, and Hungary—and if one could only travel through southern Russia freely, to parts of Latvia, Lithuania, and the Ukraine.

A visit to the camps is a trip to the major cities of Europe: Hannover, East Berlin, West Berlin, Lublin, Cracow, Warsaw, Poznan, Gdansk (Danzig), Wroclaw, Weimar, Nuremberg, Munich, Prague, Strasbourg, Lodz, Hamburg, Vienna, and Rome. To complete the story, add the cities of Amsterdam, Brussels, Riga, Vilna, Bialystok, Budapest, Bucharest, Zagreb, and Sofia.

To visit the camps of Europe is to experience the fullest range of rich cultures; wrestle with varied languages and dialects; study a multitude of art styles and varieties of architecture; hear music from Gypsy violins and sophisticated symphonies; watch the great ballets performed in magnificent opera halls and the regional folkloric dances in the open air; taste food of every imagination; view the fullest range of agricultural development; evaluate industrial growth from the primitive to the most sophisticated level; move across the entire political spectrum; and respond to a visible militarism of many shades.

A visit to the camps is a journey through the most beautiful parts of Europe and the most interesting and fascinating countryside—the Baltic Sea coast, lovely German lakes, breathtaking mountain peaks, rich farmlands and villages, a fortress city, the Russian border, industrial and railroad centers, the Hartz Mountains, the High Tatras, the Alsace ski area at the summit of the Vosges, Goethe's Weimar panorama, idyllic towns, greenhouse paradises, woods, and forests.

For the camps were everywhere.

To visit the camps is to gain at least an intellectual understanding of hanging blocks, crematoria, gas chambers, mass graves, punishment cells; lampshades made of human skin, soap manufactured from Jews' fat, mattresses stuffed with human hair, fertilizer from body ashes, gold from teeth.

To visit the camps is to put into one's mind *death:* death from gassing, bullets, torture, dogs, beatings, starvation, work, whippings, hangings, medical experimentation, freezing, drowning, burning, electrocution, despair, pain, and a need to be free.

To visit the camps is to have pictures in one's mind of *life:* of never-known courage, dignity, strength, faith, endurance, selflessness, kindness, integrity, wisdom, resistance to pain, and absolute humanness.

For the camps are in us all.

To visit the camps is to feel more kinds of fear, horror, compassion, love, pain, conflict, peace, profundity, banality, spiritualism, weariness, pessimism, hope, faith, nihilism, anger, hate, admiration, strength, weakness, loneliness, comraderie, and despair than one realized existed. It is to know God one day and deny Him the next; to meet the devil and wrestle with him, and then to lose his face in the crowd; to be filled with answers one moment, and to have only questions the next; to reach heights of wisdom in the morning and feel brutal ignorance in the evening; to search for man and find only human beings; to look for evil and find saintliness; to yearn for humanity and find only selfishness and corruption. One finishes as one began, in front of a mirror, staring into one's eyes, asking, "Why, how, who? Who are you and who are they, and what are they and why are you?"

Night and Fog
Nacht und Nebel
Nuit et Brouillard
To Each His Due
A Louse Means Death

A CONFRONTATION WITH HELL

Twentieth-century man has persisted in his zealous efforts to remove his fellow human beings from the earth in large chunks. The *chunk removal syndrome* became an *ólokauston*—a Holocaust—when the imagery of burnt sacrifice, of humans consumed by fire, grew to reality on the pyres of Treblinka and in the crematoria of Birkenau. Its victims were simply the "innocent occupiers of a certain amount of human space which henceforth will be empty."[1] The Holocaust did not erupt out of a barbarian environment. With a "perverse longing, an itch for chaos," it came out of the civilized core of modern European culture. "We know now that a man can read Goethe or Rilke in the evening, that he can play Bach and Schubert, and go to his day's work at Auschwitz in the morning. To say that he has read them without understanding or that his ear is gross, is cant."[2]

In the history of Western civilization it has always been fairly simple to understand cruelty, savagery, devastation, destruction. In every instance one finds a reason, an explanation. The Holocaust, however, confronts us with the concept of *no apparent reason.* Without heaven or hell, the world must have seemed a flat dull place to the men of the 1930s. The Nazis chose to create the easier of the two, and their hell on earth threw the Western world into a nightmare that shook the foundations of a heritage built upon reason. They corrupted the rational belief in decency and human progress, and perverted a growing faith in science and technology. The new technological civilization that had promised so much seemed to many, when Hitler was finished with it, to predict a way of life that spelled destruction and disaster. Auschwitz, Hans Syberberg reminds us, "is only a little adventure in this century."

Auschwitz was in reality the first triumph of technological civilization in dealing with what may become a persistent human problem, the problem of the waste disposal of superfluous human beings in an overpopulated world. . . .

Hitler has demonstrated how superfluous people can be dispatched with an extraordinary economy of means. He has also demonstrated that such a project need have few, if any, lasting, undesirable effects on the perpetrating group. . . . Having gotten rid of the disturbing presence of the Jews, the Germans have solved a problem.[3]

Many who read about the Holocaust find it the most fascinating and horrible event in history. Yet leaving it at that level evidences ignorance or immorality. One can become wiser by confronting the evil, the madness, and the death, but it is a terrible wisdom that haunts one ceaselessly. It scars. Acquainting oneself with hell is hard work. Initially, it requires studying the history of the Holocaust to cut away the legends surrounding the camps. Then it demands an internal, put-myself-in-their-place confrontation with the strugglers and survivors—the eyes of the camps. Finally it requires engaging the killers and challenging the indifferent. However much energy the searcher exerts, however, he remains on the outside. How does one respond to the truth that an ordinary man can bash a Jewish child's head against a wall, pick up the child's apple, eat it, and return home to fondle his own children? Nothing is left to the imagination. In the Holocaust our worst fantasies became reality.

How does a thoughtful person comprehend interplay of contrasting simultaneous experiences: that at the precise moment when the dead bodies of the gas chamber victims were being torn apart from each other to be thrust into the crematorium, men and women were eating, laughing, and going to baseball games in America? In the novel *Sophie's Choice* William Styron's narrator, Stingo, muses: "Are there, as science fiction and Gnostic speculation imply, different species of time in the same world, 'good time,' and enveloping folds of inhuman time, in which men fall into the slow hands of the living damnation?" Using imagination and energy, a reader must drive to the point

to discover the relations between those done to death and those alive then, and the relations of both to us; to locate, as exactly as record and imagination are able, the measure of unknowing, indifference, complicity, commission which relates the contemporary or survivor to the slain.[4]

Virtually all Holocaust writing becomes controversial, giving offense to someone, some group. For the subject is *death for no apparent reason*. From ancient times death as a concept has been horrible, whatever its cause. But our language is incapable of explaining, of cutting through the screams, of creating a vocabulary to adequately deal with death. It may be that no one will ever be able to clearly but compassionately pierce the "quivering flesh of reality," to live easily with a "literature of decomposition," but I think it must be tried.[5]

Elie Wiesel and George Steiner have argued eloquently for silence since it may be impossible to represent the Holocaust in works of art without denying the very dehumanization that occurred. As Steiner explains: "The world of Auschwitz lies outside speech as it lies outside reason."[6] But silence has not been what the victims have demanded. Silence, some have suggested, would be surrendering to the evil that created Auschwitz. If the compassionate and the stunned had remained silent, my students and I would not know what we know, and we have a right to that knowledge and the permanent changes it has made in our lives. In the twentieth century we must understand the Holocaust or we understand nothing. "The Holocaust demands speech even as it threatens to impose silence." That speech may be "flawed, stuttering and inadequate," but it must be attempted. In the beginning, wrote Elie Wiesel, "there was the Holocaust. We must therefore start all over again. . . . What it was we may never know; but we must proclaim, at least, that it was, that it is."[7]

HITLER—A CREATION OF TRUE FAITH

I must make war, said Hitler; I must demand the sacrifice of a holy nation. German writers like Thomas Mann proposed the concept of sacrifice as a fulfillment of Germany's destiny, and Hitler transformed the concept into actions.[8] Hitler called himself a prophet but, in fact, he was the instrument of the prophets of the past. It was in him that "these prophecies shall come to pass," whether Spengler's prediction of a new breed of men, Nietzsche's superman, or Ernst Junger's technocrat. Hitler did not prophesize; he threatened and announced plans of action. He announced the Jewish solution. Then he carried it out. And the masses supported him because he made his words come true.

To understand the intense German support of Hitler, we must, I suspect, ponder more thoroughly in the future the impact of Lutheranism and analyze Nazi Germany in the context of the Lutheran environment. Lutheranism came out of Germany. The Nuremberg rallies most closely resembled Lutheran rituals. Hitler redeemed Germany. He came from the people with a faith that moved mountains. In turn, he demanded of them faith—"through faith ye shall be free." But like Luther, Hitler also demanded works. "Faith without works is dead," intones Luther's catechism.

The German populace longed for a flesh-and-blood manifestation of God (and the spirit became man and lived among us) to save them. He who sacrifices is chosen. Out of that driving need, they felt compelled to ceremoniously select their god or king.[9] They created their own god and then turned and revered their image. Hitler cooperated by believing he could and indeed must be God. He instructed the populace that their longings were legitimate, and he created the structure and process enabling them to make him God. Both Hitler and the people looked at their creation and believed—in a moment of true faith resembling a religious conversion. The Germans created Hitler, and demanded that he save them from thought, fear, complexity, confusion, boredom. And they came to power with their new God. People do choose gods from time to time. The crux of it is not that we do it, but how well we choose. The Germans simply made a rather bad choice, that is all. Americans in the 1930s chose a Roosevelt instead of a Father Coughlin. Whatever one's view of Roosevelt, it was a choice that redeemed the Americans. Once the Germans chose their god, his will became absolute, and both choosers and chosen accepted it as absolute—for that is why humans choose gods. Hitler was ready to be absolute. He banished unemployment with one hand and human beings with the other. And when Hitlier died, when the God disappeared, the Third Reich burst apart "like a bubble," disappearing with him.[10]

THE NAZI STRUCTURE

Any investigation of the concentration camps and the concept of mass annihilation must include an examination of Nazi structure and the points at which Nazi ideology penetrated it. Germany was not a party state, not an SS state, not a state under full, coherent, authoritarian control. It is better described as a "quasi-feudal system . . . of rival baronies" deriving all power from the king, and engaged in continuous internal warfare. It lacked formal structure except in the SS. The SS gave those Germans needing and desiring order and hierarchy a home—perhaps the only available alternative to the Hitlerian chaos.[11]

Hitler purposefully created a dynamic institutional chaos. He gave no one a chance to catch his breath: no one in Germany and no one in the world. He conquered one aspect of German society and then he conquered another. He conquered one nation and then another. He never allowed a consolidation period of any length or meaning. Nothing was ever partial. He sought to gobble up everything. He intended to kill all Jews. But he was shrewd. His strategy can be defined as a "series of prudential guesses and manoeuvres," enabling him to move as fast as he could without destroying the minimal social stability necessary.[12]

The Nazi structure was brilliantly flexible and allowed very effective mobilization for short-term goals, but prohibited long-range planning except for single matters, i.e., the death of all Jews. Any project more complex dissolved into chaos. The Nazis made plans based ideologically on what must be done, not on what could be done. Since the *must* had its basis in a sacred doctrine, followers had to act as though the orders could be accomplished, even if they were impossible—such as the simultaneous co-equal orders to maintain the war effort and to kill all Jewish labor. The Nazis achieved ideological satisfaction at the one point where reality and fervor met in a nearly perfect sense—the annihilation of the Jews. The Final Solution overrode *all* other considerations and was implemented "in the teeth" of enormous difficulties. It seemed to provide a cement for the Nazis, as all else eroded away. The war produced Nazism in its purest form, and the opportunity for a total, radical realization of Hitler's most important ideological principles.[13]

THE JEWS MUST DIE

Tribes of the wandering foot and weary beast,
How shall ye flee away and be at rest.
The wild dove hast her nest, the fox his cave,
Mankind their country—Israel but the grave!
> Byron, *Hebrew Melodies,* 1815

Centuries ago the peoples of the Western world discovered the "Jewish question," and quickly raised it to the level of a persistent problem of major proportions. Whatever the term's original meaning, it soon came to reflect frustration, impatience, fear, and perhaps a grudging fascination with the cultural holding power of a stubborn "chosen people"—a group of humans the world had programmed to disappear. Strangely, however, the Jews refused to cooperate or to play by the rules. They remained a visible group whose mythical solidarity was perceived by developing nations as threatening to their very existence. No man can serve two gods. A Jew could not serve both Judaism and the nation-state, so thought both liberals and conservatives.

The Jewish question as a matter of wide consideration created a situation fraught with danger for the Jews. Germans and Jews of good will who addressed the Jewish question were talking, naïvely perhaps, about the possibility of a genuinely peaceful amelioration of a problem. The rabid Jew-haters, however, in the context in which they raised the "Jewish question" denied the possibility of a peaceful accommodation of the Jewish Germans; they demanded a *solution*. In the decade before 1933 both friends and foes of the Jews were unwittingly joined as they posed partial answers to the question, and tentative solutions to the problem. The Nazis added only two concepts to the discussion: final and total—forever and ever, done, finished—an end.

In medieval times the only good Jew was one who converted to Christianity. In the nineteenth and early twentieth century the only good Jew was one who had assimilated. By 1933 the only good Jew was one who had emigrated. But even then, a shred of goodness or virtue was possible. From Hitler, however, we learned that the only good Jew was a dead one. Between all those different definitions of the good Jew lie deep chasms, but the chasms were bridgeable, particularly by someone with Hitler's shrewdness and skill.

Hitler came to power in 1933 with two aims: to wage war against the Versailles Treaty, and to wage war against and gain a victory over the Jews. He believed he had a divine mission to purify his Germany and create a true racial community, cleansing it of its evil, its devil, its bloodsucker—the Jew.

It is well to examine Hitler's writings to determine how his anti-Semitism developed. We can believe, I think, his description of his evolution from indifference as a child to "slight dislike" as a teenager. In his Vienna days "an icy shudder" ran down his spine as he saw the Jews in a new light: "poison," "slimy jelly," "maggots in a rotting corpse." Then he took another step forward. "I gradually began to hate them," he wrote. And as the months passed, he realized that the Jews as "devils incarnate" had "the brains of a monster," instigating "the national illness." The only remaining salvation, he knew, was "a fight with all weapons which the human mind, reason and willpower are able to grasp." Hitler clarified his Vienna years: "From a feeble cosmopolite I had turned into a fanatical Anti-Semite." He committed himself then and there to a sacred pledge. "By warding off the Jews, I am fighting for the Lord's work." Hitler strengthened his vow when he moved to Munich in 1912: "He who wants to live should fight." Hitler began and ended his 1925 *Mein Kampf* focusing on the Jews. "Common blood belongs to a common Reich," he wrote in his first chapter. He charged the Jews with creating "evil legends" about him. On his final page he wrote: "A State which, in the epoch of race poisoning, dedicates itself to the cherishing of its best racial elements must some day be master of the world." Hitler sounds remarkably clear. Why, one wonders, was he not heard by us? He was, after all, intensely consistent. And when he became a dictator, he was intensely powerful.[14]

In 1919 Hitler defined the Jews as "definitely a race" and insisted on their "uncompromising removal." In *Mein Kampf* he described the Jew as a parasite, a pernicious bacillus:

Wherever he establishes himself the people who grant him hospitality are bound to be bled to death sooner or later. . . . He poisons the blood of others but preserves his own blood unadulterated. . . . The black-haired Jewish youth lies in wait for hours on end, satanically glaring at and spying on the unsuspicious girl whom he plans to seduce, adulterating her blood and removing her from the bosom of her own people. The Jew uses every possible means to undermine the racial foundations of a subjugated people. . . . The Jews were responsible for bringing Negroes into the Rhineland, with the ultimate idea of bastardizing the white race which they hate and thus lowering its cultural and political level so that the Jew might dominate.

The Aryan was the exact opposite of the Jew:

. . . the Prometheus of mankind, from whose shining brow the divine spark of genius has at all times flashed forth, always kindling anew that fire which, in the form of knowledge, illuminated the dark night. . . . As a conqueror, he subjugated inferior races and turned their physical powers into organized channels under his own leadership, forcing them to follow his will and purpose. By imposing on them a useful, though hard, manner of employing their powers he not only spared the lives of those whom he had conquered but probably made their lives easier than they had been in the former state of so-called "freedom." . . . While he ruthlessly maintained his position as their master, he not only remained master but he also maintained and advanced civilization. . . . Should he be forced to disappear, a profound darkness will descend on the earth; within a few thousand years human culture will vanish and the world will become a desert.[15]

At a Nazi party meeting in 1928 Hitler castigated the Jew as an international problem and promised his followers that "we shall not let it rest until the question has been solved." Once in power, Hitler intensified his diatribes, which were supported by the forceful Nazi propaganda machine. The publicists filled German minds with stories of filth, horror, and evil. Even children's books were vehicles for Hitler's hatred. The Nazi publication *Der Stürmer* published a book of bedtime stories called *The Poisonous Mushroom* that compared Jews to a poison that must be rooted out. The editor of that publication, Julius Streicher, spent his last seconds on earth in the Nuremberg gymnasium shouting obscenities against the Jews.[16]

In 1937 Hitler explained to party leaders that he had indeed clarified Jewish policy. But they must understand, he said, "that I always go as far as I dare and no further." He did not allow himself direct tests of strength. Rather, he maneuvered his adversary into a tight corner, "and then I deliver the fatal blow."

The outbreak of war changed Hitler's response to the Jewish question. He was now ready to annihilate the Jews, but he had one serious problem—the insistence by some that the war effort demanded the use, at least temporarily, of Jewish labor. The Reich Ministry of Occupied Eastern Territories clarified Hitler's intent in November 1941: "Economic considerations are to be regarded as fundamentally irrelevant." Goebbels commented: "The Jews will certainly be the losers in this war whatever happens."[17]

Germany's "Grand Inquisitor," Heinrich Himmler, saw the Jew as "spiritually and mentally much lower than any animal." If Germany rid itself of that degraded species, man would become nearer to God. Often, he thought, the great men of the world must step over corpses to create new life. "The extermination of the Jews," Himmler preached, "must be accomplished without harming the soul of our people." As a "glorious leaf in German history, we must do it and remain decent."[18]

Hitler's wars pitted Aryan against Jew, Westerner against Eastern Slav, in a fight to the finish. As Reich Marshall Hermann Göring declared in a Sports Palace address in October 1942:

This is not the Second World War; this is the Great Racial War. The meaning of this war, and the reason we are fighting out there, is to decide whether the German and Aryan will prevail or if the Jew will rule the world.[19]

That Hitler's rantings fell on receptive ears is shown by a brief look at the leaders of the German resistance who were going to save the world from Hitler. All of them continued to recognize a Jewish problem, even in 1944. Carl Goerdeler, who was to be the new leader, thought the Jews should be sent to "an appropriate territory with acceptable physical conditions, . . . probably in Canada or South America." Why? Because a new order for Jews "appears necessary in the entire world. . . . It is a matter of course that the Jewish people belong to a different race."[20]

The Nazis' words rang out clearly through the late 1920s and the 1930s: they were at *war* against the Jews. That war took a similar form everywhere: deception, cruelty, psychological pressure, legal harassment, the breaking of the spirit, dehumanization—and then the final pattern of sadistic torture, hunger, disease, and death for the emaciated bodies. It was intended that the victims should lose all sense of time and individuality until they denied their own humanness.

Hitler was clever in his war against the Jews. He began slowly, building step by step, placating and soothing as he went along, convincing his victims that they were not victims, and that the current stage in their humiliation would be the last one. First he took away their civil rights, but Jews had lost those rights before. He took away their right to learn and to teach, and denied them professional employment, but Jews had enjoyed educational opportunities for only a short time. He ended open relationships between Gentiles and Jews, but then, perhaps the Jews would be better off remaining with their own kind. He confiscated their companies, their businesses, their property, but surely this loss of their economic base would only be temporary, and now, at least, their neighbors would have no reason for envy. They were compelled to wear the Yellow Star, but some Jews made it a badge of honor. Hitler instituted a curfew and other "protective laws," but those would undoubtedly contribute to Jewish safety. He told Jews to emigrate, and helped them to do so. True, he kept their money—but he gave them their lives. His followers broke windows, burned books, and flamed synagogues, but Jews were long familiar with intermittent pogroms. True, there was much talk about racial purity, blood lines, a *Volk* of blood, but Gentiles had always been strange creatures, fantasizing Jewish ritual murders, desecration of the Host, and a conspiracy to take over the world.

Hitler collected groups of Jews and sent them to "labor camps." But perhaps it would be good to work. Work ensured life—*Arbeit Sie Frei Machen*—for obviously the Third Reich could not exist without the labor force of the Jews. The streams of postcards from the relatives in the "labor camps" were consoling: "Dear Auntie: The food is good, the weather is fine, the sun is shining." True, parcels sent to the camps were often returned unopened—but what could one expect from postal service in new territories? And yes, most disquieting rumors were heard—but there are always those who panic, who make misfortunes into disasters. And it was believed that the Zionists would do anything to inflame people to flee to barren Palestine. For the Germans and the Jews had lived together, side by side, for decades. The Jews were Germans. The Jews were Jewish Germans. Those were troubled times for decent Gentiles and Jews alike. But upheavals had come and gone since the beginning of time. And in the camps and ghettos at least the Jews could be together, protected by one another.[21]

And then—and then there were none left. Hitler had won. Hitler had exterminated the German Jews. And then he struck again—in Austria, Czechoslovakia, and Poland. And it became a race against time to exterminate every single Jew in Western and Eastern Europe before his world crashed down about him.

Hitler exterminated the Jews of Europe. But he did not do so alone. The task was so enormous, complex, time-consuming, and mentally and economically demanding that it took the best efforts of millions of Germans, and later of Austrians, Czechoslovakians, Poles, Russians, French, Rumanians, Bulgarians, Slovaks, Hungarians, and Dutch, with the support of the national churches. The task called for more than passive acceptance by the Gentile population; it demanded active involvement. All spheres of life in Germany actively participated. Businessmen, policemen, bankers, doctors, lawyers, soldiers, railroad and factory workers, chemists, pharmacists, foremen, production managers, economists, manufacturers, jewelers, diplomats, civil servants, propagandists, film makers and film stars, professors, teachers, politicians, mayors, party members, construction experts, art dealers, architects, landlords, janitors, truck drivers, clerks, industrialists, scientists, generals, and even shopkeepers—all were essential cogs in the machinery that accomplished the Final Solution.[22] One cannot erase six million Jews and hordes of Gentiles from the face of the earth without massive help. As Hitler moved across the continent of Europe, he found crowds of willing assistants in every country—occupied or satellite. Some countries introduced anti-Semitic legislation before Hitler asked them; and a few—like Croatia—managed to outstrip Hitler in every category from grotesque cruelty to barbaric torture to boundless zeal. And the Allies assisted with their indifference; the neutrals helped by raising immigration barriers; the British helped by closing off Palestine; the American Jews helped by their disunity, arguing, and infighting.[23]

The scientific, objective, and carefully planned annihilation of 6,000,000 people because of a cultural difference by the professional and educated members of a civilized and respected nation is an aberration in human history. The Germans killed human beings to fulfill their ideology. The means and the ends became the same. All of history's other destructions were means to an end—not the end itself. As Elie Wiesel has noted, hordes of people died between 1941 and 1945, but most were victims of World War II, not of the Holocaust. The Holocaust was not like Carthage, the Mongolian invasions, the Inquisition, the Mexican War, the Japanese relocation camps, Hiroshima, the Ku Klux Klan, or Vietnam. It was not carried out by one man or group but by a nation and a world, and not by lunatics but by ordinary citizens. There were voices of protest and alarm—but they were ineffectual. After 1941 the world knew—and it did nothing. The Allied leaders knew but remained indifferent. The remaining European Jews knew but refused to believe. The American Jewish community knew but advocated gentle persuasiveness so as to avoid the "awakening" of dormant anti-Semitism in America. And the Gentiles of the Allied and neutral countries knew but saw the spector of hordes of unemployable immigrants competing for relief and jobs.[24]

For decades following World War II, few people seemed prepared, intellectually or emotionally, to deal realistically with either the Third Reich or the Holocaust. The catastrophe seemed so unusual in modern times that the only way the historians and scholars could work with it was from the concept of insanity. Many concluded that a program of such immense grotesquerie could only have been accomplished by madmen. Therefore Hitler and his SS henchmen were judged insane. That was a comfortable thesis and it seemed to explain everything quite easily. It meant that the German had no stock-taking to do, that the Allies had no dilemmas of conscience, and Jew and Gentile alike could think in simple terms that afforded easy transition. Now, however, we know that neither Hitler nor the SS nor the Nazi leaders were insane. This is not to say that Hitler and his colleagues were either brilliant or stable. However, political scientist Hannah Arendt made a strong impact when she insisted that Eichmann was an ordinary man.

Arendt's simple thesis on the banality of evil caused a tremendous controversy that has not yet ended. One would have to conclude that the ordinary-man thesis is emotionally impossible for many people to accept. But we have actually known it all along when we think about it. There have been hundreds of descriptions of the SS camp officials as good family men who loved animals and who went home after work to putter in the garden. Numerous stories exist of the camp guards smashing inmates' children's heads against walls, returning home, and falling comfortably into the role of loving father. We have laughed cynically at that picture but refused to understand that all the stories meant was that the SS were indeed ordinary men.

But how could ordinary men annihilate millions of people in an individual fashion? The words *anti-Semitism* and *prejudice* seem to offer no help. The question troubles us to this day; and perhaps the answer will forever elude us, but the clue to understanding lies most surely in the concept of nonhumans or subhumans. If one is emotionally convinced, consciously or unconsciously, of the nonhuman or subhuman status of a group of people, almost any act by ordinary men and civilized countries then seems possible. There appears to be no real limit to an ordinary man's actions against individuals or groups deemed nonhuman or subhuman. Eichmann meant it when he said, "I do not hate the Jews."

The leaders and often the followers viewed the Final Solution as a project simply demanding completion. After all, there was a war on and the Jews were the enemy. One senses that some felt a great sense of removal from the idea of murder. The killers empathized, on reflection and on occasion, with the pain and suffering they were causing. Most leaders were clinically normal people of average intelligence who were taking advantage of the *professional opportunities* presented to them. Himmler could not stand the sight of blood. Höss was just a man doing his job. Eichmann would have performed with the same intensity and perfectionism if he had been ordered to kill all people who wore glasses. A sensitive musician, Heydrich intended to excel in all that he did. Killing Jews provided him with an excellent professional opportunity, offering wide room for advancement. Hannah Arendt concluded:

The trouble with Eichmann was precisely that so many were like him, and that the many were neither perverted or sadistic, that they were, and still are, terribly and terrifyingly normal.... [T]his normalcy was much more terrifying than all the atrocities put together, for it implied . . . that this new type of criminal . . . commits his crimes under circumstances that would make it well-nigh impossible for him to know or feel that he is doing wrong.[25]

The government organized a kill to destroy an *entire people*. The Gas Chamber Age made possible a unique massacre—total, technological, and unemotional. "Gas asphyxiation was technological genocide, coldly done, without feelings of religious, rationalist or racial hostility on the part of the perpetrators."[26] Deep inhibitions can only be removed over time, but when they slip away, the period from that point to the commission of continuous atrocities is short. Hitler was not powerful enough by himself to eliminate in one fell swoop the basic beliefs of a society. The cracks were already there, the result of centuries of myth, a history of unattained dreams, an environment of despair, anger, and frustration, a predilection to worship obedience and compliance, a conviction about the nonhumanness of a verminous group, and yes, a deep idealism.

THE FINAL SOLUTION

The Final Solution was more than extermination. Its complex program involved torture, exploitation, degradation, and the destruction of a people before they were killed. The Nazis planned it that way because it was important to them that their victims experience a life much worse than death. To die was not enough. To lose dignity and self-worth was not enough. To experience humiliation was not enough. The Solution was a package of required components. And it reserved its fullest fury for the Jews.

Germany, the motherland, was to be free of her Jews, and so must be those countries she intended to incorporate into the Reich. Hitler determined to rid Germany and then Europe of Jews. In what way, he did not know. It was a new field, a venture into the unknown. How would the Gentiles, the churches, the military, the politicians, the industrialists, the world powers, and the Jews themselves react? Until he had a clear indication of their responses, Hitler could not determine how, when, and where to eliminate the Jews. He found his answers by transforming Germany into a gigantic test center. The Jews of Germany, as experimental subjects, were the only group to be slowly and carefully eliminated. Patiently, Hitler and the SS tried out new ideas and methods, cautiously waiting for responses. They evaluated, made mistakes, changed directions, reevaluated, refined. And they became experts, specialists.

In the first period of the Nazi regime, from 1933 to 1939, Hitler planned to free Germany and the German-controlled areas of the Jews. By making life unbearable, the Germans forced the Jews to emigrate. Those who did not were barred from all normal aspects of German life. The Nazis identified the Jews, then detached them from the bureaucracy, expropriated their property, and forced them into systematic impoverishment. Later they physically segregated them, gave them new names, and forced them to wear yellow stars. When the isolated Jews were naked and exposed, they were finally deported and liquidated.

As the Nazis established their anti-Semitic programs, the nations of Eastern and Central Europe involved in a crisis of democratic institutions received Nazi support. The world's failure to react to the anti-Jewish policies of Germany signaled other countries they could safely move ahead on their own. Thus organized anti-Semitism in Europe received encouragement from the German example and from the silence of the world's democracies.

Once Hitler finished with the basic task in the Motherland, he perceived a green light at the end of the tunnel. And he moved so swiftly that the Austrian Jews had no time to catch their breaths. Gone was the patience, the care, the practice, the evaluation. As part of Germany, Austria must be freed of the Jewish menace, immediately. Before World War II began, Hitler completed his basic tasks in Germany and Austria—the ideal proving grounds for the mass administrative elimination of the Jews from the face of the earth. By the time of the German invasion of Russia, it was clear that Hitler saw the struggle against the Jews as a vital conflict, between the forces of good and the forces of evil. Hitler's war against the Jews not only took priority over his war against all his other enemies but over his military war as well. And in the Jewish case alone no inhibitions existed. Despite a critical manpower and transportation shortage, the Jews were destroyed.

Hitler carried out his war against the Jews in Nazi-occupied and Nazi-controlled territories by three means: mass executions handled by *Einsatz-gruppen* (roving killing squads) primarily in Russian and Polish territory; annihilation by labor, disease, and starvation in the camps and the ghettos; and death by gas or by shooting in the extermination camps.

The concept of the Final Solution and the technical extermination policy was evolutionary. It developed, aided by German scholarship, science, technology, and zeal and, of course, by secrecy. The leaders took care that the deliberate physical destruction of Jews was never mentioned clearly in published Nazi documents. They scrupulously guarded the secret. The very monstrosity of the crime evidently made it unbelievable. In fact, the Nazis speculated that the unimaginability of what they were doing worked in their favor.

The Jews were to die. The planners did not always know how. They were not sure what methods the captive populations would accept, and they were not certain to what lengths world opinion would allow them to go. They were not even sure what facilities were available, and they were certainly not clear about the technical expertise. But they were sure of the end—death. And the ghettos and the labor camps were but way stations on the road to destruction.

The Final Solution was a gigantic experiment in destruction and it involved an entire bureaucracy. There were problems, there were momentary pauses caused by the ordinary difficulties that burden all bureaucracies— misunderstandings, annoyances, differences of opinion—but the missionaries worked out the problems and the slaughter proceeded. The men who designed the process and created its machinery thought of themselves as sanitation engineers who were ridding the earth of vermin for a higher good.

The chief implementers of the Final Solution included the head of the SS (*Schutzstaffel*) and chief of the German Police, Heinrich Himmler; his lieutenant, Reinhard Heydrich, chief of the Security Police of the SD (*Sicherheitsdienst*); and Ernst Kaltenbrunner, Heydrich's successor. The main agency was the Security Police with its central office, the RSHA (Reichssicherheitshauptamt, the Reich Security Main Office), and its department, the Gestapo, headed by Heinrich Müller. Adolf Eichmann supervised one section of the Gestapo office. The WVHA (*Wirtschaft und Verwaltungshauptamt,* the SS Economic Office), administered the concentration camps. The *Einsatzgruppen* lead the actions. The Office of Reich Chancellery supervised the killing centers. Those were the main perpetrators. But all agencies and individuals, party and government, cooperated to implement the program, in the shadow of the Nazi structure of justice.[27]

Nazi legal expert Hans Frank proclaimed: "Justice must be that which makes the whole Nation prosper, injustice must be that which harms the whole Nation." It is not theories that cause inhumanity, but the actions coming from them. A single idea may produce varied actions, but it may also produce an identical base with varying degrees of intensity and severity. How much, after all, does the Nazi notion of the "sound feeling of the people" differ from the American concept of the Supreme Court as a dynamic, flexible institution changing with societal needs? By Nazi theory punishment depended not on the gravity of offense but on the "psychological character type" to which the offender belonged and the "national political situation in which the offence took place."[28] How different, again, is that concept from Western law in practice? I do not mean to engage here in a cynical comparison between Nazi and democratic theory and action. I only want to clarify what went wrong and where Germany started on a path of destruction.

The theory and some of the practice of the Nazi system were similar to democratic justice. Hitler revived the idea of justice as retribution. But the Nazis took that next small step by making the Gestapo—the police force— central to the justice-giving process and relegating the courts to the periphery. In this way guilt was determined more by what one was than by what one did. And the Nazis created concentration camps as the legal repositories for those to be punished within their legal structure and theory. The inmates became victims not of extralegal actions, then, but of familiar theory translated into logical, though severe, action channels.

THE SOLUTION EXPANDS

Out of Germany and Austria came the Final Solution. As Germany moved, expanded, so did the Final Solution. It went with her—with her armies, her new leaders, her bureaucrats—to be implemented in the ways most appropriate to the culture, status, attitudes, and future purpose of each country touched by Hitler, invaded by Hitler, ravaged by Hitler, allied to Hitler.

Hitler incorporated Luxembourg, Austria, and Bohemia-Moravia into the Reich. As a favor to those countries restored to the bosom of the Motherland, he purified them of their Jews, quickly and thoroughly, just as he did in the Netherlands, which he intended to add to the Reich at a later date. He occupied Norway and Denmark, two countries that he considered Aryan, and ordered them purified. Denmark, however, saved most of her Jews with the aid of Sweden, and Norway saved half of her Jews, also with the aid of Sweden. Hitler overran the Baltic states, Poland, and part of Russia (he had to destroy the home of Jewish Bolshevism). And his *Einsatzgruppen* eliminated the Jews, trapped as they were in hostile territories, surrounded by hostile people, and pursued with relentless fury.

Hitler allied himself with Finland, Italy, Bulgaria, and Hungary. Until he occupied Italy and Hungary, the Jews were safe in all four countries. He conquered a part of Yugoslavia and Greece. And the Jews died. He created two countries, Croatia and Slovakia, each ruled by a nationalistic Catholic priest evangelist; and the Jews died, the Serbs died. Hitler conquered his Aryan neighbors, France and Belgium, but he left them with military governors preoccupied with the war and with economic exploitation. Many Jews lived, and many more would have survived had he not occupied all of France late in the war.

Regardless of the degree of anti-Semitism, the creation of Jewish Councils, the strength of the resistance, Hitler killed the Jews where he conquered whenever he wished to, whenever it was his priority. He waited too long in Denmark and lost them. He vacillated in Hungary and France, because he needed the help of those countries in other ways; and he could hold off on Belgium. But when he wanted to kill Jews in those countries he conquered, he did—undeterred by strikes, uprisings, resistance, protests. He pressured his allies and satellites, but that pressure was seldom enough. To succeed, he had to conquer; and in the last year of the war, conquering was not enough in either France, Italy, or Hungary. He threatened Bulgaria and Rumania, but to no avail.

In terms of total numbers killed, Hitler did what he wished when he conquered, if he had the resources or energy to act quickly.[29]

In Western Europe the Jews were more often integrated, assimilated, dispersed, and nonvisible. They constituted a small percentage of the total population, did not live in ghettos, and joined the native resistance movements. They were hard to identify, and they enjoyed some degree of solidarity with the non-Jews. The East European Jews, on the other hand, had endured a long history of state-supported or -encouraged pogroms, language barriers, cultural antagonisms. Often those Jews exhibited visible characteristics, lived in separate communities, and found the native populations and resistance movements antagonistic toward them. Yet, ultimately, the Final Solution meant the same thing, although approaches to it differed. In the West the Germans moved cautiously, avoiding mass executions, open pits, *Einsatzgruppen,* burning pyres. But they did move and they had ample time. More Jews were saved in the West only because German control over the territory varied. When it was absolute, as in Holland, just as many Jews died as in Eastern Europe. Where the control was incomplete, as in Belgium and France, fewer Jews died.

So the location of the country mattered—some. The timing of German actions mattered—some. Indigenous political authority was a buffer for the Jews—somewhat and sometimes. The historic treatment of the Jewish population mattered—sometimes. The size and influence of the Jewish population mattered—sometimes. The degree of urbanism and agrarianism mattered— seldom. The existence and cooperation of Jewish Councils mattered—in isolated instances. The degree of Jewish sophistication and resistance mattered—hardly ever. The degree of Jewish assimilation mattered—sometimes, but not at all in Germany and Bulgaria. Jews died in huge numbers, regardless of those mitigating elements, when Hitler had complete control and wanted them dead. The mitigations made the difference of a few percentage points—significant in terms of human life but not in terms of historical evaluation and understanding.

German control is the key, but three other elements had more than a superficial impact—if dealt with carefully and within narrowly-defined limits. Hitler's future plans for a nation, an area, were significant. German occupation meant trouble of varying severity for the occupied nation's Jews, but incorporation into Germany meant a maximum drive for 100 percent annihilation. Equal partnership meant that most Jews lived. Alliance and/or satellite status meant that the anti-Jewish program bore the stamp of the native culture. Occasionally the native approach was devastating, as in Croatia, but much more often it was milder and more limited than the Nazi monomania. It usually helped for a Jew to reside in a country allied with or friendly to Germany. And, of course, Jews residing legitimately before the war in a neutral country survived the war.

It has to be said that the official and public attitudes of the churches mattered a great deal. But the issue is complex. The churches, although part of an international body, were national institutions that sprang from the soil of a particular country and bore all the characteristics and peculiarities of that area. Their varying attitudes seldom truly reflected basic Christian doctrine. In Austria, for example, the Catholic bishops openly welcomed Hitler. But in Italy the Catholic priests as individuals acted like the rest of the Italians and aided the Jews. In Poland the Catholic Church spoke publicly against the Jews; in France it spoke for them. In Bulgaria the Orthodox Church leaders spoke up for the Jews; in Greece the Orthodox leaders remained silent. In the Netherlands the Calvinist Chuch remained passive and indifferent, while in Denmark the Danish Lutheran Church made an extraordinary effort to help. In Germany Lutheranism remained energetically subservient to the state. (Protestant church behavior throughout Europe conformed more completely to the prevailing attitude in each country than did Catholic and Orthodox behavior.) Where the churches stood for the Jews, their stance helped a great deal in *one respect*: in the amount of effort, energy, and courage expended by the Christian population in helping the Jews hide or escape. But the words of church leaders, either negative or positive, seemed to fall on fertile soil. Consequently, it is difficult to separate the attitudes of churchmen from the feelings of the people in whose midst they existed, and of whom they were a part.

The fate of the Jews also hung on timing—the year or month when Germany invaded or occupied a particular country, and at what point the Nazis initiated their pressure for the Final Solution. Where that pressure came after the tide of war began to change, usually a larger percentage of Jews remained alive. As with every other general statement made about the pattern of death, however, exceptions can be found. It is probably fair to conclude from the available evidence that Hitler held the key: his intentions, his plans, his actions—and the control he exercised or wished to exercise over a nation. Still, there is no denying that different actions, responses by Gentiles, Jews, churches, and governments could have reduced the percentage of Jews who died. A reduction of 10 percent of Jewish deaths in each country would indeed have been significant in human terms, but it would not have changed the Final Solution from a unique, massive, cold-blooded program of annihilation into a mild killing operation.

THE INVASION—*THE EINSATZGRUPPEN*

Hitler tied the Final Solution program to his invasion plans for Poland and Russia. He ordered Reinhard Heydrich, chief of the Security Police, to organize the murder of Jews and communists in the conquered territories. Heydrich formed under his command a paramilitary force called *Einsatzgruppen* or special duty groups. They ranged in size from a squad to a battalion, and operated as early as 1939 in Poland and as late as 1944 and 1945 in the Netherlands and Hungary. On September 21, 1939, Heydrich issued written instructions ordering the *Einsatzgruppen* chiefs to remove the Jews from the areas of occupied Poland, place them in large settlements, and set up Jewish Councils as a preparatory stage in the Final Solution.

On June 22, 1941, the Germans invaded the Soviet Union with its five million Jews. Four million were concentrated within a few hundred miles of the June 22 border and in the White Russian and the Ukrainian republics, areas that the Nazis overran. *Einsatzgruppen* followed the troops, seized and killed the Jews, and disposed of their bodies. Their success was a function of the density of the Jewish settlement in the area and the speed of the German advance. Jews overwhelmingly constituted the largest number of victims, and in some villages and towns they were the only victims.

No more than 3,000 men killed at least 1,000,000 human beings in approximately two years. Those figures mean statistically that four *Einsatzgruppen* averaged about 1,350 murders per day during the two-year period: 1,350 human beings were slaughtered on the average day, seven days a week, for more than a hundred weeks. Each of those million men, women, and children had to be selected, brought together, held, transported, counted, stripped, shot, and buried. Every possession had to be removed from them— off them and out of them—and salvaged, crated, and shipped; and records needed to be kept on each transaction. The executions occurred by the shores of a river or a lake, sometimes in a deep wood or in the ruins of a village. And when the Germans were retreating on all fronts, troops desperately needed for military action were dispatched to complete the annihilation process. In his final opinion the judge at the Nuremberg trial wrote:

In defiance of military needs, in spite of economic demands, and against every rule of reason, incalculable manpower was being wildly killed off. . . . For a country at war nothing can be more vital than that ammunition reach the soldiers holding the fighting fronts. Yet, in one massacre in Sluzk, vehicles loaded with ammunition for the armed forces were left standing in the streets because the Jewish drivers, already illegally forced into this service, had been liquidated by the Execution Battalions.[30]

On September 15, 1947, the commander of *Einsatzgruppen D,* Otto Ohlendorf, stepped into the courtroom for the *Einsatzgruppen* trial. Handsome, poised, polite, dignified, and forty years of age—the man was a compelling personality. The killing was unpleasant to him, he said, but he knew he was destroying dangerous people. And the children? Well, the children were killed because of permanent security problems. They would surely grow up, he testified, and the children of parents who had been killed would constitute a very real danger to the State.[31]

THE GHETTO RESERVATIONS

Somewhere in a Russian ghetto, Moishe the Beadle went mad. Every day he came to the synagogue, banged his fist, and said to God: "Master of the Universe, I want you to know, we are still here." The ghetto was decimated and fewer and fewer Jews were left. Still Moishe came to the synagogue. Finally he was the only Jew remaining. He came to the synagogue, banged his fist, and cried: "Master of the Universe, I want you to know, *I* am still here . . . but *you*—where are *you*?"[32]

After the *Einsatzgruppen* finished its initial work, the Nazis ordered Jews herded into ghettos and the creation of Jewish Councils throughout Eastern Europe. They charged the councils with two duties: to obey and implement Nazi orders, and to care for their people. In the context of chaos and desperation the Nazi orders seemed cruel to the council members, but not unbearable or even unrealistic. And the orders appeared to present the possibility of preserving a narrow breathing space, a thin tunnel in which many Jews might live through the war. And so the councils prepared the ghettos, scavenged for food and supplies, organized the residents, provided social services, created labor battalions, gave special attention to children, and supported cultural and educational endeavors. And in those densely populated conclaves life continued, at a rudimentary level to be sure, but life. And with the continuation of life came hope.

Freud once wrote that no one, not any human being, really believes in the eventuality of his own death. Participation in the incredible struggle for survival in the ghettos demanded an optimistic belief in man's basic decency, demanded hope, even blindness to the possible. A novelist captures the dilemma in describing a Jewish family living in fear in a Polish village before the roundups. Rachel explains to her young sister:

Sometimes we must overlook things. Pretend we don't see certain things. And that's all right, as long as you know that *your* conduct is proper. If you know in *your* heart that what you did was right, it will have to suffice sometimes. You always must do the right thing, even if others don't. . . . But you must learn to overlook. You must.[33]

Faced with deportation, the Jews asked themselves; "How can anything be worse than what we are going through now?" The rumors of the death camps seemed ridiculous. Most Jews—and for that matter, the Western world—refused to believe in the death camps. It seemed inconceivable that the Germans would exert an immense effort to destroy human beings who had done nothing wrong. It seemed senseless to destroy a labor source critical to the war effort. It seemed irrational to systematically murder masses of people. So Roosevelt, Churchill, and the Pope received news of the death camps and rejected it as rumor, or at most, exaggeration. The British and American generals received the news and rejected it. Disbelief was so strong that some generals were able to react with sincere surprise and horror when their troops liberated the "moderate" camps. The world of the 1940s did not believe, it could not conceive. And even today there are scholars producing books that label the Final Solution a hoax.

Finding no belief, support, or aid available to them from anywhere in the world, the Jews moved to bargain with the one force left—the devil—without even the freedom or moments of pleasure of Dr. Faustus. They determined to save what could be saved, to rescue as many as possible, by any means, even if the councils had to determine who should live and who should die. No council member was a traitor, a Quisling, or a Laval. No Jew believed in or accepted Nazi ideology. No one volunteered to ship Jews to their death. All nations under occupation cooperated and some collaborated with the Germans. No Jewish group collaborated. They cooperated to gain time and save lives.[34]

THE CAMPS: A SUMMARY

The Nazis built their order on the bedrock of an enormous and highly complex concentration and destruction system. By World War II the system consisted of killing centers, extermination/concentration camps, labor camps, concentration camps, penal settlements, Jewish camps, resettlement centers, camps for foreign workers and POWs, transient camps for those waiting—usually to be killed—and ghettos.

Hitler established the camps when he came into power for the purpose of isolating, punishing, torturing, and killing Germans suspected of opposition to his regime. From 1933 to 1938 the Nazis considered the camps primarily as places for the protective custody of political enemies of the state, not as the death pits, labor extractors, and medical research stations that they became.

From 1938 until the last weeks of the war the concentration system was in a constant state of expansion. It could never succeed in becoming a stable and rationalized institution under Hitler—a dictator whose sudden moves and directives kept the nature and the purposes of the system in a constant state of flux. The system seemed always on the move, striving to catch up, gear up, to the next level. Hitler and his aides made decisions that constantly affected the system, and caused it to be characterized primarily as reactive. The system strove to develop from a primitive incarceration project to a vast, unprecedented network for the suppression, containment, exploitation, and extermination of millions of people of various nationalities who were designated as enemies of the state or as members of a nonhuman or inferior population. The *modus operandi* of the camps changed over time. In fact, if one looks carefully, one can see the camps as evolutionary units. Obviously, the initial camp without buildings, services, or facilities, and with very little food, was a different place from the camp two or three years later when all the facilities, however primitive, had been installed.[35]

The system with its major and official concentration camps and their hundreds of subsidiary camps and work parties stretched like a giant net over the whole of Germany, and then of Austria and Czechoslovakia. With World War II came changes and hundreds of additional units. The number of prisoners increased dramatically and the Nazis extended the network throughout Europe and upgraded its functions. Economic exploitation and mass murder finally reduced the security functions to insignificance. The categories and purposes of the camps differed, as did the degrees of cruelty; but in every camp the prisoners could expect brutal treatment, starvation, sickness, and/or death. The prisoners died—of murder, gassing, torture, sickness, overwork, disease, and hunger.

And who were those prisoners? The Nazis poured into their concentration camps the normal categories of people whom victors always shut away—the political dissidents, the revolutionaries, the clergy, the resisters, the criminals, people simply disliked by someone, and those whose jobs some Nazis wanted. But they also interned four groups that were different, four groups against whom they employed the severest methods: the Jews, whom they intended to totally exterminate from the face of Europe, and failed only because they lost the War against Europe; the Gypsies whom they intended to exterminate on a tribal and individual basis, and certainly did exterminate a sizeable percentage; the Jehovah's Witnesses (probably about 3,000), whom they incarcerated and ridiculed but seldom killed outright; and the homosexuals (mostly male), whom they relentlessly persecuted and incarcerated in the camps from the opening moments of the Third Reich. Historians possess well-documented knowledge about the Jews, but only minimal information about the Gypsies. There is very little written about the Jehovah's Witnesses, and no major research on the homosexuals. The four groups experienced in common the concentration system and deprivation, persecution, incarceration, and oftentimes death from 1933–1945. The first two groups faced unrelenting, inescapable extermination. Toward the Gypsies, Hitler vacillated. He wiped out some tribes and protected others. The Germans, usually articulate in such matters, neglected to say precisely why they killed Gypsies. The Nazis forced the Jehovah's Witnesses or "Bible students," as fellow inmates called them, to sign the following pledge:

I _____, born: _____ in _____
make the following statement:

1. I acknowledge that the International Association of Jehova's Witnesses advocates a false doctrine using their religious activities as a pretext in the pursuit of their subversive aims.

2. I have therefore totally rejected this organization and have freed myself emotionally from the sect.

3. I hereby undertake never again to work for the International Association of Jehova's Witnesses. I shall report any persons who approach me with the false doctrine of Jehova's Witnesses or those who in any way display sympathy for them. Should I receive any Jehova's Witness literature, I shall surrender it immediately to the nearest police station.

4. I shall in the future observe the laws of the nation especially in the event of war when I shall take up arms to defend my Fatherland, and strive to become a wholehearted member of the national community.

5. I have been informed that I must expect a further term of protective custody if I fail to observe the undertaking which I made today.[36]

But the invasion of Poland changed the thrust, especially for the Jews. Poland's military subjugation was only a first stage in Hitler's long-held intentions for the area. It was his first opportunity to implement his dream of the total destruction of East European Jewry. He tied together tightly the war on Jewry and the war on Europe. It is a mistake to assume that the military war on Europe was a first priority, for as a long-term goal, Hitler's destruction of Jewry was more important than anything else. But one war depended on the other; both wars complemented and competed with each other. They aided each other, but they fought with each other. Each was critical to the success of the other—they were cemented together. One would achieve ascendancy only to be superseded by the other. The two wars had their separate armies, and each believed its war was more important. In a curious way, the European war advanced the war on Jewry, and made possible the killing of millions instead of hundreds of thousands. But in another way, the European war prevented the completion of the war on Jewry. For the military war could not succeed without the labor of the Jews. So, reluctantly, Jews were kept alive to work—to work so that the other war could conquer more lands, with more Jews. The wider the military war, the more Jews there would be available to exterminate. But the longer that war, the greater the need for Jewish labor. And so the tensions and the turmoils came to the surface, never to be resolved, completing the most vicious cycle in history. Because of it, a sizable number of Jews survived, a group that would have been killed much earlier had Hitler's dream of *Lebensraum* (living space for the German people) been Germany's only major commitment.

No one knows exactly how many camps existed, but they numbered in the thousands. No one knows how many humans passed through the system, or how many died, for Nazi efficiency did not extend to an accurate accounting system. The Nazis transferred prisoners throughout the system continuously and destroyed as many records as they could. The sheer enormity and complexity of the gigantic system precludes a precise determination. We know that at least eighteen million Europeans passed through the system, that at least eleven million died in it, and that at least four million died at Auschwitz/Birkenau alone. We know that the Nazis murdered from six to eight million Jews. But we wonder if all these estimates are too low.[37]

The Nazis were quite precise in their official categorization of the major camps and centers. Only nineteen primary camps existed. Almost all the remaining thousands were attached to, allied with, or under the supervision of the Big Nineteen. The categories were neat and precise in original paper form, but as the war developed, as Hitler's ideas changed, the system became more complex and the functions began to overlap. Only one category retained its purity—the killing centers. This book deals with the Big Nineteen and their categories:

Category I: The Four Killing Centers

1.	Chelmno	(contemporary Poland)
2.	Belzec	(contemporary Poland)
3.	Sobibor	(contemporary Poland)
4.	Treblinka	(contemporary Poland)

Category II: The Official Concentration Camps

A. The Two Labor/Extermination Complexes (Combined Functions)

1.	Auschwitz/Birkenau	(contemporary Poland)
2.	Majdanek	(contemporary Poland)

B. The Eleven Concentration Camps Given Official Status by Himmler

1.	Dachau	(contemporary West Germany)
2.	Sachsenhausen	(contemporary East Germany)
3.	Ravensbrück	(contemporary East Germany)
4.	Buchenwald	(contemporary East Germany)
5.	Flossenbürg	(contemporary West Germany)
6.	Neuengamme	(contemporary West Germany)
7.	Gross-Rosen	(contemporary Poland)

8.	Natzweiler	(contemporary France, in former Alsace-Lorraine)
9.	Mauthausen	(contemporary Austria)
10.	Stutthof	(contemporary Poland)
11.	Dora/Nordhausen	(contemporary East Germany)

Category III: The Official Reception and Holding Center—Bergen-Belsen

Category IV: The Unique Fortress Town—Theresienstadt

Anyplace the inmates found themselves was a scene of ignominy. Anyplace where they faced death was indeed a killing center, whatever its "official" designation. But in the Nazi scheme of things the system had a symmetry to it, an official and formal structure; and it is on that structure, that system, the Big Nineteen, that this book focuses.

Three basic elements linked the killing centers with the extermination/labor centers: experimentation, technical development, and a peculiar chaos. The differences centered on the presence or absence of a single-minded purpose to kill. At first, chaos and overcrowding marked the entire system. Everything occurred on an experimental basis. No one had any experience. Nothing like that had been done before in history. Who was there to copy? What books were there to read on the subject?

The terribly slow and inefficient methods of execution and body destruction created critical bottlenecks. The early gas chambers yielded still-living bodies when the guards opened the doors. The ovens in the crematoria handled one body at a time, and nothing was mechanized. The mass graves did not work: arms and legs began to erupt from the warm earth. Each commandant ran his own show with his own brand of organization. He competed with other commandants and the generals for a share of the limited materials and money.

The very nature of totalitarianism made chaos and contradictions inevitable. There was never a clear idea from camp to camp as to the true purpose. Was it to extract labor or merely to kill? The fear engendered by totalitarianism made cooperation practically impossible. No commandant wanted to be transferred from his cushy job to the front. Achievements were not to be shared—nor were failures, as each strove to prove the former and deny the latter.

The commandants could not kill and dispose of the bodies fast enough before new ones were brought in. It was not until the final months of the war that they overcame their difficulties and became superbly efficient. Crematoria now had the capacity to hold more bodies; fat was drained off, and then added again to make the bodies burn faster; bodies could be rolled or pulled in mechanically rather than handled individually. In the gas chambers a more efficient type of gas was used, which took less time. The chambers were enlarged so that more bodies could be accommodated. Bodies were disposed of more easily and efficiently on pyres. Bone-crushing machines also helped reduce problems in the final disposal stage.

Historians and novelists alike have described the Holocaust as the capstone of modern technology. Albert Speer spoke of it after Nuremberg as the fullest use of all technical means and expertise. But we ought to have a nagging doubt about the collective wisdom of our words. The process, the system of killing, was indeed advanced, borrowed from industry. Yet what was so modern about the technology? Gas is gas. Trains are trains. And cattle cars have been with us for a century. For bone crushing, two stones will do. The Indians knew how to strip skin, and primitive societies were castrating men and removing clitorises centuries ago. And despite the ultramodern crematoria, commandants *in every camp* found that open-pit burning was more effective for large groups of people than ovens, and reverted to that method in each instance. So one wonders at the grandiose conclusions on ultramodern technology and Nazi efficiency.

1. The Killing Centers—Exclusive-Function Camps

Before the Nazis developed the killing centers and extermination camps, they used the *Einsatzgruppen* to kill the Jews and other undesirables. But those massacres showed that there were glaring problems inherent in the extermination of masses of people, among them the need for speed, efficient and complete body removal, secrecy, and disposal of belongings. Killing centers, however, provided both expediency and secrecy, and the later extermination camps made possible the full range of physical and psychological abuse that the Nazis wished to employ in the destruction of the undesirables.

Himmler designed the killing centers exclusively as places of secret and instant death. Today there is widespread misunderstanding and ignorance about the four killing centers, which were all on isolated occupied Polish territory and had short histories. Writers often confuse the centers with the camps. Very few people survived the centers, and those who did have seldom written about them; almost nothing remains of the centers; few people have visited them; all are located deep in rural Poland, and the Polish government would like them to remain obscure because they are reminders of a separate form of dying for Jews—these factors all contribute to the confusion. The key to understanding is that the killing centers were *only* killing centers—they had no other function. The prisoners there did not die on the way to death— they were killed.

In 1941 Himmler called in his gassing specialist, Christian Wirth, known as the Technocrat of Destruction, and ordered him to design and implement an extermination program with Chelmno as the pilot project. Sometime in 1941 Hitler gave the verbal order for the Final Solution, treating it as a secret of the highest order. Hitler and Himmler created Operation Reinhard—the camouflage term for the Belzec, Sobibor, and Treblinka program—under the command of Odilo Globocnik. Instead of reporting to the SS-WVHA, as did Majdanek, Auschwitz, and the other concentration camps, Operation Reinhard reported to the Office of the Führer—the Reich Chancellery Office. Although keeping control of the program close to him, Hitler delegated responsibility for the practical aspects to Himmler. The staff turned to the euthanasia program (T-4) for ideas and trained personnel. They selected the sites and sent out construction teams. T-4 construction workers helped with the buildings. And high-level T-4 personnel came to the centers after the revolts to deliver funeral orations for their fallen SS comrades.

Operation Reinhard German camp workers were not told of the program goals and their precise duties until they reached the centers. Upon their arrival, the SS officers oriented them by comparing center goals with the euthanasia program, which was very familiar to the workers. Then the SS swore them to absolute secrecy. Each worker signed a pledge that contained the following commitments:

1. I have been instructed that under no circumstances will I discuss with anyone outside of OR co-workers anything dealing with the operation.
2. I understand the top secrecy of "any of the occurrences of the so-called Jewish Relocation."
3. I may not take any pictures.
4. "I promise to keep my word to the best of my ability."
5. I understand that after completion of my service, this oath of secrecy will still apply.[38]

Operation Reinhard issued in a new phase of mass murder. Himmler replaced the mobile killing units with stationary death factories, and the gas chamber period began. The authorities had no intention of accommodating prisoners in the killing centers for any length of time—they exterminated them almost immediately upon arrival. Administrative structures were very simple. Because the centers were never linked to the war effort, only minimal industrial activity existed. And most inmates or transients were Jews, although there were some Polish Christians.

The Nazis built Sobibor, Belzec, Treblinka, and Chelmno as killing centers for the sole purpose of exterminating the Jews of Europe and as many Gypsies as could be found. All four were constructed on Polish soil primarily because of the widespread Polish railway system, which had stations in the smallest towns. In addition, the Polish countryside, which was densely forested and thinly populated, made secrecy possible. Not one killing center existed longer than seventeen months. The SS obliterated each of them, intending to remove all traces. Polish scholars estimate conservatively that in those four camps, 2,000,000 Jews and 52,000 Gypsies, one third of whom were children, were killed. Yes, the concentration camps had their gas vans, their gas chambers, their crematoria, and their mass graves. People were shot in them, given injections, gassed, and hundreds of thousands died of starvation and disease. But even in Birkenau, where some have estimated that 1,000,000 Jews were killed, there was a chance of life. In the killing centers the only inmates kept alive for a short time were those selected to process the bodies of their fellow Jews.

First came Chelmno—the pilot extermination project—rude and crude, conferring death by three gas vans, borrowed from the Eastern Front. No crematoria, just mass graves in the woods. Chelmno exemplified extermination in the primitive style. Then came Belzec with its diesel-run gas chambers, which were inefficient and time-consuming, and its primitive open-bit burning to dispose of bodies. Sobibor, in a small and obscure corner of Poland, was next. It too had gas chambers and mass graves.

And finally came Treblinka. Learning from the mistakes made at the other three, the Nazis were here able to construct an unusually efficient destruction instrument that managed to destroy the lives and bodies of 1,000,000 human beings in only twelve months—a truly monstrous carnage. In order to create a killing center with such efficiency, it was necessary to invent the killing machinery and process. And for that, the SS technicians and experts had no precedents on which to rely. They had to depend on original thinking to accomplish the task. It was at Treblinka that the technicians finally triumphed over the once insurmountable difficulties of secretly destroying the lives, bodies, and possessions of huge numbers of people in a short period of time.[39]

After the Sobibor Revolt, Himmler ordered the centers closed. He sent the German camp personnel to the Trieste area on the Adriatic Coast, to continue the operation there. Assigned to a group known as the Arm Unit, the men's task was to carry out the technical preparation for the mass killing of Jews in that area. In a rice factory near Trieste they set up a burning facility. Partisan activity, however, made program implementation impossible. On November 4, 1943, Globocnik wrote to Himmler from Trieste: "I have on Oct. 19, 1943 completed Action Reinhard and closed all the camps." He asked for special medals for his men in recognition of their "specially difficult task." Himmler responded warmly to "Globos" on November 30, 1943, thanking him for carrying out Operation Reinhard. By the end of the war, partisans had killed Wirth and Sobibor Commandant Reichleitner. Globocnik committed suicide.[40]

2. The Concentration Camps

The Nazis designed the concentration camps to house large numbers of people in a limited, structured, and defined area. Basically, the camps consisted of a series of buildings constructed or utilized to house people until they died or were killed. The camps were psychologically and technically contrived to destroy the inmates' basic humanity and, then, their bodies. Most camps were self-sufficient. They did not require local help and maintenance, for the prisoners ran internal affairs. Each camp had its own power structure—a carefully defined and ordered hierarchy. Almost all the camps were near train depots. Most were not built for permanence, and all had major problems in disposing of the bodies.

It has always been clear that concentration camps were to be camps for dying. The Germans organized them to ensure the death of the largest number of prisoners, even while extracting some useful labor from the doomed. An average healthy man in the camp, insufficiently clad, undernourished, constantly losing weight, sleeping in an unheated hut, living in disgraceful sanitary conditions, devoured by lice with no opportunity to wash, forced to work even when sick with no prospect of getting well, would fall victim to the first serious disease infecting him. From 1941 those camps were vast slave-labor markets. They varied a great deal in severity and in conditions, but even the worst of them offered a slim chance of survival.

The major difference between a killing center and a concentration camp is that in the former prisoners died quickly and with a relatively low degree of agony. In the latter they died slowly, piece by piece, over a longer period of time and in conditions that sometimes made the trip to the Auschwitz gas chamber seem almost a mercy.

As the Nazis developed camps in every corner of Europe, major complexes emerged. Each complex included the parent or mother camp and many branch units called subcamps. The subcamps were set up near factories, mines, quarries, at some distance from the parent camp, where the labor of the prisoners could be exploited.

The camps as a commercial enterprise, concentrating on the systematic salvage of goods, took time to develop. The system was a catchall until the deluge of material necessitated the development of special administrative machinery and specific jurisdictions. The Nazis confiscated all property. They used the prisoners both for labor and for experimentation. Those economic and military needs interrupted the extermination process and introduced intermediate procedures.

The two major tasks of the prisoners in those camps were to work and to die. Often they managed the dying alone, but the SS carefully planned the work in cooperation with Berlin and with Germany's major industries. For the Jewish prisoners, the Nazis always had one goal—death, in one form or another, quickly or slowly. For the non-Jewish prisoners, however, the situation was far more complex. The goals for those prisoners varied from time to time, because the Nazis could not seem to arrive at a consensus. Yet the exploitation of prisoner labor in order to advance the war effort was a major and primary short-term goal for all non-Jewish prisoners. In addition, as the war lengthened, the indirect extermination of the Jewish prisoners by work became the primary camp method of eradicating what the Nazis felt were vermin in their midst. Thus one of the most important, and at times primary, aspects of the concentration camp was the production of work—work for its own sake, work for the building of the nation, work for the war effort, and work to kill.

Still, the pressing need for labor never once diverted Hitler or Himmler from their *major goal*. They were intent first and foremost on destroying each and every Jew and unredeemable portions of the Slavic people, so they simply worked the men and women to death and replenished the labor supply from the always available pool. Inefficient, yes. Inconsistent, no. That major goal prevented Germany's total mobilization for war until it was too late, prevented the adequate servicing of the military forces, and was one of the primary reasons Hitler lost a war he might well have temporarily won.

3. The Labor/Extermination Complexes

First the Nazis deported the Polish Jews from their major centers. Then they killed a majority of them. Next they exploited the labor of the remaining Jews for private and SS industries. Finally, the SS used Jewish labor to exploit Jewish personal property. And the two major centers for the exploitation of that labor were Majdanek and Auschwitz. Both were intended to serve double duty: as extermination camps and as labor exploitation centers. Although both camps had full extermination facilities and a ghastly death rate, extermination was never their only goal, as it was in the killing centers.

The descriptions of gassing and burning can overshadow the fact that the SS decided to make a profit from its prisoners through labor and through confiscating their belongings. Plunder was a major business at Majdanek and Auschwitz. It is interesting that even though the Nazis abhorred and forbade any contact between Jews and Aryans, they had no qualms about using Jewish hair, skin, skulls, bones, and ashes for various purposes. The Nazis wore Jewish clothes, eyeglasses, and shoes. They shaved with Jewish razors, they cut with Jewish scissors, they placed their money in Jewish wallets, they lay under Jewish blankets. They used Jewish canes. They placed their children in Jewish baby carriages. They combed their hair with Jewish combs and they smoked Jewish pipes. Their wives wore the underwear of the untouchables.

Rationalization of labor had been in progress for a long time when large

German business corporations took the final step during World War II by investing huge sums in the construction of factories at the camps—for the purpose of using the pool of camp slave labor. That step made the price of labor unbelievably cheap, for once a laborer was used up, instead of turning him out into the street and adding to the unemployment rolls, they simply killed him.

The great industrial corporation I. G. Farben found itself faced with a severe labor shortage at a time when the war need for synthetic rubber was excruciating. Farben decided to build a new plant to manufacture it. Highly competent, respected corporation officials met with Nazi officials and decided, after several board meetings, on the Auschwitz site as an excellent corporate investment. It had good water, coal, and a never-ending labor pool. Farben based its decision for plant relocation on criteria used by today's international corporations: the maximization of profit and the minimization of labor costs. It undertook to "run successfully a large corporation, a death camp slave labor factory, and an extermination center. All three are part of the same world. At least in Germany, the top executives of all three enterprises often felt at home with each other."[41]

Most corporate killers went on to bigger and better positions after the war, and many of them still hold positions of responsibility and influence in Germany. The vast majority directly involved in the camp ventures were never punished, even though those men are the individuals who truly solved Germany's Jewish problem:

It was possible for respectable business executives to participate in and profit from a society of total domination and a venture involving the murder of millions of defenseless human beings without losing their elite status in one of the most advanced modern societies.[42]

In one sense, the approach was neither modern nor shrewd. Any logician would be quick to surmise that a well-fed worker could labor far more effectively than one on the brink of starvation. One must either conclude that the Germans were not very logical or that they simply were not interested in the labor the internees provided. Probably a little of both. The notion of the cool, calculating German is hard to sustain. He undoubtedly was cool and calculating in his ends, but not in his means. It was only because such a vast number of people were interned that any work at all could be accomplished. Conversely, though, if the sole desire was the elimination of those *Untermenschen,* then why bother to wait? Plainly it was the very structure of the totalitarian system based on a theory of a master race and an Absolute Idea that prevented those objectives from being clearly defined and implemented. The Nazis were not equipped to handle their own conclusions.

4. The Master Builders

In a state dedicated to concentration as a permanent function of major importance, and to extermination as a war of first priority, it would be reasonable to expect to discover an advanced and technologically efficient planning and construction system based on universal principles. One might even expect to find a few architectural triumphs. The truth, however, is that in the implementation of Hitler's most cherished dream, the famed German efficiency and architectural sophistication collapsed. Perhaps since no unified Nazi style of architecture developed for German citizens, we ought not to expect one for the camps.

Certain elements and principles did find consensus. The camp layout and buildings needed to be basic, efficient, inexpensive, and easy to construct by unskilled labor. The facilities had to serve specific purposes. They must house bodies—those of the SS and the administration, for the duration of the war, and perhaps forever; and those of the inmates until death. Facilities were needed for a wide range of productive work, both in the camp and in the outlying districts. Structures had to include a large storage and shipping center for the massive amounts of possessions brought in by inmates. Provision had to be made for effective killing mechanisms and for the disposal of the dead bodies.

Despite the simplicity of those needs, the administrators and technicians never built a truly effective camp, let alone a perfect one. Too many problems and difficulties intervened. Competing bureaucracies interfered. When the goals were clear, they were contradictory. Secrecy and uncertainty often produced unclear and vague ends. The goals shifted and changed within short periods of time. Political infighting, power politics, and the chieftain syndrome produced confusion and competition.

Practical realities intervened in all areas of implementation. The Nazis needed so many camps so quickly in specific areas that camp planners were forced to look for existing facilities that they could buy or seize and then convert. Sites had to be selected in isolated areas, often devoid of sources of building materials. And in pressing for supplies, tools, equipment, and services, the commandants and planners competed every inch of the way against the military machine. The administrators were forced to build the camps without adequate technical manpower, without prior experience or knowledge of concentration and extermination camp planning. Imagine attempting to build a vast industry without any university-trained experts. There were no specialists; any expertise was accidental. Initially the major technical problems proved too great for industry, science, and technology. Thus improvisation, experimentation, and creativity became the keys to success and productive capacity.

If every step was experimental, some progress should have been made through sharing. But no commandant wished to share success, and none dared to share failure; so the mistakes were repeated from camp to camp. Additionally, each camp was different from every other camp and varied within itself over time. The populations in each camp, for example, shifted significantly in number and ethnic composition. Consequently, architects and builders could neither predict nor count on a stable facility usage. They seldom knew how many inmates they were designing for, and they were never certain of the goals and the desired usage. The varied auxiliary services and enterprises necessitated facilities peculiar to each camp. In one a greenhouse might be needed; in another, a riding stable. Another might call for a special medical experimentation arrangement, and yet another, an advanced rabbit farm. Those special and whimsical elements created headaches for the architects. They had to design kitchen facilities so advanced that fancy meals could be served to nervous SS and guards, and gourmet dinners to a Himmler. The mass feeding requirements, however, demanded only a large primitive soup kitchen.

The architects tried to formulate some basic principles that could be applied universally. They agreed to build the camps as closed worlds, invisible from civilian populations; but Dachau, Majdanek, and Neuengamme, for example, stood in full view of populated towns and cities. Preferably the site should be unhealthy and dismal; but seashores and mountains could be made to serve equally well. Temporary structures should serve the purpose; but Auschwitz and Theresienstadt utilized old permanent brick towns and fortresses. The singular model was to be the old inefficient barracks-style horse stable, laid out in rows; but they built Natzweiler in a terrace arrangement and Sachsenhausen in the form of a large semicircle. Economic needs determined that the sites be located near raw-material sources such as quarries and forests—and near some population center, accessible by rail. By the early 1940s, however, the planners were forced to place the camps haphazardly in a variety of locations and environments, and to bring the railroad tracks to the camps. They used any available material for construction—bricks, stone, wood, logs. Even the gas chambers and crematoria differed in design, shape, size, and material. Actually, only three components were rigidly incorporated into every camp (except, of course, the killing centers): high-voltage barbed wire surrounding the camp, intermittent observation/guard boxes of varied design, and a roll call or assembly area.

The Nazis intended that Germany's major cities and small villages should "express the achievement and the nature of the German people" through architecture. They never achieved their goal, except perhaps with the camps. Ironically, almost nothing remains today of Nazi architecture except the Autobahn and the preserved buildings of the concentration system.[43]

5. The System Transport Program

Transportation loomed as a critical problem. It takes no great insight to recognize the enormous complexity of transporting quickly and efficiently millions of Jews from all over Europe to the camps and killing centers in the midst of the chaos and military urgency of a world war. Yet the brilliantly successful transportation operation seems to have been overlooked in analyses of the camps and in the legal assessment of criminal activity. Although transportation was essential to the Final Solution, scholars and judges have treated the railroads as "tools, resources, . . . possibly weapons" on "the fringes of the operation." Without the railroads, however, there would have been no successful Final Solution. One must conclude that the Transportation Ministry was central to the concentration system.[44]

If postwar officials ignored the role of the Transportation Ministry, Himmler most surely did not. Car shortages plagued him and his staff, forcing them to plead for special treatment from the manager of the *Reichsbahn* (the Reich Transportation Ministry), Dr. Albert Ganzenmüller. On July 28, 1942, Dr. Ganzenmüller reminded SS Leader Karl Wolff that one train with 5,000 Jews went daily from Warsaw to Treblinka, and twice a week a train with 5,000 Jews went to Belzec. Wolff responded to Ganzenmüller on August 13, 1942:

It gave me great pleasure to learn that already since 14 days ago, one train goes daily with 5,000 passengers of the Chosen People to Treblinka; and we even are in a position to complete this mass movement of people at an accelerated rate. I have made personal contact with the participants so that an uninterrupted accomplishment of the total undertaking seems guaranteed.

The situation, however, became troublesome enough for Himmler, on January 23, 1943, to write a letter to Ganzenmüller labeled "Urgent":

Here I need your help and support. I must—if I am to take care of these things quickly—receive more transport trains. I well understand the strained condition of the railways and that requests are always made of you. However, I must make these requests of you: Help me and see that I get more trains.[45]

The enormous transport program demanded the close cooperation and extensive knowledge of civilians, civil servants, and transportation experts in Germany and in all the countries of Europe. One of the largest Nazi government agencies, the *Reichsbahn* employed 1,400,000 people in Germany and 400,000 in Poland and Russia.

The special Final Solution trains, or *Sonderzüge,* made up of freight cars and cattle wagons, posed three areas of serious difficulty to Himmler and his staff, and to the *Reichsbahn.* The length of the war, the geographical extension of the war, and military emergencies created a serious shortage of transport. Traffic jammed the lines, and bombings repeatedly destroyed tracks. The *Reichsbahn* ameliorated the problem by lengthening the trains, packing more Jews in the cars, and using longer, more circuitous routes to destinations. The serious overloading and long time period produced unimaginable horrors inside the airless, foodless, waterless, toiletless sealed cars. Many Jews did not survive the journey. But that was considered fine by the Nazis—it simply lessened the number of Jews they needed to exert energy to destroy in the camps.

Financing that enterprise must have been extremely complex and a constant problem. The *Reichsbahn* saw its responsibility as transporting anyone anywhere for payment. For the SS, the *Reichsbahn* adopted a policy of group fares for deportees. If at least 400 people were in the shipment, the SS was charged one-half the third-class rate. Additionally, the *Reichsbahn* did not charge the SS for the return trip of empty trains, and dealt with it on a credit basis. More detailed policies and negotiations were needed when the transports originated in other countries such as Slovakia and Hungary, and when coordination was needed among several national railway systems. The *Reichsbahn* proved itself to be a brilliant negotiator.

In 1944 the Nazis deported 500,000 Jews from Hungary, utilizing critical rolling stock with the approval of the military. From October 1941 to October 1944 the *Reichsbahn* transported at least 2,500,000 Jews to their death. They also carried the Jewish loot from the camps to Germany. "Despite difficulties and delays, no Jew was left alive for lack of transport."[46]

Dr. Ganzenmüller went to Argentina after the war as a railway expert. He returned in 1955 to Germany as an expert for a major firm. Although investigated and indicted by West Germany, Ganzenmüller retired, pleaded illness, and has never been tried. During the war not one *Reichsbahn* official resigned or protested. All treated the Jewish cattle-car transports as a special business problem that they took pride in solving so well. After the war the workers and officials continued in their jobs, completely undisturbed and untouched, in a renamed agency, the *Bundesbahn.*[47]

6. Thanatology and Experimentation

The Holocaust occasioned the creation of the macabre science, thanatology—*the science of producing death*—and the camps provided the perfect laboratories. SS, military, and civilian doctors and professors performed deadly medical experiments on live bodies in most camps.

It has always been true that human beings are the most suitable subjects for medical experiments. Once the physicians realized they had an almost limitless pool of varied kinds of humans at their disposal, some very respectable professors seized upon the unique opportunity. They reported their findings at meetings and to medical societies, and no one protested. One purpose of those experiments was to discover ways in which Germans could rule Europe forever. If Germany wished to have security against real or imagined enemies, she would have to do more than win the war. Her total security could only be achieved by biological means, which meant sterilization or killing. Had the Germans won the war, mass sterilization would have been an important aspect of their program for the subject peoples. The practices of using captive, ignorant, or minority ethnic volunteers for medical purposes has been widespread, of course, even in the United States. So the Nazis were not unique in that respect (although they certainly were in the degree to which they went). During World War II the great German pharmaceutical corporation Bayer made extensive use of death camp inmates for experiments. In recent times Bayer's American counterparts, Bristol-Myers and Squibb, found a plentiful supply of subjects in American prisons, and they operated there with the approval of the federal government. It is not accidental that the American doctors selected blacks and prisoners for their experiments. If they truly believed their tests were safe, they would have used their own patients or their own labs; but instead they selected those whom they considered inferior human beings, just as the Nazis did.

Medical experiments in the camps took the form of freezing, low-pressure, and high-altitude tests; the testing of drugs on people in whom malaria had been induced; the deliberate infection of people with jaundice and typhus; the deliberate injury of prisoners and the use of mustard gas on the wounds to find effective treatment; the creation of wounds and then the inducement of tetanus and gangrene with dust and glass to test the effectiveness of sulfanamides and other medicine; the removal and transplantation of bones and muscles to examine regeneration; seawater experiments; the infliction of phosphorus burns; the ingestion of poison to find antidotes; and sterilization and castration. The concentration camps became a training field for German medicine, but even in those medical experiments the prisoners were not treated at the level of dogs. As one poet wrote:

We were not likened to dogs among the Gentiles—They pity a dog.
Caress, even kiss him with the Gentile mouth. For like a puppy
Fondled at home they pamper it, delight in it always;
And when this dog dies—how very much the Gentiles mourn him!

We were not led like sheep to the slaughter in the boxcars
For like leprous sheep they led us to extinction
Over all the beautiful landscapes of Europe . . .

Before slaughter they did not pull the teeth of their sheep;
They did not strip the wool from their bodies as they did to us;
They did not push the sheep into the fire to make ash of the living
And to scatter the ashes over streams and sewers.[48]

PART TWO

THE CAMPS

THE PRE-WAR CAMPS

DACHAU: A PERFECT MODEL

Dachau is the show camp of Western Europe. Although Nazi concentration camps dotted the continent, only one small camp on the western side of the Iron Curtain has been preserved with the intent of serving as a major visitor, education, and memorial center. Certainly, some improvements have been made at Natzweiler and Flossenbürg, and some tiny, almost offhand attempts at Neuengamme and Bergen-Belsen. But those efforts came from concerned survivors, not from the government or the German people. The West German government has put all its eggs in the Dachau basket, albeit reluctantly.

Dachau was Himmler's model camp, so why not make it a model museum? For years after the war it languished, dismal and decrepit, until survivors joined together to protest and various religious groups began to erect monuments. If an American tourist or a Western European has toured any camp, it is Dachau. And if American soldiers talked of a camp they had liberated or visited, it was usually Dachau. The American Army liberated Mauthausen, Buchenwald, Dora/Nordhausen, and Dachau. But only two of those camps now lie in Western Europe. The situation contrasts with the picture in Eastern Europe. True, East Germany has its show camp at Buchenwald and Poland has its at Auschwitz. Yet the East Germans also expended large sums of money to preserve Ravensbrück and Sachsenhausen, and the Poles built important museums at Majdanek and Stutthof. And both countries urge visitors to tour those major camps. Of course, the Poles much prefer that no one travel to the four killing centers, but at least if one manages to locate them, one finds in three instances a significant memorial park with sculpture by reputable artists.

No, the West German government has never been eager to preserve or highlight its camps, not even Dachau. And the people of that gray provincial town preferred that the camp be destroyed. But pressure from survivors mounted, and fifteen years after the war the Germans began work on Dachau. What they have created is a monstrosity. Other nations have some contrasts, some alternatives.

Dachau, only 15 kilometers northwest of Munich, is easy to reach. With approximately 30,000 inhabitants, it is a typical German provincial city, of little charm and no highlights—except the camp. And the camp obtrusively borders the town. Next to the camp is a restaurant and a large parking lot, to service the 500,000 visitors/tourists a year.

The Dachau of today would be unrecognizable to a survivor. In fact, he might well find himself scratching his head, wondering if the ugly place in which he suffered was only a fantasy. And one suspects that that is as it is meant to be, that the garish surrealism of today's Dachau is no accident.

Dachau is white, *hygienically* white. And black. Sterile, clean, perfect— an outdoor Camp Smithsonian. One large administration building housing a stark museum and small archive—white, sterile. Two prisoner barracks, rebuilt and covered with wood—white, sterile. The entire area, covered with gravel—white. The watchtowers, rebuilt—white. Concrete slabs where the barracks used to stand—white. The camp road lined with trees is gone, replaced by small stones—white. And the contrast: the long black roof of the administration building, the black roofs of the two barracks, the black barbed wire, the black roofs of the watchtowers. White, black, sterile, antiseptically clean, not a stone out of place. Even the monuments, one for each faith, blend into the new environment.

The Catholic Chapel of Atonement—an open circular semitower made of rough-hewn stones and wreathed with an iron crown of thorns—was powerful in its 1960 setting, but now it is lost among the modern sterility. The 1965 Jewish memorial is clean and crisp, but somewhat like the entrance to a subway station. The Protestant chapel, also from 1965, is a modern archi- tectural failure of questionable taste. And at the end of the grounds, through the rear entrance, lies the Carmelite Convent, built after the war. Here live twenty-one nuns who have taken a vow never to leave. The convent's prioress belonged to the group led by a Jesuit priest, Alfred Delp, who was executed by the Nazis for his part in the Hitler assassination plot.

It is all too much. Nothing disturbs the stark environment. Nothing screams out. All is in subdued good taste, and thus submerged. One piece merits attention, the recent International Monument, stretching like a stone- and-iron gate across the front of the camp ground. It was created in 1968 by the Yugoslav sculptor Glid Nandor.

In 1965 the Bavarian government established the museum. One wanders distractedly through the cold dark rooms among the artifacts and pictures. The photos are the familiar famous ones, meant, one supposes to teach a lesson; but if so, it is an elementary one, seen so often before. And so one asks: "Did that really happen here?" And the spontaneous answer is: "No, not in this park." Visitors walk away, as they do from Auschwitz, mumbling that internment could not have been as bad as they had heard. Later the more thoughtful may remark that Kafka would have been comfortable there, that the starkness, the setting, remind them of *2001: A Space Odyssey.*

It was not always like that at Dachau. Before the great cleanup in the mid-1960s, the camp was a visitor center, but no one had yet arrived with the pails of whitewash. The barracks with broken windowpanes remained standing, and the camp area, with its trees and paths, became a muddy mess in the rain. In fact, the red crumbling barracks were inhabited, with a TV antenna leaning from a roof here and there. Refugees and victims of southern Germany's housing shortage waited in the old dormitories for urban development to create "more appropriate" living space. One monument, with the rough-hewn stones stood alone. I liked it better then. It was authentic, and I could learn from it. The modern world had not yet intruded to create false images and out-of-place fantasies, messing up any mind on a search, any soul struggling for sound insight. Yes, I liked it better then. One could learn—if one wished to. In the old days Dachau was a different place. It was inadmissible, unforgettable. Now it is easy to erase from the mind, for it is unreal, it is a product of *today*.

One area remains the same, but not quite. Beyond the fence, in a perfectly preserved park, stands the old crematorium housed in a crumbling, sagging hut, the ovens still full of ashes, with dusty funeral wreaths lying on the concrete floor. Across the path lies the new crematorium, well built and more efficient, with adjacent "shower baths" and gas chamber, never used. And down the paths are the mass graves and the blood trenches adorned with red flowers leaping out of the lush greenery. A quiet place, a somber place with simple, sculptured figures—"Everyman's Grave" and a slate-gray figure of an emaciated, hollow-eyed man standing in the midst of the flowers. It is simple, serene; it makes its point. But it is not what it was. It seems out of place now on the edge of the modern camp, whose monuments dwarf the simplicity of the lone figures on the mass grave sites.

I am told that one other area remains almost the same—the large acreage inhabited by the SS. Dachau was small as camps go, but next to it the SS allocated an enormous area for their workshops and industrial activity, and almost as large an area for their living quarters—larger than the prisoners' camp. As a huge SS conclave, Dachau required luxurious officer villas with stylish and ostentatious buildings. I have always wanted to scale the fence and see what remained of the captors' camp on the other side. I have heard from survivors that the area held unused factories, attractive administration buildings, and a residential area that resembled a high-class urban neighborhood. But policemen always turned me back, telling me that the Bavarian State Special Police use the facilities as a training school, and therefore it is closed to the public. Perhaps if my desire had been great enough, I would have found a way in, as I have in other such places. Recently one author talked the police into admitting him. He noted that the structures resemble "a large resort hotel," with one exception. Today over the entrance to the largest building "a vast Nazi eagle, the swastika in its talons, spreads its wings, . . .

freshly painted black and white." Later he walked past a concrete arc, adorned with another freshly painted Nazi eagle and swastika. The guard shrugged when questioned and responded that it would be too difficult to remove the insignia.[1]

An adjunct monument has been added at the site of a new set of graves found in the hills a few kilometers from the camp, where the SS buried 6,000 of the overflow in the war's last months. Leitenberg—it too has its monument, a long way up a hill, perhaps a kilometer, lined with the Stations of the Cross. As the hill becomes steeper, the climber begins to identify with those Stations, to wait for them. At the top is a stone domed-sloped chapel with a cross. And the wind blows.

But some things never change. In the early 1960s, Dachau acquaintances over a meal in their home would hesitantly ask: "You don't think we knew, do you?" I would say: "Yes, you knew. You truly knew. Day and night the crematorium spewed its smoke, its ashes, its smell. It is only a few blocks away, and the prevailing winds never missed your town. For years the sky over the camp was gray, the houses adorned with black ash specks. And the smell. Did you ever get used to it? The inmates trudged day after day through your streets, worked in your shops, and died by the roads. Did you ever get used to the expression on their faces? Yes, you, especially you, *truly* knew." And they would redden and bow their heads over their plates. They still ask the question today. But the response no longer brings a lowered head. For the tourist business from the camp is one of the economic mainstays of the town. So the riddle remains:

From Belsen a crate of gold teeth,
from Dachau a mountain of shoes,
from Auschwitz a skin lampshade.
Who killed the Jews?

Not I, cries the typist,
not I, cries the engineer
not I, cries Adolf Eichmann,
not I, cries Albert Speer.

My friend Fritz Nova lost his father—
a petty official had to choose.
My friend Lou Abrahms lost his brother.
Who killed the Jews?

David Nova swallowed gas,
Hyman Abrahms was beaten and starved.
Some men signed their papers,
and some stood guard,

and some herded them in,
and some dropped the pellets,
and some spread the ashes,
and some hosed the walls,

and some planted the wheat,
and some poured the steel,
and some cleared the rails,
and some raised the cattle.

Some smelled the smoke,
some just heard the news.
Were they Germans? Were they Nazis?
Were they human? Who killed the Jews?

The stars will remember the gold,
the sun will remember the shoes,
the moon will remember the skin.
But who killed the Jews?[2]

It was at Dachau—the model camp, Hitler's experimental concentration station, Himmler's staff college for camp officials, the military medical experimentation center—where the Nazis developed the new field of thanatology, the science of producing death.

The town seemed to rise and fall with Hitler. It spanned the life of the Third Reich. Its prison population was possibly as heterogeneous as that found in any camp. It contained people from every segment of society, as well as the odds and ends of humanity, some whom Hitler and his cohorts disliked and feared and some on whom they focused their murderous rage and destruction.

Everything about Dachau was small—its population, its area, the percentage of Jewish prisoners, the crematorium, the number of deaths. It had no usable gas chamber. It was never intended as an extermination center, but rather as a mild camp for those prisoners who could perform only light work. Official documents indicate that of the 225,000 human beings who passed through Dachau, 31,951 died. That figure is undoubtedly inaccurate because of the poor record-keeping system. It is more likely that 50,000 died. But that number is still less than 25 percent, a low figure in major camp death statistics.[3]

Why, then, did Dachau gain such an infamous reputation in the postwar years? The American Army liberated the camp, publicized it, reeled in shock from it. But the publicity only revealed the cesspool it became in the last weeks of the war. It was no longer the so-called mild camp of former years. American troops found 30,000 prisoners, some barely alive, and 8,000 unburied corpses. Dachau's notorious reputation came, then, from its last days and from its rank as the senior member of the system.

Dachau was the first official Nazi camp, and from it evolved a large, ever-developing Concentration System. At Dachau the SS created the models of incarceration, organizational structure, codes and policies, medical experimentation, and officer/guard training that served as the basis for the years of punishment, destruction, and killing that lay ahead for the inferior peoples of Europe.

Dachau lies in a former swamp—damp, moist, and foggy. The unhealthy climate combines with long bitter winters and thick snow. On March 21, 1933, Himmler announced that the first official concentration camp would be opened in the vicinity of Dachau to accommodate 5,000 people. He initiated the action, he said, "undeterred by paltry scruples," convinced that it would help Germany and aid in restoring "calm to our country."[4] Himmler chose for his site the grounds and stone huts of an explosives factory built during World War I. Abandoned in 1919, the buildings had fallen into disrepair. When Hitler seized power, the SS acquired the ground and planned to erect a vast complex of SS barracks, dwellings, and industrial buildings. As a first step, they created a small primitive hut and barbed-wire prison to provide the necessary labor.

In 1937 the prisoners, under SS supervision, began to construct the mammoth SS complex and industrial center that had been planned for so long. The plans also included a new and advanced prison complex, which was completed on August 15, 1938. The new Dachau concentration camp remained essentially unchanged until the end of the war.

The prisoner area was about 290 meters wide and 615 meters long, linked to the SS area by a wide road. Above the main gate stood the inscription: *"Arbeit Macht Frei"* (Work Will Make You Free). As one entered the camp, the huge administration building was on the right. Painted in large letters on the roof was the slogan:

There is one road to freedom.
Its milestones are:
Obedience—diligence—honesty—order—
Cleanliness—temperance—truth—
Sacrifice and love of one's country.[5]

The SS seemed unaware of the bitter irony of the passage or their own lack of the qualities they had so brazenly proclaimed.

Dachau included the normal camp apparatus with bunkers, a roll call square, canteen, library, infirmary, barracks, watchtowers, crematorium, gas chamber, and the museum. The camp proper consisted of thirty-four barracks, called blocks. Before Dachau became overcrowded, the prisoners slept in fifty-two double-tiered bunks per barrack. Actually the accommodations were luxurious from a camp perspective. Each prisoner had a small cupboard and a stool. Each barrack contained a day room with four tables. A large stove stood in the center. At first, a single barrack accommodated only 180 persons. But later, the overcrowding became excruciating, and bunks filled all available space. The camp had been planned for 5,000, but after 1942 the number of prisoners never fell below 12,000. In 1945 over 30,000 prisoners lived in the main camp.[6]

At the north end of Dachau stood the disinfection buildings and an angora rabbit farm. The camp had a unique feature: the Dachau museum, containing plaster images of prisoners marked by bodily defects or other "odd" characteristics. Himmler's officers visited those exhibits. The large SS area included spacious officer villas and SS buildings with everything necessary for training and recreation. In 1943 Himmler ordered the creation of brothels to service the SS men in the camps. Dachau had its own prostitute and brothel service in operation by late 1943.

The builders located the original crematorium in a dingy wooden hut. In 1942 Dachau officials asked the SS Central Construction Office to build an additional crematorium. In a March 17 memo a Dachau authority explained the advantages of the planned site. It lay near the old crematorium on level ground, with access to a sewage system and power lines. He described the design in good engineering terms:

The building is surrounded on nearly all sides by trees and stands therefore relatively isolated in the surrounding country. It is enclosed by an opaque wall about 2 meters high. The building is approached on one side from the concentration camp through a gate in use for the present crematorium, and on the other side by the SS hut camp I. The building will have a celler only large enough to accommodate the heating plant and provide space for the required storage of coal. On the ground floor will be the rooms and installations asked for. The attic will be left unfinished; can, however, be made accessible by a gangway in the center, 80 cm. wide. The foundation consists of ramed concrete. The walls are built up with bricks. The floors to be laid will be, according to their requirements of concrete, tile surface or wood (vide: plan of ground floor). The roof will be supported by cantilever heads resting on joists. Heat insulation by means of glass wool resting on the ceiling boards. The roof will be covered by flat roofing tiles. Ceilings and interior walls will be given a coat of plaster. Room 8 is provided with an intermediary ceiling of reinforced concrete. The outside walls are coated with the Munich rough finish. Low pressure steam heating to be installed for heating purposes, with the plant in the basement of the building. For fire protection, foam extinguishers are provided in sufficient numbers. The water supply, drainage, and lighting will be effected by tapping the established water and sewage, likewise the main power line.

In a July 30, 1942 memo, the chief of the Central Construction Office finally approved the building: "The construction application has been examined from the point of view of construction, special technical requirements, and construction finance. Due attention is to be paid to all observations made by the examiners."[7]

The prisoners constructed the new brick structure, complete with modern ovens. To shield the crematorium workers from excessive heat, they fixed double sets of doors to the ovens. They also lowered the height of the door openings to ease the exhausting job of pushing in the bodies. Cremation was slow, taking about two hours. The prevailing wind came from the west, and consequently the smell of burning corpses filled the camp. From the color of the smoke, a camp inmate observed, it was possible to determine the length of time a victim had been in Dachau. Newly arrived prisoners, who still possessed a normal quantity of flesh and fat, produced a yellow smoke when cremated. Old-timers, who were merely skin and bones, gave off a thin green smoke.[8] During the last months the crematorium could no longer handle the number of dead despite the round-the-clock schedule. Therefore the authorities buried thousands of dead in communal graves at the Leitenberg.

While building the new crematorium, the central administration for concentration camps decided to install a gas chamber next to it. They began construction in 1942, but because of sabotage, did not complete the chamber until 1945. It was never used for killing. An attempt was made to disinfect typhus clothing in it, but to no avail. The SS took the prisoners to Hartheim in Austria for gassing.[9]

From the beginning, Himmler intended Dachau to serve as the model for camp discipline and for general regulations governing the division of duties, guard personnel, and prisoner behavior. Theodor Eicke, an ex-police officer, became Dachau's second commandant in June 1933. Adolf Eichmann served on his staff. Eicke's innovations centered on disciplinary and training camp regulations, particularly the punishment and discipline of prisoners. From Eicke came the principle "that prisoners should be treated with the maximum, though impersonal and disciplined, severity and should be shown no lenience." Eicke also created the concept of the "dangerous enemies of the state." He standardized the treatment and supervision of prisoners, and his regulations laid down the precise procedure for every activity. The general regulations drawn up in Dachau in 1933 served as the model for all subsequent camps.[10]

Himmler established a volunteer force of SS men willing to undertake long-term service as camp guards and Eicke formed those lackadaisical guards into a force to be reckoned with. He inspired his personnel with virulent hatred for enemies of the state. Insisting that feelings of pity for inmates were unworthy of any SS man, he declared that no weaklings would be tolerated. If any were present, they should race to the nearest monastery and lock themselves in—permanently. Many SS men who gained notoriety as commandants of infamous camps received their initial training and challenge at Dachau. Rudolf Höss, commandant of Auschwitz, began his career at Dachau. Dachau was indeed the "staff college" for the concentration system. Himmler rewarded the man who put it all together by appointing Eicke to the powerful new position of inspector of concentration camps in 1934.[11]

In 1942 Martin Weiss became commandant of Dachau. Previously commandant of Neuengamme, Weiss remains a man of controversy. The Allies executed him after his war crime trial, and some Dachau survivors maintain bitterly that he should have been allowed to live because of his humane camp administration. In 1943 Himmler appointed Weiss commandant of Majdanek. Majdanek survivors have never indicated that his life should have been spared!

Approximately 225,000 prisoners passed through Dachau between 1933 and 1945. Himmler originally intended Dachau to serve as the regime's permanent punishment center for recalcitrant Germans. There he would send German political dissidents and German Jews. Until late 1938 the overwhelming majority of the 6,000 inmates were politicals. But the camp composition gradually changed to include all types of "enemies of the state." When Hitler began moving into other countries, Dachau's population exploded and in came groups of criminals, racials (Jews and Gypsies), foreigners, antisocials, Jehovah's Witnesses, homosexuals, emigrés, *Wehrmacht* members, and many privileged prisoners. The Jewish group was never as large as at most other camps. The privileged prisoners or prominents, as they were known, included names familiar throughout the world. Bruno Bettelheim, the famous American child psychiatrist, spent time there before the war. Pastor Martin Niemöller, Kurt von Schuschnigg, the former Austrian chancellor, two prime ministers—Miklos Kallay of Hungary and Léon Blum of France—Churchill's nephew, and Dr. Hjalmar Schacht, the man who worked Hitler's economic miracle, are but a few of the famous who lived in Dachau.[12]

In 1941, when Himmler classified the camps, Dachau fell into the category of Grade I-A for prisoners who stood particularly in need of consideration—older persons or those almost unable to work, such as prominent political prisoners, and members of the clergy. It was, in fact, an easy camp, as camps go. Dachau inmates were given longer periods of relaxation than inmates at other camps. The SS allowed recreation and sports such as football. They also arranged theatrical entertainment, concerts, films, lectures—and, of course, they had a pool of talent from which to draw. The camp library was well stocked. And Dachau did not even have its own operational gas chamber.

Unlike at some camps, Dachau inmates could receive packages and mail, and send letters. But the rules were stiff:

Concentration Camp Dachau 3K

The following regulations are to be observed when writing to prisoners:

1. Each prisoner may receive two letters or cards per month from relatives and send two letters or cards to relatives. The letters sent to prisoners must be legible and written with ink and there may be only 15 lines per side. Only letter paper of normal size is permitted. Envelopes must be unsealed. Only 5 12 pfennig stamps may be included with each letter. Everything else is forbidden and is subject to seizure. Postcards can have 10 lines. Photographs may not be used as postcards.

2. Money sent by money order is permitted, but must include the exact last and first name of the prisoner, his birthdate and prison number.

3. Newspapers are permitted, but must be ordered through the Dachau Concentration Camp post office.

4. Packages may be sent through the mail, as long as they remain few in number.

5. Release requests from "protective custody" to the camp management are useless.

6. The opportunity to speak with or visit prisoners is absolutely forbidden.

All mail will be destroyed, which does not meet these regulations.

Camp Commandant[13]

The Nazi categorization of Dachau as a mild camp, the absence of full-scale extermination machinery, and the granting of random privileged moments were insufficient to disguise to the prisoners the enormity of the horror in which they were living. For them, it was a purgatory to be endured forever, in which they faced constant punishment, exhausting labor, starvation, and medical experimentation.

Brutal punishment was a daily occurrence. Commandant Eicke in his first regulations for Dachau defined the punishment of the prisoners in detail:

Any person who at work, in quarters, kitchens, workshops, toilets or rest places carries on politics for subversive ends, makes provocative remarks, associates with anyone else to this end, forms cliques or loiters with intent, collects, receives, passes, recounts to foreign visitors or transmits to others secretly out of the camp or by any other means lies, false or true news for adverse propaganda about atrocities in the concentration camp or its buildings, hands them on in writing or by word or mouth to released or transferred prisoners, hidden in clothes or other articles, throws them by means of stones, etc. over the camp wall or writes coded messages; in addition, any person who for subversive reasons climbs on to the huts, roofs, or trees, makes signals by lamp or otherwise or tries to make contact with the outside or incites others to escape or to commit a crime, gives advice on this or supports them by any other means, will be hanged.[14]

Included in the hanging list were inmates who attacked a sentry or an SS member, who refused to obey a command or to work, who incited or induced others to commit such acts, who complained or shouted. Anyone who caused a fire or tampered with any buildings or wires in the camp faced hanging for sabotage. The camp administration added humiliation and degradation to the physical brutality. For example, when new Jewish arrivals entered Dachau, the SS clerks asked a favorite question: "Which Jew-whore shit you out?" And the guards mocked the prisoner work group removing sewage from the open latrines by labeling them "Squad 4–7–11" after a popular perfume.[15]

All prisoners worked in compulsory labor teams. Major work assignments included rolling the streets and working in the gardens or plantation, the gravel pits, the Moor-express, and on the snow *Kommando*. The authorities laid out gardens inside and outside the camp. One huge area under cultivation, approximately 460 meters square, was labeled a "plantation" for growing medicinal plants and spices. It had been salvaged from the marshy land surrounding Dachau. On the plantation the prisoners built hothouses, shops, laboratories, and workshops.

The inmates considered the gravel pit the worst assignment, but the snow *Kommando* ran a close second. Winter was severe at Dachau, and the SS demanded that all snow within the camp be removed promptly. From 1940 to 1942 the 1,000 priests of the snow *Kommando* used shovels and boards nailed to wooden planks to pile the snow, which they dragged to the nearby river. If the snow was too much for the carts, the priests shoveled it onto large tables, which four men carried on their shoulders. Another unenviable work assignment was the so-called Moor-express—heavy four-wheel wagons pulled by prisoners. The SS harnessed the prisoners to the wagons, and four to six additional prisoners pushed the heavy wagon from behind, always at a gallop. For eight hours a day the human beasts of burden pulled and shoved the Moor-express transporting all the camp material.

The SS organized their own industries, workshops, and businesses at Dachau. Originally intended as the service sector to the camp, the workshops blossomed into a full-scale profit-making conglomerate for the enrichment of the SS. No business was too specialized for prisoner labor. The inmates produced bicycle parts, baked goods, religious objects, porcelain, electrical components, clothing, and furniture.[16]

As the war continued, the prisoners were hired out in groups to armament manufacturers and housed near the factories. They lived in conditions far worse than those that prevailed at the mother camp. By the end of the war

Dachau had about 165 outside *Kommandos*. In most *Kommandos* the working conditions were hard and dangerous, and the building of underground factories in the last months of the war claimed many victims. The *Kommandos* worked in factories, aeronautical concerns, food production, machinery shops, the metal industry, railway construction, armament, and aviation construction. One *Kommando* built a ski hut! The vast *Kommando* web spread out across southern Germany, and the ragged, starving creatures marched and labored in full view of the civilian population. Their presence in the center of the German working world obliterates any rational acceptance of the claim that the Germans did not know of the camps or of the inhuman conditions.[17]

Dachau was the birthplace of the macabre science of Thanatology. SS, military, and civilian doctors and professors performed deadly medical experiments on live bodies throughout the system. The participants ranged in skill from world-renowned scientists to political hacks. The death rate from the experiments was as high as 100 percent; the average was 33 percent. Almost every survivor of any experiment experienced permanent damage of one kind or another. The scientific problems examined ranged from a few questions of major significance coupled with a respectable research design, to a majority of simplistic questions tied to pseudoscientific research design, to many projects that were simply hobbies, curiosities, or fantasies such as skull collections disguised only elementarily under the research rubric. In no case did the victims give their consent.

The vast majority of projects were senseless, clumsy, of no value to medicine as a healing art, and often based upon superstitions and preposterous notions of superior and inferior races. Cruelty to the latter earned accolades. The researchers termed their projects medical experimentation. The Nuremburg judges called them murder. Although in a few instances the object was to determine, however stupidly, how to rescue or to cure, in most the object was simply to discover how to harm, how to sterilize, how to maim, *how to kill*.

Arthur Guett, the Nazi director of public health, wrote in 1933 that the ill-conceived "love thy neighbor" medical principle must disappear, particularly with reference to inferior peoples. It was the state's highest duty to preserve life and livelihood only for the healthy and hereditarily sound. His pronouncement became the basis for public health policy and medical ethics throughout the Third Reich. The consequent astonishing degradation of German medical ethics resulted in inefficient, unsystematic, and unscientific research projects that used the vast armies of disenfranchised slaves. As Nazi superstition spread throughout the profession, it dulled the mind as well as the morals—resulting not only in hideous crimes but ghastly scientific failures as well.

Dachau's story is the worst of its kind for several reasons. Dachau was the beginning. It served as the model, the example, the catalyst, for the camps that followed, and in time its projects became records that others tried to emulate and surpass. The researchers who began at Dachau went on to bigger and better experiments at other camps. It was at Dachau that the German Army and the German Air Force encouraged, funded, supported, participated in, and even pleaded for medical experimentation, supposedly to help their military doctors save soldiers' lives. It was at Dachau that the first timid requests for a prisoner or two, in order to move ahead with a project, received enthusiastic approval from Himmler. And it was at Dachau that those hesitant requests quickly turned into a torrent of demands for thousands of live bodies, with no attempt made to disguise the probable fatal outcome. Finally, it was at Dachau that distinguished scientists first openly discarded universal medical ethics and publicized their findings in such a way that medical personnel of all persuasions were able to adopt a new standard of medical dehumanization. Dachau opened a Pandora's box. Thanatology became acceptable and applaudable, even for famous scientists.

SS doctors under the leadership of a fanatical Nazi, Dr. Sigmund Rascher, conducted extensive medical experiments at Dachau. They investigated the impact of intense air pressure and cold on human beings, conducted seawater and malaria tests, studied the effects of new drugs, and tested allopathic and homeopathic drugs. Their projects included the usual Nazi experiments such as castration, artificial insemination, sterilization, and abortion. Dachau probably had the finest hospital installation in the system. Under normal conditions, a specialist could have treated most diseases efficiently and skillfully if he had wished. The doctors performed operations in two well-equipped theaters supported by an excellent laboratory, electrocardiographs, and X-ray apparatus. The medical unit was also equipped for dental surgery. With some additions, the facilities proved more than adequate for medical research.

High-Altitude and Freezing Experiments

From March to August 1942 Dr. Rascher, a captain in the German Air Force medical corps and an SS officer, conducted experiments to investigate the limits of human endurance at extremely high altitudes for the benefit of the German Air Force. The experiments utilized low-pressure chambers. Dr. Rascher conceived of the research project in spring of 1941 and wrote Himmler to request the use of professional criminals as subjects. Prior experiments with monkeys had failed. Himmler agreed and Rascher designed his tests. The air force supplied a decompression chamber. By pumping air out of it, oxygen and air pressure at high altitudes could be simulated.[18]

A subject involved in the experiment would begin to perspire and twist his body. Then he went into convulsions and lapsed into unconsciousness. An inmate testified that he observed through the chamber window a subject standing inside until his lungs ruptured. Prisoners in the chamber "would go mad, and pull out their hair in an effort to relieve the pressure. They would tear their heads and face with their fingers and nails in an attempt to maim themselves in their madness. They would beat the walls with their hands and head, and scream in an effort to relieve pressure on their eardrums." When that experiment was completed, top officers of the *Luftwaffe* conveyed Göring's thanks to Dr. Rascher for his pioneer efforts.[19]

Dr. Hippke, chief of the Medical Section of the *Luftwaffe,* wrote to Himmler, in "the name of German research on aviation medicine and research," to thank him for his help and interest. He found encouraging the "conclusion" that "an atmosphere with so little oxygen can be endured at all for some time." But, Hippke pointed out, no practical conclusions could be drawn, for the vital element of extreme cold had not been included. "The results in actual practice will very likely prove to be far more unfavorable than in the present experiments."[20]

From August 1942 to May 1943 Dr. Rascher, with distinguished help, examined the *Luftwaffe's* companion problem: treating severely chilled or frozen soldiers. Dr. Rascher's freezing experiments were designed to investigate two areas: first, to see how much cold a human being could stand before he died; and second, to find the best way to warm up someone who has nearly frozen to death. To freeze the subjects, Dr. Rascher used two elementary methods: he placed the subjects in a tank of ice water, or he threw the men, naked, out into the snow for the night. After holding the subjects in a water tank until they became unconscious, doctors took their temperatures and analyzed their blood as their bodies chilled. Most victims died at about 25° C. below zero. Of the 300 subjects used, 90 died.

The researchers publicized their results in German medical circles. At a 1942 medical conference entitled Medical Problems Arising from Hardships of Sea and Winter, one doctor presented a report, "Prevention and Treatment of Freezing," and another spoke on "Warming up after Freezing to the Danger Point." Ninety-five German scientists, including some who were internationally known, participated in the conference, even though the researchers left no doubt that the experiments had been conducted on human beings.[21]

Dr. Rascher invented a new kind of experiment called dry freezing. He asked for the opportunity to use Auschwitz instead of Dachau because it was colder there, but his request was denied so he continued at Dachau, praying for weather cold enough to provide effective test conditions. For dry freezing, the doctors placed a naked prisoner on a stretcher and laid him outside on the ground. They covered him with a sheet and every hour threw cold water on him, taking his temperature repeatedly. The doctors then decided that the subject should not be covered with a sheet but be left nude. The cries of those freezing men rang throughout the camp. Initially Dr. Rascher refused to allow anesthesia during the tests, but later he relented because the victims disturbed the entire camp with their screaming. If a subject survived, he was left to die on the ground or in the tents.[22]

The good doctor designed a second process to discover the best methods of thawing and rewarming German pilots. How can a frozen man, he wondered, be warmed in such a way as to save his life? Himmler asked Rascher to consider warming bodies by animal heat. At first Rascher refused and unsuccessfully tried sunlamps, hot-water bottles, and electrotherapy. He then pondered Himmler's suggestion, but decided on an innovation: the "animal warmth" would come from women, marking a new use for prostitutes. He chilled the subject in the familiar way and then placed him between two naked women on a wide bed. The experimentors instructed the women to nestle up to the chilled man and then they covered the three with blankets. Dr. Rascher found that rewarming a frozen man was accomplished faster by one woman than by two. He had difficulty accounting for that phenomenon.[23]

In Dr. Rascher's final report, "On Cooling Experiments on Human Beings," he concluded that a hot bath was the best method of treatment for a frozen aviator. Since rescue aircraft could not carry bathtubs, however, he proposed, with a flourish, that aviator suits be designed with neck protectors, that aviators wear warm waterproof boots, that something be done to rewarm a body that had floated around in icy water, that medicine be given a rescued flier, and that no medicine be given to the dead. For those startling results, 100 prisoners died.[24]

Malaria Experiments

A team of doctors at Dachau investigated immunization for malaria. They infected healthy prisoners, using mosquitoes or injections of mosquito extract. After the subjects contracted malaria, the doctors treated them with experimental drugs. Many of the 1,200 subjects died and others suffered severe pain and permanent disability. The research team leader, Dr. Klaus Schilling, was a specialist in tropical diseases who had achieved renown as a professor of parasitology at Berlin University and had secured extensive research support with the financial backing of the Rockefeller Foundation. At the postwar Doctors' Trial Dr. Schilling, by then a seventy-four-year-old man, admitted that the subjects on whom he had worked were not volunteers. He maintained, however, that his only goal had been to improve the health of mankind and he regretted not being able to finish his research.[25]

Seawater Experiments

For three months in 1944, at the request of the air force and navy, Dachau doctors studied various methods of making seawater drinkable. They divided their subjects into four groups. One group received no water; the second got ordinary seawater; the third received seawater processed by the Berka method, which concealed the taste but did not alter the saline content; and the fourth group was given seawater with the salt removed by the Schaeffer method. After experimenting with animals to no avail, Dr. Schroeder, chief of the Air Force Medical Service, asked Himmler for permission to use forty prisoners for a month of tests. He stressed the "enormous importance which a solution of this problem has for shipwrecked men of the *Luftwaffe* and navy." With Himmler's support, Schroeder went ahead. Although the Schaeffer method had been chemically tested successfully, it required substantial amounts of scarce silver supplies, to which the Technical Office of the *Luftwaffe* objected. Thus the air force needed an alternative method. The Berka method had the advantage of simplicity of manufacture and use—if it worked. An afternoon in a laboratory with a piece of jelly, a semipermeable membrane, and a salt solution would have given the air force its answer. Instead, Schroeder caused great pain, suffering, and injury to a large pool of victims.[26]

Several participating Dachau doctors were tried after the war, convicted, and hanged. But the Allies did not have to deal with the ingenious Dr. Rascher. The SS arrested that captivating and creative man and his wife in May 1944 on the charge that their children were not their own, but stolen! Some years before, it appeared that Dr. Rascher's fiancee could not bear children. Therefore Himmler forbade his SS doctor to marry her. But after the woman supposedly produced her second child, Himmler authorized the marriage. Years later evidence came to Himmler's attention that Mrs. Rascher was indeed barren and that the two children had been kidnapped. True or not, the SS hanged Mrs. Rascher at Ravensbrück and shot her husband in the bunker at Dachau.[27]

In 1975 a furor erupted in the United States over the Immigration Service's laxness in investigating suspected war criminals living in the United States. Congresswoman Elizabeth Holtzman challenged a famous scientist, Dr. Hubertus Strughold, credited as the U.S. father of space medicine. In describing his war activities in Germany, Strughold insisted that he had served as director of the Aeromedical Research Institute in Berlin, supposedly a civilian agency. His associate at the Institute was one of three scientists charged at Nuremberg with participation in the experiments. However, the three were cleared, although under "grave suspicion of guilt." Dr. Strughold maintained that he did not learn about the Dachau experiments until after the war. He spent several months as a POW before the Americans placed him at the University of Heidelberg as a professor of physiology and director of the Physiological Institute, assigned to study German wartime aviation medicines.

In 1947 he joined the staff of the U.S. Air Force School of Aviation Medicine at Randolph Air Force Base in Texas, and was named to head the school's Department of Space Medicine upon its formation in 1949.

In 1951 the Air University, which encompasses under its control all educational functions of the U.S. Air Force, conferred on Strughold the academic title professor of aviation medicine, and in 1958, the title professor of space medicine. He is the only person ever to be so honored.

Strughold worked with low-pressure chambers and other space capsule simulators which led the way to American-manned space flights.

In 1959 the school was relocated to Brooks Air Force Base, where he was assigned the additional duty as chairman of the Advanced Studies Group at the Aerospace Medical Division. In 1962 he became chief scientist when the Air Force Systems Command organized the Aerospace Medical Division. He retired in 1968.[28]

The allegations held that Dr. Strughold had been involved in the air force experiments at Dachau. Research by *Jewish Currents* produced the following:

U.S. Army translation of a top-secret Nazi transcript, placing Dr. Strughold at a 1942 scientific conference at which concentration camp experiments were discussed.

The Nazi document which proves Strughold's complicity in what the American prosecution described as "atrocities committed in the name of medical science," is Nuremberg Document, 401, October 1, 1946.

The document lists 13 scientists, including Dr. Strughold, as "persons, firms or organizations implicated" in the conference held at Nuremberg on October 26 and 27, 1942.

Strughold lectured on the high-altitude, freezing and sea-water problems that were tested for the benefit of the Nazi Luftwaffe (air force) on human beings at Dachau. Photographs and films made of the Dachau experiments were used at the conference, where the exact nature of the tests was "clearly revealed," causing a sensation among the participants, according to the Nazi documents.[29]

Dachau had the largest group of clergy inmates of any camp in the concentration system. In 1940 Himmler detailed Dachau to receive all clergy, including those scattered throughout the different camps. "During the next years Dachau was to be the meeting place for thousands of clergy of different creeds, occupying every position in the ecclesiastical hierarchy." That decision represented a diplomatic success for the Christian churches, but it deprived other camps of the spiritual help that so many prisoners needed. In all, 2,771 clergymen spent time at Dachau, and among them 2,580 Catholic priests; 700 died in the camp and 300 died in the death trains. The clergy group included 1,780 Poles, but only 445 Germans.[30]

During Hitler's time several courageous clergymen challenged the activities of the Nazis. Those men were the ones incarcerated in Dachau. The Vatican put pressure on Berlin to allow the Catholic priests there to build a chapel, to live communally, and to have lighter labor loads. The Berlin establishment agreed and in January 1941 the chapel was ready. In March 1941 the SS withdrew the clergy from work *Kommandos*. Conditions immediately improved. Clergy arose an hour later than the other prisoners and were allotted time for study and meditation. They received newspapers, library privileges, and adequate food. In October 1941, 500 Polish clergymen arrived in Dachau. The guards put them in separate barracks from the German clergy and treated them more harshly. The German clergy accepted the clear distinction made by the SS between Germans and Poles and did not resist the SS policy of restricting the chapel to German clergy.

A great plague, as the survivors described it, spread over Dachau in the last months when frantic mass transports streamed in from the Balkans and from evacuated concentration camps. It was those last months of overcrowding, of disease brought by prisoners from other camps, and of decreased availability of food that caused the horrifying conditions described by the liberation teams. Dachau in 1945 was quite different from what it had been six months earlier. Overnight, masses of starving men jammed into the barracks, bringing with them millions of lice and fleas. They threw up makeshift huts and tents in the pathways between the barracks. Bodies piled up on the ground as the small crematorium strained to keep up with the torrent of diseased corpses. Dachau had been a neat, orderly place. But in the last months the older inmates were heard to mutter that it looked like a "gypsy encampment." All services broke down. Men lay in their bunks, relieving themselves on those below. One survivor recalls lying ill from typhus. Believing him dead, the SS threw him on a heap of corpses. Using all his willpower, he crawled out of the corpse heap and back to his bunk. A Jew on the Dachau burial squad spoke of the mounting piles of bodies in the last days when anyone exhausted or sick was thrown directly into the ovens: "This was the system at Dachau: bury the dead and burn the sick."[31]

On Sunday afternoon, April 29, 1945, the U.S. Seventh Army overran Dachau, but not in time to prevent the SS evacuation of carloads of prisoners, who were sent deeper into southeastern Germany. Most of them died. The Americans had intended to bypass the camp, but a small advance party of soldiers, quite by accident, stumbled onto the railroad yard and saw the large number of dead bodies in the boxcars. Reeling with horror, they moved quickly into Dachau. Meeting little resistance, the team declared the camp liberated.

The last days of Dachau are a continuing source of controversy. It seems that two different army divisions claimed to have liberated the camp. One writer recently uncovered the story that a squad of liberating Americans, filled with rage and horror, machine-gunned to death 122 SS guards who had surrendered. More puzzling is the chasm between Himmler's extermination plans for the remaining prisoners and the rather quiet liberation of the entire camp. A few reports suggest that the SS conceived a plan to pack prisoners from other camps into Dachau and then to bomb it from the air, and that this act was prevented only by the swift movement of events.[32]

Much stronger evidence indicates that Himmler issued two types of directives for the extermination of the prisoners. Initially, Himmler and Kaltenbrunner ordered that the entire population be evacuated and sent on a death march to the Tyrol. The SS sent out the first group, the 137 prominents, on April 27. Contrary to plan, they survived. When the SS attempted to evacuate the remaining 30,000, they found themselves thwarted by the International Committee—the de facto prisoner government. That secret group knew of the SS intent and managed to halt the evacuation with its stalling tactics.

After failing in his first attempt, Himmler sent a new directive: "Not one prisoner is to fall into American hands. Exterminate every one." It was to be, as the code name said, a *Wolkenbrand,* a Firecloud. But the order came too late. Liquidation became either "impractical or inopportune," made impossible by "lack of means," "lack of time," and effective prisoner counter-measures. Many SS leaders were "no longer disposed" to stick their necks out now that Germany had obviously lost the war. It is known that Munich laboratories sent a large quantity of poison to Dachau on April 29—enough to kill in one lunchtime the entire camp. But it never arrived. The Americans appeared instead.[33]

Herbert Schowalter, a prestigious newsman, reached Dachau with the first backup teams. "Broad-winged vultures circled relentlessly above the long, low building of red brick. No smoke came from the ominous chimney, but when sudden gusts of the early spring winds reached down low to greet us, one could hardly bear the putrid, sweet-sickening odor." As a member of an ordnance squad, Schowalter had the responsibility of searching for usable war equipment left behind by the SS. His team had seen piles of unburied bodies on the battlefield, but Dachau "proved the most spine-chilling experience of all." As the Belgian guards opened the iron doors of the ovens, they saw charred leg, arm, pelvic, and skull bones lying among the corpses. The stench overpowered them. And then, behind another strongly bolted door into Dachau's morgue, they found corpses of skin and bones, looking like "discolored, dried-out, wooden fagots found on the sand of an ocean shore. These neatly arranged rows of the dead on the cement floor of this 'cooler room' represented the much touted efficiency of the Nazi mind." Schowalter and his colleagues explored the railroad track where the last evacuation train stood. It had arrived only a few hours before the troops. White lime covered the entire train. In every car naked corpses lay two or three deep in their own excreta. All were dead.[34]

The Dachau War Crimes Trial took place on the site of the crimes. Forty-two men stood accused, among them Commandant Weiss and the civilian Dr. Schilling. On December 14, 1945, the court sentenced thirty-six of the men to hang. Camp officials had seldom anticipated the need to account for their actions after the war. At the trial they denied their crimes and claimed that as loyal soldiers they had followed the orders of their superiors. They blamed all crimes on their dead colleagues. If certain excesses occurred, they were isolated incidents unknown to the officers. And, too, the visitors to the camps, whether they were high-ranking army officers or Red Cross delegations, had always reported that everything was in order. If the camps deteriorated in the last few months of the war, it was because of the Allied invasion. If trains bringing transports to Dachau arrived with everyone dead, it was because the Allies had bombed the tracks. If typhus-diseased bodies accumulated, it was because of lack of drugs. The accused claimed, essentially, that events and not men had produced those tragedies.

Immediately after the war the Americans used Dachau for the imprisonment of Nazis and SS men. The organization of former prisoners, the Comité International de Dachau, resolved to make the site something more than an army installation, to free it of its carnival atmosphere, to create a reverent place. The survivors centered their initial energies on the erection of appropriate memorials. The Dachau monuments today stand as a result of those efforts.

The most important monument was the first one, designed by the Comité International, as a stone chapel in the form of a tower. When the completed Monument of Atonement was dedicated in 1960 to the Agony of Christ, 50,000 people crowded into the main street behind the camp barracks. Three thousand Catholic young men walked from a tent city near Munich to Dachau, a distance of over 15 kilometers, carrying a heavy old cross on their shoulders. First came the youth with the ancient cross, followed by a hundred priests wearing white robes, priests who as inmates had marched on the camp street in striped uniforms. A hundred bishops and six cardinals followed. Former prisoner Archbishop Adam Kozlowiecki celebrated the pontifical mass. The congregants prayed for the sad happenings of the twelve years of the Third Reich, and then joined in a special atonement for the particularly bitter persecution of the Jews, and the hatred shown to other races:

Map 2: Dachau, 1945

Map revision by Sharon Coughran. Created from material in Barbara Distel Concentration Camp Dachau *Karl M. Lipp Publishers.*

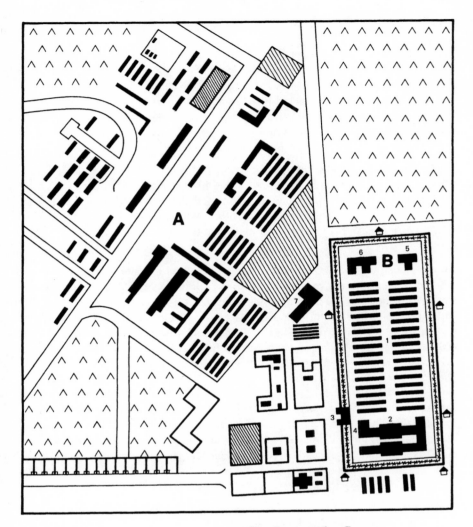

∧ ∧ ∧	Trees	**B** **Concentration Camp**
	Ditch with live barbed wire fence and camp wall	1. Barracks
		2. Parade Ground for Roll Call
		3. Entrance to Camp, and Guard Room
	Watch Tower	4. Kitchen, Laundry, Showers
A	The SS camp	5. Disinfection Hut
		6. Vegetable Garden
		7. Crematorium

Lord Jesus Christ, off-spring of David's house, deliver our people from all enmity against the Jews. Atone for the murder of many millions of the people of Abraham, the destruction of so many synagogues. Put an end to the hatred between the Arabs and the Jews. Put an end to the hatred between the Boers and the natives, between the Frenchmen and the Algerians, between the Whites and the Negroes in North America, etc. Deliver the White Race from presumption and arrogance.[35]

The former chancellor of Austria and president of the Austrian National Council reported on his imprisonment and ill-treatment. Following survivor testimonies on camp conditions, a bishop led the crowd in prayer with the admonition, "a man cannot hate his brother without being a murderer." The Bishop of Essen in his sermon grappled with the symbol of Dachau:

By completing the consecration that already existed on this site through the blood innocently shed with a consecration based upon the shedding of Christ's Blood, we try, as Christians, to face the horror hovering over this place and over all places for which Dachau—then and now—is a symbol and an example. As Christians we try to find an answer to this horror and to change this place where demons were allowed to rage into a place of blessing, supported by the belief in Him Who broke the power of the demons. . . . As we make our way through history, it is more difficult to face up to Dachau than to follow the detours which a bad conscience offers us. Dachau lies before us like an open catalogue of Nihilism. Here the craze for destruction became part of a system of the perfect machinery. Here a collective sadism was let loose and spat into the face of men, beat and kicked them without inhibitions. Here inhumanity became the law of man. It is fatal to fall into the hands of man. . . . Man was nothing more than material, a matter which could be used for the production of soap—this is a diabolic expression of soullessness.

The bishop asserted that the executioners and those in power were not the only ones responsible for Dachau. Everyone shared in the sins, showing clearly "as though through a burning lens what exactly man is and of what evil he is capable." The bishop acknowledged "the extreme gravity of guilt" for all Germans, who must accept the responsibility for the misery in Dachau of human beings from thirty-seven nations. "We have not only to ask God's pardon," he commanded, "but also that of our fellowmen."[36]

As the service ended, gazing on that stark crown of thorns, the 50,000 sang "Oh Sacred Head Now Wounded."

SACHSENHAUSEN/ORANIENBURG: THE SEMICIRCLE OF BRUTALITY

The Nazis built concentration camp Sachsenhausen in the town of Oranienburg, 30 kilometers north of Berlin. Unlike many other centers, which remained isolated and secret, Sachsenhausen was a public camp. The prisoners disembarked at the central railway station and marched the 3 kilometers from the station to the camp through residential, business, and factory districts. Civilian industries in Oranienburg made heavy use of the Sachsenhausen labor groups.

Several important camp sections remain, and the East German government has taken special efforts to restore and beautify the grounds. During the war one of Germany's most important Gestapo centers lay opposite the main entrance of the camp. There, officers trained various Gestapo and SS reserve units. That complex remains, with its barracks, clubhouse, theater, administrative building, and living quarters. Now, the former Gestapo center houses an army regiment that controls Sachsenhausen. Its soldiers guard the camp; and prisoners, under the supervision of young lieutenants, tend the flowers, rebuild buildings, and perform the manual labor necessary in such a large monument camp.

The entrance to Sachsenhausen is through a wooden structure. Inner walls ring the camp, and at intervals of 180 meters stand the small two-story sentry boxes, equipped during the war with movable machine guns and searchlights. The unique feature of the Sachsenhausen camp is its layout—it was constructed in the form of a huge semi-circle. When one steps into the camp, the first impression is of a semicircle of enormous size with the outside edge enclosed by an arched stone wall: "so large that the twenty thousand odd men who three times a day marched into it for roll call were almost lost in it."[1]

The museum officials have preserved an isolated structure near the roll call area, a barrack labeled *Pathologie*. Here was the usual vivisection, dissection, and medical experimentation hospital, complete with all the usual utensils and the draining ditches—necessary when blood flows freely. It has an unusual element, however, one not found in the other camps—a special storeroom for corpses. Underneath the barrack lie huge tiled vaults with

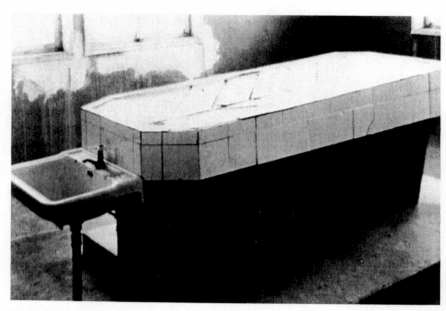

"Pathologie," Sachsenhausen. Typical dissection and medical experimentation room, with tilted table and blood draining slots.

room for 5,000 corpses. When the vaults were not in use as an overflow morgue, bodies were stored there for the dissection and head-shrinking projects performed in the building above. A concrete ramp slopes down into the vaults. The concrete is riddled like rollers so that the corpses would slide more easily down it. During one period of increasing camp population the coffin factories could not turn out the boxes quickly enough, so the corpses were brought to the *Pathologie,* slid down the concrete ramp, and stacked in the storeroom vaults. Until at least 1940 Sachsenhausen had no crematorium; it solved that problem by hiring a large city cremation company to send its garbage trucks to the camp to collect the bodies daily.

After walking across the large semicircle roll call area to reach the curved stone wall on the other side, one finds another unusual facet of Sachsenhausen: a curved shoe-testing area lines the semicircle. Local shoe manufacturers wanted their merchandise tested on a variety of surfaces, and the camp officials readily agreed. A research institute built a track with nine types of street surfaces. Each day guards forced prisoners to wear new shoes and march about 40 kilometers over a track of cement, cinders, broken stones, gravel, and sand. In 1944 officials devised a special torture: they made prisoners walk in shoes one or two sizes too small while carrying sacks filled with 20 kilograms of sand.

Originally eighty-six barracks stood in a fan shape in the semicircle. A few barracks next to the entrance have been preserved as models. Each barrack is divided into five sections. In the middle is the washroom and toilet room. Each section is divided into a day room furnished with tables, benches, and cupboards, and a sleeping room. Most concentration camps did not allow such luxuries. Even when these barracks were overcrowded, they were better than the horse stables used to house prisoners at Auschwitz. Prisoners, however, described barrack life as a "torture." In the original barracks, although already overfilled with 146 prisoners, the guards crammed an additional 300 to 500 people after 1940.

The actual camp area lay on the other side of the stone wall. It stretched for blocks, again in a larger semicircle, with row upon row of barracks arranged in a fan shape. On one side stood the industrial area and the camp workshops. They are still used today by the army and by the city of Oranienburg.

On the far side of the camp stood the *Gaertnerei* with its hothouses, flowers, and vegetables. That area also contained the commandant's prize delight, a large hog-breeding farm, which was a focus for guests and visitors. Sachsenhausen was famous in camp circles for its commandant's horticultural achievements and its phenomenal hog production. Officials sent hams throughout Germany bearing the proud Sachsenhausen stamp.

One notices flowers everywhere—of every color and variety. The prisoners saw these flowers too when they first arrived at the camp and were astonished. As one prisoner remembers:

Through many sleepless nights I had been haunted by the tragic contrast between the beautiful beds of flowers and the crime-soaked atmosphere of the camp. Often when I reflected on the loving care which the Gestapo butchers lavished on these flower beds, I thought I would lose my mind. In this place where the most cold-blooded murderers studied and practiced the murder of human beings, flowers were cherished and kept alive with the greatest affection. Numerous prisoners had been bestially murdered between these lovingly tended borders, and the flowers planted with their own hands had been watered with their own blood. Truly the German soul is a phenomenon difficult to understand.[2]

Where the SS garage formerly stood, the government has built the impressive Museum of the Anti-Fascist Struggle for Freedom by the Peoples of Europe. National exhibitions by Austria, Belgium, Bulgaria, Czechoslovakia, Denmark, France, Germany, Greece, Holland, Hungary, Italy, Norway, Poland, Rumania, Russia, Spain, and Yugoslavia tell of the underground resistance, the suffering, the struggle. Several of East Germany's

finest artists have designed extraordinarily striking murals and pieces of white sculpture.

The museum's main work is Walter Womacka's three-part stained-glass window, "International Resistance," in the entrance hall. The windows are 4.50 meters high. In the center of each window Womacka positioned a symbolic main group with side scenes. The middle window group—a Soviet soldier with a child on his arm, a liberated inmate, and a female figure with a red flag—is the work's central point. The side windows tell of illegal resistance in Germany and partisan war in Europe. The large figures are confined to clear blue, violet, and red hues so that they appear as the focal point. Womacka used lighter nuances of color in the smaller scenes and pictorial tales. Applying ancient stained-glass techniques, he created a fascinating work with easily recognizable motifs and a reserved luminosity of colors.

Next to the museum entrance a commemorative plaque is affixed to the stone wall, honoring the victims of the Sachsenhausen death march. In the museum courtyard a powerful lifesize bronze statue by the Soviet sculptor Fjodor Fiwejski, "Stronger Than Death," memorializes the 17,000 Soviet prisoners of war murdered at Sachsenhausen. It shows three inmates supporting one another in the face of an execution squad.

A group of renowned German architects, Ludwig Deiters, Horst Kutzat, Hubert Matthes, Hugo Namslauer, and Kurt Tausendschön, in cooperation with the sculptors René Graetz and W. Grzimek and the painter Walter Womacka, created the memorial site. On the central axis, shaped like a triangle with equal sides, they erected a tall three-sided concrete obelisk, the "Tower of Nations." At its top the tower bears rows of inverted red triangles—the symbol worn by the homosexual inmates throughout the Nazi camp system. The artists surrounded the former roll call square with a fence-like wall in the shape of a semicircle. The first circle of barracks stood around that area, while the other barracks were grouped concentrically. Eighteen concrete impressions in the wall in the shape of the end of a barrack indicate the former barrack places, as do flat granite blocks set in the ground throughout the site.

In front of the tower the architects placed René Graetz's stone sculpture commemorating the Red Army liberation of the camp. It is a powerful picture of a Soviet soldier leading two inmates to freedom. The massive soldier rises protectively behind the inmates with his open storm coat assuming the medieval motif of a protective mantle. One inmate radiates forceful determination, the other, timidity and hesitation.

Sculpture, Sachsenhausen, "Museum of the Anti-Fascist Struggle for Freedom by the Peoples of Europe."

Crematoria remains, "Station Z," Sachsenhausen extermination installation.

To the left of the tower lies the destroyed extermination plant. The area was referred to as Station Z, and behind that harmless name lay a large-scale annihilation installation. All that remains are broken parts of the crematoria ovens. Before the construction of Station Z, bodies were burned outside in mobile oil-fired ovens.

On the spot of Station Z, above the rubble of the annihilation center, stands an unforgettable statue, one of the most artistic camp crematorium memorials. Two prisoners envelop a body with a cloth. One bends painfully over his comrade; the other stands erect in collected strength. A strong line flows from the head of the standing figure across his arm to the cloth that carries the body, onto the torso and arm of the bending figure to the center of the group, forcing the observer to focus on the body. The faces are etched with physical and emotional pain. Sculptor W. Grzimek calls his bronze group "Liberation." The architects built a concrete roof over the memorial. Through an opening, light falls on the sculpture, and it seems to come to life.

At the April 1961 dedication of the National Memorial, attended by 200,000 people from all over the world, Premier Walter Ulbricht asked his audience to bow before the dead and dedicate the area to the martyrs, the heroes:

Every foot of this soil is soaked with the blood and the cold sweat of death of tens of thousands of martyrs from many nations, tens of thousands of people with different world outlooks. Here they were hounded and tormented to death, tortured and butchered.[3]

The East German government insists its young people acquire a thorough knowledge of Nazi history and culture, as well as the idea of a rebirth. Thus in the camps of Sachsenhausen, Buchenwald, and Ravensbrück camp restoration has become a fine art.

Under the new Nazi government in 1933 Oranienburg sprang up as the original "wild camp" and the regime's special holding center. When Hitler came to power, he appointed Göring as Prussian minister of the interior, a post that sounded innocuous enough. To achieve a Nazi revolution, however, Hitler had to gain control of Germany's police forces, pacify the military, set up his own "detective and spy branches," remove from society large groups of opponents and potential troublemakers, and create incarceration centers for such opponents. Göring's new job placed him in control of Germany's largest police force—that of Prussia—and in potential control of Berlin, the capital, and all its outlying areas. His first act was to place trusted Nazis in all police leadership positions. Then he incorporated old SA (*Sturmatteilung, Storm Troopers*) men into the ranks. With that job quickly accomplished, Göring moved to identify, capture, and intern the regime's opponents, and to be ready to house opponents captured by the other branches of Nazidom. He did not have to wait long. After the Reichstag fire, a large pool of Social Democrats and Communists became available to him.

In the summer and autumn of 1933 the Nazis sent Social Democrats, Democrats, Center party leaders, royalists, Jews, unpopular industrialists, and Communists to camps set up by the SA and SS utilizing already existing prisons. Early prisoners remember well the names of Dachau, Oranienburg, Papenburg, Esterwegen, Dürrgoy, Kemna, Sonnenburg, Sachsenburg. Until June 1933 the Prussian minister of the interior had officially recognized six camps as state concentration camps and financed them from public funds. In June the Prussian state was holding 14,000 people in "protective custody" above and beyond all the "normal" criminals in jail and prison.[4]

As the regime began to feel more secure, as the "normal excesses" of a new seizure of power waned, as confusion increased, a desire for efficiency and order began to emerge. The Reich minister of the interior in April 1934 issued a protective custody regulation that reflected the administration's desire to create order out of the confusion and do away with the exceptional institution of protective custody and hodgepodge camps.

Throughout 1934 Göring reduced the number of old "wild" camps while making a start on constructing modern official camps, where orderly procedures could be observed, where control and supervision from above could be maintained, and where efficiency and consistency among all units could be planned and implemented from Berlin. The government closed down most "wild" concentration camps in Prussia in the spring of 1934. Oranienburg, the Emsland camps, Richtenburg, and Columbia-Haus were the only SA and SS camps remaining.

Shortly after the reorganization and consolidation of the Reich's camp administration in 1935, Himmler created a special branch of the armed SS for duty in the camps. Those militarized SS guard formations bore the insignia of the SS-*Totenkopfverbände* or the Death's Head Unit. In March 1935 Death's Head units were stationed at Oberbayern (Dachau), Ostfriesland (Esterwegen), Elbe (Lichtenburg), Saxony (Sachsenburg), Brandenburg (Oranienburg and Columbia-Haus), and Hansa (Hamburg-Fuhlsbüttel). The authorities dissolved most of those camps in the latter part of 1935. Oranienburg and Fuhlsbüttel closed, as did the notorious Columbia-Haus in Berlin.[5]

Only a few meters from the former Oranienburg site the SS constructed an official camp, Sachsenhausen. It opened for business in September 1936. Esterwegen closed and its guards and prisoners became the first large group of Sachsenhausen guests. Built for 10,000, Sachsenhausen held up to 60,000 prisoners by the war's end. The SS delivered 200,000 victims to Sachsenhausen during the years of its existence. One hundred thousand died.

In 1941 Himmler drew up a new classification list. He designated Dachau, the basic Auschwitz camp, and Sachsenhausen as protective-custody camps for prisoners with good records, men capable of improvement, and for special cases and solitary confinement. Thus Sachsenhausen was an "easy camp." The president of the People's Court, the highest jurist in Germany, Judge Roland Freisler, visited Sachsenhausen in 1939. The commandant showed him the camp, including all punishment and torture facilities. Freisler's words on leaving: "Your prisoners strike me as still rather cocky. You simply have a recreation home here."[6]

Sachsenhausen housed a large number of "notables" as prisoners. Even the old Nazi guard was not immune to the possibility of having that camp for an address. When the head of the Foreign Office Department, Dr. Martin Luther, in April 1943 plotted against his boss, Ribbentrop, and lost, Hitler sent him to Sachsenhausen, where he lived out the war. The Austrian chancellor, Dr. Kurt Schuschnigg spent most of his captivity in Sachsenhausen. Dr. Niemöller, placed in "protective custody," was confined first at Sachsenhausen and then at Dachau. George Elser, who supposedly made and placed the bomb in the beer cellar in an attempt to assassinate Hitler, was placed in Sachsenhausen and then sent to Dachau. Sachsenhausen also housed the 1935 Nobel Peace Prize winner, Carl von Ossietzky, and several high-ranking general staff officers. The notables lived outside the prisoner compounds in special isolated barracks or small houses.[7]

Sachsenhausen became the school of the concentration camp system. There, the SS trained many of the leaders and junior officers who were later appointed as commandants, camp leaders, and block leaders of the 2,000 camps, subcamps and *Kommandos*. The concentration camp Inspectorate was located in Sachsenhausen's immediate vicinity in 1936, and from 1939 to 1945 it served as the seat of the central administration of concentration camps in the occupied countries.

The Oranienburg townspeople knew well of the prisoner camp in their midst. After all, it lay right on the edge of town. The inmates marched past their homes each day on their way to work, and the newly arrived prisoners disembarked at the town railroad station. In fact, the inhabitants of Oranienburg never seemed to weary of the spectacle. An avid crowd, including many mothers and children, greeted all arrivals. The entire group joined in singing their "dreadful bloodthirsty chorus":

Kill the Bromberg murderers!
Vengeance for our brothers in Poland!
Blut fuer Blut!

The crowd shrieked, howled, and threw stones, wood, and street filth at the prisoners:

Men were struck in the face, in the eyes. Many were blinded and fell down. But we were not allowed to help the fallen, not allowed to look around us; we had to keep running. Forward!

The road to the concentration camp was about two miles long. We left a two-mile trail of dead and injured behind us. Anyone who fell lay prostrate until the boots of the SS men had gotten him to his feet or he was dead. Several patrol cars drove slowly along the road behind us to pick up the victims: dead or alive, the total number of prisoners consigned to the camp had to be delivered. In Germany, order prevails.[8]

Roll calls and "welcoming addresses" were held in the huge assembly square. Scattered around the area, large white signs proclaimed:

There is a road to freedom.
Its milestones are:
Obedience, industry, honesty,
Order, cleanliness, sobriety,
Truthfulness, spirit of sacrifice and
Love for the Fatherland!

The commandant welcomed each new batch of prisoners with a stirring speech:

Here you are not in a penitentiary or prison but in a place of instruction. Order and discipline are here the highest law. If you ever want to see freedom again, you must submit to a severe training. If we are convinced that our methods of instruction have borne fruit, that you have realized how false your former *Weltanschauung* and way of life were, then the gates of freedom may open for you once more. But woe to those who do not obey our iron discipline. Our methods are thorough! Here there is no compromise and no mercy. The slightest resistance will be ruthlessly suppressed. Here we sweep with an iron broom! Dismissed![9]

The prisoners found the deputy commandant, the *Lagerführer*, a much more interesting man. The only officer who possessed a horse, he used it as his constant companion. The horse seemed to transform his puny physique and his personality. "His gloomy expression brightened: his scowling face was almost friendly." Although the horse was a wild stallion, the *Lagerführer* rode him magnificently—often into the columns of prisoners, causing broken bones and bruises they could ill afford in their weakened condition.[10]

Sachsenhausen, like the other camps, relied on prisoners to handle mundane administrative tasks and to be responsible for the direct supervision of inmates. Prisoners selected as "leaders" held the title *Kapo*. Inmates remembered well one *Kapo*, Paul:

Paul had no glimmer of native intelligence and he was barely able to write his name. But he had made a reputation for himself as a first-class brute. When Paul walked, his long arms swung at his sides as if they were feelers, eager to encounter an obstacle on which they might exercise themselves. If anyone stood in his way, he would beat that person until he could beat no more—but not because he hated us as individuals. Paul had nothing against Poles or Jews. He beat us because beating was a delight to him. And being in command of a Polish block, he could gratify his passion to his heart's content without anyone's raising an objection.[11]

The SS and *Kapos* punished and harassed the Polish prisoners ceaselessly. Prisoners feared desperately for their sanity:

The whole thing was like a monstrous witches' Sabbath, an evil dream. Confusion filled my brain. I was no longer sure whether I was waking or sleeping. Suddenly a dreadful thought struck me: I had only imagined all this; my mind was unhinged. "Dear God, don't let my mind give way," I prayed. "Only give me strength to endure patiently whatever burden you may lay upon me." The prayer worked like a miracle. I fell asleep.[12]

For months the Germans refused to allow any air in the Polish barracks. Death by suffocation seemed the goal.

The air in the barrack was close and oppressive, the heat of an unusually warm September day had collected in the room. Soon we began to sweat. The room was so crowded that we had to lie on our sides. But, even so, our bodies pressed against each other. Sweat, breath and all kinds of bodily effluvia mingled together. In a very short time the air was used up.

But all the windows and doors had to remain tightly shut. We could have opened the trap door in the roof, but Paul ordered us to keep it closed. He gloated over our struggle for breath.[13]

The Nazis housed the Jews in separate barracks and treated them with extraordinary brutality. The religious prisoners seemed to incite the guards to special violence. The Nazis formed the Jews into special labor battalions, gave them one-half the regular-food ration, and denied them medical attention. Rabbi Leo Stein lived in Sachsenhausen for one year, at a time when 1,500 Jewish prisoners were housed in two half-finished structures, in areas so small they slept crushed together on the concrete floor. He wrote:

At night, windows and doors are closed tight. Large containers serve for toilets. The air is rotten with disease. Neither water, soap, nor towels are available; washing is a forbidden luxury. Once every four weeks the Jews are given clean underwear. It is therefore not surprising that there is much more sickness and a higher mortality rate among them than the non-Jewish prisoners.

Dr. Stein's fellow inmates included rabbis, doctors, lawyers, professors, scientists. "Unused to physical activity, they suffered a terrible ordeal in the stone quarry, where they were singled out by the Nazis for the most exhausting tasks, such as carrying big rocks, felling trees, and lifting heavy loads."[14]

The Nazis focused their zeal upon the rabbis, forcing them to work in the quarry and to run with their heavy loads:

Many of the Jewish prisoners who bore their ordeal with extraordinary patience became embittered at the brutal treatment of the rabbis. Sometimes they gave vent to their indignation, but in return they were lashed and thrown into solitary confinement.

Others cried like children when they had to witness the inhuman cruelties to which the rabbis were subjected. But even crying excited the Nazis, who meted out additional beatings, since everything connected with religion seemed to upset them particularly. Prisoners of all faiths were beaten up if they showed any sympathy for the rabbis or priests, or even if they pronounced the name of the Lord.[15]

Sachsenhausen did not escape the medical experiment syndrome. Dr. Werner Fischer performed experiments on Gypsies in an attempt to show they had different blood from Germans. When the Gypsies died, he widened the experiment to include Jews. In another experiment, projectiles containing aconitine nitrate were shot into the thigh of an inmate so that Dr. Mrugowsky could prove that after such a procedure death would occur within two hours. (He was sentenced to death for those experiments and hanged in 1948.) Following the attack on Russia, epidemic jaundice became a disease of major proportions for the German forces. The *Wehrmacht* Medical Section and the *Luftwaffe* Medical Service demanded an intensive effort to discover the causes of and vaccinations against the disease. Sachsenhausen scientists responded by testing new viruses on inmates, all of whom died.[16]

Several Sachsenhausen doctors experimented solely for their own pleasure. An inmate janitor observed an operation by Dr. Schmitz in which the head physician made a long cut on the upper part of a subject's healthy thigh and stuffed into the wound pieces of cloth mixed with straw. Schmitz performed the same operation on other inmates. Afterward "their legs swelled up and turned blue. . . . The doctor tried in vain to cure the sick prisoners with some obviously newly-discovered remedy." Most victims died.[17]

The Sachsenhausen pathology department supplied universities and anatomical institutes with skulls, skeletons, and organs. The doctors murdered patients who aroused their strange medical interests. Tattooed skin was big business and the pathology department kept its eyes open for richly tattooed prisoners.

Sachsenhausen fit well into the SS and German war industrial plans. Early in its history it began supplying the armament industry with male slave labor. Sachsenhausen *Kommandos* spread throughout the region and could be found as far away as Riga and Kiev. The most feared outside work detail was the Klinker Project. Near the Oranienburg Canal lay an area of 8,361 square meters, which constituted an important military zone with numerous buildings, SS troops, and fortifications. Beyond it began the Klinker Works. A prisoner decribed Klinker as a "stretch of wasteland with working places scattered about it, where production was carried on not for its own sake, but to kill the prisoners' time and embitter their lives." The work was hard and dangerous. A 2,000-man *Kommando* was given the task of unloading the ships in the Canal:

Some of us worked in the hold of the ship, which was seven yards deep, and had to shovel up the contents onto several temporary platforms. . . .

The comrades on the uppermost platform in the hold of the ship, who shoveled their loads overboard, could not see what was going on beyond the sloping plank. So the loads of rubble and stone that they tossed up often landed on our heads and knocked us to the bottom. Since all ships had to be unloaded and sail back on the day of their arrival, we worked feverishly, and no one could stop to attend to his injured neighbors.[18]

Prisoners saw the camp work as deliberately senseless tasks designed to rob them of their dignity and humanity. Many prisoners labored daily in a tile factory outside the camp. Emil Fackenheim, at age twenty-two, described that "work":

Many a day we spent carrying sand—always on the double!—from place A to place B, only in order to be ordered the next day to carry it back from place B to place A. The senselessness of this labor was so obvious that everyone understood it. . . . We kept our morale through humor. . . .

I recall an incident early in our imprisonment (when we were still quite naive) when a well-known Berlin rabbi and I lined up outside the medical barrack for treatment for a sore or infected leg (I forget which). After a while the Nazi medical officer came out, kicked us with his jackboots and shouted, "Run, Jews!" As we were running, the rabbi turned to me and asked, "Are you still sick?"[19]

A prominent Jewish historian, Dr. K. J. Ball-Kaduri, recalled the Nazi punishment for slow workers. As a favorite amusement, the Nazi guards forced him to bellow repeatedly this "poem":

Dear old Moses, come again,
Lead your Jewish fellowmen
Once more to their promised land.
Split once more for them the sea,
Two huge columns let it be
Fixed as firmly as two walls.
When the Jews are all inside
On their pathway, long and wide,
Shut the trap, Lord, do your best!
Give us the world its lasting rest![20]

One useful form of work, central to the Nazi plot to break the Bank of England with bogus money, took place in Sachsenhausen. During World War II Major Kruger of the Nazi intelligence service initiated a scheme to wreck the British economy by flooding it with counterfeit money. He selected 140 Jewish craftsmen in Sachsenhausen for the project, intending to kill them when they finished. Those prisoners produced excellent British bank notes, which the Nazis used to pay their foreign spies. They were never able, however, to send the notes into England.

During the project Kruger established cordial relations to win the men's trust. He allowed the Orthodox group to pray every morning. The Jews even conducted a form of services on the Day of Atonement. They became a very close group. One night they produced a cabaret and invited the major. Prisoners sang, played instruments, danced, told stories, or did impersonations. No matter how they performed, however, the three prisoner talent judges turned thumbs down. Kruger realized that the prisoners were telling one another—and him—that they knew that no matter how beautiful the bank notes they produced, not one forger would survive.

By the end of 1943 the group had produced more than half a billion dollars' worth of notes. The head of the Foreign Intelligence Service told Kruger to end the project quickly and return the prisoners to the regular camps. Kruger argued against the plan. He pointed out that these were now highly skilled workers who would be highly useful for work on passports, false documents, and United States money. He won his argument. In December 1943 one of the most famous counterfeiters in Europe was added to the group, and devoted his efforts to the United States money project. The group broke the "code" and by early 1945 was ready to produce American money, but time had run out. In February the inmate forgers of Sachsenhausen, the machinery, and the plates were sent to Mauthausen. Most of the men survived the war. Although almost all the notes they produced were burned, a few fell into private hands and still turn up on the black market. The British caught Kruger and held him secretly for two years. Then they turned him over to the French, who gave him a position in their secret service. Sachsenhausen can thus lay claim to being the home of the world's greatest counterfeiters—the residents of Barracks 19![21]

The Nazis sent many political prisoners to Sachsenhausen. In 1939 and 1940 waves of Czech and Polish resistance fighters arrived at the camp. Reports exist of small resistance groups and a general camp underground. But one event, the Mutiny of the Sachsenhausen Jews, inflamed the imagination and raised the spirits of the prisoners. Following Heydrich's assassination in May 1942 the camp's Jews experienced several reprisals, ending in the shooting of at least 350. Younger prisoners reacted violently and determined to revolt, but the Communist underground administration intervened and stopped the uprising on the grounds that such an action would only lead to the assassination of Jewish prisoners and endanger the lives of the non-Jews. But the memories remained.

On October 21, 1942, the SS announced that Jews were not to report to work the following morning. The SS arrested the illegal leaders of Block 37 and shut them in the bunker. The Jews prepared themselves for the worst. About thirty-five young Jews had formed a clandestine resistance group in the previous weeks. They decided to die resisting rather than allow themselves to be taken peacefully.

At 8 A.M. on October 22 the SS burst into the huts and drove the Jews into the roll call area, where the infirmary Jews were already waiting. In the pouring rain the SS marched the men toward the disinfection hut where they were stripped of their clothes and pushed, naked, into the dressing rooms. Their new wardrobe awaited them. All assumed they were about to receive bullets in the back of their necks. The eighteen young people of the group who had not yet been taken decided to act at ten minutes after the evening roll call.

At 6 P.M. the prisoners gathered in the roll call area. The SS kept the Jewish prisoners shut in their block. Suddenly shouts were heard and pandemonium broke lose. Prisoners cried: "Shoot you cowardly dogs! Go on, shoot." The eighteen prisoners advanced through the crowd and pushed the SS guards aside.

Eighteen men had broken the iron discipline of the camp and had not been shot dead on the spot, even though they had committed the unpardonable crimes of striking the SS: and not just anyone, but the second in command of Sachsenhausen himself! The 12,000 prisoners looking on could hardly believe their eyes. The SS guards were equally stunned. The impossible had happened! And there was the *Lagerführer* in person approaching the eighteen who by this time were completely surrounded by guards brandishing revolvers and machine guns.[22]

The *Lagerführer* ordered the guards to withdraw. He told the prisoners that their fear of being killed was absurd and that they were all going to be transferred. When the camp commandant arrived, the Jewish spokesman declared: "If it is truly a matter of our being transferred elsewhere, then I must say that I have never seen prisoners in transit from this camp so disgustingly treated!" The commandant seemed to suggest that the orders had been given without his authority. He allowed the eighteen to return to their huts.

By rebelling, the eighteen had gained a tremendous moral victory over the SS. Further than that they could not go. Had there been eighteen hundred of them instead of eighteen, they still would not have been able to stop the transfers to Auschwitz. Not even the insurrection of the entire camp would have prevented that.[23]

Most of the eighteen who protested that day survived the war and thus the "riot" was a clear victory.

The Nazis focused furious energy and hatred upon four groups. We know little about the sufferings of one of those groups—the homosexuals. We do know that the Nazis collected Germany's homosexuals, threw them into jails and camps, and labeled them with a pink triangle on their striped uniforms. Most camps had homosexual inmates, but Sachsenhausen and Buchenwald housed the largest numbers. Since the only significant published memoir of a homosexual camp survivor details his life in Sachsenhausen, the Sachsenhausen environment can be used to analyze general Nazi treatment of homosexuals.

Himmler's race theory put a peculiar emphasis on homosexuals. The combination of an absurd race theory and pseudoscientific myths about homosexuals was the basis for Nazi actions against them. To the Nazis, it made pragmatic sense to destroy all the homosexuals they could find.

In the aftermath of World War I Germany suffered a severe population drop. As one of its most important missions, the government embarked on a campaign for the production of children. It coupled its pragmatic need for children with a whole Pandora's box of racial theory. Germany meant to double its population and to ensure that all its citizens had pure blood. Women had as their single mission the bearing of children, and men were required, as an absolute duty, to sire children. The population campaign began with a line of incentives, coupled with a furious crusade against contraceptives, abortion, prostitution, and, above all, against homosexuality. Eventually sterile women and women too old for childbearing were also termed superfluous to the population.

Himmler opened his war against homosexuality in 1933 on a grand scale. But the *savage* persecution began with the Roehm Putsch of June 1934. Theory and philosophy sprang out of the leaders' mouths to rejustify the actions. The Reich legal director, Hans Frank, wrote that homosexual activity meant the negation of the community. If the community did not exist, the race would perish. "That is why homosexual behavior, in particular, merits no mercy." His language concealed a simple piece of arithmetic in terms of the population policy so critical to Germany: homosexuals were considered zeroes. They negated the community by failing to produce children, and that action in a country so hungry for population was an unpardonable crime. As an SS newspaper stated, "Homosexuality was a political, not a medical, problem."[24]

The Nazis stylized the homosexually inclined male into a prototype of sexual abnormality. Homosexually inclined females seldom figured in the pronouncements of National Socialist guardians of morality. What mattered to them was the man—the warrior and the father of children. They considered a woman equipped for motherhood by nature. Even a lesbian could and must bear children, so she presented no practical reproduction problem.

Himmler dished up all the old clichés and added some ideas of his own. Besides being mentally diseased, feminine, and cowardly, homosexuals were declared by Himmler to be liars and blabbermouths, incapable of loyalty. Hitler, on the other hand, was a pragmatist, concerned about population growth. He deemed homosexuals fair game for SS actions, but the main danger as he saw it was that homosexuals would infiltrate the political leadership and constitute themselves a secret order of the third sex.

Himmler's approach was crude and dramatic. By the time he finished painting the effects of homosexuality on population growth, the "problem" had exploded to the point where it constituted a major threat to national survival. A sociologist in 1928 had estimated the number of homosexually inclined men in Germany at 1,200,000. Himmler rounded that figure off to 2,000,000 men, or 10 percent of male Germans! Himmler thought it was possible to lock up prostitutes and reeducate them, but not millions of homosexuals. Therefore he preached their total elimination. To his SS generals, he extolled the wisdom of the ancient Germans whose custom it was to drown their homosexuals in bogs. Since the bogs were no longer available, other means would have to be devised. The medieval church, he thought, had missed the point when it burned homosexuals merely as heretics.

The Nazis marched into the arena to combat homosexuality by propaganda films, decrees, repressive laws, prison sentences, incarceration in the harsher camps, and finally, by a campaign to bring the sexes together. In the autumn of 1934 the Gestapo requested local departments to submit lists of all persons known to have engaged in homosexual activities (they took serious notice of mere suspicion). In 1935 they incorporated even harsher indecency provisions into the penal code. They also began a smear campaign against the Catholic Church, attempting to tar all priests as homosexuals. Between 1934 and 1938 the prosecutions for sex crimes in all areas rose, but it rose by 900 percent for homosexuality! For homosexuals, of course, prosecution was indistinguishable from persecution. They were predestined as concentration camp fodder. Paragraph 175, a sixty-five-year-old law, punished sodomy. The strengthened statute of 1935, known as Paragraph 175a, made nine possible acts punishable for homosexuals, including an embrace and even homosexual fantasies. A man's intentions were more important than his actions in determining guilt. Under the 1935 legislation, one court brought in a verdict of guilty against a man who when apprehended for watching a copulating couple in the park confessed to having watched only the male.[25]

The campaign reached its height with the publication by Himmler in November 1943 of a decree laying down the death penalty for any member of the SS or the police who engaged in sexual relations with another man. Most of those who escaped the death penalty ended up in the concentration camps. Himmler is supposed to have had his own nephew executed at Dachau for homosexuality.

We possess statistics on the number of men brought to trial on violations of Paragraph 175. Many more homosexuals were sent to camps without the benefit of trial. Firing squads summarily executed a large number, particularly in the military. At least 50,000 were sent officially to camps, but many thousands more went. The police in one Berlin district had an index of 30,000 homosexuals. Beginning with the annexation of Austria in 1938, the SS also gathered homosexuals from the countries Germany occupied and interned them in German camps. No one has a final count of the homosexual dead, but some guesses exceed 500,000. The Protestant Church of Austria recently estimated that 220,000 homosexuals were killed during the Third Reich.

The SS brutally assaulted and sexually abused the Sachsenhausen homosexuals. Commandant Höss of Auschwitz wrote in his memoirs that the Sachsenhausen homosexuals were given as hard work as any of the prisoners at the camp. One survivor recalled the first weeks of his imprisonment: "I was the only available target on whom everyone was free to vent his aggressions." The guards referred to homosexuals as criminal deviants. They placed them in an intensified penal company and transferred them to the Klinker Brickworks. In two months the 300 men numbered 50. Recaptured escapees returned with "homo" scrawled across their clothing for their last march through the camp. Homosexuals served as prime fodder for the Sachsenhausen medical experimentation program. A survivor described an ordinary death of one of the young healthy homosexuals. The guards beat him to a pulp and then put him in an icy shower. Thoroughly drenched, he was forced to stand outside in the bitter cold night:

When morning came, his breathing had become an audible rattle. Bronchial pneumonia was later given as the cause of his death. But before it had come to that, he was again beaten and kicked. Then he was tied to a post and placed under an arc lamp until he began to sweat, again put under a cold shower and so on. He died toward evening.[26]

As in all camps, when demands for labor by essential industries reached a hysterical level, the Nazis allowed some of the Sachsenhausen homosexuals to be rehabilitated and released as civilian laborers. Rehabilitation took two forms. The guards took rehabilitation candidates to the SS brothel. If the candidate performed "properly" with a prostitute, he was released as cured. If he failed and agreed to castration, he might be released for heavy labor.[27]

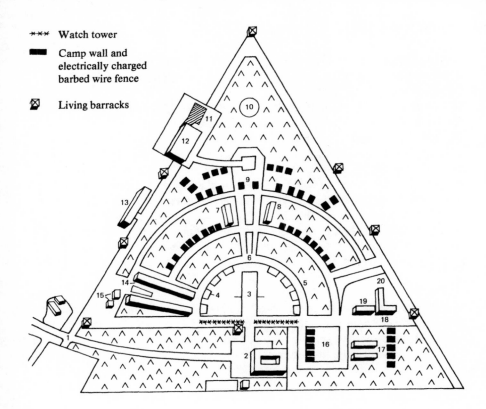

Map 3: Sachsenhausen National Museum

Map Representation by Sharon Coughran

Although the East German government revoked Paragraphs 175 and 175a immediately after the war, they remained on the books in West Germany until 1969, when the government abolished *most* provisions of 175. Although it granted some form of restitution payments to most camp survivors, the West German government defined homosexuals as criminal inmates and refused them any restitution.

It is, then, no accident that Sachsenhausen's most imposing monument, the towering obelisk, bears at its top rows of inverted pink triangles—the Nazi identification mark for homosexuals. But it also seems strange that the prestigious historians and scholars who wrote about Nazi Germany from 1945 to 1965 usually described the Nazis as predominantly homosexual, and "charged that the Nazi elite was largely made up of 'sexual perverts.'" Apparently the Himmler/Hitler propaganda on homosexuality found extremely fertile ground outside of Germany.[28]

The Sachsenhausen Death March annihilated thousands of inmates who would have lived if the SS had allowed them to remain in the camp in the last days before liberation. As the war began to grind down and the Russians moved into Germany, Himmler entered into negotiations with the Swiss with the goal of possibly placing the camps under International Red Cross inspection. Red Cross officials visited Sachsenhausen on February 2 to see what could be done. But Hitler received news of the discussion and Himmler collapsed under his anger—retreating to Hohenlychen.

When the Russian Marshall Grigori Zhukov's guns could be heard 16 kilometers to the east, Himmler ordered all Sachsenhausen inmates lined up for departure. The Red Cross delegates present in Sachsenhausen pleaded with the commandant to turn the camp over to the Red Cross. Insisting that Himmler had ordered him to evacuate everyone, the commandant pushed the 40,000 starved, sick, poorly clothed prisoners into two columns and marched them into the rain in a northwesterly direction. Those who could not keep up were shot and left in the ditches. Corpses lined the road of the march. The inmates of both Ravensbrück and Sachsenhausen experienced the pointless march of starving enfeebled human beings. Few survived it. When the Russians entered Sachsenhausen, they found only 3,000 sick inmates out of the 45,000 inmates of a few days earlier.[29]

The apparent senselessness of the last-minute annihilation of the inmates of many camps becomes intelligible when Hitler's one consistency is recalled. A popular author has his main character, SS Officer Dork, ponder about Hitler: "I even get the crazy feeling that the denial of the earth to the Jews is his *foremost aim,*" and transcends all else. How far is that fictional reaction from the words of Josef Goebbels written in his diary in the last days of the war. "The Jews must be slaughtered while we can still do it." And he seems to have meant it up to the very last hour.[30]

BUCHENWALD: A MOUNTAIN OF CULTURE, POLITICS, AND CORRUPTION

The Weimar of times past, center of humanism and culture, city hallowed by the memory of Goethe and Schiller, is known today as the site of the notorious Buchenwald concentration camp, built on the slopes of the famous mountain Ettersberg. Postwar Weimar is the cultural capital of the German Democratic Republic (DDR), and a beautiful city. A fifteen-minute drive from Weimar, Buchenwald is the show piece camp of East Germany, and a chilling city.

For an American, a visit to Buchenwald necessitates a night spent in the Hotel Elephant, where the DDR places its Western "guests" to better monitor their activities. Unfortunately, anyone who knows the history of the area has the uneasy awareness that residence at the Elephant requires sleeping in rooms formerly occupied by the Nazi brass. From 1937 on, Nazi cultural and social activities in Thuringia revolved around this hotel. Himmler and his staff stayed there on several occasions, as did Göring and other infamous men of the Third Reich. Near the Hotel Elephant stands the house of Weimar's most famous citizen, Goethe. On the short drive between Goethe's house and Buchenwald, the Russian Army intrudes with a mammoth military installation to the side of the road. Taken together, these images of Goethe, the Soviet Army, and Buchenwald exemplify the schizophrenic life of the Germans in the last fifty years.

The drive to Buchenwald follows winding roads up a mountainside. The Weimar area is lovely. Lilacs and innumerable pink and white trees of double cherry blossoms fill the green, fertile countryside with their beauty. It is at Buchenwald that the DDR has built its most impressive camp monuments. It is to Buchenwald that the DDR brings its young schoolchildren to be educated in the ways of the Nazis. During the summer months hundreds of DDR youth groups visit the camp, dressed in their colorful uniforms. In this nation children are required to understand the horror of the camps.

The panorama from the Buchenwald mountain has been called the most beautiful in Europe. Our guide, a thoughtful young woman who felt strongly about the Nazi past, spoke sadly of how her grandparents walked in these

Buchenwald entrance with the clock hands stopped at the moment the prisoners liberated the camp.

beautiful hills during the Hitler years, refusing to acknowledge the nature of the activity near them. No one who walked there then sets foot there now.

The Buchenwald National Memorial divides into two parts—the old camp grounds and the monument park. The monument area lies on the mountainside on ground formerly devoted to armament works and mass graves. To reach the camp, visitors stroll along the Blood Street or Caracho Way, so termed because the concrete road built by the prisoners was soaked with the blood and sweat of tortured men. The road ends at the entrance building. The sign over one main gate reads *"Recht oder Unrecht—Mein Vaterland,"* or "My Country, Right or Wrong," and over the iron gate at the other entrance, "To Each His Due." The clock hands on the upper gate are stopped at 3:15 P.M.—the moment when the prisoners liberated the camp.

Through the gate, I stepped out into a hilly, wooded countryside and saw the camp proper. My immediate reaction was one of desolation. Obviously, the area became thick with dust in dry weather and knee-deep in mud in the wet season. In the stiff breeze that summer day I was reminded that the winter winds surely must have been unbearable. The central courtyard contains the roll call area, administration buildings, and one large camp storage barrack. Outside that building the East Germans have erected a memorial to Stefan Jerzy Zweig, the four-year-old child who survived Buchenwald, hidden in an underground cell. Barbed wire and walls surround the camp, with guard towers at spaced intervals. Few barracks remain.

Around the camp as far as one can see on every side are the green lush valleys of Weimar. I could hear in my mind the church bells pealing, reaching the ears of the exhausted prisoners. Survivors never mention the natural beauty in their memoirs. The crematorium, the camp museum, the children's barrack, the detention center, the Jewish prisoners' area, the former canteen, and other administration buildings remain standing in the camp area. Placed randomly throughout this camp are several memorials dedicated to the tortured Polish prisoners, to Ernst Thälmann, to the murdered British and Canadian paratroopers, to the Soviet prisoners of war, and to the dead Jewish prisoners. One ordinary barrack remains intact as an example of daily life—an earth-floor hut, roughly constructed of wood, without windows or sanitation. The expanse of the camp seems large and its maximum capacity is said to have been 120,000. One building, the former prisoners' canteen, houses the Memorial to the Nations, decorated with the flags of the inmates' countries. That building also includes a library and a lecture hall. Outside the memorial—the burned trunk of an oak. Before the Nazis intruded, it was called the Goethe Oak because the poet liked to rest and meditate there during his walks. Goethe once said: "I can conceive of no crime I could not have committed."[1]

The crematorium stands as it was then, minus the bodies and the ashes: a modern complex built for large consumption and efficiency. It still reeks of disinfectant. It has a large cellar underneath for body storage, and a shooting chamber on the side. Forty-eight hooks jut out from the walls for hanging prisoners in pairs, strapped back to back. The walls are gouged and scratched where the prisoners kicked while dying. If they did not die within the permitted five minutes, guards clubbed them to death before rolling their bodies into the incinerator.

The camp museum is housed in the former disinfection rooms. The pictures, documents, and showcases emphasize the crimes of the Nazis and the resistance struggle of the inmates—naturally concentrating on the courage and leadership of the communist prisoners. In the cellar stands the Thälmann Memorial, filled with pictures and documents and dedicated to the legacy of the prewar chairman of the Communist party of Germany. The Gestapo murdered him in the crematorium at Buchenwald. The museum rooms show different phases of camp life. Pictures of the "criminals" who are now free in West Germany line one room, emphasizing the incorporation into the West German government of former Nazi leaders. The next two rooms show the inhuman conditions under which the inmates lived and worked. From large photographs, emaciated, hollow-eyed prisoners look back at the viewer. One display tells the story of the Buchenwald children—

the thousands who spent time in the camp. Another exhibit pictures the criminal medical experiments. Showcases contain bins of human hair and inmate shoes. Some exhibits emphasize the Buchenwald International Camp Committee and the contribution to resistance and sabotage by the communist prisoners.

Light comes into the museum through the magnificent stained-glass windows that portray various phases of concentration camp life in black, white, and blues. A famous German artist spent months creating these windows, which focus on the resistance, cooperation, and mutual help of the prisoners. The theme can be challenged historically, but the art is stunning. Outside the camp proper lies the quarry, a deep gouged-out cavern where prisoners died daily. The infamous stables where the SS murdered 8,000 Soviet prisoners still stand, beyond the barbed wire. Then, back out through the main gate and down the Blood Road to the Visitors Center in the middle of the former SS barracks. One brick building has been converted into a restaurant and another into a tourist hotel. A third has been set aside as a large movie house for the showing of the film *Buchenwald*. Thousands of visitors and dozens of tour buses crowd the area.

Down the mountainside on the road to Weimar in a pleasant location lie the remains of the SS residential settlements. Ten luxurious villas stood along this road, and from their wide terraces the commandants and their officers had a magnificent view of the countryside. To build these homes, long columns of prisoners dragged the stone blocks from the quarry.

The Blood Road leads to the monument area. Prime Minister Otto Grotewohl used his inauguration speech for the Buchenwald National Memorial to exhort his audience to fight against fascism and for peace:

A site of commemoration has been set up within the heart of Germany, upon blood-stained soil, in honor of all those who gave their best and most valuable possession— their lives. May this monument proclaim the immortal glory of the courageous struggle against tyranny, for peace, freedom and human dignity, to coming generations.[2]

The Buchenwald National Memorial is the most extensive, artistic, and expensive of all memorials in existence in any former Nazi camp. Several of East Germany's finest artists dedicated their best efforts in its construction. The memorial road leads from the Blood Street through the entrance gate to the landscaped plazas on the mountainside. In staggered rows moving down the hill the architects have placed reliefs, ending on the Avenue of Nations. Sculptured in stone, the reliefs show the life and sufferings, the struggles, and the victory of the living at Buchenwald. Looking out over the valley, one sees again the beautiful panorama and, at the bottom at each end, a mass grave. In the middle are a mass grave and a broad concrete street—the Avenue of Nations—linking the three large enclosed tombs that contain thousands of nameless bodies. Along the Avenue of Nations rise stone memorials for every country from which prisoners came—eighteen inscribed pillars; at the top of each pillar is an iron urn filled with ashes.

The broad Street of Freedom ends on Commemoration Square, reached by climbing up hundreds of steps from the Avenue. A huge bell tower, eight stories high, rises in the center of the square. The bell is laced at the top with barbed wire and attention is called to the Buchenwald pledge: "Our slogan is the uprooting of the Nazism. Our aim is the construction of a new world of peace and freedom." The bells toll during memorial services sponsored by the International Buchenwald Committee. In front of the massive bell tower stands a sculpture with eleven monumental figures symbolizing the disgrace of the camps, the suffering, and the invincible fighting spirit.

The building of the memorial site of Buchenwald became the most significant task of artistic monument expression in East Germany. The group that deliberated about the proposed memorial site resolved to create works of art that could bear witness to what it believed was the antifascist nature of the new state, to have ideal human figures that could speak for the new order. The planners intended to reach a new substantive level in memorial sculpture. They desired to do more than arouse sorrow, more than glorify war, more than create massively arranged abstractions. The architects wanted to honor the victim's memory, emphasize his suffering, but more important, highlight the injury done to humanity. Conceiving of Buchenwald, Sachsenhausen, and Ravensbrück as a whole, they voiced a determination to express the dignity of the people in those camps in superb works of art.[3]

Architects Ludwig Deiters, Hans Grotewohl, Horst Kutzat, and Kurt Tausendschön created the memorial site. They integrated statues, reliefs, sculpture, and landscaping into their architectural treatment of the large area, about 600 by 250 meters. In its unity of architecture and sculpture, the 1958 Buchenwald Memorial is exemplary. Buchenwald's unique character as a camp where more than 250,000 human beings were incarcerated and many thousands murdered in a place that once symbolized human culture called for an appropriate artistic solution. The planners saw Buchenwald as the triumph of international solidarity resulting in the prisoners' successful liberation of the camp. Thus they determined to focus on that "victorious resistance" as the theme of the Ettersberg Memorial. And the major memorial area would be the mountainside itself, with the monuments struggling up and flowing down the mountain overlooking Weimar.

Fritz Cremer won the 1951 competition for the central memorial group with an outline of eight standing figures. He determined to add something new to his single figures—a group tightly closed into a dynamic wedge—to create an individualization that recognized diverse attitudes and the many

Buchenwald National Memorial, "Revolt of the Prisoners," by Fritz Cremer.

facets of the inmates' struggle. He needed to develop the figures as inmates of a camp that could liberate itself. By expanding the group to eleven inmates, he was able to unite the figures substantially and formally.

Cremer arranged his figures in a wide front, and by raising them slightly, stressed the fighter with a gun, the oathtaker, and the calling figure. The inmates over whom the flag rises from the center of gravity. The motion of the flag is strengthened by the fighter with the gun. The arms of the figure giving an oath and the raised arm of the falling figure represent a compositional counterpoint. The falling figure, the fighter with the beret, and the fighter with the blanket exert supreme dignity.

The falling figure represents an essential part of Cremer's heightened message—a new quality. Cremer had changed the original wedge form to a wide front and added the falling fighter, front center, at the point of the obtuse angle, a representation of victory in death. The artist formulated a wide-ranging picture of human behavior, from a willingness to sacrifice and a determination to fight, to helplessness and negative passivity, the latter standing aside.

Waldemar Grzimek, René Graetz, and Hans Kies created the cycle of stunning relief structures that portray the camp's history from its establishment in 1937 to its liberation. Kies composed the first free-standing relief, "Erection of the Camp." Powerful diagonals—prisoners pulling a tree and setting up a gallows—dominate the composition. Torture, surrender, but also selfless solidarity are visible. In the second work, "Arrival in the Camp," Grzimek unites several groups of action in two zones, in a strongly expressive concentration of figures. The waiting group huddles fearfully, but stands opposite the inmates at the stake as a center of strength. The waiting figures, formed from large cubes, represent a core of humanity from which new resistance forces grow. Behind them, an inmate shields the "Boy of Buchenwald."

The reliefs of Kies, "Work in the Stone Quarry" and "The Singing Horses," are dominated by strong movement. In Grzimek's relief, "Exploitation and Annihilation of the Inmates," the artist divided the space into two substantive areas: the exploitation of prisoners by hard labor plays opposite the "liquidation" of those unfit for work. The worker who has collapsed in exhaustion unites the two areas. With the reliefs, "Solidarity," "Illegal Thälmannfeier," and "Liberation," René Graetz shows more strongly the ideas of political struggle and the activity of mature forces in resistance to the Nazis.[4]

Standing on the steps of the bell tower viewing the beautiful countryside of Germany so steeped with poetry and music, the viewer contemplates the monuments winding down and around a hill littered with large mass graves. The day was sunny, but the area seemed desolate and lonely to me. All the slabs of concrete were little compensation for the lost lives. The Germans have done so much at Buchenwald—the artwork is haunting and plentiful. The Russian soldiers are fond of having themselves photographed in front of the memorial, but their boisterousness is out of place. The German children were much more respectful. For in spite of the obvious propagandistic purpose of the memorial, the camp is impressive and its silence cries out for those who died.

On one monument are engraved the words: "Der Aufbau Einer Neuen Welt Des Friedens Und Der Freiheit Ist Unser Ziel!" ("The building of a new free world is our goal!"). In the nervous, closed-in atmosphere of the DDR, one fervently wishes that goal had become more than an artistic fantasy.

Goethe's Oak—and around it Himmler built a concentration camp. Not a harsh one, not the worst, but a moderate camp for protective-custody prisoners who, it was believed, could benefit from education and reform. Buchenwald quickly became a massive penitentiary demonstrating to Germans the fate awaiting those who opposed Hitler. It was not an extermination camp. The prisoners simply died there. Of the 238,980 people sent to Buchenwald between 1937 and 1945, only 56,545 expired. After all, when a government selects the cultural center of one of the world's most advanced countries—Weimar—and the site symbolizing German classicism—Goethe's famous oak—on which to build a concentration camp, that camp must not publicly offend the cultural sensibilities of the people. It cannot create an Auschwitz or a Treblinka in such a place.

In July 1937 the Nazis began the construction of Buchenwald, which would become one of the four infamous prewar camps (Dachau, Ravensbrück, and Sachsenhausen were the others). The prisoner-builders went to work on 148 hectares of hardwood and pine forest given to the SS from an aristocrat's estate, in a harsh climate unsuited for normal human living. The location itself was symbolic, with the fog-surrounded Ettersberg peak rising out of a region of tumbled trees and roots. The SS respectfully spared the Goethe Oak and designated it the center of the camp.[5]

The initial construction phase ended with the completion of the electrically charged wire enclosure, over 3.2 kilometers long and enclosing 40 hectares. The entire area within the guard line, including the work areas outside the fence, encompassed about two square kilometers. In the summer of 1938 the prisoners enlarged Buchenwald and the SS made provisions to exploit the labor they were concentrating there.

In 1943 Buchenwald held only 17,000 prisoners, but after April 1944 it became a veritable city of deportees. With the demise of Auschwitz in January 1945 and the destruction of the killing centers, the Germans dumped tens of thousands of ex-Auschwitz inmates, Hungarian deportees, and forced laborers into the other camps. Between May 1944 and March 1945 over 20,000 Jews poured into Buchenwald. In 1944 the SS opened a tent camp to take care of them.

Buchenwald was actually a series of internal subcamps with wooden and stone barracks, old horse stables, and tent cities. The "Little Camp," built beyond the roll call area, acquired the worst reputation. In one part of it the SS set aside primitive barracks for emergency needs, crowding 40,000 inmates into them. In another section the SS segregated the Jewish prisoners, forcing them to buy their water and food, and if they could not, to die. The Little Camp accommodated, in five large tents, the Polish prisoners arriving after the invasion of their homeland. Within a few months more than 1,600 Poles had died. Until quite late in the war the Little Camp had no stoves, blankets, or mattresses. When the French arrived in 1943, they found their lodging in a hastily erected tent city devoid of the most primitive necessities of life: water, cots, latrines, clothes, spoons, mess gear. Windowless, toiletless stables built for the needs of 28 horses held as many as 2,000 prisoners each. With those conditions, the Little Camp experienced several major epidemics, which raised the already high death rate. Wet, dirty, exhausted, and undernourished, men fought to remain alive under impossible conditions.

A fifteen-year-old Jewish boy, Thomas Geve, settled in the Little Camp, sleeping on the cold moist floor of Block 62. Later the *Kapo* gave him a bunk filled with a sack of straw, blankets, bugs, fleas, lice, mice, and five inmates.

One had to lie on one's side like a tinned sardine, without moving. . . . The width per person was less than a foot. On waking up—the unpleasantest moment of all in the prisoner's life—hands and feet were numb, backs aching.

He found the block a "den of wild animals, beasts that howled, robbed and killed." Inmates used their food bowls for the night latrine.[6]

The camp became a living hell in the fall of 1944. So many died that the bodies lay about in the open. The SS seemed powerless in the face of mass dying. Incidents occurred that seem beyond comprehension:

Nature's call was answered atop naked, dead bodies. On one occasion, a young Hungarian Jew asked permission of the Senior Block Inmate to extract his dying father's gold teeth, since otherwise they would be stolen by others. Savage struggles to the death took place over the pitiful daily ration. . . . Mess gear was commonly used in place of the latrines, partly from feebleness that made it impossible to leave the barrack, partly from fear of the weather outside or of theft, partly because it was almost impossible to get out of the crowded bunks. Those on top often climbed to the roof, by removing boards and roofing, and fouled the rafters. The human mind is unequal to picture these awful scenes.[7]

If Buchenwald was a moderate camp and not an extermination center, why did so many die? The answer lies in the definition of extermination. David Rousset described a conversation that he had with a friend in Buchenwald. An inmate asked why the SS did not kill them right away and Rousset's friend explained:

Because the face of death does not release enough terror. Whole avenues of hanged men are insufficient. People grow surfeited with death. But to know that a man may have to endure daily torture for years, that's effective. It took some such spectre, ever visible, to unnerve their people and finally, to stupify them. . . . To the SS we are evil incarnate. We must atone for our sins, and eke out our chastised existences until death. We are to die persuaded that we are bad, thoroughly bad, discarded by humanity. The concentration camps are high altars of expiation. Here, the SS finds its rarest gratification.

He added that they were "consecrated to death." Inmates referred to Buchenwald as the "camp of the slow death."[8]

The Nazis created a camp universe where ordinary values were destroyed and obsessive weight was placed on elemental necessities. The prisoners bestowed premiums on colleagues with technical, military, and political capacities. The title of carpenter could open the door to favor and privilege, while the laboratory professor brought only derision. But somehow the SS and the prisoners, like the ancient gods and their subjects, all shared the same world, the same nature. Thus, as Rousset has commented, a *concentrationnaire* was able to "get a grip of a kind on an SS. Also, the higher powers of the SS have their limits, as indeed the omnipotence of the gods was subject to a more profound fatality."[9]

And who were those prisoners? Until 1943 most were Germans. But with the changing fortunes of war, men from every nation poured into the camp. The politicals, the communists, and the Jews soon outnumbered the criminals. Camp policy divided the prisoners by categories and segregated the two lowest castes, the Jews and the homosexuals.[10]

Like other camps, Buchenwald had a group of "prominents," housed in an isolated barrack hidden deep in the woods opposite the SS officer residences. In the final stages of the war Himmler ordered the forty-five celebrities evacuated to Bavaria. They included the former leader of the German Social Democratic party, Rudolf Breitscheid, and his wife; the Italian Princess Von Mafalda of Hess; the business magnate, Fritz Thyssen; German industrialists; six members of the families of disgraced German officers; and at one time the former French premier, Léon Blum.

And finally, there were the children. During the war the SS separated thousands of children from their parents and sent them to Buchenwald. The first group arrived as early as 1939. Most were Jewish children or the children of executed partisans. In Buchenwald the underground succeeded in protecting many of them in a special barrack. The adult prisoners aided them as best they could, and 904 survived. A large proportion became quite spoiled. Many, who were badly used by the men, received the label "doll boys." In the fall of 1944 the SS suddenly herded together all the Jewish and Gypsy youngsters and shipped the "screaming, sobbing children" to the Auschwitz gas chambers.[11]

The youngest child in the camp was four-year-old Stefan Jerzy Zweig, a Polish boy called Yushu. The struggle of the prisoners for his life has been described by Bruno Apitz in his prize-winning novel, *Naked Among Wolves*. Apitz arrived at Buchenwald in 1937. He survived and wrote about Stefan Zweig, faithfully documenting the true story of that amazing child. The setting is Europe 1945, the Allies are winning, and the news reaches the battered and starving Buchenwald inmates. In those final weeks a small child is smuggled into the camp in his father's rucksack. A group of prisoners brave death to keep that child alive. All are touched by the struggle. During the inspections the protectors gag the little boy and tuck him underneath the floor boards. One survivor described Stefan as "the saddest character I had ever come across, abnormal in his physique, behavior and speech. He staggered along like some weak, wounded animal and uttered cries in German-Polish-Yiddish gibberish."[12]

After liberation, father and son disappeared. When the novel and the movie based on it appeared, both were found in Israel in 1964. Stefan had grown into a strong all-star player on the Israeli national handball team. In February 1964 Stefen and the survivors who had cared for him met at a reunion in Buchenwald.[13]

Those are the men then, the 30,000 to 80,000 men who lived together in some semblance of order, devoid of the necessities of life. Against the harsh enemies of hunger, cold, torture, and exhaustive labor, some united against the enemy and some divided against each other. A wealthy young French aristocrat and member of the French resistance, Pierre d'Harcourt, spent two years in Buchenwald. In picturing camp life, he emphasizes the corruption and intrigue in the prisoner hierarchy. It was a cutthroat, every-man-for-himself atmosphere spotted with rare saintly figures. The struggle to keep alive and to avoid the killing work details obsessed men's minds. Remaining alive depended on one's prior physical condition, inner attitude, politics, and, most important, who one knew. As Elie Wiesel's father lay dying in Buchenwald, the block leader gave young Wiesel some painful advice on survival:

Listen to me, boy. Don't forget that you're in a concentration camp. Here, every man has to fight for himself and not think of anyone else. Even of his father. Here, there are no fathers, no brothers, no friends. Everyone lives and dies for himself alone. I'll give you a sound piece of advice—don't give your ration of bread and soup to your old father. There's nothing you can do for him. And you're killing yourself. Instead, you ought to be having his ration.[14]

All the survivors remember roll call at Buchenwald as a daily opportunity for SS torture. Often the command would be heard after roll call: "All Jews, remain behind." The SS would then force the Jews to repetitively sing the "Jew Song":

For years we wreaked deceit upon the nation,
No fraud too great for us, no scheme too dark.
All that we did was cheat and lie and swindle,
Whether with dollar or with pound or with mark.

And now at last the Germans know our nature
And barbed wire hides us safely out of sight.
Traducers of the people, we were fearful
To face the truth that felled us overnight.

And now, with mournful crooked Jewish noses,
We find that hate and discord were in vain.
An end to thievery, to food aplenty.
Too late, we say, again and yet again.[15]

At roll call, the prisoners stood, slumped, sang songs, did exercises—whatever the SS required. Even the aged and the decrepit performed head stands in the snow.

The Nazis, with their peculiar minds, provided leisure as well as torture for their charges. They permitted moments of relaxation and recreation. Those inmates assigned to easy work were in good enough health to play soccer and asked the SS for permission to do so. The authorities found that request a fine advertisement for prisoner morale and provided the team with impressive uniforms. Prisoners also played handball and volleyball. "And the feeble wrecks, the emaciated starvlings, half dead on their unsteady legs, gleefully came to watch the fun. There are inscrutable depths to human nature."[16]

In addition to sports, the SS provided "special buildings." They forced twenty-five Jewish women prisoners from Ravensbrück to offer their services in the Buchenwald brothel. The SS brothel project was intended to corrupt the prisoners, and some it did. Prisoners with good connections and those who could steal enough food to trade for clothes for the women were allowed to spend hours in the brothel.

The prisoners formed a camp band. At first the Gypsies with their guitars and harmonicas produced the only music heard at Buchenwald. Later other instruments were added, many which the prisoners made for themselves. In 1939 the SS officers formed an inmate brass band. Whenever visitors arrived, the band played for them; and in 1941 the band members were "decked out in gorgeous uniforms of the Royal Yugoslav Guard." They looked like a group of "circus ringmasters." The band played on Sundays and during the day as the prisoners carried their dead and dying comrades into the camp from work details. Buchenwald inmates listened to radio broadcasts of German symphony concerts through the public address system. They saw motion pictures in Buchenwald's theater and made use of the prison library.[17]

The young Jewish boy, Thomas Geve, was finally sent to Block 66, the home of some 300 to 400 youngsters. The Jewish block elder had founded and made a success of a boys' choir. The day came for the choir's debut—a performance to which the SS had been invited. The program consisted of songs, sketches, acrobatics, and solo dances representing every nationality. Fortunately, the SS understood little of what the children were singing. The Polish children rose and sang about life in a new Warsaw. The Russian boys showed off their voices and their muscles with songs and dances of the Red Army. The last but largest group were the Jewish boys from Poland. They chanted about ghetto life, about mothers, rabbis, and learning from the Bible, and then went on to songs about people being led to their deaths.[18]

Labor

All leisure was shortlived, for the SS intended its Buchenwald prisoners to work and to die. Often the inmates managed the dying alone, but the SS carefully designed the work patterns in cooperation with Berlin and with Germany's major industries. Buchenwald was one of the largest labor-exploitation centers in all of Europe. The SS ruthlessly worked the prisoners to death in military and civilian factories owned by Krupp, Thyssen, I.G. Farben, Siemens, Reg, and other trusts. The government supplied those financial giants with armament orders, high dividends, and a continuous stream of slave labor. Buchenwald *Kommandos* numbered in the hundreds, and varied in strength from 10 to 6,000 to 8,000 laborers.[19]

Buchenwald was a camp for men and for boy children, although many female prisoners spoke of themselves as Buchenwald prisoners. But the Nazis sent all the female prisoners assigned to Buchenwald to outside *Kommandos*. Those women worked in the ammunition, engineering, aircraft, and mechanical industries. They built airfields and dug ore in the quarries. They suffered every imaginable horror known in Buchenwald proper, even though they spent all their time either in the underground factories or the dangerous on-site war production factories.

In 1944 the SS made 6,624,229 marks from the Buchenwald labor hired out to the arms industry. When prisoners became unfit for work in the factories, the industries requested that they be returned to Buchenwald, a move that almost inevitably meant the crematorium. Out of 15,000 prisoners shipped to Dora during two months in the fall of 1943, for example, at least a hundred bodies were returned every day, each weighing less than forty kilograms.[20]

Prisoners performed all work needed to run the main camp. The internal labor program necessitated skilled construction workers, masons, carpenters, plumbers, roofers, electricians, painters, and domestic servants. In 1943 the Gustloff works built its own armament plant inside Buchenwald to utilize prisoner labor. The camp work day lasted fourteen hours and included Sundays.

Prisoners feared assignment to the quarry *Kommando* because of its high daily death rate. In the quarry prisoners mined ore with the most primitive tools, loaded the rocks with bare hands, and transported them by human power. In 1937 SS Brigadier Eicke, the inspector of concentration camps, had issued an order forbidding the use of machinery for excavation, requiring the inmates to do that work by hand, and to carry the earth away in wooden boxes. In that manner the prisoners built the famous Blood Street and constructed the sewage plant. In another labor area the SS assigned prisoners the task of providing manure for the gardens near the SS quarters. One guard pushed thirty inmates into the cesspool and let them die. The SS found the unlimited human labor cheaper to employ than machines.

It should not be assumed that the prisoners' labor during a period when every bit of human energy was needed to further a successful war effort was always centered on the vital war industry. In fact, SS officers siphoned off major segments of the labor force for private and illegal purposes, and diverted much of the scarce raw materials needed for the war effort—such as lumber, copper, bronze, gold, and silver—to the production of a wide range of luxury goods. A survivor described the articles made by camp craftsmen for the SS:

There were whole living room suites, inlaid furniture, precious individual pieces, metalware, busts and figurines, never paid for except with a few occasional cigarettes. These articles found their way not only into the SS quarters but into the homes of friends and acquaintances throughout the land and even beyond its borders. Especially gifted prisoners were sometimes farmed out to Berlin or to other camps and headquarters for weeks at a time, to help meet the demand for luxury goods among the SS.[21]

Potters, porcelain painters, architects, stone sculptors, silversmiths, masons, painters, and draftsmen worked for the personal pleasure and economic aggrandizement of the SS.

The SS ensured that the material and tools used in its shops were of the highest quality. The photographic department spent most of its time developing magnificent portraits and albums for the SS and their families. Buchenwald had some of the great artists of Europe as inmates, and they provided valuable canvases and sculpture for the officers. The camp's print shops and binderies produced luxury books and an SS magazine. The SS also had a fetish for genealogies and family trees. Czech prisoners manufactured ancestral tables and family chronicles. Because the workmanship at Buchenwald was of such high quality, the demand for its materials spread throughout Germany. What was good for the big shots became good for the little shots, and the procedure used by the officers was followed by SS men, *Kapos,* and guards. Every nook and cranny of Buchenwald was filled with hidden contra-band, available to bribe the SS in exchange for food or even life. One SS Lieutenant General, the hereditary prince of Waldeck-Pyrmont, asked for and received a special refrigeration unit to store the deer he hunted.[22]

Punishment and Extermination

An elementary principle to follow when extensive hard labor is needed from a group of human beings is to feed them at least enough so they can do their work. It is also pragmatic to leave workers with enough of their body intact so they can achieve the most productive capacity. But these sensible principles were never followed by the SS. The absence of adequate food is well known, as is the list of punishments inflicted on every man in the camp. Probably no known punishment was left out of the Buchenwald schedule. Roll call, standing at attention, exercises; work in the quarry; tree hanging with the inmate suffering dislocation and a rupture of the shoulder joints; the detention building with its interrogation, torture, and solitary confinement; the Singing Horses, the Blood Road, the gallows in the Buchenwald disinfection room; shooting while trying to escape, beatings, trampling to death, injections—all were normal punishments inflicted upon the prisoners, usually resulting in their death. It was difficult to determine the line between punishment and execution.

And for what were the prisoners punished? For every imaginable banality, such as missing buttons from a ragged shirt, dirt on the clothes, unshined shoes or shoes shined too much, failure to salute, staying too long in the latrine, smoking in the barracks, and the slightest deviation in the roll call ranks such as coughing or sneezing. Even the most experienced survivors marvel that it was possible to survive the penalty system.

Perhaps the most serious offense was attempting escape. In the spring of 1939 a Gypsy tried to escape. He was recaptured.

Commandant Koch had him placed in a wooden box, one side covered by chicken wire. The box was only large enough to permit the prisoner to crouch. Koch then had large nails driven through the boards, piercing the victim's flesh at the slightest movement. The Gypsy was exhibited to the whole camp in this cage. He was kept in the roll-call area for two days and three nights, without food. His dreadful screams had long since lost any semblance of humanity. On the morning of the third day, he was finally relieved of his sufferings by an injection of poison.[23]

It was a blessing to be shot in the neck for an escape attempt.

Buchenwald faced the same major problem as all other camps—how to murder the prisoners and eradicate all traces of their bodies. Buchenwald had additional difficulties unknown at some of the killing centers. For example, Buchenwald never possessed a gas chamber. The SS leadership drew up plans to construct one in early 1945, aiming at the massive elimination of the Buchenwald inmates. The camp underground caught news of the project and put into operation a regular system of sabotage involving both a slowing down of construction and a tearing down during the night of what had been constructed that day. Because of those difficulties, the project ground to a halt.

Even without a gas chamber, the authorities managed, using a variety of other methods, to kill thousands of Buchenwald prisoners. The executions in Block 61 were done by injection. Each morning the SS doctors laid out a large number of syringes filled with a concentrated phenol solution, and the orderlies used them to kill prisoners. Some survivors speak of a "murder plant" located in the Buchenwald stable. It was there that the SS murdered the Soviet prisoners of war. The stable included receiving areas, medical instrument rooms, a shooting stand, killing rooms with a drain in the floor for the blood, sawdust storage, cesspools, and body storage facilities.

Many prisoners died of beatings and torture administered in the bunkers. There, the "Hangman of Buchenwald," Martin Sommer, reigned supreme. That "beast in human form" made prisoners immerse their testicles in ice-cold and boiling water, and then he painted them with iodine as the skin came off in strips. He strung prisoners up by their hands and had guards throttle them or hang from their legs. Sommer hanged prisoners in their cells, beat them to death with an iron bar, and poisoned them. In one instance, he crushed an inmate's skull by screwing an iron clamp tightly around it. When a prisoner asked permission to go to the bathroom after eating food laced with cathartics, Sommer forced him to stick his head in the filled toilet bowl. Sommer chained seven young Polish prisoners to their cots and restricted them to a diet of saltwater and pickles. They perished after the entire camp heard their screams and moans for several days. Sommer enjoyed strangling prisoners with his bare hands and trampling them with his boots until they died. That was life in the bunker.[24]

The enormous quantities of bodies produced by those methods created difficulties. Buchenwald had no crematorium until 1941. The SS piled the bodies in heaps and then in special morgues. Sometimes they placed them in camp buildings, stacked like cordwood, until they could send them to city crematoria in Weimar and Jena. As early as June 1938 Buchenwald authorities alerted the SS head office to the need for a crematorium. In a memo to Eicke the Buchenwald SS construction office presented detailed plans that would cost 14,000 marks to implement. Two days later, on June 21, Eicke, recognizing the urgency of the project, wrote to the chief of SS Administration for approval on political and economic grounds.[25]

True to form, the bureaucratic wheels turned slowly. On January 10, 1940, the formal request read more vigorously: "Construction of an *Emergency Crematorium* in the Prison Camp, cc Buchenwald." The report supplied the building specs:

As a result of the high *mortality rate* in the Buchenwald concentration camp, it has *become necessary* to supply an emergency crematorium with oil-burning cremation furnace (double muffle furnace).

For this a space *6 × 9 meters* and 4 meters high will be required. Because of the shortage of wood, the building is being erected in stone and is *not to be provided with cellars.* The floor of the room will consist of a layer of clinkers on a concrete base. The ceiling will be *faced with 2½* cm. of strong *Heraklith sheets* and plastered. The roof will be covered with a double layer of tar paper. All *visible woodwork* as well as the gutters and *wastepipes* will get a *coat of oil paint* (ersatz oil). *The inside walls and ceiling* will be painted with glue-color.

The furnace is being supplied and erected by the firm, J. A. Topf and Soehne, Erfurt, Dreysestrasse 7–9.

A description of the furnace can be seen in the estimate of the firm Topf Soehne of 21 December 1939 which has been added to the enclosure.[26]

In 1941 the contractors finished the fine modern Buchenwald crematorium. Standing in a spacious courtyard, it included living quarters for the death squads, a morgue, a dissection room, and two combustion chambers. The furnaces were equipped with the latest devices. For a camp so large, however, the crematorium was quite small. Auschwitz, for example, had six to twelve furnaces.

Medical Experiments and Other Oddities

In the isolation wards of Buchenwald SS "scientists" developed some of the worst camp experiments, with the cooperation of the German armed services, I. G. Farben, and the Behring Works. Using human beings as guinea pigs and acting on instructions received from German chemical firms, SS doctors conducted test series with typhus, yellow fever, smallpox, cholera, diphtheria, chemical warfare agents, phosphorus-rubber substances from incendiary bombs, poisoned ammunition, stored blood too old to be used on "regular patients," and other poisons. The experiments killed most subjects. The SS also rented out Buchenwald inmates to industry for experimental use. When a chemical firm requested women for experiments, it tried to negotiate a lower price for the victims:

We are planning tests with the new soporific and would be grateful if you could supply us a number of women. The price of 200 marks seeming somewhat excessive, we suggest paying you a maximum of 170 marks per head.[27]

Dr. Ding and his associates conducted incendiary bomb experiments to test the effects of various pharmaceutical preparations on phosphorus burns. A former prisoner testified that he saw photographs of phosphor burns taken at Block 46: "One need not be a specialist to imagine the sufferings of people whose flesh was burnt down to the bone. When the experiment was completed after three months, all those who survived were liquidated." The doctors experimented with poison injections, old blood plasma transfusions, and gland implants and synthetic hormones to counteract homosexuality.[28]

In 1942, at the Military Medical Academy at Berlin, Dr. Ding took part in a conference in which one topic discussed was the fatality of gas edema serum on wounded soldiers. Soldiers who had received the serum in high quantities seemed to recover but then died hours later for no visible reason. The discussants suspected it was the serum's phenol content that caused death. Dr. Ding testified in an affidavit that after the discussion Colonel Joachim Mrugowsky, chief of the *Waffen* SS Institute of Hygiene, ordered him to perform euthanasia with phenol on Buchenwald inmates and then report his findings to Berlin. He obeyed, and the subjects died immediately.[29]

The major experimental fame of Buchenwald rested on its infamous typhus experiments. The Institute of Hygiene of the *Waffen* SS in the fall of 1941 opened a clinic for typhus and virus research at Buchenwald. The bulk of the actual work was done by Dr. Ding, who committed suicide after the war. He left behind an extensive professional diary. The clinic, in Isolation Ward 46, was modern and well equipped. Famous men of German medical science participated with Dr. Ding on a consultative basis. Ding also selected experts from camp inmates for the work, including physicians, bacteriologists, serologists, and chemists. After all, the SS had at its beck and call the best medical minds in Europe.

Typhus had become a serious problem among the German troops fighting in Russia. Vaccines were so scarce that only medical personnel in exposed positions were given inoculations. After discussing the problem at a *Wehrmacht* conference, Dr. Ding wrote in his diary: "Since tests on animals are not of sufficient value, tests on human beings must be carried out." By the end of 1944 his group had conducted twenty-four series of experiments, with the number of subjects ranging from forty to sixty in each series.

In one ward technicians produced the typhus serum from mouse and rabbit livers. Some groups were given vaccine, some were not. But all were artificially infected with typhus. Every inmate selected for the experiments expected to die a slow and frightful death, for "the man-to-man passage of the typhus virus created a form of 'super' typhus." While typhus normally produces mortality rates of about 30 percent in unprotected cases, in an April 1943 experiment five out of six infected prisoners died. About 1,000 prisoners passed through the ward. The scientific value of these tests was later proven to be useless because the method of infection was unscientific, to say the least.[30]

As a kind of "kinky" sideline, the Buchenwald researchers collected and prepared human skins, heads, and skulls for the SS. The medical chief of Department D of the WVHA, Dr. Loeling, wrote several times to the pathological section director at Buchenwald in this vein: "I need immediately 10 entire skeletons, 12 skulls, or individual parts of the body, or we need some interesting bullet wounds." Hunchbacks or other persons whose physiognomy was of medical interest "excited the anatomical and macabre avarice of half-crazed doctors who were not averse to killing to obtain the skeletons to incorporate into the collections of the SS doctors or the display in the SS Medical Academy at Graz." A clerk in the pathology department testified that one day the camp physician pointed at a passing inmate and told him that he wanted that skull on his desk the next day. According to the witness, "the very same evening, the prisoner was ordered to report to the hospital and the next day he was on my autopsy table and the skull was taken apart, and it was turned over."[31]

Prisoners who had particularly well done or interesting tattoos often ended up dead on a dissecting table. Every tattooed prisoner was immediately catalogued on entering the camp, and when his order came up, the doctors called him to the dispensary and killed him by injection. They turned the corpse over to the pathology department, which was skilled at skin removal and tanning: "Production was carried out by two ways. Either it was put into a transparent form, or it was tanned so that the skin became tough, like leather." The human skin was put to several uses. The scientists sent some pieces to the tattoo collection at a special museum in Berlin. They also found that the skin made excellent lamp shades, several of which were expressly fitted for Frau Koch, wife of the commandant. One piece of skin that struck her fancy had the words "Hansel and Gretel" tattooed on it. Frau Koch's table lamp was made of human bones and had a tattooed human-skin shade. Decorators pleaded for tattooed skins for their customers.

The scientists provided special treasures for SS visitors in the form of shrunken heads. A returned traveler from Africa who understood the process of reducing a human skull to the size of a doll's head was taken into the pathology department to teach the SS staff how to shrink skulls. The SS doctors prepared a number of such heads according to requests from their clientele.[32]

And those SS men who punished, beat, experimented with, and killed the prisoners—what kind of life did they have? In every camp they received special favors, but probably in no camp were there so many added attractions as at Buchenwald, particularly for the high officials. The prisoners constructed a falconry court as a tribute to Hermann Göring, and a riding hall for Ilse, wife of Commandant Koch. They began the falconry court construction in 1938 and completed it in 1940, at a cost of 135,000 marks for the materials alone. The area contained several buildings—a falcon house, built in the ancient Teutonic style out of massively carved oaks; a hunting hall, with huge fireplaces and hunting trophies; a garden house; and the falconer's home. It also included a game preserve and a cage for wildcats. The SS and the prisoners gathered deer, wild boar, foxes, pheasants, and other animals for their preserve. The prisoners built a zoological garden, which contained at different times monkeys, bears, and even a rhinoceros. Whenever an animal died, the Jews were forced to pay for a replacement through a "voluntary collection."

As a favorite pastime Commandant Koch threw prisoners into the bears' cages. Survivors remember the excellent diet the animals enjoyed. Although the camp suffered from a serious food shortage, the zoo animals received a daily meat ration from the prisoner mess. Bears ate honey and jam, and the monkeys consumed mashed potatoes with milk, oat flakes, and other delicacies. Though the man for whom the park was built, Reichsmarshal Göring, never set eyes on it, the SS managed to profit from it by advertising the attraction through the area and charging admission to the Weimar residents to see it.

In Frau Koch's spacious and airy riding hall mirrors covered the walls. The construction materials alone cost about 250,000 marks, but the prisoner labor, of course, was free. Frau Koch used the hall several times a week for morning rides and required the prisoner band to furnish music for her enjoyment. After she went to jail the authorities turned the riding hall into a storage depot.

The SS availed themselves of a whole range of entertainment and recreational opportunities. The commandant entertained at special social evenings once a month. Inmates described those as eating and drinking sprees that ended in "wild orgies." The SS enjoyed life in Buchenwald—almost a country unto itself, wrote one inmate, with its parks and stylish villages, "all for the pleasure of the masters of the master-race. For us there was an abundance of ammunition plants, factories making parts for V2 rockets, and stone quarries."[33]

The story of Buchenwald's commandant and SS leadership is a tale of corruption, license, and punishment unusual in the annals of concentration camp and SS bureaucratic history. It revolves around Commandant Koch, Ilse Koch, the "Bitch of Buchenwald," and the Morgen Corruption Commission. Koch and his wife Ilse were an odd combination. Born in 1897, the son of a minor official, Colonel Koch served in World War I, was a clerk in the 1920s, and had married and divorced by 1931. In 1931 he joined the Nazi party and then the SS. Expelled from the party in 1932 because of an affair, he was soon readmitted. His involvement in criminal proceedings for embezzlement in 1935 did not prevent the SS from appointing him commandant of a notorious camp called Esterwegen in 1935 and commandant of Sachsenhausen in 1936. Koch had married Ilse in 1937 and they had three children. Ilse was born in 1906, the daughter of a middle-class father, and had been a stenographer until her marriage. She followed her husband to the camps.

In 1937 Himmler appointed Koch as commandant of Buchenwald. During his rise to power Koch strove for millionaire status, initially by seizing the personal belongings of thousands of Jews and not accounting for them. Additional sources of income came from hiring out camp labor to civilian employers, racketeering in food supplies meant for prisoners and guards, and taking over the camp workshop production for his private use. "The life of the Kochs and the entourage of SS officers was the phantasmagoria of promiscuity and self indulgence."[34]

Koch remained safe for several years by bribing his superior officers who wished to share in the spoils. In 1941, however, Theodor Eicke, the SS inspector of concentration camps, was sent to the front. In his absence the Thuringian Ministry of Finance started inquiries into the nonpayment of taxes. Prince von Waldeck-Pyrmont, the Thuringian SS leader and police chief, who had long been a personal enemy of Koch, stood behind the investigation. The prince met resistance from the SS officers over him. Finally, Himmler advised him that no further action was desired. In February 1942 Koch was transferred from Buchenwald to become commandant at Majdanek. When Prince Waldeck used that opportunity to reexamine Buchenwald records, he found that Koch had destroyed all the evidence of corruption and shot all the witnesses.

By March 1943 Himmler was willing to permit an official investigation, probably because a large group of Russian prisoners had escaped from Majdanek as a result of Koch's neglect. SS Dr. Morgen, who headed the investigation, arrested Koch and brought him to trial along with his accomplices and his wife. The court sentenced Koch to death, but gave him a temporary reprieve. It released Ilse because of insufficient evidence. Prince Waldeck, however, had the satisfaction of having Koch killed a few days before the liberation of the camp.

Ilse managed to survive longer than her husband. The Allies captured her and brought her to trial in 1947, by which time she was pregnant by a German with whom she had been having an affair while detained by the American troops. The court convicted her, but General Clay reduced her sentence to four years despite the fact that many witnesses had testified to her sexual depravity and cruelty and described her as a woman whose very whim could bring terrible punishment to prisoners. On January 15, 1951, another court sentenced her to life imprisonment for murder. At the Dachau trial Ilse pictured herself as a good German housewife who took care of her children, never entered the prisoner camp, and had nothing to do with the dissecting of tattooed prisoners. She told the court that it was silly to spend so much money on her when scores of war criminals had already been released.

The Kochs were not the only corrupt people in Buchenwald. The roll call list of SS officers read like a recital of criminality and corruption. One historian concludes that the Koch affair fully reflected "the all-pervading parasitism of the SS."[35]

Politics

Several aspects of the Buchenwald camp seem unusual within the concentration system. Perhaps the most striking of these were prisoner control, politics, corruption, and the strength of the underground organization. The complex situation does not lend itself to a simple analysis, and memoirs and histories of Buchenwald need to be carefully scrutinized, probably more so than for any other camp. Those who wrote them were both survivors and leaders in the underground. The leading writers—Eugen Kogon, Christopher Burney, and Eugene Heimler—fully participated in competing political groups. Consequently, the literature is filled with accusations and counter-accusations, cover-ups, defensive responses, and great gaps in factual information.

Every camp had some form of secret prisoner organization, but Buchenwald's was especially well organized, efficient, and strong. The Buchenwald underground, originally the creation of the German communists, was augmented by communists of other nationalities. As that augmentation took place, a struggle occurred. As they gathered strength and organization in the early years, the politicals began to move the criminal convicts out of leadership positions. By exploiting the laziness of the SS, by becoming indispensable to the administration, by exerting strong party discipline, they slowly gained control until they held authority over a large part of the camp's interior operations, including the transport and execution lists, the disposition of sick prisoners, and the camp police. At the same time, their basic principle became quite clear—a communist was worth more than any other prisoner.

External factors, particularly the course of the war, contributed to the success of the politicals in 1942. Hitler found himself with the dilemma of having to mobilize all remaining German males he could for the war and at the same time increase industrial production. Whether they liked it or not, in order to meet those goals, the SS simply had to look after manpower in a better fashion by providing better rations, opening up infirmaries, and changing their attitude toward prisoners. Allied bombing further complicated the problem because it made it necessary to construct underground production factories on a large scale. Such construction demanded the employment of massive numbers of workers. What better source of workers than the concentration camp prisoners? The shift in attitude substantially changed the camp regime between 1942 and 1943.

Confrontations between the communists, other politicals, the common criminals, and the SS caused great confusion and bitterness. On the top level of camp society the power relationships reflected the social, political, military, and economic changes taking place. An oligarchy of the politicals developed, achieved at great cost. Those who were not a part of the winning group found the change brutalizing. The difficulty, in the final analysis, was in the area of morality. As one survivor questioned: How much is it necessary and proper to dirty one's hands and compromise in order to save lives that might otherwise be lost? The question is a difficult one, and it was faced by many groups under Nazi control. It was certainly a common problem for the Jewish Councils. Should one struggle uncompromisingly to avoid contamination? What good is it to destroy an enemy if in the process the enemy's hated characteristics become one's own. It is helpful to remember that the prisoners forced to ask and answer those questions were starving, on the edge of dying, and constantly in fear for their lives.

Christopher Burney, the leader of one alternative resistance group, wrote about the corruption that occurred when the prisoners gained power:

These camp leaders had the unstinted and guaranteed backing of the SS guns; they had in their hands all the mechanisms of death, whether by work, by hospital "treatment," by selection for the Experiment Block, or by simple denunciation on a capital charge, and in addition, and by no means the least important, they controlled the distribution of rations and tobacco. While the SS controlled the quantity of food that entered the camp, it was the prisoners who portioned it out.[36]

Burney concluded that the communist and German prisoners abused their power seriously. Of course, as he pointed out, they had plausible excuses. If they were a bit rough, it was because the work had to be done or the SS would interfere and kill. If they lashed and beat some prisoners, it was because unless they exercised strict discipline, the SS would take matters into their own hands. If the hospital was not a pleasant place, it was because there was not enough medicine or space for everyone. There is an element of truth in every response, but Burney insists that the means the politicals employed were beyond all rules of common decency and comradeship. He judges them guilty of a grave offense in that they abused for their own ends position which they could have used in the service of their fellowmen; in that they brought death and distress to thousands when they could have saved hundreds; and that they forgot the sacred rule, that he who sets himself up as an aristocrat must first learn that *noblesse oblige.*[37]

Other leading survivors have accused the underground leaders of actions such as selecting political enemies for extermination. And they have pointed out that the politicals' positive actions were often based on self-preservation rather than charity. Still, the camp as a whole seemed to have benefited from major actions taken by the communists.

According to information now available in the DDR and presentations made by DDR scholars, the underground created the International Camp Committee in 1943, which organized a common front for all prisoners prepared to fight against the SS. The organized prisoners performed great acts of heroism on a daily basis, claim these historians. They sabotaged arms production, protected the sick and the weak against hard labor, saved patriots from execution, and raised camp morale. Their eventual aim, apparently, was to liberate the camp by armed struggle. To that end, the secret military organization trained its men carefully. It obtained weapons from various sources and made its own, and worked to ready the camp for the moment of liberation.[38]

Liberation

As the war drew to a close and the Allies moved into Germany, tension within Buchenwald increased. For the first time the SS exhibited fear of the prisoners. Unfortunately, between April 3 and April 10 Buchenwald underwent an immense and chaotic evacuation that affected 28,000 of the 48,000 prisoners. The columns of prisoners marched out of the camp were simply shot and killed by the SS. Thousand of inmates were stuffed into boxcars and sent to Dachau; cars full of dead bodies ended up on sidings or roamed around Germany until the end of the war.

Half of the last-minute deportees from Buchenwald were Jews who lived in the notcrious Little Camp where they did not receive the protection of the International Camp Committee. The SS threw 4,500 of them on the Dachau train, and most died as it wandered through Czechoslovakia in search of an unbombed track. The International Committee did not have enough arms at its disposal to fight the 3,000 guards. Thus it decided on a policy of sacrificing those whom it deemed least worthwhile, admitting that the 6,000 Jews demanded by the SS on April 2 were not worth fighting over. Similarly on April 6, when the SS needed to make up a transport of 8,000 people, the committee weeded out those Jews and Gentiles whom it regarded as worthless. Consequently, in the last days the Jews suffered the most, and received very little help from the International Committee. Yet it was in that period that the prisoner organization demonstrated its greatest power. Combining a concerted general resistance with cleverly devised acts of individual intimidation, it clearly was indispensable in saving 21,000 prisoners.[39]

While the mind of Himmler waivered in the last days, the intentions of a great many SS officers remained consistent. Himmler sent word to Eisenhower that Buchenwald would be handed over intact, and when he received word of the SS evacuation, he did stop it—supposedly. Himmler maintained that Kaltenbrunner had issued the instructions for evacuation over his head. That conclusion is still open to question. Clearly, the SS officers intended to evacuate the camp and destroy it. Later, after the prisoners gained control, they received a phone call from Weimar that the SS flamethrowers had arrived in town and needed a transport to the camp!

The International Committee carefully concealed weapons. Inmates began to refuse to go to roll call and to intimidate the commandant by different ruses. When the Americans bypassed Weimar to pursue the *Waffen* SS, the delay increased tensions. The SS evacuated more and more inmates, and it soon became clear that they intended to kill everyone. Elie Wiesel tells of waiting in the camp on April 10 with the remaining 20,000, including several hundred children. Toward evening the SS massed the prisoners in the huge assembly hall, but then the sirens began to wail, announcing an air raid alert. The guards sent the prisoners back to the blocks until the air raid was over. By then evening had fallen, so the evacuation had to be postponed to the following day. The prisoners were relieved, but tormented by hunger.

At 10 A.M. on April 11 the SS moved the 20,000 prisoners toward the assembly place. Taking advantage of the close proximity of the American troops, the International Committee gave the order for attack about noon. "Armed men suddenly rose up everywhere. Bursts of firing. Grenades exploding. We children stayed flat on the ground in the block. The battle did not last long." The inmates stormed the camp gate at 2:30 P.M., overcame the SS, and arrested them. Only the guards in the watchtowers remained. Shortly before 3 P.M., as the sounds of the general battle came closer, the guards retired to the woods. Inmates hung a white flag from the main tower and took over the camp. When the first American tanks arrived at the gates of Buchenwald, they found it already liberated, with about 20,000 survivors waiting for them.[40]

Suddenly the inmates realized they were free. For many, however—perhaps for most—liberation meant a continuation of problems. As the days passed, the liberated inmates received more food, but the change from a few grams of dry bread to unlimited quantities of goulash soup was too much too soon and resulted in uncontrollable and pitiless diarrhea:

The stagnant brown pond in the lavatory pit threatened to overflow. Everything around it, together with the footpaths leading to the blocks, was contaminated and sticky with whatever it was that the bowels of a starving man made out of warmed-up Hungarian-style tinned goulash. . . .[41]

After his liberation from Buchenwald Elie Wiesel described his feelings as he gazed into a mirror for the first time in four years: "From the depths of the mirror, a corpse gazed back at me. The look in his eyes, as they stared into mine, has never left me." And his experience came from a camp renamed for the beechwood, in the words of poet William Heyen, a soft wood "shining with sunlight falling through yellow leaves. A name, a place of terror."[42]

After a few days those who were strong enough began to explore the countryside and the villages. The German population refused to admit that they had known of Buchenwald's existence. It seems clear, however, that any Thuringian ignorant of Buchenwald "within a year of the seizure of power was either an anchorite or obtuse to the point of cretinism."[43] Inmates in their explorations found the country population frightened of them. The citizens also grumbled about being maltreated by the wanderers. Their definition of maltreatment meant the confiscation of farm goods in order to feed the sick— the survivors who were still dying of disease, exhaustion, and undernourishment.

The American Army transferred the inmates to the former SS barracks or to the main camp, and provided cupboards, blankets, books, and newspapers. The International Camp Committee became the supreme camp authority for a few weeks. Its leaders, who represented various nationalities, created army squads that patrolled the countrysize to catch former SS men and to discover Nazi supplies. Allied missions arrived to study the horror of the camps.

And then came May Day 1945. Former inmates who had settled in the surrounding towns and villages returned to celebrate with the survivors still living in the compounds. The Russians hung garlands along the streets and pasted portraits of Stalin in the barracks and along the routes. The survivors assembled in the camp square, each column behind the flag of its homeland. In front of the survivors stood a huge stage and on it a large wood construction decorated with portraits of Churchill, Stalin, and Roosevelt. The program began with a symbolic play about Buchenwald. Guests from all over the world spoke to the survivors. The survivors in turn paid tribute to their dead and affirmed their solidarity. They pledged themselves never to forget their common suffering. Then the band began playing and the columns marched past the saluting guests.

The square that, with the Nazi flag towering over the entrance gate, had for eight years of daily rollcalls been filled with helpless prisoners, now held triumphant crowds parading with the proud banners of their homelands. Its vast expanse of asphalt, which had heard the moans of thousands after thousands trudging to their death, now resounded with the victorious marching steps of the survivors.[44]

The marchers left empty spaces between them to represent those who had not survived.

Thomas Geve recalls that May Day at Buchenwald as a cherished memory. As his column drew past the guest platform his cheeks flushed with excitement. "I, the haggard shabby bearer of a little pink board with the name of some obscure province on it, I, the forgotten youngster who for years had been rotting in the concentration camps, was being saluted!" Later he described the camp as becoming very joyful and gay with nightly parties. After May Day more groups left and the time was filled with celebrations. The Russians gave their farewell performance in the huge SS theater. Singers, ballet dancers, and acrobats moved over the stage and the hall vibrated with songs of the Red Army. The Jewish youngsters from Poland also arranged an artistic evening. Performing a play called *Dance of the Machines,* the children created shadows of working youngsters. As a finale, the youngsters sang the refrain: "But machines have no hearts, know no pain and understand no jokes."[45]

A young soldier from Portland, Maine came into the camp with his fellow soldiers a few days after the liberation. His letter to his wife on April 23, 1945, is a clear description of the impressions of American soldiers. He explained that he had heard much about the camps and seen atrocity pictures. When he arrived, however, he found that the pictures, which he had thought were propaganda, fell short of presenting the unpleasant truth.

It is to be regretted that the scoffers and even more important, the legislators of all lands ... cannot all see for themselves this mute memorial to the Kultur of the Herrenvolk. It is a picture that would leave an everlasting impression and its value as a spur to remedial action would be unequalled by anything or anyone else. ... Today there are still a few thousand left not by any show of humaneness or mercy on the part of the SS Killers, but rather due to the sudden advent of our combat units which overran these places with such speed as to preclude the extinction of such life as was left in these unfortunates. I say some thousands were still alive, but some would be better dead. Too weak to even move, they lie with glazed eyes unable to move their emaciated bodies. ...

We saw piled up stacks of bodies with twitching limbs the rule, not the exception—piles of white ash with pieces of unburned bone protruding—spick and span crematoriums—immaculate "execution" chambers—products of the orderly German mind. It was said that here experiments were conducted on toxic gases, using human guinea pigs. Altogether possible since in one room I saw organs of the body floating in jars dispersed along shelves—here a brain, there a liver—this—the scientific German mind.[46]

The army brought German civilians by the hundreds from Weimar and forced them to work in the kitchens, to clean the barracks, and to dig mass graves on the mountainside. Into those graves "thousands of victims were literally chucked like old rags." There was no time for funerals.[47]

After a few days a Jewish survivor named Unsdorfer began to think about the Jewish nation, its heritage, his religion.

The face of every Jewish inmate in the camp mirrored a vivid picture of the Jewish people: a crippled and shrunken people, a race which had suffered the most tremendous spiritual, as well as physical, onslaught in the history of mankind; a race of orphans, widows, and widowers; a race of mourning fathers who had lost their sons; of saddened mothers who had their babies snatched away from their breasts; of sons who had seen their fathers, brothers, and sisters burnt to ashes while still half alive.

We had not the heroic glamour of soldiers who had died on the battlefield, or sailors drowned in the ocean; we were prisoners who had been humiliated and scorned, and now that we were free, what did the future hold?

We had lost our noblest and finest, our dearest and most precious, in the course of a callously prepared program of cold murder, destruction, and annihilation; we were a nation whose blood was shed in every country under Nazi occupation, far away from battlefields and air attacks.[48]

Unsdorfer wondered who again would want to hear of God and who would provide the religious serum. He found, strangely enough, that he received his first injection of Vitamin R—Religious Revival—in the camp. An American Jewish chaplin conducted a religious service to mark the festival of *Shavuoth,* the first postwar Jewish religious service to be held on the soil of Germany.

As Chaplin Schechter intoned the Evening Prayers, all the inmates in and outside the blocks stood in silence, re-accepting the Torah whose people, message, and purpose Hitler's Germany had attempted to destroy. Jewish history repeated itself. Just as our forefathers who were liberated from Egypt accepted the Law and the desert, so we, the liberated Jews of Buchenwald, reaccepted the same Law in the concentration camps of Germany.[49]

An amazing story comes from a group diary of Kibbutz Buchenwald, an agricultural commune formed by some survivors of Buchenwald. When liberation came, a group of Jews sat down and pondered where to go. They decided to find a farm where they could prepare for eventual transfer to Palestine and build their own kibbutz. The American military government gave them the right to use a confiscated farm. On June 3, 1945, Zionist survivors from various organizations and factions of Jewish life formed the settlement. The farm was broken down and filthy, the cattle emaciated, the land neglected. But the twenty or so survivors immediately went to work at hard labor to plant crops and bring the farm back to life. On June 9 they hoisted the blue-white flag with the Star of David onto their flagpole and invited a number of guests, including Jewish soldiers of the American Army and an American chaplain, to see their work. When it became clear that the Russian Army would occupy Thuringia, the Americans moved the group to the west and gave it another farm.

One problem that erupted immediately in the group was over the question of sexual relations with German women. One leader emphasized that he did not want blood revenge on the German citizens, but that simple human self-respect must prevent the survivors from having relations with German women. "When our beloved Jewish girls burned in the crematoria, their clothes were brought to Germany, and these very girls might be wearing their dresses, their rings." The group agreed that any member of the kibbutz guilty of such relations would be automatically expelled.[50]

Consultants arrived from Palestine and expressed surprise that a group of people with such divergent beliefs and political differences could forge such a strong bond. The survivors responded that they were comrades who had lived together on the brink of death, and had therefore developed a unity far beyond mere politics. After finally arriving in Palestine, a new Buchenwald Israeli wrote:

I feel that this moment will remain with me as the happiest moment of my life. I know that the past will not leave me, and I am a little afraid. Once I wanted to believe in the world, in people, in ideals, and life has shown me this could not be. Now the same wish begins to be reborn in me. I put away all that I have lived through in these last years. I leave it there in the depths of the sea. I go to the new life as I saw and imagined it once. Only somewhere in me I still have a fear that disillusionment will come again.[51]

The group established a successful settlement in Israel.

After the war the Buchenwald and Dora survivors formed an organization called the Buchenwald-Dora Survivors Association. Its motto: *"Qui tacet consentire videtar,"* or "By one's silence, one gives consent." The organization publishes a periodical, *Die Glocke vom Ettersberg,* which attempts to alert its members to neo-Nazi groups and actions, trial proceedings, whereabouts of old Nazis, news of the memorial. The association has branches throughout East Germany and in other countries. The Buchenwald Memorial and the association took their inspiration from the survivor's liberation oath:

OATH

of the survivors of the concentration camp

BUCHENWALD

on April 19, 1945

We swear therefore before the whole world
at this place of assembly,
at this abode of fascist horror:
We will cease our battle only then,
when the very last guilty one
stands before the judges of the peoples!
The extermination of Nazism
with its roots is our watchword.
The erection of a new world
of peace and freedom
is our goal.[52]

1. Entrance
2. Entrance gate
3. Row of prisoners' graves
4. Avenue with stelae
5. Mass graves
6. Street of the Nations
7. Group of statues
8. Bell tower

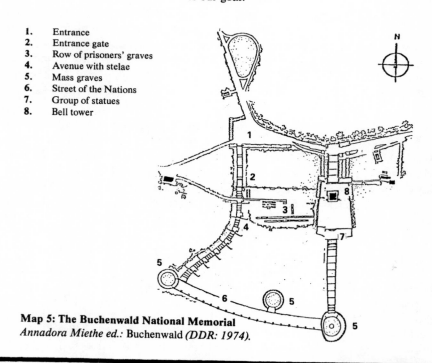

Map 5: The Buchenwald National Memorial
Annadora Miethe ed.: Buchenwald *(DDR: 1974).*

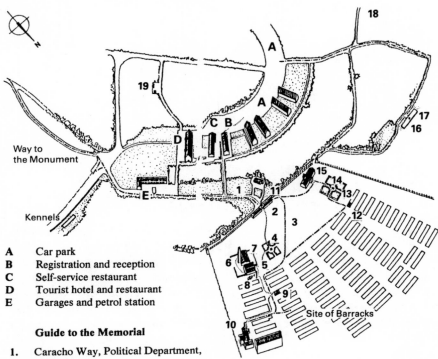

A   Car park
B   Registration and reception
C   Self-service restaurant
D   Tourist hotel and restaurant
E   Garages and petrol station

Guide to the Memorial

1. Caracho Way, Political Department, Commandatura
2. Outer buildings with entrance to camp
3. Roll-call Square
4. Memorial to Murdered Polish Patriots
5. Place where prisoners were shot in the neck (reconstruction)
6. Place where Ernst Thälmann died
7. Crematorium
8. Stake—cart—roller
9. Memorial to Murdered British and Canadian Paratroopers
10. Camp Museum and Ernst Thälmann Memorial
11. Detention center (bunker)
12. No. 8 Barrack, children's barrack
13. Memorial to Soviet Prisoners of War
14. Memorial to Murdered Jewish Prisoners
15. Former canteen, now dedicated to the nations, lecture and reading room, library
16. Stables, place where 8,483 Soviet soldiers were murdered
17. Memorial to these murdered Soviet soldiers
18. Quarry
19. Memorial tablet to Rudolf Breitscheid

**Map 4: Lay-out of existing buildings
The Buchenwald National Memorial**

Annadora Miethe, ed.: Buchenwald *(DDR: 1974).*

MAUTHAUSEN: EXTERMINATION BY LABOR IN AUSTRIA

In the dreaded Austrian camp complex Mauthausen the Nazis took the concept of extermination by labor to its fullest twentieth-century expression. The prisoners produced with their labor, but that production was a sideline, a byproduct of the killing process. Unlike the personnel of other labor camps—even Auschwitz—Mauthausen leaders displayed no nervousness because the industrious inmates died so quickly and in such large numbers. Nor did they mind that their Auschwitz colleagues sent their prisoners to Mauthausen for punishment.

Mauthausen, the term commonly used for the mother camp, must be applied to the entire Austrian labor complex that emanated from, encircled, and reported to the mother camp. That complex included sixty subcamps, some almost as large as Mauthausen proper. The subcamp designations—Gusen I, Gusen II, Ebensee, Melk—stand today as grim reminders that civilian industrial concerns often created, through their cynical demands for cheap labor, the conditions by which thousands of human beings were worked to death in surroundings far harsher than those that existed in the major extermination camps. Killing is killing by any definition. But the means to death have a great bearing on life and dignity and oppression. It was better to be shot than gassed. And it was far better to be gassed than to be crushed or suffocated in the quarries, the underground factories, or the mountain tunnels of the Mauthausen complex. Knowledgeable Auschwitz inmates paled when they received their Mauthausen transfer notices.

The mother camp lies a few kilometers off the Vienna-Salzburg Autobahn. It is reached by turning off the autobahn 26 kilometers below Linz and 160 kilometers upstream from Vienna. The road follows the Danube, passing through pretty villages and thick woods. One drives up the high hills that edge the broad valley, climbing and turning on the narrow curves to the summit—and then it springs into close view, unmistakable. From the climbing road Mauthausen looks like a typical somber-gray granite penitentiary. The air smells fresh and crisp, even in the warm summer, and the location and view are superb. From the top of the hill the visitor can catch an excellent portrait

116

of the Danube River valley below—dotted with villages—and of the Alps in the background. The view at dusk, though, is another experience. For then the walls seem to push themselves through the gloom. The white flagstones stand out in the falling light—oppressively clean and silent. The dead stillness seems to proclaim that for each stone, a human body was crushed.

Watchtowers and the tall granite wall flank the camp entrance and its huge wooden door—reminding the visitor that this view was the first seen by the condemned. Through the gate, across the roll call ground bordered by wooden and stone huts, to Barracks 5—the old quarters for the Jews and the sick. The Austrian government declared the camp an historic monument in 1949. In the center of the roll call area Austria erected a memorial to the dead of all countries. And then to the former hut village for newcomers and now a cemetery for Mauthausen victims who died after liberation. Next, the sick quarters, which now house the Mauthausen Museum. Adjacent are the gas chamber, crematorium, bunker, execution corner: simple, lonely, impartial, but so dusty and still that the past seems far away. The tiny dissection chamber, connected to the crematorium by a corridor, contains the sloping stone dissection table with its practical blood canal. Claw marks on the tiled walls of the gas chambers testify to the agony of the death struggle. The old laundry building has been made into a quiet chapel, welcomed by many visitors as a needed setting in which to begin the process of sorting out the mind's thoughts, fears, images, fantasies.

Inside Mauthausen memorials of many nations stand on the site of the SS barracks: the Russian sculpture depicting a Soviet general who died a hero's death in the camp; the Belgian granite obelisk; the Polish stone shrine; the Albanian black iron men; the Czech figure of a battered inmate raising his arms to the sky; the Yugoslavian twisted and torn iron sculpture; the German prisoner before a granite wall on which words of Brecht have been carved; the torturous Hungarian group of tall black iron inmates, with arms and clenched fists stretched above their heads; the Spanish and Italian granite walls; the French tower; the Luxembourg stone leaf. So many monuments to the courage and dying of so many different peoples.

Mauthausen was known throughout Europe as a ghastly quarry camp. The Wienergraben, as the quarries were called, survives with the 186 death steps surrounded by the steep cliffs that served as the Parachute Jump—from which the guards threw groups of prisoners. The quarry bottom is silent except for the birds, and its floor is covered with grass, weeds, and bushes. At the edge of the quarry sits a woman, a stunning form, created by the East German artist Fritz Cremer in 1961. The sculpture is an allegorical figure who turns away in pain. Her eyes are closed and in her demeanor is a silent, sorrowful endurance. The left hand points simply to the camp surroundings. Cremer tried to express German self-accusation in this sitting statue, which is a new form of a woman in sorrow. He titled his work with Bertolt Brecht's words: "Germany—Pale Mother." The facial features remind one of the falling figure in the Buchenwald memorial.

A short distance from the mother camp lies the sinister Castle Hartheim, which was used as a gassing, burning, and torture facility for Mauthausen proper. The castle rises out of the flat countryside, its heavy outline peculiar against the sky. It *is* sinister. It *does* evoke evil. And yet Austrians live there today in converted apartments.

A few kilometers west of the mother camp are Gusen I, Gusen II, Gusen III—the large labor camps with their quarries, huge tunnels dug into the hillside, and underground factory sites. Ebensee, in the wooded region of nearby Salzkammergut with its underground tunnels and factories. And Melk, built in the shadow of a beautiful monastery on the hill.

It would take a lifetime to confront the sites of the entire Mauthausen complex. A few days is sufficient to form an unwilling picture of the expanse, variety, and complexity of Germany's major labor/death institution. It covered Austria, pushing its arm into every region, every area.[1]

Mauthausen epitomizes the old slave saying: "Labor means death." Mauthausen was not an extermination camp as the Nazis defined it. The SS did not make selections when the train stopped at the station. Insteady they sent the prisoners to the labor battalions, where they were literally worked to death.

Heinrich Himmler visited Austria before Germany invaded it. He was looking for a site that could serve both for economic exploitation and as a permanent concentration camp. Himmler had in mind making the SS a "separate economic empire." The SS managed several large concerns run by camp labor; the major ones were the German Earth and Stone Works (DEST) and the German Equipment Works (DAW). At Himmler's side during his visits to Austria walked officials from the DEST works. He and his colleagues examined the Wienergraben quarries, long-term suppliers of paving stones for Vienna. The quarries lay next to a small town, Mauthausen, which had the good fortune to be on a railroad line. The group decided it would make an excellent camp site. On August 8, 1938, the SS transferred prisoners from Dachau and began the construction of the camp. In 1941, when Himmler devised his classification system for the camps, Mauthausen fell into Grade III, the only camp in that category. With the exception of the extermination centers, Grade III was the worst category—reserved for prisoners with "bad records," "criminals, antisocial elements, and those who could not be reeducated."[2]

During the camp's early months Mauthausen did not possess a gas chamber or a crematorium. As in Sachsenhausen, the SS sent the bodies to a civilian crematorium some distance away at Steyr. Because so much body traffic occupied the road between the two points, Austrian peasants and villagers began to notice, to become anxious, and to complain. Concerned about the image of the SS in occupied countries in the west, Himmler relieved Commandant Sauer and his assistant, Kramer, of their duties and sent them elsewhere.

Cruel, baby-faced SS Commandant Franz Ziereis became the new leader of the atrocity complex. His major vice "lay in his inexhaustible homicidal activities, and in this he excelled." So did his eleven-year-old son. With his father's approval, he delighted in sitting on the front porch of the administration building and shooting prisoners with his rifle as other boys would shoot rabbits. As the war ended, Ziereis lay dying in the hands of the Allies, unrepentant. He had run a concentration camp in which 40,000 people had been killed in the first four months of 1945 alone. Yet he insisted he was a substantial citizen performing his tasks well, and he spoke of himself as a good family man. He adored his wife and son. He tried to convince his disbelieving interrogators that mass killing and robbing repulsed him. On his deathbed, though, he admitted to a few charges. Dr. Richter, he said, had "murdered several hundred prisoners while operating on them without any reason and cut away the brain, stomach, and liver, . . . or other interiors."[3]

Most of the mother camp was completed by 1939. The SS planned Mauthausen for a 10 square kilometer area, divided between quarry and camp. The main camp consisted of three sections with thirty blocks. Camp I included twenty huts used as inmate living quarters, a women's section added later in the war, the sick block, and the usual maintenance facilities. Camp II included five huts that were first specified as workshops and later used as inmate housing; and Camp III had six huts for prisoners. An additional tent camp included six large and eight small military tents, erected in 1944 for the Hungarian Jews, without water and lavatories.

In the completed camp a cluster of buildings housed the kitchen, the bunker, the crematorium, the new hospital, and a double crematorium. Connecting tunnels ran underneath and between the crematorium and the double crematorium. The original two-oven crematorium functioned from the end of 1941 until liberation. The second and third double crematorium was built later. The furnace room for the crematoria contained the execution corner. Prisoners walked in and found a device for measuring heights. As they stood against the wall while the guards measured their height, an SS man shot them in the neck through a slot in the headboard. The planners camouflaged the gas chamber as bathrooms with showers. Cyclone B streamed into the chamber from the control room. The SS removed the gas chambers in 1945. The adjacent camp jail, known as the bunker, held thirty-three cells. Many prominent European politicians were imprisoned there under false names.

Mauthausen was no secret in the region. Certainly the Austrian citizens were aware of its existence. When the prisoners arrived at the small railroad station, the village children waited to throw stones at them as they began their march to the camp. The villagers also taunted them as they got off the train: "You'll soon be up the chimney on Totenburg."[4]

Work: the key word of the Mauthausen complex. The SS/prisoner ratio never fell below 10:1. Supervisory staff consisted of a large SS Death's Head Unit and 600 former army and air force personnel. Sixty subcamps emerged during the Ziereis years. Two, Gusen and Ebensee, approached the size of the mother camp. Subcamp work details spanned a full range of industrial, military, and public works activity: iron ore mining; hydropower construction; road and tunnel construction; tank, aircraft engine, and plane manufacture; armament, cartridge, and V-weapon production; and textile manufacture. Laborers worked on farms, in sawmills, and in brickworks. They forged money and helped scientists in research institutes. At Ebensee 18,000 inmates tunneled into the mountain to build underground armament plants. In Melk 10,000 labored on the tunneling/armament factory project, and in Gusen II, 12,500.[5]

The Mauthausen Quarry: For those who remained behind at the mother camp, Mauthausen *was* the quarry, notorious for its harsh conditions and the death rate. Prisoners working in the quarry seldom lived longer than three months. They used the most primitive methods and equipment to mine the granite. Following a visit to Mauthausen in 1943, Albert Speer wrote Himmler that he could not supply the SS with the materials and labor they had requested. Therefore, insisted Speer, Himmler and the SS commandants should introduce the principle of *Primitivbauweise* into Mauthausen: the prisoners should use inexpensive materials and work with their bare hands. We do not have Himmler's response, but we can imagine that he wrote back and told Speer that Mauthausen had never operated on any other principle.[6]

After raising the rocks by hand and by back from the bottom, Mauthausen inmates loaded the granite into wagons hooked to a narrow-gauge railroad line. The cumbersome carts frequently jumped the tracks, crushing workers in their path. Dangerous blasting conditions enhanced by SS perversity caused more deaths. On one occasion a guard ordered an Italian Jew with a beautiful voice to climb to the top of a rock and sing the "Ave Maria." As the guard laid the charge and connected the plunger, "the outline of the singer was silhouetted against the setting sun. The beauty of his rendering froze the prisoner onlookers with horror and grief. The plunger detonated the charge and the voice stopped abruptly."[7] Workers thought of the quarry as a death trap. They died from starvation, tuberculosis, cold, heart failure, exhaustion, accidents, and cold-blooded murder. Throughout the war stories filtered back of grizzly quarry accidents.

In 1943 Messerschmidt located a factory in the quarry. Its presence did not improve conditions or lessen the inclination of the SS to use the quarry as a routine murder machine. In one incident in 1944 a new group of NN

(*Nacht and Nebel*, Night and Fog) prisoners arrived at the quarry. The SS led the forty-seven Dutch, American, and English officers and fliers, bare-footed, to the bottom. On their first journey up the 186 steps they forced the men to carry twenty-five kilogram stones on their backs. On each successive journey they increased the weight of the load. If a prisoner fell, he was beaten. All forty-seven died of the treatment.[8]

Jews suffered from especially harsh and murderous treatment in the Mauthausen quarry. *Kapos* assigned them the worst tasks and the least food. For example, it was a Jewish job to carry the full toilet buckets on poles and dump them away from the quarry. As the Jews stumbled up the slopes, the bucket contents slopped over and covered them with excrement. The SS pushed so many Jews over the quarry precipice to their deaths that it became known as the "Parachute Jump," and the victims as "paratroopers." In 1941 a large group of Dutch Jews arrived at the quarry for special treatment. The SS denied them the use of the 186 steps for their first flight to the bottom, forcing them instead to slide down the loose stones on the side—an action that killed many. Then the SS forced the remaining Jews to load rocks on their backs and run up the steps. Sometimes the rocks rolled down the hill, crushing the feet of those behind. Those who lost their rocks were brutally beaten. For two days the SS drove the Jews up and down the steps. On the third day, driven by despair, the remaining Jews joined hands and leaped over the precipice to their death in the quarry below.[9]

The mother camp utilized a full-scale torture and punishment program with a few variations. The SS developed, as their specialty, murder by drowning. It took several forms: forcing hoses into the prisoner's mouth until the lungs burst from the water, immersing victims in barrels, and submerging them in ditches. In another torture variation the guards forced prisoners out of their blocks, naked, to stand and walk for hours in an area scattered with "fiercely jagged stones." Cold weather aided the program. In 1945, 1,700 prisoners arrived from Sachsenhausen. The SS grouped together the sick prisoners and sent them outside—nude. That night the temperature dropped below freezing. The prisoners stood in the square for four hours as they were sprayed alternately with hot and cold water. The groans of the dying rang through the camp as icicles formed all over their bodies. One remarkable prisoner, the Russian General Karbychev, walked among them, giving them comfort. He promised to set an example by dying on his feet. "At the next shower of water he leaned against the wall and immediately thick ice formed a coffin around him."[10]

Mauthausen participated vigorously in the system's medical experimentation program with the usual projects: sterilization, castration, drug tests, heart injections, and special operations. Commandant Ziereis described how the doctor who conducted daily removals of organs from living bodies bottled the organs and stored them on the dissection room shelves. One of his colleagues came up with a grotesque innovation: he used Jews' heads as paperweights on his desk. A perfectionist, he selected two men with excellent teeth. There is evidence that Mauthausen doctors operated a thriving skin business. They skinned bodies of prisoners with interesting tattoo marks and sent the skin to the Gusen pathology lab for processing into book covers, gloves, luggage, and lamp shades.[11]

Camp conditions, including the pungent sweet smell from the crematorium, drove prisoners insane, and some to cannibalism. A group of inmates stumbled across corpses with pieces of flesh removed. They caught the culprit red-handed. "He was spattered with blood and still had a piece of flesh in his mouth." Other prisoners found a body with "the stomach ripped up and the kidneys removed."[12]

When there were so many ways to die by natural causes, it seems strange that the Nazis needed gassing facilities. But as the transports continued to flow in, the officials found themselves with more workers than work. To maintain a semblance of crowd control, officials used three types of gassing facilities. One was portable—a railroad car converted to a gas van. Running between Mauthausen and Gusen, it killed thirty prisoners each way. Mauthausen had its own small chamber in the death complex, which included the execution room, the morgue, and the dissection room. Orderlies pumped carbon monoxide into the chamber, which held only 120 victims. They equipped the metal door with a "Judas opening" for interested observers, including top Nazi leaders. The gassing machinery proved inefficient, and the victims often died of suffocation rather than "dozing off." "Consequently, when the doors were opened to remove the bodies, it was found that the dead were covered not only with excrement and blood, but that their eyes protruded from their heads and their bodies stiffened into grotesque positions."[13]

The most sinister gassing facility used by Mauthausen was the nearby Hartheim Castle. It stands at Alkoven near Linz on the Passau highway. Originally, it was a home for the deranged; later it was converted into an operation for euthanasia. But Hartheim's gas chamber was used for many purposes during the war, one of which was the gassing of Mauthausen prisoners. In 1944 one prisoner, part of a work gang, had an opportunity to know the castle intimately. In the courtyard stood the crematorium smokestack, 26 meters high. Adjoining sections included carpentry and photography shops, a liquor storeroom, and the "baths":

Tiles covered the walls halfway up, and there were six showers. The next small room contained the gassing equipment—gas bottles and various meters and gauges. Then there was a larger room, also with half-tile walls; there was a table, and we found documents outlining proper procedures for research on a cadaver. A door in this room led to the crematorium, which had two ovens. To the left of the door we found a pile of ashes and human bones which would fill about sixty of our trash barrels. We also found an electric mill which was used to grind the bones left after the cremation. . . .

We tore down the smokestack and took out some of the ashes. In the "showers" we removed the tiles from the walls and dismantled the equipment used in their murders. Our work lasted eight days. The masons restored the rooms to their original layout and replastered the walls. Some of the furnishings were sent to Mauthausen, and some went to a hunting castle owned by Prince Starrenberg at Wiesenbach on Lake Ata. . . . The place was made into a children's home with room for 400. Around the end of our stay they brought in thirty-five children, six nurses, and a teacher.[14]

Witnesses estimate that between 1942 and 1945 the Mauthausen gassing facilities killed approximately 10,000 prisoners.

Conditions in Mauthausen worsened as the Allies advanced. The massive deportation of the Hungarian Jews in 1944 impacted all camps, particularly those nearby, like Mauthausen. Thousands of dying skeletons arrived daily. The SS kidnapped the son of Admiral Horthy, regent of Hungary, and sent him to Mauthausen. He described his first impressions:

I also smelled the terrible smell of bodies and burning flesh. One day, when I looked out of my cell window, I saw a lorry pulled up outside, directly outside my cell. A man had a casket in his hands and was shaking ashes and bones into the lorry, which was then deep with ashes and bones. As he finished a casket, he was handed another by his mate who was near the window. This emptying of caskets went on for several days.[15]

Other distinguished prisoners such as Hungarian Premier Kallay came with the crowded transports.

The prisoners in the mother camp describe the final days as ghastly. One survivor, transferred in the last days from Buchenwald, said that when she got on the train at Buchenwald she was told the name of the camp was simply an announcement of certain death. The imminence of defeat did not soften SS hearts or actions. From the Berlin SS office came an order to surrender Mauthausen intact to General Patton. But Commandant Ziereis showed few signs of cooperation. After his capture he told his interrogators that he had received countermanding orders from Kaltenbrunner insisting that Ziereis step up the death rate to 1,000 a day. Red Cross delegates visited Ziereis in the last days and found him surly and arrogant. One described his home: "We visited, with terrible calm, the children's room, drawing-room, hunting room with trophies and armaments, all over the house, the farmyard, the beehives, the swimming pool, but I preferred to stay in the camp with the prisoners than in the house with this monster." The delegates claimed that Ziereis planned to use the underground airplane factory at Gusen as a final coffin for all Mauthausen inmates. He intended to seal them in and blow them up. If the story is true, fortunately someone dissuaded him.[16]

At the end of April, after Ziereis formally handed Mauthausen over to the civilian police of Vienna, he ran away. Intelligence agents found him hiding in an Austrian forest. When they tried to capture him, he fired upon them and was critically wounded in the return rounds. Ziereis died in custody on May 24.

On May 8 Patton's troops entered the camp. They were simply appalled. As one soldier rolled through the gate in his jeep, he saw before him "the raw material of this torture factory—human beings by the thousands, including women and a few children, . . . in all degrees of health, some in very good condition, but the vast majority mere walking skeletons. They were mostly sitting or lying in the bright spring sunlight, or simply milling about." An American officer, George Dyer, considered Mauthausen one of the worst camps uncovered anywhere. He found "16,000 political prisoners representing every country in Europe all reduced to living skeletons and ridden with disease." One of his colleagues wrote home that the stink of the dead and dying, of the starving and the burning, was the worst part of it. He would smell Mauthausen to the end of his life. The Americans found the crematorium out of action and the communal grave bursting with 10,000 bodies. They filled in the grave and buried 5,000 additional bodies in the SS football field.[17]

The Nazi hunter Simon Wiesenthal spent his last camp days in Mauthausen and remembered liberation quite vividly. "The day was sunny, with the scent of spring in the air. Gone was the sweetish smell of burned flesh that had always hovered over the yard. The night before, the last SS men had run away. The machinery of death had come to a stop. In my room a few dead people were lying on their bunks."[18]

Although the Americans responded promptly to the survivors' needs, 3,000 deaths occurred after liberation. "Many died from sheer joy"—they had lived on hope, fear, and their nerves for so long that the relaxation of tension was too much for them. How many died at Mauthausen during its operation? The statistics are as confused as the SS organization. Prisoners were moved back and forth among dozens of camps. We know that on March 5, 1945, there were 64,800 men and 1,734 women officially listed in the camp, and approximately 15,000 unlisted prisoners. The camp authorities at the Mauthausen museum estimate that more than 206,000 lived in Mauthausen proper and that more than 110,000 perished as a result of living in the camp.[19]

The story of Mauthausen is incomplete without a description of the labor complex and the major subcamps, as they were called. Together they housed more inmates than Mauthausen proper, and in far worse conditions. The slave labor packed in the indestructible tunnels enabled Germany to reproduce what Allied bombings destroyed, and thus to continue the war at least a year longer.

The Gusen trio was the largest of the subcamps. Gusen I lies 6 kilometers from Mauthausen. It became a formal part of the main camp in 1944. Originally intended as a labor/elimination center for the Polish intelligentsia, the influx of many national groups changed its character. Its purpose became singular: extermination by labor. Its living accommodations never progressed beyond the primitive level. For example, its latrines consisted of a series of holes in the ground, covered partially by a narrow plank on which the prisoners crouched. Many fell in. The camp was without running water until 1941. Starving prisoners remember with irony that the Germans lavished the greatest attention on Gusen's famous Angora rabbits. Housed in clean modern huts, fed the best food, the rabbits received care far exceeding that given to any prisoner. Gusen's hospital was directed by the man known at Mauthausen for his special medical experiments, which he continued at Gusen. There, too, he made lamp shades of human skin and used shrunken heads for paperweights. Gusen acquired its own crematorium in 1943.[20]

In 1943 Gusen prisoners built the second camp in the complex—Gusen II. Three hundred meters from Camp I, it was originally planned as an SS site. Instead, it became the burial ground for hundreds of Hungarian Jews and French resistance fighters. After the first phase of the Gusen complex was completed, industrial concerns became interested in the area because of its superior quality of granite and potential for underground factories. Two quarries lay on a hillside at the rear of the area, and behind them the prisoners cut five enormous subterranean tunnels into the hill. Messerschmidt used the tunnels for the production of aircraft, which had been curtailed by Allied bombings. The first prisoners arrived in 1944 to find hideous conditions. No water, heat, or sanitation existed. When a convoy of Polish parents and their children arrived, a team of *Kapos* killed many of the children in a mass axing orgy. The screams carried through the camp.

Gusen III, located 3 kilometers from the other two camps, can be described simply as an underground factory. The Nazis began its construction in 1944, but the war ended before it was completed.

The SS assigned Gusen *Kommandos* to helpful tasks in the outlying areas. One *Kommando* evacuated the ruins of the Scharfenberg Castle, removing pottery, ornaments, and weapons dating back to the second century A.D. The Gusen Museum received the archeological finds. While working on a railroad line, another *Kommando* uncovered an old cemetery. When archeologists arrived on the scene, they discovered the oldest tombs in Austria. The Gusen Museum acquired those materials too. They were so valuable that after Himmler assessed them, Hitler ordered the finest objects removed to Nuremberg.[21]

The products of Gusen I, II, and III included machine guns and weapons, aircraft fuselages, and major armaments. To construct the factories, the prisoners worked around the clock and suffered a high death rate. They blasted into the mountain and then removed the huge chunks of granite. In the hole they hewed the rock with pickaxes to make standing room. Then they heaved huge wooden piles in place to support the tunnel. "The tunnels were built only by human beings pitting their strength against the unyielding mountain." The Gusen death statistics are even harder to pinpoint than those for Mauthausen proper. The official figure of 38,453 does not take into account children.[22]

In 1943 the Nazis started another subcamp, Ebensee. Situated in a secluded mountainous region, Ebensee was an ideal safe location for underground armament factories. The Nazis planned twelve armament factories to be housed in enormous tunnels, each 425 meters long and linked to a connecting tunnel—built by the Ebensee inmates. The winters in Austria are long and hard with a heavy snowfall. When the first prisoners arrived to build the tunnels, the only accommodation they found was a small barrack and an old storage hut. In that weather, without winter clothing, they worked fourteen-hour days. Snow sometimes lay 1½ meters deep. For snowboots, the prisoners wore wooden clogs, which made walking nearly impossible. No facilities for washing were available and lice soon covered the prisoners.[23]

As construction tasks go, the building of the Ebensee tunnels was a mighty feat. The mountain "towered majestically above the camp, its summit often obscured by swirling mist." When the prisoners finished with the tunnels, they installed machinery for manufacturing parts for airplanes and for the V-1 and V-2 rockets. At certain points in the tunnel staircases were built to upper-level galleries. The unfinished galleries were unlighted dank holes in the ceiling with no access to the outside world. Their purpose would be to serve as prisoner quarters. Eventually the entire camp would move inside.[24]

As the Allies advanced, the SS transferred prisoners from other camps to Ebensee. The blocks became more overcrowded and the dead bodies piled up. "Treated like a menagerie of hated animals, driven mercilessly and beyond our strength to work in a mountainside factory, we lived, each of us, on hope of imminent liberation." Three days before liberation the Germans hanged four starving inmates because they tried to buy bread. The inmates had "torn the gold teeth from out of their own mouths to get some bread from the overseers for it. For this, they were hanged." Because the furnaces were inadequate to keep pace with the deaths, the Allied liberators found bodies

Map 6: Mauthausen Concentration Camp
Evelyn Le Chene: Mauthausen *(London: Metheun & Co., 1971), 28–29.*

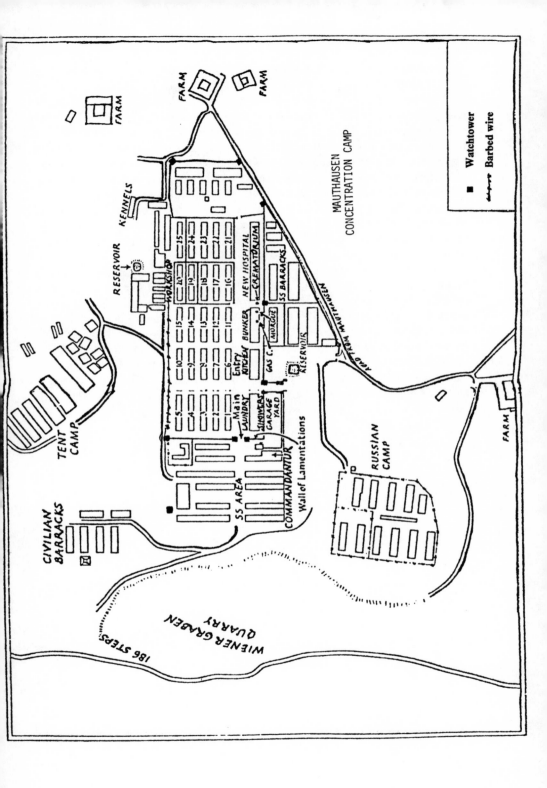

MAUTHAUSEN CONCENTRATION CAMP

■ Watchtower
▸▸▸▸ Barbed wire

FARM
FARM
FARM
FARM
KENNELS
RESERVOIR
WORKSHOP
New Hospital
CREMATORIUM
SS BARRACKS
Entry
KITCHEN
GAS C.
MORGUE
BUNKER
RESERVOIR
ROAD FROM MAUTHAUSEN
TENT CAMP
CIVILIAN BARRACKS
Main
LAUNDRY
SICKBAY
GARAGE
YARD
SS AREA
COMMANDANTUR
Wall of Lamentations
RUSSIAN CAMP
186 STEPS
WIENER GRABEN
QUARRY

lying everywhere. No administration remained and prisoners looked more dead than alive. Many died after liberation.[25]

The final camp of any large size was Melk, once famous for its beautiful monastery, which still stands near the camp site. Seventy-three kilometers from Mauthausen, Melk averaged 8,000 inmates. The prisoners worked in the tunnels in the surrounding hills building armament factories. Melk was an exposed camp established within the bounds of a large *Wehrmacht* station. Prisoners' and soldiers' quarters overlooked one another and the crematorium entrance faced straight into one of the main *Wehrmacht* streets. The tall smokestack of the modern crematorium became a landmark. Larger and more modern than any of the Mauthausen complex, the gas chamber included double walls to stifle the screams of the dying. The authorities had obviously slated Melk as a large extermination center.[26]

Added to those large camps must be the far-reaching subcamp system resulting in the deaths of thousands. Name a city or town of any size in Austria, look up its name in the Tracing Catalogues, and invariably one finds a Mauthausen *Kommando*. Thus the Mauthausen system provided one of the largest organized slave reservoirs of modern times—a reservoir used by an entire nation. The Mauthausen complex stood as an unusual experiment in the full implementation of the policy of extermination by labor. It surely was not evidence of a coordinated total mobilization for war. While Speer and the German military and economic leaders were searching frantically for labor for vital war industries, the SS labor was digging stones in the Mauthausen quarry.

FLOSSENBÜRG: A MOUNTAIN STRONGHOLD

Flossenbürg's initial impact on the visitor comes from its location in the mountainous region of western Germany, near the Czech border. The small camp lies in the heavily forested hills above the picturesque village of Floss. Floss is colorful, hilly, and innocent looking. Its central park monument honoring the soldiers and Jews from many countries can be easily mistaken for the sole remains of the camp. Certainly the townspeople would prefer that it were. Perhaps the reluctance to remember explains why no signs direct the visitor to the camp site on the far outskirts of Floss.

The road from Floss winds up a hill and around to the camp entrance. The visitor passes from the gates to a hilly park, then strolls through a well-tended garden with lovely paths, trees, and flowers. The mounds and flower beds cover the many mass graves hidden beneath the luxurious park. The path moves down a steep hill past scattered well-preserved guardhouses and views of the ominous barbed-wire wall behind the trees. The topside crematorium is the first visible building. Farther down the hill lies a garden plot designating the site of mass executions, and to the left is a small stone dedicated to the Jews who died there. Back up the stairs on the other side of the camp stands a new Christian church. It is modern, polished, and presents a thoughtful contrast. At its side is the gas chamber. A haunting statue of a prisoner stands outside the church, and scattered on the ground are boxes that held the ashes from the crematorium. The Nazis saved the ashes to fill urns sent to the unsuspecting family members in return for money. The wall around the camp still stands, as do the many quarries where the prisoners worked. No other barracks or buildings remain. A factory previously used as a prisoner work/station and an SS administration center is located next to the camp.

In 1938 an SS firm began to exploit and operate a large granite quarry works near Floss. Such an operation required a concentration camp, which the SS established as a punishment center in May 1938. Himmler's 1941 classification placed Flossenbürg in the same category as Buchenwald, Birkenau, and Neuengamme: for protective-custody prisoners with mediocre

129

records but likely to benefit from education and reform. The first inmates, German criminals, built the initial camp. By late summer 1939 Flossenbürg held 3,000 prisoners. On April 5, 1940, the first transport of foreigners arrived. Among them were Polish, Czech, Russian, and German political prisoners. Into a few small crude barracks the SS packed the prisoners, 1,500 at a time. They slept in the familiar tiered bunks on dirty straw sacks. The only means available to cut the biting cold in a barrack was one small stove. The isolated camp and the life there led to a "raw and melancholy sort of loneliness. It was wishing you weren't alive, feeling that the best thing in the world would be not to be. Feeling you're in your own way, just by being alive."[1]

After the invasion of Russia Flossenbürg became the depository for 1,600 Soviet POWs, who were placed in a special camp inside the old one. Admiral Canaris, implicated in the assassination attempt on Hitler, was also a prisoner in Flossenbürg. The SS, on April 9, 1945, hanged Canaris slowly— with a piano-wire noose. In addition, the camp held a significant contingent of Jews.[2]

Initially, Flossenbürg was a men's camp. But on January 7, 1943, the records mention female prisoners for the first time. Actually the camp was quite small. Although only 54,890 men and 10,000 women were imprisoned there, the mortality rate was very high. From February 1944 to April 1945 over 14,000 prisoners died for the usual reasons—starvation, exhaustion, and disease. The SS men killed the rest with phenol injections, medical experimentation, shooting, and hanging. As a survivor points out:

You don't die of anything
except death.
Suffering doesn't kill you.
Only death.[3]

The small crematorium worked twenty-four hours a day. When the bodies proved too many for its capacity, the guards threw the overflow into several pits dug into the hillsides. The liberating Americans disinterred hundreds of bodies of slave laborers from those pits.

The Messerschmidt factories and the DEST employed most inmates. As the war developed, the SS industrial organization transferred the quarry workers to the task of making airplane parts, and then to Messerschmidt's large fighter plane production program. At least sixty outside male *Kommandos* worked in the china, aircraft, construction, steel, and mining industries. Several female *Kommandos* worked primarily in the mechanical, weaving, optical, chemistry, and wood industries. A Jewish prisoner described his factory experience:

At this camp there was a factory that made bazookas. There was one SS man for every four prisoners. Every day 15 men died, aside from those who died from "natural causes." We ran to work. Work intended for 20 people was done by 10. We worked from 6 A.M. to 7 P.M. We collapsed. Many people committed suicide. In two weeks 500 died. Filth, no water, two days without heat, no bath, and no underwear. There was twenty-five lashes for stealing potato peelings. They called us the race gang, communists, cadets, soapbags, criminals, and bolsheviks. . . .

Because things were bad at the front, they hurried us and always beat us at the factory. . . . To load bazookas we had to use picric acid and trotil. We worked without gas masks, and after a few weeks the lungs and feet would cave in. The young were chosen for this task. SS men would kill them while they worked, so there was always a shortage of workers. . . .[4]

The *Kommandos* supplied the industrial slave labor for a large portion of Czechoslovakia.

The total strength of the inner camp divided as follows:[5]

Men	*Women*
1938— 1,800 prisoners	1943–1945—14,600 prisoners
1942— 3,600 prisoners	
1945—31,170 prisoners	

Even this isolated camp did not escape the SS Commission of Inquiry. Karl Künstler, the commandant, was dismissed for drunkenness and "feasts of debauchery." He did exercise his sense of humor before his dismissal. He erected a magnificent Christmas tree, from which six inmates were hanged on Christmas Day.

Near the end of 1944 the camp became fiercely overpopulated with four to five men sleeping in a single bed. The tempers of the SS were short, and prisoners remember the ferocity of treatment. When the Americans arrived at Flossenbürg in April 1945, they were four days too late. Just before liberation, the SS staged a typical death march for 15,000 prisoners, including children and old people. Those who could not keep up with the others were shot through the head; their bodies littered the countryside for miles. The Americans found only 2,000 living prisoners in Flossenbürg.[6]

The townspeople of nearby Namering and Floss understandably made no reference to the camp. After the American liberators dug up 800 bodies, they decided to involve the surrounding "unaware" civilian population. First, they erected a sign, which they made every citizen of those towns read: "Here lie 800 murdered bodies killed by the Nazis of Namering, Germany, in April 1945."[7] The Americans forced the citizens to view the disinterred bodies.

Those who balked were required to stand at attention for thirty minutes. Finally, the GIs kept guard while the German men and women civilians dug new graves for the corpses and buried them. A former camp inmate commented on the universal unawareness:

Germany was one giant concentration camp, with Jews marching the length and breadth of the country, but these refined, sensitive Germans never saw us. Find me a German who ever saw me. Find me one who ever harmed us.[8]

WOMEN AND THE THIRD REICH
PART I
RAVENSBRUCK: FOR WOMEN ONLY

Hitler's only camp for women, Gedenkstätte Ravensbrück, lies in East Germany, 96 kilometers north of Berlin. It is a unique facility in many ways, primarily because of the nature of its population during the war and its pastoral location in sight of the small town of Fürstenberg. The road to Ravensbrück runs through dark patches of pine woods, by lovely flower beds, and ends on the edge of a serene lake. In front of Ravensbrück a sandy beach borders a small lake across from the medieval town of Fürstenberg. Standing on the shore, one observes fishermen on docks and in small boats, old men smoking their pipes, calmly catching their fish as they have for centuries. The town so visible across the lake is about one-half kilometer away—its steeples, its trees, its quiet interrupted only by the ringing of church bells. But if one turns around and puts one's back to the lake, there, right in front, begins the high wall that separated the women in Ravensbrück from the beach and shore on the very edge of it. And over to the left is the high concrete wall surrounded by barbed wire. On one side of the lake, the church steeples and the houses surrounded by a lazy, colorful countryside; over here, the remains of that ghastly camp.

The East German government erected on a portion of the former Ravensbrück concentration camp site the National Memorial and Commemoration. It is designed as a monument to the women inmates. The entrance to the camp, made from large limestone, carries the words spoken by Anna Seghers to children about the women of Ravensbrück:

They are all our mothers and sisters.
Today they can neither learn nor play,
For them, perhaps, nothing was born;
Because those women should not have had
To place their fragile and emaciated bodies,
As strong armoured shields,
To protect us and our future from the terror of fascism.[1]

Sculpture, Ravensbrück National Memorial and Commemoration.

From the entrance the path leads to the former crematorium. Visitors pass by a narrow space between two walls that were used as a rifle execution gallery by the SS. In front of the crematorium a staircase branches off, leading to the former camp prison, today the site of the Museum of Resistance and the Archives. Over granite steps and through a new, wide entrance visitors walk into the crematorium. The ovens remain unchanged. Between the crematorium and the camp wall the architects have formed a memorial courtyard that contains an urn with its eternal flame. At the beginning of the mass grave, which runs along the camp wall in front of the lake, two bronze statues of women stand like watchguards. In graves planted with red roses lie buried the dead found at liberation. From all countries women whose relatives had suffered and died in Ravensbrück sent rose bushes. The names of those countries are written in bronze on the wall behind the graves.

The path leads farther along the ceremonial site to the edge of Schwedt

Lake. The Nazis threw the crematorium ashes into the lake. Over the ashes of the burned women wide stone plaques gradually lead down into the water. Far out into the lake on a concrete platform rises the Monument of the Resistance Fighters, a powerful statue of a woman carrying a collapsed comrade. It is the embodiment of the solidarity of the women who lived and died in Ravensbrück.

An architectural collective of national prize winners created the Memorial Camp during the period 1956–1959. Historical societies have developed an extensive museum and archives for the camp in the old prison. No original barrack remains, but the prison's old punishment cells have been remodeled into exhibit rooms dedicated by each country to its dead. It is well done and carefully planned. Soviet soldiers are presently housed in the administration building of the camp, and their families live in the SS leaders' homes, with tricycles, dolls, and sandboxes spread on the ground. Still, Ravensbrück cannot be mistaken for anything but what it was.

Ravensbrück was a special camp where 92,000 women and children out of the 132,000 incarcerated met a cruel death. That uniqueness determined the nature of the memorial created by Will Lammert and the later addition by Fritz Cremer. Even in Ravensbrück, where new arrivals often met early death, resistance was strong, although of a different character from that of other camps. Here, the artists decided to focus on the self-containment of humans, the effort to maintain human dignity, and a conscious solidarity as the most important elements of resistance. Thus Lammert did not choose a liberation theme, but tried to represent a humanistic consolidation and a retained consciousness in opposition to nonhuman, inhuman conditions. In the Buchenwald and Sachsenhausen memorials motifs of victorious resistance dominate, but at Ravensbrück sorrow for the victims prevails. In this, the culmination of Lammert's lifetime work, the representation of woman assumes a primary position. He completed his figures in quick succession and then, in 1957, he died. Lammert had matured in his Ravensbrück work into one of the most significant East German sculptors.

Lammert planned a many-figured group of women at the foot of a freestanding relief. The artist created a walking woman carrying a fallen, sick comrade. He tried to form each individual distinctly, in order to achieve a clear impression, even from afar.

The first designs were very fluid in their composition. In the final form, conceived in 1957, Lammert pulled together the gray-black individual shapes more tightly, covering the head of the carrying woman with a kerchief, which creates a unified effect of head and shoulders. He tried to make the act of carrying natural by setting both bodies clearly apart from each other. In the first version (1955) the carrying woman was embracing the body of the other. In the final version she reaches under the limp arm. The head of the body, falling forward, emphasizes the differences between erectness and physical exhaustion, powerlessness and a heavy burden. The face of the carrying woman expresses psychic and physical pain, yet is noble and constrained. Without denying knowledge of the terrible truth, Lammert's faces reveal a reserved beauty. The young woman's face reflects a certain grace despite her desolation. Under the guidance of Fritz Cremer, Hans Kies, and Gerhard Tiele enlarged Lammert's final version and placed it on a freestanding pedestal.

After completing his Buchenwald Memorial Fritz Cremer felt drawn to Ravensbrück and began to work on a sculpture that was to be an enriching extension of Lammert's work. He created a group of women fighting for the life of a sick child—a motif that expresses the women's struggle for freedom and their hope for the future, symbolized by the child. Cremer expanded Lammert's figures by adding the mother-child motif indicated by Lammert in one of his sketches.

Three women carry a sick child on a stretcher. The three concentrate on the child. The youthful woman at the end of the stretcher walks haltingly, her head lowered, abandoned to desperation. The middle woman, the mother, turns compassionately to the child. The erect front figure is the active center of the group, her face revealing a final determination. Suffering hardens her demeanor. Her face is comparable to the open faces of the Buchenwald male resistance fighters. The child seeking her protection is a strong example of socialist art. Käthe Kollwitz created similar children in graphic art and scrulpture.

Ravensbrück was one of the four infamous prewar concentration camps in Germany. Its highlights were those of the other camps: forced labor, medical experiments, individual and mass execution, murder of the ill, beatings, gas chambers, crematorium, and forced marches. But Ravensbrück was unique in that it was the only major camp for women created by the Nazis. The authorities incarcerated women in many other camps in a variety of ways. In most instances the women did not reside in the base camps with the men, but were utilized in adjunct labor camps or *sub-kommandos.*

During the first years of the Third Reich two small camps for women existed: Mohringen near Hannover and Lichtenburg in Sachsen. But their facilities were inadequate to handle the number of anticipated women. In the late spring of 1938, 500 prisoners from Sachsenhausen began constructing the only women's camp in the Nazi system. They erected fourteen live-in barracks and an infirmary, a shower room, and a kitchen. On May 15, 1939, Himmler formally reestablished Concentration Camp Lichtenburg in Fürstenberg as Concentration Camp Ravensbrück. On May 18, 1939, the SS brought the first prisoners from Lichtenburg—860 Germans and 70

Austrians, and a few women from Mohringen. By the end of 1939 the camp housed 2,290 prisoners.

The Nazis built Ravensbrück on reclaimed swamp land near Fürstenberg, intending to rent the female labor supply to the industrial firms located in the area. The region's climate is so rigorous that it has been called "Little Siberia." Planned for 15,000 inmates, by 1944 Ravensbrück held over 40,000. Approximately 130,000 women passed through the camp. About 33,000 were Polish; the other 100,000 women came from all the countries of Europe. They included 11,000 Frenchwomen, the 195 women who had survived the Lidice massacre, and, at the end of the war, women evacuated from the women's section of Birkenau. The German authorities frequently referred to Ravensbrück as a model camp, but in the last year of the war there was nothing exemplary about it. The women experienced horrendous over-population in 1945, which forced constant enlargement of the camp.[2]

Ravensbrück devoted its major labor effort to textile industrial concerns, with the camp women working primarily to produce SS uniforms. In 1941 Himmler added a small section for a few prominent male prisoners. Ravens-brück also functioned as a training center for female newcomers to the SS who intended to go into service in the camp system. The camp staff organized an extremely effective apprenticeship in the hard treatment of enemies. Irma Grese, the twenty-one-year-old "Bitch of Buchenwald," for example, was a trainee wardress at Ravensbrück in 1942.

In 1940 the inmate population reached a peak of 4,000 with a total mortality figure for the year of eighty-four. By the end of 1941 the camp held 12,000 prisoners. The year 1942 ushered in two innovations that soon became standard practice: continuous executions by shooting, and the exit of groups of women for transport to destinations unknown to them—but re-sulting in their death. In addition, 1942 was the year of the first medical experiments, the arrival of the first Soviet POWs, and the addition of sizable groups of children to the camp. In April 1943 the SS put into service a crematorium with two ovens. Until that date bodies had been cremated in Fürstenberg.[3]

In 1944, the SS enlarged its factories, separated them from the regular camp industries, and increased the exploitation of inmate labor. They built a gas chamber near the crematorium and added a third oven to the latter. They prepared the adjunct camp of Uckermark as a reception point for Jewish women. The roll call population went from 17,300 in January to about 35,000 in late July. By transporting some of the women to Majdanek for execution, the SS brought the figure back down to 34,500 in August. But later in that month 14,000 Polish women arrived from Auschwitz. In September the SS also dumped the female Warsaw evacuees into the camp in a hastily created tent city. By transport and the gas chamber, the authorities managed to reduce the swollen population to 43,000 by the end of December.[4]

The year 1945 brought continuous medical experimentation, extermination, and evacuation. Dr. Clauberg sterilized the Gypsy women and their small daughters in January; the guards poisoned dozens of inmates in February; and the SS began the extermination selections resulting in death by poison, starvation, shooting, and gas. From January to April the SS murdered 7,000 women and children in the small gas chamber. The inmate evacuation began in the last days of March, followed by the gassing of 6,000 women in the first three weeks of April. On April 27 and 28 the SS completed the evacuation of the remaining 11,500, leaving only 3,000 desperately ill women to feebly greet the Soviet Army liberators on April 30. Himmler had deported 132,000 women and children to Ravensbrück. By liberation, 92,000 of them were dead.[5]

The evacuation was one of Ravensbrück's most tragic moments. Red Cross delegates met with Commandant Fritz Suhren to attempt to prevent the evacuation and extermination of the 17,000. But they failed, and the thousands from both Ravensbrück and Sachsenhausen involved in the pointless march of starving and enfeebled women littered the roads leading to the remaining pocket of the shrinking Reich. Commandant Suhren's own famous escape with his hostage, Odette Churchill, was superseded in absurdity only by a final fitting scene. On April 28 the wife of an SS officer was observed fleeing from Ravensbrück in a carriage pulled by six female skeletons. "She was suffering from indigestion from eating too many raisins."[6]

Although a female camp, Ravensbrück's two commandants were men: first Commandant Koegel, and then, after October 1942, Commandant Fritz Suhren. But Ravensbrück had the largest contingent of women SS guards of any camp—between 550 and 600 (Gross-Rosen had 490, Sachsenhausen 140, and Auschwitz/Birkenau 60). Two held the highest women's post of Chief *Oberaufseherin*—first a woman named Klein-Plaubel and then Luise Brunner. But far worse was their first assistant, Dorothea Binz, most vividly described by Germaine Tillion in her book *Ravensbrück*:

Whenever she appeared somewhere, one literally felt touched by the breath of evil. She would walk slowly among the ranks, her crop behind her back, searching with menacing little eyes for the weakest or most frightened woman, simply to beat her black and blue.

Tillion remembers one occasion when Binz had meted out the twenty-five to fifty lashes given as punishment at Ravensbrück. After the beating the inmate lay half naked in the dirt, apparently unconscious. Binz looked at her a moment. Then she stepped on her victim's bloody legs, "her two heels on one leg, toes of her boots on the other. Binz balanced herself there for a while, rocking her weight from heel to toe. The woman could have been dead by then—she showed no reaction." After a few minutes Binz left, her boots smeared with blood. The courts in 1947 sentenced Binz to death by hanging.[7]

SS women were generally "stout, strong, and healthy," and represented all classes of society. Not all volunteered enthusiastically for the work. The Nazis selected some from among the labor conscripts and forced them to work as guards. Many were not Nazis. One would encounter "streetcar ticket takers, factory workers, opera singers, registered nurses, hairdressers, peasants, young middle-class women who had never worked before, retired teachers, circus riders, former prison guards, officers' widows."[8]

The inmates of Ravensbrück came from all walks of life and from many countries. The Polish women formed the elite and ran the camp internally. They were the senior prisoners and the majority. Although all women were badly misused, the authorities saved the most brutal treatment for the Jewish inmates, particularly the French Jews. Abused as though they were animals, the Jewesses labored from early morning to evening on the most difficult and dirtiest outside-labor details: digging, building roads and houses, chopping wood. The SS also sent to Ravensbrück all female Jehovah's Witnesses captured in Europe.

Ravensbrück housed many famous women. Among them were the relatives of the most prominent families of Europe: Madame Sarussel, wife of the mayor of Tunis; Madame Winkelkompes, wife of Cologne's mayor; Madame Renée Sintenis, a prestigious Berlin sculptress; the Austrian Countess Josephine Ptacikova, who was killed later in the gas chamber; Countess Lilly de Raubuteau, a relative of the Danish queen; Frau Wenzel, who owned fourteen estates and belonged to one of the richest families in Germany; Countess Landskoronska from Poland; Mademoiselle Geneviève de Gaulle, General de Gaulle's niece; Marie Claude Vaillant-Couturier, the widow of the French Communist leader; Frau Rosa Thälmann, wife of Ernst Thälmann, chief of the Communist party in Germany whom the Nazis executed in Buchenwald. Finally there was Olga Himmler, Heinrich Himmler's sister, sent to Ravensbrück for her love affair with a Polish officer.[9]

Adolf Eichmann sent Gemma LaGuardia Gluck, the sister of the mayor of New York, Fiorello LaGuardia, to Ravensbrück in the spring of 1944. She had been living in Budapest with her Hungarian Jewish husband. When Eichmann arrived in Hungary, he ordered her arrest, for it was his scheme to hold the relatives of Allied leaders as possible hostages. He may also have arrested her in retaliation for her brother's noisy anti-Nazism. Mrs. Gluck's husband was sent to Mauthausen, where he died. The SS sent her to the Ravensbrück special prominent section. In 1961 she was still alive in New York City at the age of eighty. Gemma Gluck had indeed been a hostage of

Adolf Eichmann. Her descriptions and analysis of Ravensbrück in her book, *My Story,* and her articles have added valuable impressions. She wrote of the conditions when she reached Ravensbrück, at the beginning of the over-crowding, when the Germans were bringing in huge transports of women from Majdanek, Auschwitz, and Sobibor. When the barracks overflowed, they put the women in a huge tent. "It was like a circus, but one without clowns—a circus where crying was heard and no laughter." The Germans packed as many as 1,500 women into a barrack. Often six women shared a bunk. As freezing exhausted hulks, they lived on watery soup, a few grams of bread, and imitation coffee. Dirt, fleas, and lice overwhelmed the inhabitants.[10]

At first housed in a quarantine block of 1,000 women, Mrs. Gluck reacted most to the noise of so many women, so many languages. The SS designated Blocks 1 and 2 for the prominents, and Block 3 for communists. They transferred Mrs. Gluck to Block 2. She was fortunate because those three blocks, holding only 400 prisoners each, were the largest and cleanest in the camp. Because she was a special prisoner, Mrs. Gluck did not have to work the twelve-hour shift and she had a bed to herself! She was also permitted an hour of rest in the afternoon, but she received the same amount of food as everyone else. For breakfast and supper women "had black coffee with a piece of terrible black bread which many times had great holes gnawed in it by the rats." They ate turnips and potato peelings for dinner. Sometimes, from the incoming loot, the cooks gave them imitation honey, marmalade, and a piece of sausage. But in her last months there Gluck remembers eating only dried bread, given out once a day. The food was awful, but it sustained her. She could never understand how the women who worked twelve hours a day could remain alive with their terrible hunger.[11]

Mrs. Gluck, in one sense, was one of the fortunate. Two months after her arrest the SS arrested her daughter, her daughter's husband, and their five-month-old son Richard. The husband they killed, and then they shipped Yolanda and Richard to Ravensbrück. They isolated the mother and child in a solitary confinement cell. Mrs. Gluck received a hint in the spring of 1945 that her daughter was living in the camp. On April 14, 1945, the commandant took her to them. The daughter remembered being frightened at her mother's appearance because she had lost forty-four pounds. Little Richard was fourteen months old. His head wobbled and he could not sit up. Toothless, limp as a rag doll, he could not grasp anything in his hands. His grandmother's first thought was: "Where am I going to bury this baby? He won't live." The SS finally sent Mrs. Gluck, her daughter, and grandson to Berlin, where they lived out the war.[12]

Ravensbrück also contained many politicals and captured members of national resistance movements. The great mixture of cultures and the disastrous living conditions swept away ordinary conventions and revealed true natures: the society women who were thieves, the patriots who became informers, the communists who resorted to cheating and hoarding. Denise Dufournier, a captured member of the French resistance, found herself in Ravensbrück in January 1944. When she first arrived, she was stunned, panicked, terrorized, and "speechless with amazement." An entire world spread out before her: the rich, poor, passive, and powerful. In a community governed by "injustice, favoritism, and corruption," Dufournier felt enclosed in an environment set apart from the human race. She was living, she concluded, on a mysterious planet, "where the macabre, the ridiculous, the grotesque rubbed shoulders and intermingled in a fantastic and irrational chaos."[13]

Because of the politicals, Ravensbrück became the scene of a resistance movement. The initiative came from the communist and French women. They began to hold secret political meetings as early as 1940 to disseminate war news. The inmates chose three women of each nationality as leaders. They exchanged newspapers, secured maps, held Sunday meetings to keep abreast of world events. The politicals used Ravensbrück's "Main Street" where prisoners walked on Sunday to pass communications. The groups helped awaken the courage to live and the will to exist; but more pragmatically, they organized a systematic sabotage of the armament factory production. Lidia Besnogowa described one political meeting:

On November 7, 1944, between the end of work and the evening siren, a number of Communist women, two from each nationality, gathered in the Soviet war prisoner block, under the leadership of Rosa Thälmann. Mela Ernst, an Austrian, spoke in German about the historical meaning of the Socialist October revolution, about the Communist organization in Europe, and about the task of the Communists in the camp. Jewgenia Klem described the situation on the front, showing that the troops had already passed the Oder and that liberation should soon take place. At the end, "Fatherland, No Enemy Shall Endanger You," was softly sung.[14]

Many children lived in Ravensbrück. They came in transports with their mothers or by themselves. Some were born there. Undernourished and with threadbare clothes, they were miserable creatures. The first transport arrived in 1939—Gypsy children with their mothers. Later Dr. Clauberg sterilized all the Gypsy women and their young daughters between the ages of five and eight. During Mrs. Gluck's residence 500 little ragged skeletons lived in Ravensbrück:

Some had no hair on their heads. Nevertheless, they behaved like children, running around and begging things from their elders. They even played games. A popular one was Appel, modeled on the camp's daily roll calls.

Eight hundred sixty-three children were born in Ravensbrück between 1943 and 1945. Without nourishment, diapers, or water, most babies died within a few days of birth by "natural" means. In addition, the midwives drowned or smothered them. One day Mrs. Gluck saw a Nazi guard carrying a bag over his arm. She asked him what it contained and he told her: "Dead babies."[15]

The Ravensbrück women wore blue uniforms with gray stripes. Later some were allowed to wear their own clothes. Gemma Gluck remembers that the women, when they had received their "new clothes," looked like beggars.

They managed to give a thin woman a fat woman's dress so that it would hang on her, or vice versa. Also, a huge X was sewn on the front and back of our dresses and coats in vivid colors, so that we could easily be caught if we ran away.[16]

Himmler was interested in the exploitation of the prisoner labor, and in profiting from Ravensbrück SS firms. Of course, all work was a means of extermination. But in 1942 Himmler insisted that the mobilization of prisoner work strength, particularly for the war program, must take precedence. The SS firms hired the Ravensbrück prisoners to work twelve-hour shifts in the factories. Private armament concerns did the same. The prisoners never saw the money. An inmate recounted that she arose at 3:30 A.M. and received a cup of black coffee for breakfast. At 6 A.M. began the hard work, and at noon the women received their first meal—watery soup, which they ate in the winter standing in the cold in front of the factory hall. When they came home from work at 7 P.M., they stood in the snow under blows and abuse for one or two hours of roll call, and only then did they receive their evening meal, again watery soup and a piece of bread.[17]

Ravensbrück not only furnished cheap labor for nearby factories, it also sent prisoner workers throughout Germany. Once a price was agreed upon, the businessman or industrialist received 500 to 1,000 women, along with wardwomen equipped with dogs and clubs. They could force twelve hours of work out of exhausted and starving women. Dead and dying slaves were replaced with fresh slaves at no additional cost to the client: the perfect cycle with no waste. The work assignment offices counted fifty-five factories and *Kommandos* throughout northern Germany. Some women worked in the airbases, at powder factories, and in the Hermann Göring Works. One transport was sent to an old salt mine to labor in a factory, 540 meters underground, making airplane parts.

By 1944 the internal camp had also become an industrial center. Articles could be manufactured cheaply because the labor was free. The dressmaking department was so proficient that "it could have held a fashion show in any large city." Of course, among the prisoners were professional "dressmakers, designers, and decorators." The dressmakers specialized in evening gowns, which were sent to the large German cities for SS wives or mistresses. The shoemaking department made shoes and the fur department created beautiful fur coat collections. Inmates even manufactured fur toy animals. The women held other trade positions, too; the normal ones found in any camp. The laundry was furnished with modern equipment and the camp officials selected nuns to work there. Polish women formed the kitchen crew, while the politicals worked in the offices and the library. According to Mrs. Gluck, women over age sixty had to knit as their contribution![18]

The Guinea Pigs or Rabbits in the Ravensbrück Concentration Camp

A major policy of all camp authorities was to disrupt as much as possible any community that might take shape. Despite that intent, the Germans created by accident in Ravensbrück a strange group drawn together over time, joined by strong ties. That group was the guinea pigs or the rabbits—the female subjects of Ravensbrück's experimental operations. The most horrifying and shameful crimes at Ravensbrück, insists one survivor author, were those experiments that used young, beautiful, healthy Polish women like rabbits in a laboratory. The Nazis infected the "rabbits," as the inmates called them, with various diseases and performed on them the most disfiguring and bizarre of all surgical operations in the long history of the Third Reich's Experimental Medical Program.[19]

At one time women whose camp numbers started with 7,000 (the *Sondertransport*) were considered doomed. The SS treated those transports in a special manner, for they contained women condemned to death by the Gestapo. As a result, no one from a transport with a number 7,000 and over was allowed beyond the camp walls. From time to time a few of those women were taken away to be shot. But a quick death was not their usual fate. They were to form the experimental nucleus.

On August 1, 1942, SS doctors summoned six women to the *Revier* (infirmary) and subjected them to surgery—these were the first experiments. Between August 1, 1942, and August 16, 1943, seventy-four Polish women prisoners were operated on, as well as an unknown number of women prisoners of other nationalities. At first it seemed that only those women who had been sentenced to death (and only the very youngest of them—under age twenty) were being subjected to the operations in place of execution. The women thought that the death sentence had been commuted for those who had surgery. Soon, however, the number of subjects increased. Their stay in the infirmary lasted from several weeks to several months. Those who had been operated on returned to the block in a crippled state and formed a new social group, the guinea pigs. The group grew; and contrary to usual procedure, it was kept together, out of the way, in a separate block. Obviously, the Germans were isolating the group from both the camp and the civilian populations. Hence, those women began to develop the features of an organized community. Since they were young and most were political prisoners, they became more courageous and determined as the project continued.

The camp inmates treated the Rabbits in an unusual manner. The overwhelming majority of the Ravensbrück inmates adopted a protective attitude toward the youngest and most crippled of their colleagues. Polish women managed to collect sheets and leather shoes for them. Cooks systematically stole cauldrons of soup for them. "Without exaggeration one may say that the entire camp tried hard to keep the guinea pigs alive."[20]

None of the experiments made scientific sense. They were sadistic and, of course, unnecessary. The reason for these most barbaric of all Nazi experiments at first glance is obscure. But upon analysis it becomes clear that the motivations were medical military need, stupidity, Nazi power politics—and a certain unique form of exhilarating sadism. The use of women subjects was not accidental. The "rabbit experiments" can be divided into the following categories:

1. Infectious Operations on Limbs—the Sulfanilamide Experiments
2. Clean Operations—Regeneration
    a. on bones: breaking, removal, grafting
    b. on muscles: removal, grafting
    c. on nerves
3. Amputation of Limbs—Bone Transplantation
4. Sterilization Experiments
    a. with surgery
    b. with Xrays
    c. with chemotherapy into the uterus
    d. with caladium seguinum

The scientist in charge of the rabbit experimentation project, Dr. K. F. Gebhardt, was one of Hitler's personal physicians and the director of the sanitarium in Hohenlychen, located about 24 kilometers from Ravensbrück. After he successfully completed the project, Dr. Gebhardt was named director of the German Red Cross by Hitler. Before his SS days Gebhardt had been a friend and classmate of Himmler. A man who trained under the best physicians in the world, he developed an experimental process to be carried out in unusually unscientific and disgusting conditions. Sophia Maczka, in her affidavit, points out that most of the doctors and other personnel used by Gebhardt were not properly trained in the medical sense.

Conditions were neither aseptic nor hygienic. After the operations the staff left the victims in filthy rooms without medicine, dressings, medical help, nursing, or supervision.

The sulfanilamide experiments or the infectious operations on limbs were directly related to the German war effort. The army had sustained heavy casualties from gas gangrene on the Russian front. The *Wehrmacht* Medical Services wanted to determine if the wounded should be treated surgically in the front-line hospitals, or by field medical officers with sulfanilamide and other pharmaceuticals and then sent down the long line of emergency centers to a base hospital. After the war medical experts testified to the absurdity of Gebhardt's research design. From July 1942 to September 1943 he directed a preliminary experiment at Ravensbrück to test the effectiveness of sulfanilamide. At its conclusion, he reported to Himmler that he intended to move ahead with a full-scale project using the Ravensbrück women:

I started on July 20, 1942, at Ravensbrück concentration camp for women on a series of clinical experiments with the aim of analyzing the sickness known as gas gangrene, which does not take a uniform course, and to test the efficacy of the known therapeutic medicants.

In addition, the simple infections of injuries which occur as symptoms in war surgery had also to be tested; and a new chemotherapeutic treatment apart from the known surgical measures had to be tried out.[21]

At his Nuremburg trial Dr. Gebhardt testified that he conducted three series of sulfanilamide experiments with each group of experimental subjects. In one he used a bacterial culture and fragments of wood; in the second he used bacterial culture and fragments of glass; in the third he used bacterial culture plus glass and wood. All operations involved the lower limbs, mainly the thigh. The staff made incisions in the legs of several women inmates to simulate battlefield infections. Then they infected the wounds with bacteria, wood shavings, glass fragments, streptococcus, gas gangrene, and tetanus. After several days they treated the wounds with sulfanilamide and other drugs.

On September 3, 1942, after experiments had been conducted on thirty-six women, Grawitz, head of the SS Medical Service, visited Ravensbrück and inspected the subjects. He asked Gebhardt how many deaths had occurred, and when he responded that there had been none, Grawitz concluded that the situation did not conform to battlefield conditions. He directed that more severe wounds be inflicted on the subjects. Therefore the doctors initiated a new series of experiments involving twenty-four Polish females. In that series they interrupted the circulation of blood through the muscles in the area of infection by tying off the muscles on either end. Into the wound they placed a gangrene-producing culture. Severe infection resulted within twenty-four hours. Operations were then performed on the infected areas and the wounds were treated with sulfanilamide. Some subjects were not given sulfanilamide in order to compare their reactions to those who received treatment. Several experimentees died. All suffered torture, and if they lived, mutilation. Postoperative care was nonexistent; most subjects were denied medicine, morphine, and bandages. Sometimes they waited for help for three or four days with a terrible odor of pus filling the rooms. One witness testified:

I felt severe pain, and blood flowed from my leg. At night we were all alone without any care. I heard only the screaming of my fellow prisoners, and I heard also that they asked for water. There was nobody to give us any water or bed pans.[22]

As a rule, the infectious operations resulted in a strong inflammatory reaction with a high temperature, in some cases surpassing 39.9 degrees centigrade. The inflammatory condition usually caused much loss of skin and affected the bones, giving rise to fistulas in the opening of wounds months after the operations. The average duration of healing was fifteen months; in some cases it was several years. Some scars opened up again several years after the operation.

Why did Gebhardt, with his excellent training, involve himself in such a reckless and unscientific project? It appears now that he may have had something quite important at stake. When assassins gunned down Heydrich, Himmler's right-hand man, Gebhardt, as one of the great doctors of the Reich, was called to the bedside. But Heydrich died a week later. Hitler was furious. He summoned Gebhardt and ranted at him. Hitler's personal quack physician, Theodor Morell, added to Gebhardt's problem when he insisted that the use of modern sulfanilamides would have saved Heydrich's life.

Consequently, Gebhardt's restoration of his own status depended upon establishing clinical proof of the inefficiency of these sulfanilamides in the treatment of certain infections caused by war wounds. And thus, the artificial "war" wounds were inflicted on our comrades' legs by this renowned surgeon, wounds which he then allowed to become infected with, for example, the gangrene baccilli. . . . And, of course, the sulfanilamides used for treatment had to be ineffective.[23]

At a conference of the Congress of the Academy of Military Medicine in May 1943 attended by 350 to 400 German doctors, Gebhardt detailed his experimental project. Not one doctor at the Congress questioned his experiments.

From September 1942 to September 1943 doctors and staff under

Gebhardt's supervision conducted experiments for the benefit of the German armed forces to study bone, muscle, and nerve regeneration and bone transplantation. Simply, they removed sections of bones, muscles, and nerves from the legs of their women subjects.

The bone operations included bone breaking, bone transplantation, and bone grafting. In the first instance the doctors used a hammer to break the bones of the lower part of both legs into several pieces. Later they joined the bones with clips and placed the legs in plaster casts, which they removed after several days. Bone transplantations were carried out in a similar manner. The muscle experiments consisted of several operations on the same spot, with larger pieces of muscle cut out each time. Most patients became crippled and suffered a great deal. One woman reported on her operation in the bunker under forced anesthesia. When she regained consciousness, she noted that both her legs were in iron splints, bandaged from her toes up to her groin. She felt severe pain in her feet and had a temperature.

The bone and muscle operations were senseless and utterly savage. The doctors covered the festering wounds with plaster of Paris despite the excessive pus. Dressings were seldom changed. Consequently a secondary and enormous destruction of the soft parts resulted. On many victims the doctors repeated the bone operations several times.

A typical example was Barbara P., the youngest female prisoner of the *Sondertransport* (she was sixteen years old when the Gestapo arrested her). The doctors operated on her on October 2, 1942. They made two incisions on the right and left legs. After the operation they covered the limbs with plaster of Paris, which ensured severe pain and swelling. After two weeks they removed the plaster of Paris from the left limb, but only to make two more incisions above the previous area. Again they applied plaster of Paris to the leg. The victim's temperature increased violently and the dressing was not changed. Two months after the first operation the plaster was taken off both limbs and dressings applied. Two weeks later the doctors subjected Barbara P. to a third operation, which opened the lower wound on the left leg. Once again the limb was put in plaster up to the knee. And again fever set in, this time lasting for two months. On January 28, 1943, the fourth successive operation opened the lower wound on the left leg. The limb was put again in plaster, and Barbara ran a temperature for a month, with severe festering. The fifth and last operation took place when the doctors opened the wound of the upper right leg. Barbara was able to walk haltingly nine months after the first operation.

In performing the large group of muscle experiments the doctors reused the same subjects. During the first operation they removed certain muscles, and during subsequent operations they cut out additional pieces, always from the same place so that the leg became thinner and thinner. Much of the surgery was conducted without anesthesia.

The operations on a special group of feebleminded or mentally ill women concerned the removal of certain limbs. The lower extremities were amputated, with a disarticulation in the hip joint. The same operation was performed on the upper extremities, with the elimination of the shoulder. The doctors wanted to determine if bones could be transplanted to German soldiers, so they sent amputated limbs, wrapped in operating sheets, to Hohenlychen. The prisoners were then killed.[24]

It is in the sterilization experiments that the destructive nature of the Nazi medical program comes out most forcibly. They were developing a new branch of medical service that would give them the scientific tools for the planning and practice of genocide:

The primary purpose was to discover an inexpensive, unobtrusive and rapid method of sterilization which could be used to wipe out Russians, Poles, Jews and other people. Surgical sterilization was thought to be too slow and expensive to be used on a mass scale.[25]

From about March 1941 until January 1945 doctors conducted several types of sterilization experiments at Ravensbrück with the purpose of developing a method for sterilizing millions of women with a minimum of time, effort, and money. The experimentors used Xrays, surgery, and various drugs to sterilize thousands.

The first series was based on the results, published in a German scientific magazine, of animal sterilization experiments using extract from the caladium seguinum plant. After reading the report about caladium, a Dr. Pokorny wrote to Himmler in October 1941 to suggest that Germany might have a new and extremely effective weapon in its hands. He proposed that the caladium drug be administered orally or by injection. In this way Germany could sterilize perhaps three million Bolsheviks and continue to profit from their labor while effectively wiping them out as a people. Pokorny proposed that the seguinum plant be cultivated in hothouses and that the experiments begin. And if the experiments proved effective, then synthetic production should proceed at once. Quickly, Himmler mobilized the SS medical service to those ends.[26]

Another sterilization method suggested by Dr. Clauberg involved the injection of an irritating solution into the uterus. Rudolf Brandt, Himmler's assistant, wrote him on July 10, 1943, that Himmler would be interested in learning how long it would take to sterilize a thousand Jewesses. He thought that the results could be checked by locking up a Jew and a Jewess together for a certain period. Proceeding on this theory, the professor injected inflammatory liquid into the uterus, and examined it with Xrays. Children were among the victims. On June 7, 1943, Professor Clauberg wrote to Himmler reporting on his research:

The method I contrived to achieve the sterilization of the female organism without operation is as good as perfected. It can be performed by a single injection made through the entrance to the uterus in the course of the customary gynecological examination known to every physician.

He needed to work out minor improvements on his method, but predicted that one adequately trained physician and one well-equipped office with ten assistants could handle several hundred if not a thousand sterilizations a day.[27] Several thousand Jewish and Gypsy women were sterilized at Auschwitz by that method. Dr. Gebhardt, of bone surgery infamy, conducted sterilization at Ravensbrück with surgical operations.

Dr. Brack's sterilization experiments used powerful Xrays. Brack made the following suggestion to Himmler in his letter of 1941:

One way to carry out these experiments in practice would be to have those people who are to be treated line up before a counter. There they would be questioned and a form would be given them to be filled out, the whole process taking 2 or 3 minutes. The official attendant who sits behind the counter can operate the apparatus in such a manner that he works a switch which will start both tubes together. . . . With one such installation with two tubes, about 150 or 200 persons could be sterilized daily, while 20 installations would take care of 3,000 to 4,000 persons daily.

Brack assured Himmler that his latest X-ray technique and research would make it possible to carry out mass sterilization with ease, though he thought that most subjects would discover later that they had either been castrated or sterilized. In June 1942 he made another suggestion to Himmler:

Among 10 million of the Jews in Europe there are, I figure, at least 2 to 3 millions of men and women who are fit enough to work. Considering the extraordinary difficulties the labor problem presents us with, I hold the view that these 2 to 3 millions should be specially selected and preserved. This can, however, only be done if at the same time they are rendered incapable to propagate.[28]

At Gebhardt's trial his lawyers' first line of defense was that there was a serious medical need for the experiments! Their second line of defense, if it can be dignified with that word, was that the Polish women had been condemned to death for participation in a resistance movement and that by participating in the experiments voluntarily or otherwise, they secured a commutation of their death sentence to a lesser degree of punishment. The court sentenced Gebhardt to death and hanged him on June 2, 1948.

It finally became clear to the victims of these grotesque experiments that their "service" to German medicine did not guarantee survival, that one could be first crippled and then be executed. A determination to resist began to grow, which finally led to open rebellion! On March 6, 1943, a previous victim was summoned for additional surgery and she told the commandant that she was not about to have another operation. The next day the doctors summoned five more experimental subjects and encountered similar resistance.

The remaining subjects wrote a letter of petition to the commandant that began with a question: Did Herr Commandant know that surgery was conducted in the camp that violated all humanitarian principles, operations that turned healthy young women into cripples, endangered their lives, and were carried out against their will? So far, they told him, seventy-one Polish women had been operated on and five had died. They wanted to know if those operations were a secret part of their sentences. Most subjects signed the petition as an act of protest. Together they marched with it to the commandant, "an entire procession of cripples with bandaged legs, some walking on crutches." At that time the Rabbit Block held about fifty inmates who had been operated upon; others were lying in the infirmary. Commandant Suhren did not come out himself, but sent *Oberaufseherin* Langefeld to hear the representatives. They would not go to the hospital, they said, because they would rather die than become invalids. Appearing unsettled by their suspicions, Langefeld claimed that the experiments would not begin again and that the summons to the infirmary had nothing to do with surgery. She also claimed (hesitantly because fifty bandaged legs stood or lay right in front of her) that their suspicions were based largely on rumor. Commandant Suhren then ordered the women back to work without punishment. The women did not suffer any immediate consequences and for a time they felt they had won.[29]

Suddenly, however, on August 15, 1943, Polish women working in the infirmary brought news that the operating room was being prepared. In the evening a guard came to the block with a list containing the names of ten women ordered to the infirmary. All the women refused, insisting that they preferred death. The policewoman left and returned with the police, who threw all the inmates out in front of the experimental block. One official told the group it was not a question of an operation, but of work. The women declared that they would go to the commandant but not to the infirmary. Surrounded by the police, the ten marched out. But then they tore away and ran back toward the block. The ranks of women opened up, the chosen ten disappeared among the others, and the ranks closed immediately. The police-woman turned the corner in pursuit and saw only the orderly ranks. Finally, those who knew the ten women by sight dragged them out and took them to the cells.[30]

The doctors subjected those ten women to one of the most disgusting operations in the entire series. Five of them were operated on just as they entered, in dirty dresses, forcibly anesthetized by the technicians without any preoperative care. A woman regaining consciousness in the dark cell exclaimed: "But I have such dirty legs!" Another victim described the ghastly scene in her affidavit:

I resisted and hit Trommer in the face and called him a bandit. He called some SS male guards who threw me on the floor and held me down while ether was poured over my face. There was no mask. I fought and resisted until I lost consciousness. I was completely dressed and my legs were filthy dirty from walking in the camp. As far as I know, my legs were not washed. I saw my sister during this time unconscious on a stretcher, vomiting mucus.[31]

Those were the last nonvoluntary operations performed in Ravensbrück.

The survivors of those last operations were sent to the so-called *Nacht und Nebel* Block, which housed inmates intended to disappear from the world. It was clear that no Nazi was interested in the medical health or well-being of the subjects after the experiments ended. Then one day the SS doctors decided to execute all their guinea pigs. Prisoners warned the women and they hid. For a number of weeks until the end of the war the women prisoners fought for the lives of the guinea pigs. Some women proposed to give the younger ones false documents and then let themselves be killed in their place. Others simply hid them. Some of the most seriously crippled women spent days buried in holes underneath the blocks. Several were sent out in transports to other camps. That action was only possible because by then nameless uncounted women prisoners had come to Ravensbrück from Auschwitz, and the camp numbers of those who had died on the way were available for disguise. So the postoperative women hid and painted the ink numbers of Auschwitz on their arms.

Clearly the experimental subjects were not supposed to live through the war. The lives of some were saved only because the camp authorities were not prepared for the rapidly advancing Allied armies and could not prevent the camp functions from disintegrating into chaos. The surviving women won their battle. At the end of the war they returned to their homes. In 1975 approximately fifty of them lived in Poland and several more lived outside of Poland.[32]

By 1945 Ravensbrück was gravely overcrowded, a situation that prevented sleep and even a modicum of hygiene. The filthy conditions killed more quickly than hunger. When the transports dumped Warsaw evacuees into Ravensbrück in late 1944, the SS threw up tents to accommodate the naked, starving women. Judith Sternberg Newman was one of those transported from Auschwitz to the tents, and she has called the Ravensbrück of 1944 "a camp of starvation and death." When women arrived, there was no food or work available so they slept in the tents and spent the rest of the time staring into space. Without washrooms, they were forced to undress and wash before the staring guards. Prisoners remember the odor of putrefaction when a typhoid epidemic swept the area and the guards allowed the dead to lie in the sun for days. Mademoiselle Vaillant-Couturier described what happened to the Hungarian Jewish women, among the very last arrivals, forced to live in a large tent:

Their condition was deplorable. There were a great many cases of frozen feet, because they had been evacuated from Budapest and had walked a good part of the way in the snow. . . . One day I passed the tent as it was being cleaned and I saw a pile of smoking manure in front of it. I suddenly realized that this manure was human excrement, since the unfortunate women no longer had the strength to drag themselves to the latrines.[33]

When a fighting woman reached the end of her strength, two symptoms came before death:

She stopped fighting the lice, and she began to believe the wild stories circulating through the camp, which until then she had been able to dismiss. . . . Did she die because she had stopped struggling? Or did she cease struggling because she was dying? But she died.[34]

Survivors remember that their physical condition deteriorated at times to the point where they did not have the strength to speak. And the feeling of total exhaustion remained with them until they were liberated. Some became *Schmückstück,* a "dirty thing." A *Schmückstück* was a human creature far past the stage called emaciation and almost at a fatal edge of starvation. Autopsies of *Schmückstück* women revealed human organs reduced to the size of rabbit organs. The *Schmückstück* were "incapable of personal or social discipline." Dirty and covered with sores, "they would throw themselves flat in the mud to lick up the remains" from soup bowls. They had no friends, no hope. All were destined for the gas chamber.[35]

How did Tillion survive? Her experience was representative of many. She owes her survival first to chance, then to anger and the motivation to reveal the crimes she had witnessed. Finally, she survived because of a union of friendship. Almost everyone in the camp was woven into that web of friendship. It bound together surrogate families—two, three, or four women from the same town or perhaps a group formed in the cattle car, all clinging to one another. Those bonds helped them prevail against the formidable organized networks of the SS.

The final six months of Ravensbrück was such an incredible period of methodical extermination, horrors, and chaos that controversy still exists over the location of the gas chamber, the number of available ovens, and the dates for each extermination phase. The Nazis added to the confusion by creating for their records a fictional place, a sanitarium called Mittwerda, to which all disappearing women supposedly were assigned. In fact, Mittwerda was nothing more than the extermination location a few hundred yards from the main camp.

For some time a small camp originally named Uckermark but which came to be known as the *Jugendlager* had existed on the edge of the main camp. A primitive compound, it had been thrown together originally as an incarceration center for German juvenile delinquents. In the fall of 1944 the Germans hurriedly evacuated the *Jugendlager* and began to ready it for use as a strange killing center, referring to it again by its original name—Uckermark. Supposedly, the commandant had received word in early fall that the Ravensbrück death rate was too low, and that unless drastic steps were taken, the camp would not be able to accommodate the anticipated transports from the evacuating Polish camps. The SS installed the gassing equipment and added a third oven to the crematorium.

Whether the gassing equipment was located several hundred meters away in Uckermark, as some sources claim, or installed in a building next to the crematorium, as East German experts insist, is a question still unanswered. Witnesses seem to remember the gas installation in both places. The issue is of relative unimportance, but let us use the East German archives and assume that the crematorium was located next to the camp, between the lake edge and the high brick camp wall. We know that the gas facilities were used in November to exterminate 1,700 Jewish women and children. We know that the guards used a white powder substance to poison inmates. We know that in early December the guards asked the ill, the aged, and the fatigued to step forward so they could be taken to a convalescent camp referred to as Uckermark. Those women who responded were gassed in December.[36]

The inability to clarify the gassing situation in Ravensbrück rests on a refusal to accept the bizarre and truly primitive nature of the means of extermination used at the camp in those last months of the war. In the first place, the gas chamber was small. It had been intended for 15 persons, and according to Commandant Suhren, it measured 9 by 4½ meters. Others estimated that at times it held 170 to 180 prisoners. It did not seem to operate efficiently. Perhaps the SS at Ravensbrück did not have the modern and fast-killing Cyclone B tablets. Whatever the reasons, gassing just could not do the job. Uckermark was an extermination center—but not in the usual sense. The guards transported prisoners by trucks to Uckermark, right down the road. They sent them there to *die*. They removed the ill and the sick to the primitive compound—to *lie there* until they died. They aided the process by long, cold roll calls, poison, beatings, the mixing of women with contagious diseases, absence of food, inadequate water facilities, shooting, suffocating, and allowing victims to freeze to death. Then they trucked the dead bodies the few blocks back to the camp crematorium, which blazed around the clock from December.

Mrs. Gluck remembers well the crematorium. Her bed stood near a window, and at night when she could not sleep, she watched the smoke pour out of the chimneys:

And oh, the terrible odor. We could force our eyes closed, but we could not keep the stench of death from our nostrils. When we were awakened at 4 A.M., the first thing we saw was the flaming smoke, the first thing we were aware of was the smell.[37]

Even so, the bodies piled up and the authorities ordered the oven temperatures raised to such a point that one oven finally exploded. But still the bodies backed up and the SS almost went frantic trying to dispose of them. They dug large graves along the camp walls; they brought in flamethrowers to burn the bodies in a nearby forest; and they continued to send bodies to the Fürstenberg town crematorium.

In January 1945, after the SS again took an inventory of the aged and ill prisoners, they sent them to Uckermark and ordered them to undress. That day the women stood naked in the icy snow of a Prussian winter for a roll call that lasted until evening. About fifty died that first day and the process was repeated daily. From the end of January there was constant movement between Uckermark and Ravensbrück. The cold and starvation did not kill quickly enough, so the SS brought in a nine-man shooting team. By April thousands of women from the overcrowded main camp had been killed at Uckermark, at the "sanitarium." One, an elderly Polish woman, escaped. She described what had happened. At one point during the winter the SS nailed shut the windows of a block's washroom, crammed in as many women as possible, and locked the doors. After a few days the SS decided it was time to bring the experiment to a close. They set up a motion-picture camera to film the emerging survivors. "These prisoners had torn away the chimney bricks to try to get air and had ripped off all their clothing; several had died or were unconscious, others had evidently gone mad." After filming the scene, the SS sent all the women to the crematorium.[38]

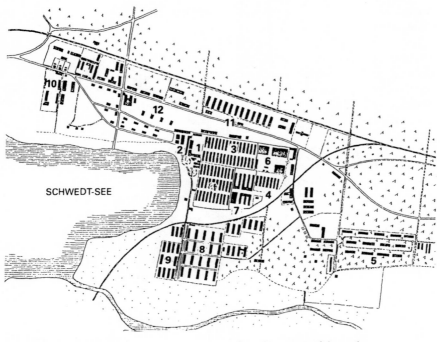

1.	Cell construction	8.	Siemens work barracks
2.	Commander headquarters	9.	Siemens inmates camp
3.	Women's camp	10.	DAW—German Construction Works
4.	Men's camp	11.	SS booty storage
5.	Uckermark	12.	SS residences
6.	SS activities work center	13.	Gas chambers
7.	SS activities work center	14.	Crematorium

Map 7: The Early Women's Concentration Camp Ravensbrück—Overall Plan
Edward Ullman: Ravensbrück *(DDR: Ravensbrück Archives, 1964).*

The women remembered the dentist who seemed to perform the hideous work of a body desecrator.

According to an established procedure, the doctor came toward his victim with an electric lamp and tongs or pliers. . . . One could hear the rattle of the tongs, the dull thud of the bodies being thrown out back. Then the booty was wrapped in paper and brought to the Commandant. The bodies lay like fish with wide open, toothless mouths, with the stamp of inspection on their shoulders.[39]

Without that stamp, the bodies could not be taken to the crematorium!
A survivor relates another story of a young healthy woman who was

placed in a group of sick and old blockmates. She was forced into the gas chamber, naked:

Somehow, she found herself regaining consciousness later—on a pile of bodies near the crematorium oven. She still had the strength to get out through a few of the barriers, then managed to remain hidden for several hours under some dirty mattresses piled outdoors. She was recaptured and gassed again the same day, but not before telling her story to other prisoners.[40]

The deputy commandant testified at his trial that he had received an order from Himmler in February to exterminate all but the young and healthy. Shooting was not fast enough, so the women were gathered by the gas chamber and told to undress for delousing. The deputy commandant related how the guards then forced the 150 women into the chamber, bolted the door, and threw in the gas capsules. "I heard sounds from the inside, mostly grunts and moans, but after a while everything was quiet." The Ravensbrück archives state that 32,000 women were killed in the gas chamber; they also point out that in no concentration camp on German soil was the share of murdered prisoners so high.[41]

Why didn't the SS kill all prisoners? They had ample time. As of April 2, 1945, the day on which they destroyed some of the gas-chamber material, they needed only forty-four days to completely exterminate the remaining 11,000 prisoners if one assumes the normal extermination rate. It could have been accomplished easily. Why wasn't it? Tillion thinks the answer lies in "Himmler's notion, crazy or not, to take power from Hitler and make a separate peace with the Anglo-Saxons through Swedish intermediaries, using us as commodities of barter. This final exploitation of prisoners as fodder for the German machine failed completely.[42]

The long-awaited liberation came on April 30, 1945; but most women who had prayed so fervently for that moment were in the groups of about 20,000 whom the SS had evacuated. The Soviet Army found their bodies strewn along the roads and stacked in the forests. Only 3,000 sick women remained in the camp. According to the Ravensbrück Archives, 132,000 women and children went through Ravensbrück and 92,000 died.

The first Ravensbrück trial, under British auspices, took place in Hamburg in December 1946 and January 1947. Fifteen people were charged. They were clean, well dressed, and nice-looking: "A dentist, doctors, a former printer, nurses, middle-level workers. No criminal records, normal educations, normal childhoods. Ordinary people." And those were the men and women who had "drowned infants in pails, poisoned the soup fed to the sick, planted gangrene in the wounds they had opened in the legs of school children."[43]

PART II
NAZI THEORY AND PRACTICE:
A WOMAN'S FUTURE

Ravensbrück was a small place and only a portion of the Third Reich's female enemies passed through it. Although Ravensbrück was unique as the only all-women's camp, it does not by itself answer the questions regarding basic Nazi theory with regard to good women and bad women. Nor does it answer questions about the different treatment the Nazis meted out to women and men within the Third Reich and without, and within the camps. Ravensbrück by itself is not very helpful.

To answer these questions, we need to look at the racial policy of Hitler and Himmler to see how it affected women particularly. We need to look at women in the Third Reich—the good German *hausfrau*. We need to assess the philosophy regarding non-Aryan women and the different steps taken to meet the problems they raised for Nazi Germany. We need to look at women in the concentration camps and incarceration centers, in women's centers within male camps, in labor details; and at SS women, at medical differences, and at children. Finally we need to look at the many memoirs written by women to see what they say about their experiences.

Aryan Women and Children in the Third Reich

The Nazi approach to women contained key elements different from the German approach during the Weimar period and the approach to women in other countries. Part of the Nazi program was based on pragmatic reasons that were blown up into a flowery propaganda effort. But basic ideological differences existed. The studies of women in Nazi Germany have indeed been sparse and many have contributed to a myth, perpetuated by historians, that can be summed up in the expression *Kinder, Kirche, Küche* (children, church, kitchen/hearth). We now know that looking at Nazi Germany in terms of that concept alone reinforces a distortion. For the Nazis might well have wanted women in the home, but the war effort did not permit them to implement that policy to the desired extent. Much of what we assume today as reality was simply propaganda. It is also true that in Nazi Germany, as elsewhere, there were strong paradoxes. The slogan *Kinder, Kirche, Küche,* however, does set the tone for Nazi ideas about Aryan German women.[1]

Himmler's new racial theory, designed to promote pure blood, needed to be coordinated with the new women's theory because at its core the racial theory rested upon women. Some object to the phrase "anatomy is destiny," but the very fact that women bore children played a vital part in determining the status and role of both Aryan and non-Aryan women. The race experts in Himmler's organization relied on the works of a well-known scholar, Dr. Wilhelm Schalmayer, whose earlier book on racial hygiene dealt with eight main points—all of which primarily affected women. According to the good doctor, all young people should be made to realize that the noblest career for a girl was that of wife and mother; that a woman's status and social position should depend on the number of children she produced; that the creation and development of a cult of the family was absolutely essential to a country; that men should be encouraged to marry young; that employment by women outside the home had to be reduced to a minimum; that the nation must fight sexual disease; and that special homes should be created for homecoming soldiers who, after being tested for racial hygiene, should become the fathers of many children. Dr. Schalmayer also insisted that the purpose of a breeding policy must be to ensure that the most unsuitable variations would not be reproduced. He believed not only in forbidding certain marriages, but also in introducing sterilization because "sex life is not just a private affair, but should be a sacred matter dedicated to a higher cause."[2]

To the Schalmayer base Himmler's SS organization added modern touches of its own. Not only was it imperative to halt the progressive deterioration of the German race caused by the mixture of inferior races—particularly Jews—but every effort would have to be made to convince men and, especially, women to reverse the directions their lives were taking. To the racial theory one must add the desperate concern that Hitler, Himmler, and the Nazi state had about Germany's population. If German was to conquer the world it would need people to settle those countries and to provide the labor for the armies and industry. Yet the birth rate had dropped sharply in the postwar period. Although the degree of social emancipation for women in post-World War I society has been exaggerated, it appears that birth control and the proclivity toward small families would have produced slow but steady changes in the social fabric had not the trend been reversed by the Nazis. It was essential, they believed, to induce women to return to traditional domestic roles and to understand that their most important mission was the bearing of children.

When Hitler came to power, German economic life had virtually ground to a halt. The country was in the throes of a raging depression. Someday we shall need to probe more deeply into the differences between actions and rhetoric resulting from general economic recovery needs and Nazi policy and belief. Although the ideology is fairly clear, the actions are more troublesome. Clearly, however, the Nazis viewed unemployment as an emergency. They simply had to remove women from the work force to provide jobs for men. Those Nazi leaders acting against women in the labor force did not need to kick down doors. The depression had done that for them. The late Weimar government had already systematically reduced the number of women allowed in public employment.

The Nazis began a major campaign to change woman's role in society. Woman was to become the guardian of the hearth, the bearer of children. The campaign against childlessness began when Hitler spoke of emancipated women as unnatural symbols.

We do not consider it correct for the woman to interfere in the world of the man, in his main sphere. We consider it natural if these two worlds remain distinct. To the one belongs the strength of feeling, the strength of the soul. To the other belongs the strength of vision, of toughness, of decision, and of the willingness to act. In the one case this strength demands the willingness of the woman to risk her life to preserve this important cell and to multiply it, and in the other case it demands from the man the readiness to safeguard life.

The sacrifices which the man makes in the struggle of his nation, the woman makes in the preservation of that nation in individual cases. What the man gives in courage on the battlefield, the woman gives in eternal self-sacrifice, in eternal pain and suffering. Every child that a woman brings into the world is a battle, a battle waged for the existence of her people. And both must therefore mutually value and respect each other when they see that each performs the task that Nature and Providence have ordained. And this mutual respect will necessarily result from this separation of the functions of each.[3]

Goebbels compared women to animals when he said: "A woman's duty is to be attractive and bear children. The idea is not as vulgar and old-fashioned as it might seem. A female bird makes itself beautiful for its mate and hatches out her eggs for him." We must not underestimate the central part played by sexism in Nazi thought and action. It was, as Schoenbaum calls it, a "secondary reason." Nazi Germany was as protective a nation toward women as we know in modern times. The leaders and the followers believed deeply that hardship should not be inflicted upon women. The concern was nice. The actions that followed for non-Aryan women were not.[4]

When the Nazi party was first formed in the 1920s, a Nazi ordinance declared that women would be excluded forever from all leading positions in the party. Party leaders also made it clear that there would be no deviation from a cardinal rule: women were basically inferior to men. The Nazis issued decrees diminishing women's status. In June 1936 they banned women from judicial office as well as from most professions. They also reduced the number of women in higher education and changed the educational directions for young women.

Once woman's status was diminished and she was back in the home, the next step was to induce her to produce large families. For that purpose, the Nazis provided benefits for childbearing. Most of their measures were primarily propaganda, but there were financial inducements in the form of marriage loans, child subsidies, and family allowances.

The program included the introduction of harsh curbs on abortion (making it an act of sabotage), undermining the idea of equality for women, mounting a major struggle against homosexuals. In addition to prohibiting the sale of contraceptives, the Nazis relaxed the divorce laws for childless couples. When it became clear that there were not enough men to go around, they initiated a campaign that gave childbearing priority: motherhood, not marriage, was a woman's duty to the state. Therefore extramarital sex was encouraged and an attempt was made to end the discrimination against unmarried mothers. None of those goals was easy to reach, but the Nazis pursued their program vigorously. When they altered their theories later to meet changing reality, they were not troubled by charges of inconsistency.

Nazi policy considered the family the cell of the nation. Success in the Battle of Births became the prerequisite for victory on other fronts. Combining harsh curbs and positive propagandistic measures, the Nazis created a cult of motherhood. When that cult was joined to a campaign to raise the quality of racial selection by developing a program of human stock breeding, they began to see results. The notion grew that infertility in marriage was tantamount to political opposition to the regime. The Nazis remembered that in the early days they had promised every girl a husband. With women overwhelmingly in the majority, however, the best they could do now was to promise every girl a baby—and somehow they must convince that girl to have at least four! They also had to encourage parents to view their daughters' illegitimate children positively. At the same time that they emphasized the family as a breeding farm, they degraded full family life. And it was to change even more when victory was theirs. Proposals for postwar actions included instituting the idea of double marriage among large groups of deserving German men. The propaganda effort strained to make women realize that the highlight of their lives was the marriage-to-menopause period, when they would be the object of public esteem. After that, it was clear they were superfluous to society.

Women in Nazi Germany were ordered to commit themselves to the battlefield of life. Anyone who produced a child was entitled to benefits—the more children, the more benefits. The birthday of Hitler's mother became the Day of the German Mother. Hitler decorated mothers of large families with the German Mother's Cross. By August 1939, 3 million German mothers possessed those decorations, which entitled them to special privileges. So great was the preoccupation with fertility that of the 18 million German mothers who were expected to devote themselves completely to the raising of children, not one was forced into a factory before 1943. The Nazi leaders insisted publicly that a decline in the birth rate was more devastating than war. And the Nazi regime, in spite of its notoriously antiwoman stance, succeeded in winning the votes, support, and loyalty of Germany's women.[5]

Himmler agreed with Hitler that after the war a fundamental change in the concept of marriage must occur. Bigamy, with all its advantages, would be introduced. In bigamous relationships wives would spur each other on. The husband, now permitted to fulfill his natural urges openly, would no longer need to practice deceit. The strife and hostility so common in monogamous marriages would fall away and more children would be born.[6] On October 28, 1939, Himmler issued an important order to the SS and the police. He was saddened that wars killed a nation's best men, but deplorable as that fact was, he said it was not the gravest result. Far worse was the loss of the children who would not be born. Therefore the high duty of German women and girls of good blood was to become mothers outside the boundaries of marriage in a spirit of "deep moral seriousness."[7]

In the mid-1930s the SS set up centers—*Lebensborns*—where racial selection and human stock breeding moved hand in hand with the political indoctrination of future generations—controlled and supervised by the SS and by Himmler. The *Lebensborn* organization, established by Himmler in 1935, provided a cradle for children and facilities for the confinement of pregnant wives, fiancées, and friends of SS males. Its purpose was to meet the urgent need of enabling racially valuable unmarried, pregnant women to have their babies and either to raise them with state financial help or to hand them over to the SS for adoption.

Himmler took a personal interest in the entire operation and little escaped his attention. He placed great emphasis on breastfeeding. Good milk producers—mothers who breastfed their babies for a long period—received awards from Himmler and were entitled to prolonged stays in convalescent homes. He made it clear to SS men that they had to produce children or forfeit their careers. He considered four children the minimum for a good and healthy marriage. A childless SS leader had the duty to adopt racially valuable children. In sum, *Lebensborn* was organized to support racially and genetically valuable large families; to look after racially valuable expectant mothers; to care for both the children of those mothers and the mothers of those children. Himmler's ambition was to populate Germany with 120 million Teutons by 1980.

The Nazi code covering reproduction had no use for the concepts of love, affection, or sentimentality. The State thoroughly indoctrinated the boys in the Hitler Youth and the girls in the *BdM* or *Bund deutscher Mädel*. Because they were only fifteen or sixteen years old and inexperienced, the *BdM* girls proved very receptive to that message and leaped into a program of reproduction in the national interest. Sexual intercourse was not a pleasure: it was a brick that every German male and female must contribute to the building of the new order. Love was contrary to the best interests of Nazi genetics and biology. *Lebensborn* also participated in a large-scale planned reproduction— or as some termed it, stud breeding—program. Himmler's dreams for the postwar period included the establishment of a system of villages for unmarried women. His fantastic plans also included his SS women. He wanted to be the founder of an original institution, "halfway between barracks and brothel."[8]

With the advent of the war, the paradoxes of the Nazis' antifeminism became blatant. The women they had destined for the kitchen and the nursery eventually formed three-fifths of Germany's wartime labor force. The contradiction of rhetorical nostalgia and the urgent need for a streamlined industrial labor force was resolved by proclaiming that although a woman's place was in the home, in wartime the whole of Germany was her home![9]

By 1938 Germany faced an acute labor shortage. Its major potential source for relief were the 3.5 million women not regularly employed who had no children under fourteen years. The Nazis turned down the idea of conscription and came up with a program urging women back to work—but only gently. The labor climate, with its nasty pay differentials and tedious jobs, was full of work disincentives and most women did not wish to go to work. The mounting labor crisis forced a tough choice on the government: conscript women or allow the Jews to live longer. The government decided to avoid upsetting their women; they hesitantly opted to allow Jews to work for a time. Essentially, they could not entice their women into the work force, so they *had* to use the Jews. Perhaps, then, the stubborn German housewife made a major contribution to the incompleteness of the Final Solution. It was not until 1943 that the Nazis moved ahead with labor registration and conscription of women. It should be noted that Nazi hesitation in this matter had nothing to do with concern over the harmful effects of work conditions on women. It stemmed singularly from concern over the bad effect vigorous women's labor measures would have on the morale of Germany's fighting men. Perhaps antifeminism lost the war for Hitler. It is certain that the anti-Jew and antiwoman core of Nazi fervor contributed mightily to the negative direction of the war.

Who were the women in the public eye? Some in the limelight were Leni Riefenstahl, the glamorous film producer and star; Hannah Reitsch, an airplane pilot and the first woman to win the Iron Cross; Gertrude Scholz-Klink, the leader of the Women's Nazi League; and Emmie Göring and Magda Goebbels. But in a nation that devoted itself to the cult of the Führer, in a nation where millions of women had helped vote Hitler into power, it is not surprising that the only real opportunities for women's leadership abilities were in the concentration camps. Perhaps one of the basic sicknesses of Nazi Germany was that the Aryan woman was degraded to the point where she could use none of her natural talent without being considered anti-Nazi— except in the concentration camps. It was Himmler himself who gave to German women their *one genuine leadership vehicle—the profession of SS concentration camp guard and concentration camp matron.* And in so doing, he perverted the concept of leadership and responsibility to the state. It should be no surprise that the end result was a scene pictured by a *Times* reporter. He described how female SS guards had tied a dead body to a living one and burned them together while dancing around the pyre, singing, with their hands joined.[10]

Non-Aryan Women and Children

The "positive" Nazi theories and programs related only to Aryan women. For non-Aryans, the Nazis developed a program aimed at destroying foreign nations and ethnic groups by eliminating and suppressing national characteristics. They implemented their program of genocide by kidnapping children, by forcing women to have abortions, by taking away the infants of Eastern workers, by severe punishment for sexual intercourse with Germans, by preventing marriages, by hampering reproduction of enemy nationals, by evacuating enemy populations from their native lands, by forcing Germanization of enemy nationals and slave labor, and by the extermination of the Jews.

When the Nazis took over Poland (considered by them to be the most inferior of nations), Himmler wrote a document entitled "Reflections on the Treatment of Peoples of Alien Races in the East." It prohibited the union of various ethnic groups located in the Government General of Poland and demanded the dissolution of the conglomeration of people living there— about 15 million. The SS were to select from that conglomeration the racially valuable and bring them to Germany for assimilation. Himmler said: "I hope that the concept of Jews will be completely extinguished." He then ordered that racially valuable children be kidnapped and the remainder annihilated or raised in ignorance and slavery. The policy in Poland, instead of *Lebensborn,* was to be *Todesborn.* Eastern Europe, particularly Poland, became a fountain of death.[11]

What did the Nazi regime in an occupied country do when faced with a population that more nearly met its critical criteria than that of Germany itself? In Scandinavia and in northern Europe generally, they pursued an unusual policy. They ordered their occupation soldiers to *consolidate their victory in the cradle!* The campaign results "exceeded the expectations of even the most optimistic race experts."[12]

Lebensborn followed the occupation armies to establish maternity homes to recover the precious German blood so desperately needed. In Norway the Nazis found the best environment for the deliberate encouragement of births between native girls and German soldiers. They embarked on an intensive propaganda campaign, set up hospitals, and introduced special legislation essential to their population policy. They abolished parental authority over female minors. Hundreds of pregnant Norwegian girls took refuge or were confined in homes in Germany, and most lost their babies immediately after giving birth to them. Some German wives were so patriotic that they warmly accepted a little souvenir from the Norwegian campaign in the form of a child. The Nazis tore the children from their Norwegian mothers with or without their consent, supported by a new law that prevented Norwegians from interfering in any matter involving a German subject! If the mother would not go to Germany or refused to give her child to the German Reich, the child was taken from her on the strength of a certificate making it a German subject. Himmler saw the pregnant Norwegian women's program as a "unique opportunity" to transplant a large group of pure Aryan women to Germany. Nowhere else in Europe did the machinery for manufacturing Nordic children work as successfully as it did in Norway.[13]

After Germany began to suffer military defeats, the need for military manpower forced striking changes in the principles governing admission to the SS. By 1944 the *Waffen* SS was made up of 80,000 young men of whom half were foreigners. Certainly most were not "racially valuable." The requirements of race experts in the matter of child selection also changed. Quantity, not quality, became of prime importance. It was no longer primarily a matter of selecting a racially qualified man and woman and encouraging them to mate; now the Nazis concentrated on an already existing product—a living child. If the child was young enough and looked and seemed racially pure, it would be brought up in Germany as a Aryan.

Thus began the extensive Nazi program of kidnapping foreign children with good racial physical characteristics and sending them to Germany to special *Lebensborn* institutions. Himmler decreed that the children be subjected to a racial and psychological selection procedure and that those found to be biologically valuable be Germanized. In 1943 he insisted that no SS man could be concerned about the fate of a Pole or a Czech.

We take those among these people who are of good blood, we steal them just as we steal their children, and we shall see to their education. The conditions in which these people live, or whether things go well or badly with them, are a matter of complete indifference to us. They interest me only to the extent that we need them as slaves for our culture. Otherwise, they do not interest me at all.[14]

He set up agencies to select, deport, evacuate, kidnap, and exterminate children, and to deport, sterilize, abort, castrate, and exterminate adults.

Who selected the children and then kidnapped them? Himmler ordered every member of the SS and the Gestapo, medical advisers, and all those employed in the major Nazi agencies to work for the cause. Those who conducted the hunt found their future little Germans in playgrounds and orphanages, among adopted and illegitimate children, children with Polish guardians, children of mixed marriages and divorced parents, children of deported or banished parents, children picked up at random, children born in camps, abandoned children, and children sent to Germany for forced labor. They were literally kidnapped off the streets.

It is estimated that the Germans kidnapped 200,000 Polish children. The boys with whom the Nazi indoctrination methods succeeded were to become SS mercenaries. The girls were intended for use on human stud farms. Young girls between the ages of eight and twelve were placed in medical centers and given hormone injections to accelerate puberty. What the *Lebensborn* organization dared not do to German women and children was done with no hesitation to racially valuable foreign girls. They were kept alive, advanced to puberty quickly, and then selected as breeding women or liquidated. Carefully selected men would mate with the chosen women, who would then have three or four confinements in an SS maternity home. When they had produced the prerequisite number of children, they would be given an injection and simply cease to exist. Thus were all traces of impure blood used in "the Nordic repopulation of Germany" obliterated.[15]

A child who survived kidnapping and the war described one of those selection camps for children. Inmates classified as valuable were assigned separate huts and treated fairly well. The rest were given a daily meal of a half liter of soup:

We swelled everywhere because of under-nourishment, which also affected the nerves, on top of which there was the cold, the blows, and the exhausting labor. Many went out of their mind. Children who wetted their beds were sent to Block 8, which had no doors or windows. The children were given blankets that were as thin as spiders' webs, and the temperature fell to minus twenty degrees in winter. During the night they froze. Next morning we had to use picks to cut the stiff bodies away from the plank beds, load them on to carts and take them to the Jewish cemetery adjoining the camp. We flung them into a mass grave, threw lime over them and covered them with earth. Sometimes they were not quite dead. When they began to suffocate through lack of air, the earth over the grave moved like a cornfield in the wind. As soon as they were suffocated the movement stopped and the earth was still again. On an average day, 120 of the 3,000 or 4,000 children died every day.[16]

In spite of the approaching end of the war and the advancing Allied armies, the Germans continued to gather children, stuff them into boxcars without food or blankets, and tried to ship them to Germany. The train would often be placed on a side track. The cars of Polish children were referred to as death trains, filled, as they were, with babies who died en route. Many little girls brought to Germany and selected out as slaves were sterilized at the age of four, five, six, or seven; the young boys were castrated. Only about 20,000 Polish children were returned to their country after the war. The Germans refer to them as "orphans of hate."[17]

Foreign women or Eastern workers who became pregnant resumed work quickly after delivery. The SS sent the babies to segregated foreign children's nursing homes. From a famous war crimes trial, the Velpe Baby Home Case, we know that conditions in those foreign baby homes were no better than in a barnyard, and perhaps worse. If a foreign worker became pregnant by a German man and the child proved to be racially pure, the child was then sent to a *Lebensborn* institution. One doctor who visited a home for racially valuable babies wrote that the babies were undernourished and asked that corrective action be taken:

There exists only one way or the other. Either one does not wish that these children remain alive—then one should not let them starve to death slowly and take away so many liters of milk from the general food supply; there are means by which this can be accomplished without torture and pain. Or one intends to raise these children in order to utilize them later on as labor. In this case they must be fed in such a manner that they will be fully usable as workers.[18]

The third policy adopted to assure the success of the Nazi racial and sexual program was the program of abortions performed on Eastern workers. Himmler decreed that where pregnancy had been caused by sexual intercourse between a member of the SS and a non-German woman, the SS must investigate, and unless the woman was of good stock, an abortion would occur. If, however, a German was not the father, then any office could order the abortion immediately—in fact, *must* order that abortion. The Nazis' systematic abortion programs were designed to keep the Eastern workers available as slave labor and to hamper and reduce their reproduction. Himmler said abortions should be carried out on a voluntary basis, but the women must be forced to volunteer! As a further step, he prohibited sexual intercourse between Germans and foreigners. A foreigner who had sexual intercourse with a German woman would be arrested. If he was a racial inferior, he would be sent to a concentration camp for "special treatment." If he was of racially valuable stock, he would be subject to Germanization. Himmler spelled out what he meant by "special treatment": "Special treatment is hanging."[19]

What happened to the leaders of *Lebensborn* after the war? The major leaders are still alive and free today! In a trial held in 1947 the court concluded that the *Lebensborn* society was a welfare organization and system of maternity homes. It also ruled that *Lebensborn* had nothing to do with the kidnapping or harming of children. Therefore it declared all defendants "not guilty."

Non-Aryan Women as Forced Laborers

The Nazi motto might well have been: Aryan women out of the factories, non-Aryan women into the factories. The good German woman's place was in her home, and the bad non-Aryan woman's place was on a labor detail or in a factory where she shared heavy labor with men. Since the work of non-Aryan women and children was critical to the Reich's labor program, the Nazis did not hesitate to use women in the most exacting labor and even in the deadly construction *Kommandos*. Pohl, head of the WVHA, sent the following telegram to Himmler in 1944:

The first transportation of Jews from Hungary shows that about 50 percent of the Jews who are fit to work are women. Since there is not sufficient adequate purely female work available for this large number of women, we must put them to work for OT construction projects. Your approval is requested.

And Himmler replied: "Of course Jewish women are to be used for labor. In this case one has merely to provide a healthy diet. Here a diet of raw vegetables is important. Be sure to import garlic from Hungary in sufficient quantity." He was, however, not entirely devoid of benevolence. When he ordered in 1943 that the infliction of punishment on Russian women must be done by Polish women, and on Polish and Ukrainian women by Russian women, he declared that "as a reward, the prisoners inflicting the punishment were to be given a few cigarettes." As further evidence of his tender regard for women, his order of January 1943 read: "Women sentenced to death shall have no previous indication of the proposed execution of the death penalty."[20]

No work was considered too difficult for women. Himmler wrote to Göring explaining that he had employed female prisoners in the aviation industry. As an example, he pointed to the mechanical workshops in Neubrandenburg where 2,500 women manufactured devices for dropping bombs and rudder controls. In one month alone they produced 3,000 devices as well as 500 rudder controls and altitude regulators. Himmler proclaimed: "We are increasing employment to 4,000 women. The performance of the women is excellent."[21]

Micheline Maurel, who spent time in Neubrandenburg, described the camp as a no-man's land. Most prisoners worked at the airplane factory. The days seemed endless as the women toiled in the windowless building. Maurel soldered small springs for bomb releases. The work inspired "hopeless weariness coupled with helpless fury." Although giving the impression of being busy, she and her colleagues tried to do their work slowly and incompetently. They spent several weeks camouflaging antiaircraft shelters around Neubrandenburg. Later the authorities sent them to lumberyards outside the camp to gather building material for barracks, and to railroad yards to unload bricks from freight cars. Many times they carried stones twenty hours a day on a daily bread ration of four and a half ounces. Their legs gave out from under them, and when they collapsed, they were beaten. Their minds blurred and their bodies disintegrated.[22]

Auschwitz and Birkenau had a huge complex of outlying factories and factory *Kommandos*. The Birkenau complex also organized difficult construction and external labor *Kommandos* utilizing the 20,000 women in their camp. Many women survivors who remember the hard labor in the camps are speaking of the incredible demands made upon them in the outside Auschwitz *Kommandos*. The SS erected critical war factories in the Auschwitz area devoted to the production of armaments. The camp complex was responsible for supplying the manpower and the womanpower for the huge plants around the camp. Most of the prisoners detailed to those factories felt themselves more fortunate than those waiting their turn to be gassed and cremated in Birkenau. Although the work was dangerous and explosions and accidents were common, at least they were in dry, lighted, heated rooms with access to some food and medical supplies.

Birkenau women were also placed in distant *Kommandos*, which meant they had as much as a 48 kilometer round-trip walk each day. Judith Newman worked in the *Kommando* that demolished houses, dug ditches, drove heavy trucks, and reclaimed swamps. Accompanied by music, the SS marched them to and from work. They allowed no rest during the working hours, and when the women returned to camp, they were covered with sores from blows and bites from the guard dogs. Once a friend of Judith's fainted. An SS man walked over and asked her if she was tired. When she did not respond, he picked up rocks and threw them at her face and body. Later that afternoon, when the group prepared to return to camp, he removed the stones and asked her if she was feeling better. The woman was still breathing. The SS guard climbed on her and placed his entire weight on her chest, stomping on her several times. Her friends heard her ribs cracking. Then he said: "Now you won't feel sick any more. You'll even be carried back to the camp."[23]

In the rain and the snow the women dug sewers, built barracks, carried rails, and laid railroad tracks. Carrying rails, one inmate wrote, was hard work! You take the old ones from the woods and you loosen the screws that hold them together. Then one woman stands between the tracks about every second or third tie and seizes a rail in each hand. The order for "up" is given: "If someone's spine cracks, what of it? There are thousands, tens of thousands of others to take her place and many more spines to be broken."[24]

Birkenau women were often given ditch-digging jobs, which they preferred. Although the shovels were heavy and the women worked for hours in the mud and marshes that covered the area around Birkenau, the effort produced a visible effect. They suffered because they "just could not avoid that all-pervasive wetness." In winter their work included demolishing houses in nearby villages. They leveled walls with their picks. "Our hands lost all strength, our kidneys seemed to be bursting, our stomachs made us ill." Pelagia Lewinska's friends modified the words *"Arbeit Macht Frei"* over Auschwitz's entrance to express the real condition of their lives: *"Arbeit macht frei, Krematorium ein, zwei, drei,* (Work makes you free, Crematory, one, two, three)."[25]

That women provided a major labor force for the entire German war effort—performing every imaginable kind of work—is evident from the list of *Kommandos* for camps spread all over occupied Europe. Buchenwald had twenty-seven women *Kommandos* and seven for men and women; they worked in war factories throughout Germany. Dortmund was a *Kommando* of Buchenwald with 600 women; Allendork was a *Kommando* with 1,000 Hungarian Jewish women working in the chemical factory. The work at Lichtenau was so dangerous that 150 women were killed by explosives. One Hungarian Jewish woman remembered well her stay there. Transferred from Auschwitz, she felt a pleasant surprise at the well-kept compound, the barracks with at least one bunk for each woman, complete with mattress, blanket, and pillow, and even rusty eating utensils. The Germans kept the women in the compound for two weeks, feeding them carrot soup, rice, potatoes, and bread because they arrived from Birkenau too weak to work. After the officials had fattened them up, they escorted the women to a train that took them every day to the munitions plant. Irén Darvas remembered that only 800 actually worked in the sulphur factory. They sat at large tables and wrapped little sulphur discs in paper. In another room other women weighed the discs. The work that at first seemed easy to Irén later injured her health severely. The sulphur dust turned the women yellow and made them ill.[26]

Of the 95,500 prisoners of Neuengamme, 13,500 were women, and they were farmed out to *Kommandos.* Dachau in November 1944 held 5,044 women out of 65,000 prisoners. But the SS leased most of those women to the sixteen Dachau female *Kommandos,* which were engaged primarily in heavy work on engineering projects. Flossenbürg in April 1945 had 14,600 women and 31,170 men on its roster. Again, few women lived in the camp. Most served in the twenty-seven female *Kommandos,* working in the chemical, motor vehicle, optical, mechanical, wool, radio, weaving, and fuel industries.

The female *Kommando* system of Gross-Rosen, located in southern Poland, was very extensive. At Kratzau a *Kommando* of 2,800 women worked in ammunitions; in Hohenelbe 400 women made airplane parts; in Gabersdorf 380 women worked in the cotton mill and dug trenches; at Bernsdorf 400 women labored in a spinning mill, as did the 2,000 women at Parschnitz. Halberstadt's cotton mill was serviced by a 2,000-woman Gross-Rosen *Kommando.* At Maehrisch-Weisswassir a Gross-Rosen *Kommando* of 900 women made ammunition, while 1,500 women at Gellenau built airplanes; 400 women at Mittelsteine produced airplane parts; 1,000 women at Ludwigsdorf made ammunition; 1,000 women at Langenbielau produced the material for army uniforms; and 500 Jewesses at Graeben served the flax mill.

Natzweiler-Struthof had many women listed on the rolls but they were out on *Kommandos,* such as the one at Geisenheim where Krupp employed 200 Polish and Hungarian Jewesses. Majdanek's 6,000 women worked in the Lublin war factories. In Latvia, at Riga's infamous Kaiserwald, one half of the roster were women working for the *Wehrmacht* and the *Luftwaffe.*

Then there were the hundreds of foreign labor camps with their "volunteer workers," like the one at Breslau where 1,500 women built roads and military fortifications, or at Lojewo where 600 women repaired the region's roads. Thousands and thousands of women from all over Europe worked and died in those labor camps.[27]

Clearly the SS and Nazi military and industrial machines were literally built on the backs of non-Aryan women. With Gretchen back in the home, someone was needed in the factories. And the Nazi leadership was loath to touch its recently created baby-producing regiments. Torn between a desperate need for industrial growth and an equally desperate need to replenish the population, the Germans met a common problem with an uncommon solution. Leaders of other nations certainly had encountered similar problems, but none possessed that incredible combination of madness and rationality that enabled them to take that next logical step. Hitler and Himmler, however, were free to design their unusual women's programs.

Women in the Concentration Camps

The Nazis and their cohorts incarcerated women throughout the Third Reich and the occupied countries. Women could be found in provincial prisons and urban jails, in Ravensbrück and the women's camp at Birkenau and Majdanek, in special confines and small groups within a few camps, in the *Kommandos,* the labor details, and the factories. Hitler treated bad women and bad men alike. The Aryan woman left the factory for her rightful place in the home and was dedicated to her rightful task, that of bearing children. The non-Aryan woman left her home for the labor squads and the factories if she was fortunate, for the gas chambers if she was unfortunate. Childbearing was forbidden. Her children who were born were destroyed; those growing in her were aborted. In many instances her pregnancy was considered such an audacity that the SS killed two birds with one stone by throwing the pregnant woman into the gas chamber.

Aryan children, as the most highly valued portion of the population, grew up in the Third Reich with all the care and attention that dedicated institutions and a committed state could give them. Non-Aryan children suffered and died or worked and died or worked and suffered and died. The master race saw as its mission the development of a world of pure blood under its control. To that end, peoples of impure blood must be destroyed. It was not a matter of morality; it was simply a matter of saving a nation, and later all of Europe, from a threat the Nazis pictured as Armageddon—the undermining of the entire Western world by bad blood. Impure children received no consideration because they would grow up and pollute the nation. Thus the medical scientists and doctors found no ethical problem in the sterilization and castration of children if they were of impure blood. Hitler preached a perverted gospel: "Suffer the little children to come unto me for theirs is the kingdom of death." If the SS treated children in the camps as things, as objects of grotesque acts of indecency, it all made sense in the Nazi scheme of things. German infanticide surpassed in brutality, callousness, and cruelty all other Nazi crimes.

Did the women suffer more than men; did they face worse conditions? The issue is complex and difficult to approach when evaluating the truly ghastly conditions for *all* human beings. Environmentally, probably women had it no worse than men. In terms of labor, women were given every kind of disgusting and demanding job. Women may have suffered more from the work level, but only because of poor physical preparation. But since the *core* of Nazi racial and population policy dealt with the woman, and since *anatomy was indeed destiny to the Nazis,* yes, women had it worse. It is fair to conclude that a pregnant woman in a camp suffers more than a man.

While the Nazi program for totally eliminating sexual activity between non-Aryans meant the castration of men, for some weird reason it meant far more severe and curious experimentation with the sexual lives and organs of women. In terms of sexual medical experiments, yes, the women had it worse. Not only were they sterilized, but all their organs were tampered with, hacked, cut up, removed, transplanted, radiated. Not only did they have to face external burns and a loss of their own pride, but the sexual operations performed on them were extremely serious and often resulted in death. In addition, German doctors seemed to be far more intensely excited by performing any kind of surgery on women than on men. Certainly, the Nazis designed some quite perverse experiments and tests for men. But in terms of maiming operations—cutting up, cutting into—it is quite clear that their subjects were far more often women than men. Because the Nazis believed that all non-Aryans were inferior, they thought they had the right to do anything they wished with those men, women, and children. But since they believed women were inferior to men, they were even less restrained in effecting the physical destruction of a woman's body prior to its death. Yes, in those respects women suffered more than men.

Because women had problems such as menstruation and pregnancy and perhaps a greater aversion to dirt, sickness, and horror, yes, perhaps they suffered more than men. Most women had not seen as ghastly sights as men. They had been protected. Now they were thrown into the same horror as the men and that made it, one suspects, a bit more difficult. But there is no evidence that they met their situation with less fortitude.

Some writers have suggested that women suffered more than men, and others have insisted that women endured that horror better than men. Perhaps both views contain some truth. But what this chapter is discussing are factual matters that have nothing to do with a woman's makeup. It is difficult to make those types of judgments because definitive books have not been written. Some eight years ago, however, I began to go through all the memoirs, notes, interviews of mine, and reactions in the first person of camp victims to assess some questions of survival and how it was accomplished. My research suggests that certain concerns were expressed by the women more often, more clearly, and more constantly than by men. The following is not an attempt to describe certain values or to judge concerns as more or less worthy than others. It is simply intended to show some constant concerns expressed by women who wrote about the camps—both those who survived them and those who left notes before they died.

Did a greater number of women survive than men? We have no reliable statistics or breakdowns that can be used to be specific about sexual differences in extermination. Did behavioral differences exist between the SS women leaders and the SS male leaders? From all descriptions, it does not seem that the women guards and SS leaders differed in any way from the men. The assumption that SS men were more sadistic does not fit the facts. Some have suggested that the SS women, once let loose, would be more sadistic. The suggestion also does not bear up under observation. Men and women SS leaders and guards were generally rather vicious, cruel, and unfeeling human beings, at least with regard to the slaves in their control.

From the memoirs, diaries, responses, remembrances, and ideas of women in the camps, the largest pool of available material concerns Auschwitz-Birkenau. But the descriptions of Birkenau are accurate representations of all the camps.

Birkenau, the extermination division of Auschwitz, was the largest camp in existence during the Nazi period, and probably the worst major camp in the Third Reich. In its first days, Birkenau was a marshy, muddy plain surrounded by electric wires, without roads, water, or sewage disposal. Garbage and excrement lay around. Seweryna Szmaglewska in her memoir, *Smoke over Birkenau,* writes that "no bird ever flies low over Birkenau though, God knows, the prisoners strain their eyes to search the skies for them during the roll calls, which last for hours. Guided by smell or instinct, the birds avoid the place." The planners did not intend that Birkenau should hold people for any length of time. It was designed as the major extermination center of the Third Reich—a kind of crematorium waiting room for 20,000 to 30,000 people.[28]

The accommodations for women were terrible. The brick barracks had four rows of stalls like small cells. Two rows adjoined in the center and the other two lined the outside walls. Each brick building housed at least fifty stalls, and the meager light came from four small windows. The horse stalls in the brick building had been remodeled for human use in a very simple way: the workers erected two wooden platforms in each stall, one about a meter from the ground, the other a meter above the first. They built the platform by nailing together two doors brought from nearby houses. That arrangement supposedly provided more than 150 sleeping bunks in each barrack, three in each stall—one on the ground and the other two on wooden platforms. On each bunk lay two straw sacks stuffed with shavings or reeds. Six to ten women occupied each bunk. Thus, eighteen to thirty women slept in a place designed for one horse. In times of great crowding a barrack held 1,200 people. One visitor from an SS commission remarked: "You can keep rabbits like this but not women."

The interior of the barracks reminded Seweryna Szmaglewska of a huge chicken coop. The worst places were the wet and cold bottom bunks. They were too low for sitting, and at night rats attacked the sleepers. Even though open to rain, the upper bunks were more desirable. But up there one could not even kneel. No artificial light illuminated the brick blocks and women returning from work at night crawled into the cubby holes in darkness:

Dark cagelike lairs—dim, flickering light from the sparsely placed candles—nude, emaciated women, blue with cold, their shaved heads huddled into scrawny shoulders, arched over a heap of filthy rags, feverishly catching the vermin and cautiously killing them on the edge of the koyts.[29]

The wooden barracks—former stables—were no better. The sign on the door read: "Mangy animals are to be separated immediately." A large brick stove divided the room into two parts. On either side of the stove stood three tiers of bunks or cages. In each cage, which measured 3½ by 1½ meters, seventeen to twenty women huddled together. When Olga Lengyel first arrived, the cages had nothing but bare boards on them. Later the SS issued the inmates filthy blankets. Lengyel, the wife of a Polish doctor and a Jew, spent her Birkenau years working as a medical aid. In her report, *Five Chimneys,* she pointed out that not all occupants could sleep at the same time because of lack of space. Some spent the entire night squatting in awkward positions. The slightest movement was a truly complicated matter. The barrack roofs let in the rain, and sometimes the internees on the top bunks literally drowned. But those on the wet mud floor were in no better condition, suffocating from lack of air. In both the brick and the wooden barracks, the filth was indescribable; but it was the women's job to keep them clean. How "ridiculous" to expect cleanliness from 1,500 women housed in old stables when they had no brooms, mops, pails, or dust rags.[30]

Life in the barracks proved a constant nightmare. Pelagia Lewinska described the dark gloom. Here and there one could see blue candles burning, and the noise and the movement reminded her of the stirrings of an awakening hive. The shed seemed like an enormous barn. In that tiny loft sleeping area women kept all their personal belongings—shoes, a bag, a comb, and a bowl.

People cannot imagine the feelings that were generated among the many residents of the same block under such conditions, despite all their efforts to remember that their fellows were three-dimensional human beings and not mere sticks of wood. How to move about, to dress oneself, to undress, to eat, sleep and go about all the essential tasks of living in this tangled mass of human beings who were swallowed in utter darkness?

After a day of labor Lewinska considered the return home a "new martyrdom."[31]

Judith Newman felt the necessity to take off her dirty shoes full of mud and dirt and put them under her head at night to prevent theft. Several shared one blanket and women slept in their clothes for it was too cold to change. Also, they had no other garments. There were no stoves until 1943. Once installed, the stoves often broke down and the women depended on animal warmth or what they called "the warm blood heating system." Seweryna Szmaglewska described the women's section as a turbulent, milling city of mud "whose numberless barracks stand and wait, like boats anchored in the port of death, for their thousands of passengers."[32]

As Birkenau was the largest extermination center, it contained a mammoth crematorium plant. *The women lived aware of that crematorium.* In the beginning the SS shot those condemned to death in the forest. After 1941, however, they put four ovens into service. When the ovens were overpacked, the Germans burned 8,000 cadavers a day in the death pits. Birkenau at its peak could handle 24,000 corpses each day.[33]

Olga Lengyel tramped past the crematorium on the way to work. "Great flames belched from the chimney, and the strange, sickening, sweetish odor which had greeted us upon our arrival, attacked us even more powerfully now." The first time Lengyel saw it, she asked an old inmate what the structure was. She was told it was the camp bakery. She learned soon that the bakery was the crematorium.[34]

By 1944 Birkenau had fourteen crematoria and deep pits, where the SS burned alive small children. "There wasn't always enough gas in the chambers," writes Lewinska, "so they economized on the children." She recalls vividly the months toward the end when endless flames leapt from the chimneys. A thick cloud lay over Auschwitz and its surrounding territory, enveloping everything in an "ashen grey shroud." Loose soot covered the inmates' bodies and clothing even when they worked in fields far from the camp. For many women, the smell of burning bodies was something they would never forget. Always the poisoned air blew over them, reminding them of filthy latrines, of the fetid hospital area, or of the crematoria. From her hut, Ella Lingens-Reiner could look across the many roofs and see the slender crematoria chimneys sharply outlined against the sky. When transports came, "a bright, sharp flame shot up, six feet high. Soon the stench of burnt fat and hair grew unbearable."[35]

Then there was the *Birkenau mud,* and no writer has failed to comment on it. Rain transformed the camp into an ocean of mud, paralyzing traffic. Mud and the crematorium became the inmates' greatest obsessions. To subject a woman to fatal suffering, the guards did not need to kill her. They only had to give her a kick that sent her falling into the mud. The SS kicked into the mud any woman lagging behind. A weak woman remained immersed in the mud and perished because getting up and cleaning herself off was an impossible task. There was no time to wash, no place to wash. Pelagia Lewinska and a friend exchanged oaths never to leave each other dying in the mud:

It seems unbelievable that tendering a helping hand to a fellow human being who falls could be the ultimate proof of devotion, and yet that was so. To help someone rise from the mud meant to risk staying with her in the mud.[36]

Almost all memoirs describe the women's reactions upon their *first arrival at a camp.* Judith Newman found it hard to believe that she was still in

Europe. She fantasized that she had been carried away to some primitive island and forced to live like a savage. Many times she woke up, thinking she was having a nightmare:

As a child I often secretly, without permission, used to read murder mysteries and adventure stories about the Indians of the Wild West, but they were tame in comparison. Never had I read about anything so horrible as what I was seeing with my own eyes and living through myself.

"We were struck," recalled a survivor, "with the impression of having entered an insane asylum. . . . It all seemed like some colony for the demented."[37]

The women recalled vividly the *physical examinations.* Lengyel calls the complete examination—oral, rectal, and vaginal—a horrible experience. "We had to lie across a table, stark naked while they probed. All that in the presence of drunken soldiers who sat around the table, chuckling obscenely." The SS rushed the women into a room where men and women barbers armed with clippers and scissors waited to dehair them. Following the dehairing and delousing, the women received their new clothing. Lengyel comments:

I cannot think of any name that would fit the bizarre rags that were handed out for underwear. . . . It was not white or any other color, but wornout pieces of coarse dusting-cloth. And still we could not be choosy. Only a few of the select were awarded underwear.

The SS did not care whether the dresses fit. Large women wore dresses that were too short and tight; and "slender women were given huge dresses, some with flowing trains." In many camps the Germans painted an X or an arrow on the back of the dress to complete the style. Lengyel drew a rather "ordinary assortment." Her attire consisted of an elegant tulle dress, now tattered and transparent without a slip. She also received a pair of men's striped drawers. The dress exposed her in the front to her navel and in the back to her hips. In spite of her situation, she could not help but laugh when she saw how ridiculous the bald and absurdly dressed women looked.[38]

No one was laughing a year later at the unrecognizable women they had become and at the gnawing hunger tormenting them. By 1944 Micheline Maurel's hunger had destroyed her flesh, leaving her with old hanging skin:

The skin at the waist level was so drawn and shrunken it seemed to be sticking to the spinal column. None of the muscles that go to form the buttocks, the thighs or the calves were left. We had no breasts. Nothing but brownish, ulcerated skin.[39]

Szmaglewska never forgot a scene of women standing naked before their delousing session. A nude body, she thought, could be beautiful against the background of nature, bathed in sun and the forest. It could also be beautiful in the cozy interior of the home. "But I cannot imagine anything uglier than that big naked mob standing five abreast, . . . a strange, shapeless mass of nakedness covered with gooseflesh and blue from the cold."[40]

All women remembered the *administration of the camps and the class structure,* which encouraged the development of a "small sovereign state." The *Kapos,* the ward mistresses, the camp policemen, and officials chosen from among the inmates (usually they were of the criminal class) stood at the top of the hierarchy. Their rank entitled them to better food, rooms of their own, and other life-saving privileges. At the bottom lay the Jews and the laborers. The higher-ranking women treated the lower ones with arrogance and contempt. "We often had the impression of drowning in moral excrement." The immorality of relations among some prisoners gave women deep pain. "This, the most terrible thing of all, was what constituted our veritable martyrdom." Before arriving at Birkenau, Dr. Lingens-Reiner had assumed that an absolute equality in misery would exist there. But class differences unfortunately played a major role. It was usually helpful to belong to a higher social stratum. It could, in fact, save one's life. Working in the fields was the worst possible situation; but to be a doctor or speak several languages certainly put one at an advantage. Quite simply, one might stay alive a little longer.[41]

The treatment of the women in Birkenau was probably a bit better than that meted out to the men in one respect: their punishment treatment was not as sadistic. Only infrequently were non-Jewish women executed. If they attempted to escape, they were usually flogged, but heavy corporal punishment was not a constant. Jewish women, of course, were treated horribly and their struggle was a fight for survival. Dr. Lingens-Reiner, a Gentile, insists that "the survival of a Jewess in Birkenau was twice as improbable as the survival of a non-Jewish prisoner—improbable as that was too." More important to the women than the ill-treatment, though, were *camp conditions.* Their accommodations and hygiene were of a far lower level than the men's.[42]

In their memoirs women focus on *water and washrooms.* In Birkenau only two barracks were turned into washrooms. Across each building ran two metal pipes carrying water to taps placed about 100 centimeters apart. Beneath the pipes a trough caught the water. But usually there was no water. The SS turned it on once or twice a day, for about an hour or two. And it was in that washroom, that place, that trough, where the women washed and rinsed their mouths, clothes, and hair. It was impossible to accomplish cleanliness. Every day a dense crowd swarmed outside the building. "This herd of dirty, evil-smelling women inspired a profound disgust in their companions and even in themselves." Sometimes a woman was able to clean up in the washroom after a fashion; but then she would find that her clothing had been stolen while she washed. Women saw little point in making the cleaning effort without soap, toothbrushes, and combs.[43]

The water ration was so small that the women, tortured by thirst, never missed a chance to exchange their meager rations of bread for half a pint of water. Better to endure their hunger than that hellfire gnawing at their gullets. The water flowing through the rusted pipes was evil smelling and hard to swallow. But the washroom water was better than the rain that stagnated in the puddles, "liquid" that some internees lapped up. "What prices we paid for half a pint of water!" On her first Sunday, Lewinska saw women squatting outside cleaning their soup bowls with snow. Others washed their hands, faces, and bowls in a green and foul ditch because it was the camp's "all-purpose sewer."[44]

The latrines! Dr. Lingens-Reiner called the latrines one of the worst features of camp life and she never grew accustomed to them. The shed which served for the defecation of 6,000 to 7,000 women was 10 by 5 meters, with a cement gangway in the middle. A 1¾ meter deep trench drained into a sewer. At the other end of the trench two iron pipes came down to the height of the wall and from there a small jet of water fell into the ditch. Although their function was to flush excrement into the sewer, they were the only additional sources of available water. When women took water for tea or for washing from those pipes, the sewage system blocked up. In the finest movie yet produced on the Holocaust—the 1980 documentary, *Return to Auschwitz*, survivor Kitty Hart still shudders when she recalls the latrines and the terrible water problem.[45]

Jewish and Gentile writers describe different latrines because they were segregated and could not use each other's. For Lewinska, the latrines were appalling with their horrible filth. In the Jewish section the latrine was simply a large ditch bisected by a narrow board. Filth covered the two-sided perch, and the women often soiled each other. Lewinska believes that the Germans purposefully condemned the Jewish women to drown in their excrement. One day Olga Lengyel was assigned to the latrine-cleaning squad. In the morning each woman took her two buckets to the pits. They pulled up full pails of excrement and carried them a few hundred meters to another pit. They did that all day—day after day for two weeks. In the evenings they tried to clean themselves and went to bed. The odor reeking from Lengyel's co-worker sleeping beside her sickened her.[46]

The women never forgot the *rats and the mice*. Birkenau was a rat's paradise. They were everywhere—in the barracks, in the hospitals, running through the camp. It seemed at times to Lewinska that only crows, rats, and mice remained her companions. The hordes of mice hid in her bunk, shared her bread, brushed past her face, waking her during the night. Rats chewed on the human cadavers lying on the ground. When night fell, the huge rats scurried from their holes and attacked the women in the bottom bunks. In Block 25 the rats chewed the fingers off the corpses, gnawed at their faces, and even attacked dying bodies. They ran up to the patients in the hospital. Someone would call out, "A rat, a rat," and they raced away. There were so many of them that while hallucinating, some feverish patients saw them as a huge army of bacteria. All night long the scurrying, leaping, and squeaking disturbed the women's sleep. Dr. Lingens-Reiner saw women with toes gnawed by the rats while they were asleep and one whose nose had been bitten. In the hospital the rats crawled up to the third level of bunks where the very weakest patients lay, bit into the buttocks, and chewed off pieces of their noses and limbs. The night nurses tried to drive the rats away from the sick women. They took turns sitting up. But the hospital rats had grown fat eating on the corpses until they reached the size of big cats. They were not afraid of people. When driven away with sticks, they only hid their heads and drove their claws into the bunks, readying for the next attack.[47]

And then *the lice*. Every camp had them. In one labor camp the ritual of the louse hunt became such a normal occupation that it was carried on during the literary sessions that the women held in their bunks. Perched on the topmost bunk, Micheline Maurel recited poetry with her friends "while crushing lice with their nails, just as in other gatherings we might have knitted while we talked." The lice plagued the women so mercilessly that they resorted to desperate scratching for relief, an action that created ugly sores. As they did not have enough water to wash themselves, every woman contracted scabies. Vermin filled their unwashed garments. They invented special methods to kill the lice, but all their work was undone the moment new inmates arrived. The women were helpless in the face of such infestations. They had neither the time nor the means to free themselves of the parasites. Delousing did no good. The gas was too weak. It is hard to imagine how overwhelmed the women were by lice—not only by their bites, which carried typhus and death, but by the way, night and day, they irritated the skin and kept the body full of sores and pus. Thousands of inmates died from the lice.[48]

The women suffered *constant hunger.* The inedible soup smelled rotten and contained junk in it: buttons, tufts of hair, rags, keys, mice. The black bread was 60 percent sawdust. As a hospital nurse, Judith Newman watched the prisoners march into the gas chambers, some holding on to their last pieces of bread.

The survivors ate any remaining bread that was left behind, even if the sick had lain on it and it was covered with excrement. I confess that oftentimes I myself pulled a piece of bread from under a dead body, even though the corpse had laid on it all night. So great was our hunger that we were even capable of eating dirt.

Newman often nibbled at her own skin and her nails because her stomach was growling so badly; and she pictured people elsewhere living in freedom, sitting down to tables laden with wonderful meals. She would have given almost anything just to have had the stale leftovers from her fantasy table. Relating two indelible scenes, Gloria Goldreich writes of an inmate who choked to death on a piece of bread. Another inmate had rushed to the dead woman, reached her hand into her throat, "removed the masticated hunk of food, and eaten it hungrily." In another incident, a dying woman vomited: "Someone picked clots of undisgested puke that lay on the floor and swallowed them."[49]

How difficult it was to *sleep at night.* Huddled bodies crowded into 1½ square meters on hard boards fought for a sleep that would deaden all sensations. But the nights were short and true sleep was really out of the question. When the women lay down, the lice swarmed out of the crevices, so gorged with blood that their tight skins burst at the slightest touch. When the whistles blew, the barrack began to stir. Waking was the hardest moment, remembers Szmaglewska: "Each morning reminds you that you lack strength to begin a new day, a day identical with all the previous days."[50]

Almost every woman had *Durchfall*—a deadly kind of dysentery, aided by the ingestion of saltpeter, a product of the munitions factories. After two or three weeks in the camp "most prisoners had intestinal tracts so stripped of natural lining that terrible epidemics resulted," called *Durchfall* or "fall-through." What was eaten came out quickly in the original form, for the body could absorb nothing. The lack of washing water and the impossibility of changing clothes created a "monstrous trial for the sick woman." The disease combined many symptoms of typhus and dysentery, and proved deadly in many instances.[51]

No woman wanted to become so ill that she had to enter the *hospital.* But it was difficult to avoid it because every inmate was sick in one way or another. Everyone suffered from a swelling in which the body periodically puffed up and the face became like a mask. The eyes could hardly be seen and the thick legs became "heavy loads to drag along." Dr. Lingens-Reiner worked with cases in which the edema became so bad that the skin could not stand the tension and burst, leaving deep gashes from which liquid poured. Most women's bodies were covered with sores and abscesses. All women had lice. And most were starving. Every sickness and contagious disease attained epidemic proportions once it occurred in the camp: tuberculosis, malaria, typhus, scarlet fever, measles, diphtheria. Surgical cases included scores of women mauled by dogs and smashed by rifle butts. "One might have thought oneself in a human slaughter house."[52]

Unlike most camps, a *women's hospital* existed. Inmate doctors and nurses have described it: no electric lights, one makeshift brick stove for heat, four buckets for toilet facilities, a floor damp and slippery from excrement and urine. The sick women lay unwashed. The lack of water made it impossible for those sick with typhus and dysentery to quench their thirst. A hospital barrack designed for 200 to 250 sick people had 600 to 800 bed-ridden patients and sometimes more. The overcrowding prevented setting up isolation wards or dividing the patients according to their diseases. Maria Nowakowska, who worked in the hospital, provides a stark picture: "Sleepily sitting figures, of course only those who had the strength to sit, looking for vermin and killing them with their fingernails." Most women had traces of rat bites, and some were even eaten to the bone. Women made very primitive compresses from kerchiefs and their own urine. The scanty stores of medicine were used for all diseases and proved satisfactory for none. The nurses were afraid to identify the diseases for fear the SS would send serious cases to the gas chamber.[53]

The constant reinfection of starving patients with the various diseases raised the already heavy mortality rate. The sick had little opportunity for recovery. Because they were unable to work, they received smaller food rations. The food, according to one prison doctor, was "rotten potatoes, weeds and without exaggeration one may state that it contained about 20% rat's feces." Irene Schwarz remembers the first time she walked into the hospital to work: "The dense air filled with chlorine, and the groans of people begging for water in diverse languages, made a Dante's Inferno."[54]

Birkenau's hospital population never fell below 2,000 and during epidemics the number of patients rose to 7,000. Yet the SS allocated supplies for a maximum of 600 people, the number the hospital was supposed to accommodate in a camp designed for 20,000 women. If the inmate doctors complained, the SS told them that the average medication per patient was the same as for the civilian population! One major difficulty for Dr. Lingens-Reiner was the incredible dirt—so bad that she often did not dare touch a patient. In the diarrhea room the women lay on bare boards. *Durchfall* patients evacuated liquid fifteen to twenty times a day in their bunks, even when they received large doses of opium. After they soiled their beds the nurse wiped the mattress and the blankets with a damp cloth. New patients lay down on the filthy bunks. One patient happened to glance over at the next bunk and saw diarrhea dripping slowly from the upper bunk on the woman below. The sick woman calmly wiped off her face with her hand. Usually two or three women shared a bed. Often the top bunks broke under the weight and the patients fell on the women lying underneath. Many patients were naked, for there were no gowns.

After all this it is scarcely necessary to say that a patient who once entered the hut, perhaps with nothing worse than a septic throat, would not leave until she had passed through most of the diseases assembled within the four walls. But the stamina of some women was incredible.[55]

Szmaglewska described her first days in the clinic: "Here is an emaciated woman with legs so swollen that the skin over them is taut and shiny. The face is so puffed up that all features are lost. White, unhealthy flesh like a batch of raised dough effaces the features, hides the eyes." In another bunk huddles a woman whose bony knees and legs are covered with gray skin and "at each slight move a terrible odor emanates from her. The dirty clothes sticking to her body bear irrefutable evidence that this patient probably fainted over an open latrine pit and fell into it. . . . Here is a beautiful Russian girl racked by fits which make her limbs shudder convulsively. A dark face, eyes wild with fear, blackened lips, from which issues a whine, bay, giggle or sob? It may be malaria." In a corner a young girl suffers from dysentery with her face greenish white and every now and then down her legs "trickles a stream of black parched blood or of foul greenish excrement." Over in another corner "large beautiful eyes luminous with fever lighten a skeleton-thin face. The sharp features, fallen chin, prolonged nose, almost transparent skin, blue shadows under eyes tell too plainly of rampant t.b." Other women are scratching and tearing at their skin. Blood oozes through the filthy rags bandaging the hands, feet, and head of a woman who had been mauled by a dog. Just imagine, challenges Szmaglewska, a waterless hospital with two people to a bed lying on filthy blankets or boards.[56]

Micheline Maurel lay in the infirmary at the labor camp in Neubrandenburg with other fleshless creatures, two to three to a bunk. Many were awaiting death. "Walking skeletons in short gowns wandered between the bunks in search of pails. The noise was infernal." Patients loudly recited recipes or sang hymns. Still others prayed.

Scores of voices clamored plaintively for a basin that was unavailable. The charwomen stormed, screamed and slapped the sick. The chamber pot overflowed. Frequently there would be two or three skeletons struggling for the same pot. Above all this noise and dominating the tumult of the *danse macabre* resounded the measured, rhythmic, victorious recital of recipes for potted hare or scalloped potatoes *au gratin.*[57]

But what other impressions fastened into women survivors' minds? They remembered the noise, the crowding, the sickness, and the crematoria. But they also remembered their *red bowls*—for the meaning of life seemed to focus on possessing them. Without a bowl, a woman descended quickly to the animal level. It was her only worldly good. Eating depended upon the bowl. There was no place one could leave it without having it stolen. "Imagine having to carry a basin about with you wherever you went. You would find that holding a basin under your arm and carrying a spoon would be awkward at first." A woman looked around for a piece of string to tie the bowl to her waist. As time went on, she secured that piece of string, fixed a makeshift bag around her waist, and began to believe that she belonged. And just at the moment when she felt somewhat "normal" because the bag carried a comb, a piece of soap, and a bowl, the guards would run in and clean out the barracks to delouse the inmates. The woman would be stripped of everything and have to start over again.[58]

The women remembered the *constant uproar,* living in the midst of a stinking, teeming hole, the shrill voices, the crowd. "There was never any solitude, never any silence." Maurel believes that most women who had experienced solitary confinement in prison soon longed for it, because "living in a crowd prevented one from thinking, from dreaming and even from being one's self."[59]

All women recalled scenes that were especially ugly to them. Reska Weiss, a survivor of eight camps, spent most of her time in the Neumark women's labor camp. She never forgot the women called *Stutthofers.* The SS named them as a joke: the very sick, those about to be shot, were told that they would be "transported to Stutthof." No one was allowed into the tents of the *Stutthofers.* They were seldom given food. Stumbling accidentally into the *Stutthofer* tent one day, Weiss was overcome by what she saw. "I screamed in horror and shut my eyes to the sight. My knees trembled, my head began to swim, and I grasped the central tentprop for support. It was hard to believe the women on the ground were still human beings." Their eyes blazed from their starved skeletons. For two months they had lain naked on the ground. Their own urine and excrement covered their straw mats. Wounds, bites, and blood covered their frozen limbs, and lice had found a home in the short hair on their head.

No stretch of the imagination, no power of the written word, can convey the horror of that tent. And yet . . . they were *alive.* . . . They were hungry and they tore at their skeletal bodies with their emaciated hands covered in pus and dirt. They were beyond help.[60]

Olga Lengyel could never forget the agony of a woman forced to undress her daughter and then look on while the girl was violated by specially trained dogs. Others remembered the frightening *medical experiments.* A favorite experiment was conducted with newly arrived women who still were menstruating normally. During their periods they were told that they would be shot in two days. The Germans wanted to ascertain the effect of such news on menstrual flow.[61]

Perhaps the most awful scenes in the camp involved pregnant women, *childbearing women,* and the women who brought children with them to the camps. The procedure for Aryan women differed somewhat from that for non-Aryan women, but for both it was inhuman. Two days after Christmas Judith Newman remembered her joy over a Jewish child born in her block. Three hours after the birth she saw a small package lying on a bench. Suddenly it moved. It was the baby. A clerk took the infant and submerged its body in cold water. Newman wanted to shout "Murderess!"

> The baby swallowed and gurgled, its little voice chittering like a small bird, until its breath became shorter and shorter. The woman held its head in the water. After about eight minutes the breathing stopped. The woman picked it up, wrapped it up again, and put it among the other corpses.[62]

The clerk turned to Newman and told her the only way she could save the mother from the gas chamber was by killing the child. When the crematoria became overcrowded, the staff abandoned each baby to its fate, leaving the umbilical cord untied until the infant choked.

An inmate midwife in the Aryan hospital recalled that about 3,000 children were born with her help. Thirty isolated bunks near the stove constituted the so-called maternity ward. Rats, mice, and dirt filled the ward, and the newborn babies quickly became their victims. A woman preparing to give birth was forced to trade her bread rations for a sheet. She tore it into strips and prepared diapers and shirts for the baby. Without water, laundering the diapers was especially difficult. The mothers dried the diapers on their own backs or thighs, because if they hung them up, they might be seen and killed. As an SS principle, babies received no food rations, not even a drop of milk. The dried-out breasts of the starved women only irritated the babies and intensified their hunger.

The midwife reports that until 1943 all newborn babies in Birkenau were drowned in a small barrel. Two midwives sent to the camp for the crime of child murder performed the task. After each delivery loud gurgles and the splashing of water would be heard in the next room. Later the new mother would see her baby's body thrown outside and torn apart by rats.[63]

The guards tracked down Jewish children with "ruthless severity." Hiding a Jewish child was impossible, said the midwife. The two midwives under Nazi control watched Jewish mothers in childbirth, and once the child was born, they often drowned it in the barrel. The fate of the infants who survived was worse. "They died a slow hunger death. Their skin turned thin, like parchment, transparent, so that one could see the tendons, veins and bones." Of the 3,000 babies born in her section, only 30 survived. Several hundred were deported, 1,500 were drowned, and over 1,000 died as a result of cold and hunger. That number applies only to the period after 1943.[64]

When the transports came into Birkenau Judith Newman and her friends sorrowfully watched the children climb out, run about, and play in the sand while their parents undressed. When the children asked about the flames leaping out of the chimney tops, they were told that it was a factory where they would be working. "Nobody would have thought it possible that in civilized Europe this was possible—the murder of innocent children and women." When the gas chambers were full of adults, the children were not gassed. Instead the SS dug pits and threw many children into them alive. The guards grabbed a child's arms and legs, and hurled the baby through the air "like a length of wood, to land in the blazing pit, while the murderers watched the results of their bravery with great pleasure." They also laughed as they threw live children into the pond next to the crematorium. Witnesses testified at the Nuremberg trials that several thousand children were burned alive in Birkenau in 1944. When an SS man felt pity toward children, "he took the child and beat the head against a stone first before putting it on the pile of fire and wood, so that the child lost consciousness." But most SS killed in the regular manner by simply throwing the children on top of the piles.[65]

Dr. Janina Kosciuszkowa in her writings divides the children into four groups: the children burnt directly after their arrival, the children murdered in their mother's womb or murdered immediately after birth, the children born in the camp who were left alive, and the children brought into the camp as prisoners. Most Jewish pregnant women were sent to the gas chambers. Occasionally a mother would save her child, somehow, for four or five months. Then it would be found and she would have to hand it over to be killed. "I remember one case when the mother pressed her son to her breast and they went together to the crematorium." One transport brought 100 pregnant women who were taken into the hospital and immediately aborted. Some died.[66]

At Birkenau the women also fixed in their memories the *"cyclone," or the mass transports and extermination in 1945,* particularly of the Hungarian Jews. During the mass Hungarian extermination the SS began to clean out the women's camp, dragging the women out of barracks and hospitals and stuffing them into garbage carts headed for the gas chambers. Birkenau was in the process of full-scale liquidation at the same time that new trains continued to arrive from Hungary. The furnaces burned day and night at maximum capacity. The sky was blood red and ashes covered the camp—the "cyclone" had hit. The smoke filled the mouth and throat and permeated the food.

Sometimes in the dark the lava burst into active flames, the fire belches powerfully from the throat of the chimney, tearing through the blackness to the deep-blue sky and disappearing after awhile. Sometimes—especially in the evenings—the crematories vomit flames for long hours, often until morning.[67]

For days and weeks on end the road adjoining the rail crossing was filled with crowds of people walking tightly as if in a religious procession. By January 1945 the entire Auschwitz complex, Auschwitz I, II, and III, did not exceed 20,000 inhabitants.

Was there nothing good the women remembered? Did they find a positive way to describe *how to survive*? The women here too have interesting memories of the careful strategies they worked out to live. After the war survivors pondered their camp lives and pulled out special memories. Seweryna Szmaglewska remembered Christmas, the one day in the history of the camp that did not start and end with a roll call but culminated instead with the first appearance of the women's orchestra directed by Alma Rosé, a brilliant woman conductor. The assembly of women artists from all over Europe begin to play a melancholy tune, so sad that a woman singer pours out her cry.

The orchestra senses the passion of the song. Their playing becomes a cry of despair, wrenched from the bowels of their instruments and from the depth of their hearts. The jungle of yearning, as a rule so carefully evaded by the prisoner, suddenly opens and begins to sing with many voices. Forte, fortissimo, the orchestra plays. It is as the thunder of a herd of stampeding wild horses who race on.

Judith Newman also recalls the Sunday prisoner concerts. The violins seemed to cry within her as she felt her heart breaking.[68]

Many camps had male inmate orchestras, but Birkenau possessed the only female orchestra in the system. Alma Rosé, the Jewish daughter of the first violinist in the Berlin Opera Orchestra, niece of Gustav Mahler, and a fine violinist, conducted the Birkenau Women's Orchestra. Fania Fenelon, an orchestra member, wrote of her unique experience in *Playing for Time*. Started by Commandant Höss to provide music for the prisoners to march to work by, the group played twice a day—for the inmates and the SS. The orchestra included an odd conglomeration of instruments: ten violins, three guitars, one flute, reed pipes, drums and cymbals, two accordions, five mandolins, and Fania as the singer. For the SS, the orchestra played symphonies, arias, popular songs. For the inmates, the women played marches from a cold, wind-blown bandstand. The orchestra did not make Fania's experience forgettable. Thirty years later she wrote: "I've never left the camp; I'm still there, I've spent every night of my life there, for thirty years." All was madness. "Death, life, tears, laughter, everything was multiplied, disproportionate, beyond the limits of the credible."[69]

Each woman remained alive in a different way. Some lived for each day, walking like blind women groping from object to object, from morning to evening, putting all energy into the maintenance of daily life. Their sense of security depended upon the acquisition of a red bowl, a scrap of turnip, or a piece of soap. The life of the healthy was a continuous struggle against danger. The life of the sick was a continuous struggle against death.

A healthy person in the camp is like one riding on the step of an overloaded trolleycar, holding on with one hand and hanging by the toe of one foot. The sick are the sons who fall off during the ride. The healthy ones see them fall and might have time to scream in alarm, but not always to save them.[70]

To those who managed to remain alive for as long as six months, it seemed like a bestowal of the gift of immortality. The old-timer welcomed the new generations and bade farewell to the departed. Perhaps she would allow herself to become attached momentarily to the passersby and the passers-through, creating in brief friendship and out of imagination a world called tomorrow.

Life itself depended on *friends and friendship*. Possibilities for love remained for those few who could sneak across briefly to the men's camp. A woman with a lover enjoyed a rare distinction because of the difficulty of reaching men. Women grew attached to each other. Some memoirs refer to them as perverts, others regard them in a warmer way. One woman wrote about a small group of lesbians who gave parties with dancing and music. She remembers feeling disgusted, but realized that the parties provided a few hours of forgetfulness for the devastated women. Dr. Lingens recalls one day when Dr. Mengele sent for her and said he had an "astonishing" piece of news: "Do you realize there are lesbians in your hut?" "Of course," Dr. Lingens said. When she wrote of the incident, she emphasized that the Nazis had inhumanly imprisoned young women in surroundings where there was nothing for them to love, not even a flower. Pressed together into bunks, when the women "clutched at each other trying to find joy, the SS doctor reproached the prisoner-doctor for 'not doing anything about it.'" The Nazis acknowledged male sexual needs by providing them with brothels. It did not occur to them that women also had sexual needs. Dr. Lingens-Reiner commented on the close friendships of a lifesaving nature that emerged in the camp and thought it unlikely that an isolated woman would survive for long. Lengyel wrote that love in the degraded atmosphere of the death camp was "but a distortion of what it was for normal people, for society in Birkenau was but a distortion of a normal human society."[71]

For some women, strength came from a *belief in God*. Jewesses tried in the midst of the horror to create an atmosphere of Sabbath holiness. Friends working in the warehouses gave them candles. Or they hollowed out a potato, inserted a rag for a wick, filled it with margarine, and used it as a Sabbath candle. Women in the arms factories brought back screws and filled them with machine oil to make the candles. Horse grease served for candles. If nothing was available, the Jewesses lit their candles symbolically. Many gave their lives for Kashruth. They refused to work on the Sabbath and were tortured for it. Jewesses celebrated the festivals by praying and lighting the candles and even by fasting! In one camp on the eve of Rosh Hashanah the Jewish women walked from tent to tent with tears in their eyes, sadly wishing each other a "good year." They held Yom Kippur services at Bergen-Belsen and other camps. Women remembered Hanukkah: lighting candles, singing Jewish songs, and dancing the Hora. At a labor camp Jewesses baked cookies for Purim from bread, margarine, and carrots. Many refrained from eating levened bread during Passover, trying to live on raw carrots or cooked mashed potatoes. They even managed to hold a Seder with 300 women attending.[72]

Writers have carefully documented the deeds of the male SS leaders, but the actions of the women SS guards and leaders have been less publicized, except in cases considered bizarre. The SS women were, however, no more bizarre than the men. It should be kept in mind that no camp was *run* by SS women. They simply served under male commandants. The Allies and civilian governments held several trials of women guards and SS leaders. The Belsen Trial involved the largest number of women. Most Belsen women had also been guards in Birkenau and/or Ravensbrück. The court tried twenty-one women. It found five not guilty. It gave eleven women terms of imprisonment from ten to fifteen years. One received a three-year term and another a one-year term. The court sentenced three women to death by hanging—Juana Borman, Irma Grese, and Elizabeth Volkenrath.[73]

The courts charged SS women with all categories of crimes: beatings, torture, and killing. For the SS women to receive the death sentence, it appeared necessary for them to have been involved directly in the selection process at the station resulting in the deaths of large numbers of women and men in the gas chambers. The court considered all other actions to be lesser crimes, and gave the women light sentences or set them free!

The trial transcripts sum up the arrogant and unfeeling responses of the women guards. Juana Borman denied being present at any gas chamber selections. When prisoners disobeyed orders, she admitted to boxing their ears or slapping their faces, but never violently. Elizabeth Volkenrath denied making selections and beating anyone. She took food away from the women only when they had too much. When women needed strenuous exercise as punishment for wrongdoing, she ran them for a few hours around the camp—but that, she claimed, was only ordinary procedure. Herta Ehlert testified that she was not cruel to prisoners; she slapped prisoners' faces only for serious infractions, such as cutting up blankets to make clothes.

Ilse Lothe insisted that she did not carry a weapon, did not beat prisoners with a stick, did not knock them to the ground. Stragglers on her work

Kommando may have been slapped, but not beaten. Hilda Lobauer had been a *Kapo* for only four weeks and lost her position because she was not severe enough. At Auschwitz, she said, she became a *Kapo* again and carried a wooden stick. She denied that she ever used a whip. She admitted to striking prisoners with her wooden stick, but never so hard as to draw blood. She never beat a woman without reason, she insisted, and she never beat a woman so severely that she died.

Charlotte Klein maintained she never beat the prisoners on the bread *Kommando*. If she found a woman trying to steal bread, she merely took the bread away and slapped her face. Herta Bothe admitted to beating inmates with her hands for stealing, but never with a stick or a rod. She claimed she had never killed anyone. Frieda Walter agreed that she hit a woman once with her hands because she stole potatoes. She hit with her hands prisoners who stole, but she never used a stick or rubber truncheon. Irene Haschke admitted that she had beaten prisoners with her hands when they took food from others. Gertrude Fiest agreed that she had on occasion hit prisoners with her hands, but denied that she had ever marched them rigorously or that she had kicked anyone.

Gertrude Sauer hit prisoners near the kitchen with her hands when she caught them stealing vegetables, but, she said, she always endeavored to make the regulations more lenient, and never used a riding whip or a stick. She denied that she ever beat prisoners without reason. Hilda Lisiewitz admitted that if she found a woman stealing, she took away what she had and slapped her face; but she had no stick. Johanne Roth claimed she never beat any prisoners without reason, and she never beat old women under any circumstances. She hit women in Belsen during food distribution, she said, because they tried to get second helpings or crowded around the containers.

Anna Hempel never beat her kitchen staff. She might have slapped them when they worked too slowly or stole food. But then, they begged her to slap them rather than remove them from the kitchen detail—so she obliged them. Stanislawa Starotska said she found it difficult to control some of the inmates because they were all criminals with long sentences and no moral principles. She tried persuasion to no avail, and was forced to resort to beating with her hands.

In 1948, in a mood of either despair or lucidity, Micheline Maurel, survivor, wrote a moving invocation that encompasses the feelings of so many:

True God, let there be no more camps! I weep because there have been and still are camps. Because there are people now who are preparing for war and for new camps and who do not know what this means. . . .

I weep because the human beings who were in the camps have never been freed. They have never known a joy which would make up for the suffering endured there. The deported are either dead or have brought back within themselves their camps, where no one has entered and very few have even tried to enter, where they are alone, wretched *schmustics,* surrounded by the crawling crowd back there. Those who have come back vainly try to recapture the gift for happiness which other people have: the camp sets them apart from the world, just as it did when they were there. They cannot leave it. . . .

I weep for all those who died in the camps, because no one has ever understood or ever will understand what they suffered. For their sakes, I hope that their death is a total death. . . .

Confronted by this immeasurable, this irreparable, misery, the mind is shattered by rage and despair. No problem of evil, no philosophy, no religion can account for the suffering of the camps. No crime committed by men can justify it. No cause is great enough to warrant such stakes. No vengeance is possible or desirable. The only way to avenge would be to re-create the camps for those who made them, and it would begin all over again. . . .

And yet, how can I be happy now, my poor comrades, when I find again in photographs or in my memory, just as you were back there, as you were found, as you are, forever etched in the present? I feel that there is a staggering sum of suffering to be made up. I am torn by that suffering. I feel the camp around me. There is someone who walks in Geneva, who goes by my name: it is a phantom, a dream of the other me, the real me, who remains seated back there because she can no longer walk, holding out her empty bowl. My poor, my dear companions, all alike, all wretched, you the survivors and you the dead, I know it well: the camps have not been liberated. Each survivor has brought his camp back with him; he tries to obliterate it; he tries to stifle in the barbed wire and under the straw mattresses all those despairing *schmustics,* but suddenly a date or a photograph brings back the entire camp around him. He would like to run away, shielding his eyes with his arm in order not to see, howling in order not to hear. But the entire camp rises again slowly, for it has not been destroyed and nothing has made up for a single day of suffering.[74]

THE
POLISH
CAMPS

STUTTHOF/SZTUTOWO: THE BALTIC SEA RESORT

Sztutowo is the name of a fisherman's village, located at the Fleche de Sable de Vistule, 34 kilometers northeast of Gdansk (Danzig) and 3 kilometers from the Baltic coast. With the German invasion of Poland, Sztutowo became Stutthof and entered the halls of history as the wartime site of one of the most strict and primitive of the official concentration camps. It was the first camp established on Polish territory and the last camp in occupied Europe to be liberated. The first prisoners arrived on the morning of September 2, 1939. The last prisoners were not freed until the day after the official ending of the war, May 10, 1945.

The Baltic Sea coast is the major resort area of Eastern Europe. We were told throughout Eastern Europe that if one had a choice, a vacationer would pick either the Baltic Sea coast or Lake Balaton in Hungary. In the spring, summer, and autumn tourists fill the wide sandy beaches. On any highway leading toward Gdansk, the modern tourist buses with their Baltic Sea patrons from every Iron Curtain country far outnumber the automobiles.

Gdansk has always attracted Europeans: for industrial, shipping, vacation, and maritime reasons. It is an old town, rich in history, with deep cultural roots and traditions. North of the city lie the beautiful beaches of the Baltic Sea. No signs along the narrow roads mention that traveling to the coastal area includes a journey through the vicinity of the infamous concentration camp. Every Pole over age forty knows of Stutthof, for it was the concentration camp for Polish prisoners. The Poles had good reason to avoid it.

The drive along the coast from Gdansk to Sztutowo into Stetna Port is one of the loveliest in Europe. The road winds through small villages onto a ferry, across the Vistula, past miles of brightly colored tent cities and cabanas. The country roads, filled with cars, horses, and wagons, seem almost taken over by bathers walking to the beaches. Driving down the narrow roads to the beach, one passes inns, camping grounds, eating booths. Tourists stand in line for every variety of food imaginable—Belgian waffles, steaming fish freshly caught in the morning, sausages, potato pancakes.

Then to the beach where fishermen have pulled up their beautifully colored boats: every 9 meters traditional open Polish fishing vessels rest on the sand. Characteristically, at each boat stands an old fisherman dressed in black, mending his yards of net. Brightly colored buoys and floats hang over his boat or lie on the sand. His wife, also dressed in black, is mending nets on the other side of the boat. That scene is repeated a hundred times as far as the eye can see. Thousands swim, lie on rafts, sun on the sand; and children surround the fishermen, watching them work. Such is Stetna Port; such is Sztutowo.

I have been told that the SS had mixed feelings about being assigned to Stutthof. The camp was as primitive as any, but the beach and the resort region was the loveliest place SS troups could be stationed if they were on concentration camp duty. To lie in the summer on one of the finest beaches in Europe after a long hard day at work in the smelly, diseased, and depressing camp was a welcomed relief. Himmler had special seaside buildings constructed for the camp staff "for recreational purposes." The survivors never mention the ocean beaches in their memoirs.

Just as summer is gorgeous in the area, winter is brutal and the residents begin praying in February for spring to come. When that cold Baltic wind blows off the water, the citizens of Gdansk huddle in insulated homes with numerous stoves and fireplaces, heavy furs on their backs and large comforters on their beds, and shiver and shudder through the six winter months. They did not need to be reminded during the war that their discomfort would be deemed luxury by the Stutthof prisoners who worked each day in the gruesome weather, clad only in ragged cotton pants and shirts, hardly adequate even for the summer. To survive in any concentration camp was difficult, but to survive a winter in Stutthof required a miracle of the finest order. The weather was a more effective killer than any expensive gas chamber.

Stutthof was no secret to area residents or to vacation visitors. The labor gangs did not creep to the forests; they marched to their destinations on the highways. The camp stench and the crematorium smoke were oppressively noticeable for miles, and obviously a constant discomfort to the sun bathers. Little doubt could have remained about the nature of the establishment behind the trees bordering the sea. The most fashionable resorts in Poland—Sopot and Gdansk—are nearby. Rich vacationers traveled to that area from all over Europe. The less monied tourists, the campers, and the hitchhikers, came to the beaches next to Stutthof. The contrast between that area of fun and sun and the primitive terror of the lone crematorium and its adjacent gas chamber stiffens the observer's backbone.

The camp makes a stunning impression because of its extreme contrast with the locality. The Poles have taken great efforts to preserve Stutthof. The administration building and the commandant's villa are lovely, and an unusual fountain lies in front of the headquarters. At the far end stands the crematorium and the gas chamber. The aura of both dominate Stutthof today.

The tiny gas chamber, Stutthof.

The walk to the open-air ovens by the inmates offered no possible fantasy because the buildings were undisguised.

The gas chamber is unique because it is so small—only 7¾ meters by 3¼ meters by 2¾ meters. The chamber has two entrances. Somehow it could hold 100 persons. Death occurred in about one hour. With the stench of the crematorium and the screaming from the gas chambers, the Stutthof inmates must have realized that each day might well be their last.[1]

Prisoners worked in the large greenhouse still situated on the camp grounds—famous in Nazi days for the quality and beauty of its horticulture. Others labored in the factories next to the camp, factories now run by Poles. The administration building is in full use for camp staff and museum personnel, as is the villa, the former commandant's residence. A few barracks remain, and serve as part of the camp museum. With their dark weather-beaten wood, they contribute to Stutthof's grim impression.

The Polish government dedicated the Stutthof Museum on March 12, 1962, "for the purpose of an everlasting commemoration of that place of crime and murder of the Hitlerism." In all Polish camps, except for the Jewish killing centers, the museums are administratively responsible for the entire area. At Auschwitz, Majdanek, Lambinowice, and Stutthof the museums are central to the reconstruction of the camps and the education of the Polish people. After liberation, the Polish government became sharply interested in commemorating the camps that had a predominantly Polish Gentile population. No camp that held primarily Jewish populations has received much attention, and none has any museums.[2]

During the first years after the war, even though Polish society was impoverished, many groups in the Stutthof area tried to conserve with limited funds what remained of the camp. They formed an organization to coordinate those efforts called the Council of the Protection of Monuments of the Battle and Martyrdom. In 1961 it certified Stutthof as a museum and began the reconstruction process. The highest levels of government approved and guaranteed the project's funds.

By 1962 the crematorium building had been put in order with the aid of the famous artist Wiktor Tolkin. He divided it into eight exhibition halls. In one hall stand the furnaces and on the wall is a large picture of the heap of bodies found in Stutthof. Flags of the inmates' nations ring the room. The halls and their exhibits tell the chronological story of Stutthof. The museum authorities planned the walking route for visitors in such a way as to represent the camp during the war years. The barracks hold documents, pictures, beds, straw mattresses, bowls, basins, and the large map of the camp.

The central point of the reconstructed camp is the monument standing near the gas chamber and crematorium. In commemoration of the twenty-third anniversary of Stutthof's liberation, the government unveiled the powerful sculpture created by Wiktor Tolkin. Projected as a huge mausoleum in the form of a long horizontal block with carved reliefs, the elements of the abstract symbolize struggle. In a crevice inside the block the artist placed the ashes of victims. Piles of steel taken from the camp and flag poles line the road. On ceremonial days the flags of the inmates' nations wave in the wind. Although the Nazis destroyed the so-called new camp, the monument area commemorates it too, with architectural elements of white stone engraved with barrack numbers.

In 1967 the state placed the Stutthof Museum under the Ministry of the Culture of Art and that status gave the museum the framework and sphere of activity as a center for research. The museum includes two major sections staffed with experts. The Section for Science and Research is charged with recovering Stutthof's history. It made contacts with former prisoners and gathered their memoirs and testimonies. It established a library and archives in the Nazi administration building and continues to upgrade the camp's history. The collections include the prisoner files and pictures, and an extensive library of 1,500 books dealing with the occupation period. As a result, the Research Section has produced several books, articles, brochures, information sheets, and movies. The second section, for Science and Instruction, serves visitors, and takes seriously its responsibility for informing the Polish population of the problems of the war years.

Interest in the Stutthof Museum has increased significantly. In 1962 it had 62,000 visitors; in 1963, 93,000; in 1966, 209,000; in 1968, 257,000; in 1972, 400,000; in 1974, 650,000. The museum carries the camp to the people with movies, lectures, and photographic exhibits in towns and villages across Poland. The Polish government has stated that the museum has had a "stimulating effect," particularly on Polish youths, "keeping them alert to the problems of fight and martyrdom of the people of most of Europe during World War II."[3]

On the museum's advisory councils serve some of the most prominent professors, scientists, and government figures in Poland. Stutthof survivors have formed clubs that have taken the lead in collecting memoirs and statements. Part of the motivation for this successful effort stems from a strange fear expressed most clearly by the president of the Committee for the Protection of Monuments:

We do not forget those days of the Polish people and their fight. It is from their sacrifice, fight and martyrdom that our reality could be born. We recall our crimes, committed on the land of Gdansk, among others; because in Western Germany today the same forces are regenerated which prepared this cruel destiny of the people of the whole of Europe in the past. This monument should serve as both a commemoration and a warning that what happened can reoccur.[4]

Concentration Camp Stutthof dates its existence from the moment when the Germans crossed the border at Gdansk/Danzig and fired the beginning shots of World War II. As German troops moved through the town of Gdansk on September 1, 1939, the Gestapo followed and began to arrest Poles previously identified by Germans living in the area. The SS established Stutthof on September 2, 1939, as a civilian internment camp under SS jurisdiction. The next day the *Gauleiter* of Gdansk, Albert Forster, visited it, taking with him Stutthof's first commandant, Lieutenant Max Pauly, chief of the Gdansk SS troops. By September 13 the Poles initially arrested by the Gestapo inhabited the camp. On that day a Nazi regional newspaper complained: "One thing is sure, those who are imprisoned behind the barbed wires are too well treated." For a camp in which the inmates were too well treated, the total death figure of 85,000 seems unusually high. From the day of its founding until liberation on May 9, 1945, about 120,000 men and women passed through its gates, citizens of more than thirteen countries of Europe.[5]

Most people realize that Hitler intended to exterminate all the Jews of Europe. What seems little known, however, is that he harbored a great distaste for the Poles and outlined specifically the steps he would take in Poland when the war ended. He decided that some Poles should be kept alive because they could be of value. He resolved, however, to eliminate many of them, especially the intellectual class. Poles for whom Germanization was either impossible or undesirable, were to be reduced to an animal state.

In a secret report of 1940 Hitler described carefully the future fate of Poles. In several regions, including Gdansk, he would halt Polish education at the fourth grade. Instructors would teach Poles to count up to 500 and to write their names. They would learn that obedience to the Germans was God's will. They would not be taught to read. As a first step, Hitler closed Polish schools and banned newspapers and books.[6]

In the second phase of his program Hitler decided to clear large areas of Poland to provide *Lebensraum,* or living space, for Germany's population. He wished to settle Germans in Poland and Germanize the area. Immediately following the invasion, mass evacuations began, and with them the mass murders. It was the Stutthof camp that played a major role in the extermination and incarceration of the Polish people.

The Stutthof camp lay in an area with a North Sea climate of biting cold, heavy rain, and fog—the same area of marshes and forests where the East Prussian Junkers hunted stag and boar in a past century. The Nazis selected the site because of its isolation, its easy access by highways and railroad, its unfavorable situation for escape, and its unhealthy weather. The climate, plus overwork, starvation, and inadequate clothing, would ensure pneumonia and hasten the death of the inmates.

The early 1939 camp, remote and primitive, was simply a collection of leaky, decrepit, freezing huts. Prisoners built the camp from scratch. They tore down a forest, ripped up the stumps, leveled the ground, and built the buildings—in the biting cold Baltic winter, with living conditions less adequate than those of the Arctic Eskimos. In the early days sanitary conditions were terrible. For thousands of prisoners, the Germans provided one latrine. No pipes or water existed. Only 200 soup bowls were available for all prisoners.[7]

From Stutthof's first day it was in a continuous process of enlargement. As more transports arrived, the barracks became impossibly overcrowded; even the cemetery outgrew its capacity. With no space left for the living and the dead, and with the prospect of increasing shipments of prisoners, it seemed to the SS that the time had come to build a new camp, to give Stutthof the designation of "concentration camp" and put it under the jurisdiction of the formal Nazi concentration system.

The process of expansion involved long negotiations and the best efforts of top SS brass. Fortunately, we possess documents that detail the laborious process. The reports and letters read like those of a group of businessmen putting together a hush-hush real estate deal or plotting the takeover of a company.

SS officials held a conference on December 12, 1941, to discuss the transfer of the Stutthof civilian internment camp to formal camp status. They evaluated the December 10 report of an investigation of the civilian site, which stated:

The camp is situated in an area which has been acquired from the county of Danzig. It has been bought in order to erect an SS School for SS Main Sector Vistula. But in September 1939 it became necessary to find quarters for civilian prisoners (antisocial persons and Poles). That is how the camp Stutthof came into being. The main building is massively built. Camp headquarters and the guards are billeted there.

At present the camp has 1,024 inmates; out of which 100 are women; 650 are employed in the camp, about 250 thereof in the workshops. The remaining 376 prisoners work in outside [of camp] labor detachments in Elbing with contractors, normal wages for unskilled workers being paid to camp headquarters. The prisoners are accommodated in barracks. The workshops, viz, tailor shop, shoemaker shop, tinsmith shop, electrical workshop, locksmith shop, smithy, carpentry shop, upholstery, and painters' shop are also in barracks.

The camp is very neat and properly equipped. After the Reich Leader SS has ordered the camp to be taken over as a regular concentration camp and the accommodation there of about 25,000 Russian prisoners of war, I consider the completion of the existing workshops and the taking over by the German Equipment Works Ltd. as very favorable.[8]

The investigator recommended the purchase of the Werdershof estate located near the camp. Thus the camp would gain 20 horses, 40 cows, 60 pigs, and 100 hectares of heavy soil on which wheat, rapeseed, and turnips were being cultivated. The investigator mentioned that he had visited the brick plant, one kilometer from the camp:

The plant employs 41 men, 14 of them are provided by the camp. The plant is situated directly on the river bank. Shipment of the stones [bricks] is done by water. The clay deposit is said to be sufficient to produce 8 million bricks a year for 80 years, according to the manager. In addition, the plant produces tile and pipes.

According to information by the manager, the county asks 800,000 marks. The plant makes a faultless impression.[9]

SS officials responded quickly with a lengthy memo to Berlin on January 9, 1942: "Subject: Concentration Camp Stutthof, Inspection on January 8,

1942." High-level representatives of several SS offices and organizations held an inspection conference at Stutthof. They examined the "real estate of the CC Stutthof including the brickworks and the estate Werdershof." The group made several suggestions. In order to house 25,000 prisoners at Stutthof, the SS should purchase the existing site from the Prussian Forest Administration: "The value of the real estate of Stutthof, lock, stock, and barrel . . . is said to be appraised by the competent agencies at 1.4 million, not including living or dead inventory." The memo indicated that Himmler had ordered that the large school remain as an officers' club and head-quarters building. In exchange, the contractors would erect a new school building near the sea. The SS should acquire the brickworks and the farm, Gut Werdershof. "In order to ascertain a permanent employment of the prisoners . . . , it appears necessary that the Reich obtain the brickworks, which have a clay supply for 50 years and a yearly output of eight million perfect bricks."

On January 17, 1942, General Pohl notified the Gdansk SS Office that the Stutthof land had been purchased, that the camp would be enlarged, and that the nearby brickworks and farm should be acquired or leased. In February 1942 the camp received its new status, and by September, the construction was finished.[10]

The "new camp" contained thirty large barracks and a separate section of ten buildings identified as workshops for a German weapons establishment. Those included locksmith, gunsmith, saddle, tailor, and shoemaker workshops. The Germans built large shops on the east side of the "new camp" where they established the Focke-Wulff plant for the construction of airplane parts, and the Deltahella, for the manufacture of submarine machinery. The prisoners added two villas for the commandant and his assistant.[11]

Initially the Germans reserved Stutthof for the concentration and extermination of Poles. First came the Polish activists arrested by the Gestapo at the beginning of the war; then the Polish prisoners from the rest of the area: postmen, railroad employees, firemen, soldiers, activists, eminent professors, journalists, writers, judges, mayors, and 250 priests.

Thus Stutthof began as a small, primitive, parochial camp for the work extermination of regional Poles: erected by Poles for Poles. It went international when Hitler invaded additional European countries. Norwegian policemen, Danish Communists, Lithuanian officials, and Russian war prisoners arrived. After them came the English, the Austrians, the Belgians, the White Russians, the Czechs, the French, and the Spaniards. In 1943 about 8,000 prisoners lived in the camp. The great influx began in the summer of 1944; within four months 37,000 people had passed through the camp. After July 1944 Jews formed about 70 percent of the population. Although Stutthof was initially a male camp, women of different nationalities began to arrive, and after the construction of the new camp, the SS reserved several barracks in the old camp for them.[12]

As in other camps, Jews were put into a separate group for special treatment. Their conditions were the most severe in the camp. Most Jewish prisoners were young people between the ages of thirteen and twenty-two. They became the victims of mass killings, special treatment, and medical experiments. The Jewish women who arrived in the 1944 transports from Hungary lived in horrible sanitary conditions with few beds, mattresses, or blankets, and little water or food. A witness mentions that one SS man "selected Jewish female victims personally, and when the gas chambers failed to work, killed them with his own hands. During August to November, 1944, some 1,500 were killed in this way, most of them women."[13]

Labor was a more serious feature of Stutthof than most Polish camps. In the early days inmates worked at three main tasks: clearing the forest, fencing the camp, and constructing barracks. As the camp grew, the SS expanded the work gangs. The most important ones employed on the camp site were groups of craftsmen, electricians, carpenters, locksmiths, masons, gardeners, and cooks. Prisoners built subcamps in the region, including brickworks, sawmills, wood yards, machine shops, synthetic benzine factories, airfields, wagon and railway shops, and shooting ranges. Other groups constructed roads, prepared building materials, and kept order on the premises.

The most exhausting and damaging work was done by the forest group known as the *Waldkolonne*—the men who cleared the trees and leveled the ground in preparation for the enlargement of the camp. The SS used the inmates in place of horses, forcing them to pull carts and drag trees. During the first period of the camp employment in the forest gang meant inevitable death. Even in the following years the mortality rate was highest in that group. In the tough transport division the SS harnessed the prisoners to huge heavy wagons, and with those wagons they dragged bricks, construction machinery, and logs.

Survivors maintain that starvation caused the highest mortality. Since Stutthof was a heavy labor camp, the number of calories necessary for survival was quite high, probably about 4,500 a day. Yet the prisoners who did not receive packages from home earned an automatic death sentence.

The inmates were beaten, tortured, killed, and exterminated. The SS developed "a system of organized bestiality, planned to break the body and spirit." Those not killed by torture and punishment died from contagious diseases, which were even more common. The mass sickness of the prisoners, called edema or phlegmon, was caused by insufficient food, lack of vitamins, and water without calcium. In addition, Stutthof suffered through many typhus epidemics. During December 1944, 5,000 prisoners died of the disease.[14]

There was nothing in the camp to counteract disease. "Witnesses agree that washing was very difficult because of the shortage of water and soap (one cake lasted at the utmost ten days)." It was only in 1941 that the construction of washing facilities was started; but even in 1942 the taps were not widely available. The prisoners always had lice. And, of course, the hospital was of no help. It contained ten prisoner doctors and 1,000 patients in a space that could hold a maximum of 600. Two or three sick patients occupied one bed. The mortality rate was 50 percent.[15]

But still the inmates did not die quickly enough to satisfy the SS. For a variety of errors, the SS hanged them in the trees, drowned them in the mud, killed them by hitting them with sticks on the head, broke their ribs, and jumped on their breasts "until the mouth of the tortured was full of blood." Inmates remember the Germans drowning prisoners in sinks and burning them alive in wood furnaces. "Legal" executions usually took place in the crematorium.[16]

Survivors tell of one unforgettable execution that took place in 1944. It was the first time that the prisoners had been permitted to celebrate Christmas. In the middle of the camp stood a tall Christmas tree. On December 28 a hanging stand was placed near the tree. The SS hanged one young Pole there for sabotage.

As at Belzec, the SS had backup gas mechanisms. They kept specially equipped railroad cars on the sidings for use as gas chambers. From the exterior these wagons looked normal and the SS men dressed in railroad uniforms and ran around with whistles and flags. While loading the prisoners, the guards informed them they were going to another work area. Then they slammed the doors and blew in the gas.[17]

The original wooden crematorium burned down and was replaced with a brick structure with a larger capacity. Still, the capacity was insufficient to handle the bodies. Thus in January 1945 the prisoners dug mass graves north of the camp. After stacking bodies in piles with wood interspersed between them, they poured benzine on the corpses to fire them. "Such a pile burnt constantly during the days and nights and the wind blew away the ashes, the smoke and the bad odor."[18]

Like all camps, Stutthof had its special attractions. Its gas chamber was the smallest of any camp, almost like a toy. The commandant's administrative villa was large and lush, fronted by a beautiful fountain. A major source of pride, the large greenhouse produced flowers and vegetables of every description. In addition, the SS opened a rabbit-raising farm that became known throughout Nazi administrative circles.

It seems that Stutthof manufactured soap. Some historians claim that the Nazi manufacture of soap from human fat is just a grim rumor. However, cakes are on display; and witnesses have testified that soap was made at Stutthof from the fat of dead Jews.

At the War Crime Trials Sigmund Mazur, laboratory assistant at the Danzig Anatomic Institute, testified that the institute conducted experiments in producing soap from human bodies. The professors collected bodies, bones, and human fat in a building called "a laboratory for the fabrication of skeletons, the burning of meat and unnecessary bones." The chief, Professor Spanner, gave Mazur the soap recipe:

5 kilos of human fat are mixed with 10 liters of water and 500 or 1,000 grams of caustic soda. All this is boiled 2 or 3 hours and then cooled. The soap floats to the surface while the water and other sediment remain at the bottom. A bit of salt and soda is added to this mixture. Then fresh water is added, and the mixture again boiled 2 or 3 hours. After having cooled the soap is poured into molds.

The prosecutor presented Mazur's description of the process:

I boiled the soap out of the bodies of women and men. The process of boiling alone took several days—from 3 to 7. During two manufacturing processes, in which I directly participated, more than 25 kilograms of soap were produced. The amount of human fat necessary for these two processes was 70 to 80 kilograms collected from some 40 bodies. The finished soap then went to Professor Spanner, who kept it personally.

The work for the production of soap from human bodies has, as far as I know, also interested Hitler's Government. The Anatomic Institute was visited by the Minister of Education, Rust; the *Reichsgesundheitsführer,* Doctor Conti; the *Gauleiter* of Danzig, Albert Forster; as well as professors from other medical institutes.

I used this human soap for my personal needs, for toilet and for laundering. For myself I took 4 kilograms of this soap.

Two British POWs gave the prosecution staff testimony on the soap experiments:

Owing to the preservative mixture in which they were stored, this tissue came away from the bones very easily. The tissue was then put into a boiler about the size of a small kitchen table. . . . After boiling the liquid it was put into white trays about twice the size of a sheet of foolscap and about 3 centimeters deep. . . . Approximately 3 to 4 trayfuls per day were obtained from the machine.

A machine for the manufacture of soap was completed some time in March or April 1944. The British prisoners of war had constructed the building in which it was housed in June 1942. The machine itself was installed by a civilian firm from Danzig by the name of AJRD. It consisted, as far as I remember, of an electrically heated tank in which bones of the corpses were mixed with some acid and melted down.

This process of melting down took about 24 hours. The fatty portions of the corpses and particularly those of females were put into a crude enamel tank, heated by a couple of bunsen burners. Some acid was also used in this process. I think it was caustic soda. When boiling had been completed, the mixture was allowed to cool and then cut into blocks for microscopic examination.

The prosecutor showed the court soap samples.[19]

Stutthof adds a special chapter to the history of the notorious Nazi death marches. As the Red Army approached Poland, Himmler ordered the Polish camp commandants to evacuate their prisoners. Polish and Russian resistance units in Poland had been in touch with the camp underground. All units readied for a full-scale revolt. That revolt failed to take place, for the evacuation of the camp came as a surprise. On the day of evacuation the register showed 25,000 to 30,000 persons in the main camp, about half of whom were Jewish women. The guards divided prisoners into groups of 1,500 persons each and gave them provisions for the road—a half loaf of bread, a half piece of margarine, a piece of cheese. The 30,000 prisoners were marched out under a strong convoy at regular intervals.

It was winter; the snow often came up to the knees of the marchers, and the cold wind made the walk more difficult. Because the prisoners could hear the sounds of the guns in the east, the first day was one of courage, for they believed the Soviet Army would liberate them. The next day the SS started to machine-gun the straggling prisoners, and then the race against time began. The residents of the region tried to help, and the news of the march spread through the villages. The death march lasted ten long days during which prisoners died from hunger, cold, sickness, blows, and dirt. And among the marchers diarrhea, typhus, and lice increased the number of dead. The Germans did not intend for the march to end in life. As the prisoners of Stutthof termed it, "the road of torment" is marked by thousands of common tombs still tended by residents of the region.[20]

The Nazis took several groups to the sea to place them on boats. The destinations of those prisoners varied. Some boats sank; others were found by Swedish patrol boats. Many who shipped out on boats shared the same fate as the Neuengamme prisoners of *Cap Arcono* fame. The tragedy of the boats in the Neustadt Bay did not end with the bombing by the British planes, however, for the Germans did not intend for any prisoners to live through the war. Those who swam up on the shore were hunted down and machine-gunned by the SS. The corpses of the unfortunate lay for days around the port.

Any civilian who in those days saw the miserable train of starved figures clothed with rags being driven with rifle butts and kicks . . . will never be able to forget the sight. . . .

The exact number of survivors can hardly be determined. Some years later school children discovered a grave with nine skeletons. Bone fragments have also been found. Along the beaches of the Baltic Sea graves are still being uncovered by the tide.[21]

One group received an early consignment of death on January 31, 1945. The Germans took those Stutthof prisoners to the beach. A survivor reports:

Darkness all around—we did not know where we were going. We were divided into groups. Then we were led through bushes and undergrowth . . . we were promised that we would not be shot—we should just walk along quietly, we were being brought by sea to Estonia to work there . . . no need to be afraid. . . . Then a Jewish prisoner came and said under his breath: "You do not know what they are doing with us . . . we are being separated off into groups and thrown into ice holes. . . ." Then a German ran up to me, took me by the collar and threw me into the sea. Our whole group was already inside the water. Several women were shot . . . I lay on a block of frozen ice and the body of a woman who had been shot was thrown on top of me. . . . It turned out that the people were being thrown into the sea, alive. . . . At shallow spots along the shore there was a cover of ice . . . but people screamed, begging to be shot.[22]

Not all prisoners or SS were evacuated in the death march. On the grounds by the old camp remained sick people, cooks, German criminals, resettled Germans, and members of the *Wehrmacht*. The *Wehrmacht* set up its defense around the camp. When the end of World War II was proclaimed on May 9, 1945, the Stutthof camp was still in the hands of the Germans. The commandant surrendered the camp and on May 10 a detachment of the Soviet Army entered Stutthof.

At the end of May 1946, in front of a special jury in Gdansk, Stutthof SS men answered for their crimes. The court sentenced several SS members, *Kapos,* and guards to death, and the executions were performed on June 4, 1946. In October, in Gdansk, ten Stutthof SS men were tried and executed. Others were condemned to long years in prison. In April 1948 the court condemned to death Gauleiter Albert Forster, one of the creators of Stutthof. *In absentia,* the Polish Court condemned to death the first commandant of Stutthof, Max Pauly. In 1945 the English courts also condemned Pauly to death and executed him. The courts in the Federal Republic of Germany that tried Stutthof criminals gave them sentences of from three to nine years. At the war's end the British arrested Paul-Werner Hoppe, commandant from late 1942. He escaped and went into hiding. The Germans arrested him in 1953. After years of trials, in June 1957 the German court sentenced Hoppe to nine years.[23]

GROSS-ROSEN: A EUTHANASIA ACTIVIST

The Polish nation, caught as it was in a vicious vise between Russia and Germany, experienced both the wrath and disdain of Hitler and the terror of Stalin. The Soviets incorporated the northern districts of Wilno, Polesie, Bialystok, Wolyn, Tarnopol, Lwow, and Stanistawow. After reducing the population to destitution, the Soviets began to obliterate the Polish past and tradition. Implementing a policy of terror, they deported 1.7 million uncooperative Poles, intellectuals, and leaders to Siberia. The Nazis, however, kept their Polish "criminals" on Polish soil—either in graves or in Gross-Rosen, Stutthof, Majdanek, and Auschwitz. Hitler incorporated the western territories into the Reich on October 8, 1939—the districts of Poznan, Pomerania, Silesia, parts of the Krakow and Kielce districts, most of the Lodz district, and the northern part of the Warsaw district. He stripped the Poles in that area of all rights and enacted special legislation for them. Intending to erase Polish culture from the western territories and resettle Germans there, Hitler ruthlessly suppressed churches, forbade the use of the Polish language outside the home, closed schools and libraries, gave German names to towns and villages, confiscated homes and businesses, and applied a bare subsistence rationing program.

On October 12, 1939, Hitler created the Government General (GG). He carved it out of the Lublin district, most parts of the Warsaw, Krakow, and Kielce districts, and part of the Lwow district. The GG contained one third of Poland's former territory and 45 percent of her population. It was to become the gathering place for Poles and Jews—a reservoir of slave labor, a dumping ground for undesirables, and an extermination reservation. The GG contained the two huge labor/extermination complexes, Majdanek and Auschwitz. The German occupation lasted longer in Poland than in most other countries and was by far the most severe. From the incorporated territories Hitler moved 2 million Poles to the GG to make room for his German colonizers. To eliminate leadership potential, he executed leaders, intelligentsia, and priests. His plan was to subjugate the Poles and reduce them to slavery and exploitation forever and ever. Poles in the western territories whom Hitler did not execute or deport lived under the shadow of Gross-

Rosen and Stutthof. For those were their camps, their places of incarceration, their torture and death stations.[1]

Gross-Rosen became a major Polish camp, active in the euthanasia program and in Hitler's subjugation of the Polish people. Even so, its history is clouded because of the limited records. The Nazis established Gross-Rosen in August 1940 in Lower Silesia. The determination of the SS-owned DEST to work the nearby granite and marble quarries catalyzed its creation, as it did Flossenbürg and Natzweiler. SS bureaucrats identified a serious labor requirement for the quarries, and space needs for the overflow of Polish prisoners from older camps. Later Himmler also designated Gross-Rosen as one of the two camps (the other was Natzweiler) to accommodate most *Nacht und Nebel* (Night and Fog) prisoners. Although the camp's normal capacity was between 10,000 and 12,000 inmates, at its top strength the population reached 20,000.[2]

Prisoners sent to Gross-Rosen climbed out of the cattle cars at a small village. On the road to the camp they trudged past large stone quarries to the camp gates. Their first impression was of large flower beds beautifully tended. Those flower beds divided the SS buildings from the prisoners' shacks.[3]

Inside the camp a long road separated the men's compound from the fenced-off women's camp. The crematoria stood next to an internal gate, and on the other side lay the extension camp, a group of fifty widely spaced barracks dotting the rough hillside.

Zdenka Fantlowa arrived late in the war and found the thick woods surrounding the camp comforting—"like a warm bandage wrapped on a wound." A veteran of several camps, she remarked on the strange hair style created at Gross-Rosen: "Down the center of their scalp ran a shaven strip."[4]

The prisoners slept on bare wooden floors in primitive barracks. One inmate explained barracks life:

People were nervous, irritable and unwilling to cooperate. In the evenings, when after the noisy, troublesome issuing of blankets we were looking for a place to sleep, the floor never seemed big enough. At night when we groped our way to the lone pit in the loamy ground that was the lavatory, we risked being shot at. On coming back we would find our sleeping place occupied by someone else. Then, unless we felt strong enough to be aggressive, we could only wait at the door until the next lavatory-goer had to give up his place.

Even those hugging their precious part of the floor without ever budging from it, had anything but a quiet night.[5]

Prisoners existed on a daily ration of 300 grams of bread and a spoonful of jam. As extra sustenance, *Kapos* doled out a cup of lukewarm soup made of flavored water and salt three times a week. The "hilly, stone-littered camp site" and starvation took its daily toll of victims. Those who remained alive worked at the appalling jobs in the quarries. As Zdenka Fantlowa observed: "They were no longer human beings. In long, striped coats and wearing prisoners' caps on their heads, they crept along like human shadows, out of which they had sucked the last drop of life. Only their eyes still lived, telling of hunger and endless suffering. I shall never forget those eyes. I understood them."[6]

The commander of the Gross-Rosen SS killed 65,000 Russian inmates in six months by feeding them soup made of grass, water, and quantities of salt, followed by quantities of cold water. "They contracted dysentery and died like flies." He also awakened inmates in the middle of the night, drove them naked into the icy cold, and forced them to do three or four hours of gymnastics.[7]

In the camps construction plans moved through the same kind of bureaucratic process as they did in industry and government. In correspondence, Gross-Rosen officials emphasized the need for a "delousing plant" (extermination chambers) and complained about the delays. Finally, the SS construction management chief advised that "a rather long term for the delivery of the machinery required has become likely." To fill the gap, he ordered that Neuengamme turn over "the machinery existing there as well as the accessories." The language is neither unusual nor, at that late stage, used primarily for the purpose of secrecy. The Nazis had become habituated to using words like "louse" for Jews over a period of years, so they found it natural to refer to extermination as delousing.[8]

In August 1941 negotiations proceeded for securing the two extermination chambers. The SS Construction Management Office of Gross-Rosen dealt with the major company in the field: Tesch and Stabenow, International Vermin Extermination Corporation, Ltd. That company was engaged in a brisk business operation with the SS, and expressed its gratitude in an August 25, 1941 letter: we "thank you very much for your order for the delivery of circulation equipment for *two extermination chambers of 10 cubic meters each.*" The letter also noted the unusual request for "heat registers for electric heating instead of for hot water heating. We have informed our delivery plant accordingly and have requested a price estimate. . . . To your question regarding the chamber doors, we reply that the doors must extend beyond the door opening." Unfortunately, Tesch and Stabenow could not meet the previously stated delivery date for the chambers "due to the loss of further skilled workers to the armed forces." The company suggested that the SS office secure priority certificates so that the chambers would be considered top military orders instead of civilian orders. In that way, the equipment could be quickly supplied.[9]

On the day Germany attacked Poland Hitler unveiled the euthanasia program by charging SS Dr. Karl Brandt with "the responsibility of enlarging the authority of certain physicians to be designated by name in such a manner that persons who, according to human judgment, are incurable can, upon a more careful diagnosis of their condition of sickness, be accorded a mercy death." Brandt created a complex organization and process to implement the new program. Although carried out with elaborate subterfuge, the project was no secret to top Nazi officials. It was common knowledge in Germany as early as the summer of 1940. Under the program, thousands of prisoners were transported to euthanasia stations, particularly Bernburg and Hartheim, and murdered. In addition, Hitler's order gave camp SS doctors a free rein in the systematic phenol injection euthanasia program. Before the project was curtailed, Gross-Rosen had participated in it more actively than any other camp.[10]

The purpose of the program was to eliminate undesirables, the "useless eaters." Every German mental institution as well as several concentration camps received questionnaires from the Reich Ministry of the Interior to complete for each inmate. Ministry experts evaluated the completed questionnaires to determine if the patient should be sent to a "killing station." The Ministry then sent lists of doomed patients to the different insane asylums and camps, ordering the directors of the asylums and the commandants to hand over the "patients" to the General Sick Transport Corporation for transfer to the killing stations.

On December 10, 1941, the Inspectorate of Concentration Camps advised the commandants of Gross-Rosen, Dachau, Sachsenhausen, Buchenwald, Mauthausen, Auschwitz, Flossenbürg, and Neuengamme that they could soon expect a visit from a doctors' selection commission that would pick prisoners for "special treatment 14 f 13." Five days later the Gross-Rosen doctors carefully selected 293 inmates as eligible for screening under headings such as "Poles or Czechs in Protective Custody," "Shirkers," "Jews in Protective Custody," "Jews who were Habitual Criminals," "Jewish Shirkers," "Jews Who Defiled the Race." Out of that pool the SS expert in euthanasia, Dr. Mennecke, on January 16, 1942, selected 241 Gross-Rosen inmates for extermination. Most were Jews. One hundred twenty-seven were sent to the Bernburg euthanasia station, thirty-six died before the transport left, and forty-two were not transported because after a thirty-day rest they were able to resume work.

That speedy recovery brought a sharp reprimand! Obviously if forty-two inmates selected for special treatment could so quickly become fit to work again, their initial selection was stupid and unnecessary. The camp commandants were asked "to give their special attention to this matter."[11]

It is apparent from the available documents that one of the main purposes of the euthanasia program was the extermination of Jews. Aryan prisoners at least received a perfunctory medical examination before selection, but

Jewish inmates received none. On the back of a series of pictures of sixty-three Jews selected for euthanasia at Buchenwald Dr. Mennecke had written his reasons:

One Jewess was noted as having a "derogatory attitude toward the Reich; continuous race defilement by keeping her Jewish descent a secret and rendering the Hitler salute." Another had made "incredibly impudent and spiteful remarks toward Germans; on the train made acquaintance of soldiers coming from the front, introducing herself as Jewish, gave them bread for coffee and cocoa, then insulted the soldiers in the meanest possible way." A third was said to be an "anti-German eastern Jew agitator; in the camp, lazy, impudent, recalcitrant."[12]

Another purpose of the euthanasia project was the killing of "mentally and bodily deficient children" and large numbers of insane Russians and Poles. Included in that group were patients with arteriosclerosis, tuberculosis, and cancer. The program defined persons no longer of any value to the state as "useless eaters."[13]

Under the euthanasia project, from 1939 to 1940 the doctors killed about 100,000 humans by a variety of means: gas, injections, starvation. *Aktion* T-4, as it was called, met with such vigorous protests on behalf of Aryan Germans that at the end of August 1941 Hitler scratched the project.

When one examines the extermination program and the euthanasia project together, it is understandable why writers have seen the Nazi era as a riddle of evil and the Germans as the "most flagrant of Evildoers." They were "simply a horrifying, horrible case history to serve as a warning to all mankind."[14]

THE GERMAN CAMPS

NEUENGAMME: A GARDEN OF EDEN

The town of Neuengamme, so near bustling industrial Hamburg, appears as an oasis in a desert. One of the garden spots of Germany, Neuengamme's major industry is the production of flowers. The townspeople make their living from the millions of multicolored flowers that grow in its more than one hundred translucent greenhouses. A quiet, slow-moving river winds through Neuengamme, and a variety of small boats moor along its banks. Lush, idyllic, the town is a kaleidoscope of every color known to flowers.

The concentration camp of Neuengamme is named after the village and clearly visible from the town's center. The townspeople do not wish to be reminded of the camp's existence. They tear down signs directing people to the camp and have fabricated an effective falsehood to keep people away. Few markings for the camp are visible. An arrow points to "Gedenkstätte Neuengamme," but the so-called camp, when found, turns out to be simply a small well-kept park, perfect for an afternoon stroll, a bike ride, or for just sitting among the flowers. Children race their bikes through the park and older people wander on the paths in a small area no more than a block square. The paths through the park are well laid out and the rose bushes are beautifully tended. In the center stands a large rectangular memorial reaching high into the sky, and next to it is a haunting sculpture of a suffering camp inmate, in his dying agony making one last desperate effort to rise.

The markings and the townspeople identify this park as the sole camp site, but if one challenges that identification, a surprise awaits. One half block down the road stands a large modern youth hostel—on the grounds of the former SS barracks. And one block from the youth hostel is a large brick encampment. When curiosity pressed me to walk through the gates and into the office, I found that I was standing in one of Germany's largest maximum-security prisons, holding 400 murderers and incorrigibles. Initially, the prison warden denied that the prison was part of the camp. It soon became clear, however, that the major part of Concentration Camp Neuengamme was indeed this maximum-security prison. The Germans tore down the most ramshackle prisoner barracks, back where the park is, but left the major portion intact. Here, on this side of the youth hostel, is the real camp, the

"The Unknown Prisoner," by Francoise Salmon.

barracks and administration buildings, in good condition and now used as a prison. And it makes sense: Germans do not destroy perfectly good buildings. The guards and the warden, if pressed, will admit that they are standing in the middle of a former concentration camp. It is possible to drive around the maximum-security prison. The road and Nazi barbed wire encircle the installation. The narrow dirt road is ringed on one side by wire and on the other by lush fields. Obviously, the camp prisoners tilled the fields, tended the dairy, and looked after the cows wandering on the outskirts. From the prison/camp the panorama of flowered colors is as prominent to the eye today as it was to the prisoners in Gedenkstätte Neuengamme.

That the residents of the small village do not want to acknowledge the camp site so near their town is understandable, for during the war the residents had numerous opportunities to observe Neuengamme's 10,000 inmates. The trains unloaded their cargo at the station in the center of town. The cargo walked through the town to the camp, an hour's march. The labor squads worked throughout the area, in particular on the canal running through town. A Neuengamme survivor talks of the intimate knowledge possessed by the citizens:

From Neuengamme we had to take care of some canal there by the name of Dove [sic]-Elbe. That place of work was approximately one hour and 15 minutes to one hour and 30 minutes from our camp. We had to walk that distance. In their desperation some of our comrades would commit suicide rather than go to work. Sometimes you could find 3 or 4 inmates on the road from the concentration camp to the working place. These inmates had broken through the line, or had fallen out, or had broken through the chain of guards, and these guards shot them. They committed suicide this way. All those things were seen by the population there. That was in the morning, but they also saw our return when we came back from our place of work. I don't see how such a return march could possibly pass unobserved in other countries such as France or in Sweden without speaking, of course, of a highly democratic country like America. A long column of one thousand inmates is jogging along the road. All men are tired. At the end of the column we have 30 or 40 pushcarts. We have one dead inmate on each pushcart pushed by an inmate half dead himself. The head of the dead inmate is banging against the wheel of the pushcart. The SS men spur on the inmates; the SS men let their bloodhounds loose on the half-dying inmates in order to spur them on; teams of four men carry inmates who are about half dead. Nothing but a long mournful column, day after day, for one hour and a half. On the left and right side of them, were the German people.[1]

In June 1940 Himmler established the concentration camp of Neuengamme. From 1938 a detachment of the Sachsenhausen camp had been using the area for the production of bricks for the SS firm DEST. The German campaigns in Norway, Holland, Belgium, and France created a serious and immediate need for a large center in western Germany to accommodate the political prisoners from the newly conquered countries. That need became the decisive factor in the designation of the Neuengamme facilities as an independent concentration camp. In 1941 when Himmler divided all camps into graded categories, Neuengamme, along with Buchenwald, Flossenbürg, and Birkenau, fell into Grade II: for "protective-custody prisoners with less good records but who are likely to benefit from education and reform." Until the end of the war French, Belgian, Dutch, and Norwegian prisoners composed the bulk of the population.[2]

Little is known of actual camp operations. In fact, today Neuengamme is seldom remembered as a camp. Even so, Neuengamme had its share of horrors. It was a center for "scientific" medical research. The most important medical research carried out at Neuengamme focused on tuberculosis experiments. They paralleled a tragic accident in the city of Lübeck three years before Hitler seized power. In the laboratory of the municipal hospital three researchers sifted the BCG vaccine for use with infants in the children's clinic. After the vaccine was administered orally three times to 251 infants, it was discovered that it was contaminated with the virulent Koch bacillus. Seventy-three of the babies died. That accident almost halted the use of the BCG vaccine for several years, even though it was the most effective method known at the time for the prevention of tuberculosis.[3]

Fourteen years later at Neuengamme Nazi physicians repeated the Lübeck tragedy by experimenting with little children. Dr. Stanislaw Klodzinski, a Polish scientist, has researched the issue and described it in detail for his colleagues. As he recalls, in November 1944 the SS brought a transport from Auschwitz to Neuengamme containing twenty-five children between six and twelve years of age. A Dr. Heissmeyer in Berlin had previously selected those children for experiments for "the benefits of progress in medicine." The doctors placed the children in an isolated block under the care of prisoner professors and Dutch orderlies. All the children showed some evidence of tuberculosis.[4]

The researchers started the experiment three weeks after the arrival of the children. The project's originator, Dr. Heissmeyer, came from Berlin every ten days to work with the children. He made incisions in the skin and rubbed cultures of tubercular bacilli into the skin of the left or right arm. After a few days redness and swelling appeared on the arm and the auxillary glands enlarged; the child's temperature rose sharply for a few days, and then returned to normal in a week. The process was repeated several times. After administering a local anesthetic such as novocaine, a doctor made a long incision under the armpit to remove the lymphatic nodes of each child, an operation lasting about fifteen minutes. He then plugged and dressed the wound and sent the sterile test tubes, numbered and named, to Berlin. There, technicians bred new cultures of tubercular bacilli, made an emulsion, and sent the mixture back to the camp. Every two weeks each child was given an injection of the vaccine from his own lymphatic node. After four or five months the majority of the children ran high temperatures. In the third month enlarged lymph nodes appeared in 80 percent of the children. The doctors noted serious lung changes by the fourth month. By the sixth month cavities had formed in the lungs of almost every child.[5]

While secretly giving sweets and toys to the children, adult prisoners had an opportunity to observe the experiment. Dr. Kowalski, one of those prisoners, provides us with descriptions of the disposition of the tubercular children. In April, when the allies were nearly at the gates of Neuengamme, Dr. Heissmeyer proposed that the children be transferred to a subcamp of Neuengamme called Bullenhausendamm. He wanted all traces of the experiment eliminated, including the children. General Pohl gave the order and the doctors moved the children to Bullenhausendamm, where they were taken down into the basement. After administering morphine, the doctors put ropes around the children's necks and hanged them, as one prisoner observed, "like pictures hung up on a wall on hooks."[6]

Dr. Kowalski recalled a similar experiment with the tubercular bacilli, also carried out in Neuengamme. Dr. Heissmeyer had selected twenty-five male prisoners with evidence of tuberculosis, conducted an experiment on them similar to the one with the children, and then killed them all.

Neuengamme had fifty-five subcamps serving one of Germany's major industrial areas. Firms employed prisoners within the camp for gun manufacture, reconstruction, and brick production. Neuengamme *Kommandos* spread over northern Germany, particularly to service industry in Bremen, Hannover, Hamburg, and Kiel. The *Kommandos* worked in the steel, chemical, engineering, aircraft, fuel, ship, motor vehicle, and wood industries.[7]

Approximately 90,000 prisoners (77,000 men and 13,000 women) passed through Neuengamme, and 40,000 of them died. Germans numbered 10 percent of the prisoners; 50 percent were criminals. The others were primarily political prisoners from the occupied countries. Of the 13,000 Frenchmen imprisoned in Neuengamme, only 600 lived to return to France.[8]

Count Folke Bernadotte, an influential Swedish noble, played a part in the Neuengamme story. In 1945 he used his influence to try to persuade high Nazi officials to free Scandinavian camp prisoners before the war ended. On February 12, he met with Himmler in Berlin. Himmler did not accede to the count's requests, but he did agree to move all Norwegian and Danish prisoners in the camp system to Neuengamme, and also to allow the Swedish Red Cross to enter and care for them. Women and children, the old and the sick, were allowed to return home from Neuengamme.

The commander of the Swedish Army immediately ordered a strange mobilization: thirty-six buses, twelve trucks, a number of motorized kitchens and ambulances, together with Swedish Army personnel and buckets of white and red paint. The soldiers painted the buses white with large red crosses. The eighty-seven vehicle convoy, known as the White Buses, moved into Germany on March 12, and then scattered to pick up inmates from several camps to bring them to Neuengamme. By April 21 Neuengamme had grown by 5,000 Scandinavian transfers. To house them, the Nazis evicted less fortunate inmates from their barracks.

The feelings raised among non-Scandinavians as they watched the Danes and Norwegians leave from their camps must have been excruciating. The unhoused Neuengamme inmates also reacted bitterly. To make matters worse, the SS used the White Buses to move inmates to other camps to make room for the Scandinavians. It is painful to imagine the joy felt by the inmates as they climbed onto the Red Cross vehicles, and then their devastation when they were deposited at another camp instead of being freed.

The Scandinavians were aware of the trauma they created, but the "law of survival operated with full power." A Buchenwald prisoner testified: "When they were fetched by the Bernadotte buses, they put all the bread and food they could carry in their bags to take it along from the camp. Before the eyes of starving, dying half naked prisoners they carried food, clothes and blankets with them.

Beginning on April 3, Himmler implemented a staggered release plan and the White Buses made daily trips to Denmark. On April 19 Himmler ordered the freeing of all Scandinavian prisoners. The Danish Jutland Corps added its vehicles to the convoys and in two days transported 4,255 Danes and Norwegians from Neuengamme to Denmark. Why did the Germans allow such strange goings-on during the last days of the war? A German official gave a ready answer. It was time, he said, "to save the best of the remaining people of Western Europe."[9]

Neuengamme is perhaps best known for the unusually tragic end of most of its prisoners immediately before liberation. As the Allied armies neared Neuengamme, the Red Cross intervened in an attempt to convince the commandant to turn the camp over to the Allies intact. On the first of April Count Bernadotte was allowed into Neuengamme, but he was unsuccessful in his negotiations. As a result, Commandant Max Pauly evacuated the camp almost at the moment of liberation on May 3, 1945. In what became known as the "tragedy of the *Cap Arcona*," 10,000 prisoners were loaded on a ship of that name and on two others and sent out to sea. The ships sank, and 8,000 of the 10,000 prisoners who had managed to hold on so long to life died. Not only Neuengamme prisoners suffered. Since April 14 the *Cap Arcona* had been anchored in Neustadt Bay. The *Athen* sailed up on April 27 with 2,500 prisoners from Neuengamme and Stutthof, which she transferred to the *Cap Arcona*. A second shipment of 2,500 arrived the next day. The *Athen* sailed back to Neustadt Bay on April 29 with 3,000 prisoners. The *Cap Arcona* raised anchor on May 2 and sailed to Neustadt harbor. Early in the morning on May 3 three towed barges with 1,200 prisoners from Stutthof arrived in the bay. The tugboat guards fastened the barges to the *Thielbeck* and left. The prisoners cut the ropes and drifted off to Neustadt, landing and taking shelter in the town. However, at 3 P.M. on May 3 RAF Typhoons moved in and in one hour sunk the *Cap Arcona,* the *Thielbeck,* and the *Deutschland.* Only a few prisoners survived.[10]

NATZWEILER/STRUTHOF: A SKIER'S PARADISE

As the French say, "Struthof is a favorite resort in both winter and summer. In summer it is notable for its views and promenades. In winter it attracts skiers from every part of Europe." One guide told us: "Struthof is regarded by some as having the most beautiful view in the Vosges. In summer it recalls the words of Goethe when he lived in Strasbourg: *'Ueber allen Gipfeln ist Ruh.'*"[1] The concentration camp, named for the mountain area— Le Struthof—offers a panoramic view of the surrounding country. Le Struthof has been famous for its skiing for many decades. On a small mountain road a sign nailed to a tree abruptly announces the camp: "Struthof, Zone of Silence. Be silent in memory of our martyred dead." And suddenly, out of the quiet mountains, Natzweiler bursts into view.

The winter winds must have stunned the inmates, because the camp flows down, in a series of terraces, from the top of a large hill, unprotected from the elements. The barbed wire, the wooden watchtowers, and four of the initial seventeen barracks remain. Those barracks contain the museum, kitchens, cell building, and crematorium—surrounded by the eight guard towers and the barbed wire fence. The foundations of the razed barracks climb the hill, and the steps are crude and barren. Barbed wire encases the large wooden gate entrance. In front of it a woman sells camp mementos. Before the summer of 1976 the first sight upon entering the camp was a barrack building converted into a museum that contained all the memoirs and records gathered during the years and many camp artifacts. But an arsonist burned down the building and all its relics in May 1976. The French government is in the process of rebuilding a new fireproof museum.

The French did not finish the renovation of Natzweiler until 1960. For many years after the war France, unlike other countries, did nothing about restoring any camp in its territory. Although Natzweiler was considered by Hitler to be on German territory, it is the only large-scale camp intact in France today—the single native spot that can serve as a significant memorial to dead Frenchmen. After receiving considerable pressure for several years, the French government finally restored its one official Nazi camp as a monument, a memorial, a warning, a remembrance. DeGaulle personally dedicated Natzweiler on July 23, 1960.

Natzweiler: sculptor, architect, Bertrand Monnet; sculptor, L. Fennaux.

The Natzweiler memorial in addition to the camp itself includes the National Graveyard and the National Camp Memorial. The graveyard holds 1,120 corpses of Frenchmen brought back from several concentration camps in Nazi Germany. According to the inscription engraved on its stone front, the unusual and stunning memorial was dedicated "To the heroes and martyrs transported. The French Republic is grateful." Designed by the French architect B. Monnet and erected in 1950, the 40-meter-high memorial is a simple shaft, pointing like a sword to the sky. It rises like a great boat with white sail from the rows of symbolic crosses. On its curved face the sculptor Fennaux carved the ghostly shadow of an emaciated prisoner. At its base lies buried one of the unknown dead.

The entire camp area is small, approximately three-fourths of a kilometer square. The August wind blows chilly and stiff. In orderly, steplike fashion the barrack foundations descend to the restored barracks at the bottom of the hill. The French, in the process of rebuilding portions, are dedicating each barrack foundation to the dead from a particular country or from a special group. The construction cranes lend newness to this miniacre of death and torture. On all sides one is struck by the breathtaking mountainous view: dense forests, lush shrubbery, hills dotted with towns.

Natzweiler is truly a place from which escape was impossible. It is isolated, in the center of a sky resort area that remained active during the war period. The skiers found the brisk winters exhilarating, but to the starving, unclothed prisoners, they were bitter cold, desolate, death-producing. Over the crest of the hill are the remains of the brush-overgrown quarries where the inmates labored. There is a certain stark beauty to this camp. The dark-brown weatherbeaten wood of the buildings contrasts with the deep green forest and the bright blue sky. Natzweiler was a place without hope, without sight of salvation, to those enclosed by that barbed wire with the locked gate. Screams, cries, would be lost in the wind—not even an echo could be heard.

Four well-scrubbed disinfected huts remain standing. One barrack is preserved with its wooden bunks, tier upon tier, where men slept, crushed and stifled. Another barrack holds the dissecting room, and next door is a special chamber with bunks for vivisection subjects. This part of the camp was a mecca for visitors—professors from Strasbourg University who came with their medical students to study the vivisection experiments. Natzweiler is the only camp that exhibits crematorium urns. Although common during Nazi years, the urns seem to have disappeared from the other camps. *Kapos* filled the urns with ashes from the ash pit and sent them to relatives of dead inmates, who had been told that for a sum of money they could receive the remains of their departed relatives. Thus the Nazis made a profit from every part of the human body, including the ashes. In one room at Natzweiler there are dozens of red clay pots for the final remains.

Natzweiler's death rate necessitated a crematorium, and it remains intact.

The prisoners cremated there died from labor, hunger, torture, punishment:

In their thin uniforms, toiling in the bitter cold in the autumn and winter, beaten and starved, they sickened and died in the thousands. The furnaces at Struthof never stopped burning. Day and night the prisoners went "up the chimney." The stronger men, chosen for torture and death, were doused alternately with scalding and freezing water, then forced to do exercises to music, stripped to the waist in the open air.[2]

Natzweiler has another unique feature, again centering upon the Nazi insistence on avoiding waste. Obviously, the heat generated by the bodies burning in the crematorium should be of some value. And, unlike in any other camp, the commandant of Natzweiler found a use for it. He built a shower room for SS men next door to the ovens. Its water was warmed by the hot gases produced by the burning bodies. Even in the dead of winter the SS guards did not lack for hot water.

After leaving the camp, I drove 3 kilometers down the road back to Struthof, took a short turnoff, and found a small lovely *gasthaus* called Le Struthof. During the war the Germans took over this ski lodge, famous for its view and comfort. Immediately across the road from Le Struthof, not more than ten yards from the *gasthaus,* stands another building, which originally housed a washroom, kitchen storeroom, extra dormitories, and additional showers. Inscribed on its door are the words *"Chamber à Gaz"*—the SS had converted the building into Natzweiler's gas chamber. The efficient but small gas chamber, accommodating only twenty persons in the reconverted shower and dormitory rooms, contains another feature unique to camp gas facilities. The Germans built into the floor of one room three tiled pits, each perhaps 4½ meters deep and 2½ meters square, and filled them with a preservative solution. Into the pits they placed gassed bodies. Two days a week the research professors would arrive from Strasbourg, check in at the little hotel, and in the morning stroll the 9 meters across the street to look over the pickled bodies. They immediately dissected those of special interest, removing unusual heads and placing them in jars. Intact bodies were loaded on trucks to be used as cadavers by the Strasbourg medical students. This little gas chamber was considered an exciting medical research facility.

Today the hotel has recovered its prewar fame. Its dining room is in demand for fancy wedding parties by the elite of Strasbourg and surrounding towns. A visitor sees wedding parties drive up to the hotel and park in front of the gas chamber. The wedding guests walk into the hotel dining rooms, sparing not a glance for the gas chamber, clearly marked only a few feet away. And they dine and celebrate a new marriage—so very close, so very, very close to that spot where many human beings lost their lives. Hotel guests during the war had perhaps a more unnerving experience, because the men and women to be gassed stood nude outside that plain building across from the restaurant, in full view of the luncheon patrons and the visiting professors. The victims' screams in the gas chamber were easily heard in the hotel and provided the background noise for the diners and sleepers. On the other hand, the hotel guests may have been simply reflecting sentiments like Himmler's when he told his men that the SS was built on honor and decency "to bearers of our own blood, but to no one else." That chamber, a startling study in the barbarites of civilization, remains today as it was during the Nazi years.[3]

After leaving the *gasthaus* area, one drives back down through the beautiful mountain region, heavily frequented today by the ski crowds. By concentrating on the marvelous skiing available, it would have been simple then, as now, to ignore or deny the existence of the concentration camp up the road. Today's travel brochures for the area read: "For the poets and sportsmen, there ranges a succession of savage and uncultivated spots conducive to calm, contemplation and relaxation."

In May 1941 the Nazis erected a new concentration camp in the Alsace region near Strasbourg. In the middle of the famous ski area the SS-owned DEST Works discovered a valuable source of rare red granite. That discovery determined the establishment of Natzweiler. The Germans constructed their only French-situated camp near a charming village on the summit of the Vosges at an altitude of 800 meters. Three hundred German prisoners, living in shacks, built the camp in 1941, while suffering dreadfully from the foggy, cold climate. As an early inmate reflected, it was a contrast of the romantic versus the Germanic: a curtain pulled up on a tragedy of degradation, destruction, and debasement of human beings by other human beings. Five to eight thousand prisoners eventually inhabited the camp; an additional fourteen thousand served in the external *Kommandos*.

The curious "NN shipments" began to arrive at Natzweiler in 1943. NN stood for the German *Nacht und Nebel*—Night and Fog—but the true meaning became evident: "Never-Never shipments." Those shipments contained several hundred Dutch, Belgians, and French who had been given "racial-biological examinations" and then shipped to Natzweiler, from which they were to disappear quietly. Natzweiler and Gross-Rosen handled the bulk of Germany's NN prisoners, most of whom had been members of the resistance movements of their various countries. Distinguished by clothes marked with a large cross and red patch, the NN were forbidden to receive correspondence and packages or to circulate inside the camp. Living in seclusion in a block encircled with barbed wires, they were even denied use of the infirmary.[4]

In the beginning Natzweiler was an "ordinary" place, but later in the war it became an abomination—"a house of insanity." The small, grim camp either worked its prisoners to death in the granite pits or killed them through unique medical experiments. The prisoners arrived at the little station after a long cattle car trip. They walked the kilometer to the top of the mountain and, at first glance, took in the magnificent spectacle with the strong wind swirling the snow. The camp appeared as a collage of contradictions: the white snow, the black night, the bright stars, the bright moon. Prisoners soon contrasted the natural beauty of their surroundings with the atmosphere of brutality in the camp.

The days were the same. Up at 4 A.M., wash in the cold water, dress, throw down the half a liter of tea, roll call—often for hours, standing and freezing in the snow. Then to work. Noon: return to camp, another roll call, and food—one liter of soup. Back to work. At 6 P.M.: return to camp, the last long roll call, food—half a liter of coffee, 300 grams of bread, 20 grams of margarine, one spoon of marmalade—and then bed. The routine was broken only by a memorable Christmas with two days of rest from work. The commandant provided a large Christmas tree and then a special treat. But first came a performance before the tree: the slow hanging of two prisoners, whose strangling lasted ten minutes. The prisoner audience filed slowly by the grinning commandant and the hanging lifeless bodies—to receive their surprise, an extra ration of three potatoes and a weak meat broth. And then, sitting in the snow, they sang Christmas carols in many languages.

The prisoners' work was a form of extermination. The SS sent some out on armament *Kommandos*. Others worked in and around the camp or on the neighboring farms. The interior *Kommandos* dug up the mountainsides, excavated the stones by hand, leveled the ground, and pulled the wagons. An unusual story has circulated about one *Kommando*. It left each morning with twenty men but was expected to return with only seventeen:

The *Kapo* had the freedom to achieve this reduction by whatever means he cared to use: a blow of a club or shovel, strangling, or perhaps burying some of his charges alive. If he managed to do so by noon, he would have three extra soups to eat—his personal profit. "And during the afternoon, one felt a little more at ease," one of the few survivors told me. Theoretically, the *Kommando* would be wiped out within a week, but since there were continuous arrivals of more or less exhausted men, some of the new ones died the first day, while some of the veterans managed to last several weeks, during which they might be transferred to another *Kommando*, then from there perhaps sent to another camp needing manpower.[5]

Newcomers remarked on the faces: shaved, burned by the sun, expressionless. The weather was severe, the work crippling, and the punishment unending. As official punishment, prisoners who committed minor infractions received three days in an isolation cell without food. Those who committed more serious crimes earned thirty-two days in an isolation cell, where they were provided with food and water every four days. Any repeater was placed foodless for three days in a bunk designed so that a stoop was the only possible position—no lying, standing, or sitting. And God help those who fell sick! In the so-called hospital they lay uncared for, without even as much as aspirin. In Block 5 of the hospital the SS put the very sick, whom they killed by injections, and the experimentees, whom the Strasbourg doctors sterilized, subjected to typhus, and used for mustard gas experiments. They added the gas chamber in the summer of 1943. Until the crematorium was finished in October 1943, the guards cremated the bodies in furnaces on a farm. After the new crematorium was built, the camp orchestra played throughout the burnings. The bodies' previous belongings yielded a valuable return. During one forty-seven day period the SS sent to Germany 99,992 suits and children's clothes and as many women's outfits.[6]

The University of Strasbourg pointed proudly to its world-renowned faculty—several scientists whose interest in new medical and anthropological discoveries was exceeded only by their excitement on finding human bodies (alive) that could be obtained easily for that research. As Natzweiler was the camp nearest the university, the scientists conferred on those prisoners the honor of dying for medicine.

In 1942 University of Strasbourg Professors Hirt and Bickenbach, with several of their colleagues as assistants, agreed to perform a secret and urgent medical experiment at Natzweiler for the benefit of the German Air Force. The experiment dealt with finding the most effective treatment for wounds caused by Lost gas, better known as mustard gas. Colonel Wolfram Sievers, Reich manager of the *Ahnenerbe* Society and director of its Institute for Military Scientific Research, convinced Hirt that he could provide excellent research facilities at Natzweiler. He offered Hirt (Strasbourg's director of anatomy) significant research subsidies from the SS society *Ahnenerbe* if he would accept the project.[7]

The name *Ahnenerbe* means "ancestral heritage." The SS started the Society and charged it with devoting its efforts to research "concerning the anthropological and cultural history of the German race." Later the Institute for Military Scientific Research was organized within the Society. Himmler served as the Society president. On July 7, 1942, he wrote Sievers asking that the *Ahnenerbe* "support in every possible way the research carried out by SS Haupsturmführer Professor Dr. Hirt," to "make available the required apparatus, equipment, accessories and assistants, or to procure them," and to charge the costs to the *Waffen* SS.[8] Sievers followed Himmler's "request," and wrote that Hirt and his colleagues would receive official automobile transportation from Strasbourg to Natzweiler, and that 20 liters of gasoline would be made available to camp authorities each month for that purpose. He also made several demands of the SS Construction Office:

The experiments which are to be performed on prisoners are to be carried out in four rooms of an already existing medical barrack. Only slight changes in the construction of the building are required, in particular the installation of the hood which can be produced with very little material. In accordance with attached plan of the construction management at Natzweiler, I request that necessary orders be issued to same to carry out the reconstruction. All the expenses arising out of our activity at Natzweiler will be covered by this office.[9]

Professor Hirt supervised the Lost/mustard gas experiments from 1942 to 1944. Initial difficulties slowed down the experiments. On November 3, 1942, Sievers needed to step in again to secure the help of Himmler's personal administrative officer, Colonel Rudolf Brandt. Sievers wrote of his particular ire at the Natzweiler commandant's insistence that money be paid for the use of the experimental subjects:

When I think of our military research work conducted at the concentration camp Dachau, I must praise and call special attention to the generous and understanding way in which our work was furthered there and to the cooperation we were given. Payment of [for] prisoners was never discussed. It seems as if at Natzweiler they are trying to make as much money as possible out of this matter. We are not conducting these experiments, as a matter of fact, for the sake of some fixed scientific idea, but to be of practical help to the armed forces and beyond that to the German people in a possible emergency.[10]

Brandt settled the matter and Hirt began his experiments. In one set the doctors inflicted wounds on the victims and then applied the gas directly to the skin. They recorded symptoms until death intervened. In another set of tests the doctors applied one drop of liquid to the lower arm of thirty subjects. Ten hours later burns appeared and spread over the body. Some subjects went blind, and all suffered terrible pain. After the sixth day the first victim died. Seven more followed him. The gas had destroyed the lungs and organs of the subjects. In a third set of experiments the doctors placed two subjects together in Natzweiler's tiny gas chamber. They forced the subjects to smash ampules of the Lost liquid and inhale the resulting vapor. The gas ate away the breathing organs of 150 inmates in that manner. Fifty died. Other subjects were forced to take the gas by injection and by mouth. None of the 250 experimentees had volunteered for that ordeal.[11]

Dr. Eugene Haagan, also a full professor at Strasbourg, designed typhus and other disease experiments to investigate the value of various vaccines. Researchers injected 300 healthy prisoner subjects with an antityphus vaccine and then infected them with typhus. Even worse, they infected some inmates with typhus "with the sole purpose of keeping the typhus virus alive and generally available in the bloodstream of the inmates."[12]

Hirt conducted experiments for the armed forces on the causes of epidemic jaundice. He infected subjects with jaundice, some of whom died and all of whom suffered great agony. For the benefit of the armed forces, scientists also conducted spotted fever vaccine experiments. One of Dr. Hirt's private hobby experiments necessitated the removal of testicles. None of those experiments, however, matched Dr. Hirt's major fascination. Because Hirt's major fascination coincided with Himmler's, they joined forces and Natzweiler became the center for one of the most bizarre projects of the Third Reich. What happened next reminds one of the words of Thomas Hardy: "While much is too strange to be believed, nothing is too strange to have happened."[13]

In early 1942 Dr. Hirt lay sick in the hospital with bleeding lungs and circulatory asthenia. Nevertheless, he was able to write a preliminary report on his new project: "Securing the Skulls of Jewish-Bolshevik Commissars." Dr. Sievers forwarded that report to Colonel Brandt on February 9, 1942, expressing his keen interest in the project. To obtain a collection of Jewish skeletons, Dr. Hirt advocated murdering Jewish Bolshevik commissars, "who personify a repulsive, yet characteristic subhumanity," and thus can provide "tangible scientific evidence" of a little known race. The *Wehrmacht,* said Hirt, should turn over all living Jewish Bolshevik commissars to the field police, who would then inform a central office. A team of experts would arrive to take photographs and anthropological measurements.

After the Jew had been put to death, without in any way injuring his skull, the physician severs the head from the trunk and sends it to its place of destiny in an hermetically closed tin box, especially adapted to this purpose, filled with a preserving solution. As soon as the dispatch is received by the scientific laboratory, it will be possible to record on a photographic plate the results of comparative and anatomic examinations of the skull, to define racial features as well as the pathological features based on the shape of the skull, the shape and size of the brain, etc., to make measurements and obtain a number of other data regarding the head as well as the skull itself.[14]

Dr. Brandt communicated on February 29 Himmler's eager support of Hirt's work as soon as he was well.

Hirt regained his health and returned to his research. But Jewish Bolshevik commissars were hard to find. After extensive correspondence among Himmler, Sievers, and Brandt, they decided to use 125 Auschwitz Jews. Dr. Bruno Berger, an *Ahnenerbe* official, went to Auschwitz to "work on" 115 inmates, including 79 Jews, 30 Jewesses, 2 Poles, and 4 Asiatics. When danger of infectious diseases at Auschwitz interrupted his work, Sievers rescued the project by transferring the subjects to Natzweiler. Approximately eighty arrived, only to be gassed (at Hirt's request) in August 1943 in the Struthof gas chamber supposedly built for that purpose. After gassing, the bodies were stored in the tile preservation pits that Hirt had ordered built within the newly converted gas chamber. At intervals, he shipped the bodies to the Strasbourg Anatomical Institute and preserved them in tanks in the cellar.[15]

Joseph Kramer served as deputy commandant and then commandant of Natzweiler from April 1941 to April 1944. In 1944 Himmler appointed him commandant of Belsen, where he presided over that camp's horrible last days with extraordinary immunity to human suffering. Though he became infamous for his role at Bergen-Belsen, he obviously learned his trade at Natzweiler. That warm family man, a bookseller before the war, came a long way to the indifferent person peering through the peephole of the Natzweiler gas chamber. In his memoirs he described his part in the Hirt project:

I went to the Strasbourg Anatomical Institute, where Professor Hirt was based. He told me that a group of prisoners were to be executed in the gas chamber at Struthof, and the bodies to be taken to the Anatomical Institute for his use. He gave me a bottle containing about a quarter liter of salts—I think they were cyanide salts. . . .

Early in August 1943 I received eighty inmates, and one night, around nine o'clock, I made a first trip to the gas chamber with fifteen women in a small truck. I told them they had to go into the chamber to be disinfected. With the help of a few SS I stripped them and pushed them into the gas chamber completely naked.

While I closed the door they began to scream. I placed a certain amount of the salts in a tube under the peephole and then watched what happened inside. The women breathed for about thirty seconds before falling to the floor. After turning on the ventilation I opened the door. I found the women lying dead on the floor, covered with excrement. . . .

I had no particular feelings in carrying out these operations because I had received an order to execute the eighty prisoners in the manner I have described. In any case, that was the way I was trained.[16]

When the Allied armies began to threaten Strasbourg in September 1944, an alarmed Sievers telegraphed Colonel Brandt for instructions as to the disposal of the Jewish bodies stored in the institute cellar in Strasbourg. Hirt had informed him that the "collection can be defleshed and rendered unrecognizable," but that action would mean that the long efforts would be wasted and that "this singular collection would be lost to science." Sievers offered Himmler three options: preserve the collection because it could be made to appear "inconspicuous"; dissolve the collection in part and declare

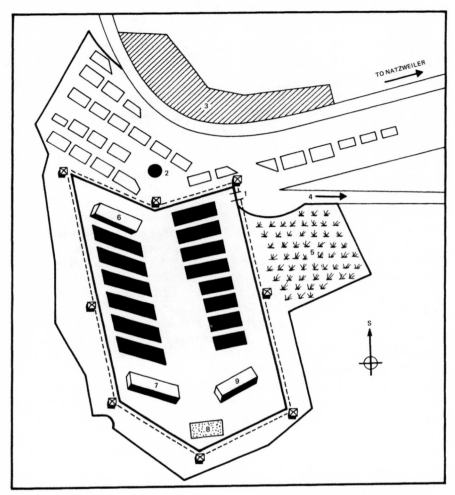

TO NATZWEILER

S

- - - - - -	concentration camp enclosing wall
————	general enclosing wall for Natzweiler
▰	living barracks
⊠	watch tower

1. Entrance to camp
2. Monument
3. Sandpit
4. Road to gas chamber
5. Former garden of commandant
6. Kitchen
7. Crematorium
8. Grave site
9. Cells

Map 8: Natzweiler Concentration Camp Memorial

Map Representation by Sharon Coughran

that the flesh parts had been left by the French; dissolve the collection completely. Himmler ordered the collection dissolved. But the task was never completed:

Hirt had ordered Bong and his assistant, Meyer, to cut up the 86 corpses and have them cremated in the Strasbourg crematorium, but these two men alone were unable to carry out this enormous task. A number of corpses remained undissected and were left in the tanks, together with partially dissected corpses, in order to create the impression that they were used for normal anatomical research.[17]

In August 1944 the camp was declared a zone of war. Prisoners expected liberation, but instead a great influx of new inmates occurred. A camp meant for 4,000 now held 7,000. The first evacuation convoy left on August 31, 1944. The convoy of 2,000 barefoot prisoners, SS men, soldiers, and dogs struggled down the mountain. At the bottom the commandant drove up and ordered the convoy back up the mountain because the train had not yet arrived. The prisoners dragged themselves back. At 5 A.M. the whistle blew and down the mountain they fell again, to be loaded into animal wagons without water or food. At 10 A.M. the train began to move; it reached Dachau the next morning. That convoy was lucky for only two men died. The other convoys deposited more dead than living at their destinations. The French First Army liberated Natzweiler on November 23, 1944. But the SS had finished its "evacuation" by early September. SS Dr. Hirt disappeared and was never seen again.

DORA/NORDHAUSEN:
THE NAZI ROCKET FACTORY

Dora/Nordhausen, a former center for Nazi rocket production, lies in the midst of the Hartz Mountains of Thuringia. Rich farmland and thick forests surround the East German town of Nordhausen and its nearby camp, Dora. No foreigner gains free access to the camp and tunnel area. Only with the assistance, guidance, and "companionship" of a member of the state police could I visit the barren camp. An examination of the extensive tunnel system is "not possible." Clearly, the tunnels dug in the mountains for the V-1 and V-2 rockets and the armament factories created during Nazi years are used in some fashion by the East German government today.

In 1943 the SS organized Dora as a Buchenwald sub-*Kommando* to build, in tunnel factories, the V-1 and V-2 rockets. Subcamps engaged in the manufacture of secret weapons, construction of factories, and the maintenance of war materials dotted the Hartz Mountains during the war years. Tunnel systems crisscross the entire area. Buchenwald, adjacent to Weimar, supplied the labor for the rocket industry, and a trip to Dora requires the same tedious 50-kilometer drive through the mountains taken by apprehensive prisoners thirty-five years ago.

Before the construction of the Dora living facilities in the latter part of 1944, the prisoners, some 12,000 to 14,000 of them, lived in the tunnels. Dora had none of the amenities of the other camps. On the ground one saw nothing but rows of shabby barracks. There was no hospital and no gas chamber. They were not needed—it was enough to work the prisoners to death in the tunnels. The Germans built the crematorium in 1944 to avoid the long trip to Buchenwald, where they had been sending the bodies. There are several mass graves in the area, and the Allies found piles of bodies stacked throughout the mountains.

After liberation the Allies razed Dora. The East Germans are now in the process of reconstructing it. What remains of the original camp is a single building: the modern crematorium, 120 steps up the mountain, with its chimney thrusting through the trees. The crematorium platform provides a startling view of the beautiful Hartz Mountains. A sensitive German

Sculpture, Dora Memorial Plaza, next to crematorium.

sculptor, Jurgen Woyski, created next to the crematorium the stark sculpture of Dora slave laborers. A life-size squad of prisoners stands on the platform, expressing in their faces and bodies the suffering and determination of the inmates.[1]

On the lower camp ground the East Germans have created a setting with eternal flames, benches, and rose bushes to commemorate those who perished. In the summertime the mountains are beautiful as they must have been during the winter—but for the weather. As many prisoners died from the bitter climate as from the impossible workload and starvation. Science has always demanded a severe price for the implementation of its research. But when one stands on the crematorium platform at Dora/Nordhausen and looks at the hazy mountains, one knows with certainty that this time the price was extraordinary.

The development of Dora/Nordhausen and its subcamps parallels the development of the famous German "secret weapon," the V-2 rocket and the V-1 flying bomb. Circumstances tied that production to Dora and explain why the Nazis kept that camp and its subcamps a secret, even from the German people. Dora was the cover name for the concentration camp established in the Hartz Mountains.

Rocket experimentation began in Germany after World War I with the testing of rocket automobiles and military rockets. In 1936 German army ordinance rejuvenated rocket research and founded the major army research station, Peenemünde, on the coast of the Baltic Sea near the island of Rügen. As was true of all Germany's experimental weapons, rocket research developed slowly. The production of the V-2 rocket did not begin until the middle of 1943. Allied intelligence, however, located the rocket production site, and in the summer of 1943 intensive bombings by the Allied air forces almost destroyed the Peenemünde Research Station. Clearly, the Germans had to look for other locations for those plants.

Sites selected for the new installations centered in the so-called SS "Closed Areas," each encompassing many square miles. For the rocket program, the Germans settled on the Hartz mountain region. They developed Closed Area B, employing 150,000 prisoners to construct the underground plants for armament and military industries.[2] For centuries, companies had mined calcium sulphite in Kohnstein—a hill 6 kilometers from Nordhausen. I. G. Farben in 1938 maintained a small branch mining operation at the site. The government research firm WIFO was searching for bombproof storage for gasoline and oil. Farben joined with WIFO, and Kohnstein became a cooperative venture. WIFO used the tunnels as storage and helped with the excavation, and Farben gained an inexpensive calcium operation.[3]

The original plan of excavation and tunneling provided for two long tunnels that would parallel through the mountain from north to south and be connected by forty-six smaller tunnels. By 1943 WIFO had completed Tunnel B and had partially finished the Tunnel A opening on the northern side of the hill. The project yielded an excellent site for underground rocket production in the two main tunnels—each 1,800 meters long and 12½ meters wide—and twenty-three connecting tunnels. The Germans used the main tunnels for rocket testing. Railroad tracks ran the length of the tunnel, with sufficient space remaining at the side for huge pieces of machinery. The Junkers Company used the small northern section to manufacture airplane engines.[4]

To meet the demand for additional underground space as Allied bombing accelerated, government firms began constructing three tunnels on the other side of Kohnstein and one on the mountain, called Himmelsberg. They designed the huge parallel tunnels with ten connecting units as factories for the production of liquid oxygen, synthetic gasoline, and new rockets—the A-3 and the A-9. By the end of the war the Germans had completed 80 percent of the tunnel work. The plants were operable.

In 1943 a new government firm, the Mittelwerk, took control of the administration of the tunnel system and the tunnel industry. All of Mittelwerk's physical installations were called the Mittelbau. When any camp became independent, it was organized under the term *Mittelbau*. Later Dora received the official title Mittelbau CC.

The completion of the tunnel system and the subsequent weapons production called for an extensive labor force. To procure that labor, the SS founded Dora as a subcamp of Buchenwald in September 1943. The Buchenwald *Kommandos* labored in the tunnels under dangerous conditions, performing most work manually. Even the rocks broken loose by blasting were removed by hand. As there were no facilities in the region to house the prisoners, they lived in the tunnels where they slept on cots and wooden bunks in dank, damp rooms without ventilation and light. The sight of daylight was a special privilege. Since blasting occurred twenty-four hours a day, the prisoners endured dust so thick "it was impossible to see five steps ahead." Food rations were limited and no water for washing or sanitary facilities existed. Prisoners secured drinking water from leaks in the water pipes.[5]

With thousands of prisoners packed together in those impossible conditions, dysentery, tuberculosis, and other diseases ran rampant. The death rate in Dora rapidly accelerated, but because so much labor was available from Buchenwald, it scarcely mattered. The SS simply shipped the dead bodies back to the Buchenwald crematorium. Buchenwald received at least fifty bodies daily from Dora. "The bodies were filthy, louse-infected, neglected. Their weight was seldom as much as ninety pounds. They were intertwined into knots that could hardly be separated." The Nazis were nowhere much concerned about the death rate, let alone at Dora where Hitler's demand for quick production of the secret weapons became the only goal that mattered.[6]

The Germans built the external Dora facilities in March 1944 on the sloping southern edge of the Kohnstein. Near the tunnel entrances they erected wooden barracks. Because of the hurried construction, they made no provision for ordinary camp amenities. Food, sanitation, and medical treatment were poor in all the camps, of course, but they were worse in Dora than elsewhere. With the completion of the barracks, Dora became an independent camp—Mittelbau I. The new brick crematorium on the hillside was the only concession to modernity.

Dora survivors recalled that the worst period of camp existence began in November 1944. New guards and officers came from Auschwitz and other evacuated camps where they were accustomed to using arbitrarily cruel methods on inmates. They quickly took out their anger and frustrations on the Dora prisoners. The prisoners remember one day when the guards hanged fifty-seven inmates:

They were hanged in the tunnels with the help of an electrically controlled crane, a dozen at one time, their hands bound behind the back. A piece of wood was put in their mouth, and held fast by a wire tied at the back of the head in order to prevent shouting. All the prisoners had to attend these mass-hangings, which were allegedly a result of sabotage. Sabotage, by the Gestapo and the SS, was a very extensible word! Sometimes the use of a paper cement bag to keep warm, the use of a piece of scrap metal to make a spoon, the use of a piece of electrical wire to hold wooden shoes on the feet, or other trifling measures were considered as sabotage, and resulted many times in death by hanging or being beaten to death in the bunker.[7]

Shortly before the war the Germans established another major subcamp called Nordhausen, which assumed the formal name of Boelke Kaserne. Several *Luftwaffe* barracks lay on the outskirts of the town of Nordhausen. In January 1945 the SS converted those barracks into a "recuperation camp" for inmates of Dora and its outcamps. Prisoners from Dora, Ellrich, and Harzungen "recovered" at Boelke Kaserne. Since the SS expected labor from the recuperating prisoners, they daily sent labor details into Nordhausen. Even though the recuperation camp contained a hospital, the obvious goal was slow but sure extermination. With little food and no medicine, death rates of 35 to 50 people a day were usual, and toward the end of the war 75 people a day died out of a camp of 4000 inmates. The corpses kept the Dora crematorium operating around the clock. The Allied bombs that fell on Boelke Kaserne in April 1945 killed many inmates. Then, leaving the sickest prisoners behind to die, the SS evacuated the camp.[8]

Sixty kilometers southwest of Buchenwald was another labor subcamp, Ohrdruf, known as one of Hitler's underground headquarters. Twelve kilometers from Ohrdruf huge underground mountain tunnels housed V-weapons factories. Ten thousand prisoners built the tunnels, working in conditions similar to those at Dora. "Only a fraction survived."[9]

Ohrdruf's medical facility could be called a hospital in name only. Most of the ill inmates lived in animal quarters. A prisoner, Dr. Bernhard Lauber, testified to the conditions:

They were accommodated in the stables. There were no beds in those stables. It was a concrete floor. The sick people lay on the bare floor, without straw, without covers and blankets; no drugs; and these ill people were given 50 percent of the food which we were given. They were so ill that they couldn't eat very well. They lay there with open wounds, they were not dressed, and they died there by the thousands.[10]

American troops evacuated Dora and its subcamps on April 5, 1945. The soldiers reported sights that filled them with revulsion. At Nordhausen they found piles of dead and dying bodies in the same hut, lying in their own excrement and filth. Among the dead they discovered emaciated children. In the cleanup that followed, the Allied troops forced SS officers to dig trenches and fill them with the nameless bodies. Bulldozers leveled the mass graves. Finally they set fire to the filthy typhus-filled barracks. On April 11, 1945, when U.S. Army troops liberated Boelke Kaserne, they found piles of naked bodies under the staircases—when a prisoner died, the guards stripped him and threw him beneath the stairs, like stacked wood.

A U.S. congressional delegation inspected three concentration camps in May 1945. At Dora they found piles of dead bodies and thousands of dying inmates. One representative said of the SS: "They reached depths of human degradation beyond belief and constituted no less than organized crime against the civilization and humanity for which swift, certain, and adequate punishment should be meted out to all those who were responsible." The survivors called Dora the "Hell of all concentration camps."[11]

Walter Farr, a member of the First Army, came in with the Dora liberation force. At Nordhausen he saw "a series of long sheds with wooden racks reaching to the ceiling. On the racks were laid hundreds upon hundreds of men, shrunken with starvation, wanting to die." Farr described them as "living flesh—not men." As he wrote, hundreds were still dying under Allied care every day. Piles of bodies awaited cremation but the camp had run short of coal. Not enough labor existed to dig the graves, so the bodies lay rotting. Although the SS attempted to erase the evidence, "whitewash could not obliterate the blood stains nor putty conceal the holes where the 'hanging hooks' had been removed." According to Farr, a camp designed to hold 8,000 inmates housed 59,000 at the end. Germans living near the camps told Farr that they "had no idea that such things were being done." "But Nordhausen young men, out for a walk with their girls, used to go near the 'extermination center,' point out the prisoners, and crack jokes at them."[12]

No one knows exactly how many inmates went through the Dora/Nordhausen Mittelbau Camp. The International Tracing Service has determined that the average strength at Dora was 15,000. At least forty additional sub-*Kommandos* existed, ranging in strength from 15 to 7,000, with an average of 500. Reports indicate at least 200 women worked in the Mittelbau.[13]

When Dora became an independent concentration camp with numerous subcamps, it had responsibility for 32,000 prisoners. In the last months—after the arrival of the evacuation transports from Auschwitz and Gross-Rosen—the number of prisoners grew to 40,000. Probably about 60,000 persons passed through Dora during its existence. The best estimate is that about 22 percent, or 13,000, died in that short period. The death lists show 56 percent died from unknown causes, 13 percent from tuberculosis, 9 percent from pneumonia, 8 percent from exhaustion, 7 percent from diarrhea, and 3.5 percent from beatings. Most prisoners delivered to the hospital were already dead, which made it difficult for the doctors to ascertain the cause of death. It should be understood that the figure 13,000 dead quoted above comes from official records. Experts believe that easily another 5,000 people died without death certificates or without being recorded.[14]

It is perhaps understandable that a government cannot give the needs of workers highest priority in wartime. Certainly, the foreign laborers who volunteered to work in Nazi Germany or who were forced to work there lived a most unpleasant existence. It is also true that those picked for work *Kommandos* in the concentration camps were seldom envied by their fellow inmates. But in the history of the Nazi concentration camps there is probably no place of labor that bears the same stigma of wretchedness as Dora/ Nordhausen. There the slaves labored to implement some of Germany's greatest wartime scientific experiments, but they labored late and in vain, for the products they yielded made little impact on the war.

The laborers of Dora might have made a difference if Hitler had not so thoroughly depleted the ranks of Germany's scientists—particularly physicists—in the 1930s. He dismissed 25 percent of Germany's physicists from their posts in 1932–1933 because they were Jewish. The group of dismissed Jews included twenty Nobel Prize winners. Hitler's racial policies always came first—they even took precedence over winning the war. He used Jewish bodies to aid in the war effort but not Jewish minds.[15]

The destruction of the slave laborers cannot be attributed solely to a war-generated need for speed. The Nazi government marked certain classes of human beings as available to be worked to death. Goebbels thought that exterminating prisoners by labor was ideal—killing two birds with one stone.

THE CZECHOSLOVAKIAN CENTER

TEREZIN/THERESIENSTADT: THE FORTRESS TOWN OF PRETENSE

Heinrich Himmler converted the nondescript military fortress town of Terezin into Theresienstadt—the one truly unique German concentration camp facility. Terezin became a symbol of pretense and games that allowed the world, the Germans, and the Jews to convince themselves that the Nazis held to a code of human decency after all. Himmler created his model ghetto in Theresienstadt; and visiting International Red Cross commissions obligingly gave it their stamp of approval. Terezin was one of the Nazis' great public relations effort—characterized by a complex pattern of "lies, deceit, camouflage, swindle, falsehood, ruse."[1]

Terezin acquired its infamy during World War II when the Nazis created there and in nearby Litomerice the largest complex of Nazi camps in Czechoslovakia. They selected for the core of that complex one of Czechoslovakia's best preserved fortresses. It was at Terezin that the Nazis destroyed the bulk of the proud Prague Jewish community, one of the oldest in Europe. It was at Terezin that the Nazis made Czechoslovakia *Judenrein.* So one begins one's Terezin journey in Prague.

For seven centuries the Prague Jews experienced tension, brief expulsions, separation into ghettos, anti-Semitic laws, plague; but still, the community flourished. The state completed the process of legal emancipation of the Jews by 1867 and abolished the Prague ghetto. In 1896, because of unhealthy conditions, the municipality pulled down the old Jewish quarter, leaving only the important historic sites. Most Jews from the area dispersed throughout the city. Many historic buildings with priceless collections remain today, veiled by the melancholy beauty of a world belonging to the past and marked by the tragic fate of its creators' descendants. Their memory is consecrated in the Pinkas Synagogue which has been converted into a monument to the 77,207 Prague Jewish victims of Nazism.[2]

The buildings constituting the famous State Jewish Museum of Prague are located in the old Jewish ghetto area, a medieval enclave in the heart of the city. Recently, on the edge of the old ghetto, businessmen erected an elegant Intercontinental Hotel with a Penthouse Restaurant. Sitting in the restaurant,

234

staring through the vista windows, one looks down upon the entire ghetto—a stunning confrontation of the new and optimistic with the very old and desolate.

A strange tale accounts for the greatest collection of Jewish art, quantitatively and qualitatively, ever brought together—housed today in the Prague Jewish Museum. During the war some Nazi party intellectuals made plans to combine the annihilation of a people with the memorialization of their artifacts. Determined to establish a Museum of Extinct People to commemorate the extermination of a decadent race, they set up the Institute for Jewish History in Munich, gathered together groups of Jewish scholars, and ordered them to research and record the huge collections of Jewish material amassed from the occupied countries.

The knowledgeable Jews painstakingly catalogued the treasures: gold and silver ornaments, vestments, pictures, books, manuscripts, and ritual objects. Each piece of loot, identified, numbered, and noted for its town of origin, was later stored in Prague. The museum dream became a reality in one of the oldest Jewish centers of Europe—after the destruction of the Third Reich. The collection includes more than 200,000 art objects.

The postwar Communist takeover of Czechoslovakia introduced a period of stagnation for the Jews remaining in the country. Under the state's general antireligious policy Jewish religious activity ceased (until 1965). For example, the state allowed worship services in only two of Prague's nine synagogues. Peculiarly, the Czechoslovakian government in 1950 created the Jewish State Museum, using the other seven synagogues as exhibition halls and warehouses. At great cost, they restored the historic buildings and made the museum into one of Czechoslovakia's major tourist attractions. But so few Jews remain in that hostile country that most museum officials and guides are Gentiles.[3]

The story of the wandering Torahs deserves special mention. More than 1,500 abandoned Torahs lay in piles in Prague for two decades following the war. With the cooperation of the Czech government, a Jewish group arranged for the acquisition and transfer of those Torahs to the Westminster Synagogue in London. The scroll committee cleaned and refurbished the Torahs, researched each one's history, devised a system of cataloguing, and divided the scrolls into five grades. They worked diligently at repairing the middle grades, and sent the best ones to universities and synagogues across the world as sacred memorials. And the work still continues in London. At age twenty-one, Shel Bassel bends over his craft as one of the youngest *sofers* or Torah scribes in the world. His task is so exacting that he cannot work for more than a few hours at a time. As he writes, he repeats: "I am writing the name of God for the Holiness of his Name." He can erase mistakes in the scroll with a knife and pumice stone, unless it is an error in the writing of any of God's names. In that case the parchment must be discarded and the Torah repaired.

American Jews heard of the abandoned Torah scrolls. A prominent businessman in North Boston gave a donation to the Westminster Synagogue in return for the loan of a scroll. Irving Brudnick waited at Logan Airport with Rabbi Liebschutz to receive the Czech scroll. As they unwound it, the clear outlines of a bootmark emerged. Written at the bottom, a simple line: "Austerlitz-Slavkov," dated 1890.

Rabbi Hugo Stransky left Czechoslovakia in 1936 and came to New York where he served as the spiritual leader of Temple Beth-Israel for twenty years. Scroll 66 from a synagogue in Bohemia finally arrived at Temple Israel. At the first ceremony the old rabbi, moved by the faces of the people in front of him, wiped the tears from his eyes. Before him was the very Torah he had used in his first congregation in Europe! Seated in the sanctuary was another member of the early congregation, Mrs. Vera Bunde, who survived a concentration camp while her husband and children perished. When asked what the occasion meant to her, she replied simply: "I am here."[4]

The preserved buildings in Prague are as important as the collections they hold. The legendary *Old-New Synagogue,* the oldest in use in Europe today, was erected in 1275 as a twin-nave hall in the Cistercian Gothic style. It is the most significant monument in the museum complex. The synagogue's roof rises into a peak of carved slated material. The light in the two-aisled early Gothic hall is dim, giving the interior a misty appearance. The eighteenth-century flag of the Prague Jews hangs from the wall.

By a stroke of fate, the Jewish Town Hall, the oldest in Europe, has been preserved. A wooden spire and cupola cap the structure. At the spire top is the famous Town Clock with its Hebrew numerals and hands that run backward. The planners created the hall in Renaissance style. It acquired its Rococo likeness in 1765. The adjacent *High Synagogue* was originally a part of the Town Hall; its rectangular hall is in the Renaissance style of 1568. In the nineteenth century the Jews separated the synagogue from the Town Hall and gave it a new staircase and a street entrance. The Ark inside is done in an almost Chinese style, reminiscent of some interiors of Schöenbrun—light, delicate, airy—in sharp contrast to the heavy solemn bareness of the Old-New Synagogue. The High Synagogue contains valuable art and artifacts, including the guild sign of the Jewish *Ceremonial Hall* built in 1906 and now the museum administrative center. The last time I was there, the hall held a comprehensive but numbing art exhibit from the museum's major gallery of artists who had been imprisoned in Terezin, plus the incredible collection of children's drawings from the camp.

The unforgettable *Old Jewish Cemetery* contains 12,000 gravestones and the tombs of men whose memory is still alive today and for whom Prague was the "crown of the world." The cemetery was used until 1787. It has far more graves than gravestones, however, because the community was forced to bury its dead in several layers in the small area allotted by the city for a cemetery. The Hebrew inscriptions on the gravestones, including the name of the deceased, the deceased's father's name, the death date, and burial date, provide an important historical source. The larger portions of the inscriptions describe poetically the family's grief and the good deeds of the deceased. The oldest gravestone (1439) is that of the poet Avigdor Karo. The legendary scholar and pedagogue Rabbi Löw, who died in 1609, is also buried here. He is connected to the legend about the creation of an artificial man—the *Golem.* Visitors come from all over the world to place small stones on his grave.

The Jews installed the *Pinkas Synagogue* in the Horowitz family house at the end of the fifteenth century and finished the reconstruction in 1535. It borders the cemetery on the southern side. After World War II the synagogue was designated a memorial to Nazi victims. In 1955 the names of the Prague victims were inscribed on the walls, and next to the Ark, in large black letters, the name of each concentration camp.

In the years 1590–1592 the Jews built in Renaissance style the *Maisel Synagogue* for Mordechai Maisel, the *primas* of the Prague Jewish town. After the great fire in the Jewish area in 1689, they rebuilt the synagogue in Baroque style. It was reconstructed one more time, in neo-Gothic style in the 1890s. The interior is soaring, delicate, full of light. It houses a magnificent silver collection including Torah crowns and extensions, Torah shields, Bohemian glass, candlesticks, spice boxes, goblets, Seder bowls, pitchers. The Jews built the *Spanish Synagogue,* with its stunning exterior, in 1867 in the Moorish style, and later decorated it with stucco ornaments. It contains a vast and rich synagogue textile exposition with draperies, Torah covers, embroidered material. Finally there is the *Klaus Synagogue*, built in Baroque style at the end of the seventeenth century, with its beautiful barrel vault.

The Jewish State Museum cannot be replicated anywhere in Europe. Its collections are rivaled only by Jerusalem's Israel Museum and perhaps the New York Jewish Museum. The museum displays a rich culture now gone—along with its people. The Nazis ripped up the history and destroyed the Czech Jews, creating Terezin as their first stop on the journey to destruction.[5]

SS Colonel Heydrich established a Jewish concentration camp in Terezin on November 24, 1941. The SS expelled the Czech population from the town, transformed it into a transient concentration camp, and officially labeled it, for propaganda purposes, a ghetto. Terezin became the largest camp on Czechoslovakian territory. In the same area, in 1944, the SS established an auxiliary branch of Flossenbürg at Litomerice. Prisoners from Terezin constructed an underground factory with the cover name of "Richard" in the vicinity of the Litomerice camp, on the site of a former limestone mine.[6]

Himmler referred to Terezin as a model camp. It contained all the

The Terezin Ghetto today, used as a Czechoslovakian military barracks.

Protectorate Jews, plus privileged Jews from Germany, Austria, Holland, and Denmark. In that "luxury camp" prisoners were not actually exterminated. They died instead of hunger, torture, beatings, and disease. At one point nearly 60,000 individuals were concentrated in a town with a "normal" living space for 7,000. Whenever the authorities wished to reduce the congestion, they mercilessly dispatched large convoys to the gas chambers of Auschwitz and Majdanek. 200,000 people, most of them Jewish, went through the three-camp complex—the ghetto, Small Fortress, and Litomerice/Richard. Only a third lived to see the end of the war. 34,000 Jews perished in Terezin from "natural causes." As the ghetto became a funnel to the killing centers, the Nazis sent 83,000 Jews, including small children, to the extermination camps in the east. The Russian Army liberated the complex on May 8, 1945.[7]

Today Terezin has reverted to its status as a fortress town, holding a contingent of the Czechoslovakian Army garrisoned in the barracks where so many Jews starved to death. The dark ramparts separate the town from the countryside and from the outlines of the Bohemian Mountain range in the distance. Terezin's center is a rectangular square enclosed by trees—rebuilt by the Jews thirty-five years ago to impress the Red Cross Commission. The

Church of the Resurrection borders the square, with two military head-quarter buildings guarding both sides. Old apartment houses line the streets and cast their shadows over them, leaving precious little room for the sun and no room at all for trees. The neatness of the dun-colored buildings is very like that of army and prison barracks.

Terezin is no longer a camp but traces of its infamous past remain. The authorities have fenced in the ash deposit on the bank of the Ohre. The plat-form from which the Jews stepped into the death trains is used now for civilian travel. The hotel that housed the Nazi leaders and guests serves the few tourists who wish to stay there. And the children's pavilion, a highlight of the farce, remains, decrepit and rusted, in the park. The café where the Jews drank brown-water coffee is a restaurant, doing a bustling business with Czech soldiers. The scene beyond the moats and bunkers is dirty yellow, seedy and grim—in contrast to the blue mountains and serene rolling hills in the distance. But Terezin has a new element—the tourists. Hundreds of thousands come to visit the Big Fortress, the Small Fortress, and Richard.

The Small Fortress seems to be a tourist highlight, especially for children. It remains today much as it was then, but without the SS and the prisoners. With its moats, catacombs, tunnels, and bunker cells, it fascinates the young. Adults, however, find it difficult to avoid images of the decades of torture and killing in that space. A walk through the fortress takes in the crowded communal cells, the solitary and torture cells, the bunker infirmaries, the barber shop, the kitchen, the delousing equipment, the bridge to the massive fortress construction, the ugly mortuary, the underground corridor to the execution place, the women's yard, the scaffold, the mass graves, the SS swimming pool, the SS cinema, the cells for special prisoners. Actually the whole place is terrible.

In 1945 the Czech Republic built a symbolic national cemetery in front of the Small Fortress to commemorate the fate of the thousands who perished there and in the ghetto. Every year on the anniversary of liberation the Czechs hold peace meetings and ceremonies at that symbolic spot.

About a kilometer outside Terezin lies the monument cemetery park, whose highlight is the white crematorium building. The area includes the Russian cemetery, the Alley of Nations, the symbolic graves and small monuments, and the cemetery for 8,903 ghetto dead in 217 mass graves and 1,250 individual graves. The crematorium is the most modern remaining in any camp. Housed in what looks like a new apartment building, it has white internal walls in dramatic contrast to the black gleaming ovens, incinerators, and ironwork. The four ovens are of the most advanced and mechanized design. Each could accommodate from two to four bodies. The building is so constructed that the furnace area is light, "cheerful," and airy. The usual medical/disinfection rooms are attached. It is an especially ugly place, partly because of its stark modernity.

The Terezin crematoria.

At the Terezin Museum the government has sponsored significant art festivals. The most important one, held in 1972–1973, was called *Kunst in Theresienstadt 1941–1945.* The collection is extensive and the work stunning. The faces and scenes that stare out from those pictures tell of a life much different from that presented to the Red Cross commission. There, in a dark tiny room with cracked ceilings, sits a ninety-year-old woman playing solitaire. And over there lie three emaciated skeletons on their three-tiered bunk. Here is a picture of an attic crowded to such an extent that nothing can be seen but a mass of miserable people. There are portraits of loved ones and dignitaries, and pictures of little children. Over there is a scene of a burial party and another of a transport line. And then the many pictures of costume designs for the various theatrical productions, and even sketches of the set designs. It is a critical collection, for it also includes manuscripts, books, poems, and the scores of music compositions created in Terezin.[8]

In 1977 an unusual message came howling out of that fortress abyss. This message from the grave was in the form of an opera, *The Emperor of Atlantis,* written in Terezin in 1944 by the distinguished Czech composer Viktor Ullman and a twenty-five-year-old librettist, Peter Kien. The Nazis encouraged the original work, but when it was well into rehearsal they banned it because of its antiwar sentiments and its thinly disguised satire of Hitler. Before being shipped to their deaths in Auschwitz a month later,

Ullmann and Kien were able to hide the manuscript with a fellow inmate who survived, Dr. H. G. Adler.

In 1973 Dr. Adler interested a conductor, a young Englishman named Kerry Woodward, in the reconstruction of the opera. Woodward pieced together the torn and ragged manuscript, typed on the back of inmate arrival forms, and he conducted the opera's world premier in Amsterdam in December 1975. The American premier opened April 28, 1977, in San Francisco, with the English translation by the American poet Aaron Kramer. The Brooklyn Academy of Music's New Opera Theatre staged its version the next week. Performances were also scheduled in Paris, Jerusalem, Mexico City, and Germany. Woodward spoke recently of the opera's two strong, deep elements—desperation and hope. Reviewers have written of the work's "shattering impact." Ullmann and Kien, like "dying men whose last words cannot be denied," converted their agony "into a universal hypnotically theatrical drama that exalts death as the ultimate liberation."[9]

I found the San Francisco production an artistic masterpiece, but almost too much to bear when one carries mental pictures of Terezin. The opera, an ingenious allegorical fable, centers on Death. The Kingdom of Atlantis is a joyless world whose people have been hopelessly subjugated by the Emperor, who speaks to them only through a loudspeaker. In order to recycle corpses into phosphorus, the Emperor declares universal war and orders Death to lead it. In protest, Death, personified by an old military veteran, abdicates. And, a singer explains; "A very strange disease has broken out; no one can die, no matter how ill or in pain."

Unable to kill each other, a boy and a girl from enemy camps fall in love instead. The chorus pleads: "Death, where is thy sting?" Death's sardonic aria about the good old days with Hannibal and the cruel Attila the Hun is sung to a saucy dance step. On a stage designed as an expressive wasteland and filled with the debris of flight (old mattresses and empty trunks), the singers and drummers move with irony through macabre songs and a goose-step roll.

After failing to convince his people that immortality is desirable, the Emperor begs Death's return: "Without you, we cannot live." Death resumes his work only when the Emperor agrees to become his first victim. The opera closes with a chorale, a final hymn of praise to Death sung to the familiar music of Luther's "A Mighty Fortress is Our God": "Death, our worthy, honored guest, into our hearts descending. Lift all life's burdens from our breast; lead us to rest, our sorrows ending."

The Austrian Emperor Joseph II built Terezin in 1780 and named it after his mother, the Empress Maria Theresa. It consisted of the Great Fortress and the Small Fortress, lying on the Ohre River. A tightly designed fortress town, Terezin was considered unconquerable. It never had to meet the test, however, for hostile armies bypassed it. The government converted the Small Fortress into a military and political prison and, after the 1848 revolution, imprisoned several Prague revolutionaries there. The Czechs turned the so-called Large Fortress—the whole town of Terezin—into an army garrison, and abolished its fortress status in 1882.

After the 1914 Sarajevo assassination, the Austrian government jailed at Terezin several of the murderers, including the ringleader, Gavrilo Princip, who died of tuberculosis in 1916. During World War I, Terezin became the largest Czech POW camp. The prisoners' bodies were buried in an open field known as the Russian cemetery.

Under the Czechoslovakian Republic the Small Fortress remained a military prison and a penitentiary for dangerous criminals. When the Nazis occupied Bohemia and Moravia, they arrested their opponents and jailed them in the Small Fortress. It took on the character of a transit prison whose inmates either died or were sent to German camps. During the war years the Nazis tortured thousands to death in the Small Fortress: members of the resistance movement, playwrights, composers, outstanding scientists, physicians, and politicians. Included in the prison after 1941 were Jews from the Great Fortress whom the SS wished to punish. As the number of inmates increased, the Small Fortress assumed the more formal features of a concentration camp. In 1945 about 5,500 prisoners resided there. From June 1940 to May 1945, 35,000 prisoners passed through. Twenty-five hundred died in the bunkers.[10]

Although the Great Fortress, as the town was known, was formally abolished in 1882, Terezin remained a grim garrison whose chief features were deep moats, concrete bunkers, fortress walls, and huge gray barracks. It was laid out as a large square with all streets intersecting each other at right angles. The population remained static, and "architectural and technical progress bypassed the town as had the hostile armies in the past."[11]

The old dark dismal homes were indistinguishable from the barracks. Water mains were not laid until 1930, and then only for the barracks and a few new buildings. No industries located in Terezin. Once it had had a population of 8,000 soldiers and peasants. In 1940, looking very little different from the town of a hundred years earlier, it housed 3,700 people living in 219 homes, plus the barracks with a normal capacity of 3,500 soldiers. It was this town that became the famous ghetto.

Pre-Ghetto Phase

In Western and Central Europe the Germans approached the solution of the Jewish problem in a different manner than in Poland and Russia. They used prohibitions and laws rather than public massacres—hoping to allay

Jewish fears. The Germans moved slowly but continuously in their attack. The position of the Jews "was not unlike that of a man in a sealed room with water flowing in all the time." Large-scale deportation from Bohemia and Moravia did not begin until the autumn of 1941.[12]

The campaign against the Jews in the Protectorate can be divided into two periods. In the first months after they seized power the Germans concentrated on economic liquidation. The second stage began in the summer of 1939 when the Nazis made an agreement with Russia to repatriate German minorities and resettle them in the newly acquired Czech territory. To make room for those Germans, the Jews had to be expelled.

When the Nazis proclaimed the Protectorate over Bohemia-Moravia, three main Jewish organizations existed in Prague—the Supreme Council of the Union of Jewish Communities, the Prague Jewish Community, and the Joint Social Commission. They cared for the thousands of refugees from Germany, Austria, and the Sudentenland, and played an important role in Jewish emigration. Two years later those same groups drew up the deportation lists for the Theresienstadt ghetto.

The Prague Council, which held superficial jurisdiction over Czechoslovakian Jewry, meant to avoid the fate of the Polish Jews. At first, its policies seemed to offer positive results. The leaders managed to persuade the Germans to use Jewish labor within the boundaries of Czechoslovakia and no transports left for Poland. In September 1941, however, a regime of terror began with the appointment of Heydrich as acting protector of Bohemia-Moravia.

The Prague Council invented the idea of a lifesaving ghetto. It asked the Germans to set up a ghetto within the boundaries of the Protectorate. The Germans felt a Prague ghetto would keep the Jews too visible to the outside world. After considering several Bohemian and Moravian towns, the Germans finally selected Terezin, renaming it Theresienstadt. When the Nazis announced an "autonomous ghetto" for Jews in Terezin, the Prague Jewish leaders expressed relief. They looked upon the plan as a means of rescuing Jews from deportation to unknown places. The Germans proclaimed Theresienstadt a model ghetto—but used it as a station to Auschwitz. It came to be called "a funnel with only one hole"; but in Prague it was pictured as a protected place for Jews. Czech Jews bribed Gestapo agents for the privilege of moving there.[13]

Before the first departures for Theresienstadt, the Jewish Community Organization set up a special Department G to procure supplies. The leaders drew up plans for the organization and self-sufficiency of the ghetto and readied a work team to prepare the barracks. On November 24, 1941, the first transport to Theresienstadt gathered at the Prague railroad station, a work squad of 342 young men. The opening of the gates to the Jewish volunteers marked the beginning of the history of the Theresienstadt ghetto. The Jews of Prague remained hopeful. The Prague community contributed money and energy to refurbish the old barracks. Playing their part well, the Nazis made masterful use of the normal human yearning for safety and autonomy. They notified the leaders that the ghetto would have its own currency bearing the effigy of Moses holding the Tablets of the Law, and its own technical, legal, and financial departments. Those first transports became symbolic:

They were the earliest puppets in a gigantic play, staged by the Nazis at the expense of more than 150,000 people of Jewish origin who, within the forty months to follow, were sentenced to serve some time in this "privileged ghetto."[14]

October 1942–June 1942: A Czech Retreat

By the end of 1941 the 7,365 Czech Jews in Theresienstadt were living like prisoners in the barracks, forbidden any association with the other 7,000 residents. Life in the model ghetto soon changed.

On December 4 the Germans created a Jewish camp administration composed of Jakub Edelstein, head of the Council of Elders who received the official title Elder of the Jews, and thirteen council members. The Germans identified the council's first priority as the organization and administration of the ghetto with all its attending problems. The council tried to mitigate the distress caused by the Germans and to enable the maximum number of persons to survive the war:

In doing so, the Jewish camp administration was faced with tasks more complex and difficult than those carried out by the administrative machinery of any modern state. Yet these tasks had to be mastered regardless of the fact that external pressure affected the inhabitants created abnormal internal conditions which greatly hampered the work of the camp administration.[15]

The original housing conditions were strikingly inadequate, and in time they disintegrated. Fifty persons in the Sudeten barracks occupied one room, which under normal conditions housed twelve soldiers. Twenty to forty women shared each room in the women's barracks. The Germans placed children under twelve with their mothers, and housed the older ones with father or mother according to their sex. Many male teenagers lived in the stables. The SS allowed the children in children's homes to visit their parents only on Sundays.

The scarcities encountered by the Jewish administration made life virtually impossible. Bunks, vehicles, medicine, equipment, cook houses, offices, and stoves were nonexistent. Because of inadequate cooking equipment, people began to starve. Decrepit funeral hearses became the sole form of transportation. Jews, harnessed to the worn-out carriages, transported old people, living and dead, as well as supplies.

On January 5, 1942, an event occurred that changed the basic nature of Theresienstadt. Notification came that a transport of 1,000 persons would leave Theresienstadt in January for Riga. So Theresienstadt would no longer be the journey's end for the Jews. The Nazis dispatched transports to the east from January 1942 until October 1944. Thus the ghetto became one of the links in the chain of concentration camps: "a genuine floodgate between two different levels of the same river, of which one was represented by those Jews still expecting deportation while the other was represented by the death camps in Poland."[16] By the middle of 1942 the Nazis had removed all Czechoslovakian Jews from their homes, including the officials of the Jewish community of Prague. In July of that year they evacuated all the civilian residents of the town of Theresienstadt, readying it for the next phase.

The Arrival of the Germans and Austrians

The special classes of Jews remaining alive in Germany posed a problem to the Nazis. Hitler had declared that Germany was *Judenrein,* but it was 1942 and that order had not yet been fulfilled. SS Colonel Heydrich and Himmler went to work on the problem. They set their sights on Theresienstadt, which had already received publicity as a "model ghetto." Surely, then, it would prove salable to privileged German and Austrian Jews.

In a conference on the Final Solution on January 20, 1942, Heydrich announced that all Reich Jews over sixty-five would be sent to an old people's ghetto and allowed to die a natural death. He added a second privileged group, Jewish war veterans who had been seriously disabled or who had received the Iron Cross First Class. Later he made other categories eligible—prominent Jews whose disappearance in a killing center might cause alarm; Jews married to Aryans who had lost their exemptions; and privileged Jews willing to buy their way into a model setting. Heydrich expected that the number of Jews in those categories would total 85,000. The old Jews would die quietly without much fuss. And the war veterans would be tucked away so that no one could intervene in their behalf.[17]

The Germans promoted Theresienstadt as a spa for aged and privileged Jews. In fact, it was known in Germany as "Theresienbad." Because of its aura of safety and privilege, many Jews purchased the right to go there. "They had signed fraudulent contracts for accommodation in the ghetto for old persons and had paid tens of thousands of marks for the privilege of going to Theresienstadt. Old German Jews brought with them their top hats, tails, lace dresses, and parasols."

The ones to profit from the prisoners' unrealistic approach to life, their credulity, and political naiveté, were the Nazis who did not have to exert themselves to delude their victims. Elderly invalids, arriving in what they expected to be a comfortable Old Age Home for Jews, innocently asked for rooms with a southern exposure.[18]

Within one year, 1942, almost 90,000 Jews were sent to Theresienstadt to occupy the normal living space of 7,000. By the end of 1942 over 85,000 Jews were crowded into the ugly quarters, "wasting away or being readied for Auschwitz."[19]

From Ghetto to Transit Center:
The Organization and Administration of Theresienstadt

Unknown to the leaders of the Theresienstadt Jewish community, January 1942 marked the beginning of a new phase that would last until the middle of 1944. During that period deportations would be very much a part of ghetto life, and would transform Theresienstadt into nothing more than a transit center. The Germans, however, kept their secret plan from the Jews and ordered them to get about the business of organizing a normal ghetto. Three tasks faced the Council of Elders: to prepare the town for the reception of new arrivals; to reorganize the administration to handle the influx of people; and to provide housing and health care for an expanding group of older, sick people. The new arrivals were the so-called privileged persons, most of them sixty-five years old or war invalids. Those who limped into the station with their luggage believed they were being resettled in an old-age home. The Germans soon destroyed their illusions by taking their belongings from them and throwing them into lofts or small cubbyholes.

In July 1942 further transports arrived, including eleven from Bohemia and Moravia and forty-six from Germany and Austria. That influx increased the population by 25,000. At the same time, transports began to leave for the east. On July 1, 21,000 prisoners lived in the ghetto, and on July 13 there were 43,000 prisoners. In August transports carrying 13,000 persons reached the ghetto and three transports of 1,000 each left for the east. In September 18,000 persons arrived and 13,000 were deported. In October 5,000 arrived and 9,800 left. On December 31, 1942, 49,400 prisoners were living in the ghetto. In January and February of 1943 the purge of Bohemian and Moravian Jews was completed with the arrival of five transports. On February 1, 1943, a transport of 1,000 deportees left for Auschwitz. Then the deportations halted for seven months.[20]

With the arrival of the new people and the deportation of the old, the ghetto population and structure changed and national rivalries sprang up. By January 1943 German and Austrian Jews equaled the Czech Jews in number, and the population shift necessitated changes in the composition of the Council of Elders. In January 1943 Edelstein, a Czech Jew who had been chairman of the council, was replaced by the Nazis with a member of the German-Austrian group, a Dr. Eppstein.

The Jewish Council faced a continuous problem—housing scarcity. The problem was made all the more difficult by the need to conceal it from the Germans lest they remedy it by ordering additional deportations to the east. The camp administration reduced individual dwelling space, separated married couples, and segregated the sexes. They introduced three-tier bunks and converted lofts into rooms. Old and sick people, the primary inhabitants of the lofts, lay on the bare floors in misery and squalor. Many died of pneumonia, diarrhea, and undernourishment. In November 1942, 988 lavatories were available for 53,000 people—that is 54 persons to one lavatory. In August 1942 the living area figure of 1.6 square meters per person included all the additional lavatory, cookhouse, and washhouse space. To clarify the problem even further: the average density of the population of Prague was 5,500 persons per square kilometer; but if Prague had been as densely populated as Theresienstadt, its population would have totaled 22.5 million, instead of 1 million!

Food was also a major problem. The prisoners' diet consisted primarily of moldy bread and rotting potatoes. The council opened a cookhouse for children only, where the food was better and more varied. Eventually the acute food shortage forced the council to introduce a rationing system whereby the biggest rations were allotted to workers doing heavy labor—their increase came at the expense of the aged and the infirm. Thus the food shortage caused enormous suffering, particularly among older people:

Starving elderly men and women begged for watery soup made of synthetic lentil or pea powder, and dug for food in the garbage heaps rotting in the courtyards of the barracks. At a certain period the main characteristics of the Ghetto were a combined stench of decay and chlorine from the latrines, and groups of aged people shuffling through the streets until they collapsed and died of starvation.[21]

The mortality rate rose quickly. By September 1942 the daily deaths averaged 131. In September 3,941 persons died. Many times a day the residents watched the carts loaded with plank coffins passing through the streets on their way to the mass graves. To ease the situation, the Germans completed the crematorium outside the town in September 1942. It was capable of handling 190 corpses a day.

As the ghetto became a real town with a semblance of administrative rules and regulations, the Germans required it to create a productive economic area to manufacture commodites for itself and goods ordered by the Germans for export. It set up workshops for engineering and metalwork, woodworking, manufacture of furniture and huts, paper and cardboard processing, production of lamp shades and artificial flowers for export, splitting of mica for the war industry, boot and shoe repairs, bandage manufacture, a laundry, and a bakery. The prisoners were also in charge of an extensive German livestock project that included horses, pigs, sheep, goats, rabbits, poultry, and bees.

Once the Germans sealed off the ghetto and it became a productive economic unit, they permitted some vestiges of civil and religious life. Prisoners could marry, and limited religious services were allowed. Included among the population at Theresienstadt were some Protestants and Catholics, even a few nuns and priests, and they also were permitted to hold services.

Standing in the background but always exercising a heavy hand were the camp commandants. SS Colonel Dr. Siegfried Seidl, the first commandant, left Theresienstadt in 1943 for Bergen-Belsen and later was transferred to Budapest, where he organized the deportation of the Hungarian Jews. After the war the Austrian government hanged him. His successor, SS Major Anton Burger, a former Austrian schoolmaster, hated the Czechs, tortured the Jews, and visibly enjoyed being present at the deportation proceedings. SS Major Karl Rahm succeeded him as the last commandant. Later the Allies sentenced him to death and hanged him.

Theresienstadt, like all towns and societies, had its social structure in the form of a pyramid of many layers. The old and the sick fell into the bottom layer. They received the least food, the worst rooms, and the poorest service. Because the black market flourished there, for a time the most privileged members of the community were the smugglers. Later those who had some contact with food such as the cooks or bakers became the privileged class. In the more sophisticated stage the power of the bureaucracy increased and the ghetto emerged as a community with a ruling class, a middle class, and a slave labor element. But no society like Theresienstadt could remain stable because of the deportations. All privileges were temporary and almost all high officials eventually died in Auschwitz. Nevertheless, unlike at most concentration camps, a measure of self-administration and even normal cultural life did exist at Theresienstadt.

From January 1942 to October 1944 the reality of the deportations hung heavily over every aspect of the ghetto. Altogether, sixty-three transports totaling 86,934 persons left Theresienstadt; and only 5 percent of the deportees survived. Each transport pushed the inhabitants of Theresienstadt into a desperate state of mind. The threat often produced wishful thinking and self-deception, with many Jews trying to ignore the spectre of Auschwitz.[22]

Each time Berlin ordered the organization of a transport, the commandant instructed the Jewish Council that a specific number of persons must be deported on a certain day. Who would go was left up to the council. The Germans issued general directives giving the size of the transport and a list of the exempted persons. Those exemptions changed from week to week. Age, once a reason for exemption, became a reason for deportation. Youth, at one time a reason for deportation, later became a reason for exemption. And so it changed.

The preparation of the transports raised agonizing moral dilemmas. Deporting the sick and old people, for example, violated the Fifth Commandment, but it also meant saving, for a time, the healthy, strong, and young. One survivor, Zdenka Fantlowa, described the deportations as coming suddenly, like a natural disaster: "A cataclysm had struck the city, and within a short time, it had swallowed 25,000 sacrifices. The streets were transformed into human rivers." As she noted, the ghetto never recovered.[23]

Children

Between 1942 and 1945, 15,000 children passed through Theresienstadt. One hundred survived. Those children live on today in the remarkable poems, stories, and paintings they created in that ancient fortress. The children of Theresienstadt never saw butterflies or trees, but they painted them and they wrote about them. After the war the authorities found the drawings and the poems of the children in cardboard folders. The State Jewish Museum in Prague holds the 4,000 drawings.

The Jewish children in Theresienstadt were doomed. The Germans did not take much interest in children when they arrived at the camps, but they tried to prevent all births. When Burger became commandant he insisted that all pregnancies be interrupted. The council finally managed to persuade him to allow a small number of births. Only 207 children were born in the ghetto. The situation faced expectant mothers with a difficult question: Should they bear their children and expose them to a hazardous future or should they have abortions? Most chose the second alternative.

The children arrived in Theresienstadt, sometimes with their parents and sometimes alone. One fourteen-year-old wrote:

When a new child comes
everything seems strange to him.
What? On the ground I have to lie?
Eat black bread, no not I.
I've got to stay? It's dirty here!
The floor—why, look, it's dirt, I fear!
And I am supposed to sleep on it?[24]

The Jewish administration tried to create a bearable situation for the young inmates, but the descriptions left by the children do not picture a livable life. As a teenage girl, Zdena Berger waited at night in her bunk for the bugs—the lines of marching bugs, a "patrol of soldiers" surrounding her fortress. A fifteen-year-old boy, Peter Fischel, who died in Auschwitz in 1944, left his thoughts:

We have gotten used to getting up at 7 o'clock in the morning, standing in a long line at midday, and at 7 o'clock in the evening, holding a plate into which they pour some hot water tasting a trifle salty, or perhaps with a suggestion of coffee, or to get a small portion of potatoes. We have got used to sleeping without beds, to greeting any person wearing a uniform, to keeping off the footpaths. We have got used to have our faces slapped for no reason whatsoever, to getting hit, and to killings. We have got used to seeing people wallowing in their own excrement, to seeing coffins full of dead people, to seeing the sick lying in filth and stench and to seeing the doctors powerless.[25]

The children seemed to pick up the realities of the ghetto. One youngster wrote:

Death after all claims everyone.
You find it everywhere.
It catches up with even those,
Who wear their noses in the air.

And another:

In the ghetto at Terezin,
it looks that way to me,
is a square kilometer of earth
cut off from the world that's free.

A nine-year-old had just one wish:

I'd like to go away alone
where there are other nicer people,
somewhere into the far unknown
where no one kills another.[26]

Peter, a young friend of the teenager Zdena Berger, lay dying in his bunk. Instead of telling fairy tales in the normal sense to calm the boy, Zdena asked him to close his eyes and "I will tell you things you will see one morning when you wake up." She described the bedroom in which Peter would awake with his puppy wagging his tail, and how he would play ball with the puppy on the lawn. "How do you like that morning?" she asked. Peter whispered: "Please. Tell me another morning."[27]

Though the Nazis forbade school, many inmates risked their lives to teach the children. Determined to keep some spark of hope alive in the children, they bribed the guards for crayons and paint, stole paper, and helped the children discover that by writing and by painting they could escape from the misery in which they lived. And that discovery seems to have created a quiet determination within the young people:

The world's a-bloom and seems to smile.
I want to fly but where, how high?
If in barbed wire, things can bloom,
Why couldn't I? I will not die!

And from another:

No, no, my God we want to live!
Not watch our numbers melt away.
We want to have a better world.
We want to work—we must not die.

The children discussed God. One child noted: God "is the chemical in your cells." When hungry or hurt, God leaks out of a child. "The cells break. Just pain or hunger is left and no space for God."[28]

Several children's diaries have been preserved. The following excerpts come from them:

It's terrible here now. There is a great deal of tension among the older, sensible children. They are going to send transports to a new ghetto—into the unknown. And something else, 1,500 children will arrive tonight. They are from Poland. We are making toys and little bags and nets for them, etc. I have diarrhea. Of 27 children, 19 have diarrhea and 16 are sick in bed. Two toilets for 100 children aren't enough, when there is infectious diarrhea in every "Heim." What those toilets look like!!!

The old people's transport, the young people cannot volunteer. Children have to let their old parents go off and can't help them. Why do they want to send these defenceless people away? If they want to get rid of us young people, I can understand that, maybe they are afraid of us, don't want us to give birth to any more Jewish children. But how can these old people be dangerous? If they had to come here to

Terezin, isn't that enough, can't they let them die in peace here? After all, these old people can't hope for anything else.

Everything here is so strange—different from anywhere else in the world. . . . We sleep in bunks and everywhere lots of people are packed in. Husbands and wives do not live together and their children live separate from them in homes, or whatever you call it. . . . I am here completely alone. Without Mommy and Dad and without my big brother whom I miss so much.

I was fourteen years old not long ago and I had never been away from home before. . . . So this is my first trip away from my parents and it's so strange. I should be glad that my folks are not here, and actually it's better that way. They will send me parcels and that's fine and dandy, and soon the war will be over and I'll go home. Everyone said that I'm going for only a couple of months and perhaps I can hold out that long.

I've learned here to appreciate ordinary things that, if we had them when we were still free, we didn't notice at all. Like riding in a bus or a train, or walking freely along the road, to the water, say. Or to go buy ice cream. Such an ordinary thing and it is out of our reach. . . .

I should like to perform some great deed, so that my name would not die out, but I'll not be able to do anything. I know it is stupid, and so I don't tell even Tonicka anything about it. . . .

It is rumoured that they are building gas chambers here. People whisper about it and they really are building something mysterious in the fortification catacombs with airtight doors. They say a duck farm. What for? Might it still be gas? I can't believe it. It is too terrible. Never before have I truly admitted the idea of death, and now gas all of a sudden. It's terrible, even if the longed-for end of the war is coming closer. Oh how stupid I was when I was unhappy over silly little things! For example, that I was unlucky in love, or that I didn't want to get up in the morning. Everything is so petty compared to this thing. Here it is a question of life and we have only one single life. . . . I won't give up. I am not a bug, even though I am just as helpless. If something starts, I'll run away. At least I'll try, after all, what could I lose? It would be better to be shot while trying to escape than to be smothered with gas. . . . I want to live, I want to go back home, for after all I've done nothing to anyone, who why should I die? It's so unjust![29]

One day a transport consisting of 1,500 children between six and fifteen years old arrived in Theresienstadt. The Germans closed off the streets and prohibited the Jews from making any contact with the newcomers. From the station came a heartbreaking procession of children in dirty rags, marching to the brewery for delousing. Here and there a little boy would support a tired little girl. Some looked like adults, others like trapped animals, and still others seemed apathetic or indifferent. All whispered and none smiled. Evidently they had lived through horrors. At the delousing station they suddenly panicked when they saw the notice "Danger Gas," and they had to be dragged into the rooms. One orderly learned from the children their story. They had come from Bialystok where the SS had gassed their parents and many children.

For six weeks the camp authorities kept the children in strict isolation. They transferred nurses and physicians to their encampment to treat their injuries. One day, just as suddenly as it arrived, the transport left again. The healthy children rode away in trucks together with the nursing staff. After the war nothing was heard of the fate of the transport and none of the children or the fifty-three nurses were ever seen again.

The plight of the little Polish children is the basis of a stirring novel by Michael Jacot, *The Last Butterfly*. It is the story of a Czechoslovakian comedian, Antonin Karas—a fussy, peculiar man with unusual spurts of courage. In his last impromptu act on the legitimate stage, in the middle of a bow, for example,

his hair fell over his forehead, and when he straightened up, the hair had placed itself like a dark shadow just over one eye. His body slumped slightly. . . . When he stood up again he was Hitler. The reaction from the audience was slow, but when it came it was mingled with fear. With his left finger posed as a toothbrush mustache, Antonin broke the hushed silence of the theater by raising his right arm in the Nazi salute. . . . Then he said, "That's how high my dog can jump." For a moment there was dead silence. Then it broke. Wave after wave of laughter and applause.

Because of that incident the Nazis send him to Theresienstadt and force him to entertain the children. When the Polish children arrive in the transport and are placed in isolation, the Nazis throw Antonin in with them. Soon he is performing for them, making them laugh and forget. As he and the children move closer to death, Antonin comes to life. He joins the death train with this message:

There once lived a king who hated butchers. So he had every butcher in the kingdom put to death.
Then he began to hate all cyclists, and he started a program to exterminate them all too.
Someone asked, "Why cyclists?"
To which he replied, "For the same reason as butchers."[30]

The Edelstein Brutality

An episode occurred in the ghetto that no survivor forgot. Called the Edelstein brutality after the former council chairman, it began when Dr. Edelstein concealed irregularities he discovered in the population register. No inmate had escaped, but someone had erred in the count of a transport. Commandant Burger found out about Edelstein's concealment. On November 9, 1943, he sent Edelstein to a prison bunker, accused of falsifying daily reports and aiding in the escape of fifty-five prisoners. Later Edelstein and his family were killed in Auschwitz.

To ascertain the total number of prisoners, the Germans determined to take a general census and ordered all inmates to assemble early in the morning. The guards drove 40,000 shaking people outside Theresienstadt to a large field. Because it is impossible to count that many people in an open field, it is conceivable that the incident was meant as a perverse show of Nazi strength. By noon all inmates were assembled on the drill ground, in the rain. Most had not set foot outside the ghetto for years. No one knew what the Germans intended, and some of the more cautious brought along their luggage. The counting continued until 5 P.M. Old people sat on the damp ground and children cried. Confusion expanded when the results would not tally. The guards and SS men disappeared. Darkness fell. The situation disintegrated into total confusion in the drizzling rain. The "desperate and miserable mass of humanity" pressed from the drill ground toward the gates of Theresienstadt. It was now 9 P.M. Collapsed Jews lined the road, but still no order came permitting the prisoners to leave. "It was an ironic situation—all these people pushing, pressing, longing to be allowed to return to the misery of the Ghetto." Finally, a few volunteers succeeded in organizing a return of the prisoners to the ghetto. It took another two hours to empty the grounds. It was learned later that the SS had argued over whether the people should be left there until morning. Although they decided to bring them back, someone forgot to issue the orders to the guards. Three hundred prisoners paid with their lives in the census.[31]

The Farce

The Germans established a grotesque "model ghetto" in Theresienstadt. Their exceptional skill at deception was assisted by the gullibility and optimism of most of the German and Central European Jews. The Jews assumed that they would be able to survive at the price of their property and perhaps a few lives. They made that assumption out of a long history of persecution. They could no more comprehend the horror of the camps than the rest of the world; and they profoundly misjudged Nazism. Obedient to orders, they helped the Germans carry out their aims; and the Germans exploited that attitude, encouraging the victims to dream of salvation. Although the Inquisition and the Crusades had been cruel, the Jews had survived and maintained their vitality. They had, therefore, a realistic faith that they could survive this persecution as they had all the others down through the centuries: not by fighting for their lives, but by having the strength to suffer without physical resistance.

Deportations temporarily ceased in February 1943 and the process of stabilization inaugurated earlier by the Germans resumed. It looked as though the Germans actually were going to use Theresienstadt as a showpiece for the benefit of public opinion throughout the world. Himmler had begun to believe his own propaganda and was willing to conduct diplomatic tours through his "model ghetto." He actually thought that those visits would discount the gas chamber rumors abroad. As late as April 1945 he was using Theresienstadt as his passport to respectability, saying: "Theresienstadt is not a camp in the ordinary sense of the word but a town inhabited by Jews and governed by them, in which every manner of work is to be done." The first tour came in August 1943 when a German Red Cross delegation visited. But no non-Germans had yet been allowed a look.[32]

Three hundred and sixty Danish Jews resided in Theresienstadt. The Danish Jews "lived a relatively charmed life in the camps," particularly in Theresienstadt. When the first group arrived, the commandant and SS officials gave them an official reception and special ceremony. The Danish government followed the internment immediately with inquiries to the Nazi government about the welfare of its citizens. The Nazis allowed the Danish government to send clothing, medicine, and food—which gave the Danish Jews a much higher chance of survival. Eichmann also promised that no Danish Jews in the ghetto would be sent to a killing center.[33]

The Danes continued to place unrelenting pressure on the Nazis for permission to visit their Jews. By 1943 the Germans seemed open to the representations made by the Danish and Swedish Red Cross, and finally agreed that a Danish Red Cross commission would be able to visit in the summer of 1944. It was an important decision, for it made a deep impact on the prisoners.

To prepare for the commission visit, the Germans zealously went to work on a major beautification program—with Jewish labor, of course. The Jews painted the walls, washed the sidewalks, and constructed new barracks. They tore down the fences and barriers, dug flower beds, painted the house fronts, and cleaned the streets. They were transforming a ghetto into a bright and gay town with the appearance of a happy holiday resort. The prisoners reequipped the café, improved the park square, erected a playground for the children, and built concrete benches in the park and sand paths surrounded by flowers. The project took many months.

Soon there were a station, a park, and actual street names. There was a pavilion on the square for the newly created municipal orchestra. High-quality goods stocked the store windows. Prisoners laid green turf throughout Theresienstadt. One bastion became a large sports ground. All buildings went through a final spring cleaning. The Jews upgraded lighting, repaired the roads, refurbished the bank, and transformed the former sports hall into a community center with a stage, prayer hall, library, and verandas. They also renovated large halls in the municipal buildings for artistic and cultural performances. Even the mortuary and the urn repository had face lifts. The walls were whitewashed, the doors replaced, and the entrance spaces bordered with flowers. Outside the urn repository, the commandant ordered the planting of trees and the erection of a monument in memory of the dead Jews. He opened a cemetery with imitation graves.

But still there too much visible misery in the camp and too many people crowded in together to make a good impression on the Danes. What would the visitors think of so many huddled groups of old people? To solve the problem, Rahm deported 12,500 prisoners to the Auschwitz gas chambers. In one transport he sent young and healthy Jews so that the image of Theresienstadt as an old age home would not be spoiled. With a wave of his hand, the town had changed.

Some finishing touches needed to be added to the picture. The commandant supplied the hospitals with white sheets and pillows and gave the nurses new uniforms. Ground-floor apartments were vacated, allocated to elderly prisoners, and furnished with real beds, tables, and chairs. The authorities issued lamp shades, hung curtains, and put flowerpots on the window sills. The words "Boy's School" were painted over the entrance of a former hospital, but a poster added: "Closed during the holidays." The Jews built a mess hall; the waitresses wore spotless white aprons and tables had tablecloths, silverware, and flowers. The commandant even canceled the order requiring the prisoners to salute the SS and the guards.

Then Theresienstadt was ready. When the Red Cross commission members arrived, they would see an unusually tidy and attractive town. To ensure success, the Nazis organized concerts, lectures, and sporting events. They created a sham self-government, for a day, at least. And then that day arrived, June 23, 1944. The Nazis were about to begin Act I of a terrible farce called "Model Jewish Settlement," played out to deceive world opinion.

A diplomat from the Danish Foreign Ministry headed the commission. A Jewish burgermaster, impeccably dressed and furnished with a car and chauffeur, greeted the guests. It was the poor Jewish elder, who a few days earlier had been beaten brutally. He said what he had been told to say and did not talk about the thousands of inmates who had seen sent earlier to their death to make the town appear less crowded. He did not tell the guests that the cripples and sick persons were hidden away in a barrack.

The Germans welcomed the visitors in the former Victoria Hotel. Then the guests toured the town, visiting some of the barracks, specified workshops, mess rooms, the bakery, the children's home, the sports ground, and the sports hall. They were shown the quarters of the privileged. But they viewed none of the general housing. What the commision saw were well-known Jews relaxing and conversing together at the Community House, forced to do so by the Nazis. They heard the happy slave band playing in the café, the streets, and the music hall. They saw famous artists giving concerts for a group of well-dressed retirees in the luxuriously furnished café.

Commandant Rahm provided special entertainment for the guests:

All along the route orderlies, well out of view, ran ahead of the commission and started off various embellishment devices as one starts off a jukebox by dropping a penny in its slot. Thus some handsome girls working in the fields outside Theresienstadt shouldered their rakes at the appropriate moment and marched singing along the road; bakers in white overalls and white gloves started loading loaves of bread: it was a mere coincidence that they did it just when the honoured guests appeared.[34]

At the Community Center a performance of Verdi's *Requiem* was in full swing when the visitors arrived, and on the ground floor the children were listening spellbound to a children's opera, *Brundibar*. The visitors saw vegetables unloaded at the grocery shop and a football game on the sports field.

Josef Bor wrote a novel called *Terezin Requiem* that tells the story of the Red Cross visit. It deals with that incident of Verdi's *Requiem*, emphasizing the eighteen-month effort of the well-known conductor Schächter to produce the performance. Schächter's major problem, besides the need to smuggle in instruments, was that the Nazis continued to deport members of his orchestra and chorus to the death camps. In the end he managed a triumphant performance. As he intended, the premier performance portrayed to his audience of prisoners and dignitaries a theme of strength: "Listen, you inhabitants of the camps, we endured, we never gave way, we never succumbed. And we've lived to see those others, the damned, near the final accounting."[35]

The delegation returned from its mission extolling the good treatment of the inmates. In Stockholm the delegates delivered a glowing report, describing Theresienstadt "more as an ideal suburban community than a ghettocamp." The Danish Jews benefited measurably from the good report. They received better food, permission to remain in their showcase apartments, and exemption from deportation. After the war the commission leader tried to defend his actions by maintaining that the commission purposely exaggerated the ghetto picture in order to ensure that the Germans would continue to allow Danes to receive food and medical supplies.[36]

Following that extravaganza, the Nazis seemed convinced of their own fantasies. The SS ordered that a film be produced of life in the model ghetto, showing how well the inhabitants lived. After securing the services of a well-known actor and director, the Germans ordered them to film the picture during the summer of 1944. Filming began in mid-August with a cast of thousands—inmates forced to join in that next-to-last fraud. One scene pictured an open-air stage in a field where music was performed in the presence of 2,000 spectators. The SS had force-marched the audience to the field and ordered all to smile. One sequence caught inmates swimming and splashing merrily in the SS pools. Another scene placed Jews at the bathing beach, sunning themselves on the riverbanks. The Germans forced the Jews to drink tea in a "coffee shop" and sway to jazz music, under watchful camera eyes. "A transport of children from Holland was photographed, with Rahm tenderly lifting each child out of the cars. The Nazis intended the film for foreign consumption, hoping to show a model life with good food, pleasant apartments, and continuous entertainment. The closing scene showed a family sitting around a bountiful dinner table.[37]

When members of the newsreel staff returned to synchronize the musical scenes in February 1945, they were a bit bewildered to find the setting changed and some of the prisoner musicians gone. But as the war thundered to a close, Commandant Rahm had nothing better to do than help the film-makers finish the project. After it was completed in March 1945, Himmler personally censored several of the scenes. Today only 36 meters of the film are preserved in the Prague Newsreel Archives. No one knows what happened to the rest.[38]

Theresienstadt was a strange camp because of the pervasiveness of the fraud. But the Germans were caught up in it to the depths of their subconscious. Photos of the time show the growth and expansion of the model ghetto accompanied by a good deal of hearty German laughter:

Lots of creamy Pilsen beer and *Braunschweiger* must have been gobbled as they dreamed of Terezin—the *nice* concentration camp. . . . Rarely does one encounter such bubbling joy, such gaiety, as manifests itself in German planning vis-à-vis the Jews. How thoroughly they enjoyed their work! Explosive guffaws, flat smiles, blue eyes rolling and winking.

Theresienstadt and its farce appears to have been "an interminable bloody joke." Perhaps the fraud was partly a product of the unconscious suspicion by some Nazis that punishment would be inevitable for them. "The truly outrageous thing is that Terezin worked marvelously for them. It deceived its inmates. It prolonged the deception of many neutrals and many in the West."[39]

Art, Culture, Education

Perhaps the most amazing element of Theresienstadt was the high-quality artistic, cultural, and educational life that emerged in that peculiar ghetto. It would be difficult to find an equal to that phenomenon in history. The fine arts produced in Theresienstadt have made some impact on Czechoslovakian culture.

The inmates of Theresienstadt included some of the most prominent intellectuals and artists of Czechoslovakia, Austria, and Germany. Famous writers, artists, scientists, jurists, diplomats, ministers, professors, actors, musicians, and poets gathered together in that little town. The astounding achievement of the ghetto were the masterpieces produced by its scholars and artists in a climate considered devastating to creativity.[40]

From the end of 1942, when the Germans stabilized the conditions, cultural life prospered. The Germans sanctioned the establishment of a cultural department to further their propaganda. Clandestinely it grew into a focal point for artistic achievements:

In particular during the final stages of the embellishment, Theresienstadt probably was the freest town in Europe . . . [in terms of] culture. Since the Germans at first did not trouble to impose any restrictions or censorship, words were spoken on Theresienstadt's stage which, outside the Ghetto, would prove the undoing of writers and actors.[41]

The Germans remained indifferent. What did it matter? The Jews were going to die anyway. Cultural freedom was a type of drug administered to keep them content.

Somehow Theresienstadt developed an atmosphere that fostered a rapid maturing of valuable literary, musical, and artistic works. The instability, dreariness, boredom, monotony, and danger of the Theresienstadt life frustrated basic needs, but still the inmates were determined to create. Theater performances, concerts, and lectures were an everyday occurrence.

The hunger to take part in cultural undertakings was certainly no less abnormal than the structure of the whole ghetto society. There was something of a morose greatness in it. It would not be going too far to take it as a measure of the unbroken will to live. But we must not forget that there were also objective conditions that made possible a proliferation of culture that would be unthinkable in Dachau or Auschwitz.[42]

The oddity they created fascinated the Germans. "Who but Jews would bother staging *Carmen,* the *Bartered Bride,* or performing Verdi's *Requiem* on a diet of stale bread and thin soup, in a place where your first violinist or leading soprano might be at rehearsal one day—and in a filthy train bound for Auschwitz the next?"[43]

Theresienstadt had a bookshop, which was eventually transformed into a lending library stocked with German books confiscated from Jewish homes. A private library collected by the Germans consisted of 60,000 Hebrew books brought to Theresienstadt from dissolved museums and libraries throughout German-occupied territories. After the war the Germans intended to open a Jewish museum, of which the library was to be a part. In Theresienstadt rabbis and Hebrew scholars labored at compiling a book catalogue for the Germans.

The artists of Theresienstadt: Ungar, Fritta, Haas, and Fleischmann. Unger died after liberation; Fritta died from beatings; Fleischmann and others were gassed. Leo Haas survived. "They were the main actors in a revealing footnote to the Nazi era known to Czech graduates of Terezin as 'the incident of the artists.' . . . In the simplest of terms, these men died for daring to tell the truth through their art." The Nazis constructed a special drafting room for the artists. They ordered them to prepare reproductions of famous works and paint pastoral scenes of their lives. The artists obeyed, but also painted secretly and bartered their work for bread. The hidden pictures that have survived portray some of the worst realities of the camp.[44]

Fritta, the head of the art section, refused to make his pictures pleasant, so the SS arrested him in January 1944 and sent him and his family to the Auschwitz ovens. He had concentrated on Theresienstadt's dreadful reality; his paintings showed the hopeless resignation on the faces of the deportees, emaciated old men and women close to death, sordid overcrowded barracks. Professor Otto Ungar, another fine artist, had the fingers of his right hand chopped off and was sent to Buchenwald. The two men had something in common—their Theresienstadt works were better than their prewar paintings.

Alfred Kantor was twenty-two when he compiled one of the most moving documents of our time: a book of watercolors of Terezin and Auschwitz. While a prisoner at Terezin, he sketched constantly, and his pictures show the small details in the larger network of horror—a step-by-step process. His shattering pictorial account speaks of: the barracks where each human marks out his personal "space" with his suitcases; sick people lying in clouds of dust in attics; starving people searching in the garbage for rotten potatoes; the busy streets; a hundred ill and hunched inmates lined up to use the one toilet provided for 1,000 people; a secret *Carmen* performance in an attic sound-proofed against the SS by blankets; the Terezin café and the band "The Ghetto Swingers"; an inmate soccer game on Sunday.[45]

In a powerful memoir Zdenka Fantlowa describes the cultural life and its most valuable components, theater and music. "The concerts, arranged by former members of the Prague Conservatory or of foreign conservatories, were invariably sold out." Zdenka participated in the first theatrical efforts and she remembers building a tiny stage in an attic. For a curtain, a sheet; for chairs, planks. And they played to a sold-out house! Three additional theaters were opened, she reported, accommodating 250 to 300 people. The council put the necessary facilities at their disposal, and equipped the theaters with lamps, lights, costumes, and decorations. Of course, they had splendid actors in residence.[46]

Writers have commented that the highest level of musical achievement was reached in Theresienstadt. Composers-in-residence Pavel Haas, Gideon Klein, Jan Krasa, and Viktor Ullmann worked with the conductors, Karel Ancerl and Rafeal Schächter, as well as with many musicians and singers. In an attic Pavel Haas composed choral works, a suite for pianos, a study for strings, and many songs. The winner of the Czechoslovakian State Prize for Music, Jan Krasa, created a trio for strings and a quartet for strings. A disciple of Schoenberg, Viktor Ullmann composed many pieces for the piano and an opera.[47]

Several music groups existed in Theresienstadt but the largest was a mixed choir conducted by Schächter. Schächter adapted several operas for concert performance, including the *Bartered Bride,* the *Marriage of Figaro,* and the *Magic Flute.* He also produced the children's opera *Brundibar.* Stage artists and designers helped with the performances. In the evenings, in a small café selling a dark-brown beverage, inmate customers listened to band music. Five popular cabarets performed in the courtyards.

Once the Red Cross commission left the camp, the Germans no longer saw the necessity of continuing the cultural activities or the lives of those who had contributed to them. Most artists died in the camps or in the gas chambers.

Resistance and culture were intimately linked at Theresienstadt. Evidence exists of a resistance movement in Theresienstadt formed as early as 1942. Its members attempted to warn the ghetto in 1944 when the real truth about Auschwitz was known, but most refused to believe. The Nazi camouflage thwarted any major action by the prisoners. Thus the primary form of resistance in the ghetto was drama, poetry, music, and literature.[48]

A few writers have wondered if the Theresienstadt Jews submitted too readily, if they were cooperative victims, if they thought so much of survival that they refused to die with honor. A student of Theresienstadt ghetto art insists (as do many historians) that the manner in which the Germans went about murdering the Jews precluded anything but the most feeble of protests. But Gerald Green adds: "I keep thinking of Fritta's old people in the attic or Fleischmann's new arrivals, and the wide-eyed ghost children of Bialystok, and I have great difficulty envisioning them at the throat of some fat, healthy blond SS sergeant." If the Jews had followed Bettelheim's advice, the 15,000 children would have been "organized in Commandos, taught karate and knife-fighting, formed resistance cells, sabotaged the Germans' industries, and when the time came for the transport, died tearing at the throats of the SS guards." And what does one do with those Czechoslovakian Jews in Theresienstadt who spent long hours in the classroom drawing Passover Seders of a long-gone world, arranging musical evenings, dutifully attending lectures on Plato, and teaching their doomed children to read and write and add. Most died. "Would they have been better off dying a year, a month, a week sooner, in some bold, defiant act?"[49] Rather, Green concludes, the Germans should be asked why they behaved as they did.

The Last Days and Liberation

As the Allied armies advanced into Germany and the occupied countries, the fate of the Jews was closely linked to that advance. As fast as the Allies moved, so did the Germans in transferring the Jews to the gas chambers. The Jews were losing their race with time. At a time when every man, truck, and gun was needed on the front, those in charge of the camps found ample transport and supplies to send the Jews to their places of death. The Red Army liberated Theresienstadt on May 8, 1945. They did not arrive soon enough to prevent a mass deportation effort.

By the summer of 1944 Theresienstadt was the last major Jewish community in central Europe with the exception of Budapest. The Germans decided to liquidate the ghetto in the face of the hope raised for the inmates by the rapidly advancing Allied armies. They had sufficient time to carry out their extermination schemes. In September 1944 the SS stepped up the Theresienstadt deportations. In eleven shipments to Auschwitz from September 28, 1944, to October 28, 1944—just one month—the SS transported 16,902 persons. Of that number, approximately 1,495 survived the war. Only the Danes, a small Dutch group, the mica employees, part of the transport staff, a few agricultural workers, a few individuals protected by powerful Germans, and prisoners over sixty-five were able to weather the storm.[50]

Deportation spread a deadly chill over the town; no one knew when his turn would come. The Jews kept their luggage packed, because the SS gave such short notice that they often had no time to switch off their lights or turn off the water. They left their washing on the clotheslines and their trunks scattered on the floor. The eleventh and final major transport included room for the special deportees such as the members of the council and other important persons. Although the prominents traveled in greater comfort than those in the cattle cars, they died like all the others immediately upon arrival at Auschwitz.

The Germans kept one small group of prisoners, twenty young strong men, apart from the rest. When the trains had gone, those young men were taken to the Small Fortress to carry out the commandant's scheme to erase all traces of the German crime and remove the ashes of the dead. The group emptied 8,000 urns into a pit near Litomerice and 17,000 urns into the Ohre River. Then they went to the courtyard of one barrack and dug up the remains of the prisoners executed in 1942 and put them into coffins. Once those coffins were incinerated, the commandment killed the twenty prisoners. When it was all over in the space of a month, 18,402 prisoners had been deported. Most victims were young and healthy. The potential leaders of any resistance movement and prisoners familiar with the German crimes were deported.

With most of the population gone, gloom descended on Theresienstadt. Another period of stabilization followed, and then the floodgate from the other camps opened and into Theresienstadt poured the residue of the extermination centers of the east. They came by train, truck, and foot. They arrived half dead and provided a most startling sight for those in Theresienstadt who still wished to believe that the stories of Nazi crimes were propaganda.

The approach of liberation created tension and turmoil for both Jews and Germans. The top levels of the SS could not agree on the final disposition of camp inmates. Some thought that sparing the Jews and their attractive ghetto would help disprove rumors of atrocities and ensure better treatment for the Germans. Himmler leaned toward that view. But Eichmann and others knew better and wanted all the Jews to die, to complete the Final Solution. The SS pursued Eichmann's plan until the commandant made the decision to spare the remaining inmates of the ghetto.

In February the top SS made their first attempt to deceive the Allies when they put together a transport of 1,200 persons with Switzerland as the destination. Those who gathered in the Theresienstadt station were given food parcels and they climbed suspiciously into a comfortable train. A few days later ghetto residents heard on the radio that the transport of former prisoners had reached Switzerland.

In the same month the advocates of extermination laid their plans and began to improve upon underground passages in the bastions in the gates. Work on enlarging and ventilating the pits went on for a few weeks. It looked as though the whole underground area was being converted into gas chambers. On March 5 Eichmann visited Theresienstadt to see whether it was fit to be presented to an international commission. After he left, the work on the massive gas chamber was discontinued.

High-ranking SS officers carried on negotiations with the International Red Cross, which had requested that its representatives be admitted to Theresienstadt. The Germans bought time until April so they could cover up the evidence of the high mortality rate and mass deportations. The officials intended, once again, to present the ghetto as a community of Jews living in comfort! They refurbished it, planting flowers and painting barracks.

On April 6, 1945, Eichmann escorted Paul Dunand, Swiss Red Cross, through Theresienstadt. In the evening General Frank, protector of Bohemia-Moravia, gave the Red Cross delegation a reception in the Prague Palace. Eichmann promised Dunand that the deportations were over, and after Dunand left, the Scandinavian Red Cross obtained from the German authorities the release of the Danish Jews. On April 15 the white coaches with the Red Cross emblems drove into the ghetto. The crowds bid the Danes farewell and the convoy left. The SS, however, were readying another transport. The elder had been asked on April 19 to supply Rahm with a list of the ghetto's 600 most important prisoners. Rahm told him that he wanted to send those Jews away from the fighting and bombs. The elder complied; but suspicions grew, and finally the members of the council made a secret appeal to Dunand in Prague. He visited Theresienstadt again on April 21. In truth, Rahm had planned to hold the Jews in a camp in the Tirol as hostages for negotiations with the Allies. Dunand succeeded in getting the departure of that transport postponed again and again until he extracted a promise that no further deportations would occur.

On April 20 more transports of prisoners from other camps, some 2,000, arrived in open-air railroad trucks. A few had been original deportees from Theresienstadt who had come all the way home! The exhausted prisoners finally gave their Theresienstadt friends a full report of what had happened, and that reality destroyed any remaining belief in "propaganda" about the Nazi camps. The Germans had not provided food and medicine for the new flood of humanity. Dunand assured the elders that the Red Cross would take care of Theresienstadt and would place it under International Red Cross protection. Rahm and his staff prepared for flight and the Jewish administration prepared for the horrible danger of a major typhus epidemic. And their fears were realized. The final deaths in Theresienstadt came from typhus.

Dunand placed the ghetto and the Small Fortress under the protection of the International Red Cross on May 3, 1945. Rahm left on May 5 with the last of the SS. That day the ghetto simply ceased to exist and its prisoners were human beings for the first time in years. On May 8 the first Red Army tanks passed through the town on their way to Prague. And on May 11 Theresienstadt, with its 32,000 inmates, more than a third of whom were non-Jews, was formally delivered to the Russians. The "model ghetto" complex and its outlet, Auschwitz, had claimed more than 120,000 lives.[51]

One tragedy remained: a typhus epidemic that spread through Theresienstadt, the Small Fortress, and Richard during the last days of the war. Over 12,000 recent arrivals from German camps had to be isolated in barrack blocks because of typhus. Approximately 3,000 persons contacted typhus in those last days, and 500 died of it.

Thus ended the unusual history of an unusual place: Theresienstadt, proposed by the Jews as a refuge, heralded by the Nazis as a spa, becoming in turn a prison, a ghetto, a reloading station, and a "mask for Auschwitz."

THE KILLING CENTERS—EXCLUSIVE FUNCTION CAMPS

CHELMNO/KULMHOF: THE SECRET CAMP

Unlike Auschwitz, the name "Chelmno" did not bring terror to the hearts of the Poles or to the Jews of the Lodz ghetto exterminated there. For Chelmno, the first of the killing centers, was a *secret*. All camps were secret if that term is used to identify something the human mind refuses to accept, because it is repulsed or fearful. But Chelmno was truly secret. Its geographical isolation veiled its existence. In their pilot extermination camp, in deep secrecy, the Germans gassed as many as 340,000 human beings at Chelmno, 99 percent of whom were Jews, and burned their bodies in the nearby woods. The entire Jewish population at Lodz, the second largest Polish city, went up in smoke at Chelmno in 1939. Chelmno has no international survivor organizations, for of the more than 300,000 people brought there for extermination, less than 10 escaped. When the Polish government dedicated the monument, only four survivors stood in the crowd.[1]

The village of Chelmno is located 14 kilometers from the town of Kolo, and 50 kilometers from Lodz. Not a stick of wood or a piece of concrete remains of the camp. The Germans destroyed all traces of Chelmno, excavating the buried corpses and burning them. The bones were crushed and together with the ashes dumped into the nearby river or thrown to the winds.

Chelmno today is a place or a group of places where something was. The original village no longer exists, nor does the manor house that was located in its midst, appropriated as the reception center for the "relocatees." No killing center had more than limited housing accommodations, but Chelmno had none. It was truly a camp on wheels. Why would food or housing be needed? The relocatees were exterminated the day they arrived. So add a few huts for the Jewish extermination squads, and house the soldiers in the village. No fuss, no costly building operation, no need for large Jewish labor squads. The only extermination machinery needed were the large trucks in which the victims were gassed as they rode from the manor house to the mass graves in the forests 4 kilometers away, or later to the crematoria. The best one can hope for today is to retrace the routes of doomed Jews, walk in the forests that held the graves, and ponder on the probable site of the vanished crematoria.

Sculpture, Chelmno Killing Center site, Buskievicz and Stasinski, architects.

It is difficult to find the Chelmno sites, for they are not marked. The Poles built the camp memorial in the heavily wooded area that harbored the mass graves. The monument stands large and stark in the clearing. Fashioned by a famous Polish sculptor, it is a striking stone edifice. Underneath it, Poles continue to lay fresh flowers. It may be that the monument stands on the crematorium site, but no one really knows. The memorial park is untended and has a primitive wild look. There are no guidebooks, no souvenir shops— the quiet speaks loudly for itself. Memorial stones dot a second small clearing where a few makeshift huts formerly stood. The scene is a somber one, but any fantasy one might have of the sinister is unfulfilled. The sky is too blue; hundreds of birds break the noisy quiet with their talk; and a cool breeze moves the leaves.

The village of Zawadki lies 2 kilometers from the main road to the camp. During Chelmno's existence trains brought the Jews to nearby Powiercie, and then the soldiers marched them down the dusty road to Zawadki, where they spent the night in a large mill building. Zawadki townspeople walk in the memorial park on Sundays. Peasant houses encircle the woods and Polish farms dot the rich farm area. On the road to Zawadki stands a complex of buildings, said to have been the SS barracks.

Chelmno marked the beginning of the gas chamber decade and owed its existence to an order by Himmler creating a new phase of mass murder. The mobile killing units turned into stationary death factories and gas replaced bullets. In the autumn of 1941 SS administrator Arthur Greiser asked Himmler and Heydrich for a group of trained executioners to clear his Warthegau area of Jews. He was particularly concerned about the 100,000 Jews still remaining in the Lodz ghetto. Himmler dispatched SS officer Fritz Lange, and with him went gas vans previously used in Russia. In the small village of Kulmhof (250 people) Lange discovered an old, isolated mansion that seemed perfect for his purposes. With the addition of three gas vans in late December 1941 or early January 1942, Chelmno opened for business as the first Nazi killing center.

Chelmno was not a camp in a true sense—the Germans had no intention of accommodating the prisoners for any length of time. Since Chelmno was the first operable killing center, it borrowed both personnel and techniques from the euthanasia and Russian campaigns. Because it was a killing center, Chelmno had few Gentile victims, was separate from the war activity, and served no labor needs. It recognized no other purpose than speedy and thorough killing.[2]

A vacant country house owned by the state stood in the village. Surrounded by an old park, it was the site that Lange selected for the extermination camp. He enclosed the park with a high wooden fence and expelled the local inhabitants, retaining only a few workers. The enclosure contained the manor house, an old grainery, and two wooden huts. The entire area measured less than 2 hectares.

Chelmno's primary aim was the extermination of the 450,000 Jews living in the Warthegau area. The process began on December 8, 1941, with the ghetto populations of the small towns and villages, and then the larger cities, and finally Lodz. The first Lodz Jews arrived in January 1942. Chelmno accommodated approximately 1,000 Jews a day until April 1943. In addition to the major transports from Poland, Jews came from Germany, Austria, France, Belgium, Luxembourg, and Holland. The dead included 5,000 Gypsies and a 1,000 Polish and Russian POWs. A German historian insists that Chelmno was used also as a euthanasia treatment center. Evidence does show that Gauleiter Greiser proposed to Himmler that 25,000 tubercular Poles be admitted to Chelmno.[3]

Chelmno had a carefully picked Special Commando of eighty to ninety men pledged to absolute secrecy, a Code of Silence, on Hitler's orders. At first, the guards changed every few months. The commandant required squad permanency, however, after he discovered that soldiers on leave talked of their experiences. The Special Commando received extra monetary bonuses, special treatment, and free alcohol and tobacco. The Polish workers were allowed to select Jewish women from the transports to serve them for a few days before being killed. Though well compensated, the Special Commando found the original killing method of shooting too hard on their nerves, necessitating a quick shift by the planners to gas vans.

The Germans managed to dim the reality of extermination. They told rural Jews they were being taken for military work on fortifications in the east and explained to urban Jews that they would be resettled in the Ukraine. Trucks and trains transported the victims. After unloading the train, the soldiers marched the victims down the road to spend the night in a large mill building in Zawadki:

> Everyone brought his dearest possession because you must
> not leave what is dear to you when you go far away.
>
> Everyone has brought his life along, above all it was his
> life that he had to bring along.
>
> And when they arrive
>
> they think they have arrived
>
> in Hell
>
> possibly. Still they did not believe it.
>
> They did not know that you could take a train to Hell but
> since they are here, they steel themselves and feel ready to
> face it.
>
> with women, children, aged parents
>
> with family keepsakes and family documents.
>
> They do not know that you do not arrive at that station.
>
> They expect the worst—they do not expect the unthinkable.[4]

In the morning trucks transported 150 people in each load to Chelmno, about a kilometer away. By keeping the process going, 1,000 victims could be disposed of by early afternoon.

The trucks drove into the camp ground and stopped before the manor house. An officer told the visitors that they were going to work in the east. He promised them fair treatment and good food. He explained that first they must take a bath and give up their clothes to be disinfected. From the courtyard the Jews moved inside the house to a heated room where they undressed. Then they walked down a corridor with signs directing them "to the bath." At the end, through the front door, a large van awaited them. Guards explained that they were taking them in the van to the bathhouse. They climbed into the van, the door clanged shut, and the van drove away.

Theoretically the victims died in fifteen minutes. The van would then drive to the Rzuchow woods, 3 kilometers away, where the corpses were unloaded and buried. While those trucks were unloading the bodies into the mass graves, other trucks were bringing in the next batch from Powiercie.[5]

In the woods a special detachment of Jews threw the dead victims into the graves after they had removed their valuables. As payment for their services, those Jews earned a few more weeks of life. One observer, Herman May, described in his journal a trip he took in late 1941 to Kolo, traveling in the car of the Nazi coordinator for the region. The official remarked that the trees grew well now, and when asked what he meant, he answered: "Jews make very good fertilizer." Later May saw enough so that the remark made some sense. "He observed truck after truck, loaded with Jews, speeding along the roads in the direction of the abandoned manor house that had been ringed by a high palisade of logs. It was here that the Jews he had seen were suffocated in the portable gas chambers and dumped into mass graves in the woods." As a forester, May was later requested to plant trees over the mass graves. But the ground over the graves began to ferment and heave, necessitating the destruction of the entire forest.[6]

The Nazis used three gassing vans, each capable of holding from 80 to 100 persons. The primitive process was neither efficient nor workable. The liquidators had trouble with the trucks, the gassing did not always work, the vans broke down. The van instructions said the process should be over in fifteen minutes, but sometimes it lasted for hours. Occasionally, the victims were still alive when the doors were opened. One van called the "ghetto autobus" got "embarrassingly lost"; it was finally located in a repair shop in a neighboring city. An SS doctor complained to his superiors:

The application of gas is usually not undertaken correctly. In order to come to an end as fast as possible, the driver presses the accelerator to the fullest extent. Thus the persons executed die by suffocation and not by dosing off as planned. My directions had proved that by correct adjustment of the levers death comes faster and the prisoners fall asleep peacefully. Distorted faces and excretions, such as could be seen before, are no longer noticed.[7]

Those trucks were officially named *Sonderwagen.* At one point the trucks needed to be overhauled, and the Polish mechanics who repaired them reported on their construction. The large truck measured 6 by 3 meters, and smaller ones 4.8 by 2.4 meters.

The outside was covered with narrow overlapping boards, so that it would look as though it were armored. The inside was lined with iron plates and the door fitted tightly, so that no air could get in from outside. The outside was painted dark grey.

The exhaust pipe was placed underneath and discharged its gas through a vent in the middle of the floor, which was guarded by a perforated iron plate, to prevent it from choking.[8]

News of the successful killing center reached the ears of high officials. One day the Gestapo chief summoned his Jewish expert, Adolf Eichmann, and ordered him to visit Chelmno to observe the process. Eichmann later told his story:

I followed the van and then came the most horrifying sight I've ever seen in my life. The van drew up alongside a long pit, the doors were opened and the bodies thrown out; the limbs were still supple, as if they were still alive. They were thrown into the pit. I saw a civilian pulling out teeth with a pair of pliers and then I took off. I rushed to my car and departed and said no more. I was through. I had had it. A white-coated doctor said that I ought to look through the peephole and see what went on inside the vans. I refused. I couldn't speak. I had to get away. Frightful, I tell you. An inferno. Can't do it. I can't do it.[9]

The mass grave problem continued to haunt SS officials. Not only were they alarmed by the unanticipated underground activity of the corpses, but they began to suspect that the bodies might be responsible for recurring typhus epidemics. In June 1942 Gestapo Chief Müller ordered *Einsatzgruppen* Commander Blobel to eliminate the graves in the occupied territories. In late summer Blobel came to Chelmno to see what he could do.

He employed ovens, explosives, and funeral pyres in his effort to destroy the graves. Once the corpses had been excavated and burned, Blobel still had problems with the bones. He ordered the Lodz Jews to send him a bone crusher. Evidently the ghetto had no bone crusher. Blobel finally secured one from a major industrial firm and extolled its virtues to Commandant Höss of Auschwitz. On his visit in September Höss was unimpressed by the Blobel process. He observed that dynamite was ineffective in eliminating mass graves. Finding to his distaste that bodies were putrefying slowly and fitfully in the open air, Höss also noted that the stench was difficult to hide from the next batch of victims.[10]

Blobel finally discovered an efficient method of body disposal. He constructed a vast pyre of iron rails and wooden sleepers, built in the form of furnaces. They were laid deep in the ground so they did not project above the surface. The furnaces measured at the top 6 by 10 meters and were 4 meters deep. A channel to the pit below facilitated the removal of ashes and bones.

In the furnace were alternate layers of chopped wood and corpses: to facilitate combustion, space was left between the corpses. The furnace could hold 100 corpses at a time, but as they burnt down, fresh ones were added from above.

The ashes and remains of bones were removed from the ash-pit, and ground in mortars, and, at first, thrown into specially dug ditches; but later, from 1943 onwards, bones and ashes were secretly carted to Zawadki at night, and there thrown into the river.[11]

High Nazi dignitaries personally inspected Chelmno. The region's *Gauleiter,* Greiser, visited the camp on several occasions, and at one banquet honored the members of the burial detail. Greiser found the enterprise quite profitable. He controlled the Chelmno loot and established a central inventory station near Lodz where all the victims' belongings were sorted and sold, or sent back to Germany. On September 9, 1944, his staff sent 775 wrist watches and 552 pocket watches to the SS center. They sold the victims' clothing for the benefit of the Winter Assistance Program. Those who received the material, particularly the clothes, were not always pleased. An industrialist complained that the textiles from Chelmno were badly stained and "partly permeated with dirt and blood stains." In a shipment of 200 jackets the Jewish stars on 51 of them were still embarrassingly attached. In another case, the Chelmno warehouse sorters demanded danger money because of the risk of infection.[12]

One of Greiser's most productive and profitable projects was the salvaging of gold from the live pockets and dead mouths of the deported Jews. The enormous SS enterprise dealing with gold from the mouths of millions of dead humans received its impetus at Chelmno. The operation, a first in modern times, started slowly and crudely. But the profits that began to fill the Reich bank vaults were so encouraging that the removal of dental gold became a normal first step in all camp body-salvage operations. Each camp developed efficient removal and collection procedures. The gold secured in that manner was significant enough to make a noticeable difference in the Reich monetary condition.

The removal of dental gold from the mouths of the dead has been an idea resisted by modern civilization—in part for pragmatic reasons. To be profitable, such an operation needed to be done in bulk—which was, of course, no problem for the Nazis with their millions of victims. The operation also required ignoring the customary reverence surrounding death, the shame a family would feel knowing of that type of demand on their dead relative's last personal possessions. But here again, the Nazis had no problem, for they had already shockingly violated all normal sensibilities about the dying and the dead. Thus no obstacles stood in the way of initiating a successful dental gold-salvage project. Actually, good sense dictated it.

The SS authorities who organized the project at Chelmno had read a much-discussed article, "The Gold of the Dead," written in 1925 by a distinguished scientist. The thesis was based on a phrase from *Faust:* "All that lies quietly buried beneath the earth." The doctor suggested, and the SS agreed, that the burial of dental gold was an archaic practice that no modern state could afford. From the date of the initiation of a gold-salvage program, he estimated that 150 million marks in gold would be in use again over a thirty-year period. Detractors insisted that few medical personnel willing to perform the extractions would be found, but the writer pointed out that teeth removal is no more revolting than the postmortem dissections that medical people consider their conscientious duty. The state, he thought, should legislate the removal of dental gold from all bodies before burial, take the gold as a contribution to the state, and make it clear to medical personnel that gold extraction was their conscientious responsibility: "In any case, the simplest way of getting back the gold and platinum would be to cremate all corpses." No decency would be outraged if the gold could be taken from the ashes.[13]

Himmler intended that Chelmno be liquidated in spring 1943 after the elimination of as much evidence of mass murder as possible. Gauleiter Greiser came to Chelmno to thank the Special Commando for its outstanding performance. He told the men they would be entitled to a four-week vacation after the camp was dissolved. Greiser wrote Himmler of the excellent job done by those men, who "represented truly the best German soldiery." In April 1943 Chelmno closed, and Himmler awarded the War Service Cross to SS Leader Bothmann and the Special Commando, and sent them to Yugoslavia to serve in the SS Prinz Eugen Division.[14]

Himmler, however, ordered the camp reopened in April 1944. He brought back SS Leader Bothmann and members of the Special Commando from Yugoslavia to reduce the number of Jews remaining in the Lodz ghetto. The victims were brought by a local branch line directly to the village and spent the night in the church. The next day trucks transported them to the woods. Not far from the crematoria two wooden huts had been constructed, one as a dressing room and the other as a storage room. The victims undressed in the huts and climbed into the gas vans under the impression that they were being taken to the bathhouses. After the gassing, the trucks drove to the nearby crematoria. The number of persons killed in 1944 numbered about 10,000.[15]

In late 1944 the camp in the woods and the crematoria were completely destroyed. The workers tore down the huts and leveled the ground. The *Sonderkommando* and a group of thirty-seven Jewish workers stayed at the camp site to work on the grave demolition project. From a poem entitled "Mass Graves":

Those digging up the dead
had to be careful:
no hair or piece of bone to be left
or even a piece of paper—

everything to be burnt
so that nobody would know there had ever been a grave there.
The heap of the dead sometimes had as many as two thousand bodies,
but an exact count was kept of the number of bodies burnt;
in the evening those working at it had to report the number to the
    commander in charge—
and were forbidden to tell it to anyone else.
If one of them was asked, even by the man who kept the account,
"How many bodies were burnt yesterday?"
he·always answered, "I forget."
Otherwise, his body would be added to the dead.[16]

On January 17, 1945, the *Sonderkommando* began to execute the last of the Jewish workers, intending a final liquidation of the camp. The Jews resisted and killed two guards. The *Sonderkommando* trapped the Jews in a building, ignited it, and opened fire on the forty-seven workers. Two survived.[17]

Chelmno is the story of how the Nazis depopulated a corner of Poland of its Jews by the use of a secret but primitive facility for large-scale killing. Chelmno served as a prototype for the huge death factories that followed. The ancient Jewish communities reached back into the thousand-year history of Poland. Chelmno ended that history—permanently.

BELZEC: A GASSING NIGHTMARE

Set in a dismal corner of southwestern Poland, the Belzec killing center lies on the edge of the small industrial town of Belzec. Everything about the town and the camp site is dirty, dingy, dilapidated. They seem to share a single character.

If it were not for the Belzec municipal railroad station, the camp site would be difficult to find, for the townspeople are reluctant to give directions to it. The Nazis enlarged the railroad complex, widening it to eight tracks. Its unusual size for such a small town serves notice that a camp is nearby. Indeed, the camp site lies immediately beyond it. Raw-materials factories and a large sand pit border the area.

Visitors to Belzec during its productive period—and, of course, the townspeople—were overwhelmed by the stench from the putrefying corpses lying on the ground or in the uncovered pits. The camp was located on a barren flat plain, about 2½ kilometers square, surrounded by barbed wire. It contained a few shacks and the gas chambers. Grim Nazi humor labeled the gassing facilities the "Heckenholt Institute," after the mechanic who ran the diesel engines. When the Nazis destroyed the camp, they planted groves of pine trees. The trees, the barbed wire, and the stone fences remain, enclosing the smallest of all the official camp areas.

Because Belzec had no crematorium, the SS buried the bodies in open pits dug deep into the ground. Near the war's end, Jewish workers cleaned out most pits and burned the bodies. But they were never able to eliminate every grave. Underneath the ground of the existing site thousands of corpses lie, twisted into each other.

Belzec was surely the least secret and only visible killing center. Because the area is so small, the victims had to be exterminated quickly. The camp provided dying rather than living space. Immediate extermination of crowds of people by primitive methods in a tiny space created serious problems for Nazi officials.

On October 10, 1945, a Polish court visited the site. They found bones, women's hair, false teeth, hands, and children's body parts. A terrible smell

Sculpture, Belzec Killing Center site.

of dead human bodies still came from the ground. They discovered that local people had been digging for gold throughout the area.[1]

The central camp monument is out of place. Its yellow sandstone fits into the environment but its high quality does not. It is a fine and striking sculpture of two victims, one holding the other. Someone has tried to build a series of monuments up and down the hill in the shape of large urns. Although the original idea was interesting, neighborhood residents have desecrated the monument sections. The sculptured stone urns or dishes are broken in half and lie scattered along the sides of the paths. The area is isolated, silent, and wild. No one cares for it now. The gate to the camp tilts on broken hinges. It is a miserable site, rising as it does out of a dirty, nondescript industrial neighborhood. But then who would remember? Only *one* person is known to have survived the camp.

Belzec, the first of the River Bug chain of killing centers, opened on March 17, 1942. Located 160 kilometers southeast of Warsaw, it had the advantage of lying within a few meters of the main railroad line between

Lwow and Lublin. It was not a camp in the true sense. The Germans built it exclusively as a killing center to exterminate the Jews of southeastern Poland. It occupied a small area and contained few facilities. The authorities had no intention of accommodating prisoners for any length of time. Belzec was separated from the war effort; only minimal industrial activity occurred there. As with other single-purpose centers, virtually all its victims were Jews (the exception was 1,200 Poles). Because of the chaos that can attend the continuous arrival of large crowds of people in a small area and the attempt at their immediate extermination with inadequate facilities, a large guard force of Ukrainians, numbering in the hundreds, served the camp.

The first camp to be equipped with *permanent* gas chambers, Belzec used primarily six carbon monoxide chambers with a capacity of 15,000 a day to reach its final death number—as many as 600,000 Jews. As no crematorium existed, the disposal process centered on open-pit burning. After one and a half years of operation, in fall 1943 the authorities ordered all traces of the camp destroyed. They leveled the premises and planted the area with pine trees. Belzec's functions had been replaced by the new modern killing facilities in Auschwitz.[2]

Belzec was not a model of efficiency. Its primitive process and machinery broke down constantly. Out of action completely between May and June 1942, the camp handled only two transports a week in July. Its killing days ended in late November 1942, but the Jewish *Sonderkommandos* worked at destroying the mass graves until June 1943. In 1944 the heaving ground forced the Germans to return and reopen the mass graves, pour gasoline on the corpses, and burn them. They ground the bones to a fine meal and distributed it over neighboring fields. According to historical reports, few except the SS and the townspeople knew of the camp, and it has remained something of a mystery since the war. But one of the few observers, a courier in the Polish underground—Jan Karski—maintained that news of Belzec traveled throughout Poland: "The common report was that every Jew who reached it, without exception, was doomed to death."[3]

Under the direction of the first commandant, Christian Wirth, a Jewish labor brigade built Belzec and became the first victims of its extermination machinery. Ten wooden barracks and one wooden building occupied the small area. The camp included the following structures: the guard house, across the railroad siding, and immediately behind and to the left of the entrance gate; farther to the left, the staff barracks; a large yard bordered at the end by a barrack; beyond the yard, two barracks for Jews working with the liquidation of the transports; and the extermination center behind the central cluster of trees surrounded by a wooden fence. Ditches lined the eastern side, used first for the burial of corpses and later for the burial of the ashes. The SS offices and the property warehouses lay immediately outside the main camp.[4]

The slaughterhouse, however primitive, in its very limited time of operation managed to gas several hundred thousand Jews primarily from the Galacia, Lublin, and Cracow areas. Although the death rate never reached the level planned by its dreamers, at its height Belzec claimed 10,000 bodies a day. It was so thorough that few escaped: thus we suffer from an absence of personal accounts and depositions by survivors. The camp information, gathered by Polish commissions, comes from guards, railway workers, and civilian workers.[5]

In 1942 Jan Karski, a secret courier of the Polish Underground, who later became a professor at Georgetown University, escaped from Poland and presented his testimony to the Polish National Council in London and then to Roosevelt and Churchill. His was the first eyewitness testimony. Before his escape from Poland, he visited Belzec, disguised as an Estonian guard. As he walked toward the camp, still a mile away, he heard shouts, shots, and screams. He asked the guard at his side what the noise was all about. The guard grinned. "The Jews are hot."[6] The noise and stench overwhelmed Karski as he neared the camp. He turned the corner and there it was:

the loud, sobbing, reeking camp of death . . . completely covered by a dense, pulsating, throbbing, noisy human mass—starved, stinking, gesticulating, insane human beings in constant agitated motion. . . . The Jewish mass vibrated, trembled and moved to and fro as if united in a single, insane rhythmic trance. They waved their hands, shouted, quarreled, cursed and spat at one another. Hunger, thirst, fear and exhaustion had driven them all insane.[7]

The guards seemed "bored and indifferent." As men doing a routine job, they had tired and disgusted appearances like "shepherds bringing in a flock to market."[8]

The weather was cold and rainy on the day of Karski's visit and the stench was suffocating, made up as it was of "sweat, filth, decay, damp straw, and excrement." Karski and the guard pushed through the mob to reach the other post. He found it a ghastly ordeal:

I had to push foot by foot through the crowd and step over the limbs of those who were lying prone. It was like forcing my way through a mass of death and decomposition made even more horrible by its agonized pulsation. . . . Distracted and clumsy, I would brush against people or step on a figure that reacted like an animal; quickly, often with a moan or a yelp. Each time this occurred I would be seized by a fit of nausea and come to a stop.[9]

When the Jews arrived at the camp, the guards opened the train doors and dragged them out. Once the crowd had gathered in the yard, an SS officer told them they were to be taken east as laborers; but first they must be bathed and disinfected. The guards drove the victims to a building identified as a bathroom. They packed the Jews into the room and turned on the carbon monoxide gas. Often the diesel engines failed and the victims in the chambers waited hours for their death. In a primitive manner the *Sonderkommando* removed the bodies. "Leather belts with buckles were put around the arms of the dead which were dragged like carcasses over the sand road to the pits." Before the bodies were buried, dentists removed the teeth. A prison orchestra played during the entire process. The Nazis added a final touch: a flowerpot at the entrance of the gas chamber.[10]

The SS burned the corpses in the pits: "Within an area of fifty kilometers huge stakes are burning Jewish corpses day and night." Treblinka's Stangl described one pit problem: "One of the pits had overflowed. They had put too many corpses in it and putrefaction had progressed too fast, so that the liquid underneath had pushed the bodies on top up and over and the corpses had rolled down the hill . . . oh God, it was awful." While the bodies went up in smoke, workers sorted the loot. They stored the clothing, footwear, and valuables and then periodically sent them to Germany.[11]

SS Lieutenant Gerstein also visited Belzec, and his famous description of the gas chambers is as horrible as any. Gerstein, an expert in Cyclone B gas, delivered a load of the experimental gas to Belzec. What he witnessed during the carbon monoxide gassing of Jews stunned him. Later he tried to convince papal officers and diplomats, but no one believed him.[12] His report follows:

In the hot August weather the whole place smelt like the plague and there were millions of flies everywhere. . . . In front of us a sort of bath-house with geraniums, then a few steps, and then three rooms each on the right and left, 5×5 m., 1.9 m. high, with wooden doors like garages. . . . On the roof, as a "witty little joke," the Star of David! In front of the building a notice: Heckenholt Institute.

The next morning a transport arrived, containing 6,700 people, of whom 1,450 were dead.

200 Ukrainians tore open the doors and drove people out of the wagons with their leather whips. A big loudspeaker gave further instructions: undress completely, take off artificial limbs, spectacles, etc. Give up valuables at the counter without credit notes or receipts. Tie shoes together carefully (for textile salvage), otherwise in the pile of shoes, which was a good 25 m. high, no-one could have found a pair that matched. . . .

Then the procession began to move, a long line of naked men, women, children. An SS man calmly told the crowd to take a deep breath in the disinfection chambers to expand the lungs. Inhalation would prevent disease and infection.

When asked what was going to happen to them, he answered: "Well, of course, the men must work, building houses and roads, but the women don't have to work. Only if they want to, they can help with the housework or in the kitchen." This gave some of these poor people a glimmer of hope that lasted long enough for them to take the few steps into the chambers without resisting. The majority realized—the smell told them what their fate was to be! So they climbed the steps and then they saw everything. Mothers with babies at the breast, naked little children, adults, men, women—all naked. They hesitated, but they went into the gas chambers, pushed on by those behind them, or driven in by the leather whips of the SS. Most of them without saying a word. A Jewess of about 40, with eyes blazing, called down upon the heads of the murderers the blood being spilt here.

She received six lashes in the face from the commandant's riding whip.

Many people in the packed chamber were praying, and Gerstein prayed with them. The doors closed. But the diesel engine did not work. The people waited in the chamber, some weeping, some standing quietly. Finally, after three hours, the diesel fired up:

Up till then people were alive in these four chambers, four times 750 people in four times 45 cubic metres! Another 25 minutes went by. True, many were now dead. One could see that through the little glass window through which the electric light lit up the chamber for a moment. After 28 minutes only a few were still alive. At last, after 32 minutes everyone was dead!

The Jewish work squad opened the doors and faced the standing upright dead pressed tightly together, unable, even in death, to fall down or bend over:

One could tell the families, even in death. They were still holding hands, stiffened in death, so that it was difficult to tear them apart in order to clear the chamber for the next load. The corpses were thrown out—wet with sweat and urine, soiled with excrement, menstrual blood on their legs. Children's bodies flew through the air. . . . The naked corpses were carried in wooden barrows just a few metres away to pits. . . . After some days the putrefying bodies swelled up and then, a short time later, collapsed violently so that a new batch could be thrown on top of them. Then 10 cm. of sand was strewn over it so that only a few single heads and arms stuck out.[13]

If that method of execution was not bad enough, the Nazis had a unique process in reserve for those times when the gas facilities broke down or were overcrowded, which seemed often. The deportees who had been standing in the open without food for days were crammed into the train cars and sent a mile away. The floors had been covered with lime, and the victims suffocated—in time.[14]

Karski viewed that method of killing and reported on it. He described the guard marching the Jews to the waiting freight cars. A guard told the assembled victims that they would be taken to a labor camp. Freight cars may carry 40 soldiers or 8 horses, but the Germans jammed 120 to 130 Jews into each car. The policeman slammed the doors across the arms and legs that protruded:

The floors of the car had been covered with a thick, white powder. It was quicklime. Quicklime is simply unslaked lime or calcium oxide that has been dehydrated. Anyone who has seen cement being mixed knows what occurs when water is poured on lime. The mixture bubbles and steams as the powder combines with the water, generating a searing heat.

The lime served a double purpose in the Nazi economy or brutality: The moist flesh coming on contact with the lime is quickly dehydrated and burned. The occupants of the cars would be literally burned to death before long, the flesh eaten from their bones.

The Jews would die in agony. The lime was also an efficient and inexpensive preventative against the spreading of disease by the decomposing bodies.

Not until evening were the forty-six cars packed. The train "with its quivering cargo of flesh seemed to throb, vibrate, rock and jump as if bewitched." After a period of calm, the train began "to moan and sob, wail and howl." A few dozen dead bodies remained on the ground.

In the now quiet camp the only sounds were the inhuman screams that echoed from the moving train. Then these, too, ceased. All that was now left was the stench of excrement and rotting straw and a queer, sickening, acidulous odor which, I thought, may have come from the quantities of blood that had stained the ground.

Karski, hearing the dwindling cries, pictured the journey in his mind. After a 13 kilometer trip, the train would halt in an empty field:

Then nothing at all would happen. The train would stand stock still, patiently waiting while death penetrated into every corner of its interior. This would take from two to four days.

The disposal process took from three to six days. Then the train would return to begin the process again.[15]

Few inmates escaped from Belzec and only one survived the war.[16]

The ghastly scenes of Belzec raised questions in Gerstein's mind of the essence of man and God, Satan and evil. He did not live long enough to probe them. Others have, but no one with the impact of Elie Wiesel. In his recent play, *Trial of God,* Wiesel carries on where Gerstein left off. The setting is Poland, but the year is 1649.[17]

On the eve of Purim—"the annual day of fools, children and beggars," when Jews play games and let loose and drink—three Jewish minstrels stop at a roadside inn owned by a bitter, angry Jew, Berish. To their horror, they discover they are in a town recently devastated by a pogrom that had killed all but a few Jews. Berish has given up on God—"I resigned from God." His stance is firm: "Let Him find another people, let Him push around another Jew."

An Orthodox priest enters and warns the innkeeper that another pogrom is building. How can that be true, questions Berish, when no Jews are left but him and his daughter. The priest assures him that as long as any Jew is left, he will inspire hate. A minstrel addresses the priest: "What would you do if you had no Jews to hate, to vilify, to murder? You Christians would turn on each other, having practiced on the Jews."

Berish wants to know why God stands with the killers—giving them strength. "Every man who suffers or causes suffering, every woman who is raped, every child who is tormented implicates him." He challenges the minstrels on Purim (when anything goes) to stage an honest and sincere trial—the trial of God. Berish selects for himself the role of prosecutor. No one wishes to play the role of defense attorney. A stranger, Sam, enters, listens to the conversation, and volunteers to defend God. The trial is on.

Berish charges God with "hostility, cruelty, and indifference," because God hates Jews or is not interested in them. Sam, in defense, agrees that pain and sadness erupted in the town; but, he maintains, it was done by men to men. Why involve God? The dead witnesses belong to God's community, loving Him. Sam informs Berish that since God spared his life, he should honor God, rather than hate God.

The priest breaks in to tell the group the inn is surrounded and they will all die. Sam reacts by choosing God. "I'm His servant. He created the world and me without asking for my opinion; He may do with both whatever He wishes. Our task is to glorify Him, to praise him, to love Him—in spite of ourselves." But how, asks a minstrel? Because of boundless faith, responds Sam.

The trial must be interrupted, but it will continue, in a later decade, without them. As they prepare to die, they admire Sam for his faith. Then he smiles and pulls off his mask. They realize before they die that he is Satan.

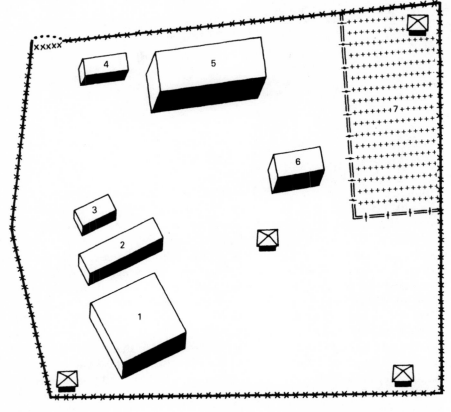

 Guard Tower

1. Administration buildings and barracks of Jewish workers
2. Barracks
3. Stripping rooms
4. Guard house
5. Barracks of the crews
6. Gas chambers
7. Graves

Map 9: Belzec (Second Stage of Existence)

Map representation by Sharon Coughran

SOBIBOR: A DESPERATE REVOLT

Killing center Sobibor claimed 250,000 lives. It lies tucked away in a tiny, sparsely populated corner of Poland 70 kilometers southeast of Warsaw, near a nondescript village of the same name. Rich, lush farmland surrounds the area; Chelm, one of the most colorful Polish towns, is nearby. No more than a kilometer from the river Bug on the Russian border, the camp site could easily be missed if a large railroad yard did not jump out of nowhere, testimony that a camp must have been nearby. At the edge of the narrow highway stands a small stone monument denoting that this spot was Sobibor. On it are the words: "In this place from May 1942 until October 1943 there existed a Hitler extermination camp. At this place 250,000 Russian, Polish, Jewish and Gypsy prisoners were murdered." An enormous watchtower used as a fire observation post stands on the edge of both the town and the camp. The town itself is on a dead-end road. The large railroad station and yard are used for some kind of large logging operation. The station building seems to have been renovated. A small cottage in which the Sobibor commandant stayed remains unchanged, so the villagers tell me.

A long road runs from the railroad tracks to the site. After half a kilometer, the road ends at a large meadow clearing that resembles a pastoral masterpiece. The camp area, now empty of everything but nature and a monument, is isolated and beautiful, its silence broken only by the chirping of birds and the talking of the crickets. It is an idyllic scene in contrast to the railroad center only a few meters away. The territorial area of the camp is not large, and it had no need to be. Its sole purpose was to kill quickly. In the center of the clearing, the monument, a large mound of earth, rises out of the ground as would a mass grave. The huge circular mound must be at least 9 meters high. Stones form a surrounding rim. The mound marks the place where the gas chambers stood: appropriately it is covered over with multicolored weeds. A glass-plated box filled with human ashes is embedded in the bottom of the stone ridge. In front of the mound lies a small bed of tended flowers.

If one knows the layout of the camp, one can walk its entire area, certain on one level that this is an isolated place for nature lovers, and aware on another level that one is literally walking on bones and ashes. The descriptions of the camp have been too stark to leave anything to the imagination.

Sobibor, from the mass grave mound.

Although the immediate impression is one of beauty, vastness, isolation, quiet, the visitor knows that here lay a small but efficient center for the final processing of Jewish human beings.

Sobibor opened its doors on May 8, 1942, and ceased to exist at the end of October 1943. The famous Sobibor Revolt of October 14, 1943, hastened the camp's demise. Two days after the revolt Himmler ordered the camp destroyed. Its existence had to be kept a secret, and the fact that one or two hundred witnesses were now at large must have been embarrassing. Sobibor was razed to the ground, without leaving a trace. No papers, records of victims, or railway documents pertaining to Sobibor have been found. The estimates of the Sobibor dead range from 250,000 to 600,000. Probably the most accurate information comes from the Jewish Historical Institute in Warsaw. According to its analysis, in the seventeen months of operation the Sobibor extermination machinery killed 350,000 human beings.[1]

Of the six labor/extermination camps and killing centers in Poland, Sobibor and Chelmno are the least known. Before the war Sobibor was a small obscure railroad station. Himmler picked the site for the second extermination camp of the Wirth River Bug Chain. In March 1942 the Germans brought a squad of Jewish laborers from neighboring towns to build the camp, an area of about 60 hectares. Under the supervision of Ukrainian guards and

SS officer Christian Wirth, the Jews erected the gas chamber buildings, with an intended output of 20,000 bodies a day. They surrounded Sobibor with four rows of barbed wire fence, a ravine filled with water, and a mined field. Like Belzec, Treblinka, and Chelmno, Sobibor was not a camp in the true sense of the word. Only twenty barracks existed for all prisoners and workers. The Nazis built Sobibor as an advanced killing center, and most Jews died shortly after arrival. Himmler ordered one special enterprise, the dissembling and salvage of captured ammunition. It does not seem to have been put into operation.[2]

The opening of Sobibor in 1942 enabled Hitler's resettlement scheme to continue even though Belzec was overworked and out of action for six weeks. Sobibor truly "filled the gap" until Auschwitz and Treblinka reached full production. Himmler's visit in July 1943 resulted in an acceleration of the extermination to a high of 15,000 buried in a single day. For Himmler's dinner party, 300 Jewish girls were gassed in his honor.[3] Thus the words in Revelations 6:8 seem to provide an accurate description of Sobibor:

And I looked, and behold a pale horse: and his name that sat on him was Death, and Hell followed with him. And Power was given unto them over the fourth part of the earth, to kill with sword, and with hunger, and with death, and with the beasts of the earth.

The victims came from all over Europe. From the Vüght camp in Holland in late spring of 1943 the Germans shipped out children, aged one to sixteen, with their mothers. They told them they were joing to a "special children's camp—Sobibor." The majority of victims were Jews from Poland and German-occupied USSR. Transports of 1,500 to 2,000 Jewish deportees arrived daily from Poland, Czechoslovakia, Holland, France, Austria, and other occupied countries. The Nazis excelled in deception. Many Jews from Western Europe arrived in luxury trains. So deceived were they that they offered the train personnel tips as they climbed down the steps. The SS kept a small number of Sobibor Jews alive to cook, clean, launder, polish, and sew for them, and to pander to their special tastes such as performing music and making jewelry. They also used them to sort, store, and ship victims' remnants, run the gas chambers, cremate the bodies, and bury the remains.

SS leader Globocnik administered Sobibor. The procedures of his commandants—first Richard Thomalla, then Fritz Stangl, and finally Franz Reichleitner—differed little from those at other killing centers. While being driven from the trains, the men were separated from the women and children. After the prisoners undressed, barbers cut their hair while others took away their clothing and belongings. The victims died in five carbon monoxide gas chambers. Although writers disagree on the total capacity of the chambers (from 400 to 2,000), they agree they were housed in a massive building with "stone inside-walls and wooden outside-walls." Witnesses testified that death took about fifteen minutes. Chains pulled out the corpses through a specially constructed door; and railroad cars carried the bodies to the cremation sites. Inmates tossed the victims' bodies into pits and sprinkled them with lime. The stench was terrible.[4]

As in all camps, the procedures never worked quickly and efficiently enough to satisfy the annihilation demands or meet the tasks of disposing of mountains of possessions. Often one transport was kept waiting on the tracks while the workers completed the gassing of the previous transport. The SS tried to solve the bottleneck problems by increasing the number of Jewish work squads and by introducing a specialized work procedure. At one time the squads had stored so many Jewish valuables in the available buildings that the walls had to be strengthened to prevent the buildings from bursting.[5]

The pit method proved slow, difficult, and very noticeable. The summer heat of 1942 produced a terrible smell and polluted water. A new process went into effect which spread the smell of burnt flesh and the sight of smoke and fire throughout the region. The workers placed the bodies in layers on grates made of rails and supported by stone foundations:

The device was very simple. Two parallel rows of concrete posts supported the rails, on which the corpses were placed, and a fire was lit beneath the bodies. Easily combustible materials were used for this purpose. By the time this system of burning the bodies was introduced, a great number of corpses was already amassed in the ditches. They were dug out by means of excavators and subsequently burned on the grates.[6]

Toward the end, burning in large open pits took care of most of the body disposal.[7] A few sources speak of the unlikely use of crematoria. It may be true that such ovens were built, but too late to be of use. Following cremation, workers pulverized the bones with mallets, stuffed the powder into sacks, and sent them to Germany to be sold as fertilizer.

The SS made good use of the victims' belongings. Ber Feinberg, a Warsaw wigmaker, spent seventeen months in Sobibor and recalled that every day a trainload of ten cars left the camp for Germany filled with clothing, shoes, and sacks of women's hair:

Later I was transferred to other work. In Camp II three barracks were erected especially for women. In the first they took off their shoes, in the second their clothes, and in the third their hair was cut off. Being a wigmaker I was assigned to the third barracks. We were twenty wigmakers and we all cut the women's hair and stuffed it into sacks. The Germans told the women that their hair was cut for hygienic reasons.[8]

The SS committed their usual atrocities in Sobibor. They stomped on little children and smashed in their skulls. Their dogs tore chunks of flesh from prisoners' bodies. Any sign of disease or illness meant instant death. The Jewish workers found a child among the clothing rags. A guard rushed over, took a shovel, and "split open the baby into pieces." Babies born were thrown directly into garbage pits or "were torn apart down the middle by their legs, or just flung up and shot in the air."[9]

In 1972 Gitta Sereny interviewed Stangl, the notorious Treblinka commandant, who had also been commandant of Sobibor. Stangl described the gassing area as a three-room brick building fifteen minutes from the camp center.[10]

Sobibor had a gassing trial run, with the aid of a chemist consultant from Belzec—Dr. "Blaurock" or Dr. "Blaubock." He measured the concentration of gas in the mechanism before the thirty-five Jewish victims entered the chamber; and he regulated the motor activity during the gassing.

In spite of testing, the flimsy chambers sometimes failed. One day the following incident occurred:

When the people were already in the "bath," something went wrong with the apparatus supplying the gas. The victims broke down the door and started to run out. The SS killed some of them in the yard; the rest were driven back in again. The mechanic repaired the machine and everything proceeded according to schedule.[11]

When Stangl became the Sobibor commandant, he said he lived on two levels of consciousness. His overwhelming memories centered on sandflies:

I was walking from the forester's hut—my quarters—to one of the construction sites and suddenly I began to itch all over. I thought I was going crazy—it was awful; I couldn't even reach everywhere at once to scratch. Michel said, "Didn't anybody warn you? It's sandflies, they are all over the place. You shouldn't have come out without boots." . . . I rushed back to my room and took everything off—I remember just handing all the stuff to somebody out of the door, and they boiled and disinfected everything. My clothes and almost every inch of me were covered with the things; they attach themselves to all the hair on your body. I had water brought in and bathed and bathed.[12]

All SS officers at Sobibor tortured and killed prisoners. Each seemed to have his own special technique. Frenzel murdered children for crimes as small as stealing a can of sardines. When Groth sent a young Jewish boy to retrieve an umbrella from a barrack roof, the boy fell off and received twenty lashes. That incident catalyzed the new SS parachute game—pushing Jews with umbrellas off roofs. The notorious Gomerski stabbed workers in their behinds with a pocket knife when they bent over to pick up branches while cutting trees. Other SS officers sewed up prisoners' trousers, threw rats inside, and beat any rat victims who moved an inch. Bauer broke a bottle in his private bar one day. He ordered a prisoner to clean the floor with his tongue—cutting his face to shreds from the glass.[13]

One of the most vicious SS officers was Gustav Franz Wagner, known to the victims as "Wolf," the "Camp Sword," or the "Hangman of Sobibor." Wagner earned his various titles because he hit, killed, trampled men to death, and practiced marksmanship with both bottles and Jews as his targets. Considered a demon, that "strong-as-a-bull" German tested his muscles by ripping children out of their mothers' arms and tossing them into the air until they died. He became joyous at the sight of a cattle car full of naked, frozen women and took delight in photographing them. After a young woman gave birth, Wagner ordered the baby thrown into the latrine. Later prisoners found the baby floating in the excrement. Wagner learned his trade, along with his friend Stangl, in the euthanasia program, and had served an apprenticeship at Castle Hartheim.

Wagner and Stangl escaped capture after the war by fleeing together to Brazil. Wagner became a servant in a Brazilian household, and was known for being happy, helpful, well-behaved, and loving toward children. In 1967 Simon Wiesenthal (the Nazi hunter) discovered Stangl, and the Brazilian government deported him to Germany to stand trial. After Stangl died of a heart attack following his trial, Wagner proposed to his widow. She refused him because she considered him vulgar and sadistic.

Wiesenthal also found Wagner in Brazil. Brazilian courts heard the testimony against Wagner from many witnesses claiming he had killed 150,000 people. Wagner insisted at first that he had worked in construction at Sobibor. When faced with witnesses, fingerprints, and documentary proof, however, he collapsed. At his questioning, Wagner said that Sobibor was a "work paradise." Only mentally ill people were killed there, he claimed, because the overburdened hospitals in Germany could not handle them all. The Brazilian court released Wagner in 1979, after failing either to convict him or to order his extradition. His file was closed. In October 1980, Gustav Wagner committed suicide at age 69 on his isolated farm eighty kilometers from San Paulo, Brazil. He knifed himself in the chest.

The Sobibor Revolt

On October 14, 1943, an amazing revolt took place in Sobibor. At its end the camp was evacuated and destroyed. At the time of the successful revolt, 600 prisoners resided in the camp. What is extraordinary is that the underground movement that organized the revolt was but three weeks old! Several escape plans had previously been formulated at the camp, and some unsuccessful escapes had been attempted.

A Russian by the name of Alexander Pecherski, a former political commissar of the Red Army, arrived at Sobibor three weeks before the revolt, and provided the leadership. After the war he wrote his memoirs, *The Revolt of Sobibor,* published in Moscow. He described how he had designed a plan that, had it been implemented fully, would have saved more inmates.

Pecherski enumerated the details of his plan to a small group of aides. First the SS officer group had to be quietly eliminated. That process should take no more than an hour. He assigned the killing of the German officers to dependable men selected from the Soviet prisoners of war. At 3:30 P.M. a *Kapo,* Brzeki, who had agreed to cooperate in return for his life, would take three men to Camp III. Those men would kill the four Nazi officers working there. At 4 P.M. prisoners would cut the telephone wires connecting the camp with the guard reserve, signaling the beginning of the killing of the officers in the main camp. The officers would be invited individually to the workshops, where two prisoners would be waiting to kill them. At the same time two co-operative *Kapos* would line the inmates up as though they were taking them to work, and the column would head for the exit. One group would attack the weapons arsenal; the others, the guards. Once the weapons had been seized, the guards at the gate would be removed and the watchtower attacked. Although the fields around Sobibor were mined, Pecherski assumed that the field next to the officers' houses contained signal mines, which were not dangerous. It was at that point that the wire fence would be broken through; and those in the front lines would throw stones as they ran in order to clear the mine field.

When the day for the escape came, plans went according to schedule, for a time. The prisoners cut the phone wires and killed some of the German officers. Pecherski gave the signal for the full revolt. Those who had military training proceeded as planned, but the rest of the prisoners seemed to run helter-skelter throughout the camp. The attack in the arsenal did not succeed because a barrage of automatic fire cut off the attackers. Most inmates rushed for the central exit. Trampling the guards, they pushed through the gates and made for the woods. One group hacked its way through the barbed wire on the wrong side of the camp and perished in the mine fields. Pecherski and his group ran through the unmined field behind the officers' house and escaped. Fifty-seven of his group took to the woods, joined the partisans, and survived.

When the revolt was over, eleven SS guards were dead, thirty-eight Ukrainian guards were dead or wounded, and forty Ukrainian guards escaped rather than face the Germans. Historians have muddled the issue on how many escaped, but some facts are certain: 600 inmates made a break for freedom, and 400 actually succeeded in breaking out of the camp, though about half of those were casualties of the land mines. Some were killed by

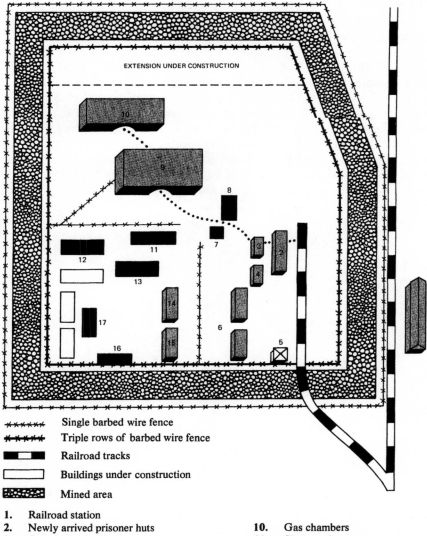

EXTENSION UNDER CONSTRUCTION

✗✗✗✗✗✗	Single barbed wire fence
✗✗✗✗✗	Triple rows of barbed wire fence
▬▬	Railroad tracks
☐	Buildings under construction
▨▨	Mined area

1. Railroad station
2. Newly arrived prisoner huts
3. Garage
4. Arsenal
5. Guard tower
6. SS officers' villas
7. Water tower
8. Ukranian barracks
9. Undressing sheds
10. Gas chambers
11. Shops and storage
12. Men's barracks
13. Women's barracks
14. Tailor and furrier shops
15. Carpenter shop
16. Lavatories
17. Kitchen and baths

Map 10: Sobibor Death Camp

Map representation by Sharon Coughran

pursuing aircraft and by the SS, police, and troops numbering in the thousands. More were murdered by Polish fascists of the Home Army. The rest, probably a hundred, reached freedom and/or the Soviet partisans. Perhaps only thirty-five survived the end of the war.

Four days after the revolt a special *Kommando* arrived in Sobibor on Himmler's orders. They dynamited all the buildings and the watchtowers, and pulled down the barbed wire fence posts. The big cranes evacuated the pits, and the SS burned the bodies. They sent in thirty Jews for final cleanup. They plowed the earth and planted pine trees. The revolt resulted in the closing of a camp that had already claimed the lives of hundreds of thousands of Jews, and would have killed many more.[14]

TREBLINKA: THE VICTORY OF THE TECHNICIANS

In the middle of nowhere is the experimental killing center of Treblinka. The "Big Factory of Death." Graveyard for a million souls. Isolated. Stark. Lonely. Desolate. The forgotten railroad station of the tiny village of Treblinka rises unexpectedly out of the sandy plain dotted with pine woods, marshes, lush farmlands, fields of bright wild flowers. The transportation of one million condemned required a large depot. And there it was. In the center of a sparsely populated, backwoods area, a railway collection point. No buildings, but several sidings in use, then—yet. Dozens of empty cattle cars wait on the tracks, precisely as though each had just disgorged its frightened Jewish contents.

Treblinka may be an important national monument, but it is difficult to find. Although the distance in kilometers from Warsaw is short, the drive takes five hours round trip because of the cows, ducks, wagons, and peasants using the narrow roads. There are no markings or road signs to the town or the camp—until one is right on top of it. And then, a lone sign stands in peculiar relief against the countryside.

The Germans liquidated Treblinka and destroyed all traces, except for a few bones. But in the dirt are the ashes of at least 800,000 dead. Out of those ashes grow the pine trees planted by the Germans, and the wild grass and flowers planted by no one. The camp area is so large that it includes a mixture of green forest and sandy barren clearings, and is well hidden from everything except the peasant farms encircling the area. No buildings remain. *Nothing* of the old remains except the grounds—a flat expanse broken by the large holes, now empty, that once contained the bodies of the dead.

Treblinka with its yellowish sand, reflecting the dry hot summer sun beating down out of an unusually blue, cloudless sky. The smell here is strange. I knew by my nose when I had reached the camp. And that strange odor did not come from imagination. It almost, but only almost, conjures up the all-pervading stench of former times. In the empty silence, broken only by the rustle of the wind and the voices of flocks of birds, one can imagine the pounding of the excavator engines, the whines of the scoop shovels, the shouts of the guards, the cries of the prisoners, the bustle of a busy place. The silence is so deep, it reverberates.

Treblinka, rock monument symbolizing the death of the Warsaw Jews, by F. Duszenko.

Walking along the site of the former railroad tracks, represented now by great concrete slabs stretching into the distance, one wonders what the condemned saw, felt, believed. And then one enters the camp area and trudges down the Road to Heaven to the gas chamber location, a spot (like all others) to be guessed at, for there are no markers, no traces. One stands at the excavation holes, knowing that hundreds of thousands of humans died there, but believing none of it, or perhaps too much of it. Where huts and watchtowers and piles of clothing and barbed wire stood, nature has taken over and recovered the land to herself.

But the memorial—the sensitive, *strong,* unique memorial—brings it all back through the shape and the thrusting of thousands of stones pointing to the sky like a vast field of arms reaching upward, imploring. The majesty, the awesome dignity of the silent stone field encircling the central monument. The stones, everywhere, go on forever, creating an eerie but beautiful aura around the ash field.

In 1961 the Polish government set up a Civilian Committee for Commemoration, which determined to build a memorial area somehow worthy of the past. "We want to enshrine these buried memories in the redemption of the yearnings of those who died in despair with only an imperishable hope that they would be remembered." Through public subscription throughout Poland the committee raised the necessary funds to build the symbolic railway and cemetery created by Polish sculptors Adam Haupt and Franciszek Duszenko. The memorial was unveiled in May 1964.[1]

Trains brought the stones to the Treblinka station. Trucks with cranes conveyed the stone blocks, cement, and brick to the area. And there they created a symbolic cemetery with thousands of granite slabs, all different sizes, representing the humans killed from the cities, towns, and villages of Poland. Thousands of natural rocks in a symbolic cemetery scattered in a random way around a central monument. Stones—some blunt, some ragged, most moving in the shape of a triangle from a base to a sharp point. Each small stone seems to represent a village; the larger stones, towns; and all are dwarfed by the towering rugged rock symbolizing the 300,000 Warsaw Jews who died at Treblinka. Many stones have inscriptions designating a place, a town. A pit of small black stones lies near the main monument. And back toward the entrance the former path of death is covered now with hundreds of 30-pound rounded rocks—a cobblestone road in relief. At the end of the road is a memorial to the 10,000 non-Jewish Polish prisoners who died at the labor camp nearby—a burial ground with hundreds of crosses.

The Germans snatched Treblinka from oblivion. Nature and time have handed it back.

In July 1942 the third killing center in the River Bug Chain, Treblinka, opened its doors for business. Because of its location 120 kilometers northeast of Warsaw, Himmler carefully selected Treblinka as the site for the extermination of the Warsaw ghetto Jews. The sandy region he chose was overgrown with pines and far from major centers of human habitation.

Himmler sent Dr. Irmfried Eberl to Treblinka as its first commandant to direct construction. The SS began the project on June 1, 1942, using Jewish workers from the surrounding area. They killed them when the camp was finished in the middle of July.

Designated by Himmler as a killing center, Treblinka proved to be an unusually efficient destruction instrument. From 800,000 to 1,000,000 Jews of central Poland, particularly Warsaw, and from Germany, Austria, Czechoslovakia, Holland, Belgium, and Greece met their deaths at Treblinka. That extermination record was accomplished in a little over a year. Treblinka had the shortest life of any camp: from July 1942 to the fall of 1943, when it was destroyed following the famous August prisoner revolt.[2]

Several years before the war the Poles began operating a gravel pit 4 kilometers from the small station of Treblinka and connected to it by a long railroad siding. After the occupation of Poland the Germans took over the pit as a source of raw materials for army fortifications. Later, when military exploitation of the gravel ended, a German officer in Sokolow Podlaski erected a concrete factory to utilize the raw material. The need for a low-cost labor force inspired the idea of founding a forced-labor camp near the gravel pit named Arbeitslager Treblinka I. Although the beginning date cannot be fixed, an order exists, dated November 15, 1941, establishing that penal colony. During its life 10,000 Poles passed through it. Seventy-five percent of them died.[3]

Because of its single-minded purpose, Treblinka had few of the accouterments of a regular concentration camp. Most visitors were exterminated on the day of arrival, which eliminated the need for major housing facilities. Seven to eight hundred guards ran the death factory and supervised the one thousand worker Jews. Although minor industrial activity existed, it was not linked to the war effort. For death purposes, thirteen gas chambers utilizing carbon monoxide gas produced a body count of 25,000 Jews a day—30,000 if everything went perfectly.[4]

Treblinka *was* different. In its time it was the largest and most efficient killing operation the world had ever known. No subsequent camp could destroy both the lives and the bodies of nearly a million people in one year. It was a truly monstrous carnage by any criteria. But Treblinka was different in another way, perhaps much more important. It was at Treblinka that the technicians finally triumphed over overwhelming odds and against problems never before encountered. It was at Treblinka that the technicians struggled mightily to overcome the impossibility of secretly destroying the lives, bodies, and possessions of masses of people in a short period of time—and succeeded. No wonder those experts and specialists who tested their technical skills at Treblinka came away proud and highly respected by their colleagues. For it is no easy task to kill, destroy all traces, and profitably dispose of all possessions of hordes of people in a process that ensures quiet, efficiency, calmness, and surprise—and do it at a low cost and high profit, utilizing available materials in a wartime economy. The technicians met all these problems with daring, creativity, and genius.

As *the* extermination center experimental station, Treblinka developed methods of using limited manpower to handle large groups of people; to keep thousands of humans facing death unaware of their sentence until the last moment; to discover the maximum body condition at which gassing would be most quickly accomplished; to design such complex and sophisticated assembly-line techniques that all processes in every category proceeded like clockwork; to burn completely 25,000 bodies a day without the use of scarce gasoline or wood; and to dispose of possessions in an organized and financially lucrative manner. The technicians succeeded beyond their wildest dreams. Every experiment produced conclusive answers to major extermination problems. And then the job was done. The SS destroyed Treblinka in 1943 and left it almost without a trace.

Treblinka consisted of an area of 16 to 20 hectares. Barbed wire divided the camp into two parts. Camp I had a railroad siding, a fake train station, a fake hospital or *Lazarett,* undressing barracks, stores, warehouses, ammunition magazines, workshops, offices, the yard used for roll calls, concerts, punishments, and sports events, living quarters for the SS, Ukrainians, and some of the Jewish workers, pig stys, food depots, garages, a kitchen—and later, a number of fancy additions and renovations. On first glance, it looked like a genuine labor camp.

Camp II was a different matter. It was the extermination area and contained two buildings with thirteen gas chambers, living quarters for the Jewish burial and burning squads, a laundry, a laboratory, a small women's cabin, the trenches or graves for the bodies, the primitive pyre cremation arrangements made from rails and concrete supports, and the three mechanical excavators for the exhumation of corpses. The "tube" that led from the "undressing barracks" in the lower camp (Camp I) to the gas chambers in the upper camp (Camp II) was a 90-meter-long fenced-off path. The SS called the tube the "Road to Heaven."

In the summer of 1942 Himmler ordered the final resettlement of Polish Jewry. Treblinka's first task was the extermination of the Warsaw ghetto residents. The process proceeded slowly because Treblinka had only three gas chambers—the major gassing facility was still under construction. Nevertheless, the Nazis transported three-fourths of the Warsaw ghetto inhabitants to the camps between July and October. Most went to Treblinka. Mass deportations from Warsaw to Treblinka began on July 22. Trains transported 5,000 Jews a day; and within two months Treblinka had exterminated 300,000.[5]

Several people attempted to warn the Warsaw Jews of their fate. The Bund sent a young Jew, Zalman Friedrych, to Sokolow, a small village outside Treblinka. He learned that all Jews arriving at Treblinka met immediate death. The Bund published his report and an escapee confirmed it later. But the Warsaw Jews refused to face the truth. They believed that Treblinka was a horrible place, but that Warsaw was special; the Nazis would not dare to do in Warsaw what they had done in the rural areas.[6]

The death train to Treblinka normally consisted of forty to sixty standard boxcars. Some days there would be no trains. Karl Wolff, a leading SS official, wrote to one of his superiors on August 13:

... I was especially pleased to learn from you that already for a fortnight a daily train, taking 5,000 of the Chosen People every time, had gone to Treblinka, so that we are now able to carry out this shifting of population at increased speed. I have contacted the departments concerned myself, so that the smooth carrying out of all these measures seems to be guaranteed.[7]

The Polish citizens in the area knew the truth. Initially, they had heard rumors that the place was a camp for Jews working on damming the River Bug, or a military installation, or a control area for a new secret military weapon. But a Polish railroad man spread the real description of the camp, and by the end of the summer railroad men were selling photographs of the Treblinka "bathhouse." Survivors insist that the true nature of Treblinka could not have been a secret. "The Poles between there and Warsaw must have known about it, and lived off the proceeds. All the peasants came to barter, the Warsaw whores did business with the Ukrainians—it was a circus for all of them."[8]

The remaining ghetto Jews composed a ballad that was sung throughout ghettoland, telling the story of the transports to the Treblinka death camp:

Our brothers across the ocean
Cannot feel our bitter pain.
They cannot feel our bitter anguish
As death lurks over us every moment.
The war will end some day.
The world will realize the unheard-of horror.
Our Jewish heart is filled with pain:
Who will be able to heal our hurt?
Rivers of tears will flow,
When they will find some day
The biggest grave in the world
In Treblinka, in Treblinka.[9]

During the days of increased tension in the Warsaw ghetto a young boy who had heard the horror stories of Treblinka wrote to his younger sister in Palestine:

Dear Tamara, Where should I begin? I will start with mother. She was taken to Treblinka. Everyday thousands of mothers, fathers and children are being dragged away. Why should our mother be an exception? . . . Do you know how people die in Treblinka? The boxcars are shunted into a special track up to the murder house. . . . Then the people have to undress. *Nagaikas*—submachine guns. Everyone has to put his clothes bundle on a special spot. Then he gets a number. So he is being sent to work, of course. But before he goes to work he has to be deloused (the camp commander usually says: "the most modern delousing plant in Europe"). They go inside. After a minute there suddenly resounds horrible screaming. But only very briefly. A lever is turned over and a huge maw opens and swallows the people that are later burned in the crematorium. The entire process only takes a few minutes. (Friends of Wanda, "good" Germans, say: "What is so horrible about that? Our people are dying at the front. And it doesn't hurt here, either. It's over quickly.") Jews, who have been especially selected beforehand, collect the clothes under the supervision of Ukrainians and load them into wagons. They also take the ash out of the crematorium. And then they too are sent to be "deloused." Sometimes one of them succeeds in hiding under the rags. And someone like that will tell you everything afterward. And so mother has died also.[10]

A small group of SS men administered Treblinka. Himmler had removed Dr. Eberl because he had failed to kill the victims efficiently and quickly and replaced him with the Sobibor commandant. Fritz Stangl brought with him his Sobibor assistant, Kurt Franz. In 1972 Gitta Sereny interviewed him extensively and published her study in an astonishing book, *Into That Darkness.* Stangl seemed like a "decent enough" man, she wrote, a good father, an excellent husband. He remembered his first impressions of the camp. Driving along the road, he could see corpses lying on the railroad track and at the station—hundreds of corpses that had obviously been sprawling on the ground for several days in the heat. Stangl had never seen anything like it, not even in Sobibor; and he remembered that day as his worst during the Third Reich—a "Dante's Inferno." The thousands of decomposing, putrefying bodies produced an indescribable smell. His first action was to try to reduce the odor. In the gas chamber waiting area, where the women defecated from fear, Stangl suggested to extermination expert Wirth that he place buckets. Wirth responded: "I don't care a damn what you did with shit in Sobibor. Let them beshit themselves."[11]

Stangl reflected that he soon became accustomed to the liquidations. He repressed his thoughts of them by building a special retreat with gardens, zoos, and new buildings—and by drinking. Finally, he concluded that Jews were cargo, garbage, nonhuman—a mass of rotting flesh. Although he detested what was happening, he said, he made no protest because he was convinced that such a protest would be a useless gesture, resulting only in his death. Stangl insisted he did not hate the Jews, but only felt contempt for their weakness, their passivity.

Although fully aware and supportive of camp operations, Commandant Stangl was more a figurehead, an observer, than one of the actual experts who identified the problems, analyzed them, and solved them. It was his technical assistants who put into motion the industrial models to develop Treblinka as the world's first major killing center. In creating a killing center, it was first necessary to invent the killing machinery. Since the SS experts had no precedent on which to rely, they had to use their imaginations.

There must be a better method than small mobile vans, they reasoned. A fixed gassing facility could be of unlimited size, they thought. They built one. Once the gas chamber was in place, "amateurism, guesswork and the mistakes inherent in all innovations came to an end. The Final Solution entered the era of modern technology. The machine came to man's aid; engineering took over where good will left off. An almost perfect system had been created. A new world was about to be born."[12]

At first, Treblinka operated with the same chaos noticeable at other killing centers, but the vast numbers to be disposed of from the Warsaw ghetto forced the SS to smooth out the killing process. The camp's three small gas chambers were inadequate. The situation demanded efficiency, organization, and specialization. It also required the aid of a sizable work force. The only help available were the Jews. Capitalizing on the hopes and fears of their victims, the planners sought to develop a slave society whose members would labor for their masters as compliant, obedient workers.

The technicians split the extermination process into four tasks: handling the live bodies, handling the bodies' possessions, handling the dead bodies, and taking care of camp upkeep. They broke down the first task—handling live bodies—into two categories. In the first they needed to remove the Jews from the train, collect the baggage, and clean the cars. One *Kommando* handled that function. The staff also needed to undress and shave the victims and get their clothes into the square. The "Jews of the Square" performed that second job.

The second task, handling the possessions, lent itself quite easily to the assembly-line process. Each object had its own sorting *Kommando:* there was a separate *Kommando* for trousers, shirts, toothbrushes, eyeglasses, and so on. The SS gave special status to the Jews who sorted the gold and the money, calling them *Goldjuden* or Jews of Gold.[13]

To dispose of the dead bodies, the SS placed the *Totenjuden* or Jews of Death in Camp II and sealed it off from the rest of the camp. That

Kommando removed the bodies from the chambers, extracted the teeth, threw the bodies into the ditches, and covered them with dirt. The Jews labeled the road to Camp II the "Road of No Return."

The Court Jews, the aristocrats among the victims, were responsible for camp upkeep. They lived west of the chamber, in the roll call compound, on land sloping downward. Their area was therefore called "Below." The compound was called "Above" and Camp II was termed "Down There."[14]

The SS planners were obsessed by the goal of perfection. For a perfect system to evolve, the camp would have to run itself, and that requirement would necessitate serious reforms. The reforms came from the creative mind of Kurt Franz. His ideas predated the advanced computer in a robot/ automation format. "We must reach the point where we no longer have to do anything, not even press a button when we get up in the morning. We create a perfect system, then we watch it work. As masters, our role is not to do but to be."[15]

Franz did not have his way—entirely. The prisoners, awakening from their initial shock, were humans, not robots, whatever their outward appearance. First, they discovered a free act—suicide—and their ability to select death limited the authority of the planners. From that point, a process of living, struggling, watching, cooperating, challenging, and waiting emerged and the game became more complex.[16]

How did the residents and the prospective arrivals describe Treblinka? The ghetto historian Emmanuel Ringelblum pictured Treblinka as "the slaughter house of the European Jewry."[17] Survivors always talk of Treblinka as a dismal place. The weather itself was a killer. One witness told of the significance of the outside undressing method in the winter. When the temperature reached 30° to 35° C. below zero, mothers and children stood naked outside. The victims seemed to realize death was waiting for them.

Some of them suffered nervous shock, crying and laughing alternately. Irritated guards made use of their whips. Babies who interfered with the shaving of their mother's hair were grabbed by the legs and smashed against the wall. Upon occasion, the guard handed the bloody mess to the mother.[18]

Yankel Wiernik was transported to Treblinka from Warsaw in August 1942. He escaped and soon after wrote his story. The underground smuggled a copy out of Poland, which was relayed to New York, where the Jewish Worker's Union published it in 1944. As a member of the Jewish death squad, Wiernik had intimate familiarity with the three small gas chambers. Each chamber, measuring 25 square meters and 2 meters high, was situated in a brick building separated from Camp I by a wooden wall. Walls of wood and masonry formed a corridor.

The victims were ushered through the doors from the corridor and their bodies were dragged through the doors facing Camp Two. Along the gas chamber stood an electric station, about as large as the chambers but somewhat higher. This station provided light for both camps. A motor from a Soviet tank pumped in the gas, which reached the chambers through inflex valves. The speediness of the execution depended on the quantity of the gas intake.

Two Ukrainians operated the death machines. One was called Ivan, a tall man with pleasant eyes, but nevertheless a sadist.[19]

On his first day, when Wiernik saw men, women, and children running to the gas chambers, he nearly went mad. He said that he tore his hair and wept unceasingly. His description of the death scene is as vivid as any:

I suffered most when I looked at the little ones walking beside their mothers, or at the others walking alone, who had no thought of the quick and cruel death impending. Their eyes were wide with fear and wonder. . . . When they saw the stoney faces of their parents, however, they kept silent and prepared for whatever might come. They remained stock still or nestled against one another or cuddled up to their parents, awaiting the ghastly end. Suddenly the entrance doors would swing open. Ivan would appear with a thick gas pipe, a meter long. Nicholai was with him, swinging a sword. At a signal the victims would be driven in, clubbed and lashed without mercy. To this day the fearful screams of the women and the crying of the children ring in my ears. There was despair and agony in the screams. . . .

Into the chamber of twenty-five square meters 450 to 500 people were jammed. The congestion was unbelievable. The victims carried in the children, somehow hoping thus to save them from death. On their way to die they were beaten and driven by truncheons and gas pipes. Dogs were set upon them; barking, they threw themselves upon the victims. Everyone, eager to escape the blows and the dogs, rushed screaming into the lethal chamber. The stronger pushed the weaker. But the tumult did not long endure. The doors closed with a clang on the packed chamber. The motor was connected with the inflow apparatus and switched on. In twenty-five minutes, at the most, all lay dead. But they did not really lie, for they had no room to fall. They died standing, their legs and arms entangled. There were no more screams. Mothers and children were clasped in death's embrace. . . . No one was more beautiful or ugly—all were suffocated, yellowed by gas.[20]

Wiernik recalls that 10,000 to 12,000 people were asphyxiated each day.

Martin Gray went to Treblinka in a cattle car. He observed men covered with welts, prisoners killed with shovels, inmates attacked by dogs, and his entire family sent to the gas chambers. For him, human time ceased. Another category of time had been created without clocks, marked by the arrival of the trains and the assemblies. "I wasn't aware of how the sky might change during a day: my eyes saw only the yellowish sand and their boots."[21]

Gray was a member of the burial squad and his description rings with grim authority. In the area of the graves the sound of the digging machines was overwhelming. A giant excavator plunged its arm into the sand. Guards shouted and prisoners rushed around carrying stretchers. "The bodies were naked, entwined tendrils; the bodies were yellow and blood had dribbled down their faces and their noses. They were my mother, my brothers, . . . all my people." Prisoners threw the bodies into the ditches and the excavator pushed the sand over them. Sometimes Gray found living children among the dead, the warm bodies still clinging to their silent mothers. The squads strangled them and threw them back. One group encountered by Gray and his fellow workers were the children, staff, and director of the Warsaw Jewish Orphanage. Janusz Korczak, a true hero of the Warsaw ghetto, refused all offers of escape and led his children through the silent streets to the Treblinka train. Did he know what awaited in Treblinka? Perhaps, as someone has suggested, his mission was to remind the world "that no child should ever be allowed to die alone."[22]

Yankel Wiernik remembers the day he arrived at Treblinka. By late afternoon the camp yard was littered with corpses: "their faces distorted with fright and awe, black and swollen, the eyes wide open, with protruding tongues, skulls crushed, bodies mangled. And, blood everywhere." The SS assigned Wiernik to the squad that handled the corpses. The men dragged the corpses on the run—bodies that had been lying around for some time. The stench was overpowering. Sometimes an arm or a leg fell off while they were moving the bodies. The Ukrainian guards, drunk and bored, often selected the best-looking Jewish women from the transports, dragged them to their barrack, raped them, and then delivered them to the death chambers.[23]

In early autumn 1942 the prisoners finished the new gassing facility located between Camps I and II. The ten chambers—five on each side of a corridor—measured 50 square meters. The outer walls were large trap doors that could be raised to facilitate corpse removal. The floors of the chambers sloped toward the outer side.[24]

The new structure had five terraces with hedges and flowers set around them. On the roof was a large Star of David. Although new, the chambers functioned poorly because of the inadequate motor; and the Jews inside often suffered interminably. Some were still alive when the SS reopened the doors. When all thirteen gas chambers were in operation, Wiernik remembered that on some days 20,000 people were killed. Several Jews who worked on the gas chamber *Kommando*, as many as fifteen or twenty each night, would hang themselves upon returning from their "work."[25]

Kurt Franz's dream of a perfect system was not yet a reality, for while the facilities were modern, the organization was not. Getting the Jews from the train to the chamber took too long. Franz asked his top aide, Lalka, to solve the bottleneck. The root of the problem was the arrival of the train. The Jews sensed or saw destruction and contributed to the disorder. If they could be given concrete hope of life, perhaps they would quiet down and cooperate.[26]

The planners designed a false colorfully painted railroad station surrounded by flowers. Its timetables, posters, and curtains put the Jews at ease. So did the signs to different doors: "Station Master," "Toilet," "Infirmary." The door to the undressing room was labeled "Bialystok." To the eye, it seemed a "pretty station in a little provincial town." So the arriving Jews took hope. The *Kommando* politely but firmly escorted them from the car, and cleaned the car in five minutes. So far so good.

The undressing and shaving stage of the process needed attention. Lalka grouped the victims and conducted the sick and old to the "hospital," where the guards seated them on a long bench facing a trench. Standing behind the bench, they shot the victims in the back and their bodies fell into the trench. Lalka set up a clothing production line so that each prisoner would drop a piece of his clothing at each station until he was naked. To process the women whose heads would be shaved, the SS created a "beauty salon" where nude women sat on long benches. Behind each bench the barbers waited. Lalka perfected a technique that he called "the Treblinka cut." "With five well-placed slashes the whole head of hair was transferred to a sack placed beside each hairdresser for this purpose. It was simple and efficient."[27]

The SS abandoned deception at the next stage of the process—the 90-meter run down the Road to Heaven to the gas chamber. Since winded and frightened victims inhale more gas and die quickly, it made sense to create panic in the victims and force them to run to the chamber. Guards stationed along the road with whips ended all sparks of hope. Any leftover victims were forced to do calisthenics in an adjoining area until it was their turn.[28]

The leaders could point with pride to their streamlined system: it took forty-five minutes from cattle car to gas chamber. The new procedures made it possible to handle twenty trains of twenty cars each or 24,000 Jews between 7 A.M. and 1:30 P.M. if everything went right.

Prior to the final tightening of the process, Commandant Höss of Auschwitz visited Treblinka in the summer of 1942 to study the extermination process before he completed the Auschwitz plant. In his Nuremberg testimony Höss indicated he did not think Treblinka's gas chambers were very efficient because carbon monoxide gas took so long to kill. But he learned from the Treblinka process and adopted it with some changes. Besides using Cyclone B instead of carbon monoxide at Auschwitz, he built his gas chambers to accommodate 2,000 victims at a time. At Treblinka, he stated, the ten gas chambers could only accommodate 200 people each. Höss also decided to fool his Auschwitz victims into thinking they were merely undergoing a delousing process, because he noted that the Treblinka victims almost always knew at some point that they would be exterminated.[29]

The Treblinka body-disposal process remained chaotic until the experts devised an assembly-line technique. The body carriers raced double-time to the ditch. Instead of having the same workers carry the bodies to the ditch and also go down and stack them, the SS created a body-stacker squad that remained in the ditch. The carriers threw the bodies into the ditch and ran back for the next load.

From a primitive operation producing chaos and panic, Treblinka developed into a well-oiled machine capable of handling efficiently a large number of deportees with two hours' notice. That machine depended on trained prisoners. Thus Franz did not exterminate his Jewish work squads as early as other camps did. "By unremitting effort Franz succeeded in turning the camp into an extraordinary machine whose every wheel, perfectly oiled, turned smoothly, processing convoy after convoy, without a cry, without a hitch, with fantastic rapidity." So in a way Franz contributed to the survival of the work squads.[30]

How did the prisoners describe their own survival efforts? Richard Glazar, a survivor of the Treblinka revolt whom Sereny interviewed, speaks of an intangible quality that enabled one to survive. He insists this quality was not ruthlessness. He described it rather "as an overriding thirst—perhaps, too, a *talent* for life." He also speaks of the need for friendship. *Few loners survived.* He thinks perhaps that prisoners did develop an internal numbness to allow nightmare events to become routine in the mind. Only a very few prisoners committed suicide or willingly helped the SS.[31]

The Treblinka staff designed a well-oiled machine whose capacity was far greater than its achievements. German war requirements created a lack of transport, preventing Himmler from dealing with far vaster numbers at Treblinka. Treblinka alone could have handled more than six million Jews. "Given adequate rail transport, the German extermination camps in Poland could have killed all the Poles, Russians, and other East Europeans the Nazis planned eventually to kill.[32]

In April 1943, when few transports were arriving, Commandant Stangl embarked on his magnificent (or monstrous) building program. The survivors of the camp believe that the Germans started the reconstruction to keep the prisoners preoccupied and sedated until the deportees arrived.

The work squads built a wide avenue, cleared the forest, created a zoo, spruced up the railroad station, and landscaped the area. Treblinka began to resemble a "luxury spa." At the end of the avenue prisoners constructed a gate resembling a "medieval city door." They decorated a guardhouse in medieval style. "Treblinka was becoming a fortress of Teutonic knights." After tearing down the old barracks, the prisoners reconstructed them in the style of the Middle Ages. They designed gardens, an athletic field, and a park. The landscapers created little paths with white gravel, decorated the lawns with colored stones, and constructed a birch log building in the park. In the center of an ornamental lake they placed a sculptured stone frog.

Treblinka had become a complete, self-sufficient world. The right side of the main street was reserved exclusively for the Germans. . . . To the south, lay the German gardens complete with tables, chairs and even umbrellas. On the other side of the paved area rose the German buildings flanked by a high tower in which water was stored and on which a huge flag bearing the swastika was planted. A wing was added to the original buildings, and the whole interior was redesigned very luxuriously with guest rooms, bar and bathrooms.[33]

Treblinka had its own orchestra conducted by a noted Polish musician, Arthur Gold. It played lively tunes while the victims ran down the tubes; and it played during roll call. It performed for the SS at major functions and galas. With the completion of the project, "the first town of the Thousand Year Reich was born. It had everything: a history, music, cruelty, science, horror, lies and madness."[34]

Himmler visited the camp in March 1943 and ordered the complete destruction and burning of the corpses. After his visit the SS planners and experts put their minds to the difficult but urgent project. Yankel Wiernik was one of the first picked to help with the task. He described it in his usual clear fashion:

Whenever a grave was opened, a terrible stench polluted the air, as the bodies were in an advanced stage of putrefaction. It turned out that women burned easier than men. Accordingly, corpses of women were used for kindling the fires.

The sight was terrifying, the worst that human eyes have ever beheld. When corpses of pregnant women were cremated, the abdomen would burst open, and the burning of the fetus inside the mother's body would become visible.[35]

The incredible complexity of the mass-grave problem frustrated the Germans. Their dismay was legitimate. Treblinka's soil contained 700,000 bodies—a volume of 69,000 cubic meters weighing 35,000 tons, the same as a medium-sized battleship. Even if 1,000 bodies could be burned each day, 700 days would elapse before Himmler's order had been obeyed.

Franz and Lalka tried many approaches to the problem. They poured buckets of gasoline on the bodies in one ditch—producing huge flames and slightly singed corpses. They piled one hundred bodies into wide but shallow ditches, and dumped in gasoline again. The resulting fire did not destroy the corpses. They experimented with varying sizes of piles and quantities of gasoline—to no avail. At the end of the first testing period they concluded that Himmler's request would take 140 years to fulfill.[36]

As a second experiment, they built huge pyres—alternating bodies and wood and soaking the whole with gasoline. The fire destroyed the bodies but the test could not be repeated, for it was wartime and gasoline and tree trunks were not available in the quantities necessary to burn 700,000 corpses.

Finally, the planners were forced to bring in an expert, Herbert Floss. When he arrived, he saw in a detached way what survivors have described:

To the left yawned an immense ditch and moving around it were three excavators, mechanical giants which jerkingly plunged their long jointed arms to the bottom of the pestilential pit and lifted them more slowly, loaded with dismembered bodies. The bodies seemed to lean forward as if to escape or to dangle their heads like drowned men. Each long steel arm ended in a monstrous set of jaws which closed gradually as they rose, inexorably eliminating anything that was too long, severing heads, torsos, and limbs, which fell heavily into the ditch. After that the mechanical arm would describe a wide circle, pause, shutter, and brutally open its jaws, hurling to the ground its cargo of damned.

In the pits the dead seemed to come back to life. "They twisted and grimaced as if contorted by unbearable pain. The liquid fat and lymph that suddenly exuded covered their faces with a kind of sweat that further reinforced the impression of life and intense suffering." But the expert knew that Himmler's orders to wipe away all traces before closing down the camp had to be achieved. He also knew that the camp officials had failed in their attempts.[37]

Floss had the prisoners erect four cement pillars, 76 centimeters high, forming a rectangle 19 meters long and 1 meter wide. On top they laid railroad rails, and on the rails they piled several hundred bodies. Inmates called the two huge iron pyres "Roasts." A witness suggested that the primitive grills could hold 2,600 bodies.[38]

But Floss knew that all bodies do not burn at the same rate, so he came up with a second idea:

There were good bodies and bad bodies, fire-resistant bodies and inflammable bodies. The art consisted in using the good ones to burn the bad ones. According to his investigations . . . the old bodies burned better than the new ones, the fat ones better than the thin ones, the women better than the men, and the children not as well as the women but better than the men. It was evident that the ideal body was the old body of a fat woman. Floss had these put aside. Then he had the men and the children sorted too. When a thousand bodies had been dug up and sorted in this day, he proceeded to the loading, with the good fuel underneath and the bad above. He refused gasoline and sent for wood. His demonstration was going to be perfect. . . .

The mounting flames began to lick at the bodies, gently at first, then with a steady force like the flame of a blow torch. Everyone held his breath, the Germans anxious and impatient, the prisoners dismayed and terrified. Only Floss seemed relaxed. . . . The bodies burst into flames. Suddenly the flames shot up, releasing a cloud of smoke, a deep roar arose, the faces of the dead twisted with pain and the flesh crackled. . . . Floss beamed. This fire was the finest day of his life.[39]

Wiernik, who witnessed that successful cremation, saw the possibility that 10,000 to 12,000 corpses could be cremated at one time. He described the German reaction to the huge pyre burning:

The Germans stood around with satanic smiles on their faces, radiating satisfaction over their foul deed. They drank toasts with choice liqueurs, ate, caroused and enjoyed themselves near the warm fire. Thus, even after death, the Jew was of some use. Though the weather was bitter cold, the pyres threw off heat like that from a stove.

The result was a huge inferno, "which from the distance looked like a volcano breaking through the earth's crust to belch forth fire and lava. The pyres sizzled and cracked. Smoke and heat made it impossible to remain close by."[40]

The Germans celebrated that day with wine, women, and song. "Treblinka, abandoned to the madness of men of another age, seemed to have become the sanctuary of terrible pagan rites. The Technicians had been transformed into barbaric and blood thirsty demigods arisen from some mythology." And obviously the SS were pleased. The whole project was successful beyond anticipation. The planners brought in two more machines for exhuming corpses and constructing many more fire grates, thus speeding up the process.[41]

One final problem needed the attention of the experts—excavation and body transportation. Now reorganized into another assembly line, each of the three excavators had its own squad. Instead of prisoners clumsily carrying pieces of dismembered bodies under their arms, they carried stretcher crates filled with the body parts. With production rising to 2,000 a day, Floss made a stirring speech at roll call:

Today we burned two thousand bodies. This is good, but we must not stop here. We will set ourselves an objective and devote all our efforts to reaching it. Tomorrow we will do three thousand, the day after tomorrow four thousand, then five thousand, then six thousand, and so on until ten thousand. Every day we will force ourselves to increase the output by one thousand units. I count on you to help me.[42]

Still, the essential goal of 10,000 a day could not be reached. Again, the experts applied assembly-line techniques:

When the carriers reached the piles of bodies, they stopped and rested while their litters were being loaded. This represented an enormous loss of time. To offset this disadvantage the excavators were ordered to lay their bodies not in a compact pile but in the form of an arc. The loaders were arranged along this arc and the carriers were instructed to walk along the line of the loaders.... The loaders were no longer responsible for one crate, but instead they threw a piece of a body into each crate that filed by.[43]

Herbert Floss had succeeded. Kurt Franz and Lalka had succeeded. Stangl had succeeded. The experts, planners, and technicians had triumphed. And then, the graves were dug up and the corpses burned to eliminate every last trace of what Treblinka had been. The workers filled the empty graves with the ashes, mixing them in with the earth. They experimented with planting vegetation on the ash area, and the soil proved quite fertile.

Then, suddenly, the situation changed. The prisoners revolted! Historians, novelists, and survivors herald the Treblinka revolt as the most impressive of its kind. On August 2, 1943, thirteen months after the opening of the camp, and 800,000 or more victims later, the 850 to 1,200 resident worker Jews of Treblinka staged an uprising. They killed several of the guards and broke through the barbed wire defenses to freedom—for most, temporary; for a few, permanent. The revolt was not spontaneous; it was carefully planned by committees formed within the Jewish death squads. In spite of the weaknesses in its implementation, the insurrection was one of the most heroic feats of Jewish or Gentile camp resistance to the Nazis.

Where did it begin? The exact course of events cannot be reconstructed, for every leader of the resistance organization died during the revolt. When some working Jews finally realized that no amount of cooperation or labor would prevent the wholesale extermination of the resident prisoners and the total liquidation of the camp, they created a Committee of Resistance, which executed plans to procure escape weapons. The first attempt in the late winter of 1943 miscarried. But spring arrived and with it the visit from Himmler, coming to sign Treblinka's death sentence, to catalyze the project to eliminate all traces of the camp before its close-down. A few days after his departure when the body burning began in earnest, the committee realized that the hourglass had just been turned over. It moved quickly to determine exactly how fast the squads were burning the bodies, and therefore precisely what day the camp would be liquidated. As the bonfires roared, the countdown began.

And then it was summer, July, and Treblinka celebrated its first birthday party.

Born out of chaos, Treblinka was sinking into madness. Eight hundred thousand men, women, children and old people, sane and mad, beautiful and ugly, short and tall, had been exterminated. Their bodies were almost all burned. The curtain was falling on the next-to-the-last act of the drama. As in ancient tales, the adversaries were fraternizing before the showdown.[44]

On July 20 Camp II sent a message to the committee warning that the workers were starting on the last ditch of bodies, that in two weeks they would be finished and so would the camp. The committee responded by upgrading the machinery of revolt. The Jewish camp workers, stokers, grave diggers, camp cleaners, and gas chamber attendants extended the bonds of solidarity. The first step, the procurement of arms, took a leap forward when a Jewish locksmith made duplicate keys to the armory, which enabled a work squad to steal guns and grenades.

The leaders set the date of revolt for August 2, 1943, at 5 P.M. Their plan was to ambush and kill the chief SS men, disarm the guards, cut the telephone wires, destroy all the extermination facilities, free the Poles from the detention camp, and finally flee into the forest to form a partisan band. A shot was to signal the beginning.

August 2 dawned a very hot day. At 2 P.M. an order came from the committee that no more Jews would be allowed to die. Suddenly, about two hours early, a shot rang out and the revolt began prematurely. The accidental change in schedule meant that several hundred prisoners outside the camp were unable to participate. It also meant that the meager supply of arms had not been adequately distributed, so the Ukrainians in the watchtowers were not killed as planned, and they shot the prisoners down "like ducks." Survivors remember the revolt as utter confusion. The first moments were "madly exciting; grenades and bottles of petrol exploding, fires almost at once, shooting everywhere. Everything was just that much different from the way it had been planned, so that we were thrown into utter confusion." It quickly became a case of each man for himself. Hundreds struggled over the barbed fence.[45]

Accounts vary considerably over the number of escapees and survivors. Two hundred to six hundred people reached the forests. More than twenty Germans were killed. Perhaps sixty escapees survived the war—some accounts say only twenty. The Polish peasants, partisans, Ukrainian fascist groups, *Wehrmacht* deserters, and the Gestapo killed the rest.[46]

Himmler transferred Stangl to Italy and replaced him as commandant with Kurt Franz. After the revolt small transports continued to arrive, though at a slow rate. Finally it appeared that the Germans had had enough. They blew up the remains of the camp in November and built a farmhouse on the site. The remaining *Kommandos* cleared the area of its mass graves, leveled it, and planted it with pines. However, the job was done in such a sloppy manner that when the Russians began exhuming Treblinka in March 1944, they found mass graves that had been hidden rather than destroyed. Photographs of Treblinka in the summer of 1945 show several earth depressions containing bleached bones—skulls, legs, pelvic bones, arms, spines. As late as 1957 a Jewish visitor to Treblinka wrote that bones and skulls were still scattered everywhere. Eventually the Polish government removed the bones, covered the pits, refenced the area, and built the controversial monument.[47]

How many died there? The Polish authorities adopted the figure of 750,000 right after the war ended. When new evidence emerged in 1971, however, the West Germans raised their official estimate to 900,000. Other experts place the figure as high as 1,200,000. Whether it was 800,000 or 1,000,000, Treblinka as an experimental killing center performed a mighty technical miracle in one short year.[48]

When it was over, a few realized they had survived. At least they were still physically alive. Yankel Wiernick lived to write of his experiences. But he spoke of himself as a "homeless old man . . . without a family, without any next of kin." While alone, he talked to himself and answered his own questions. When he looked in the mirror, he saw a nomad.

It is with a sense of fear that I pass through human settlements. I have a feeling that all my experiences have become imprinted on my face. Whenever I look at my reflection in a stream or pool of water, awe and surprise twist my face into an ugly grimace. Do I look like a human being? No, decidedly not. Disheveled, untidy, run-down. It looks as if I were carrying a load of several centuries on my shoulders. The load is wearisome, very wearisome, but I must carry it for the time being. . . .

Time and again I wake up in the middle of the night moaning pitifully. Ghastly nightmares break up the sleep I so badly need. I see thousands of skeletons extending their boney arms toward me, as if begging for mercy and life, but I, drenched with sweat, feel incapable of giving any help. . . . Phantoms of death haunt me, spectors of children, little children, nothing but children.[49]

Because so few survived the killing centers and because they lay far from Germany in isolated rural Poland, the International Military Tribunal paid little attention to the killing centers, hearing evidence only on Treblinka.

Eberl committed suicide. Stangl was arrested but escaped to Brazil in 1948 and he was not extradited until 1967. Franz went back to Düsseldorf after the war, living there under his own name until he was arrested in 1959. His captors found in his quarters a photo album of Treblinka that he had titled, "The Best Years of My Life."

The Germans held two Treblinka trials. The first, which began on October 12, 1964, tried Kurt Franz and nine others. The accused usually admitted participating in the killings, but claimed that they had only acted "under orders." The Düsseldorf court handed down its verdict on September 3, 1965, sentencing Franz and three others to life imprisonment, sentencing five defendants to three to twelve years, and setting one free.

In the second Treblinka trial, held May 13 to December 22, 1970, Fritz Stangl claimed he was only responsible for collecting the victim's valuables. The court found him guilty of participation in the killing of 400,000 Jews and handed down a life sentence. Stangl died of a heart attack before he was remanded to prison.[50]

THE LABOR/ EXTERMINATION COMPLEXES

MAJDANEK: IN MEMORY OF A HUMAN TRAGEDY

Majdanek: a vast memorial camp with the Lublin skyscrapers visible in the near distance. Majdanek: in Edgar Snow's words, reflecting the Nazi's "most brilliant success in perverting the very virtues of a once great people into the service of a machinery of crimes almost too monstrous for the human mind to accept." Majdanek: *the* symbol of the Nazi regime's perversion of the old adage: "Waste not, want not." Majdanek: a planned technological system devoted to the reduction of a human being from an upright energetic animal to a kilogram of gray ashes, with the complete utilization of all by-products. Majdanek: today an impressive collection of preserved buildings and artifacts, including an accumulation of over 800,000 dusty, decaying shoes. At Majdanek, *nothing was wasted, everything was salvaged*—ashes, gold fillings, bones, clothes, wooden arms, legs, and crutches, toothpaste, nail files, children's toys.

Majdanek was a uniquely urban camp, in the suburbs 4.8 kilometers from the center of Lublin, chief city of a major Polish region. Bordering one of Poland's main highways on flat treeless ground, standing like a gigantic grotesque billboard, lies the only large Nazi camp constructed in the midst of things, without secrecy or subterfuge. The Nazis built many camps with a special purpose, and liquidated or planned to liquidate them once that purpose had been met. But Majdanek was different. From its inception, the camp grew and expanded. Had the German construction plans materialized, Majdanek would have become a large city housing hundreds of thousands of slaves forced to work in the mammoth SS industrial complexes of the future.

Because Majdanek stands on level ground at the edge of a major highway, its past functions intrude on the mind of the traveler and the Lublinite peering from his high-rise apartment. Surrounded by rich farmland, much of the original area remains. The tall crematorium smokestack observable to any passerby is silhouetted against the bright cloudless summer sky. Rows of brown weatherbeaten wooden barracks sprawl over the ground, enclosed by watchtowers and barbed wire. The major SS complex remains across the highway from the camp, in use today as a Russian-Polish military training base.

Majdanek camp.

In 1970, to commemorate the twenty-fifth anniversary of the camp's liberation, the Council for the Protection of Memorials of War and Martyrology erected an imposing memorial honoring the Majdanek victims. The council commissioned one of Poland's foremost sculptors, Wiktor Tolkin, to create the memorial. It consists of two parts: the Monument of Struggle and Martyrdom, with the adjacent Homage Road; and the Pantheon-Mausoleum.

The Monument of Struggle and Martyrdom rises in the forefront of the camp. From a 2-meter-high monolith with two swords carved into its surface, the broad Homage Road leads to the monument. Designed in the shape of a huge gate, the massive block of interweaving irregular stones dominates the area. The inscription on its steps reads: "In homage to victims of Hitlerite homicide." In front of the monument stands a replica of the Order of the Grunwald Cross, built by the Council of State to honor the Majdanek martyrs.

Tolkin's second sculpture is the massive mausoleum built in the shape of a rotundal urn covered by a lifted stone dome. Located along the road leading to the crematorium and covering what was a mound of human ashes, it reflects the old Slavic custom of burying body ashes in urns. The raised dome allows visitors to enter under the roof to the interior, which contains the ashes of the dead. The inscription reads: "Let our fate be a warning for you."

Majdanek crematoria.

The Polish government has created five state museums dedicated to the memory of "a human tragedy" located at Pawiak prison in Warsaw, at Auschwitz—the center of concentration camp scholarly research—at Stutthof, at Lambinowice, and at Majdanek. The Majdanek Museum is the Polish Center for the Art of War and Atrocities, organized jointly by the Consultative Group of the Five Museums of Martyrology. The museum curators have presented a full picture of the crimes committed in Majdanek with displays, photostats, camp objects, and rows of preserved barracks. To complete the museum complex, the authorities retained the crematorium and gassing facilities. Take the stench, the disease, the life, the misery, the massive inhumanity. Add the large gas chambers, the disinfection barracks, the washrooms, the well-preserved crematoriums, and the discarded cans of Cyclone B. What emerges is a comprehensive visual picture of mass extermination.

Each of eleven museum barracks houses historical exhibits, including 820,000 pairs of shoes, candlesticks, teeth, shaving mugs, hair, disinfection tables, and grinding machines that turned bones into ashes. One barrack is devoted to the story of extermination. Daniel Siegel recorded his poetic response:

Once you have seen displayed
in cases
thousands of the brushes
prisoners surrendered
with their hair and bodies
at the gates,
your hands will never hold
a toothbrush
without pyres of memories.
Soap forever resembles
your uncle from Derevno
disappeared in 1934
   (thought about before
   theorized before
   nowhere in the bitsandpieces cases).
Glasses irk your nose and ears
because you saw some 50,000
thrown together at Majdanek.
The most common objects
of our everyday
become a desecration
in the run of 30 years
of memories.[1]

Majdanek's art museums and exhibitions are central to the educational and cultural mission of the camp. In addition to the magnificent juried exhibitions in which some of Poland's finest artists compete, the museum prepares portfolios and catalogues of the collections. The exhibit catalogue for the superb 1976 exhibition, for example, focuses on the misery of war and torture. Many of the artists are survivors of the camp. Some developed their talent and created their masterpieces while in Majdanek; others gained renown before imprisonment. They have attempted to communicate their deepest feelings in works using the materials of everyday existence: thread, string, wire, toothbrush handles, pieces of wood, dishes, and even bread.

Some pieces in the exhibition had been commissioned by the SS; a few were created under the ignorant eyes of the SS. One prisoner, with the agreement of the SS, made a sculpture of a large tortoise. As was well known during the German occupation, members of the resistance painted the tortoise on the walls of houses to symbolize deliberate slowness in carrying out work for the Nazi occupiers. In this defiant manner an artist expressed a precise but hidden message understood only by the inmates. Exhibition works include art prepared by survivors after liberation, from their memories.

The 1976 exhibition was the most complete picture of the war tragedy and the hope for peace. The titles of the works of art, taken together, convey an idea of the vast scope of concentration camp culture: "Shot at Work," "Extermination," "Tomb of Nations," "March of the Aggressor," "Father and Son Sharing the Bread," "Spilled Soup," "Sadness," "Execution," "Transports," "No More," "Crematorium," "Gallows over Poland," "The Kapo." One canvas pictures dark starving women in vague form, blown by the wind, trudging down the road. Another pictures a roll call in the driving snow. And yet another in exact detail recaptures the prisoners dragging their colleagues to their feet on their return from work. The sculpture includes a prisoner pushing an ill friend in a wheelchair, two starving children holding each other and looking into each other's eyes, thin and stark metal figures standing at roll call, stone people rising out of the ground begging for food, and a wood tree trunk with the agonizing face of a woman carved into the top, labeled "Shout."

The 1972 exhibit included such works as "Mother," "The Gas," "The End of the Winters," "Never More," "The Anxieties of the Alive," "The Final Despair," "Terror," "Hunger," "Gas Chamber," "It Was a Man," "Hunted," "Nobody Will Rest," "The History of Cruelty," "The Ghost of War," "Violence," "Bread," and "Memories." Majdanek: a stark cultural and artistic tribute to the men and women who worked and died in this this special Nazi center.[2]

Himmler inspected the Lublin area in July 1941, looking for a site for a new camp large enough to hold 50,000 inmates. When the main area filled, he anticipated setting up additional camps in the vicinity. On December 8, 1941, the main SS office designated Majdanek for 150,000 prisoners of war and civilian internees. The SS departed from their general rules of secrecy for economic reasons. They planned large industrial complexes in the Lublin area to be served by the labor force from Majdanek. Construction began in the fall of 1941, with Polish Jews and prisoners of war brought in from the camp on Lipowa Street in Lublin, and with civilians and peasants from nearby villages. Construction halted at the end of 1942. Most accommodations found by the liberating Soviet troops date from that period.[3]

Once the planned internment fields had been encircled with barbed wire, the first transport of 5,000 Soviet POWs arrived. Majdanek bore the official name of a POW camp and remained such for a time. The first prisoners found no barracks, no water, no latrines. They lived under the open sky. While constructing the barracks, most Soviet POWs died. At the end of 1941 additional groups of prisoners arrived, causing Majdanek to lose its character as a POW camp, though its official designation was not changed until February 16, 1943.

Majdanek came into its own in 1941 as a forced-labor settlement. It was intended as the central camp for the Government General. The Government General was the official name for that part of Polish territory, representing about one-third of prewar Poland, that formed a separate administrative unit created by Hitler's decision of October 1939. Inhabited mainly by Poles, the Government General was viewed as a reservoir of labor for German industry and agriculture. As the Government General's major camp, Majdanek had four branches in Blizyn, Budzeyn, Random, and Warsaw, as well as two camps in Lublin: one on Lipowa Street and one on the territory of the former airport.

The Nazi's second largest camp, Majdanek was one of two (Auschwitz was the other) with a large inmate population. Contrary to public myth, Majdanek was not created primarily as an extermination camp. Although Auschwitz and Majdanek had full extermination facilities and ghastly death rates, extermination was never their primary goal as it was of the killing centers. But in the fall of 1942, by adding gassing machinery, the extermination specialist Wirth made Majdanek the final link in the extermination chain. By the end of the war, after less than three years of existence, the mass shootings and the gas chambers had claimed at least 360,000 victims.[4]

Although the original scheme envisioned 150,000 prisoners for Majdanek, plans changed to allow for 250,000 people. The developing front-line needs of the German Army, however, meant the curtailment of supplies for the construction. Thus only 20 percent of the plan came to fruition, and consisted of the administrative buildings and the prisoners' camp with 144 barracks, each built to house 300 persons. The whole area covered 275 hectares. The SS referred to each section or sector as a prisoner field. On each field they built twenty-two barracks and two workshops. Free space between the barracks constituted the roll call square. West of the prisoner section the SS located workshops and storehouses. Future camp buildings and industrial installations were to occupy over 880 hectares of agricultural land belonging to the farmers of the neighboring villages.[5]

Majdanek had a standard concentration camp organization. The turnover in camp commandants was quite high. Karl Otto Koch (November 1941–August 1942), Max Koegel (August 1942–September 1942), Herman Florstedt (September 1942–November 1943), Martin Weiss (November 1943–May 1944), and Artur Liebehenschel (May 1944–July 1944) served as commandants. An SS squad of 1,200 personnel constituted the support staff. Koch, one of the famous commandants, became a victim of the RKPA/Morgen SS Commission of Inquiry. That commission, set up to investigate cases of corruption and arbitrary killing, reached heavily into Majdanek. It condemned to death Herman Florstedt for murder and executed him. Koch, the first commandant of Buchenwald, husband of the famous Ilsa, and then commandant of Majdanek, was also sentenced for murder by the commission and executed.

Although populated primarily by Jews, Majdanek's national mix was quite varied, representing over fifty nationalities. Poles constituted the second most numerous group. A large proportion of the population included Soviet Union war prisoners. As the war progressed, transports came in from everywhere. In 1942 the SS sent 1,000 farmers from the Lublin province to Majdanek for failing to supply the required quota of agricultural products! When Polish villages were destroyed to accommodate Hitler's plans, Himmler sent the inhabitants immediately to Majdanek. Many women and children made the trip. Near the war's end, transports flowed in from other camps.[6]

The transport trains stopped at the station in Lublin. The prisoners lined up on the platform and marched out to the camp. Upon arrival they went through all the procedures used by the camps to denigrate, degrade, and destroy human beings. Once the prisoners had been shaved, they were taken to the baths. Initially, there was no bathhouse, only a primitive building without doors, windows, or floors. And there, in the cold, wrote one survivor, "stood several big barrels filled with lysol stinking water into which the prisoners were made to jump in turn, and SS-men amused themselves to force the bather's head under water. Thus disinfected, the prisoner climbed out of the barrel, cold and stinking with lysol, from a water thick with dirt into mud up to the ankles, hurried by the SS-men's knouts."[7]

The SS lodged the prisoners in wooden barracks with tiny skylights instead of windows. The air was close, and the winter temperature frigid. Before 1943, when the barracks were provided with tiered plank beds and sleeping boards, the prisoners slept on straw spread in thin layers on the bare ground. Each block measured 40 by 9 by 2 meters and contained 250 bunks. However, 500 to 800 people slept in them, and the figure shot up to 1,000 at certain times. The barracks leaked and the floors were covered with mud. The barracks had no sewage system until 1943.

An unknown Polish poet inmate composed the unofficial anthem of the prisoners, the "Majdanek Song," which they sang everywhere:

There never has been,
Nor will there ever be,
Anywhere on earth,
A sun like that which shines
Upon our Majdanek . . .[8]

Understandably, most prisoners were ill. The SS provided a "hospital," but it certainly resembled no hospital the civilized world knows. The doctors possessed no drugs. *And Majdanek suffered from the highest mortality rate of any German concentration camp in its middle years.* The camp also had its share of experiments, although these were not as extensive as at most other camps. The infamous Professor Rascher of Dachau fame obtained permission from Himmler to carry out his freezing experiments at Majdanek.[9]

Brutality at Majdanek is perhaps best exemplified by Anton Tuman, the "Beast of Majdanek." Carrying himself proudly and usually imitating a Napoleonic pose, Tuman struck fear in the hearts of the prisoners whenever he appeared. He flogged and beat them relentlessly. One day a female prisoner called out to her husband in the men's sector. For the crime, Tuman ordered her to stand at attention for the day. At evening, he commanded the camp prisoners to surround her, forming a huge square into which had been placed a flogging bench. Tuman tied the woman, naked, to the bench, and his henchmen flogged her until the pain caused her to lose control of her bowels. Laughing, Tuman kicked her and forced her to clean up her excrement with her hands.

Tuman loved Majdanek. It was his camp and he cared for it with a zealous devotion. He would tolerate not the slightest deviation from the rules. For some infraction, he forced a group of prisoners to stand naked in the cold without food for three days and nights. Then he shoved the twenty-six men into the freezing water of the camp pool. They froze to death at once. After Majdanek's demise, Anton Tuman went on to Auschwitz. On liberation day the Russian prisoners stoned him to death.[10]

Extermination was big business at Majdanek. Rather than focusing on one process, the SS used several. In the first stages of the camp's existence mass shooting was the major method—during 1941 and 1942 the SS exterminated the Soviet POWs in that manner. Mass executions often included several hundred or even a thousand victims. In addition to shooting, prisoners were killed by hanging. Each field had a gallows, and between Fields One and Two the staff erected a special facility with a row of nine hooks for collective hangings. Frequently the SS drowned inmates in the small reservoir. Others were strangled, beaten, or trampled to death. Many prisoners died from the living conditions in the camp.

The most common method of mass murder was gassing in special chambers. Technicians built seven such chambers, equipped with carbon monoxide and Cyclone B, the latter used mainly for experimental purposes. They erected the first two chambers in 1942 in the space between Fields One and Two near the small crematorium. The next three chambers were adjoined to the bathhouse by one roof, and the inscription at the entrance read: "*Bad Und Desinfektion.*" The guards gave the prisoners a shower before driving them to the chambers. Two chambers measuring 5 by 3.5 by 2 meters were adapted for the use of Cyclone B. Thick metal doors sealed in the 150 victims. Two additional chambers were lighted so that the SS men could watch the gassing through peepholes. The seventh chamber was installed in the large crematorium facility. Gassing usually occurred at night when the prisoners were asleep, and those who worked at the gas chamber were isolated from the other prisoners. Mass gassing reached its height from May to July 1943, when thousands of Jews brought from the Warsaw ghetto were executed. Often the authorities sent complete transports of prisoners directly into the gas chambers.

Majdanek was an important enough camp to invite the attention of Eichmann, and he went there to view it. He recalled: "A German police captain there showed me how they had managed to build airtight chambers disguised as ordinary farmers' huts, sealed them thermetically, then injected the exhaust gas from a Russian U-boat motor. I remember it all very exactly because I never thought that anything like that would be possible, technically speaking."[11]

Many prisoners remember the largest camp execution, a mass slaughter of the Jews that occurred on November 3, 1943. On that day the SS shot 18,400 Jews in ditches near the crematorium. The massacre started early in the morning and went on until evening. First, the guards herded the Jews into Field Five and ordered them to strip. Then they drove the naked Jews to the ditches and forced them to lie, face down. The SS machine-gunned them. The next group of victims had to place themselves atop the layers of corpses before they were shot. That process went on until the ditches filled. "It was a breathtakingly beautiful day on God's earth," remembered a witness, "but we did not see the beauty." Loudspeakers played "Rosamunde, Give Me a Kiss and Your Heart" throughout the day to muffle the sounds of the shooting and the cries of the dying. The SS code name for that execution was "*Erntefest*," or "Harvest Home Festival"; inmates called it "Bloody Wednesday." One witness termed his reaction "superhuman shock."[12]

Following the massacre, prisoners covered the graves with thin layers of dirt. One witness, named Vrba, was ordered to help eliminate all traces and burn the dead. The squad brought in wood and started the cremation. When the ashes cooled, they cleared the graves. A special mill ground the remaining bone pieces into powdered fertilizer. The squad shoveled the fertilizer into sacks and took them to the SS warehouses. As Vrba recalled: "Had I stayed at Majdanek, I surely would have ended up as fertilizer." Prince Christopher Radziwill, an original prisoner who had been at Majdanek since 1939, described the massacre: "I shall never forget the day the Nazis killed 17,000 Jews at Majdanek, while I was in another part of the concentration camp. That evening, many of my Polish fellow prisoners got drunk to celebrate."[13]

Bodies once killed then had to be destroyed. For some time no cremation machinery existed at Majdanek so squads buried the corpses in a ravine beyond Field Five. As the camp population increased, however, mass graves no longer proved sufficient. The solution came in the form of crematoria. Corpses were first incinerated in a small crematorium operated from June 1942 in the area between Fields One and Two. Its two small ovens borrowed from Sachsenhausen had a limited capacity of 100 bodies a day. The shortage of fuel and crude oil caused further difficulties. When the small crematorium became totally inadequate, body squads burned the corpses in the open air on specially made pyres. Iron chassis from old trucks were placed in a gratelike fashion over deep pits on which alternate layers of bodies and logs were piled. Squads poured petrol or methanol on the bodies and set them afire. The method was borrowed from Treblinka's successful experiment. At the end of 1943 the SS constructed a large crematorium with five ovens, each capable of handling three bodies at a time. Coke heated the furnaces and the temperature reached 800°C. The big crematorium probably had a capacity for 1,000 bodies daily. By 1943 the only limits on extermination in all the camps (except for labor needs) were administrative and technical: breakdowns of machiney, corpse-disposal difficulties, disruptions of the railroads.

The descriptions of gassing and burning can overshadow the fact that the SS needed and decided to make a profit from its prisoners through labor and also through the accumulation of the prisoners' belongings. Plunder was a major business at Majdanek. The new arrivals were always stripped of everything they brought with them, and they brought many things. Jewelry, money, shoes, clothes, dentures, toys, utensils, toilet outfits, their hair (used for knitting warm socks for soldiers), gold teeth, and their bones (crushed in electric grinders for fertilizer): those are only a few of the uses to which the prisoners' bodies and their possessions were put.

Labor battalions formed an important part of the Majdanek structure. Because the camp retained large numbers of living Jews and also had a significant number of non-Jewish prisoners, it contained a sizable inmate population, necessitating an elaborate administrative structure and a full battalion of guards. The Germans linked the massive camp industrial activity to the war effort. The camp contracted out large prisoner battalions to work in Lublin's food, cement work, and wood product industries. Others built barracks and camp facilities; installed electricity, water, and sewer lines; or labored in the camp workshops. The camp had its own garden and its own agricultural farm. If there was not enough legitimate labor available, the SS personnel detailed the prisoners to do purposeless work with the aim of producing physical and mental exhaustion. One prisoner described the return from work: "On their way back to the camp, the kommandos dragged heaps of corpses on sledges; the living were led by the arms; left to themselves inside the gate, they would crawl to the blocks, using their hands and feet to cross the ice-covered assembly area; those who managed to reach the barracks, tried to get up with the help of the wall, but they could not keep standing for long."[14]

The Majdanek population included a large number of women and children. In 1942 several German female wardens arrived from the special training camp at Ravensbrück. Elsa Erik was appointed superintendent of the women's area, while four others, including Hermine Braunsteiner, became deputy wardens. They designated Field Five, close to the large crematorium, as the women's quarters. The first female prisoners were Jewish and Polish women rounded up on the streets of Lublin. Lena Donat, who managed to survive the Warsaw ghetto, Majdanek, and Auschwitz, described the sadism and perversity of the SS wardresses in Majdanek. During roll call, for example, a typical wardress would select an inmate with a shapely figure. She then savagely whipped the woman on the breasts and abdomen and kicked her in the pelvis with her boots. "The girl, howling like nothing human, would crawl away on hands and knees, leaving a trail of blood behind her." The victim usually died.

The authorities transferred many women to the subcamps to manufacture garments or to make grenades in ammunition factories. The largest number were employed in sewing workshops. The women's camp usually contained 6,000 to 8,000 inmates, but the figure rose in 1943 to 11,000. Several children also lived in Majdanek. Jewish babies were murdered immediately upon arrival, or at birth if they were born in the camp.[15]

A resistance organization existed in the camp, and its actions took many forms, some as original as found in any camp. The prisoners were able to maintain cultural, educational, and artistic activities. As one example, the prisoners constructed and erected the Column of Three Eagles in Field Three, the first monument to be built in homage to the victims of Nazi Germany. The prisoners raised the column in 1943 under the pretense of improving the appearance of the field. They also created the sculpture of a tortoise, which symbolized the watchword: "Work slowly." The most daring forms of resistance were flights from the camps. Many well-prepared escapes succeeded.

Prisoners living in Majdanek often referred to it as a place set apart from civilization. They saw themselves as troops in a weaponless army, subject to discipline more severe than anyone had known. Scientists calculated that food rations were sufficient to keep a person alive for three months. They were inaccurate, however, because few men lived that long. Only a tiny number who stayed in Majdanek survived. A transfer to Auschwitz actually raised an inmate's life expectancy.

The Exploitation Story

The extermination of the Polish Jews began at the moment of invasion. According to Hitler's plan, the Jews of Poland were to be quickly exterminated, and then their property and possessions were to be exploited for the good of the Reich. But conditions soon necessitated the injection of a new element into the plan—the exploitation of Jewish labor. The SS did not despair at being thwarted from their final goal. Not only did they rent out Jews to industry and to the military, but they conceived of a plan to exploit Jewish labor themselves so the SS could become economically independent of both state and party. Besides using Jewish labor in SS industries, they exploited Jewish property and possessions. That brilliant enterprise enabled the SS to become a state within a state, industrially and economically, as well as politically and militarily. Himmler entrusted the development of SS industry to *Amtsgruppe W* of the WVHA, which was headed by fanatical Nazis who had transformed themselves into fanatical businessmen.

First the Jews of Poland were deported from their major centers; second, a majority were killed; third, the labor of the remaining Jews was utilized for private and SS industries; and fourth, Jewish labor was used to exploit Jewish personal property. And the two major centers for the exploitation of that labor were Majdanek and Auschwitz. It was Majdanek that received the bulk of the Jewish possessions of Poland and, in particular, Warsaw. Every watch, gold fountain pen, and pair of shoes represented a dead man, woman, or child—and monetary profit for the SS.

On September 26, 1942, SS General Frank issued basic instructions to the WVHA agents in Majdanek and Auschwitz on the "utilization of property on the occasion of settlement and evacuation of Jews." Frank informed the agents that Jewish property in the future would be referred to as "goods originating from thefts, receipt of stolen goods, and hoarded goods." He divided the goods into categories and clarified the final disposition of each category:

1. Cash money: pay into Reich bank account.
2. Foreign exchange: deliver to German Reich Bank.
3. Rare metals, jewelry, precious and semiprecious stones, pearls, gold from teeth, and scrap gold: deliver to German Reich Bank.
4. Watches, clocks, pencils, electric razors, scissors, flashlights, wallets, and purses to be repaired: then deliver to front-line troops.
5. Men's underwear, men's clothing: first, cover the needs of camp inmates and troops. Then hand them over to the racial Germans, against payment.
6. Valuable furs, raw and cured: deliver to SS WVHA.
7. Ordinary furs—lamb, rabbit: deliver to clothing plant at Ravensbrück.
8. Women's clothing and underwear, children's clothing and underwear: hand over to racial Germans, against minimal payment.
9. Pure silk underwear: deliver to Reich Ministry of Economics.
10. Featherbeds, quilts, woolen blankets, cloth for suits, shawls, umbrellas,

walking sticks, thermos flasks, ear flaps, baby carriages, combs, leather belts, pipes, sunglasses, mirrors, tableware, suitcases: deliver to racial Germans, against minimal payment.

11. All linen: deliver to racial Germans, against minimal payment, and to troops.

12. Spectacles and eyeglasses: deliver to medical office.

13. Furniture and household items: recondition and deliver to racial German settlers, and German Army agencies.

From all clothing, ordered Frank, the Jewish star must be removed.[16]

Prior to December 1943 the WVHA collected, primarily at Majdanek, personal property of Jews in the Lublin area alone valued at more than 180 million Reich marks—or, at the exchange rate of 2.5, $72 million! That figure included foreign currency of forty-eight countries, with $1 million in U.S. money. The list numbered 262,711 articles of considerable value; and the Lublin area loot included 2,000 freight cars of clothes, linens, and rags! Much of the money went into a revolving account used to finance SS economic enterprises.[17]

The author of the report on collectible materials was exhibiting "some of that grisly Nazi humor" when he wrote that the goods seized were "accounted for with the greatest of expediency and *without defrauding.*" The War Crimes prosecutor, in evaluating the reports, remarked that it was a boast of a famous Chicago packing house "that when a pig goes through one of their slaughterhouses, nothing is wasted except the squeal. These defendants can without any immodesty make the same claim."[18]

On February 6, 1943, SS General Pohl sent a statement to Hitler showing the delivery of 825 additional cars of textiles from Majdanek and Auschwitz. Himmler was fascinated by the operation and became involved in it down to the finest detail. After inspecting the Warsaw and Lublin warehouses, he wrote to SS Obergruppenführer Krueger and Pohl:

I again request SS Obergruppenfuehrer Pohl to arrange a written agreement with the Minister of Economics regarding each individual category; whether it is a question of watch glasses, of which hundreds of thousands—perhaps even millions—are lying there, and which for practical purposes could be distributed to the German watchmakers; or whether it is a question of turning lathes, which we need for our workshops, and which we can either have legally given to us by the Minister for Economics or buy from him; or whether it is a question of sewing machines to which the same thing applies; or common furs, or superior ladies' furs. I believe, on the whole, we cannot be too exact.[19]

Again, on February 27, 1943, the Majdanek officials sent a report to Himmler listing additional goods and money delivered up to February 1, 1943. Portions of that report follow.[20]

REPORT BY SS STURMBANNFÜHRER WIPPERN, 27 FEBRUARY 1943, CONCERNING VALUE OF MONEY, PRECIOUS METALS, OTHER VALUABLES, AND TEXTILES OF JEWS, DELIVERED UP TO 3 FEBRUARY 1943

Valuation of Jewish belongings delivered to 3 February 1943
File No. Secret 115

1. *Cash* Delivery SS Econ. Krakow SS WVHA Berlin (R.B.)	Total . . . . RM			53,013,133.51
2. *Foreign currency* *in notes*	Total . . . . RM			1,452,904.65
		[Rate of Exchange]		
USA Dollar	505,046.00	2.50	RM	1,262,615.00
3. *Foreign currency in* *minted gold*	Total . . . . RM			843,802.75
		[Rate of Exchange]		
USA Dollar	116,425.00	4.20	RM	488,985.00
4. *Precious metals*	Total . . . . RM			5,353,943.00

5. *Other valuables*

5	pieces gold automatic pencils	at RM	30.00 RM	150.00
17	pieces gold fountain pens	at RM	70.00 RM	1,190.00
4	pieces ladies' platinum watches	at RM	300.00 RM	1,200.00
2,894	pieces gold gentlemen's pocket watches	at RM	500.00 RM	1,427,000.00
579	pieces gentlemen's gold wristwatches	at RM	300.00 RM	173,400.00
7,313	pieces ladies' gold wristwatches	at RM	250.00 RM	1,828,250.00
19	pieces platinum watch cases with brilliants and diamonds	at RM	1,000.00 RM	19,000.00
280	pieces bracelets with brilliants and diamonds	at RM	3,500.00 RM	980,000.00
6,245	pieces gentlemen's wristwatches	at RM	10.00 RM	62,450.00

13,455	pieces gentlemen's pocket watches	at RM 20.00 RM	269,100.00
1	piece gentleman's gold pocket watch with brilliants	at RM 600.00 RM	600.00
179	pieces ladies' gold watches with brilliants and diamonds	at RM 600.00 RM	107,400.00
7	pieces ladies' gold ring watches	at RM 150.00 RM	1,050.00
4	pieces ladies' lapel watches with pearls	at RM 200.00 RM	800.00
394	pieces ladies' lapel watches with brilliants	at RM 600.00 RM	236,400.00
228	pieces ladies' watches, platinum and brilliants	at RM 1,200.00 RM	273,600.00
293	pieces ladies' gold watches	at RM 250.00 RM	73,250.00
22,324	pieces spectacles	at RM 3.00 RM	66,972.00
3	pairs cuff links with brilliants	at RM 150.00 RM	450.00
11,675	pieces gold rings with brilliants and diamonds	at RM 1,500.00 RM	11,675,000.00
7,200	pieces ladies' wristwatches	at RM 10.00 RM	72,000.00
40	pieces gold brooches	at RM 350.00 RM	14,000.00
1,399	pairs gold earrings with brilliants	at RM 250.00 RM	349,750.00
169	pieces pins with brilliants and diamonds	at RM 100.00 RM	16,900.00
1,974	pieces gold brooches with brilliants and diamonds	at RM 2,000.00 RM	3,948,000.00
27	pieces gold bracelets with brilliants and diamonds	at RM 250.00 RM	6,750.00
49	kg. pearls		4,000,000.00
7,000	pieces fountain pens	at RM 10.00 RM	70,000.00
130	pieces large single brilliants	at RM 1,000.00 RM	130,000.00
2	pieces necklace, with brilliants and diamonds	at RM 1,500.00 RM	3,000.00
1	piece gold cigarette case	at RM 400.00 RM	400.00
1	piece mother-of-pearl box	RM	20.00
3	pieces gold compacts	at RM 50.00 RM	150.00
2	pieces binoculars, mother-of-pearl	at RM 50.00 RM	100.00
1.44	kg corals	RM	150.00
51,370	pieces watches, to be repaired	at RM 5.00 RM	256,850.00
1,000	pieces automatic pencils	at RM 3.00 RM	3,000.00

350	pieces razors	at RM	2.50 RM	875.00
800	pieces pocket knives	at RM	1.00 RM	800.00
3,240	pieces purses	at RM	1.50 RM	4,860.00
1,315	pieces pocketbooks	at RM	2.50 RM	3,287.50
1,500	pieces scissors	at RM	0.50 RM	750.00
230	pieces flashlights	at RM	0.50 RM	115.00
2,554	pieces alarm clocks, to be repaired	at RM	3.00 RM	7,662.00
160	pieces alarm clocks, in working condition	at RM	6.00 RM	960.00
477	pieces sunglasses	at RM	0.50 RM	238.50
41	pieces silver cigarette cases	at RM	30.00 RM	1,230.00
230	pieces clinical thermometers	at RM	3.00 RM	690.00
1,315	pieces pocketbooks	at RM	2.50 RM	3,287.50
	Total .... RM			26,089,800.00

6. *Textiles*

462	boxcar rags	at RM	700.00 RM	323,400.00
253	boxcar feathers for bedding	at RM	10,000.00 RM	2,510,000.00
317	boxcar clothes and linen	at RM	33,000.00 RM	10,461,000.00
	Total .... RM			13,294,400.00

FINAL TOTAL RM 100,047,983.91

[Signed] Wippern

Lublin, 27 February, 1943 *SS Sturmbannführer*

The Majdanek shipments kept rolling. On May 14 Frank delivered another list to Himmler that included 132,000 watches, 39,000 pens, 4,000 wallets, 3,500 purses, 28,000 scissors, 230,000 razor blades, and 12,500 razors. He reported that special goods had been distributed as follows: free scissors to *Lebensborn,* surgical scissors to camp physicians, barber scissors to army barber shops. He recommended the following distribution: 500 watches to each SS combat division, 3,000 watches to the submarine service, 200 watches to camp guards, 300 fountain pens to each SS combat division, and 2,000 pens to the submarine service. Frank also asked what to do with 33,000 ladies' watches, valuable old gold and silver coins, four boxes of valuable stamp collections, and 5,000 expensive Swiss watches in pure gold cases and fitted with precious stones. Himmler's aide responded:

The Reich Leader SS has agreed that you, according to your proposition, distribute pocket watches, wrist watches, and fountain pens among the individual divisions. He merely requests that the police division should not receive 700 pocket watches, but only 500. Those 200 watches are to be distributed, 100 watches each, among the divisions, "The Reich," and "Death Head."

I have reported to the Reich Leader SS immediately because I thought that it would be better that you suggested to put the watches and fountain pens in his name at the disposal of the divisions for the yuletide celebration. . . .

Of the ladies' watches about 15,000 shall be given on yuletide to the racial German resettlers now coming from Russia, in accordance with SS Gruppenfuehrer Lorenz.

Furthermore, the Reich Leader SS is requesting that the coins be delivered to the coin museum of the Reich Bank. Likewise, the watches with the most precious Swiss works in pure gold and platinum cases, etc., and also pure golden fountain pens and propelling pencils have to be put at the disposal of the Reich Bank for sale abroad.[21]

On November 30, 1943, Himmler acknowledged the final reports on Action Reinhardt: "I express to you my thanks for the great and unique merits you have earned by the performance of operation Reinhardt for the benefit of the entire German nation."[22] The Yiddish poet Chaim Grade reflected on the activity from a vastly different perspective:

Since at the death camp of Maidanek I saw shoes
But not the feet, nor any footstep traces,
Just shoes and dust and ashes, and dry camomile growing loose
As if to cover footsteps, to erase them,
Since then I walk with my head down. . . .
. . . .

Adorn your head with the camomile's bitter flower
And let it as the herbs of Paradise to you be sweet,
Put on the rotten shoes from death camp of Maidanek
And go to Heaven, saint, to search for burned feet![23]

Liberation

The Nazis began the evacuation of Majdanek before the Russians liberated it. Since it was the most eastward camp, the evacuation started when the Eastern Front was still far from Polish borders. The first prisoner transport left for Germany as early as April 1943. When transportation facilities became scarce, the Majdanek prisoners marched on foot across Europe. The advancing Russians liberated only a few. SS personnel had little time to destroy the camp installations, though; everything was left intact, including gas chambers and crematoria. When the Red Army arrived in July 1944 the soldiers found huge warehouses spilling over with goods. They discovered dead bodies and further evidence of a full range of atrocities, which they publicized immediately to the world presses. *Life* magazine of September 18, 1944, carried a description by one of its stunned correspondents, Richard Lauderbach. He found his experience "grim":

It was not the gas chambers where victims were snuffed out standing up, or the crematorium where they were chopped up and then burned in construction ovens. This part of the "death factory" didn't get to me somehow. Too machine-like. It wasn't even the open graves with skeletons or skulls or stacks of fertilizer made from human bodies and manure. The full emotional shock came at a giant warehouse chock-full of people's shoes, more than 800,000 of all sizes, shapes, colors, and styles.

In some places the shoes had burst out of the building like corn from a crib. It was monstrous. . . . I looked at them and saw their owners: skinny kids in soft, white, worn slippers; thin ladies in black highlaced shoes; sturdy soldiers in brown military shoes.[24]

Lauderbach attended an SS hearing where camp witnesses testified against the guards. One described a scene in which he saw a truck of prisoners arrive. A Polish woman, twenty-eight years old, refused to undress as ordered. The commandant began to beat her and she scratched him. The commandant roared that he would burn her. He called two assistants. They grabbed the young woman and dragged her by her hands and legs to a crematorium, where they strapped her to an iron stretcher. Then they slid her into the fire. The witness recalled: "There was one loud scream. Her hair went up in the flames momentarily. Then I could see no more."[25]

In September 1972 Majdanek leaped into the headlines in America because an American court was considering extraditing for war crimes Mrs. Hermine Braunsteiner Ryan of Queens, New York, a housewife. She had served as deputy warden of the women's quarter in Majdanek. The government prosecutor charged her with beating inmates to death and contributing to the murder of many others. Dozens of Majdanek survivors from all over the world streamed into the courtroom. On the witness stand they described the camps much as the survivors had described them in 1945 and 1946.

One witness explained what he meant by the term "horse." The prisoners were horses. They hauled the food wagon. The SS had a team of twenty prisoner

Map 11: Majdanek Concentration Camp

Map originally appeared in German Crimes in Poland, *Central Commission for the Investigation of German Crimes. Revised by Sharon Coughran*

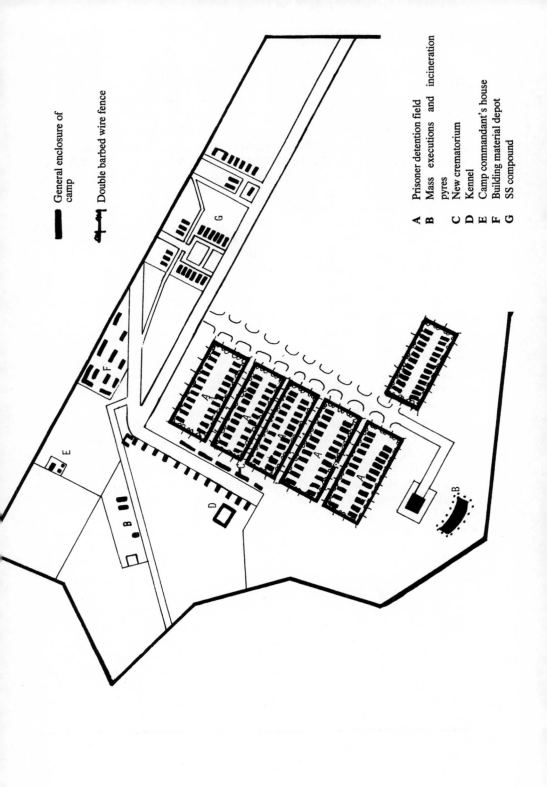

General enclosure of camp

Double barbed wire fence

A Prisoner detention field
B Mass executions and incineration pyres
C New crematorium
D Kennel
E Camp commandant's house
F Building material depot
G SS compound

horses pulling the front and twenty prisoner horses pushing the back. In that way, the witness and his colleagues dragged food into the women's camp and were able to see how the "Queens housewife" treated the women. On one occasion Mrs. Ryan was trying to convince women to relinquish their children to be exterminated. She told them that the children were being sent to a summer camp. Suspicious, some mothers refused to let them go. "Braunsteiner began to beat an old woman holding a child of about two or three in her arms. The old woman was not the mother of the child she held in her arms, but its protector. Braunsteiner hit the woman again and again and then both woman and child were on the ground." Afterward the witness had to carry away their corpses.[26]

When Mrs. Ryan was young, she dreamed of becoming a nurse. When that ambition did not materialize, she went to work in a munitions factory in Berlin. One day she received the opportunity to become a camp guard. The SS trained her at the Ravensbrück center, and there she began a career that resulted in a war crimes conviction, a prison term, and, twenty-seven years after the defeat of the Nazi regime she had served so well, the deportation proceedings brought against her by the United States government.

In 1949 in Vienna the People's court had convicted her for her work at Ravensbrück. It charged her with kicking and trampling on Ravensbrück prisoners, including old women, until they bled and died. But that court did not have the charges and evidence from Majdanek, and so it gave her a light sentence. After release from prison in May 1950, she went to Canada, where she met her husband, and emigrated to the United States. Mrs. Ryan failed to mention on her applications for immigration and citizenship that she had been convicted of crimes. She had told her husband that she had worked in a rehabilitation and education camp.

The American court proved her guilty of sending Jewish children to the crematoria. It deported Mrs. Ryan to West Germany, and her husband followed her, protesting that this was just one more piece of evidence of the Jewish conspiracy in America.

In 1975, under long-term pressure, the West German government finally agreed to try fourteen camp guards, including Mrs. Ryan, in what is now called the Majdanek Trial. She is one of five women and nine men charged with murder. In 1979 the chief of Poland's war crimes investigation commission told the Associated Press that the proceedings represent "a phantom trial, a classic case of stalling." He predicted that the court would not return a verdict until late 1980. Harassment of Polish witnesses in the courtroom—reported by the press—had so devastated those testifying that many survivors have refused to appear in person. Finally, in June 1981, a West German court sentenced the Queens housewife to life imprisonment for murdering two of the 250,000 people killed at Majdanek. In the longest and costliest German war crimes trial, the court served the highest sentence possible because Germany has no death sentence.

AUSCHWITZ/BIRKENAU: THE CORE OF THE HOLOCAUST

The symbol of all camps. The mother camp. A way of dying for all seasons, for all people. An empty void where four million once lived. Not even a graveyard honors their lives; for the bones and ashes have disappeared, blown to the winds, scattered as fertilizer, made into trinkets.

Auschwitz/Birkenau, a gigantic extermination center secluded on the edge of a quiet, drab Polish town, Oswiecim. From the medieval center of Polish art and learning, Cracow, to the epitome of death and dying, just a brief 50 kilometers—a stunning contrast. The birch trees—the beautiful birch woods surrounding Birkenau which for four springs observed the worst pesthole on earth—grow strong, nourished by human blood and ashes.

After the war prospectors descended on the area with their shovels and pans, and were joined by a new professional class of grave robbers who specialized in excavating the remains of the dead and their hidden treasures. They dug up the camp area again and again, looking for gold and treasure and finding it. Early visitors saw clusters of men hunched over a creek, sifting, panning, washing the day's haul of bones and ashes—a Polish Klondike.

Auschwitz/Birkenau covered 40 square kilometers. Auschwitz I, the base camp, lay in the area's southeastern part. Three kilometers to the northwest stood Auschwitz II, or Birkenau—several times larger than Auschwitz. I came early to the area in the old days, looking for Auschwitz, not knowing then that Birkenau had ever existed. I have returned several times and left with different thoughts and feelings. It was not the first camp in which I had stood, nor was it the last. But I cannot forget the old Auschwitz and my initial reactions, my primary lessons.

It was a barren landscape then, gloomy and secluded. One entered through a hotel that served also as a reception building. I was never able to understand how anyone could stay overnight at Auschwitz, how anyone could sleep in those beds contentedly, knowing just a little. All is there now as it was, but not really, only in form. The substance, the essential senses are missing: the noise, the smell, the sight, the taste, and the faces—the faces of the SS and of the victims. First come the fences, the double-cordoned, unending meshwork of wire. The inside wires on the light poles with insulators bear signs meaning "Attention: High Tension Danger." And interspersed, the deserted watchtowers. It is quiet: the tramping of the sentries' boots and the shouts of the guards—gone. Then through the famous main gate: *"Arbeit Macht Frei."* And finally, the surprise: the perplexity upon realizing the *small size* of Auschwitz. Silly, is it not, to expect infamy to be housed in a large space?[1]

Down the street: first the long low barrack with the chimney, the building that dominates internal Auschwitz. Another surprise. It is not the expected crematorium, but the kitchen. Auschwitz is a garrisonlike camp with two- and three-story red brick buildings arranged in monotonous rows. The streets are wide and cobblestoned—every pebble trodden into the ground by the feet of thousands. Tall trees and lawns line the sidewalks, and fall leaves in brilliant color cover the ground. The layout is like a chessboard of life and death. But the thousands of emaciated inmates in striped prison clothes no longer stand quietly, waiting.

At the edge lies the old crematorium, a small nondescript structure built into the ground, only partially visible from the surface. But the tall chimney alerts. It contains the original equipment: the furnaces and the iron body carts. The chimney—smokeless, cold. Behind the crematorium stands the gallows from which the Poles hanged former Commandant Höss in 1949. A crematorium that could not cope: too small, too makeshift, too old-fashioned. It became an air raid shelter because it could not handle the volume of corpses. Body-burning functions were shifted to Birkenau.

Most blocks or barracks were open to visitors in the early days. They were dirty, drab, and "unspoiled." The Poles had turned Auschwitz into a museum, but it was an unusual museum then because it was highlighted by the warehouses full of loot that the Russians found when they liberated the camp. Each museum block contained a specific category of confiscated goods. Whole rooms were packed with vestiges of human life. Behind the partitions, behind enormous glass cases the size of boxcars, lay the remains of the Final Solution. One huge glass case contained what looked like steel wool at first. But it was simply a barrack of hair—wagons of hair: pigtails, curls, tufts, black, blond, gray. Oh, God, the hair. Mountains and mountains of women's hair, baled, packed, and labeled for shipping to a Bavarian firm that manufactured insulation material for submarines.

Another barrack held mountains of worn shoes, and clothing—piles of children's clothing. The mounds of shoes must have been 3½ meters high. A whole building full of valises, luggage, piled haphazardly, each with the name of its owner written on the outside. One could almost have written a history of death from that roomful of labeled baggage. A large display case stretching along the building held toothbrushes; another, 30,000 spectacles in a massive collage of wire, almost as though eyes were staring out of the metal piles; and another, millions of combs. Yet another long case contained kitchen utensils:

piles of cans, metal bowls, pots, cups. One case held dentures of all kinds. And in another were thousands of moldy shaving brushes. I never knew that there were so many brushes in the whole world. At first from a distance, to a nearsighted person, it seemed like a mound of rotten potatoes.

Perhaps the most shocking of all, a large display, an entire barrack-side filled with artificial limbs purposely broken and torn open by the guards looking for gold and currency: steel corsets for cripples, plastic and wooden feet, arms, legs, hands. I realized suddenly that out of four million people, a certain percentage certainly would be crippled. But that picture is almost impossible to forget. One building held rooms of faces hanging from the walls, all dead now. The eyes out of those thousands of photos stared blankly. Two or three were smiling.[2]

Auschwitz in the late 1970s is different from what it was in the early 1960s. Its parking lot is filled with hundreds of brightly colored buses and cars. On the lawn people are sunbathing. There is a bustle to it. The same hotel in the old barracks has been redone and the receptionist tells me it is always full. So is the adjoining restaurant. Outside it stands a little store selling a variety of food: hot dogs, ice cream cones, candy. Everyone walking through Auschwitz seems to be eating something.

The Auschwitz Museum is now tidy, contained, sterile, clipped, professional, detached, and small. The realness and magnitude are gone. Everything that took place is softened by the sterile atmosphere. The real Auschwitz is replaced by a gallery of photos, films, and documents, a teeming tourist attraction boasting its own splendid facilities. Much is preserved at Auschwitz still—but it is diluted, neatly arranged, so clean and orderly. It is truly like visiting just another historical museum. And the groups that tramp through are totally irreverent; they wore my patience thin. In a few buildings small dignified cases contain neatly organized exhibits—as though a department store window dresser had been at work. The walls are whitewashed and somehow most of the smell has been removed. The museum now includes only a few barracks, and everything from both Auschwitz and Birkenau is placed there.[3]

Block Fifteen holds an historical introduction, showing the history of Nazi Germany and the war. Block Four contains the Cyclone B cans, a few bales of hair, just a few—with only one open—a small pile of teeth, a few carefully selected and arranged suitcases, and a small collection of artificial legs behind glass. That block also stresses the extermination process, and houses the Hall of Nations with its flags and urn holding a handful of ashes.

Documents, pictures of prisoners, scenes of death, and maps detailing the extermination places fill the downstairs. From those maps every killing place in the complex is clear. Auschwitz had three such places. In the cellars of Block Eleven the commandant first experimented with gas; and in the yard of Block Eleven the guards shot 20,000 prisoners. Crematorium I—the old crematorium—was used to burn bodies, but it could only cremate 340 in twenty-four hours. The SS gassed in the mortuary attached to it. For Birkenau and Auschwitz, two farmhouses took care of the bulk of the gassing before the construction of the new Birkenau crematoria. And then, at Birkenau, the officials built four huge gas chambers and crematoria with a very modern design—resembling manor houses. On immense pyres they also burned bodies. The pyres were so vast that the strong stench carried for many miles. Before the erection of the new crematoria, thousands of bodies were buried in common graves dotting the countryside. When the Nazis, toward the end of the war, were forced to exhume all bodies from the graves, they dug huge open pits, threw in the rotted corpses, poured methanol over them, and set them afire: the pits burned night and day, a total of 107,000 former people.

The infamous Block Ten (closed to the public) was the place where the guinea pig and medical experiments were performed. The Nazis had boarded up the windows so the inmates could not see the Courtyard of Death separating Blocks Ten and Eleven. Its yard with a high wall at the end was the execution plaza. A birch tree still stands behind it. Metal baskets covered the basement windows of Block Eleven to suppress the groans of the tortured and starved prisoners in the basement cells. Blocks Thirteen through Seventeen contain the Exhibition Pavilions of East Germany, Belgium, Denmark, Russia, Hungary, Czechoslovakia, and Yugoslavia. None of these national pavilions are impressive; they are simply there.

The tourists of today with their candy bars miss the misery, the torture, the despair, the degradation, the suffering, and the sadness. They will never know the sardonic laughter and the indifference that were part of the daily camp life. Although no outsider could have ever felt it fully, today it can hardly even be sensed at all. Auschwitz is too much like a Polish Disneyland with crowds of tourists shepherded about by guides. Many times I overheard groups of visitors who had viewed the exhibits remark that it really did not seem like such a terrible way to live, or that things were not as bad at Auschwitz as they had heard!

Yet every day visitors arrive from all over the world for a variety of reasons. Too many come out of curiosity. In the old days, at least, they walked quietly. Now they do not bother. After all, it no longer seems like hallowed ground. One realizes there is no place to pray at Auschwitz.

When I first saw Birkenau it was by accident—but it remains the most terrifying accident of my life. It was nearly two decades ago on my first trip to Poland. I was driving my car to Auschwitz, and did not know that Birkenau was a separate place. I went to Oswiecim from Cracow, lost my way, arrived late, went through Auschwitz. I was stunned. It was not my first camp but it was the symbol of all the camps. The warehouses overwhelmed me. From them, I learned. Although I felt the degradation and the horror, I could not place it in the context of that neat orderly little camp. I did not know that the real extermination center was down the road.

We left Auschwitz when it was dark, but a full orange Polish moon stood in the sky. Wrong turn, and suddenly, silhouetted starkly against the sky, the strangest, eeriest sight I had ever seen. No one was around. It was silent. We got out, walked to the gates, and then peered through the fences. I did not know what I was looking at, but it frightened me to my depths—a young American girl standing with a friend in Poland in the deserted countryside, at Birkenau. I felt an overwhelming sense of evil—not horror, as in the Auschwitz warehouses, but evil. God, it was awful. I stood with my eyes wide and my mouth open, speechless. I had no idea what it was, but I felt evil, and that moment, that time, has never left me. Now, whenever I am there, I still tremble at that vivid, decades-old picture in my mind, afraid if I close my eyes and open them again, it will be night, deserted, and that unyielding feel, smell, of being in the midst of evil will completely overpower me again. But it doesn't happen. Now I arrive early in the day and leave by midafternoon and drive as fast as I can back to Cracow, almost as though I must put miles between myself and Birkenau before night falls.

The Nazis began to build Birkenau in 1941 and much of it remains. The main administration building and camp gate through which the trains rolled stands sentry duty now. The planners had divided Birkenau into three sectors. Part of Sector I—the brick barracks for the penal colony—and another part of the same sector—the brick building for the women—are still standing. Sector II contains rows and rows of wooden horse stables divided by mud streets. A section of those huts remains. The railroad track rolls through the administration building, divides, and stretches for hundreds of yards to its end—the extermination plant.

All that remains of the crematoria and gas chambers are piles of ruins. The ruined concrete slabs jut up sharply, with their twisted cement and broken steel. And at the end of the railroad tracks lies the International Monument dedicated to the former prisoners of all nations. An urn with an eternal flame burns on each rail. The monument is not significant—it could not be in a place like Birkenau.

Whenever I see Birkenau, I walk away with my mind full of tales. For Birkenau is more awe-inspiring than any other camp. It is worse than imagination, beyond fantasy. I have been there in every kind of season. When the weather is warm and dry, the camp stands quiet and desolate, populated only by hordes of flies and mosquitoes. I have seen it in the fog and the cold with the stinking mist hanging over it: dismal. Whatever the season, the dead always seem to be present. The low dark barracks stand in a row, dirty and deserted. Each was wooden-built to hold 48 horses, but housed 800 humans. The barbed wire fences surrounding Birkenau run for miles. It is a bleak, silent world. Even the tourists, or most of them, seem to avoid it.

Crematoria remains, Birkenau.

Grass covers the rusty railroad tracks. The roads are usually muddy and they crisscross the camp. Hundreds of barracks have been torn down; only the ruined barrack chimneys jut out like gravestones. The air seems to be full of the cries of the murdered and the shouts of the executioners; but even here it is impossible to estimate the pain and death of just one man.

Borowski grasped the significance of the barracks in his literary picture:

If the barrack walls were suddenly to fall away, many thousands of people, packed together, squeezed tightly in their bunks, would remain suspended in mid-air. Such a sight would be more gruesome than the medieval paintings of the Last Judgment. For one of the ugliest sights to a man is that of another man sleeping on his tiny portion of the bunk, of the space which he must occupy, because he has a body—a body that has been exploited to the utmost: with a number tattooed on it to save on dog tags, with just enough sleep at night to work during the day, and just enough time to eat. And just enough food so it will not die wastefully. As for actual living there is only one place for it—a piece of the bunk. The rest belongs to the camp, the Fatherland. But not even this small space, nor the shirt you wear, nor the spade you work with are your own. If you get sick, everything is taken away from you: your clothes, your camp, your "organized" scarf, your handerchief. If you die—your gold teeth, already recorded in the camp inventory, are extracted. Your body is burned and your ashes are used to fertilize the fields or fill in the ponds. Although in fact so much fat and bone is wasted in the burning, so much flesh, so much heat![4]

Words seem useless when faced with an inscription scratched on the wall of a barrack by a young man before his death: "Andreas Rapaport—lived 16 years." One visitor wrote an article reacting to that single line; and I remember feeling the same thing he had when I saw that simple sentence written in despair by a child knowing he was going to die. I, too, think it says all there is to say: abandonment—fear—hunger—pain—gas-filled lungs—naked corpses—burning flesh—black smoke—ashes—eternity.

There seems to be no end to Birkenau, but actually most of it is gone, at least the substance of it. The wind has erased it. The rain has washed it. The sun has bleached it. In my mind I can still see the prisoners walking, and the SS men standing, watching, smiling. And I know as I pause there that in all that misery some men from the master race enjoyed participating in a *process* that we find so terrifying: committing atrocities for *pleasure*.[5]

Before I left this last time, I saw the tourist film at Auschwitz and I found myself crying in shame at the pictures of the hopeless empty eyes. For the film contains footage shot at the time of a procession of 150 children dressed in clothes too big, walking unsteadily in their rags. They hold each other's tiny hands, their little faces emaciated by starvation, mortally serious with big questioning eyes. Some still have the courage to scowl. The children pass by without toys, parents, a home, childhood, and soon without breath. Tears are rolling down the cheeks of some. And then I cry. Because of the murder of the children? No, I don't know them. No, I cry because I, too, belong to the human race.

Auschwitz/Birkenau brought the rational and orderly extermination of human beings to a point of efficiency and magnitude unknown in the modern world. Not only was it the largest mass killing installation in history, but the number murdered there exceeds the combined population of several small European nations. In the record of what men have done to other men there is no place where so many people have been put to death so quickly: 4,000,000 in an area of 39 square kilometers in less than five years. Auschwitz/ Birkenau became the most renowned of all camps. During the war years the immense Auschwitz complex also became one of the largest Jewish communities in history:

More Jews arrived at Auschwitz from all over German-occupied Europe, more Jews lived in Auschwitz, more Jews perished in Auschwitz in a shorter period of time than anywhere else in the world.[6]

Before the war Oswiecim, a small Galician town in Upper Silesia, had 12,000 inhabitants, about one-half of whom were Jewish. It was unhealthy, malaria-ridden, and industrialized: located 286 kilometers southwest of Warsaw, and 50 kilometers west of Cracow. Any renown it may have had came from its location near the rich Silesian mines. The town lay in a perpetual mudhole on flat land formed like the bottom of a flat basin. Moisture, water, sat on the land, draining nowhere. It was a foggy area with stagnant, poisonous pools and damp air. (The water was so unsuitable that the SS men were forbidden to use it, even for washing.) As an old Jewish community on the Vistula, Oswiecim was one of the first Silesian towns in which Polish Jews settled during the Middle Ages. It was a spiritual center for Judaism.[7]

Auschwitz was to become a vast establishment with thirty-nine camps divided into three main groups: Auschwitz I, the main camp, which included the central administration, the Gestapo, and various armament firms; Auschwitz II, officially known as Birkenau, dedicated to the destruction of prisoners in the gas chambers; and Auschwitz III, or Buna, the labor camp for the construction of the vast synthetic rubber and petrol works at Monowice (Monowitz). The vast complex also included a network of smaller labor camps.

The Nazis set up a closed zone around Auschwitz serving an area of over 50 square kilometers. They evacuated several nearby towns as early as 1940 and subsequently used them for subsidiary camps within the huge establishment. Auschwitz I, the only part of the complex with a long history, had as its nucleus an Austrian cavalry barracks.

In January of 1940 a conference took place in Wroclaw in the office of SS General Erich Bach-Zelewski. SS Colonel Richard Glücks, inspector of concentration camps, and several SS officers were present. They discussed plans for a new concentration camp. Only six camps then existed in the Greater Reich: Dachau, Sachsenhausen, Buchenwald, Flossenbürg, Mauthausen, and Ravensbrück. Because the Polish underground was growing in size, the SS needed a camp for large numbers of Polish prisoners on a site central to the territories the Nazis planned to conquer. The site would have to be isolated from population centers, yet have good railroad access. After examining the map, their eyes fell on Auschwitz. As a result, in February 1940 two examination commissions went to Auschwitz. Both issued negative reports because of the foul water and marshy ground. But commission member Rudolf Höss, then manager of the Sachsenhausen camp, and Glück prepared a report suggesting that the Auschwitz site could be used. Himmler accepted their opinion and established the camp by order on April 27, 1940. He appointed Rudolf Höss commandant and ordered him to create quickly a transient camp for 10,000 prisoners.[8]

Initially the camp consisted of the Austrian military barracks and several buildings of the Polish tobacco monopoly situated on the left bank of the Solo River. Expansion began immediately. Auschwitz opened for business on June 14, 1940, with the arrival of the first transport of 728 Polish political prisoners. The camp grew rapidly. By the end of 1941 it could accommodate 18,000 prisoners, and by 1943, 30,000. The Germans made laborious preparations for the erection of a mammoth city devoted to the death industry—"a great Himmlerstadt"—that would hold 750,000 prisoners and have a daily crematoria capacity of 40,000. Those prisoners would be employed in factories run by the SS and large industrial concerns.

In the summer of 1941 Himmler summoned Höss to Berlin to discuss a major problem. He told him that Hitler had ordered the SS to solve the Jewish question permanently. Himmler explained that he had earmarked the Auschwitz complex, especially *Birkenau*, for that purpose because of the good communications and the ease of camouflage. A few weeks later Eichmann visited Auschwitz and exposed to Höss the plans for the Final Solution. They discussed together how to destroy millions of people and decided on gas. Höss and Eichmann inspected the area and made plans to gas inmates in a peasant farmstead in the corner of what became Birkenau. Thus it was decided that Auschwitz/Birkenau would be the center for the extermination of the Jews. That decision led to the permanent extension of the camp.

The Auschwitz complex became very much like Majdanek—built first as a concentration camp before advanced machinery gave it an extermination purpose. It also retained a core of Jewish prisoners for labor purposes. Because Auschwitz contained a large inmate population, it had a serious maintenance problem—the provision of shelter, food, and medical care. In the end it also experienced a body-disposal problem and had to shift to open burning. Thus the Auschwitz complex, including Birkenau and Monowitz, was both the largest of all camps and, with the added gas chambers, the largest installation for extermination.

Two conflicting aims characterized Auschwitz for much of its history: the extermination of the Jews and the exploitation of labor. Each function lay with a different Berlin bureaucracy. Auschwitz and Majdanek were the only camps where schizophrenia of purpose remained fairly constant, and where the selection procedures involved most arriving transports. On the Birkenau ramp the SS doctors and officers separated from the mass of arrivees those persons capable of working: young people, middle-aged men, and healthy women. They exempted them from extermination and sent them to the camp, where they had a slim possibility of survival if they remained fit. Selection meant extermination, of course.[9]

From an organizational point of view, Auschwitz I was the main camp. At the same time it had an unusual mission—to be a showpiece for the public if and when that became necessary. Since it was deliberately designed to allay suspicions, it looked very different from most camps. The twenty-eight one- and two-story brick buildings with spacious washrooms and the careful landscaping did not conform to normal camp appearance.

About 91 meters from the end of the small compound stood the crematorium. It had originally been used as a storage shed for geese. Camp officials closed the brick building with earth on three sides and planted grass, small trees, and flowers. They reinforced the roof with special concrete. A high wall enclosed the space in front of the entrance. At night the small ovens produced a thick black smoke and a high flame shooting out of the chimney. The interior of the crematorium consisted mainly of the oven chamber, a vestibule, and the big mortuary with its six covered air vents and exhaust mechanism. The SS executed the inmates inside the mortuary:

Heart breaking scenes took place. Mothers had to part from daughters; men of military bearing shook hands for the last time; others said a last prayer. While all this was going on, murder most foul was being committed in the mortuary. The groups of ten nude prisoners were led into the chamber whose walls were covered with blood. The bodies of the dead prisoners were piled up in the rear. A wide ribbon of blood ran through the center of the room into the drain. The prisoners were ordered to go up close to the dead bodies and line up. Their feet became stained red by the blood in which they stood. Some of them recognized close relatives, perhaps fathers, among the dying.[10]

Filip Müller, a young Slovakian, arrived early in Auschwitz—April 1942—and survived! He did so, however, because of his forced work assignments as a stoker in the Auschwitz crematorium and then as a jack-of-all trades in the Birkenau extermination plant squad, the *Sonderkommando*. His descriptions of the facilities and of the process are the most precise and chilling accounts we have. In the antiquated Auschwitz crematorium the procedure was remindful of the Stone Age. The stokers dragged the bodies across the floor to the ovens. A main rail track ran across the room, with six branch tracks leading to the six ovens:

On the main track was a turn-table which enabled a truck to be moved onto the branch tracks. The cast-iron truck had a box-shaped superstructure made of sheet metal, with an overall height and width of just under 1 metre. It was about 80 centimetres long. An iron hand-rail went right across its entire width at the back. A loading platform made of strong sheet metal and not quite 2 metres long jutted out in the front; its side walls were 12 to 15 centimetres high. Open at the front, the platform was not quite as wide as the mouth of the oven so that it fitted easily into the muffle. On the platform there was also a box-shaped pusher made of sheet metal, higher than the side walls of the platform and rounded off at the top.

The stokers brought a truck to the branch rail, poured water on the truck to keep it cool, and loaded three corpses on it.

Now the time had come to open the oven door. Immediately one was overcome by the fierce heat which rushed out. When the wooden prop had been removed, two men took hold of the front end of the platform on either side pulling it right up to the oven. Simultaneously two men pushed the truck from behind, thus forcing the platform into the oven. The two who had been doing the carrying in front, having meanwhile stepped back a few steps, now braced themselves against the hand-rail while giving the pusher a vigorous shove with one leg. In this way they helped complete the job of getting the corpses right inside the oven.

While the corpses burned, the stokers stripped the waiting bodies. At the most fifty-four bodies could be cremated in one hour. The continuous over-loading and operation of the ovens caused the inner fire bricks to crumble. The staff built a new modern chimney in the summer of 1942. But it soon evidenced crumbling; and the extermination process, never very effective, began to disintegrate. Himmler soon became dissatisfied. The process moved too slowly; the stench contaminated the surrounding countryside at night; and the red sky over Auschwitz could be seen for miles.[11]

The gassing process generated enormous piles of corpses, and the number grew daily. The small crematorium could not cope, so the squads buried the corpses in mass graves in the Birkenau woods. Although the corpses were covered with chlorine, lime, and earth, after a few months the inevitable decomposition began to poison the air, causing an intolerable stench throughout the entire neighborhood. Doctors found deadly bacteria in springs and wells, and predicted serious epidemics. Experts at the fisheries began to complain that the fish in the ponds in the vicinity were dying, which they attributed to the pollution of the ground water through cadaveric poison. The bodies, rotting under the summer sun, swelled up and a brownish red mass began to seep through the cracks to the surface. Quick action had to be taken.

Colonel Blobel arrived from Eichmann's office with Himmler's orders that all bodies be exhumed and burned and the ashes removed. Working in two shifts, the prisoners dug up the 50,000 decaying corpses, took them away on trucks, and burned them—first on wood pyres, 2,000 at a time, and later in pits. The fires raged day and night until December 1942 when the anti-aircraft defense service protested because the fires could be seen for great distances. Himmler also found fault with the process because open-pyre burning could hardly be kept a secret. Therefore the top SS bureaucracy became aware of the vital need in the future for an efficient process of final body disposal.

Following Himmler's expansion order, Birkenau's construction began in 1941. The SS moved prisoner teams into the area to raze the empty houses and prepare the ground for new huts. Each day the work squads covered an area of many kilometers—demolishing depopulated villages, leveling the ground, filling in the marshes, constructing primitive sewage systems, marking off camp roads and fields, and collecting old stones to build "new" barracks. The primitive camp (no more than a collection of brick and wooden huts) covered 175 hectares, divided into three main sectors.

By October 1941 basic Birkenau was ready, the largest of Hitler's camps. It served simultaneously as a center for extermination and a center for industrial exploitation. The Nazis continuously expanded Birkenau; by the end of the war they had completed Section BI, Section BII, and part of Section BIII. At its peak in 1943, Birkenau housed approximately 100,000 inmates. Planned to hold a population of 250,000 eventually, the total area was 2 square kilometers. It required about an hour and a half to walk around it. Section BI was the oldest, built in 1941, and it housed 20,000 inmates. It contained two camps, BIa and BIb, the majority of the blocks built of bricks. After the summer of 1942 BIa became the camp for women. Later in 1943 the rest of the sector took care of the overflow from the women's camp. Section BII was a men's camp for 60,000 prisoners. It also contained the hospital, Canada, experimental stations, and facilities for quarantine, Czech Jewish families, women criminals, and Gypsies. Höss began Section BIII, intended for 60,000 inmates, in 1944, but failed to complete it. He started the dismantling process in October 1944 and moved many buildings to Gross-Rosen.

At Birkenau inmates were not accommodated. Instead, they died or managed a bare existence in the 250 primitive stone and wooden huts originally intended as cavalry stables for the German campaign in Africa. The SS usually packed each hut with twice its *possible* capacity. The wooden stables had no windows. The sole ventilation and light came from the skylight in the roof. Three-tiered bunks lined each side. A block housed from 400 to

500 people. In good times an inmate had about 8 square feet in which to eat, live, and sleep. There was neither a lavatory nor a washbowl. At night two tubs were placed against the back walls among the sleeping prisoners. Those often overflowed. The prisoners carried out the tubs and emptied them into the main lavatories

which will remain for all time as a noble testimony to Nazi inventiveness in the field of hygiene—a wooden hut, 30 × 130 feet, with six rows of holes sunk through the concrete floor to serve 250 people. The crush in the morning after reveille was indescribable and the stink unbearable.

Until 1943 the only drinking water for the entire area came from a single tap in the lavatory. Clothing was inadequate. "Summer and winter," wrote an Auschwitz woman, "we have but one type of clothing. Its name is 'rag.' "[12]

The brick blocks of Camp BI accommodated 1,200 people, without water, washrooms, or lavatories. Prisoners described the conditions as below animal level:

The block was filled to capacity by four rows of low berths, looking like a three-tier chicken house. It was always damp and cold inside, even in hot weather, and the aisles between the berths were covered with slimy mire. The straw on the berths came from thatched roofs of the adjacent farmhouses which had been pulled down. The straw was rotten and stinking in the lower berths where it was mixed with mud and looked like dung. The best thing was to find an upper berth, but these were already taken. . . . The stink, thirst and hunger made sleep impossible.[13]

The SS found such huts unsuitable for housing their camp cows; for those animals, they erected special cow sheds. For their dogs, they constructed a dog kennel complex. The animals never would have survived in the prisoner huts, they concluded.

On November 25, 1944, the SS incorporated Birkenau into the base camp. The transformation caused no real change. Its object was to camouflage Birkenau's existence by centralizing its administration. On paper the complex appeared as two camps: one at Auschwitz and the other at Monowitz. The name Birkenau disappeared from the public list of Nazi camps, even though the camp remained the largest one in the system. The nameless camp killed its inmates by starvation, inadequate diet, disease, injections of phenolic acid, beatings, torture, and execution. The prisoners met death in unspeakably primitive, unsanitary conditions as medical guinea pigs, and as victims of sadists. They died from overwork, degradation, sadness, and despair. The SS gassed the majority of them.

Modern society, whatever it has thought of its grown-ups and however it has decided to treat them, has usually considered its children special, demanding for them care and devotion. Few comments about an adult can be more disparaging than to remark: "She is a bad mother" or "He is a bad father." Nazi Germany was no different. The model SS father took special care of the large group of inmate children in the Auschwitz/Birkenau complex: special brutality, cruelty, experimentation—beyond even the ability of the hardened prisoners, so used to death, to watch and tolerate. The conditions led one woman to pledge: "Together we will endure death. Even life." Examples of child cruelty are unlimited. When the Gypsy children died of starvation, they were thrown in heaps. A witness at the Auschwitz trial testified: "I saw a mountain of corpses, children's corpses. And scurrying among them the rats." Another witness recalled seeing a little boy jump off an incoming truck of Jewish children. He held an apple in his hand. Boger, one of the SS terrors, and another officer were talking nearby:

The child was standing next to the car with his apple and was enjoying himself. Suddenly Boger went over to the boy, grabbed his legs, and smashed his head against the wall. Then he calmly picked up the apple. And Draser told me to wipe "that" off the wall. About an hour later I was called to Boger to interpret in an interrogation and I saw him eating the child's apple.[14]

Others testifying at the Auschwitz trial remembered seeing SS men killing children by bending them over their knees like sticks of wood and breaking their spines, then throwing them into ditches. Often, when the *Sonderkommando* pulled the dead from the chambers, the hearts of some children were still beating. The SS shot those. SS Sergeant Moll tore a child away from his mother, took him over to the crematorium, and threw him into the boiling fat of recently cremated victims. Then he turned to a colleague and said: "I have done my duty. I am satisfied." When transports arrived, the SS made selections among the children. During the selection process an SS man would place a rod at the height of 1.2 meters.

Children who had passed under the rod would be gassed. Small children, knowing only too well what was waiting them, tried hard to push out their necks when passing under the rod, in the hope to escape gassing.[15]

Usually, the Nazis did not allow children to be born at Birkenau. Pregnant Jewish women went to the gas chambers; any children were killed. In 1943 Aryan children born in the camp could remain alive with the unofficial consent of the SS. After they were entered in the camp register, their camp numbers had to be tatooed on their behinds or thighs because their little arms were too tiny. Most died within a week. From some transports, the selectors spared young boys from the gas chambers because they could use them as building apprentices on crematoria construction. After their work was finished, the boys were killed by phenol injections. The Soviets found only 156 children when they evacuated Birkenau in January 1945. Historians estimate the number of murdered young people below the age of eighteen at one million.

The Auschwitz complex copied every type of torture and punishment used in the earlier camps and created forms of its own. The guards wielded severe punishment for the slightest infraction, with twenty-five lashes a minor penalty. One guard invented the infamous necktie torture. He would order the victim to lie on his back. Then he placed an iron bar on the victim's throat and stood on the bar with both feet placed on the ends. His colleagues gathered as an appreciative audience. Auschwitz had a special starvation cell. A prisoner thrown into such a cell recalled the horrible smell of decaying corpses. After accustoming himself to the darkness, he noticed a corpse in the corner with its intestines pulled out "and beside him in a half recumbent position—a second body, also of a prisoner. He was holding in his hand a liver he had taken from the body of his dead companion. Death struck him in the act of devouring this liver." The SS extracted nails from fingers, inserted needles into particularly sensitive parts of the body and into women's breasts, and poured water through funnels down throats.[16]

One of the most famous tortures was the "Boger Swing." The SS forced the victim to sit on the floor, tied his hands, and pulled them over his raised knees. A heavy rod was then pushed between his bent legs and knees and rested on two tables. The victim now hung with his head above the ground, swinging back and forth, receiving a blow on his buttocks and genitals at each swing. Sometimes he was hit with a bull whip so violently that he would make an almost complete somersault. If he yelled too vigorously, the guards put a gas mask over him. After fifteen minutes, blood drenched his trousers and he lapsed into unconsciousness. His backside was already so bloody that further beatings could not increase the pain. After reviving him, the Gestapo proceeded to the next step: dripping hot water into his nose, which resulted in unbearable burning pain.

Anyone familiar with Auschwitz knows the meaning of Block Eleven. It looked like any other block from the outside. The upper windows were sealed off and the basement windows barred. The crimes of the inmates isolated in the narrow, crowded, stinking cells included stealing a few potatoes, smoking a cigarette, and other minor infractions. Most Block Eleven residents were later taken outside in the yard to the so-called Black Wall. For thousands of innocent people, that wall of black cork became their last moment of life.

Medical experimentation, an intriguing operation in all camps, was big business at Auschwitz/Birkenau, which had excellent experimental facilities, a massive pool of experimentees, and the growing attention of business, industry, science, and Himmler. Scientists used the inmates as guinea pigs for the widest variety of experiments, including military hygiene, sterilization, and artificial insemination. Doctors removed sex organs from men and women and sterilized them by various methods. In Dr. Mengele's secret lab he murdered twins, dwarfs, and hunchbacks to provide the Berlin Institute of Anthropology with human organs. Mengele was obsessed with the hope of discovering a foolproof method to enable every German mother to bear twins. He stood patiently, day after day, at the selection ramp and picked out pairs of twins suitable for his work. One day a child he had under observation died a natural death. During the autopsy it was discovered the child had a peculiar chest disorder. Dr. Mengele raced out to find the other twin. He located the child, lured him into his car with a piece of chocolate, and drove him to the crematorium yard where he shot him. Then Mengele ordered a postmorten to determine if the second twin had the same chest trouble as the first.

I. G. Farben designed a full-scale lethal nerve gas test program that utilized Auschwitz prisoners. Originally Farben used guinea pigs and rats, but found they had little relation to human beings. The scientists moved to apes, but apes were hard to secure in large numbers and the cost proved prohibitive. Finally the lab directors turned to much more satisfactory subjects—Auschwitz inmates. As human beings, they were perfect subjects, and they came very cheap. According to British intelligence and one Farben leader, the top echelon at Farben knew of those experiments. They justified them on two grounds: (1) the inmates would have died anyway; and (2) the tests were humanitarian because they would save German lives. Farben's conduct seems to have reflected Himmler's attitude when he remarked: "What does it matter to us? Look away if it makes you sick."[17]

The Nazis were determined to kill Gypsies. They sent convoys of Gypsy families from all over Central Europe to Birkenau. It overflowed with Gypsy children. About 21,000 Gypsies passed through the camp. Himmler ordered the liquidation of the surviving Gypsies on August 2, 1944.

From all the brutalities, though, the Jews suffered the most. Lena Donat worked as a pharmacist in the Auschwitz hospital for almost two years. She survived mentally because she did not see, hear, or know. She had already developed a heart of stone as a graduate of "two great universities of human suffering," the Warsaw ghetto and Majdanek:

"I who had formerly almost died of fright at the sight of a mouse now slept at Auschwitz with enormous rats crawling back and forth over my face. I handled corpses without either fear or disgust. I trampled on human ashes but refused to permit myself to be aware of it. Not only my nerves, but my very senses were blunted, and I succeeded in creating in myself an induced amnesia: I simply did not dwell on the horrors I was living through."

Lena also drove away memories of her loved ones. "Like a snail, I curled up inside my shell." She was determined to survive to return to her little boy. Deafness and blindness were her armor. She lost forever the "notion that man was created in the likeness of God." When their close friends died, the women tried to give them Auschwitz funerals: they wrapped them in sheets and placed them on the corpse pile behind the barracks.[18]

Max Garcia, a nineteen-year-old Dutch Jew, made up his mind to win "the Survival Game." He learned to outplay the SS. Hope kept him going, hope that he would be alive the next day. "What's the future?" he pondered. "The future is tomorrow; the future is an hour from now; the future is the next bowl of soup." For him, "breathing, being alive" was the motivation. He joined a group of fighters—other arrogant men who knew that somehow they would beat Dante's Inferno. They could "never die again because they were dead there." Beating the selection gave Garcia and his friends "moments of joy, exhilaration." He "out-Germaned the creeps." Germans clicked their heels; so when Garcia's turn came to stand before the SS doctor, "I clicked hard in naked heels, but the sound was stronger than those in the boots."[19]

Led by a trumpet player in the Auschwitz orchestra, Max Garcia and several Dutch prisoners formed a unique camp group—a cabaret to entertain inmates with music and jokes. The SS, for unknown reasons, gave it their stamp of approval. Garcia assumed the dual role of MC and Maurice Chevalier, while his friends played instruments. The prisoners and the SS roared with approval during the performances. The group gave regular Sunday programs, and included the women's camp in Birkenau on its list.[20]

A former inmate told the story of a group of 2,000 interned American Jews brought to Birkenau in the summer of 1943. In Italy the SS had told them they were going to Switzerland to be exchanged. Instead they ended up at Birkenau. The Jews were not really American. They were wealthy Polish Jews who, led by a business magnate called Mazur, had all been issued false American passports obtained through the SS by one of them, a woman dancer named Horowitz, for millions of dollars. Furnished with the passports, the group did in fact leave for Hamburg; they even embarked on a ship, but it never left harbor. The SS continued the farce to the bitter end, using the period of enforced waiting at the harbor to obtain documentary letters from the so-called Americans for propaganda purposes. They continued to blackmail the relatives of the victims. When they had tapped all the financial sources available, they allowed the travelers to get under way—but not to America. They sent them straight to the gas chamber at Birkenau. The overseer at the crematorium where the women were gassed was a guard named Schillinger. When the dancer, Horowitz, appeared in line, Schillinger ordered her to take off her brassiere. Instead she snatched up her dress, threw it in the man's face, seized his pistol, shot him in the stomach, and wounded another SS man. Pandemonium broke out; then the group was driven into the chamber and killed.[21]

Taking that story as his base, novelist Arnost Lustig, in *A Prayer for Katerina Horovitzova,* tells the tale of twenty harassed Jewish men in rumpled business suits and one beautiful young Jewess playing out a game in Poland. In the Lustig version the twenty men are rich European-born Jews with American passports who fall into the hands of the Germans in Italy in 1943 and who expect to be exchanged. Commandant Brenske fans that hope as he collects more and more money from the men, and even allows Katerina Horovitzova, a young Jewish girl who wept on the loading ramp, to join the group at the request of Cohen, one of the men. The lengthy negotiations take time and each delay costs more money to resolve. And through it all, listening silently, allowing herself to hope from time to time, sits Katerina. Commandant Brenske calls the camp a culmination as he admonishes the group:

If new arrivals are welcomed, there must also be goodbyes. It's as though one, two, a thousand, even a million flames were merged together into one single bonfire. Thanks to magnificent organization, we can handle everything.

Katerina finally understands about the indestructibility of the ashes. They would neither freeze, nor burn, nor dry up:

No one living would ever be able to escape them; these ashes would be contained in the milk that will be drunk by babies yet unborn . . . the ashes will linger in the flowers which grow out of them . . . they will be contained in the breath and expression of every one of us.

It is Katerina, fully comprehending the totality of it all for the first time, who manages to wrest a gun from Schillinger and shoot him in the stomach:

She could feel her heart beat, but she had heard nothing. Not even the dry crack of the bullet. She simply understood and killed.

Later, after all have been killed and gassed, Brenske orders that the girl's body be exhibited in the warehouse beside the oven where hair cut from the heads of dead women was usually dried. The book ends with Rabbi Dajem of Lodz's prayer for Katerina, sung as he watches her body burn:

... A hundred times courageous, a hundred times good, a thousand times just, a thousand times beautiful.[22]

As in other camps, at the Auschwitz complex, the Germans determined to profit from the victims before and after death. They built thirty-five special huts called Canada to sort and patch clothing and other articles, and to store the victims' belongings. They sent valuables as gifts to German families and gold to the state treasury. Before their evacuation, the Germans burned twenty-nine stores and their contents. In the remaining six stores the Russians found the following: "368,820 complete men's suits of clothes, 836,255 women's complete outfits, 5,525 pairs of women's shoes, 38,000 pairs of men's shoes, 13,964 carpets and large numbers of toothbrushes, shaving brushes, spectacles, artificial limbs, all kinds of kitchen utensils, and also children's clothing." From camp records, it appears that over a period of one and a half months, for example, 100,000 suits of clothing and children's underwear, 200,000 suits of clothing and women's underwear, and 225 sets of men's clothes and underwear were sent to Germany from Auschwitz. The liberating army also found 7,000 kilograms of human hair packed in paper bags, only a small portion of the hair that the authorities had not yet sent to the Bavarian factories for processing. Hair sold at the price of 50 pfennigs a kilogram.

The German Energy Crisis

The story of the Auschwitz labor and extermination program is intricately tied to the history of the giant chemical firm I. G. Farben, and joined with the vital German energy crisis that plagued the country during the first forty-five years of the twentieth century. Because of that constant and grave problem, I. G. Farben got away with murder during the Nazi years. It became "a mighty industrial colossus," a collection of brilliant Nobel Prize scientists charged with creating the economic self-sufficiency that would enable Germany to move into world politics, and the organizer of a vast slave-labor program. The Farben/military alliance began in World War I. No nitrate— no gunpowder; and Germany had no nitrate. It also needed poison gas. Farben threw its industrial might into the "Chemists' War," and out of that war precedents for a successful Holocaust emerged. (It would seem, after all, that everything is based on prior experience.) From World War I emerged poison gas, the deportation of foreign labor (in cattle cars, no less), and the lies regarding labor. Farben told news reporters in 1917 that humanitarianism prompted the deportation of the Belgian workers—they were only protecting able-bodied men from the ruin of unemployment (an idea not far from *Arbeit Macht Sie Frei*). In 1919 the Nobel Prize committee awarded the poison gas creator, Dr. Haber, the Nobel Prize in Chemistry at the very moment the Allies were trying him for war crimes. As after World War II, the War Crimes Trials against industrialists became pointless.

Carl Bosch, head of Farben, dreamed during the 1920s of solving Germany's energy crisis with synthetics—by making coal into a "torrent of gasoline." To do so, he steered Farben into partnership with Standard Oil of New Jersey, an alliance that caused Standard to drop its own research into the development of synthetic rubber. The Farben-Standard Oil marriage was ahead of its time. The discovery of enormous oil reserves in Texas lowered the price of oil and Standard lost interest in hydrogenation and synthetics— and did not regain it until 1974. That action stunned Farben, which had counted on Standard Oil's participation in the costly research (synthetic gas cost seven times more per gallon to produce than natural gas). Farben then turned to the government for help.[23]

1933 saw the development of the strange alliance of Farben and Hitler devoted to the synthesization of gasoline. When Farben's Bosch warned the Führer that destroying Jewish scientists would set physics and chemistry back a hundred years, Hitler roared: "Then we'll work a hundred years without physics and chemistry!" He never again appeared in the same room with Bosch.[24]

Farben and Hitler reached an agreement on December 4, 1933, signaling a "monumental technological achievement in modern power politics." Farben would expand synthetic oil and rubber installations and the government would guarantee the company costs plus a 5 percent return. In return, Farben promised to free Germany from dependence on foreign oil and rubber. That military-industrial alliance required the complete Nazification of Farben—which was accomplished by 1937.

As Hitler took over country after country in Europe, Farben rushed to get in on the kill. It compiled lists of "prospective booty" in reports such as "The Most Important Chemical Plants in Poland" and "The New Order for Austria's Chemical Industry." Farben board member Baron Georg von Schnitzler followed the German troops. Farben took over the entire management, for example, of Polish chemical plants—on its own terms. It drew up detailed plans to absorb the chemical industries of France, Norway, Holland, Denmark, Luxembourg, Russia, Switzerland, England, Italy, and the United States.[25]

Desperate to solve the energy crisis, Farben looked to Silesia for sites to build mammoth synthetic oil and rubber plants. In early 1941 Himmler proposed to Farben that it construct a huge synthetic rubber plant next to Auschwitz and exploit the inmate labor. Göring gave his support and ordered that Auschwitz prisoners be rented to Farben as slaves. On March 1, 1941, Himmler visited Auschwitz to explain to Höss that he had a new task for him. He wanted a special camp for 100,000 prisoners. Auschwitz I would be expanded, and new areas added. Himmler wanted to transfer important branches of the armament and energy industries to the area and add agricultural research stations and farms. Höss moved immediately to evict and evacuate the local population and clear the neighboring villages—over an area of about 14 square kilometers.

I. G. Farben was the first Nazi monopoly to obtain permission from the Göring ministry to construct a factory near Auschwitz. Because synthetic petroleum and rubber were urgently needed, the industrialists intended to erect the plant with lightning speed. Hitler promised that Farben could derive its essential labor force both to construct the plant and work in it from the inmates. The SS pledged to deliver the requisite number of strong and healthy prisoners and also agreed to replace its exhausted and ailing work force with fresh prisoners without delay.

The construction of Buna in the village of Monowitz, about 8 kilometers from Auschwitz, began. Inmates built the plants and roads and constructed barracks and two company villages. Because of bottlenecks and lagging schedules due to its most "vexing problem"—inmate labor—Farben set up its own concentration camp at Monowitz. The foremost researcher of Farben maintains that Monowitz definitely belonged to Farben, and that the SS only provided security, punishments, and a ready supply of inmates. Farben adopted SS methods in its factory. One survivor recalled the Farben practice of throwing corpses of dead workers into ditches that had been dug for cables. Then Farben employees poured concrete over the bodies. Carl Krauch (a Farben board member) led the way in the creation and completion of Monowitz in September 1942. (For his crimes, the Nuremberg tribunal sentenced him to six years.)[26]

Buna Camp was a "human slaughter-house," with the workers dying in the thousands. By March 1943, 15,000 prisoners worked at the camp. Regular weekly convoys arrived with fresh prisoners to replace those who died or were too sick to labor further. Civilian commissions from Berlin visited regularly to review the work. When the Farben representatives were dissatisfied with low output, the prisoners were punished or killed. Several thousand civilians also worked on the project—forced labor from the occupied countries of Europe. They lived in a special section of the camp.[27]

Farben netted considerable profits from the work of the prisoners. It paid the camp administration 4 marks for one day of skilled labor and 3 marks for unskilled labor. Child laborers cost 1½ marks a day. The camp administration received more than 12 million marks during a period of seven months. One Farben branch, Degesch, manufactured Cyclone B, the gassing material. It received 300,000 marks from the sale of the gas in the years 1941–

1944. Auschwitz alone used about 20,000 kilograms. One member of the Farben board wrote that the firm's cooperation with the SS had been "a blessing." During the war the vast network of outside camps formed an industrial empire run by Krupp, Farben, Union Werken, and other German industrial giants, which starved and worked the slave laborers to death.

The Nazis intended eventually to concentrate all chemical production of synthetic materials, especially gasoline, at Buna. In 1944 Buna turned out four truckloads of gasoline a day. By 1944 sixty-three chemical laboratories in Buna engaged in experimentation with various medicines. Farben purchased prisoners from the camp authorities for medical experimentation.

A prisoner who considered Auschwitz hell, after transfer to Buna called Auschwitz a mild form of purgatory. He recorded his first impression:

Piles of wood, cement mixers, and all the paraphernalia of buildings. Half-built houses thrust towards the sky and everywhere hundreds of men were scurrying, ant-like, driven on by the bellowing of the gangers. It was a grim vista even from a distance; but as we drew nearer the entire canvas unrolled before me, revealing awful detail.

Men ran and fell, were kicked and shot. Wild-eyed Kapos drove their blood-stained path through ranks of prisoners, while SS men shot from the hip, like television cowboys, who had strayed somehow into a grotesque, endless horror film; and adding a ghastly note of incongruity to the bedlam were groups of quiet men in impeccable civilian clothes, picking their way through corpses they did not want to see, measuring timbers with bright yellow, folding rules, making neat little notes in black leather books, oblivious to the blood-bath.

They never spoke to the workers, these men in the quiet grey suits.[28]

On January 8, 1945, the SS hastily evacuated Buna prisoners before the advancing Soviet Army. On January 27 the Soviet Army occupied the entire network of Farben factories. While Buna was in use, over 150,000 prisoners from the occupied countries died there:

Such were the sacrifices that were necessary to maintain the profits of the vast international I. G. Farben concern using cheap slave labor hired from the SS. After extracting the maximum labor power from the prisoners, the firm turned them to the SS for the gas chamber, for which the same concern supplied the poisonous gas, Cyclon B.[29]

The prosecutors at Nuremberg charged "the Devil's Chemists" with murder. The court judged twelve guilty. Guilt under the worst count—slavery and mass murder—brought the longest sentence: eight years. The verdicts and the astonishingly light sentences came down on July 29, 1948. Three years later not one of the convicted was still in prison. The West forgot Nazism in its obsession with communism.[30]

The Extermination Factory

Himmler had ordered Commandant Höss to build an extermination factory. But Höss had a problem because he was reaching into an unknown world, traveling farther than any man who had gone before him. Without precedent as an aid, he had to depend on invention, and that process demanded time and experimentation. One of the first attempts occurred in the summer of 1941. Into the cellar of one Auschwitz block the SS packed 250 hospital patients and 600 Soviet POWs. They covered the cellar windows with earth and an SS man wearing a gas mask poured Cyclone B on the floor. They waited—until the next afternoon. When they opened the door, they discovered that some prisoners were still alive. So they pumped in more Cyclone B and locked the doors. The following evening they opened the doors again and found everyone dead. A witness at the Auschwitz trial talked about these experimental gassings:

I saw people clutching hair in their fists which they had torn from their own heads or those of others. I saw people locked in a tight embrace. I saw fingers that had been bitten through. The victims were kept in the bunker for about two days, so the bodies were already in a state of decomposition. The skin of the dead stuck to our hands.[31]

Next, Höss developed a small gas chamber adjacent to the crematorium in Auschwitz. But that facility proved so limited that he was forced to systematically extend the gassing operations. In autumn 1941, near Birkenau, the SS converted a small peasant cottage into a primitive gas chamber. They referred to it as Cellar II or the "White Cottage": there they gassed 800 victims at a time. A mile away they converted another cottage—Cellar I, called the "Red Cottage"—which could handle a group of 1,200. The SS brought the Jews in trucks, made them undress, and told them they were going to be disinfected. The Jews handed over their valuables and went into the gas chambers. After about a half an hour the SS opened the doors.

It was a ghastly sight. Naked women and children were convulsed into the most horrible attitudes, their skin lacerated, their fists clenched and their limbs bleeding from biting each other in their pain. The victims died standing up, for they were so wedged together they could not fall.[32]

Rudolf Vrba tells a story of Yankel Meisel who died because three buttons were missing from his striped prisoner's tunic when Heinrich Himmler visited the Auschwitz camp on July 17, 1942. It was probably the first and last time Yankel had ever been untidy in his life. He was a quiet old man who seemed to have one goal—to be invisible. The Himmler entourage approached the gates; they swung open; the orchestra broke into an excerpt from *Aida*; and a long black open Mercedes moved slowly into the camp. Seated in the back were Himmler and Rudolf Höss. The Mercedes stopped before the orchestra. Himmler got out, paused for a moment, smiled at the musicians. The prisoners were lined up in rows before him. He moved through them "with the grace and easy charm of someone from the upper-middle echelons of English royalty, relaxing in an atmosphere that was as benevolent as that of any English garden party." He seemed to have the knack of putting others at ease. He acknowledged salutes and smiled at the SS men. Photographers scurried before him with their cameras clicking. Himmler walked up and down the rows eyeing the prisoners with polite interest. And that is how Yankel died when Himmler spotted the buttons missing from his tunic. A *Kapo* clubbed Yankel to death.[33]

Himmler watched the selection of the Jews and he visited all the barracks—looking at the cramped quarters, the absence of latrines, and the deficient water supply. In the women's camp he observed the whipping of a female criminal. That evening he attended a dinner given for the visitors and the officers. He met them all and chatted with them about their work and their families. But he was not satisfied with what he had seen. Horrified by the grossly inefficient methods used to exterminate the Jews, Himmler ordered the creation of the largest and most efficient extermination factory ever known.

After lively competition the contract for the construction of huge crematoria was finally given to J. A. Topf and Sons, manufacturers of heating equipment. On February 12, 1943, Topf wrote to Auschwitz regarding Crematorias Two and Three: "We acknowledge receipt of your order for five triple furnaces, including two electric elevators for raising the corpses and one emergency elevator." Installations for stoking coal and one for transporting ashes were also on order. But other German businessmen continued to compete for the business of corpse disposal. One of the oldest companies in that field offered its drawing for other crematoria. They suggested using a metal fork moving on cylinders to get the bodies into the furnace. Another firm, Kori, seeking the Belgrade business, emphasized its great experience in the field; it had constructed furnaces at Dachau and Majdanek, and given "full satisfaction in practice."[34]

Construction of the Birkenau extermination plant began in the summer of 1942. By January 1943 it was far enough along for Himmler to view the first results. He arrived for the special event. Once more the neat and clean prisoners lined up, with the band playing. The crematorium "was truly a splendid affair, one hundred yards long and fifty yards wide, containing fifteen ovens which could burn three bodies each simultaneously in twenty minutes, a monument in concrete." It had been built by a man named Herr Walter Dejakco, who was still practicing his craft in 1977 in a town in the Tyrol. In 1963 the Innsbruck Bishop praised Dejakco for the parish's new presbytery which he built.[35]

Himmler arrived in camp at 8 A.M., and by 8:45 the new gas chambers were packed to capacity. By 8:55 the tension was almost unbearable. The SS man with the pellets stood on the roof of the chamber. Then the phone rang with the message that Himmler had not finished his breakfast. Everyone relaxed. Inside the chamber a different scene was occurring:

... frantic men and women, who knew by that time what a shower in Auschwitz meant, began shouting, screaming and pounding weakly on the door; but nobody outside heard them because the new chamber was sound-proof as well as gas-proof.

Even if they had been heard, nobody would have taken any notice of them, for the SS men had their own worries.... By ten o'clock the marathon breakfast was still under way.[36]

At eleven o'clock a car drew up and Himmler and Höss stepped out. Himmler ambled over to the sealed door, glanced through the observation window at the bodies inside, and then asked some questions. Finally, the time for action was at hand and the gassing began. Höss invited his guest to have another peep through the observation window, and for some minutes Himmler peered into the death chamber, obviously impressed. When it was clear everyone inside was dead, he took a keen interest in the procedure that followed. Although complicated, the special machinery and process worked well. "Himmler waited until the smoke began to thicken over the chimneys and then he glanced at his watch." He turned, shook hands, saluted, and left. Auschwitz was finally in business as an extermination center.[37]

Leaders of the Third Reich and industrialists had the opportunity to view the entire operation on the formal inauguration day, a bright March morning in 1943. With prominent guests present at the ceremony, the program "consisted of the gassing and burning of 8,000 Cracow Jews. The guests ... were extremely satisfied with the results and the special peephole fitted into the door of the gas chamber was in constant use. They were lavish in their praise of this newly erected installation."[38]

The extermination plant with the most advanced design available anywhere in the world consisted of two large crematoria/gas chambers and two smaller ones. Crematoria Four and Five were built on the surface of the ground. Crematoria Two and Three had subterranean gas chambers and reception areas. They were about 102 meters long by 51 meters across. The basement consisted of two main rooms—the undressing area, which also served as a mortuary, and the gas chamber. Victims climbed down the steps into the basement. Those who could not walk were pushed down a concrete slide. The gas chamber, about 225 square meters, looked like a large communal bathroom with shower heads:

The Zyclon B gas crystals were inserted through openings into hollow pillars made of sheet metal. They were perforated at regular intervals and inside them a spiral ran from top to bottom in order to ensure as even a distribution of the granular crystals as possible. Mounted on the ceiling was a large number of dummy showers made of metal.

The largest room in the factory, the changing chambers, accommodated 1,000 people. Notices throughout the room contributed to a "cunning . . . and clumsy deception"—telling victims they were in disinfection rooms, urging cleanliness, reminding them to remember their clothing hook number.[39]

The extermination plant contained a hair-drying loft run by fifteen Orthodox Jews. Spread over the floor, noticed Müller from the extermination staff, was women's hair of every color:

Washing lines were strung across the room. Pegged on these lines like wet washing were further batches of hair which had first been washed in a solution of ammonium chloride. When the hair was nearly dry, it was spread on the warm floor to finish off. Finally it was combed out by prisoners and put into paper bags.[40]

The SS set up a gold-melting room in the plant. There two dental technicians soaked the teeth for hours in acid to remove bone and flesh, and used a blowtorch to melt the gold into molds. They produced as much as 5 to 10 kilos a day.

As in Treblinka, the stoking gangs sorted the bodies into combustibility categories: strong men, women, children, and *Mussulmans*. The SS staff had performed earlier experiments to find ways to economize on fuel—with the help of Topf and Sons, civilian experts:

In the course of these experiments corpses were selected according to different criteria and then cremated. Thus the corpses of two *Mussulmans* were cremated together with those of two children or the bodies of two well-nourished men together with that of an emaciated woman, each load consisting of three, or sometimes, four bodies. Members of these groups were especially interested in the amount of coke required to burn corpses of any particular category, and in the time it took to cremate them.

During these macabre experiments different kinds of coke were used and the results carefully recorded.

Afterwards, all corpses were divided into the above-mentioned four categories, the criterion being the amount of coke required to reduce them to ashes. Thus it was decreed that the most economical and fuel-saving procedure would be to burn the bodies of a well-nourished man and an emaciated woman, or vice versa, together with that of a child, because, as the experiments had established, in this combination, once they had caught fire, the dead would continue to burn without any further coke being required.[41]

As early as June 13, 1943, all was not well with the new installation. The Central SS Construction Management of Auschwitz sent a letter to a German equipment firm urging the completion of carpentry work in the new crematoria. The chief requested the delivery without delay of the doors for the crematoria, "which [are] urgently needed for the execution of the special measures; otherwise, the progress of the construction would be jeopardized." In addition, he demanded the completion of the windows for the reception building. If the carpentry work could not be done, building operations would have to be suspended for the winter. Eventually, the ovens seemed to fall apart. Crematorium Four failed completely after a short time and Crematorium Five had to be shut down repeatedly.[42]

The plans for the crematoria have been preserved by an architect who stole them from the Birkenau plant. The one-story buildings looked like large bakeries with steep roofs and dormer windows. The grounds were well tended; lovely flowers bloomed on the lawn. The underground gas chambers rose 51 centimeters above the ground to form a grassy terrace. No one would know at first glance what they were. Crematoria Two and Three were close to the camp and visible. Pine trees and birches hid Crematoria Four and Five. Around the crematoria lay large piles of wood for burning the corpses in the nearby pits. All chambers had doors with thick observation windows. In 1942 and 1943 alone those chambers used 27 tons of Cyclone B. The gas chambers and the crematoria of Auschwitz were called "special installations," "bath houses," and "corpse cellars."[43]

Each day the trains rolled into the camp through the passageway constructed in the far gate, down one of the three tracks to the selection platform. As they fell out of the trains, the victims were sent one way or another, with tearful parting scenes. The procession moved to the crematoria yard where the SS told the Jews they were going to take disinfection baths. An orchestra of attractive women played gay tunes from operas and light marches. Then to the dressing room or reception center with numbered clothing pegs driven into the walls. The SS ordered the victims to undress and to remember their numbers. Sometimes they gave them towels. Then the SS drove the victims through the corridor to the heated gas chamber. The heating was provided not for the comfort of the prisoners but to create a better setting for the evaporation of gas. The gas squads packed the 2,000 victims into the room. From the ceiling hung imitation shower heads. The doors were closed, the air was pumped out, and the gas poured in. Cyclone B, or hydrogen cyanide, is a very poisonous gas that causes death by internal suffocation. In sufficient concentrations, it causes death almost immediately. But the SS did not bother to calculate the proper quantities, so death took anywhere from three to twenty minutes. While the victims were dying, the SS watched through the peepholes.

When they opened the doors, they found the victims in half-sitting positions in a towerlike pile. Most were pink, others were covered with green spots. Some had foam on their lips, while others were bleeding at the nose. Many had their eyes open. The majority was packed near the doors. The squads in special clothing moved in with hooks to pull the bodies off of each other.

The SS physicians and scientists monitored the selection and the gassing, watching the procedure through the special airtight door. The doors could not be opened until the doctor gave the sign that all victims were dead. The doctors assumed their monitoring of the killings on a rotating basis.[44]

Two German firms, Tesch/Stabenow and Degesch, produced the Cyclone B gas after they acquired the patent from Farben. Tesch supplied two tons a month, and Degesch three quarters of a ton. The firms that produced the gas already had extensive experience in fumigation. "In short, this industry used very powerful gases to exterminate rodents and insects in enclosed spaces; that it should now have become involved in an operation to kill off Jews by the hundreds of thousands is not mere accident."[45] After the war the directors of the firms insisted that they had sold their products for fumigation purposes and did not know they were being used on humans. But the prosecutors found letters from Tesch not only offering to supply the gas crystals but also advising on how to use the ventilating and heating equipment. Höss testified that the Tesch directors could not help but know of the use for their product because they sold him enough to annihilate two million people. Two Tesch partners were sentenced to death in 1946 and hanged. The director of Degesch received five years in prison.

The scientifically planned crematoria should have been able to handle the total project, but they could not. The whole complex had forty-six retorts, each with the capacity for three to five persons. The burning in a retort lasted about half an hour. It took an hour a day to clean them out. Thus it was theoretically possible to cremate about 12,000 corpses in twenty-four hours or 4,380,000 a year. But the well-constructed crematoria fell far behind at a number of camps, and especially at Auschwitz in 1944. In August the total cremation reached a peak one day of 24,000, but still a bottleneck occurred.

Camp authorities needed an economic and fast method of corpse disposal, so they again dug six huge pits beside Crematorium Five and reopened old pits in the wood.

Thus, late in 1944, pit burning became the chief method of corpse disposal. The pits had indentations at one end from which the human fat drained off. To keep the pits burning, the stokers poured oil, alcohol, and large quantities of boiling human fat over the bodies:

The sizzling fat was scooped out with buckets on a long curved rod and poured all over the pit causing flames to leap up amid much crackling and hissing. . . . The air reeked of oil, fat, benzole and burnt flesh.

Müller described the ghastly scene:

The corpses in the pit looked as if they had been chained together. Tongues of a thousand tiny blue-red flames were licking at them. The fire grew fiercer and flames leapt higher and higher. Under the ever-increasing heat a few of the dead began to stir, writhing as though with some unbearable pain, arms and legs straining in slow motion, and even their bodies straightening up a little, hesitant and with difficulty, almost as if with their last strength they were trying to rebel against their doom. Eventually the fire became so fierce that the corpses were enveloped by flames. Blisters which had formed on their skin burst one by one. Almost every corpse was covered with black scorch marks and glistened as if it had been greased. The searing heat had burst open their bellies: there was the violent hissing and spluttering of frying in great heat. Boiling fat flowed into the pans on either side of the pit. Fanned by the wind, the flames, dark-red before, now took on a fiery white hue: the corpses were burning so fiercely that they were consumed by their own heat. The process of incineration took five to six hours. What was left barely filled a third of the pit. The shiny whitish-grey surface was strewn with countless skulls.[46]

At intervals, flamethrowers were brought in to destroy the rotten remains. In the center of Nazi industrial might it was the open pits that finally broke the bottleneck of bodies: a technique from ancient times.

Burning that many bodies produced an enormous amount of ashes. To finish the task, the labor squad cooled the ashes with water, shoveled out the ashes, piled them in heaps, removed remaining bones and limbs with special tools, reburnt the limbs, pulverized the ashes, and buried them in pits or threw them into the marshes. Later they threw the ashes into the Vistula and Solo rivers. A small, carefully sifted quantity was kept in a shed. Sometimes families were notified of the death of their loved ones and in return for money they would receive urns filled with the ashes.[47]

Before her death, an unknown poet wrote three poems on March 8, 1944, near the crematorium. One was entitled "We, the Dead, Accuse!":

No crosses rot upon our graves,
No headstones gently lean;
No lattice wrought or twined wreaths,
No bowing angels' screen.

No willow tree or gold-writ rhyme,
No candle never quenched.
We rot in pits, white-splashed with lime,
With rain our bones are drenched.
Our whitened skulls without defense
Tremble on barbed wire fence,
Our scattered ash fills many an urn,
And still the bodies burn.

A chain we are, which the earth wears
And the wind blows like seed;
We count the days and months and years,
We know not time nor speed.
Our numbers grow by day and night,
We swell beneath your ground,
And upward press, until our might
Will burst our earthly bound.
Then skull to skull and bone to bone
We'll mount the judgment throne
And bring to all the fearful news:
Lo! We, the dead, accuse![48]

In his first book, *Night,* Elie Wiesel wrote of the darkness of the concentration camp universe. A young boy saw his mother and sister go up in smoke at Auschwitz:

Never shall I forget that night, the first night in camp, which has turned my life into one long night, seven times cursed and seven times sealed. Never shall I forget that smoke. Never shall I forget the little faces of the children, whose bodies I saw turned into wreaths of smoke beneath a silent blue sky. Never shall I forget those flames which consumed my faith forever. Never shall I forget that nocturnal silence which deprived me, for all eternity, of the desire to live. Never shall I forget those moments which murdered my God and my soul and turned my dreams to dust.[49]

In early 1944 camp officials converted the old Crematorium One into an air raid shelter. Crematorium Three burned down on October 7, 1944, during the *Sonderkommando* revolt. The SS dismantled the technical parts of Crematoria Two and Four in November 1944 and sent them to Gross-Rosen. Then they dynamited the buildings. Crematorium Five was burned and blown on January 20, 1945.

Auschwitz, like all Nazi camps, had a resistance movement. The most active organizers were the Communists and the Socialists. The movement took the form of an international committee led by Polish Socialist lawyer Josef Cyrankiewicz, the future prime minister of the Polish People's Republic. Two Auschwitz inmates escaped and brought with them a report from the resistance organization. The report reached government leaders of the major Allied nations. It proposed that the governments issue a warning to the Germans and the Hungarians that the Allies would take reprisals against the Germans living in their countries if the exterminations did not stop. Auschwitz and Birkenau—particularly the gas chambers and crematoria, which were recognizable by their high chimneys—should be bombed from the air, along with the main railroad lines. The reports should be given the widest publicity on the radio and in the newspapers so that the Nazis would know the world was informed of what they were doing. The public warnings should be repeated over and over again, and the Pope should issue a strong condemnation of the crime. After receiving the report, the Vatican began various efforts in Hungary to halt the deportations. Pope Pius XII intervened directly at one point with Horthy, the Hungarian regent, which turned out to be an ineffective move. Although public disclosure seemed the only remaining hope, the Pope decided against so firm an action. It was the British Broadcasting Corporation that finally made the report public. Many people, however, called it mere propaganda. Then the War Refugee Board in Washington published the report and President Roosevelt, through the Swiss delegation, urged Hungary to halt the deportations. But no country bombed the camp or the railroad lines.

The only bombing of the camps during the war was done by a desperate group of prisoners in the Auschwitz *Sonderkommando* who were armed with weapons of their own making. Because Jews were not included in the resistance group, the hard-core Jewish resistance occurred in the *Sonderkommando. Sonderbehandlung,* or special treatment, in the Nazi terminology meant putting to death. *Sonderaktion* (special action) in Nazi terms meant massive execution. *Sonderkommando* was the name of the special squad responsible for aiding the extermination. The *Sonderkommando* men knew they were destined for ultimate execution. They decided to prepare a last stand. The leader of the revolt was a French Jew by the name of David.

Four courageous Jewish women from the Krupp works delivered explosives for grenades. Equipped with that material, the *Sonderkommando* mined the crematoria with dynamite.

Although the *Sonderkommando* was supposed to synchronize its revolt with a general uprising, the Jews were forced to act without warning when they discovered they were going to be liquidated. On October 7, 1944, they blew up Crematorium Three, tossed a sadistic overseer into the oven, killed several SS men, and wounded a number of others. The other explosives did not go off. Finally they cut the barbed wire and tried to escape. Two trucks of soldiers and troopers with hounds pursued the escaping prisoners. One document lists one survivor, Dr. Charles Bendel, a Paris physician and medical officer of the *Kommando*. Supposedly he tried to commit suicide by taking an overdose of drugs, but he was miraculously brought around by his fellow doctors and hidden in the infirmary. The report says he lived to tell his story at the trial of the Belsen guards. Most reports, however, deny the existence of any survivors. Filip Müller seems to have emerged only recently.[50]

The Gestapo tortured the Jewish women who helped, but they betrayed no one before they were hanged. That one revolt had profound moral and political significance. In addition, it showed the world:

that a small group of prisoners, determined to put up a fight, could tie down an SS garrison several thousand strong. Since the SS by this time were unable to bring the garrison up to proper strength, they had to drop their plans for the mass liquidation of the prisoners at Auschwitz in favor of evacuation.[51]

During the last phase of the war Himmler altered his policy toward the Jews. He asked that the selection and gassing of the Jews cease on November 2, 1944. On November 26 he ordered the gas chambers and crematoria destroyed to eliminate all evidence of the mass murders. The last transport arrived at Auschwitz on January 5, 1945. On January 18 the camp administration sent 58,000 freezing and starving inmates off on their death march. The Germans burned down twenty-nine of the thirty-five storerooms before they left. The survivors of the death march were dumped into German camps in the interior. At least 80,000 inmates died in those internal German camps in the last two months of the war. On January 22 the Soviet troops entered Auschwitz and saved the 5,000 sick prisoners left behind by the retreating Nazis.

We will never know exactly how many died in the complex. Accurate records were not kept and documents were destroyed. Historians estimate that between one and five million died at Auschwitz. The official Auschwitz Museum figure is four million. Three different tribunals in Western and in Eastern Europe have said that at least, no less than, or more than four million perished. Probably half of those were Jews. About 80 percent of the arrivals to the camp went straight from the train to the gas chambers without being counted or listed. One-third were women.

After the war the Allies tried the criminals of Auschwitz. On April 2, 1947, they sentenced Höss to death in Warsaw and executed him near the old crematorium at Auschwitz. Several trials against officials of the firms of Farben and Krupp were held. Gerhardt Peters, general manager of Degesch, which supplied the poison gas, was acquitted at his Frankfurt trial. Camp Dr. Kramer was tried in 1960 after his release from a Polish prison. The court judged that he did not have to serve any further time. On December 20, 1963, after five and a half years of preparation, a lengthy Auschwitz trial began in Frankfurt (it ended on August 20, 1965). Twenty-two former SS men went on trial and witness after witness recited their record of brutality and mass extermination. For two years the defendants reiterated that they themselves had done nothing and could remember very little of what went on at the camp. The judge remarked that he had never yet met anyone who admitted to doing anything at Auschwitz. Six of the accused were sentenced to life imprisonment; three were acquitted; two were released for ill health; and the rest received prison terms ranging from three and a half to fourteen years. None of the defendants took the trial seriously. Perhaps they were right because *all* went free on appeal.[52]

The world's profound disinterest in Auschwitz continued throughout the decades. After the Six Day War in 1967 the Poles closed the Auschwitz Jewish Pavilion "for repairs." The repairs took eleven years—until April 17, 1978, when the Polish government finally reopened the pavilion with a ceremony attended by a large, diverse, and distinguished audience: delegations from nine countries, Jewish survivors, Israelis, Polish officials. The event heralded a change in Polish-Jewish relations. Yad Vashem officials (Gideon Hausner and Itzhak Arad) in an adjunct ceremony awarded scrolls and emblems to twenty-two Poles who had aided Jews during the occupation. The ceremony occasioned a visiting survivor, David, an elderly Jew from Israel, to recall the prayer of Reb Yitzhak of Berdichev:

I do not ask You, Lord of the Universe, to reveal to me the secrets of Your ways—I could not comprehend them. I do not ask You to know why I suffer. But I do ask you, Lord of the Universe, do I suffer for Your sake?[53]

The Bombing of Auschwitz

After the war survivors and writers began to question whether Auschwitz needed to have claimed the lives of so many. Could a substantial number of people have been saved? The answers they gave equaled a resounding *yes*.

Yes, they wrote, the 400,000 Hungarian Jews could have been saved by a variety of means, not the least of which was the Allied bombing of the crematoria and gas chambers and the railroad tracks leading to Auschwitz. The Allied governments had been deluged by pleas and requests from all over the world to take such action. Yet they did not. After the war those governments responded to the charges of inaction with various excuses about the impossibility or impracticality of the action, and absence of information. The challengers, without technical military information in the immediate postwar years, did not effectively rebut the claims. The questions came up occasionally in the 1950s and 1960s, but the issue remained relatively quiet.

In 1978 the question of the bombing of the camp death apparatus and the tracks blazed forth again, in part because of the CIA's release of clear aerial photographs of Auschwitz that identified the chambers and crematoria. The challengers raised the old questions; the U.S. government and its agencies pulled out the old answers—and the trap closed once more on the energies of the researchers. Again, the challengers answered the officials on their own terms, attempting to disprove their responses. Round 2 has resulted in the same silliness as Round 1. Senator William Proxmire asked innocently on the floor of the Senate, "Why didn't America bomb the death apparatus at Auschwitz and the railroad tracks leading to it?" as if this question were an agonizing one without any answer. Wrong. The question is not agonizing and the answer is simple and clear—as long as the trap of responding to U.S. officials in their own terms is avoided. The arguments used in 1944 and 1978 against bombing are the same and break down into crisp categories:

1. *The most effective relief for the Jews,* according to official U.S. War Department policy, *was the speedy defeat of the Axis.* But there are numerous examples of the Allies designing raids on targets not central to the speedy ending of the war. Those raids occurred whenever the Allies, for some reason, believed they were important.

2. *The bombing of Auschwitz was impractical because it required the diversion of considerable air support.* The statement is true. Any bombing anywhere diverted bombing from someplace else. The Allies bombed many places when they felt it important for some reason, and diverted air support in the process. Additionally, since the Auschwitz area from August 7 to August 29, 1944 was a "hotbed" of U.S. bombing activity, we are discussing a diversion in terms of a distance of 16 kilometers— hardly significant.

3. *Auschwitz was too far away.* Auschwitz was far away. But the Fifteenth Air Force in Italy possessed the necessary range and capability. The Allies flew several successful raids to bomb the oil refineries near Auschwitz. It was a long trip, but the Allies undertook such dangerous

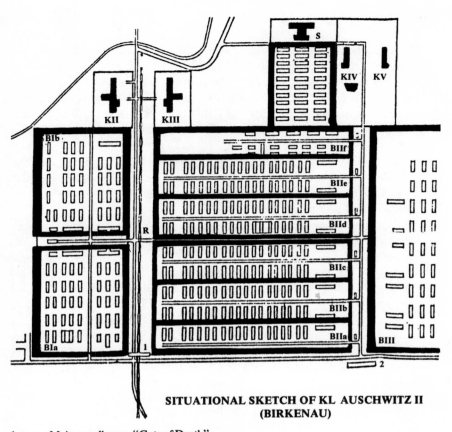

SITUATIONAL SKETCH OF KL AUSCHWITZ II
(BIRKENAU)

1	Main guardhouse–"Gate of Death"		*erlager*); from Nov. 1944 women's
2	Commandant's office		hospital camp
BIa	Women's camp	**BIIf**	Men's hospital camp
BIb	Men's camp; from Aug. 1943 wo-men's camp	**BIII**	Jewish transit camp *"Mexico" (Durchgangs Juden Lager)*
BIIa	Quarantine–men's camp	**R**	Railway ramp
BIIb	Family camp for Jews from There-sienstadt	**KII**	Gas chamber and crematorium II
		KIII	Gas chamber and crematorium III
BIIc	Camp for Hungarian Jewesses; from Sept. 1944 women's camp	**KIV**	Gas chamber and crematorium IV
		KV	Gas chamber and crematorium V
BIId	Men's camp	**S**	Baths–*"Sauna"*
BIIe	Family camp for gypsies (*Zigeun-*		

Map 12: Birkenau

German Crimes in Poland, *Central Commission for the Investigation of German Crimes. Revised by Sharon Coughran* projects, before they had control of the skies as they did in 1944, whenever they considered it important to do so.

4. *Bombing railroad tracks and bridges is difficult and ineffective because of quick repair.* That concern is certainly valid. But, however unproductive the bombing of tracks, the Allies bombed bridges and tracks, and requested the Resistance to do likewise, whenever they deemed it important.

5. *The Auschwitz crematoria and chambers presented difficult precision bombing problems.* They certainly did; and so did the hundreds of other targets, some more difficult, which the Allies tried to bomb when they considered it important to do so.

6. *The Allies did not possess adequate information.* This claim is the only one that is a clear lie. By 1944 the Allies possessed extensive topographical information, as evidenced by the recent discovery of aerial photos of Auschwitz. They also had the report from escapees Rudolf Vrba and Alfred Wetzler, with its detailed plans of the crematoria and gas chambers.

7. *Prisoners might die during the bombing.* True, bombs might have killed some inmates. The gas chambers were certainly killing inmates. Allies bombed many areas without undue worry over the inmate deaths they caused whenever they considered it important. Because Nazi *Kommandos* were spread throughout occupied Europe, it was impossible to bomb anywhere without killing inmates. Yet the Allies bombed everywhere—except Auschwitz—with little concern about death. Half a million Jews died in Auschwitz after August 1944. It is unlikely that a few bombs would have killed that many.

We know the answer to Senator Proxmire's question: The Allies did not consider the saving of Jewish lives to be of any importance. We do not know why they put no value on those lives, but we do know they did not give the salvation of Jewish lives any priority. The idea did not catch their fancy as did some other projects to which they devoted time, energy, and money. They refused to become interested enough to do even a quick feasibility study. They simply said a simple and steadfast *no*. Their response was consistent with their responses to requests since 1933 for governmental action on behalf of the Jews. That concern did not exist and it is a dreary matter for anyone to suggest it did. Energy would be better spent acknowledging indifference, accepting it as fact, and building bridges to mitigate that killing type of disinterest in the future.[54]

Map 13: Auschwitz/Birkenau Complex
German Crimes in Poland, *Central Commission for the Investigation of German Crimes.*

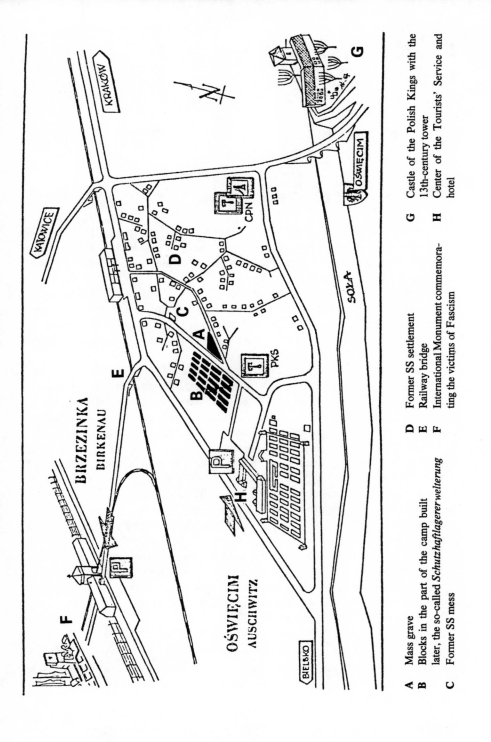

A Mass grave

B Blocks in the part of the camp built later, the so-called *Schutzhaftlagererweiterung*

C Former SS mess

D Former SS settlement

E Railway bridge

F International Monument commemorating the victims of Fascism

G Castle of the Polish Kings with the 13th-century tower

H Center of the Tourists' Service and hotel

LIBERATION

BERGEN-BELSEN: THE LIBERATION OF A GRAVEYARD

In a familiar film picturing the liberation of the Nazi camps, a British soldier pushing a mass of emaciated corpses to a pit with his bulldozer wipes the tears away from his eyes. That scene was Bergen-Belsen, a monstrous typhus graveyard.

Belsen is located in a sparsely populated area near Hannover, Germany. Fertile farmlands surround the area; and brightly colored flowers and neat farmhouses fill the landscape. The Belsen site is simply a graveyard. Nothing remains of the original camp. Belsen has blended into the peaceful rural countryside.

Though Belsen ended the war in an explosion of mass death, it played a comparatively modest role in Hitler's extermination plan. If it had not been for a typhus epidemic and overcrowding, the word *Belsen* might never have entered our vocabulary of the Holocaust. Unfortunately, near the end of the war prisoners from every part of Europe were trucked, marched, or taken by cattle car to Belsen to escape the advancing Allies. Thus the camp doubled its size in the last months. Food became scarce or nonexistent. Because of the influx of diseased evacuees, one of the worst typhus plagues in the history of the camps broke out, sweeping through Belsen in almost demonic fury. Most of the camp population died either from starvation or typhus, or a combination of both—so quickly that thousands of bodies piled up all over the area.

Belsen had none of the modern crematorium equipment found in other camps. Consequently, the mess that greeted the British liberating army was as gruesome as could be found; and the sights transcribed on film and in photographs became known throughout the world. As one of the incoming officers described it:

There were people dying in the compounds, dying in the mass before our eyes. There was one crematorium, but the Germans did not use it because they could not cope with the number of deaths.

We saw enormous covered death pits. One was uncovered. It contained a great pile of blackened and naked bodies. There was typhus in every compound, and in one compound typhus cases were not even separated.

People were lying dead in gutters outside the huts to which they had gone to rest more comfortably, and died as they lay. In the women's compound, in full view of the children's compound 50 yds. away, we saw an enormous pile of naked dead women which stretched about 60 yds. by 80 yds.[1]

Starvation caused more deaths than typhus; and many prisoners still breathing at the time of liberation were alive in spirit only. The first night after the British arrived, several hundred more inmates died. Their emaciated fellow sufferers, many themselves already doomed by typhus and starvation, dragged the naked bodies from the huts and laid them in piles at the entrance to the compounds. The British gave the task of burying the 10,000 corpses to the SS men and women guards. Then they set afire the huts and SS installations. Nothing but ashes remained. Because the British had never seen anything like it, because their government had obviously not prepared its soldiers for it, the well-meaning army arrived without medicine or proper food, unprepared to face a reality they could not have imagined. 28,000 typhus-ridden and starved human beings died after liberation.

Bergen-Belsen is named after the town of Bergen, 4 kilometers from the camp. The town provided hospitality and entertainment for the SS during the war. A hygienic German village with perfectly kept buildings and small houses, it is sustained now by farming and the NATO base nearby. One kilometer from Belsen, between the camp and the town, stands the British army base—one of the largest NATO training centers in Germany. In the past it housed a large SS division, the Panzer Training School, and the Belsen guards. Much of the land previously on the edge of or part of the camp has been taken over by the NATO firing ranges.

Three kilometers from Belsen stands an isolated railroad track and small station. The Germans built it as a loading dock for the Belsen prisoners, hidden behind a grove of trees next to the road. The guards unloaded the prisoners on the railroad ramp and marched them the 3 kilometers to the camp, past the SS Training School. Clearly, the existence and the nature of the camp were no secret to the Bergen residents. It is even difficult to imagine ignorance by the residents of Hannover.

After liberation the SS Training School was immediately taken over by the British for the medical rehabilitation of the prisoners. For five years it served as the Bergen-Belsen DP Camp. Prisoners and camp inmates who describe Bergen-Belsen from 1945 to 1950, and the amazing political, civic, social, and cultural life that developed there, are referring to the grounds of the former Panzer Training School, where the NATO base is now situated. That Bergen-Belsen from 1945 to 1950 was perhaps the most advanced

Belsen, International Obelisk by Falke, and the Jewish Memorial.

camp for displaced persons in Europe. And Belsen boasts the only large-scale survivor organization, the Bergen-Belsen Association.

At the entrance to the Belsen site, a desolate open field, the sign reads: "A Place of Graveyards and Tombstones." On the treeless field, black and white markers rise to symbolize tombstones. The mass graves contain 300 to 5,000 bodies. Some are still raised and marked; others have been leveled.

A year after liberation the Belsen survivors dedicated a monument to the memory of the murdered, a simple 1.2-meter stone town decorated by a Star of David, with the inscription: "Earth conceal not bloodshed on thee!" At the far end the International Memorial, a tall obelisk made of great hewn stones, pierces the sky. The concrete platform and wall at its base contain inscriptions in various languages honoring the unknown dead. Here and there, flower wreaths decorate the area, some labeled for Anne Frank who is buried in one of the mass graves. Belsen has a rare quiet beauty to it amid the sounds of birds and gunshots—a colorful panorama with the green of the surrounding trees. The grass is prickly and the graves are rough. Anything that is atop the ground now is postwar vintage. Belsen was never that large but the whole area is virtually a mass burial ground, topped by a few monuments built primarily by the Bergen-Belsen Association.

In a poem entitled "T. S. Eliot at Bergen-Belsen" Leslie Mittleman described his thoughts on visiting the site:

He never came. The railroad tracks abruptly
stop, broken at the ties, where iron
crosses the rolling grass. Several nuns
shade their eyes before the memorial plaque.
Jews from New Rochelle on a synagogue tour
shuffle their feet. A lady coughs. For what
can even the gossips say? Knowing that here
in cattle cars and stinking boxcars came
Bleistein, sans his celebrated cigar,
to do his burning act; and Rachel, born
and died Rabinovich, "with murderous paws"
her daughters outraged at her breast; also
that absent landlord, Antwerp entrepreneur
whose lease was death—they came, those caricatures,
pranksters, nasties, Levantine buffoons
the poet "spawned" (as what is not?) to indulge
his harmless wit.[2]

When the British Army liberated Bergen-Belsen in April 1945, it was accompanied by a stunned Jewish chaplin, Leslie Hardman, who spent the following months attempting to help the survivors. He recorded his response that first day:

Toward us came what seemed to me to be the remnants of a Holocaust—a tottering mass of blackened skin and bones, held together somehow with filthy rags. "My God, the dead are walking!"

On that liberation day the British found 10,000 unburied dead and 40,000 sick, starving, and dying prisoners. The medical officer described Belsen as a "dense mass of apathetic scarecrows." The women, in the worst condition, wore only "filthy rags." The camp had no running water or electricity. It was "riddled with typhus and tuberculosis." British medical personnel were forced to deliver many babies of women suffering from typhus.[3]

Ironically, Bergen-Belsen had never been given formal concentration camp status. Created as a model repatriation and transit center, it was known as a center for the privileged. But then in the last months of the war a fierce typhoid and typhus epidemic and tuberculosis devastated the camp—with an inmate population that had grown fourfold in two months. As a result the area looked like a charnal house from ancient times when the British arrived. The incredulity with which the British grasped the reality of their first liberated camp created of Belsen a metaphor for horror.

Belsen's beginnings were far milder. In 1943 Himmler purchased half of an old *Wehrmacht* POW camp for wounded prisoners and ordered its reconversion to an interment, transit center. Initially, he had in mind a model camp that could stand up to the scrutiny of visiting inspection teams. That aim was never achieved, for Belsen's purposes became confused at the outset. In the early months five different uses were made of Belsen: as a small Russian POW camp, as a convalescence camp, as a transit center, as an exchange camp, and as a collection center for interned American citizens.

In September 1943 Eichmann's office ordered three classes of Jews sent to Belsen: exchange Jews, Jews with Palestinian relatives, and Honduras and Paraguay Jews. Himmler's top aides created the concept of the exchange Jew when they discovered the existence of a sizable business in Switzerland for the sale of Honingrasian and Paraguayan passports to Jews. They also knew that many Germans had been interned in the United States and Latin America, while Germany had few citizens of those two areas in her internment centers. Obviously from the Nazis' point of view, an exchange medium could be quite valuable if Germany ever wanted to recover some of her valued citizens.

Instead of killing the bogus Jewish foreign "citizens," why not group them in one location, formally term them "exchange Jews," and use them for negotiations with American and Latin American officials? To avoid duplication, the same camp could be used to house legitimate foreign nationals throughout the war or prior to their use in repatriation deals. Thus on August 2, 1943, Belsen's first inmates arrived—367 Jews with Spanish passports. They were followed by a shipment of exchange Jews from Warsaw, and then a group of 305 Dutch Jews with foreign passports. By September 15, 2,000 exchange Jews lived at Belsen.

Then, somehow, the official categories became mixed or altered. The SS began to send to Belsen any privileged group, any group that might conceivably be used in negotiations, and any persons who might have some special usefulness—but still, mostly Jews. For example, on January 11, 1944, the authorities diverted to Belsen a Dutch transport headed for the crematoria at Auschwitz, containing a hodgepodge of "special" Dutch Jews: diamond workers, Iron Cross holders, half-Jewish members of the Dutch Confessional Christian Church. For some reason, Eichmann sent one-fourth of the Slovakian Jews to Belsen. Operating under the convalescent category, authorities moved the sick from Birkenau's women's camp to Belsen. And in 1944 the "privileged" Hungarian Jews, the subjects of the Kästner-Himmler negotiations, also landed in Belsen. Fortunately for them, Himmler allowed a token shipment of 318 across the Swiss border on August 21. After continued negotiations, the 1,368 remaining privileged Hungarian Jews were sent to Switzerland on December 6.[4]

The commandant divided Belsen into two rigidly separated areas. Camp I was an area of dilapidated huts reserved initially for Russian POWs. Camp II, or the Star Camp for privileged Jews and foreigners, was handsomely laid out and contained some good permanent buildings. Until the last months food seemed to be adequate in that section and no typhus existed. In the winter of 1944 the SS administration brought to Camp I huts from the evacuated Jewish camp of Plascow in Poland. They crammed all nonprivileged newcomers into that area.[5]

At the end of 1944 Himmler ordered the purchase of the other half of the *Wehrmacht* camp and used that area to expand Camp I—for the nonprivileged. Josef Kramer, who had been supervising Birkenau's 1944 mass slaughter season, became commandant on December 1. He was a "dull unimaginative brute" who soon made another Birkenau out of Belsen's Camp I. In a way, however, Kramer inherited a bad situation. The tragedy had already begun.[6]

Germany's front lines began to disintegrate in February and March of 1944. As more army groups surrendered and major cities capitulated to the Allies, the SS moved quickly to evacuate the camps. Belsen was handy and still safe. By summer 1944 it was serving as a receptacle for the evacuees from other camps. It had accommodations for only 7,000, but that limitation did not deter the SS. In May 1944 the killing centers began closing down and the old established camps received the bulk of those prisoners, but the SS dumped the overflow in Belsen. It became more and more difficult to move the remaining Dutch Jews to distant Auschwitz because of Allied bombings of the railroads. Thus many were unloaded at nearby Belsen. Rosemarie Brenner, a young Dutch girl, arrived in January 1944 in a transport from Westerbork, where she had spent two years. She found life at Belsen unbearable:

I closed my eyes and I saw the camp days stretching before me—day after day of hunger and dirt and boredom and pain. Had I ever known things like a real bed, a warm bath, an easy chair—or a clean, neat tiled washroom like this? Had I? In this life—or in another?

It scared me to realize how I had sunk into passive acceptance of an intolerable situation, bearing everything meted out to me, living only for the next breath, the next heartbeat, for another moment of life.[7]

Belsen became so crowded in late 1944 that the SS sent some of the Star Camp residents to Auschwitz. But the worst was yet to come. From east and from west, from all over Poland and from Germany, transports with forced laborers and camp inmates drove toward the remaining three camps. Belsen alone received thousands of Jews from the southeast defense lines, and thousands more from the western sector. From January 1945, Belsen became a dumping ground for the survivors of the other camps, and finally of Auschwitz.

In January Belsen received large groups of female prisoners from Buchenwald and Auschwitz; and Commandant Kramer opened a new *Frauenlager* in an area quickly becoming notorious—Camp I. Zdenka Fantlowa arrived in that Auschwitz shipment. Having survived three camps, she was certain that nothing worse could happen to her, sure that she had experienced every possible horror. She was accustomed to hunger, and death did not frighten her. But Belsen was a horror that even she could not have imagined. The accommodations were worse than at Birkenau:

We slept in groups of twelve, forming small human skyscrapers. Those on the lowest level were almost on the ground. They could not sit up, because there were boards over them. Those who slept on the highest level had the ceiling on their heads. We slept crowded together, uncomfortable, contorted. If four sensible people could get together, they made arrangements for taking turns, so that two of them could stretch their legs until midnight and two after midnight. Otherwise, sleep was impossible.

And there was no food. She remembers coming across a barrel filled with stinking bones on which there were bits of raw meat and yellowed fat:

Avariciously we gnawed these bones clean, like starved wolves, not even thinking of the poison such food might contain. Nothing happened to us. On the contrary, it tasted so good that when several days later our section was changed, we thought regretfully of the bones and the greenish meat, and our mouths watered.

It was in Belsen that the female wardwomen talked of having so many new "pieces of prisoners per day."[8]

In the last days Belsen contained 500 children ranging from a few days old to sixteen. Some were dying; many had tuberculosis. Most were shocked or dazed. Although their experiences must have been especially devastating, some children appeared to have a basic strength, a reserve of calm, that external events did not destroy. Laszlo and Eva, a brother and sister five and eight years old, were orphans when the camp was liberated. They came to

Belsen with their mother six months before the end. Eva somehow avoided the typhus. But the pictures in her mind were gruesome:

She saw the piles of dead around. She saw the other women and children in the hut cough out their life-blood, die moaning, or just seem to fade away. She saw people murdered and flogged so that their bones, already almost through the skin, broke loose, showing raw or white bones. Always the awful stench was in her nostrils. She saw the horror, smelt it, knew it.

Each day her mother told her it would not last much longer. Each day she did what she was asked, nursing her brother and shutting the death scenes from her eyes.

Corpses were just shrivelled things to her now. They no longer shocked her senses. She did not cry or scream at any awful spectacle that now met her eyes. She trusted her mother so completely that nothing that happened in the raging world around them really mattered. The world she was in was mad, and dangerous, but her mother was there and told her what to do. Besides, there were so many tasks that it did not leave her time to try to think. She worked, slept, woke, and worked, and so was able not only not to think consciously, but even not to notice much that happened.[9]

Before liberation her mother died in the eight-year-old's arms.

With the flood of new prisoners, camp administration broke down. And then the typhus hit. In the "nonprivileged" area, Camp I—a rectangle measuring 1½ kilometers by 365 meters, the British found 40,000 people, some still alive. They estimated that 39,000 Polish and Hungarian Jews had died in that plague compound.[10]

Rudolf Höss of Auschwitz, an old hand at sickening scenes, remarked that in all his experience he had never seen anything like it. Zdenka Fantlowa wrote of her battle for life. The weapons—"only our undermined health and our inconceivably strong will." The well-armed enemies—"hunger, thirst, filth, germs and lice." She and her sister became ill with typhus. The disease fell on them "treacherously, like a destructive and evil enemy who puts a knife to one's throat." Their bodies burned with fever, their heads roared, they could not eat. In spite of their indescribable thirst and severe diarrhea, they were forced into labor squads. At work, they dropped with fatigue, and at roll call, they fainted. The disease spread to the most remote sections, increasing each day the number of dead and decreasing the number of living. No one came to clean the filthy quarters or deliver food. Finally, the camp was cut off from all supplies. The neglected victims lay in hopelessness, sustaining themselves on water and air. Then the water disappeared:

In our dreadful despair we made our way to a tank in which dirty underwear was washed and which was unclean with every possible kind of filth, and here we quenched our thirst. Despite the fact that the water was disgusting, there was such a scuffle around it that it might have been nectar. Within a few days the tank was half empty. Quart after quart of this dangerously fetid water ran down the throats and into the intestines of the sick, where the germs began and finished their destructive work. We called it intestinal typhus. And although we all knew what was ahead of us if we drank the water, we voluntarily chose death in preference to the maddening torture of thirst.

But the situation worsened. Inmates lay on the dirty floor waiting for death. Dozens of women died each day in agony:

The cadavers remained in the room, mixed with the living. It was hard to ascertain who was dead and who was still alive; we all looked so much alike. Our bodies were scrawny to the bone, and a puzzling, disgusted expression was in our eyes. Ours were the eyes of those who had seen death. No one buried the dead. At best they were thrown out in front of the barracks, and here, within a few days, towered mounds of human bones. The number of dead assumed astronomical proportions.[11]

On March 1 Commandant Kramer informed his superiors that there were 42,000 people in the camp, and that typhus was killing 250 to 300 of them a day. On the 19th of March, when the Belsen population surpassed 60,000, SS General Oswald Pohl arrived with an order from Himmler to Kramer that no more Jews were to be killed and that the death rate must be reduced. Himmler told a leader of the World Jewish Council a few days later that he had taken steps to deal with the typhus epidemic. On March 23 Heinrich Müller, head of the Gestapo, informed one of the emissaries from the World Jewish Community that things were under control.[12]

But the transports continued to pour in. In two weeks, April 4–18, the trains dumped 28,000 new prisoners into the camp. The food supply was cut off and roll calls stopped. The starving, sick inmates were on their own. Corpses rotted in heaps; rats attacked living inmates; starving prisoners ate their dead acquaintances. A survivor, Rudolf Kustermeir, cannot quite believe now that he really experienced the things he recalled:

I well remember a day at the end of February, 1945, when I heard for the first time of people have eaten the flesh of dead bodies. There were lungs, hearts, and livers missing from some corpses, and pieces cut out of the thighs and buttocks![13]

No camp endured a more horrible situation in the last days. Some historians speculate that Eichmann himself was responsible for what happened. Himmler had promised that the Belsen Jews would be saved; and Pohl had visited Belsen on March 19. Why, then, did transports pour into Belsen for another three weeks? One report suggested "that this was the last leering gesture of the man who was going to 'leap into his grave, laughing because he had five million deaths on his conscience.' "[14]

On April 10 Himmler appointed Kurt Becher special emissary for the concentration camps and sent him to Belsen. From the camp, Becher phoned Himmler and persuaded him to turn the camp over to the British intact. Although Colonel Harries (area commander stationed at the SS Panzer Training School) refused, agreement was finally reached on April 12 permitting the guards to surrender in order to keep the typhus area under control. Not until three days later, however, did the British enter the camp.

Himmler had been shocked, Pohl was shocked, Becher was shocked, even Höss was shocked, and now the British were shocked. But the British found an inconceivable situation: down the road at the Training School, they discovered 800 tons of food and a bakery that produced 60,000 loaves of bread a day. When Kramer's civilian supplies stopped, the SS sent him 10,000 loaves a week. Kramer did not ask for more. From his own testimony, he said that would have meant filling out special forms. "Used as he was to seeing human beings die in their thousands in the Buchenwald infirmary and gas chambers, he was not used to taking the simplest action without signing on the dotted line."[15]

While prisoners died by the hundreds in the hours before liberation, a few still hoped for a miracle. When Zdenka Fantlowa was informed that the British had arrived, she reacted with disinterest, without emotion. "It is strange and paradoxical that this longed-for moment for which we had been awaiting throughout the war, of which we spoke constantly, which our imaginations depicted in every form, whose distant luminosity lit our path for us like a lighthouse—this moment for which the whole world was waiting, left us cold." A few hours before liberation her sister died in her arms and she herself was near death: "I could be no more interested in the fact that the British had come than the fact that it was raining on the equator."[16]

Sara Berkowitz was lying on a filthy bunk recuperating from typhoid on April 15. When the first British soldier walked into her barracks, she realized she had survived. "I was free—free to start life again. But how? I was sick, lonely, and alone; it seemed certain that no one from my immediate family had survived."[17]

The liberation of the camp was not uneventful. Agreement had been reached between German and British army commanders over the transfer of Belsen. Both sides were worried that the 60,000 prisoners, ill with typhus, would break out, stream over the countryside, and infect British troops and German civilians. The German forces agreed to leave Bergen-Belsen, and then the SS wardens would hand over the camp. When Derrick Sington, a member of the British Army, drove up the road to the camp, he found the SS officers drawn up in front of the main gate. Commandant Kramer was particularly friendly. Sington described it as a "grotesquely uncongruous" drama:

For just over the shoulders of these gay young officers with their almost knightly bearing were 10,000 unburied dead piled in twisted heaps; mass graves containing 40,000 bodies, and survivors perishing at the rate of 500 a day—all civilians dead or dying from starvation or ill-usage. I could not, of course, see the unimaginable back cloth to the cheerful performance at the gate.

Later Sington drove into the camp with Commandant Kramer standing on his running board advising the British how to act. As Sington rode along the main track of the camp, thousands of shaved heads gathered behind the barbed wire while others surged onto the highway. "We drove on past a throng of women whose hysterical joy broke out like the sobbing and screaming of the damned. Kramer watched as if he were in a menagerie of ill-trained leopards; and when a birch branch, flung instead of garlands for our welcome, lighted on his shoulder, he brushed it disapprovingly away." The SS and Hungarian guards continued to shoot prisoners for venturing beyond the lines.[18]

In September 1945 the criminals of Belsen were brought before a British military court in a trial that lasted fifty-five days. Forty-four persons were charged. Three, including Commandant Kramer, were officers. The court sentenced the three officers and eight others to death, and acquitted nineteen. The trial made this fundamental distinction between the conditions at Belsen and those at Auschwitz:

... the conditions at Belsen were caused by criminal and inexcusable neglect coupled with an administrative breakdown, while the conditions at Auschwitz were the direct result of a carefully designed and executed policy of long standing.

The defense pleaded that the state, not individual jailers, must bear the responsibility; they also used the soon-to-become-familiar argument of "superior orders." Kramer, in his testimony, came across as a fanatical Nazi, always obeying orders.

His type was that of the perfectly obedient underling with no scruples of any kind. If 500 men were ordered for execution at 0900 hours, they would be there to the minute and to the man. . . . But this efficiency and the acts to which it led him sprang from his desire to keep a safe, comfortable job, rather than from any deep-rooted Nazi conviction.

Little evidence was presented of Kramer's personal cruelty. What stood before the court was a man with "an almost unbelievable disregard for the suffering of his prisoners. . . . They just did not make any impression upon him at all; they were all part of the day's work."[19]

Irma Grese, the infamous "Bitch of Belsen," had been captured with other SS women. When questioned, she insisted that it had been her elevated duty to exterminate antisocial elements. In prison, when a British investigating officer reinterrogated her, he found her convinced of the righteousness of her actions. At the Belsen trial Irma Grese was a prominent figure. She was by any standard a pretty girl:

Her hair was blond, with fair ringlets bursting around each shoulder. Her eyes were a clear blue under a high, broad forehead. She might have been a handsome young nurse, a secretary, or even the headmistress of a girl's school.[20]

In a recent memoir an Auschwitz woman remembers Irma well:

How else could Irma Grese have been so perfectly beautiful? Flawless skin. A head of natural blond hair. Almost perfect features. Who made this beautiful beast?[21]

Those who testified against Irma Grese accused her of beating inmates with a riding crop and then shooting them. They charged her with forcing the women to stand for hours in the cold and the snow without food. She beat and kicked inmates until they were senseless. One testified that Grese set her dogs on prisoners, who chewed them until they died. Repeatedly, the witnesses charged her with killing and cruelty.

Irma Grese denied all charges. She was only twenty-one years old! The daughter of a farm laborer and one of five children, she grew up in the farmland area of Prussia. Hitler came to power when Irma was ten years old and she was eligible for the young women's youth group. Her father disapproved of the Nazis and tried to keep his daughters out of any group associated with the Nazi regime. At age fifteen, Irma went to work in the infamous hospital at Hohenlychen. In 1941 she came into contact with Dr. Karl Gebhart, famous for his obsession with research on healing gangrenous war wounds, transplanting bones, and regenerating nerves. As his guinea pigs, he used Jewish women from the nearby concentration camp of Ravensbrück. Ravensbrück was only 16 kilometers from Hohenlychen.

In 1942 Irma Grese left Hohenlychen to become an apprentice warden at Ravensbrück. After eight months in Ravensbrück, she transferred to Auschwitz, where she advanced rapidly because she was good at her job. And then she came to Belsen. The British courts sentenced her to death, and in December of 1945 she was hanged—a hardened, experienced killer at age twenty-one. The courts also sentenced Kramer and Borman to hang. Then on December 22, 1951, five Belsen female guards and *Kapos* who had been sentenced to ten years for beating and killing prisoners were suddenly released from prison.

The attitude of the British toward the War Crimes Trials has mystified casual observers. In their courts the accused received the fullest benefit of any doubt. Those who murdered many received the death sentence, but those who only murdered a few drew two to seven years and early release from custody. Martin Gilbert, Churchill's official biographer, cites one trial official as saying that sentences erring on the side of leniency are on the side of right. Gilbert suggests that his government's trial policies reflect the same absence of human concern evidenced early in the war. In one example, Britain denied 20,000 Polish Jewish children permission to emigrate to Palestine because their emigration would aid the Nazi war effort—by freeing the Germans of the economic responsibility of feeding them![22]

A Photographic Survey of Belsen's Liberation

The conditions of the Belsen camp and the activities of the days following liberation are probably the most photographed events in concentration camp history. The *London Daily Mail* in 1945, and later the Bergen-Belsen Association, published collections of photographs shot by British army photographers and accompanying newsmen—pictures of the camp, the dead, and the survivors.[23] Those hundreds of photographs speak more clearly than any words that have been written. As a collection, they convey an agony and a horror seldom found in the annals of history. What follows is based solely on the photographic collections.

It is true that on Sunday, April 15, 1945, at 3 P.M., the victorious British army liberated Belsen. It is true that a few days later that army erected a large sign with white lettering on a black·board:

This is the site of the infamous Belsen concentration camp; 10,000 buried dead were found here, another 13,000 have since died. All of them victims of the German new order in Europe. And an example of Nazi culture.

But those words are neither accurate nor helpful. To say that Belsen was liberated is stretching the point. And to proclaim that the British Army was victorious is true in terms of its war effort, but not in terms of the men's faces burying the dead and shoveling the bodies with bulldozers. It is also questionable that the horror there was created by a culture, any kind of a culture. It had to have its roots in something else.

The camp was not a camp on liberation day. It was a large area, foggy, steamy, and muddy, crammed with barracks, huts, tents, and makeshift dwellings and bodies and living dead and creatures stumbling about and cooking fires and puddles of water. The pictures show Commandant Kramer dressed in his Sunday uniform surrendering the camp to the puzzled British soldiers. As the military police round up the German guards, a group of emaciated women in striped uniforms actually smile—some raising their thin arms in a greeting. But another view that day shows an old woman hunched in the mud wearing an SS officer's coat and a shawl around her head trying to keep warm, surrounded by the bodies of her friends who have not made it to that hour. Behind her are tents made from sheets or blankets, and little fires over which inmates are roasting potatoes or weeds or grass. Everywhere the mud. Several women with striped skirts and light blouses, shawls on their heads, wash themselves from their bowls; and the water for the wash is coming out of a puddle of muddy water steaming with fetidness in the center of the camp.

In a crowded barracks 100 women rest on the floor as the British walk into the room. All are thin, a few are smiling, many are just sitting. Some look stunned; others have their heads in their hands and they are crying. Each is too weak to rise or even to wave. Over by trees in front of dead naked bodies sits a smiling woman peeling a potato with a sliver of wood, and next to her is another woman cutting up the potatoes into a wooden bowl. Near her on the ground with her legs drawn up lies a woman, still alive, whose eyes open in disbelief and hopelessness.

Everywhere that day sparks of life are flickering faintly in the proximity of the dead. Between the barracks a few survivors have the energy to pick their way among all the piles and pieces of bodies to get to the other side of the camp. The squalor is as unbelievable as that of any scene photographed in the twentieth century. Those are not just piles of bodies. They are naked bones wrapped and twisted around each other in tortured stances, eyes open and looks of horror on each skull. Near a barrack door a little orphan girl, no more than eight years old, with a shawl around her head, cries quietly in despair a few feet from a group of dead bodies who must have been her friends because they, too, are naked children. Outside another barrack a few energetic survivors are carrying out the bodies of those who died the night before, or perhaps during the moments and hours in which the camp was being liberated. In the clearing six women with expressions of agony on their tortured faces, some even with looks of deep hatred, surround a naked woman with a lovely face and long black hair who has obviously just died.

Those alive seem to be resting, gathering whatever little strength is left in them in order to live long enough to remain alive. Some wash with the little water available. Others sit picking the rows of lice from their rags. So many, too weak to stand, are lying with bowls of food next to them, too ill to eat. Still others are sitting, rocking, crying in agony, knowing that they too are dying and that this day of liberation is their last. A group of men sprawl on the ground dressed in nothing but skin and bones, but still alive. Everywhere are the dead, their eyes open: the awful looks of awful deaths in awful shells that were human bodies. Little victims lie unburied over by a tree: a little girl stretched tightly around a little boy, two children who died holding each other. Two older living sisters clutch each other and gaze at each other with looks of surprise: two members of one family surviving together! Throughout Belsen the survivors rest, sleep, think, cry, and eat in the presence of stinking bodies. Many are in the process of dying, and those who are still living sit by their side, holding their hands, crying, pleading, trying to breathe just another day of life into them. The dying have the looks of individuals who have already left this earth.

Life must go on and so they cook what food they can find and draw water from the mud. A huge pile of boots has been gathered from the dead; and the survivors in their new but desperate fight for life are using the shoes as fuel to build fires for warmth and to warm the soup they are making. Those without garments are taking clothes from the corpses. The looks on their faces are not heartless, but realistic, for they need the warmth more than the dead. The soldiers, still stunned, begin to talk to the prisoners, but the prisoners are too hungry to speak. The British bring in water and food and the prisoners line up, knowing at this point that even a gulp of water might save their lives.

Within just a day or two the British realize that typhus is the first enemy. They put up signs: "Typhus, no entry, no exit." Every day 1,700 die of the disease. Inside the hospital the patients know that few will emerge alive. Children sit in the beds, their large piercing eyes filled with the knowledge that they are dying. One barrack is transformed into a sick bay for those children. Soon the British take over the SS camp down the road for an improvised infirmary. They start to carry out the bodies. As the nurses and doctors come in to move the utterly emaciated prisoners, they have difficulty telling if they are alive. As one asked, "Can these bones live?"

The commandant and the SS officers no longer look so confident. Commandant Kramer, after the fourth day, is unshaven, stunned, his eyes staring in disbelief. The SS staff line up without their uniforms, ready for work. The SS women, who were undisturbed for the first few days, are now marched out of the barracks to view the dead. Two look frightened, one looks grim; and unbelievably, two are smiling.

In different parts of the camp some makeshift chapels are set up. A tent with a small cross on the top, an altar, a priest kneeling before small groups of prisoners. In another corner a small synagogue with the Star of David, and groups kneeling or sitting before it.

But what to do with all the bodies left to rot in the camp? The British excavate large pits for the bodies. There is nothing else to do. No one knows who they are and they cannot even be disentangled from each other. Occasionally, a living creature is found under a corpse. One such human is a tiny girl, wasted away to nothing, lying on a blanket, her eyes wide, a wisp of a smile on her face. Into the communal death pits go the unburied bodies, frozen in a state of horror. The British assign the SS the task of burial; and they load trucks with the dead. Arms hang over the side of the trucks, heads bump in the wind. The SS women unload the emaciated dead women, whose sex can scarcely be determined. As the loading process goes on, a crowd of prisoners gather, hate in their eyes, crying for vengeance. In the woods the British find a forest of death—endless piles of bodies waiting for some end. They also find open pits already dug for them filled with the tangled bodies of prisoners.

The British go through the crematorium and find more piles. There are so many bodies that they must bring in bulldozers to scoop them into mass graves. German youths from neighboring towns carry, in open coffins, bodies of victims scattered over the road outside the camp. For many days the survivors witness the same gruesome scene until the mass burial is completed under the eyes of brokenhearted survivors.

Finally all the bodies are lying in the graves. The British force the infamous SS physician Dr. Klein, who killed thousands with his death injections, to stand among the corpses of his victims in the pits. Emotions break out from the survivors as they witness the mass graves. Some come to the microphones crying and eulogizing the dead. Others are praying quietly. The chaplains stand with their Bibles; and Rabbi Leslie Hardman recites the Kaddish at the grave. The bulldozers shovel the dirt into the grave and the rollers level the ground. Most graves are left raised as large mounds. A sign identifies each grave with the approximate number of people buried in it. A flat mound marks the site of a mass grave of thousands of Jewish men, women, and children. Here lie 800 bodies, there lie buried 5,000 bodies. Only the mass graves remain as a witness to the tragedy.

Once the dead are removed, both the British and the survivors must prepare for the next stage—to house, clothe, feed, and care for those remaining so that they may live. One picture shows such joy on the faces of young women as they hold loaves of fresh bread in their arms, an experience almost forgotten over the past years. They carry soup and sausage and have their first warm meal. A temporary kitchen is opened near the old barracks. The prisoners build improvised baths and showers. They wash for the first time in months. Rehabilitation begins. The survivors in the pictures seem determined to help themselves. One or two have found combs, one more new experience. Another man is shining his shoes and women are doing an old, but almost forgotten chore, the laundry. Strength is slowly returning to many inmates. Women are helping each other dress. Some are standing still, wondering if liberation is a dream or a reality. The British remove the typhus cases to the Panzer School. They disinfect the survivors in the first attempt to eliminate the typhus. Many survivors are in such a state of exhaustion and emaciation that they will hover between life and death for several weeks. The British send nurses and voluntary aids into the crowded Panzer School hospital. Wards are set up in the rooms. Thousands still die because it was too late for them. But the survivors seem to feel some gratitude toward the British and their commander, Brigadier General Hughes.

And then the remaining prisoners are moved to the Panzer School. General Hughes orders the Belsen barracks burned to the ground to prevent the spread of typhus. Big British flamethrower tanks go into action against the barracks and the camp begins to blaze and blaze and smoke. The flames symbolically wipe the earth clean of an abomination. The survivors watch as the entire camp burns down. Soon nothing but ashes remain of Bergen-Belsen. A lone tree stands to mark the site of so much suffering and agony. The British chaplain, Dr. Levy, exhorts the watching group, "You must choose life." The survivors turn from the burning camp and prepare to struggle for a new life.

1945–1950

The history of the second half of Bergen-Belsen occupies a longer time period than the first. For there was another Belsen—the post-April 1945 Belsen, "which proved that the flames consuming Jewish flesh and bone, were powerless to kill the sources of . . . dreams and regeneration." A large group of heterogeneous Jews survived Belsen. They came from every culture, land, and religious background, and spoke many different languages. But a strong feeling of common fate joined them together. "When the day of liberation arrived, all the Jews had a common language, common hopes, aspirations, and dreams." And it was that group that formed a most unusual survivor organization. It was that group that took the lead across Europe in demanding, and finally securing, some modicum of decent treatment for the victims of the Nazi horror.[24]

When the Jews speak of Belsen after 1945, they are referring to the DP camp created down the road at the SS Panzer Training School. That entire complex, renamed Belsen, is where the Belsen Jews lived until it was liquidated in 1950. The survivors immediately began to organize themselves.

Two days after the arrival of the British, 200 Jews met together and elected the first Jewish Committee of Belsen. The committee assumed the task of caring for the survivors.

When the typhus epidemic had run its course (about 28,000 had died of typhus after liberation), 13,000 Jews remained alive in Belsen, including several hundred Jewish children. But Belsen soon experienced growing pains, for when Jews in other camps heard of that unusual concentration of Jewish people, they streamed in from all over the British Zone. They came to find their children and members of their families and to be with their own kind.

The Belsen survivors faced serious problems. While the British tended to the bodily needs of the survivors with some dispatch, they were no more ready to minister to them as human beings with a workable future than any of the other national liberating groups. There were political factors in Germany, and unfortunately in the Allied camps, that caused the denial of the Jewish character of the problem. The Allies steadfastly continued to define the survivor problem as applying in the same measure to all victims. Governments took the initial stand that the Jews were to be given no special help: they were simply war victims, displaced persons. Britain, joined by other Allied nations, designated the nationality of each Jew by the country of his origin. Obviously the Jews knew what the results of that policy would be.

The fight of the Belsen Jews to remain in the new Belsen was not an easy one. The British intended to use the barracks for their own soldiers and to remove the Jews by sending them to Lingen, an international camp near the Dutch border—desolate and primitive, without utilities.. They were surprised at the fuss started by Josef Rosensaft. He had been at Belsen only a week before liberation, having spent the earlier years in Dora. After surviving the Nazi camps, he and his friends were certainly not afraid of the British. Rosensaft decided that no Jew should go to Lingen, and he stopped the evacuation. He also stood in the forefront of those protesting the British effort to change Belsen's name to Hohne in an effort to erase the bloodstain that Belsen had left. The Belsen Jews successfully protested the removal of the symbolic name.

For a time, liberation became a lesser of two evils in which "Nazi torture has been supplanted, not by freedom and renaissance, but by the frustrating and bureaucratic combination of the military government and UNRRA, the latter of which often seems to need more spiritual relief and rehabilitation than the bodies of whom it is supposed to succor." But the city grew and stabilized and normal life began. People married and had children. Rabbis prayed and conducted services. Jewish police and judges maintained order. Newspapers, Hebrew schools, and libraries appeared. Rosensaft pictured the new Belsen as a *shtetl:*

Perhaps it was—the last shtetl in Europe, whose inhabitants, teeter-tottering between despair and exhilaration, were suspended between past and future. Their memories pursued them, waking or dreaming. . . . Public events were occasions for processions to the cemetery, and the Deuteronomic text "Remember what Amalek did unto thee" became commonplace.[25]

Under the direction of Rosensaft, Belsen became an organized community with 10,000 Jews as its citizens. He and his colleagues set up a tracing service to find survivors and relatives. The Joint Distribution Committee provided supplies.

The DP camp Panzer School, although better than most DP camps, still conferred unbearable indignities on the survivors. They were crowded, huddled into small rooms, denied privacy and dignity. And those humans needed to rebegin their lives. A survivor had to decide the role of formal religion in his life. He needed to search for any living family. He needed to find meaning for his life, and to decide where he was going next. But as one man pondered, the theme was noble:

It is a story of a shipwrecked crew who are braving the storm to get back to port. It is the romance of a group who, though scarred and wounded in body and spirit, have risen above their ugly situation to fight for an ideal—home. In this sense then, the drama is religious, godly, and moral.[26]

One of the most important memories to which the survivors point was the children's school. The heterogeneous children had in common a few basics: all had been denied an education as well as a home and parents. Belsen gave 200 children an opportunity to receive a normal education, even though there were no textbooks and the teachers had to improvise each day.

The children's thirst for knowledge was insatiable. They devoured every bit of information, every scrap of learning. The only spot in the whole school that was deserted in the early weeks was the playroom. Much energy was spent to create the conditions and atmosphere for play to quicken the child's pulse and to restore his capacity for pleasure and fun. It was some time before laughter was heard.[27]

Later several hundred children left the camp for Israel.

And to the Belsen "city" came more and more refugees from Poland and other countries behind the Iron Curtain. Jews from the east told of new pogroms and anti-Semitism. Most newcomers strengthened the ranks of the local Orthodoxy. Soon a yeshiva, a Talmud-Torah, a Bet-Jacob School and Seminary grew up. Belsen had its own rabbinate, which formed a strong core of the community. The Central Committee grew stronger in influence and impact:

All the multi-colored threads of Jewish endeavor wound towards it. The Committee represented *all* the community and not any one part. It acted as a laboratory in the unique effort to weld and unify the remnants of a shattered people and make of it a goal-conscious entity.[28]

That city, that community, was such a remarkable place that it cannot be overemphasized. Here were people attempting to live again in an area that had formerly housed their killers. Some survivors returned home immediately, but most remained, homeless, facing an uncertain future. Josef Rosenşaft was elected head of the Belsen Jews and then chairman of the Central Committee of the Liberated Jews in the British Zone of Germany. Eventually he became president of the World Federation of the Bergen-Belsen Survivors. In 1945 he traveled to America to participate in the conference of the United Jewish Appeal, and his work with the American Jewish leaders made a tremendous impact. Belsen became known throughout the world and many persons of authority and fame visited it. In July 1945 Dr. Schwartz, the European director of the American Joint Distribution Committee, and Earl Harrison, President Truman's representative, came to Belsen. David Ben-Gurion arrived in November 1945. Fiorello LaGuardia joined with the Belsen survivors in a ceremony. Any occasion was used to march to the Belsen camp site to place wreaths or to commemorate the dead. The Belsen Jews began traveling throughout the world to Zionist and Jewish conferences.

Many couples married and had children. Soon there were birthday parties for the young. The survivors, with help from abroad, organized a modern hospital with dedicated doctors and nurses from the Allied countries. Determined that the world should not forget, the Belsen survivors produced newspapers, books, pamphlets, biographies, bibliographies, poetry, photographic exhibits, posters. In Belsen they began what they called the concentration camp theater. Survivors performed various works such as Shalom Aleichem's *The Bewitched Tailor,* Emile Berhart's *Redeemer,* and the play *The Eternal Wanderer.* In their tent theater the survivors also performed concentration camp plays written by them. The Belsen theater toured and impressed Europe with its exceptional performances. Belsen inmates also started an amateur orchestra and a symphony. The city developed its own trade schools where young people learned tailoring, machine work, mechanics, dentistry, and other occupations. Belsen residents did not content themselves with culture, education, and music. They also participated vigorously in sports. Chess, soccer, volleyball, and boxing teams played each other and teams from elsewhere in Germany.

Zionist groups of every persuasion organized at Belsen and responded constantly to the twists and turns of British policy in Palestine, often not to their own benefit. The survivors organized protests and demonstrations against the British, and clashed with the British soldiers using tear gas. The Jewish police and the survivors fought back. On September 7, 1947, the Belsen demonstrators displayed their solidarity with the "Exodus" passengers on their return to Germany. They demonstrated for several days in the Belsen camp: speeches, flags, crowds. And many passengers arrived back in the Belsen camp, again behind bars.When the United Nations, in November 1947, voted to partition Palestine, the Belsen Jews danced in the square. Of course, on May 15, 1948, Belsen celebrated when the state of Israel was proclaimed.[29]

Then they began to build the monuments in their former place of residence. The first monument, made of wood and meant to be temporary, was unveiled at a ceremony before the opening of the first Congress of Liberated Jews on September 25, 1945. On April 15, 1946, the first anniversary of liberation, the Central Committee, surrounded by survivors and guests from all over the world, unveiled the Bergen-Belsen's Martyrs Monument. On its side are printed the words: "Israel and the world shall remember 30,000 Jews exterminated at the camp of Bergen Belsen at the hands of the murderous Nazis." And further down: "Earth conceal not the blood!"

The old Belsen camp today is what it is because of the Bergen-Belsen survivors. They made it indeed a Camp of Memory. The International Monument was erected in 1953 with help from abroad. The center is a tall tower visible at a distance. Stone walls replace the wooden markings on the mass graves. The German descriptions denote the number of buried victims. The committee also placed symbolic tombstones throughout the camp, and at the gate they built a stone wall and sculpted in the name and date of the camp. Many visitors came to the unveiling of the International Monument in 1953. On the wall opposite the column are inscriptions in fourteen languages, including Hebrew and Yiddish. The English words read: "To the memory of all those who died in this place."

In 1950 Belsen came to an end. On the occasion of the closing of the camp, Josef Rosensaft wrote a eulogy to the living and the dead of Belsen. He entitled it "Farewell to the Martyrs of Belsen."

There are no wreaths or flowers in our hands as we stand before you, our dearly beloved and hallowed dead, to bid farewell to you, without ceremony or celebration, as we leave the spot in which are buried the stubs and embers of your sacred Jewish bodies; we whisper and sigh our *Shalom* as we depart never to return.

Map 14: Camp Belsen

A portion of this map originally appeared in Holocaust and Rebirth: Bergen-Belsen, 1945–1965 *by Sam E. Bloch (NY: Bergen-Belsen Press, 1965). Map revision by Sharon Coughran.*

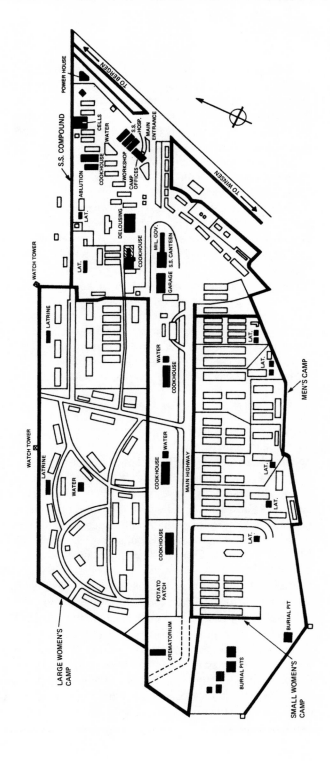

The monument of our Central Committee, the few crumbling tombstones, the hurriedly thrown up mounds untidily hiding your tormented bodies—these will from now on become even lonelier and more sadly forsaken, more orphaned; no longer will there congregate around you weeping kinsfolk and groups of worshippers reciting muffled prayers; there will be no more memorial services; no crypt, no vault or mausoleum will be erected; nor will an eternal light burn over your burial place. . . .

That Valley of the most terrible Gehenna . . . is now to be converted into a "scented paradise" with beds and roses and leafy trees, a veritable mingling of "butchery and springtime." . . .

Our eyes are offended by this contrived panorama, this bucolic pastoral landscape lining our brothers' and our sisters' mass-graves drenched by our bloody tears. The aroma of these flowers remind us of the incense which used to be burned in deference to the "sensitive" hangmen to save their delicate nostrils the smell of the victims' blood. . . .

Our hearts are heavy and choked with tears as we recall our last stay here, at this "resting-place" of our martyrs, in this alien wild desolation and we are speechless. We are as mute as mourners and can think only of the words recently spoken here, that these dead would not be abandoned amid a hostile surrounding and that, meantime, care would be taken that the graves were not tampered with.

It is with these words of promise that we take leave of those "remaining" in Camp 1 in Belsen. The day of new visitation shall come when your bones will find their true rest.[30]

And so they dispersed to Israel, to America, and throughout the world. They healed themselves, they went to work, they started new lives. They became successful, but they never forgot—joined together by their Belsen experience. The Belsen ties still bind them. And each year in many places of the world, whether it be Chicago, New York, Tel Aviv, hundreds of Belsen survivors gather at a hotel where they hold an anniversary liberation dinner to honor the martyrdom of their colleagues. And to those dinners have come the most famous Jews alive, to speak to this special group of survivors: Golda Meir, David Ben-Gurion, Gideon Hauser, Josef Rosensaft, Abba Eban. These gatherings are attempts "to involve the whole Jewish community in the memory of Belsen, and, against all odds and despite the incongruity of the setting, he [Rosensaft] has somehow succeeded."[31]

Josef Rosensaft and his colleagues in the Bergen-Belsen Association have organized an annual pilgrimage to the Belsen site and ceremonies of remembrance in cities across the world. They have seen to it that Belsen memorials have been established in Israel and in Canada; and they watch over the mass graves in Belsen. They established scholarship and loan funds for Belsen survivors and created Belsen Memorial Libraries in several cities. They subsidized the publication of commemorative books. The

Bergen-Belsen Association made Belsen a camp of memory; and the survivors have maintained their close association for some thirty-five years to challenge the world to remember what it wishes to forget.

POLAND

GENTILE POLAND: THE GRAVEYARD OF THE THOUSAND-YEAR KINGDOM OF JUDAISM

Poland, the cultural center and home of Eastern European Jewry with its 3.5 million Jews, is now *Judenrein,* the result of a historical process pressed by the Polish government and the majority of Poles between the World Wars, taken to the next logical step of extermination by the Nazis in their five years of havoc, and finished by the postwar Polish government and people with pogroms, anti-Semitic campaigns, and forced emigration. One way or another, the Jews are gone, unless one counts the 8,000 to 10,000 scattered throughout the country. The Jews had lived longer in Poland than anywhere else in Europe. The Yiddish world, the Yiddish kingdom, had stretched from Amsterdam to Vilna and from Strasbourg to Odessa. It has been called the largest empire in the history of Europe, lasting almost a thousand years, without a king, a parliament, or an army.

After World War II many Poles acknowledged without regret, that Hitler had solved their Jewish problem. The Polish government sealed the verdict in 1968. And most Poles take the disappearance of the Jews for granted. Of those few Jews who remain, most are aged and dying and many pass as Gentiles in hope they will be left alone. Although the Preservation Council has erected and affixed at least 2,500 monuments and tablets throughout Poland in commemoration of Poles killed by the Nazis, the government has exerted great effort to eradicate all memories of the Jewish martyrdom. It has effectively prohibited the special identification and citing of Jews as victims of the Nazis in writings about the period, in monuments, in camps, and in commemorations. The Warsaw Ghetto Uprising, for example, is not identified in specific terms, but described rather as a revolt of the national Polish resistance. The exhibitions in the camps conform to the rules; the role of the Jew hardly figures in them. And not one of the four killing centers (with almost exclusively Jewish death counts) contains a state museum; not one is publicized; and all are virtually impossible to find. No official guidebook or information exists on those four.

Poland today seems vast compared to other parts of Europe, and its varied climate and geography make it a fascinating country to tour. One is constantly reminded that its economy is still a rural one, based on peasant farms and lush pastures. And each year I return, the life of the peasant has obviously improved. Where there were no highways, there are now many forms of transportation. Where the communities were isolated, buses now stop every hour. Where in the 1960s I drove through dark villages at night, I now travel through electrified rural communities. Rural lands that in the past were dotted with decrepit farmhouses now have new farm buildings and homes. The farmers, the peasants, still look the same during the week in their traditional black clothes. They walk the highways and they toil in the fields. They still drive their horse wagons down the roads. But more and more, one sees tractors and combines and mechanization. On Saturday nights in the small towns the traditional black dress has given way to more modern clothing.

I am also impressed by the immense growth, modernization, and industrialization of Poland's cities. Each year they seem to become more modern and to resemble the metropolises of the West. One could not ask for a more advanced city in Eastern Europe than Warsaw. But Poland is building up its other urban areas as well. Poznan, for example, such a dismal place in the early 1960s, is now a modern industrial city with intercontinental hotels and classy restaurants. The resorts in the 1960s were primitive places; now they have the most modern, elegant motels and accommodations in all of Eastern Europe. Poland is a strange country, with so many contrasts. Its people work hard and its government is obviously intent on fostering some kind of freedom and advantages for them. They speak more freely and they seem more prosperous in every respect than their counterparts in the other Eastern European countries. While the greatest economic miracle may have been the recovery of East Germany, an advanced economy is not as evident there as in Poland. One must remember that the Germans nearly leveled Warsaw to the ground. One must remember that many other parts of Poland were devastated in the war. Now, the countryside seems peaceful, although food riots occur; and in the cities the inhabitants resemble in their needs and goals people in other major European cities. But it is still hard to buy meat in Warsaw, and without reservations it is virtually impossible to obtain hotel accommodations. There is still a serious housing shortage throughout urban Poland and my friends there are cramped in small apartments. Still they work hard and are paid for it, and they save their money to buy a car.

Poland is witnessing a final chapter in the thousand-year history of the Polish Jews. There is irony in it, even now. Poland's Jews are vanishing through attrition. It is hard to tell how many remained after the last major emigration triggered by the 1968 purge. At that time 14,000 Jews moved to other countries. Scholars assume that there are 10,000 to 12,000 Jews left, including the offspring of the many mixed marriages. One count has 3,000 practicing Jews, another 17,000 in the eighteen congregations left in all of Poland. Those congregations are united under the Congregations of Moses

Denomination. No rabbis remain in Poland and it is hard to form a *minyan* anyplace at any time.

Anti-Semitism lingers even without the Jews, but it breaks out on the surface only at times. Differences do exist between the urban and the rural population. In some parts of Poland, stopping in a town near a camp, one feels as though it is 1920 or 1930. It is no surprise if people shout out at the foreign car, "*Juden, Juden!*" The visible Jews are very, very rare—one sees a few men with skull caps or notes an occasional Jew walking through the cemeteries. The only place one sees the traditional dress is in craftshops that sell Jewish dolls as folklore.

Warsaw—thirty-eight years after the Germans entered and thirty-two years after they left. In 1945 most of Warsaw had been systematically destroyed. Certainly during the Warsaw Ghetto Uprising the ghetto had been leveled and 85 percent of the rest of the city had been destroyed during the Warsaw Uprising. The Poles built it up very quickly. In 1964, 1965, 1966, it was a dismal, quiet city, its silence broken by music and a few autos. The government had opened up memorials and parks and every Sunday in the 1960s one could sit by the Chopin Memorial and hear the music of the famous composer played by national artists. On the adjoining islands of the lake in Warsaw, the military band and the orchestra played old Polish tunes. In renovated Old Town elderly men and women sat rocking in the square. New buildings of Stalinist-type architecture seemed to crowd together in the center of Warsaw. Cars were few and far between and so were restaurants. I remember one night sitting in the big ballroom of the Europa Hotel watching the floor show, Poland's most expensive extravaganza. The tunes were from the 1950s. I remember, too, inadequate accommodations, even in the newest motels. A missing towel in the room meant for the occupant five days in jail, regardless of whose fault it may have been. Buying money on the black market was a scary prospect, almost certain to land one in jail. Gas stations were scarce, and traveling in the rural areas was a risk without a full tank of gas.

Today it is different. The magnificent new Forum Intercontinental Hotel rises through the skyline of Warsaw, surrounded by other modern buildings. The streets are wide and clear and crowded with traffic. Goods are available throughout the city. It is still hard to purchase gasoline, but it is not so difficult to buy money on the black market, and no one really seems to care. There is very little left in Warsaw to remind one of the devastation of the war. It is a stunning view from the top floor, many, many stories above the rest of Warsaw, of the Forum Hotel: one gazes on a never-ending landscape of buildings, knowing that few existed twenty years before. It is perplexing to wonder what America, one's own country, would have done had it been so utterly destroyed. If one had to describe Warsaw in a word, the term "bustle" comes to mind. Everyone seems in a hurry, running and rushing. The old

Polish inefficiency has given way to efficiency and modernism. Things work. Things are in order. It can even be a pleasure to visit and travel there—that is, if one has no memories. The hotels are filled with American and European businessmen who act as they do in any New York, San Francisco, or Washington hotel.

In the city of Warsaw the Council for the Preservation of Monuments to Resistance and Martyrdom has created, from my count, 225 memorials to the victims of the Nazis—from tablets to monuments. Only three refer to the Jews. Not even the Jewish cemetery has a monument in it.

The most familiar Polish monument commemorates the Polish Warsaw Uprising in the form of a sculpture of a woman brandishing her sword. Another of Warsaw's impressive monuments is housed, somewhat ironically, in what is now Poland's huge Ministry of Education Building. During the war it served as the Central Gestapo headquarters for the entire Warsaw District. The Museum of Struggle and Martyrdom is in the basement where the prisoners waited for interrogation, were tortured, recovered, were tortured again or died. The Gestapo burned their victims bodies in the courtyard; the dust and ashes were found after the war. The isolation and torture cells in the basement have been kept intact. Inscriptions written by the prisoners are still visible on the walls. Those inscriptions read in different ways: "Oh Lord, how do they beat!" "Let our agonies and sufferings cause the coming of better Poland." "Nobody thinks of me and nobody knows. I am so alone. Girl of 21 years of age and must die guiltless." And finally: "It is easy to talk about Poland, it is harder to work for her, harder still to die, yet the hardest to suffer."

The infamous Pawiak Prison at Dzielna 24/26 stood during the war as a symbol of terror and dread. It was leveled by the Nazis and the only authentic part of the prison remaining is the gate. But the Poles have recreated Pawiak and made it one of the Museums of Martyrology, together with Lambinowice, Majdanek, Auschwitz, and Stutthof. The cells and the beating rooms have been reproduced, but they now hold a collection of artistic work by the prisoners. Materials that were given artistic shape include pieces of thread, string, wire, toothbrush handles, wood, tissues, and even that which was most precious of all—bread, from which various figures were made. During the war the Germans kept over 2,000 political prisoners in Pawiak, including hundreds of women. But the turnover was high because the condemned were quickly executed and their places taken by newcomers.

When the Germans began the final liquidation of the ghetto, they destroyed the entire district. On the devastated side of the ghetto there remained only Pawiak, the prison for the Poles and the Jews. The complete isolation of the building in 1943 from the rest of the city and the many acres of completely desolated ghettos surrounding it gave the Germans favorable

Warsaw Ghetto remains, 1960s.

conditions for committing fresh crimes there. In May 1943 the first mass shooting of Poles from Pawiak took place in the surrounding ruins. The Gestapo then burned the victims on the spot in order to keep the affair secret. The Warsaw Poles remember the uprising and torture times, those who survived. They intersperse conversations about the period with complaints about inflation, insufficient consumer goods, and the high prices of everything.

The Poles, with some formality, have recognized three places in Warsaw of historical Jewish interest. On Mila Street, No. 18, is a mound of dirt topped by a small memorial stone inscribed in Polish and Hebrew honoring Mordechai Anielewicz, leader of the Warsaw Ghetto Uprising. The stone stands at the summit of the ruins of the former bunker where he died. On Stawki Street stood the railroad loading ramp the Jews climbed to reach the cattle cars taking them to Treblinka. A memorial tablet on a nearby building highlights the spot, in Polish, Yiddish, and Hebrew. And the third official recognition is the Warsaw Ghetto Uprising.

The Jewish ghetto once covered one-third of Warsaw. It was systematically leveled by the Germans and in many places even the stones were crushed. By the 1960s the Poles had built apartment houses on the old ghetto site, but a Jewish memorial—the Monument to the Heroes of the Ghetto—stands near Zamenhofa Street, in what was once the heart of the ghetto. It is at the end of a large park where mothers walk with baby carriages in the sun. The small memorial, made of large stone blocks, contains at its center impressive carved figures beside a *menorah.* It was created by the Jewish-Polish sculptor Nathan Rapaport and dedicated on the fifth anniversary of the rebellion. Standing on the spot where the young Jews threw crudely made firebombs at the German tanks, Rapaport's sculpture is intended to portray the agony of the ghetto victory. He freezes an instant of time. But his sculpture is not a realistic work because the figures have muscles and strength and sturdiness, and those who fought in the ghetto were ragged, starved, and diseased. Perhaps the artist transformed the fighters into figures larger than life because by their own deeds they had in fact transformed themselves. An inscription reads: "We may all perish in this fight, but we will not surrender. We are fighting for your freedom and for your human and national pride—and ours."

Standing in the ghetto, it is hard to envision this spot as the same place where General Stroop commanded its bloody liquidation and ordered photographs taken of the final days. The Stroop Photographic Album, still available, portrays moments and scenes from the life-and-death struggle of the last days. After studying the material, the pictures become engraved on the memory forever. There are the starving, skinny, crying, and swollen children; the smiling German officers talking over liquidation plans; and army soldiers shelling the walls of the ghetto. In another picture a number of Jews who cannot escape from the third floor of a burning house are jumping to the cobblestones on the road. Corpses litter the pavement; and in one picture an old woman hangs from a balcony, trying to escape the death and flames. There is a picture of a bunker where Jews are forced to pull out their brothers from their hiding places. There are Jews leaving the cellars with their hands raised; another picture shows a family found in a bunker—one old lady, two women, a little boy, a little girl. In the corner are corpses of Jews previously shot, left to be burned. The ghetto today bears no resemblance to that ugly past, not with the monument and the park filled with flowers and baby carriages, encircled by high-rise apartments.

Other parts of Jewish Warsaw remain, and these are probably more striking than the monuments. One remaining fixture of Jewish culture is the Yiddish Theater, run by Ida Kaminska until she left the country in 1968. It is still open, costs the state considerable money in annual subsidies, and for what? I do not think more than half a dozen in the audience understand Yiddish; most of the theatergoers used earphones for a simultaneous translation. People come to see the acting. The Theater tours Poland and goes abroad. It is difficult for the players to maintain contact with an audience that cannot understand a word they are speaking. More and more of the plays are using music, cutting down on words. Perhaps in the end the Yiddish Theater will end up wordless.

The Jewish Historical Institute is government supported and holds a collection of Judaica assembled from Jewish libraries and museums looted by the Nazis. In the past it was an exciting, scholarly place, but no longer, at least to me. Today it is dusty, dirty, and quiet, and not terribly impressive. Its once famous director, Ber Mark, is in the cemetery in one of the few shiny new graves. The upper floors of the institute known as the Martyrs Museum portray the story of the Warsaw ghetto, but not very well. They do contain Dr. Emanuel Ringelblum's milk cans in which he kept the daily records of *Oneg Shabbat.*

Some small remnant of a Jewish communal life still remains. The Jewish observant community is afraid, dying, aging, and almost gone. No rabbis are left in Warsaw or in the rest of Poland. A few kosher restaurants still exist, supported by outside funds. One, Ameca, is government supported. Some say 1,000 Jews live in Warsaw. One man argued there were 2,000 between eighteen and thirty. I doubt it. There is a state-run Jewish Social Cultural Society under the Ministry of Interior, but what it does is hard to tell. All Polish-Jewish schools (state-run, of course) closed in 1967. The community has its matzoh for Passover, its kosher flour produced at a special mill as a state enterprise, and its two kosher slaughterhouses. One wonders if they would meet any religious standard. The center of the living community seems to be an old cafeteria or a soup kitchen. Most people sitting there are over sixty and the food is simple, good, and kosher. They all seem to be seeking companionship, not in the freezing or steaming synagogue, but in the cafeteria.

The gravedigger at the cemetery said he was the president of the Jewish community and that we should come down to the synagogue. He gave us directions. Perhaps he *was* the president of the Jewish community. He told us that there were 1,000 Jews left in Warsaw. We went looking for a synagogue in a square, but all we could find was a large Catholic church. Assuming that the priests there would know the location of the synagogue, we asked them in Polish and in German. When the first four walked away from us, we decided to count and see how long it would take. We asked fourteen priests where to find the synagogue and from not one did we get an answer. They all turned on their heels and walked away from us. It must be the wrong question to ask a Catholic cleric in Warsaw.

Who knows how many Jews remain? They say one body goes to the cemetery every week but no one remembers a birth or a Jewish marriage. A man in the Historical Institute said, "Anyway, who is a Jew?" He suggested that only the keeper of the cemetery knows, and he is probably right. The Poles believe all the Jews have left, but they disclaim any responsibility for the exodus. In discussing the 1968 purge, Poles insist that the government

The famous desecrated Jewish Cemetery, Warsaw.

was not after the Jews but only the Zionists. They do admit, though, that the government might not have been able to tell the difference.

But then the single most important place or monument for someone like me in all of Europe is the Jewish cemetery on Genzia Street. During the war it stood at the end of the ghetto, actually outside the walls, and was reached by a wooden bridge. It was a huge cemetery then and had housed dead Jews for centuries. It became a center of smuggling, resistance, and death. It stands right next to the Catholic cemetery; in fact, the two cemeteries are joined by one large wall, and both are several blocks square. The Catholic cemetery is beautifully attended. Across the narrow wall, however, the Jewish bodies rest in a jungle: probably the most terribly desecrated, lonely, ruined, isolated, and overgrown burial ground that exists anywhere in Europe. Its size, its vastness, and its junglelike atmosphere drive home forcefully the fact that Poland is *Judenrein.* Not only are there no more Jews to bury in the cemetery, but there are no Jews left to visit the graves, to care for them, right in the heart of what was the largest center of Judaism in the world. I spent many hours there on a summer afternoon walking down one path after another, pushing bushes and debris aside. But much of it is impenetrable. The paths are overgrown. There is evidence of age and abuse, yes, but also

"The Jews of Poland Are No More," Jewish Cemetery, Warsaw.

something more. The Hebrew tombstones are green with age and they lean in all directions. Some are topped by the roots of trees; others have been knocked down and broken by desecrators and graverobbers. At least half the graveyard has been totally desecrated and broken up, probably looted years ago. The ground is mossy and wet, and if one walks over it, many times it will open and one falls into the hole below. I stood there, knowing I was surrounded by the history of a dead people in a land where the natives allowed them to die and to bury their dead, but never to live in peace, or even to live.

The tombstones are a proud tradition and they speak of struggle and agony. In the less ruined part of the cemetery there are some newer graves, but not very many. I am told that occasionally a body is carried in, followed by a small group of mourners. Some of the bodies are just brought in without any mourners. There are no rabbis to read the service, so a member of the community must. Sometimes there is just the gravedigger to bury the body. Soon there will be no one left to do that.[1]

One gravedigger digs the grave. He is a little old man and one always finds him down in the hole with a shovel. When he finished one afternoon that I was sitting there, he went back to a little building and came out dressed in an old brown suit, carrying a briefcase. He smiled and offered his gnarled hand. I got up from the edge of Ber Mark's grave. He asked me if I was Jewish. We spoke in German and I said no. He asked me why I had been there so very long and I told him I was thinking. He smiled and talked about the Warsaw Jewish community. As its president, he was very proud, he said, that there were still some Jews left, but he was worried. He apologized for the condition of the cemetery but explained that there was no one left to help. He also was aware of the contrast with the Catholic cemetery next door and he understood its meaning.

Such was Poland. Epitomized by that startling never-to-be-forgotten cemetery jungle that makes its point far more clearly than any camp monument. Done. Finished. Over. The Polish Jews. Gone.

PART THREE

THE INDIFFERENT, THE SLAUGHTERERS, THE STRUGGLERS

A FEW QUESTIONS

The time comes at the end of a long journey through the Holocaust to reidentify the major questions. How was it possible for a civilized modern state to carry out the systematic step-by-step face-to-face humiliation, degradation, deportation, and then murder of massive numbers of ordinary-acting and ordinary-looking citizens in their midst simply because in some precise, yet absurdly defined manner, they were Jews? How was it possible that in most countries taken over by Germany, attached to it, made satellite to it, or pulled into treaties with it, the citizens, the state—regardless of how far removed from Berlin, the center of Final Solution planning, or from Auschwitz, the center of Final Solution implementation—picked up with alacrity and excitement the imported ideas of vermin exorcism, and, in fact, performed that exorcism in many instances with far greater speed, efficiency, and thoroughness than even the mother state, sometimes with such gusto that *Hitler himself* had to caution against excesses of enthusiasm?

How was it possible for Allied nations that proclaimed they were fighting to save democracy and to preserve Western civilization together with a group of self-righteous neutral nations to ignore the Final Solution, when they *knew* from 1935 of the degradation of the Jewish Germans, and from 1940 had precise and extensive information about the concentration camps? How was it possible for them to remain silent, and to speak publicly only to the subject of the postwar punishment which would await the perpetrators? How was it possible for the *St. Louis* to sail unwanted by the ports of these nations; for the Evian Conference in Switzerland to result in a *total increase in Jewish quotas from these nations of 5,000*; for the doors of these nations to remain closed to Jewish emigration—even of doomed Jewish children? How was it possible for Great Britain, which had created the idea of a Jewish homeland in Palestine, to renege on its commitment, and then to blow up the boats carrying those pitiful few Jews who had somehow managed to escape the concentration camps of Europe only to die in the waters off Palestine or to be washed ashore on the beaches and then interned in Cyprus?

How was it possible for the Polish Government-in-Exile in London (with British support) to drop arms to the Poles with the proviso that none be given to Jewish resistance fighters or the Warsaw ghetto defenders—because "it was known Jews could not fight" and the guns would be wasted on a lost cause? How was it possible that the tracks to Auschwitz remained unbombed even in 1944—the tracks over which the 400,000 Hungarian Jews traveled to their cremation in the last months of the war? How was it possible that the military units of these nations operating under fully informed generals arrived at the camps as rescue teams without proper food, medicine, doctors, or Jewish chaplains, so that at least 60,000 camp inmates had to die *after* liberation?

How was it possible that the knowledgeable leaders of the major world churches, particularly the German bishops and even more seriously the Vatican, failed to make a committed effort to aid the Jews but comforted themselves instead with platitudinous expressions about their "sorrow" and "prayers for all victims"? How was it possible for the Vatican to identify, until 1945, Bolshevism as the real peril, to meet with the killers and give papal audiences to the most spirited exorcists of all—the Catholic priest-leaders of Croatia and their priest SS men who led the massive gorge-dumpings of Jews in Serbia, and to support the Polish Catholic pogromists "in their travail" as they responded to the Warsaw ghetto burning on their Sunday after-church walks with such comments as: "It is good that the Germans are taking care of this problem for us"?

How was it possible for a heterogeneous people of all nationalities, languages, religions, classes, cultures, tied together by a grandfather clause and faced with a new phenomenon in human history—a Final Solution—to so consistently and constantly attach themselves to life? How was it possible for a powerless, humiliated diverse group which, like the rest of the world, underestimated the threat of National Socialism to expend enormous human and financial energy to gear itself up for the emergency, build morale, and organize self-help? How was it possible for a starving conglomeration of Jewish nationals crammed into ghettos designed to destroy to rally with energy, inventiveness, and optimism to face each day, usually with decency and fraternal solicitude, and exhibit a will to live that contrasted dramatically with the passivity and resignation characterizing the populations of most occupied countries and many prisoner-of-war camps? How was it possible for a ghetto people devoid of even the barest necessities to place a first priority on satisfying educational, cultural, and intellectual needs? And how was it possible for the group of Europeans with the very least opportunity to determine their fate to be so actively and constantly involved in resistance to the enemy?

Are there any answers to these questions? Possibly not. Perhaps one can only search; but it must be a search among human beings: the indifferent who saved lives, the indifferent who slaughtered, the strugglers who died, and the strugglers who lived. The indifferent, the slaughterers, the strugglers.

THE INDIFFERENT

From here we are driven out
And there we may not enter
Tell us, dear Father [in Heaven]
How long will this go on?

—Hassidic Folk Song[1]

The Allied participation in the Holocaust is the story of the contribution of vigorous international indifference to the death of large numbers of Jews and other undesirables. That activity makes the *indifferent*—the Allied and neutral nations—largescale contributors to the final death figures. Only two categories of countries existed for Jews: countries where they were forbidden to live and countries where they were forbidden to enter. The Jews, as a universal minority, had no national representation and protection. If a state revoked a Jew's citizenship or protection, he became an isolate. As a German-Jew or an Austrian-Jew, he stood out as a hyphenate a legal freak in international diplomacy. The true *noncitizen* of the world, he was ignored by the Allied nations, by those who professed a desire to *save* him.

Fear, deceit, insecurity, vacillation, and cruelty highlight America's response to the plight of the European Jews. From 1938 to 1945 America was not a haven for the oppressed. Her people never matched their condemnation of Nazi persecution with zealous activity on behalf of the victims. Roosevelt and his colleagues reacted to concerned requests for action with the shopworn rationalization that "we must put our energy into the war effort." In 1943 the military shipped more than 200,000 German and Italian POWs to America. But in that same year America admitted fewer than 5,000 Jewish immigrants. The War Department constructed 155 camps in 45 states to hold the 400,000 POWs, but bureaucrats worried about the cost of building a few refugee camps for Jews if any more were allowed to enter. America refused to take steps to rescue the Jews; and none of the twenty-eight nations fighting Nazism at her side deviated from her leadership.[2]

The basic question is a simple one: Were saving Jews and winning the war completely incompatible ends? The answer for a thoughtful person is a clear *no*. But the governments of the United States and Britain insisted they were and took no effective steps to mitigate Jewish suffering and to constrict the Final Solution process. They even went so far as to conceal their knowledge of Nazi atrocities against the Jews. The United States initiated no substantive measures to ensure that fleeing Jews had at least a temporary haven. And the Allies imposed no sanctions against Germany for the Final Solution.

Great Britain

In the 1930s British leadership, aware of the plight of the Jews, worried about "an unmanageable flood" of Jews into Britain if they opened the doors. Although Britain's prewar record toward Jewish immigration was "relatively generous"—about 50,000 Jews were admitted—her wartime record was as miserly as that of her allies.[3]

The British attitude derived in part from Britain's involvement in Palestine—a relationship that made the "Jewish question" a continual element in British politics, much more so than it was for her allies. Britain considered the Suez Canal her "jugular vein" and a highest-priority item. Between 1933–1935 the Jewish population in Palestine increased by 80 percent, from 192,000 to 355,000; and the Jews because 28 percent of the total population. Between 1933–1939 Jewish immigrants to Palestine numbered 215,000. The Arab reaction to that influx of Jews took the form of a long revolt that bled Britain's economy and diverted her military resources. Britain became both irritated and frightened by her "Achilles' heel." In wartime, she thought, her military strength depended on oil, the Suez Canal, and at least the neutrality of the Arab states.[4]

During the war the British government knew it had the automatic support of its Jewish citizens. Thus Jews were of no political interest. Britain felt free to lead the fight against illegal immigration to Palestine and to seal off the escape routes from Europe—thus ensuring the fate of the Jews. Most important, during and after the war British policy refused to recognize Jews as a distinct entity, but insisted instead on grouping and treating them as nationals from their country of origin.

So Britain maintained a consistent policy of limiting Jewish emigration from Europe to appease the Arabs in return for their wartime support. To the British, appropriate wartime policy necessitated considering the extermination of millions of Jews (whom the upper-class British leaders did not much care for anyway) as a side issue that must not be allowed to interfere with the thrust of British action.

Anthony Eden in December 1942, speaking as the secretary for foreign affairs, tersely informed the House of Commons of Hitler's implementation of his intention to exterminate the Jews of Europe. Governmental response was brutal. For example, in January 1943 a government document sent to the U.S. State Department regarding refugee policy recognized the following "complicating factors":

(a) The refugee problem cannot be treated as though it were a wholly Jewish problem. . . . There are so many non-Jewish refugees and there is so much acute suffering among non-Jews in Allied countries that Allied criticism would probably result if any marked preference were shown in removing Jews from territories in enemy occupation. There is also the distinct danger of stimulating anti-Semitism in areas where an excessive number of foreign Jews are introduced.

(b) There is at present always a danger of raising false hopes among refugees by suggesting or announcing alternative possible destinations in excess of shipping probabilities.

(c) There is a possibility that the Germans or their satellites may change over from the policy of extermination to one of extrusion, and aim as they did before the war at embarrassing other countries by flooding them with alien immigrants.[5]

Throughout the war British policy remained firm and undeviating: placation of the Arabs by blocking or limiting both Jewish emigration and immigration. True, Britain could not have stopped the Holocaust nor could it have prevented the death of a significant percentage of Jews. But to firmly refuse to save some because of an irrational fear of a flood of "alien immigrants" evidences an indifference, a distaste for Jews, an attitude best exemplified by Anthony Eden—"he loves Arabs and hates Jews." It is that *attitude* that helps to explain the British government's persistent refusal to persuade British colonies and possessions to open their doors; to involve itself in any Axis deals to save the Jews; to help Jewish orphans; to allow the formation of a Jewish fighting force; to approve retributive bombing of Germany; to agree to massive propaganda warfare emphasizing the atrocities against the Jews; to bomb the camps; and to provide the same kind of food and medical rescue help readily made available to the Gentiles of Europe.[6]

The attitude in the military and civil service stiffened to such a degree that the prime minister's orders to bomb Auschwitz or to aid Jews were simply not implemented. In spite of Winston Churchill's repeated efforts to push his government to help the Jews, British official responses to the Jews can be characterized by insensitivity, callousness, distrust, distaste, animosity, hysteria, and, yes, hatred.

The United States

In dealing with the difficult problem of Jewish persecution between 1933 and 1939, President Roosevelt attempted the impossible: to demonstrate strong disapproval of Germany's actions while at the same time protecting and strengthening America's economic interests abroad. The State Department responded with words of sympathy to the constant demands from representative Jewish groups for official American protests to Germany. Secretary of State Hull, a proper Wilsonian, assumed that in the early 1930s, as in the past, American intervention would only make matters worse for the German Jews. Deluded by the belief that correct diplomacy and noninterference in internal affairs would give conservatives in the Nazi government the time they needed to moderate German policy toward the Jews, the State Department restrained public demonstrations of opposition to Germany.

The American Jewish community split over the issue. The American Jewish Committee and B'nai B'rith struggled with the American Jewish Congress, which, under the leadership of Rabbi Wise, desired to take action in the form of mass protest meetings and boycotts. When Hjalmar Schacht, president of the German Reichsbank, visited the United States, he informed Jewish leaders that outside pressure could only harm the German Jews. In the middle of 1935, however, when the futility of American restraint had become evident, the State Department withdrew its opposition to public criticism of Germany. When Germany seized Austria, relations worsened; and 1939 brought a turning point, the Crystal Night, causing Washington to reconsider its policy of official silence. Informal diplomacy had failed to help the Jews.

If the Allies, particularly the United States, had simply remained passive, more Jews would have been saved. But by their vigorous indifference they actually sabotaged rescue plans proposed before the eruption of the war. Obviously, the raising of immigration quotas would have been helpful during the period when Germany was eager to expel her Jews. To probe that possibility, Roosevelt catalyzed the infamous Evian Conference in Switzerland in 1938, which was supposed to deal with the problems of refugees. It was doomed to failure because few countries would agree to admit additional refugees, particularly penniless Jews, who were unwelcome everywhere.[7]

In 1937 the German government inaugurated a plan to exploit the Jews by holding out the prospect that they could be ransomed, but still Latin America and Britain did not open their doors. A search began for areas suitable for mass colonization—British Guiana, Madagascar, Ethiopia, and Angola—to no avail. The United States urged other nations to open their colonial territories to refugees, but it refused to set an example by opening the Philippines and Alaska.[8] Both the British Foreign Office and the American State Department knew that the Germans could be bribed, but the Allies would not pay the cheap price: from $2 to $10 for a human life. A few million dollars would have redeemed hundreds of thousands of children. The Allies said they had no money, no personnel, and no place to put the children. Thus it seems incontrovertible that Allied lethargy encouraged the Germans to believe that their diabolical method of dealing with the Jews had strong underlying support in the rest of the world.

Roosevelt's policy between 1933 and 1938 did nothing to ease entry into the United States. During that period 45,940 quota immigrants from Germany entered, two-thirds of them Jews. But the German quota *on an annual basis* was 25,957! By the end of 1941 only 104,000 Germans had immigrated to the United States; 75 percent of them could be classified Jews. The official restrictionist policy reflected American public opinion.

The Wagner-Rogers Bill, introduced in February of 1939, authorized the admission, beyond the quota, of 20,000 German refugee children under age fourteen for a two-year period. Openly aimed at rescuing Jewish children, the bill made the children's admission contingent upon the receipt of written guarantees pledging financial support from relief agencies or foster parents— pledges that the government received. Although it was supported by powerful political, religious, and civic groups, the bill met with formidable opposition in Congress. Groups such as the American Legion opposed it, clouded the issues, and developed a mass hate campaign. In their propaganda they went so far as to assert that the bill would assist Jews who were known to be mental deficients and Communist infiltrators.

As a theologian has pondered, was there much difference between the murderers of those children and those who refused to save them?

Can one think of a more hypocritical reason for not saving children from persecution and death than the one put forward by the American Legion that "it was traditional American policy that home life should be preserved and that the American Legion, therefore, strongly opposes the breaking up of families, which would be done by the proposed legislation."[9]

Those Americans somehow felt more moral than those cruel Jewish parents who would part with their children rather than take them with them to the camps. And one congressman, Carl Mundt, argued against the Wagner-Rogers Bill because granting special privileges to one group violated the American way of life. The president took no public position on the bill. The Senate Immigration Committee reported it out on June 30, 1939, with a crippling amendment charging the 20,000 to the quota. It failed to pass.

The outbreak of World War II immediately altered the situation—all refugee questions were viewed strictly in light of war objectives. The Allies believed that military needs prevented any "further" international action to save the Jews.

America and Britain shamefully contributed to the Final Solution by their grim actions in the well-known *Sturma* and *St. Louis* incidents. The British conferred the death penalty on the *Sturma* passengers when they denied the ship access to Palestine. The American President and his State Department cleared the way for certain death for the *St. Louis* refugees when they denied them sanctuary. For two weeks while the *St. Louis* first sailed by the Florida coast and then waited hopelessly in Havana Harbor for help, headlines in *The New York Times* blazoned the hideous story:

700 JEWISH REFUGEES AWAIT FATE OFF CUBA

UNABLE TO LAND IN CUBA, REFUGEE TRIES SUICIDE

FEAR SUICIDE WAVE ON REFUGEES' SHIP

RUMOR THAT US WILL PERMIT ENTRY TO AVERT SUICIDES

REFUGEE SHIP IDLES OFF FLORIDA COAST

HAVEN STILL SOUGHT FOR 907 ON ST. LOUIS

The Secretary of State withstood the pressure to grant asylum to people whose forced return to Germany meant certain death. With great patriotic conviction, he said: "I took an oath to protect the flag and obey the laws of my country and you are asking me to break those laws."[10]

Throughout the war the Allied governments steadfastly refused to issue an official condemnation of the Final Solution. They stifled, whenever they could, significant rescue proposals and attempts. It seemed as though the "soul had gone out of the majority of the Western nations." Perhaps most important, they took no action to disrupt the flow of prisoners to the extermination plants and the operation of those plants. The Nazis joked about it: "The safest way to get vital military transports to the front was to put some Jews in them and write on the cars in large letters: This is a Jew transport to the extermination camp. Thus it was sure not to be molested by the Allies."[11]

And then the British closed Palestine. The British White Paper of 1939 fixed the Jewish national home in Palestine at permanent minority status by limiting Jewish immigration to a maximum of 75,000 up to May 31, 1944, or 15,000 a year, and thereafter suspended immigration altogether unless the Arabs consented to its continuance.

Washington preferred to postpone consideration of the Palestine problem until the war's end, but the Zionists challenged that reluctance. The State Department saw Zionists as harmful to American Middle East policy. In 1943 the British warned Washington that Zionist agitation in America "constituted a danger to the Allied war effort." The members of the World Zionist Executive met in an extraordinary assembly in New York in the Biltmore Hotel on May 9–11, 1944, to devise a plan of action. The Biltmore Program condemned the British White Paper and demanded that Palestine be constituted a Jewish commonwealth and opened to unrestricted Jewish immigration and settlement.[12]

The Zionists knew how unfavorably the State Department and the White House viewed their position on Palestine, but they continued to press their cause. In 1944 a bipartisan resolution was introduced in both Houses of Congress in support of free entry of Jews into Palestine and its ultimate constitution as a Jewish commonwealth. Seeing the overwhelming support in the Congress for the resolution, the State Department turned to the War Department to provide adequate military reasons or excuses. The War Department reluctantly testified that a high degree of tension existed in Palestine and that military need required peaceful conditions. It would be much better, said one of the testifiers, if we "let sleeping dogs lie." Congress then shelved the resolution.[13]

Because of the efforts of American Zionists, in the summer of 1944 both the Democrats and the Republicans adopted a plank supporting a Jewish commonwealth in Palestine in their party platforms. The reelection of Roosevelt raised the spirits and hopes of the Zionists, for Roosevelt had pledged to implement the commonwealth concept as soon as practicable. When, however, Congress moved to reconsider the Palestine resolutions, the State

Department interfered again with the claim that the war situation had so changed that Roosevelt's statement of support was no longer viable. But had anything changed so radically between October 15 and December 6? At the international level, no. But the political scene had indeed changed. The president could ignore his pledges following his successful presidential campaign.

The vigorously indifferent informed the American Jews that rescue attempts would surely undermine the war effort. A speedy Allied victory was the only way to help, they scolded. Sensitive to the ugly charges of nonpatriotism thrown around so easily in the war climate, American Jews found themselves in a delicate position. If rescue efforts would seriously interfere with Allied war aims, how could they press for energetic lifesaving efforts? Rabbi Wise raised a gentle question to the politicians: "What would victory mean to the dead?" His logic was ignored. But other fundamental questions emerged.

What was the effect of Allied disinterest on the captive peoples of Europe who might shelter the oppressed at the risk of their own lives . . . or on axis troops weighing the commission of atrocities . . . or on churchmen in German-occupied lands, wrestling with their consciences . . . or on German commanders contemplating their own futures?[14]

Concerned Americans flooded Washington with proposals to help the Jews. They suggested a direct appeal to the Nazis to release the Jews; the suspension of immigration quotas and the relaxation of the Allied blockade; the shipment of food and clothing to the camps in emulation of the Danish program; and the catalization of the American Red Cross. But Washington remained asleep and lost important opportunities to save some Jews.

According to the Morgenthau Report, State Department officials not only used governmental machinery to prevent the rescue of the Jews but failed to cooperate with private organizations in their efforts to implement nongovernmental aid as well. The department even tried to halt the programs already worked out by the organizations. Not only did they fail to facilitate the obtaining of information concerning the extermination of the Jews, but they suppressed the information they received. The officials concealed, misrepresented, and gave false information. Morgenthau's report to the President ended:

The matter of rescuing the Jews from extermination is a trust too great to remain in the hands of men who are indifferent, callous, and perhaps even hostile. The task is filled with difficulties. Only a fervent will to accomplish, backed by persistent and untiring effort, can succeed where time is so precious.[15]

On January 22, 1944 the President responded to Morgenthau's report by establishing the War Refugee Board. By then, most Jews were dead.

The Allied leaders single-mindedly upheld the principle that the best way to save the Jews was by a general victory. The contradictions of that approach leap forward. One example: the Allies in April 1944 bombed the rubber works 7 kilometers from Birkenau, and in July they bombed the town of Auschwitz, 3 kilometers from Birkenau, but took no action against the smoking fires of the crematorium. Another example: the State Department claimed as an obstacle to rescuing the Jews a shortage of ships, but U.S. troop transports to Europe and ships bearing food to Greece often returned empty.

Saul Friedman, a specialist on American policy toward Jews, notes that President Roosevelt could have ordered reprisals against German-Americans as he did against the Japanese—and with more cause. He could have threatened that America would use gas in Germany. He could have ordered the bombing of crematoria and railroad tracks. He could have thrown his prestige behind a demand for the lowering of immigration barriers. One might suppose he could have simply said: "We know, and we will avenge you."[16] As one survivor asked me: "Couldn't he have done something?"

Hitler declared war against the Jews. The evidence is plain enough that the Allies rejected entrapment in that war by refusing to acknowledge its existence. In a sense, they declared themselves neutral in the Jew War, took no compromising stands, refused to separate the Jews from the general group of war victims, and escaped the odious image of Jew-savers.

The lives of the European Jews had been written off by the time of Pearl Harbor. Any later action in their behalf was considered pathetic, a waste of effort. The leaders and the citizens of the Allied nations, in one of the most painful errors of the twentieth century, gave up on the Jewish strugglers, but those people did not give up on themselves.

Shanghai: The Anti-Semites Who Saved Jews

While the countries of Europe were trying to eliminate the Jews, while the Allies and neutrals exerted energy to keep them out of sight and mind, one nation began a lifesaving operation—Japan. That strange story born of absurdity, myth, fear, arrogance, and misunderstanding can only be told here in brief. It is a story of Hitler's only ally who did not share his dream of *Judenrein*. The Japanese made it possible for 18,000 German and Polish Jews to survive the war in the only place left open to them in the world— Shanghai. Japan became a "miniature and short-lasted Open Gate, a small but significant exception in the history of the Closed Gate Period."[17]

The Japanese policy goes back to the late 1920s and early 1930s when a few energetic Japanese officers became "Jewish experts" after reading and accepting as fact such anti-Semitic forgeries as the *Protocols of Zion*. They believed in the economic conspiracy claim and concluded that Japan could either be destroyed by it, like every other country, or use it to her advantage. Those experts actually believed that Jews controlled finance, the media, and politics in America and Britain. They thought the Jews, intent on creating a world empire, "were so wealthy and powerful that they controlled and manipulated governments at will." Although anti-Semitic, the Japanese were strangers to the Christian tradition that associated Jew and devil and necessitated elimination. They thought they could harness Jewish wealth and power to their own ends. Japanese policy toward the Jews evolved from indifference to "marked friendliness" (1931–1935), to pro-Jewish developments (1936–1938), to an Era of Good Will (1939–Pearl Harbor), and finally to hostility during the war years. But never did Japanese anti-Semitism reach Nazi extremism. Japan's single purpose was to utilize international Jews in her own best interests and to tap American capital.[18]

The so-called Fugu Plan centered on enrolling the talent/skills of European Jewry and the capital/influence/sympathy of American Jews in building Japan's Greater East Asian Co-Prosperity Sphere. In exchange, Japan would offer a safe haven. Although Japan's Fugu Plan was based on gross misunderstanding and a form of anti-Semitism, it saved 18,000 Jews.[19]

Not a very appealing place to European Jews, the Shanghai of 1938, nevertheless, was an open city requiring no visa—the only such place in the world. Although Shanghai was 11,000 kilometers from Germany in an alien Oriental environment, it seemed more attractive to many Jews than a concentration camp. Immigration began in 1933 and tapered off in 1939. Initially the Shanghai Sephardic and Russian Jewish communities responded generously to relief needs. Later they relied financially on the American Joint Distribution Committee.

In 1939 fear and hysteria gripped the old Shanghai Jewish community. It was certain it could not absorb the influx of immigrants in the future; and the severe housing shortage exacerbated a fear of economic competition. The Jewish community clamored for restrictive action from the Japanese with such energy that it "took on the character of a universal conspiracy to prevent further immigration from Germany (and Poland) of thousands of potential refugees." Sir Victor Sasson, president of the Jewish Community and Shanghai's leading Jew, promised the Japanese that the Closed Door would not result in widespread international Jewish opposition. Heeding the pleas of the Shanghai Jews, America, France, and Britain applied pressure to halt the flight of the Jews from Germany. Japan closed the door on August 9, 1939.[20]

After Pearl Harbor the Japanese occupied Shanghai and Jewish life changed radically. The American Joint Distribution Committee responded to their plight by cutting off all funds, thus going even further than the law demanded to avoid "trading with the enemy." To the shock and dismay of the

Shanghai Jews, the Joint made no significant contacts between 1942 and 1943. Reacting to Nazi pressure, the Japanese created a ghetto in February 1943 and installed a Japanese official *ghoya* as "King of the Jews." Even at his worst moment, however, he neither shot a Jew nor ordered anyone shot.

The Shanghai immigrant Jews reacted as they did in the other ghettos by setting up a "culture amid want," developing a religious, educational, and communal life. The Joint, in December 1943, breathed life and hope into the ghetto with renewed funding—enabling the Shanghai Jews to survive the war.

Knowing versus Knowing

The question of knowing arises repeatedly: Did they know of the Final Solution? Did the Jews know, the Poles, the Germans, the Allies? How could they not have known? If they knew and did nothing, then perhaps they can be charged with a crime. If they did not know, then the focus shifts to the success of SS secrecy. As with most important matters, simple answers are attractive, but they hardly improve our understanding. What is knowing for an ordinary person, a leader, a Gentile, a Jew? Because human beings hear and read about ugly things, do they then know? "Not wanting to know," a philosopher reminds us, "always means knowing enough to know that one doesn't want to know more."[21] At the very least, we can agree that considerable information was available to Jews, the German people, and the citizens and leaders of the Allied nations. But research shows that groups of people respond to information with different mechanisms, and their basic reasons vary.

What we can say, I think, is that the Allies and their peoples possessed all the information about the Holocaust they could possibly need to act. Before action is possible, however, people must accept the information as fact. Information became fact in American minds by 1944. Most Jews were already dead. To save the Jews, or a portion of them, demanded more than the possession of information, more than accepting the information as fact, more than knowing becoming *knowing*. It demanded nothing less than the mobilization of the American spirit. That spirit had been mobilized before with less time, less threat, less information, and less horror. But in this instance America's spirit would not be mobilized. Why? Perhaps because America had its own suffering to deal with. We can never underestimate the chilling hold the Great Depression had over America's mind and spirit. Her frozen spirit created a wall of active indifference that was not breached during the war with regard to the Jews. It was too soon. One suspects it was virtually impossible for the American people—imbued as they were with a low-level pervasive anti-Semitism—to move in less than a decade from general negativity to sacrifice *for* the Jews.[22]

Liberation

After liberation the Allied attitude toward the Jews continued. Out of Washington came the policy that surviving Jews should remain in Europe, and that policy was zealously enforced by General Eisenhower, who ordered the DPs to return to their place of origin. Roosevelt ignored the particularly Jewish nature of the refugee problem—a precedent set earlier by London. In 1945 he told King Ibn Saud of Saudi Arabia: "The Germans appear to have killed 3,000,000 Polish Jews, by which count there should be space in Poland for the resettlement of many homeland Jews." After returning from his meeting with Saud, the president informed Congress of an unusual insight: "Of the problems of Arabia, I learned more about the whole problem, the Muslim problem, the Jewish problem, by talking with Ibn Saud for five minutes than I could have learned in an exchange of two or three dozen letters."[23]

The Allies liberated the camps and gave the survivors food and medicine, but they told them to be grateful and not to push to the head of the line. When the Jews objected to the barbed wire and German guards, the liberators reacted by calling them insolent. And here and there people were heard to say it was a pity that Hitler had not finished off the job. They told the Jews that it was their duty to stay and help in the rebuilding of Germany and Poland, the countries that had destroyed them. Palestine was to remain a forbidden land. The Jews tried to leave in leaky vessels, but the Royal Navy watched the sea and blew the boats out of the water.

The nations of Europe did not welcome back the liberated Jews. In country after country the leaders and the people made no secret of their hatred and disdain. Pogroms and murders erupted in Poland. Finally rid of the Jews, many Poles vehemently protested any efforts to bring them back. On September 14, 1945, Leopold Kunschak, president of the Austrian parliament, in a public speech attested to his undeviating anti-Semitism. The Jews, he said, had been responsible for all of Austria's troubles. A year after liberation, "students of the University of Vienna (where the Jewish enrollment was 20 of a total student body of 8,000) staged an anti-Semitic demonstration and a 'welcome home' party for a professor who had been a known Nazi." In March 1946 Jewish spectators at a soccer game were attacked, amidst shouts from the crowds: "Throw the Jews into the gas chambers."[24]

The attitudes of the Allies and of the German population carried over into the subsequent War Crime Trials (or lack of), and the imprisonment of former killers (or lack of). The camp strugglers had united in their misery on one conviction—that the victorious nations would move swiftly to punish those who had created and those who had aided and abetted in the slaughter. Perhaps their assumption of vindication was naive. Perhaps they granted the world a compassion, a steadiness of purpose, and a clarity of insight it had never possessed and could never engender. But clearly the strugglers who survived were unprepared for the disinterest, disdain, and downright hatred they encountered. And they were stunned by the light sentences many of their tormentors received and the reemergence into public and corporate life of officials and industrialists who had played such a large part in the Final Solution.[25]

So much has been written of the struggles of survivors to put their lives together while accommodating the experiences and pictures from the camps. Dita Saxova in Arnost Lustig's novel "found herself judging people by whether or not she would want to be in the camps with them." She and her friends soon realized that those ugly memories were no protection "in the slightest against what still lies ahead." Impressed with "the enormity of their desecration," some experienced a "victim's shame at being victimized." "The years have passed," a survivor quietly muses, "and I have not been comforted." Normality seemed to escape the grasp of one who explained: "To love you need life and we had only death between us." Jack Eisner, in his memoir speaks of being haunted:

I am never truly alone. Thousands of people are always with me. My head is so crowded with ghosts I sometimes think it will burst. My ears ring with cries from the voices of the dead. My dreams flame with horror. My memories are gray with ash. I am a survivor.

In one of Elie Wiesel's novels Michael, a young man and a camp survivor, returns to his native country and his home. He walks past a square where, a decade before, Jewish men, women, and children were brutally herded together and shipped off to the death camps. He remembers having looked up and seen the face of a man at a window staring with indifference at the agony beneath him. Ten years later Michael finds that same house and enters. He meets the owner of the face and confronts him: the man remembers well and is still indifferent. Michael concludes:

Finally! Everything was clear, stark. There, then, was the reason, the *real* reason, the reason behind all the other reasons. . . . This, this was the thing I had wanted to understand ever since the war. Nothing else. How a human being can remain indifferent. The executioners I understood; also the victims, though with more difficulty. For the others, all the others, those who were neither for nor against, . . . those who were permanently and merely spectators—all those were closed to me, incomprehensible.[26]

THE SLAUGHTERERS

For centuries it has been assumed that ordinary people are basically decent. For that reason historians have found it extremely difficult to view the Nazis as ordinary people. What they did seemed to negate human nature. But the Nazis claimed normality. Though they may have believed in their arrogance that they should win the "best of breed" prize as the most advanced of the Aryans, they saw themselves as logical, sane human beings. Their actions, they assured themselves, came not from sadism or perversion (concepts with which they were familiar), but from the logic of the situation in which they found themselves. They looked at what men had done in the past and at what nations and people were doing in the present; and they concluded that they acted no worse than others, that they were victims of social forces and currents set in motion by others. In the 1930s the rulers of the European democracies were convinced that Adolf Hitler was a respectable man who desired peace, someone with whom they could deal. Ordinary Germans placed their trust in him. Prominent citizens of the democracies visited with Hitler and his staff, toured the country, and returned extolling the German "miracle." They read his books and his speeches, but dismissed his unrelenting theme of destruction as political propaganda. And then Hitler and his people unleashed a fury of devastation upon the world. In the case of the Jews, Hitler allowed the democracies the opportunity to be saviors if they so chose. The Pope, the American president, the British prime minister, and the world's leaders did not elect to be Jew-savers, so Hitler became a Jew-killer. Is there any connection between the two acts? Of course.

There must be some *reason,* some unusual circumstance, that triggered the Holocaust, else are we to believe that unrestrained violence is a given for the future? If we can understand in at least a shadowy way the slaughterer, perhaps the complementary figure—the vigorous nonactivist—will be more explicable. Clearly, bases do exist from which to gain an insight into the Final Solution. Because it was, in fact, not final, and because it did not solve anything for anyone, it is worth probing into the complex interrelated structure of the mutually interdependent contributors. That journey is a double-faced coin, for while it reveals a fearful side of midnight, it also overwhelms with an explosive magnificence. The probing must begin with theological anti-Semitism and the myth of deicide.

The Anti-Semitic Base

Since the time of Christ, institutionalized Christendom has flooded the Western world with diatribes against the Jews, insisting at a minimum that Jews do not deserve and must not receive equal human treatment; and at the most that they are subhuman or nonhuman and ought to disappear either as individuals or as a cultural group or both from the face of the earth. For centuries the Christian Church taught its captive audiences to picture the Jew in a consistently negative manner: as Christ-killer, agent of the devil, profaner of the Host, powermonger, member of an evil worldwide conspiracy, bloodsucker drawing off the lifeblood of nations, magician, and communist. In the Middle Ages hatred of Jews became a fundamental doctrine, and oppression of them a sacred duty. The least one could say is that over the centuries it is not possible to find one fully positive or accepting statement from the institutionalized Church regarding the Jews.

Only exceptionally wise and mature human beings seem to be immune to the strong infantile fears and hatreds to which such striking myths appeal, particularly in times of exceptional strain or disorientation. The strongest people wonder if they could withstand the pressures of what is now known as "brainwashing." Most humans intellectually understand the danger of constant exposure to one-sided propaganda. Yet few wish to recognize the simple notion that 2,000 years of continuous negative, emotionally charged images paved the way for the indifference to, acceptance of, and even enthusiasm for the Nazi War against the Jews. The primitive, vicious Nazi propaganda did not appear to appall the sensibilities of the civilized world. The world's leaders were not crushed by the sheer knowledge of what was taking place, as Elie Wiesel would say.[27]

It would be difficult to assert rationally that the complex anti-Semitic superdome constructed so carefully over the centuries created the Final Solution. Cause-and-effect is never, unfortunately, that simple. But that superstructure did indeed render the Germans numb and desensitized when their acceptance and participation were requested. Theological anti-Semitism did create a social and moral climate energetically receptive to the Final Solution, and it did prepare the civilized world to react with hardened and righteous indifference. In the most moderate view, the Nazi assault upon the Jews did not erupt in a vacuum. It came steadily and patiently out of 2,000 years of animosity and hatred actively cultivated by Christianity. "Theologically, legally, and culturally Christianity had effectively rendered the Jews hateful." Thus when the Nazis excoriated the Jews, they did not have to be inventive. They only had to reach into an old reservoir of Church teachings, papal pronouncements, pulpit sermons, Jesuit writings.[28]

While the anti-Jewish myth had its origin in ancient times, it gained momentum in Christian antiquity. It was the early Church fathers who proposed the theme of the Jew as Satan's agent, and that theme inspired the persecutions and massacres of the Jews that ran all through medieval history. Through the teachings of Christian theology, the conviction that the Jews have no right to exist as Jews became woven into the intellectual and emotional fabric of the Western world—in every country, every century, then and now. In a range of languages—English, French, German, Spanish, Italian, Russian, Bulgarian, Polish, and Hungarian—the ministers of God's work on earth have reviled the Jews from their pulpits for more than a thousand years. The Christian determined to make the world more Christian. The Jew never thought of making the world more Jewish, only more human, so that he and the oppressed minorities and classes might remain alive in it.

It has long been evident that greater emphasis must be placed upon the concept of deicide, or the Jewish crime of killing the major religious figure of the Western world—Christ, the Son of God and the Son of Man. Even those of us in postwar middle America who grew up in the Christian Church, whether Catholic, Lutheran, Presbyterian, Baptist, knew that the Jews killed Christ. Every year we mourned that crime on Good Friday, in a symbolic yearly funeral service, preceded by the Lenten weeks of reminders and fasting. The intensity of reaction to the deed has surely decreased, but the mythical knowledge remains. It is in our bones. It is a most serious matter for one's God to die, and it is even more distressing that He should be killed, regardless of whether He arose again. A mature person, with assistance and encouragement, can discard those kinds of intense myths so that they no longer operate as an active element in his life. But he must know enough to do this, and he must wish to. It is unlikely that most of Christendom in the 1930s and 1940s knew or wished to.

The popular tradition of deicide finds little justification in the New Testament. Saints Matthew, Mark, and Luke made clear that their people— the Jews—were unaware of the crime and were not responsible for it. As one writing from outside the Jewish world, however, St. John repeatedly used the phrase "the Jews" in his gospel. Although he emphasized that the Roman soldiers, not the Jews, crucified Christ, in his story about the trial he laid responsibility on the Jewish people. Biblical scholars have suggested that St. John made use of the phrase "the Jews" to avoid repeating the words "high priests and Pharisees." Whatever may have been his reasons, from that time, the Christian Church conferred the crime of a few priests and elders and Roman officials and soldiers on the entire Jewish people, and its literature consolidated the theme.

Throughout the centuries, Christians have treated the Jews as though they were of another species. To justify persecution, they claimed self-defense, or they maintained they were carrying out God's will. The early church fathers made an enormous contribution. The mighty St. Ambrose told his congregations that the Jewish synagogue had been condemned by God himself. As a result, the people of his congregation went out and set fire to one. In the fourth century St. Gregory of Nyssa composed against the Jews a comprehensive indictment:

Slayers of the Lord, murderers of the prophets, adversaries of God, haters of God, men who show contempt for the law, foes of grace, enemies of their father's faith, advocates of the devil, brood of vipers, slanderers, scoffers, men whose minds are in darkness, leaven of the Pharisees, assembly of demons, sinners, wicked men, stoners, and haters of righteousness.[29]

A leading Church father, St. John Chrysostom was known as a compassionate reformer. Called a bright, gentle soul with a sensitive heart by Cardinal Newman, St. John preached a doctrine of hatred that has seldom been duplicated; and the violence of his language has never been exceeded in any recorded sermons. St. John informed his congregants that Jews were possessed by evil spirits and that they were habitual murderers, destroyers, robbers, and assassins of Christ. All were guilty, every single one of them. God had punished them and that punishment would last forever. St. John's ugly sermons thrust a hatred into the minds and hearts of Christian congregations. The priests taught his ideology in seminaries and schools, transmitting the vicious sickness from child to child, mind to mind, generation after generation.

The condemnation of the Jews by the early church fathers in the name of God, and the spreading of that condemnation throughout their congregations, their seminaries, and the entire Christian world, created a tradition of hatred that grew in strength from the Dark Ages to modern times until it reached its apotheosis in the Nazi Holocaust. For hundreds of years, Christians informed Jews: "God hates you." As an example, French bishops in one district urged their parishioners in their Holy Week sermons to avenge the killing of Christ. They complied; and stoning of Jews became an integral part of that area's Lenten ceremonies. Toulouse Christians created the equally vicious Easter custom of dragging a Jew before the altar and slapping his face vigorously.

The First Crusade, in 1096, catalyzed in a symbolic manner the darkest days of European Jewry until the Holocaust. The Crusaders began their first mission for Christ with a massacre. Before setting out to wrest the Holy Lands from the infidel, and after receiving Holy Communion, the Crusaders devoted the day to the slaughter of 10,000 Jews. And when they captured Jerusalem in 1099, they spent the first week slaughtering the inhabitants. They shut the Jews in their synagogue and set it on fire, and wrote home that they were up to their knees in blood. When they believed that their Savior had been sufficiently revenged—hardly anyone in the city was left alive—they washed up the blood and went tearfully to receive Holy Communion. It was Peter the Venerable who first wrote about the duty of the Jews to pay for the Crusade. Why should they not contribute more than anyone else to the expenses of the Holy War, he asked? And centuries later Göring asked why the Jews should not pay the expenses for the Crystal Night, the evening when the Nazis went on a rampage throughout Germany and destroyed billions of dollars' worth of Jewish property.

Popes in the Middle Ages usually defended the Jews against personal violence but seldom condemned the hatred behind the violence. In France the Jews in the twelfth century lived in some prosperity until 1182, when King Philip drove them out of the country. His action resulted in an economic slump, however, and in 1199 the king decided for business reasons to ask them to return. Pope Innocent III, however, did not concur. The picture of wealthy Jews with serene family lives was not consistent with his view of the Jews as slaves in perpetual misery. So he wrote two letters of reprimand in 1205. The first, addressed to the French hierarchy, reminded them that God had condemned Jews to perpetual slavery and allowed them life only because of His grace. Innocent complained that Jews showed no appreciation for that mercy. But his chief concern was Jewish employment of Christian female servants. Jews, he heard, forced their Christian nurses at Easter to eject their milk into latrines for three days before allowing them to return to the nursery.

Innocent's second letter to King Philip contained more serious accusations. The Pope charged the Jews with blasphemy, usury, and murder. Innocent urged using every means available—boycott, ostracism, expulsion, and disgrace—to make the Jews objects of universal contempt and hatred.

The Fourth Lateran Council approved the Pope's plan in 1215. It produced a number of humiliating and restrictive orders, which forbade Jews to walk in public on certain days, prohibited them from wearing their best clothes on Sundays, turned them out of all public offices, and required them to wear distinctive badges on their clothes. The Council "settled the destiny of the Jewish people for many centuries." From that point, the European Jews possessed one universal historical theme: endurance, resistance, and survival as permanently displaced persons.[30]

Through the ages, the Church has accused the Jews of being perfidious, obstinate, ungrateful, and insolent. They were obstinate because they refused to be impressed by the miracles of Christ and to convert. They were ungrateful because they did not appreciate being allowed to live. And they were insolent because they did not accept their inferior status. Many clerics and Church leaders insisted that it was a Christian's duty to hate the Jew.

The Protestant Reformation did not enhance Jewish life, for Martin Luther's hatred of the Jews was as devastating as the animosity of the popes. His intellectual vanity and the vigor of his groundbreaking faith intensified his hatred. Luther believed that anyone who did not agree with him was an "obstinate enemy of the Holy Spirit." He assumed that the Jews would readily accept his amended version of Christianity and join with him in the fight against Catholics. When they refused, he bombarded them with the full blast of his hatred.[31]

Luther published a series of anti-Semitic pamphlets in which his demands read like the later Nuremberg Laws. The synagogues should be burned and the ashes covered by dirt "for the honor of God and Christianity." Jewish homes should be destroyed and the Jews gathered together in stables so they could realize they were "miserable captives." His followers should destroy the prayer books, forbid the rabbis to teach, remove all Jewish passport and travel privileges, and take away the Jews' cash and valuables. They should be driven out of the country for all time. "God's rage is so great against them that they only become worse and worse through mild mercy and not much better through severe mercy." Luther urged the Protestant princes to free him of "this insufferable, devilish burden—the Jews."[32]

Luther's attacks were highlighted by a special brand of vulgarity. He told the Jews that the only Bible they had any right to was that concealed "beneath the sow's tail; the letters that drop from it you are free to eat and drink." In a famous passage his ravings sound like those of a lunatic with much less sophistication and control than Hitler:

When Judas hanged himself and his bowels gushed forth, and, as happens in such cases, his bladder also burst, the Jews were ready to catch the Judas-water and the other precious things, and then they gorged and swilled on the merd among themselves, and were thereby endowed with such a keenness of sight that they can perceive glosses in the Scriptures such as neither Matthew nor Isaiah himself . . . would be able to detect; or perhaps they looked into the loin of their God "Shed," and found these things written in the smokehole. . . .

The Devil has eased himself and emptied his belly again—that is a real halidom for Jews and would-be Jews, to kiss, batten on, swill and adore; and then the Devil in his turn also devours and swills what these good pupils spue and eject from above and below. . . . The Devil, with his angelic snout, devours what exudes from the oral and anal apertures of the Jews; this is indeed his favorite dish, on which he battens like a sow behind the hedge.[33]

For centuries Christian hysteria centered upon a growing package of unspeakable crimes laid at the doorstep of the Jews. When they finally defined the odious acts, the *blood libel myth* erupted into the history of the Christian and Jewish world. The Christians accused the Jews of kidnapping little children, killing them after torturing them, and using their blood for a religious rite. The myth supposedly began in the twelfth century when an English monk informed the populace that the Jews had tortured and crucified a young boy, William, and hidden him in the woods. Using the story to excite their people to attack Christ's killers, the rural clergy created the emotionally charged Cult of the Blessed William—for Christendom's popular child martyr.

The Cult spread to France and in 1171 the first "ritual murder" under that myth occurred. One man said he had seen a Jew throw the body of a child into the river. Even though no corpse was found and no other evidence produced, the parishioners tortured and burned at the stake fifty-one Jews, including seventeen women. By the century's end all of Christendom had heard the tale and from the pulpits the Church Fathers bemoaned the Jewish custom of celebrating their hatred of Christ by crucifying a Christian child once a year. Every country of Europe celebrated its cults of little children murdered by Jews with statues, miracles, and pilgrimages. The bloody child symbol deepened the hatred of Christians, and blood libel accusations became the activity of the day.

In 1758 the Vatican condemned the cult of the so-called child martyrs and reaffirmed the falsehood of all ritual murder accusations against the Jews. But that year Christians in Poland revived ritual murder trials. They tore off the skin of the accused, cut out their hearts, and amputated their hands and feet. The Nazis continued the story. In 1936 the Jew-baiting periodical *Der Stürmer* published illustrations of Jews feasting on the blood of Christian children.

During the fourteenth and fifteenth centuries hatred of the Jews combined with fear of their commercial competition and Christian competitors decided to eliminate their Jewish rivals. When the Nazis later offered to sell the Jews or to allow them to emigrate in exchange for their property, here again, they were inventing no new ideas. When the Black Death hit Europe in the fourteenth century the Christians accused the Jews of making special journeys to India to bring back the plague. As a result, they burned thousands of Jews and robbed them of their goods. The Nazis acquired Jewish possessions in a similar manner.

Individuals living in the twentieth century have difficulty understanding the lengths to which anti-Semites went and the widespread belief in the myths they engendered. One has only to look at early caricature art to see the depth of impact the myths must have had on adults' minds, let alone children's. One of the worst symbols was the *Jewish sow.* An early German libel that gained popularity associated Jews with the unclean pig forbidden them by their own laws. It originated in the thirteenth century and appeared first in three-dimensional form in churches and town halls, and later in illustrations in books. It took the form of Jews sucking from the sow. Often a rabbi straddled the animal backward and sucked its tail. In one woodcut a Jew is sucking from the sow while two others feed it. In an eighteenth-century drawing two libels are combined: the horned Jewish devil is urging the Jews to drink the sow's milk and to eat its excrement, "since they are, after all, your best delicacies!'' It was no difficult feat to move from that revolting myth to blood libel and pictures of children having their blood sucked out by Jews, and long-nosed Semites eating pork in secret, violating Christian women, and committing adultery.[34]

In the thirteenth century the Church found a new catalyst for mob violence against the Jews: the myth of the *desecration of the Host.* Jews, they said, stole Communion bread from the churches to use in magical ceremonies in which they stabbed and mutilated the Host, causing it to bleed, and then called forth vengeance on Christ. That simple myth stayed alive for centuries, leaving destruction in its wake. Wherever it erupted, the neighborhood Christians apprehended the so-called criminals, forced them to confess under torture, and killed them; and then rounded up all the Jews in the area, burned them alive, and took all their property. Whatever else varied, appropriation of property remained a constant in all myth eruptions through the centuries. Jews were animals from which Christians profited economically. The Nazis perfected the process; their technology allowed them to make money from the bodies as well as the possessions.

Finally, the Christian world produced the most modern of the myths—a Jewish international plot to destroy the world detailed in *The Protocols of the Elders of Zion.* That forgery, of the late eighteenth or early nineteenth century, consisted of a secret book of rules and strategy whereby the elite Jews in every country would join together to take over and control the world. Amazingly, the book became a bestseller. In the United States the popular right-wing priest Father Coughlin reprinted it in his periodical, *Social Justice,* and Henry Ford published it in his *Dearborn Independent.* It is printed and sold in Arab countries today.[35]

In the modern era of nationalism European societies were unable to accept the Jews as a distinct separate group. Even the liberals demanded that Jews efface their traits and Jewish identity if they wished to be included in the nation. Just as the Christian Church had viewed the stubborn separateness of the Jew with alarm, as a challenge to the very truth of Christianity, so did the modern nation-states view that separateness with loathing, as a challenge to the very strength of the nation, the *Volk.* German liberals, though they pushed for Jewish emancipation, demanded as an indispensable condition complete assimilation into the enlightened liberal society of Germany.[36]

German conservatives saw the state as essentially Christian and constitutional. Therefore Jews who did not convert could not expect to be treated as full citizens. But as the conservatives began to perceive that most Jews would agree to convert in bad faith, as a means for social and professional advancement, they became antagonistic to the concept of conversion. The conservatives also adopted a positive attitude toward political Zionism: If Jews wanted to exist as a separate group, they ought to leave Germany.

Finally, the German conservatives concluded that there was really no way to integrate or assimilate the German Jew into German society. Christian charity and love had proved ineffective, and even conversion had failed to redeem them. At that point, conservative Protestantism was in agreement with racial anti-Semitism.

The liberals, on the other hand, viewed the Jews' desire to retain their identity as a severe blow because they had based their program on the liberal Protestant principle of unity. They began to feel that Jewish recalcitrance prevented their attainment of national unity. By 1900 the liberal Protestants and the Jews recognized the complexity and fragility of their relationship. As long as both sides insisted on retaining their identity, the contradictions would grow.

The relationship between Christian or theological anti-Semitism and modern anti-Semitism is not as simple as many have supposed. In some ways, the two seem to have opposing elements. Christian anti-Semites held that Jews could be saved if they converted. Modern racial anti-Semites, however, held that all Jews were irredeemable. Traditional Christianity offered conversion, and with it a hope for some kind of life. But modern anti-Semitism aimed to destroy all "racial" Jews no matter what religion they professed. Once Christian anti-Semitism with its hope is rejected, nothing is left to convert to and only one option remains logical—disappearance and/or destruction. One might say that what happened during the twentieth century to Christian anti-Semitism is that the anti-Semitism persisted and the Christianity disappeared. By the time that modern anti-Semitism took hold, however, there was nothing the Jews could have done that would have satisfied anyone. When that modern anti-Semitism became politicized, it aided all other groups in their efforts to increase their political and economic power and to integrate into modern Germany.[37]

Anti-Semitism of every kind—Christian teaching about the Jews, volkish anti-Semitism, doctrines of racial superiority, economic theories about the role of the Jews in capitalism and commerce—combined with the insecurities of post-World War I Germany to produce an emotional milieu in which it was possible for masses of normally rational Germans to yield themselves to pathological fantasies about the Jews. In medieval days entire communities had been seized with witchcraft hysteria. In modern Germany the mass psychosis of anti-Semitism rooted in a hysteria of fear deranged a whole people so that they were willing to accept Hitler as their redeemer. One curious paradox is the contradictory image of the Jew as vermin, something to be rubbed out, and also as the mythical, omnipotent superadversary against whom war had to be conducted on a large scale. But one must remember that the Germans themselves had a dual self-image. On the one hand, they were the vigorous superhuman Aryans, invulnerable to Jewish poison, the people destined to rule the world. But on the other hand, they were aggrieved victims outwitted by the Jews, destined to spend their entire resources struggling against the Jew in order to destroy him so that they could live.

Theological anti-Semitism played a vital role in the destruction of the Jews. The teaching of contempt furnished the stereotypes that enabled the Nazis to be successful in using the Jews as a scapegoat. It created a residue of anti-Semitism in Europe which affected the local population's attitudes toward the Jews. It even enabled some Christians to feel they were doing God's duty in helping to kill Jews. In 1942, for example, a rabbi pleaded with Archbishop Kametko of Nietra to intervene against the deportation of the Slovakian Jews. Tiso, the Slovak head of state, had been Kametko's secretary for many years and the rabbi hoped that Kametko would have some clout in persuading Tiso to stop the deportations. He did not know, yet, about the gas chambers. The Archbishop replied:

It is not just a matter of deportation. You will not die there of hunger and disease. They will slaughter all of you there, old and young alike, women and children, at once. It is the punishment that you deserve for the death of our Lord and Redeemer, Jesus Christ—you have only one solution. Come over to our religion and I will work to annul this decree.[38]

As late as 1941 Archbishop Gruben of Germany in a pastoral letter blamed the Jews for the death of Christ. When the Vichy government inquired of the Vatican about the law of 1941, which isolated and deprived Jews of rights, it received this response: "In principle there is nothing in these measures which the Holy See would find to criticize." In fact, throughout the Holocaust period the few forthright church protests focused on the converted Jews—the Jewish Christians. Prominent Christians who resisted at great cost the Nazi takeover of the German Evangelical Church did not speak out on the Jewish question. Most Protestant clergy "joined with the new masters and tolerated or welcomed anti-Semitic campaigns." At the war's end the Vatican and circles close to it helped thousands of war criminals to escape, including some of the most murderous commandants.[39]

This thing called anti-Semitism—how to understand it, inside, at one's core. We Catholics and Protestants should have an easier time with deicide and Christian anti-Semitism at the gut level. Yet the so-called modern anti-Semitism, in its raw form combined with blood and race, presents danger and difficulties, as an explosive mixture of many things. One could try, I thought, immersing oneself in it for a short intense period, keeping an open mind, trying to be as that German and accept the words "without prejudice." For one month I sat down with Treitschke, Nietzsche, and Spengler; Richard

Wagner, Houston Chamberlain, Count Gobineau, and Theodor Fritsch; Adolf Stöcker, Ernst Renan, Max Brewer, Eugene Dühring; and Wilhelm Marr, Otto Glagan, Hans Blüher, Bruno Bauer, William Stapel—and *The Protocols of Zion* and the *Dearborn Independent.* Everyone should try it sometime. I think I now understand anti-Semitism. I still do not understand the Holocaust.

A Summons to Perfection, Obedience to Authority, Conformity, Submission, Malignant Aggression

Anti-Semitism, existing among civilized people for centuries, and dei-cide—the conviction that the Jews killed Christ—do not produce a Final Solution. Scholar George Steiner in *Bluebeard's Castle* adds one more piece to the structure of understanding and causation. The claims of the ideal, insists Steiner, were forced upon Western consciousness in three supreme moments: monotheism at Mt. Sinai, primitive Christianity, and messianic socialism. Three times *Judaism sought to impose perfection* on Western life. Three times Western civilization has felt impossible, agonizing demands upon its normal, ordinary, mundane fabric of common instinctual behavior. "Surmount yourself. Lose your life in order to gain it. Give up property, rank, worldly comfort. Love your neighbor as you do yourself, no, much more, for self-love is sin. Make any sacrifice, endure any insult, even self-denunciation, so that justice may prevail." The "blackmail of perfection" worked its power because the ideal was "profoundly desirable," its supreme value fully acknowledged. It could not be rejected. But its perpetrators, the Jews, could.

"Deep loathing" and "murderous resentments" derived from the failure to reach perfection built up in the subconscious of the Western mind and were directed in primordial fury against the "bad conscience of Western history," the Jew. Because of the intolerable pressures, claims Steiner, the European world turned on "the incarnation of its own best hopes." "We hate most those who hold out to us a goal, an ideal, a visionary promise which, even though we have stretched our muscles to the utmost, we cannot reach, which slips, again and again, just out of range of our racked fingers."[40]

Still, resentment because of failure to realize a stern ideal does not lead automatically to the construction of a killing center. And however powerful the wishful thinking and pervasive indifference, anti-Semitism and theological vindictiveness can be no more than a base to which intersecting constructs must be affixed. Christian anti-Semitism is the basement of the structure. The beams come from elsewhere—from man.

For thoughtful social scientists, the basic questions still remain—why, why man, and how? The future search for reasons will most surely include a look at the way normal people behave under abnormal and unusual circumstances. That research direction is already opening the door of understanding—a bit.

Social scientists received Stanley Milgram's book, *Obedience to Authority,* as a bombshell. Milgram had designed a simple experiment at Yale University to test how much pain an ordinary citizen would inflict on another person simply because he was ordered to by an experimental scientist. The experiment pitted stark authority against the subjects' strongest aversion to hurting others. With the protests of the victims ringing in their ears, a majority of ordinary men and women gave in to authority. The experiment found that many adults are willing to go to almost any length on command. The first experiments used Yale undergraduates as subjects; and about 60 percent obeyed the command to deliver lethal shocks. In the next experimental series Milgram drew subjects from every stratum of New Haven life. The results were the same. When the experiments were repeated in other countries, the level of obedience was invariably somewhat higher. A Munich scientist found 85 percent of his subjects obedient.[41]

A few years ago the psychology department at Stanford constructed a mock jail in the basement of the department. They advertised for volunteers for an experiment at $1.75 an hour. The department head participated, along with the psychology faculty and the paid student volunteers. A coin was flipped and half the group became guards and the other half prisoners. Anyone, of course, was free to leave at any time. The experiment was to last two weeks. The psychologists were expecting to find mild behavioral changes under conditions of tension and confinement, group pressure, and an authoritarian structure. After four days the experiment was halted because the behavorial changes in both faculty and students were so great that crackups occurred and the situation became dangerous. No "prisoners" thought of leaving. Several volunteer prisoners became weak and submissive. Some volunteer guards became brutal and cruel. Stanford faculty and students![42]

Several years ago S. E. Asch carried out a series of brilliant experiments on *conformity.* He showed a group of six apparent subjects a line of a certain length and asked them to say which of three other lines matched it. All but one subject in the group had been secretly instructed beforehand to select one of the "wrong" lines on each trial or in a certain percentage of the trials. The naïve subject was so placed that he heard the answers of most of the group before he had to announce his own decision. Asch found that under this form of social pressure, 75 percent of the subjects went along with the group rather than accept the unmistakable evidence of their own eyes. Although three-quarters of Asch's subjects *conformed* to the group norm, they always understated the degree to which their actions were influenced by members of the group—they minimized their *conformity.*

Psychiatrist Eric Fromm reminds us that animals display viciousness when their environment is disturbed, as in overcrowding. But modern man acts destructively even in uncrowded situations and feels intense satisfaction in doing so. His "biologically nonadaptive, *malignant aggression*" is not a defense against threats; it manifests itself in killing, is pleasurable, and is rooted not in instincts but in the human condition.[43]

Hannah Arendt and Douglas Kelly have insisted that the Nazis were normal, ordinary people. Arendt argues convincingly that evil thrives because of the *banality of ordinary men*: after all, Eichmann did not hate his victims. Fromm insists that man's aggression manifests itself in pleasurable spurts of killing. One might also conjecture, however, that an invitation to do violence has a greater effect than the so-called obedience to authority:

The social lesson to be learned from this is not that in a wicked world decent people will act in a wicked way, but that in a wicked world people with a penchant for wickedness will freely indulge it, justifying themselves (when called upon to do so) on the grounds that they were merely obeying orders.[44]

The Jews whom the Nazis murdered were, after all, not perceived as likable, mild-mannered people. They were viewed as less than human. I suppose that one can say with Hannah Arendt that a man may kill large numbers of people without feelings of hatred; and with Eric Fromm, that modern man periodically takes satisfaction in vicious destruction; and with Stanley Milgram that ordinary, decent people are quite able to inflict pain or even death on helpless people when ordered to do so; and with S. E. Asch that group pressure exerts tremendous force. Thus, on top of the basement of deicide and Christian anti-Semitism, we have placed beams at intersecting points of perfectionism, ordinariness or banality, obedience to authority, submission, conformity, and malignant aggression. Are we finished? Do we have a Final Solution? I think not.

A Cumulative Betrayal, Nonaccountability, and the Unfettered Leader

One cannot help but be impressed by the scope of betrayal by the entire world. When an enormous number of men carry the concept of indifference to such an extreme, it may mean madness, or a curious kind of nonaccountability. Perhaps Eichmann was an ordinary man, but he and the Germans knew one thing—that they would never have to account at any time in the future for the fate of the Jews, because that fate interested no one. The Jewish question did not weigh on mankind. Eichmann said ironically that no country was interested in saving the Jews, and he also pointed out that if he tried to sell Jews, no one would buy. He was correct; no one was interested in having them. It was different from the days of the Middle Ages. In those times the expelled Jews had someplace to go. The Jews living under Hitler had no place to go in the entire world. Those who did escape were often driven back into the darkness and the furnaces. The Germans were not so certain of world reaction at the beginning of their war against the Jews. They expected some outrage, but never once did they hear it. The absence of response told them that at least in one area they had a green light: they could destroy the Jews. It seemed to them that someday all the peoples of the world would be grateful to them. A cumulative betrayal. Is that insanity?

We will have difficulty, I think, attributing the Holocaust to insanity unless the definition of sanity is so narrowed that it would include only the angels. But it is as difficult to believe the reverse—that the *leaders* of the Third Reich were ordinary men. (Perhaps the followers were.) How can a Holocaust, such an extraordinary circumstance, be the work of an ordinary mind? It seems inconceivable that the enormous breadth of vision necessary to undertake the destruction of an entire people could be the product of an ordinary mind. The theories about obedience to authority have some bearing on the Holocaust, but the leaders were not obedient to anyone. The leaders of the Final Solution felt themselves subordinate to few. It is hard to believe that their motivation came from a desire to please.

No one is automatically human except in a biological sense. Only when a person strives to think for himself can he approach his potential as a human being. It would seem that in order for a person to feel responsible for his actions, he must realize that his behavior stems from his inner self. During the Holocaust the vast majority of Germans perceived their actions as originating in the motives of some other person, usually a leader. When an individual sees himself as the embodiment of someone else, as merely a vehicle for carrying out that person's orders, he no longer takes responsibility for his actions and blind obedience can follow. It is indeed ironic that the Jews have been condemned for allowing themselves to be led like sheep to the slaughter, when it is actually the German people and their collaborators who acted like sheep.[45]

All people in their history have related to a god or an authority figure. If people live under a god or an authority figure who does not protest against their actions, they feel a release from restraint that equals a dynamic approval of bad things being done. If the god or the authority figure not only does not protest those actions but says that it is all right to do them, then those people feel a release from restraint and an approval of actions that results in worse things being done more often to more people. If that god or authority figure not only refrains from protest and scolding, not only acknowledges and approves, but in addition *orders* the actions to be done, then those people can feel a righteous zeal in doing the worst things all the time to everyone of an identified group because they are operating under a holy command.

The forces that move people are complex and difficult to fathom. No one would deny the extraordinary complexity of the modern world; it should therefore come as no surprise that those human beings living in that world have developed an equal complexity. Consequently, any sure analysis of the forces that came together to produce the Holocaust configuration must use multifaceted and interrelated concepts.

In the basement of mankind's greatest outrage stood theological anti-Semitism and deicide, which produced an all-encompassing, overwhelming fear of the caricature of the Jew. They prepared the way. But what led to the commitment to full and total destruction of the Jew? We now suspect that those who watched and those who followed and those who remained silent were evidencing the rather common character traits of obedience to authority, conformity, submission, and nonaccountability. They were also evidencing what may be a developing phenomenon—the capacity to kill and to dismantle large groups of people by ordinary men. But those ordinary men were not led by followers or other ordinary men. They were led by committed and thoughtful leaders—a master race of men who shook the world by their destructive deeds, or by their indifference to the destructive deeds of other leaders unless those deeds affected them and their own kind. Perhaps for the first time in modern history we saw the presence on the world scene of the unfettered leader, seemingly accountable to no one on earth, unrestrained by any morality or societal rules.

After examining characteristics or tendencies or possibilities of modern man that contributed to the Holocaust, we must still place that unprecedented deed of destruction in the context of the time in which it occurred—at the breaking point of modern technological society. Technology knew no limits. Suddenly, anything was possible if only a nation had ample resources, money, and time. The Holocaust was driven by the elation and the glory of the unrestrained machine and the men who made that technology possible. Its masters were like curious children left alone in their parents' home for an hour or so without supervision. There were no restraints, no morality, no sermons, no divine laws, no social tensions constraining the technological age in its infancy. When modern technology finally broke free, it smashed the restraints that had always held back, in the last analysis, the actions of men, groups, and nations. Just as technology developed a spirit of nonaccountability, so did the human beings playing with it. The leaders were not accountable, and since the followers were accountable only to the leaders, they were not accountable at all. In fact, the whole world was nonaccountable. That nonaccountability, evidenced by vigorous indifference, led to a cumulative betrayal of humanness, integrity, and all feeling toward one's fellow man outside of one's own special group.

The intimate, particularized, face-to-face, steady, careful annihilation of masses of people has not been repeated, but the elimination of sizable groups of people continues. It is almost as though the potential in man to kill massive numbers of people willfully and easily became a bad habit in the time of the Holocaust. Society continued to develop, for the next three decades, the bad habit of massively killing massive amounts of masses of humans. Additionally the nonaccountability phenomenon engendered by the Holocaust began to permeate entire societies. It may be, though, that nonaccountability or unrestrained killing has run its course. Bad habits, once learned, can be discarded; and perhaps we are beginning in a short period of time in human history to learn to deal with the technology of destruction and extermination. As a psychiatrist recently wrote:

Tragic times have a perfume of their own, and smiles of hope, and traces of charm, and offer olive branches and late warnings that may not be too late.[46]

THE STRUGGLERS

How can any normal human being remain sane and whole in spirit and strive unceasingly to live while suffering devastating mental and physical torture and damage? Humans have asked this question down through the centuries, but few have found satisfaction in the responses. It should come as no surprise, then, that we have difficulty in understanding the art of struggling, the philosophy of survival in the camps, and the struggler. It is linked to our difficulty in facing and understanding death and dying. We honor the deed of the martyr—the individual who sacrifices himself for his beliefs, or who dies so that others may live. It is a truly heroic vision. To many, it makes sense to die for the highest principles. But when human beings die in the hundreds of thousands, how can death have dignity, how can death have courage, how can death be heroic? In Elie Wiesel's *The Oath* an old wanderer, Azriel, implores a young friend not to kill himself:

I only ask you not to offer death one more victim, one more victory. It does not deserve it, believe me. . . . There is no beautiful death. Nor is there a just death. Every death is absurd. Useless. And ugly. . . . Whether life has meaning or not, what matters is not to make a gift of it to death. All you get in return is a corpse. And corpses stink.[47]

The strugglers in the camps shouted: We shall not make a gift of our lives to death!

The struggler is not a likely hero. We do not include him in our heroic classifications and myths. We even suspect those who survive calamities. The struggler is "anyone who manages to stay alive in body *and* in spirit, enduring dread and hopelessness without the loss of will to carry on in human ways. That is all." The struggler lies at the core of the story of the camps—the story of the struggle to live. Struggling to live is a process hard to pin down and understand. It is virtually impossible to fathom an intensive total effort that results in nothing except perhaps staying alive, for one more moment. The struggler makes a decision to stay alive but he is never assured of success. In fact, everything around him tells him that he will fail.[48]

The Nazis asked for everything: the mind, the human spirit, and finally—and only finally—the death of the body, in an environment which they defined as eternal. They trapped the strugglers in a landscape created for death in every practical and symbolistic way. They ensured "a permanent state of dying."[49] In those extreme conditions there was no escape, no end in sight except the grave. There was no single battle to be fought, just a boring, almost mundane continuation of the effort to remain alive.

Clearly, the struggler was much more than a victim. Whatever his facade, he was a rebel: he was supposed to die; he did not or had not yet. The strugglers went forward simply because they considered it their human responsibility to do so. Perhaps they *needed*, in that environment, to struggle to remain human. And that struggle took so much effort that it simply would not be worth it to give up or die out. The struggle went forward without drama, dignity, excitement, or victory. To the martyr, death is a victory. To the struggler, death is defeat.

"In surviving," remarked one struggler, "you are not so afraid of Death, because Death becomes commonplace." "Death was like a fellow prisoner who walked alongside, behind, or in front of us. We were so aware of his presence among us that we hardly noticed him." Since death was more common than life, it became an "accepted resident."[50]

We are afraid, we humans, of the strugglers. We are afraid of the strugglers who died and the strugglers who lived. They all bother us terribly. Their very struggling and their surviving frightens us. We are terrified of what we believe must have been their breakthroughs in strength and humanity and wisdom, breakthroughs that our minds cannot even begin to perceive. These struggler survivors who walk among us minimize us, frighten us because we know they were ordinary men and women, not giants. It is because they were ordinary that we are so very terrified of them. We are afraid of the fantasies they force upon us, afraid of thinking about a real hell. It is too much.

In our world of ordinary men and women, when a mother dies, we mourn. We mourn divorce, the lack of a child, the absence of a job. Society tells us to mourn over our troubles. When we are upset, we see a clergyman or a psychiatrist. When we are sick, we see a doctor. But *they* endured so much more with no help. Thus we become weak and ashamed in our own eyes and, we think, in *their* eyes. So we search for their weaknesses and we find them in the very proof of their strength—survival. We ask them how they could possibly have survived, or we tell them that they must have debased themselves to the level of animals, and emulated in their actions their SS guards. We attack their survival. We make the survivors an enigma to themselves. Why do we denigrate the twentieth century's greatest act of heroism? I would propose two possibilities: our necessary myth of the heroic, so outlandish now that most individuals avoid it; and our inability to tolerate what we imagine to be our own weaknesses.

When a struggler remains alive, he achieves one goal: he simply loses less, to use Des Pres's phrase. He wins no victory. He achieves no release. He finds no respite from fear. In fact, his fear may accelerate as the odds against him rise. And to have that one more day or that one more hour, he has had to struggle with all his will. When the struggler becomes a survivor and returns to civilization, he feels guilty for surviving; and we do nothing to relieve that guilt.

What did the strugglers do that was so extraordinary? Primarily they resisted. They resisted conditions and situations unknown before in modern history. The Nazis intended that they rot alive, that they be defiled; and they rotted alive and they were defiled—but still they lived. What else did they do? An exhausted, near dead group of humans actually arose in the morning. That must have been the hardest act of the day. What they overcame defies the biological and psychological theories of modern civilization. Humans *need* sleep, sex, food, rest, gratification, hope—or they become senile, insane, or die. But the strugglers did not. In fact, the gas chambers attest to this phenomenon. The strugglers struggled so hard to live that the Germans realized that they had to *kill them to get them to die.* For many of the planners of the Final Solution, that factor was the most unexpected facet of the Holocaust.

In a death world the strugglers allowed the desire to live to return to them. In fact, they brought it back. It takes time to wake up from a dream to face evil; but they did it, and in less time than most of us can appreciate. They also had to deal with chance. One easily notices the tension in a gambling casino, the almost heart-attack-producing tension for a few hours because of chance. The strugglers learned somehow to live in such an all-encompassing chance environment without relief.

The strugglers also repudiated logic and rationality. Had they not, they would have died instantly. It was logical to be hopeless, so they resisted logic. It was rational to collapse with despair, so they became irrational. They stood on the razor's edge of disaster. Each day they began life all over again. In ordinary living we humans despair about the prospect of starting over again. We do not believe that we could begin again, over and over. We worry that we would choose death. "Take life day by day." Only strugglers know the true meaning of the phrase. For them the past was gone, the present hell, and the future denied—and yet they lived.

In staying alive, the majority did not take on the souls of their oppressors, as some have claimed. To the contrary, the strugglers were dealing with "men of damaged souls" and needed to structure their behavior accordingly. They learned to act. They gave dramatic performances that should have won the Academy Award a thousand times over.

It was the SS who had the damaged psyches, and to stay alive, the strugglers learned to play the Survivor Game with them. A nineteen-year-old Jewish boy, in his early days in Auschwitz, succumbed to tears. "Don't cry," warned an older inmate. "It won't help." *Everyone,* he reminded the young boy, had a sad story to tell. So forget the past. "Just figure you dropped out of the sky into this awful place." And learn to survive. "Toughen up. Learn their games and outsmart them." The captors' game was intended to end in the ultimate degradation of the struggler. To beat him, "you go as far down as he wants you to go without letting him know you are still cleverer than he is, and can come out of it. That's the game. That's the whole thing." The player prepares for the game by learning their habits, their language: "Learn how they think and start thinking that way."[51]

The strugglers also learned to save life by being willing to use "death strategically." They gathered to themselves, somehow, the strength to accept the fact that each day they lost less rather than gained more. They learned a commonplace—that receiving help and helping another were acts that existed side by side, intertwined. They prepared to run risks to live, knowing that by doing so, they were also courting death.

Existence at the limit, then, is beyond the imagination of any human being who has not lived such a life. It necessitates an entirely new psychology even to understand it. The struggler's goal centered on keeping life going, not merely staying alive. One has an active element to it, the other, a passive core. It was not enough to remain alive one more day because one more day was never enough.

The Germans designed the camps as experiments in a closed environment. Using the inmates like Pavlov's dogs, they applied the standard negative reinforcements. But the strugglers refused to die when the bell rang each day. They pushed to stay alive. *They struggled to survive for the sake of survival.* Modern society views that type of struggle with disparagement. How often do we hear the accusation: "He merely survived." We would rather see some cataclysm in the life of a human being than witness mere boring survival. But we have never lived in a concentration camp. There was no such thing as mere boring survival or struggle. For example, one inmate spoke to friends about killing herself. One of them asked her: "Why hurry?"

Death was so simple, so real, in an environment where the question of "Why not suicide?" brought only the response "Why hurry it?" When the SS came to take Dr. Jacob Edelstein away to the gas chambers, they shouted at him to hurry up. His response? "I am the master of my last moments."[52]

Hungry, battered, sick, dying, the strugglers retained their humaneness and their respect for one another in the most horrible of all situations. For the strugglers, holding on was the phenomenon. It was not to die of hunger in spite of little food, to economize to the last drop of water, the last piece of bread. It was not to die of cold on the ground in the snow and the rain; not to freeze during long hours of roll call. It was not to die of blows and kicks from the SS. It was not to allow despair to enter into the spirit and penetrate the heart. It was to say: I am not hungry, I am not cold, it does not hurt. From the strugglers, we learn that they exerted energy to answer a universal question, posed so well by Saul Bellow: How should a good man live in that environment? What does it mean to be "exactly human"? Clearly, many calmly answered: "Exactly human: standing neither too stiffly upright nor with unduly bowed shoulders; recognizing that though one is an imperfect creature this is no cause for self-laceration; it is no cause for self-inflation either."[53]

The concentration camp strugglers found themselves in hell—not a mythical, symbolic, or imaginary hell, but a real one. Ordinary men and women struggled to live. The strugglers thought it enough. We do not. We wanted them to perform a heroic act according to our definitions of heroism. Neither surviving with dignity nor dying anonymously with dignity is a positive symbol in our conceptual realm. It embarrasses us, they embarrass us, and in turn we embarrass them. We do not recoil from studying the Holocaust because of the death theme. War movies and violence fascinate us. We recoil because this situation is a distasteful and unfamiliar form of death.

Premeditated, devastating, destructive violence is an everyday occurrence, and humans can understand and interpret it. It has a beginning and an end, and it has a reason. But pure atrocity, for no apparent reason, defies comprehension. It violates our intellectual and emotional definitions. The Holocaust explains to us that everything forbidden is possible; and that the obscene, the hellish, the unimaginable, the sickening can become ordinarily routine. The Holocaust tragedians make dying uninteresting, and violation of humans, pedestrian. Man and animal merge into each other. The Holocaust befouls values and precious concepts. It destroys the supposedly iron link between civilization and decency. It is a black hole without limits, without boundaries, without parameters. Its statistics defy reason. The Holocaust and its sufferings reach beyond imagination, beyond fantasy, and beyond prayer. The intense internal pressure to close our minds to it is understandable. But there is more to the Holocaust than a message of defeat and desolation.

If we only listened to the survivors and gazed forcefully at the strugglers and their struggle, we would learn so much more about hope and life than about death and hopelessness; but we are afraid to look. It is like the closed doors of Bartok's opera in *Bluebeard's Castle.* We are afraid to look through those archetypal doors because we are so certain we will see simply death without hope. But, in fact, the strugglers, those who died and those who lived, may have taught us far greater meaning. We owe it to them and to ourselves most particularly, and to the future especially, to at least speculate, ponder.

In "Visitor from Buchenwald" by the American poet Virginia Mishnun-Hardman, a struggler spirit who died in Buchenwald visits the narrator and exhorts her to remember the Warsaw ghetto, "where Jews, slated for slaughter, kept their schools, And made new rules whereby they lived and died."

Terror shared is terror halved;
The oppressor faced is in that act defaced;
When all hope's gone, defy and dignify.
Their wills were weapons, their deeds
Seeds on which the brave will feed.

They knew they could not win, those strugglers. Yet, as the poet says, they gave a new commandment to the world: *"Thou shalt prevent the torment of the innocent."* Remember, the guest commands:

Remember that small, skinny Jew
Who, in the last few seconds of his life,
Lifted a battered head,
Like a defiant giant said to his tormentors:
"You'll yet choke on my smoke."[54]

They struggled to live, preferring to stand on Dostoyevski's "square yard of space all their lives . . . , to live, to live life,whatever it may be!"

We need to speculate on the struggler's primal scream—"I intend to live!" It was not a scream of desperation but of rage, determination, dignity. It took time for it to come out of each struggler, but when it came, so did calm, a reach to the essence. The Orthodox did it; the Reformed did it; the Conservatives did it; the Catholics did it. Some called it finding God. Others knew that they may well have been finding themselves. To the Jewish strugglers, the admonition of Elie Wiesel's grandfather, Dodye Feig, in 1944 would have made sense: "You are Jewish, your task is to remain Jewish. The rest is up to God."[55]

Human beings are still agonizingly vulnerable to the presence of death. We ignore, we transcend, or we go insane when it becomes an element among us. We are just beginning, with the new science of thanatology, to understand the potency of death and our civilization's failure to confront it. We are not yet able to stare at it, but we do sneak glances. Those camp strugglers may have been the first modern humans to *stare* at death. Because they stared at it, now we know that we must also. But as we approach the survivor and the struggler, we respond to them as symbols of suffering and death, and thus react with nonrecognition, apathy, and fear. Our reaction is more than anti-Semitism, verminism, nonhumanness, or indifference. I suspect it has to do with our very very deepest and most pulsating fear, which no modern man has yet addressed—except, perhaps, the struggler. His actions during the Holocaust overwhelm with an explosive *magnificence.*[56]

The Madness of the Holocaust

There is a kind of madness about the Holocaust—a madness that passes all understanding. To each person who suffered in it, to each who lived through it, and to each who now agonizes over it, its meaning is different. To some, it has meant that God is dead. But God did not die at Auschwitz. If He is dead, He died a long time ago. If He is not dead, His presence simply means that it would take more than any human event to kill God. After all, it was man, not God, who created the Holocaust. To a few, the Holocaust is simply God's will on earth, conceived to teach a lesson impossible to learn by any other means. But again, it was man who destroyed, man in his fullest and greatest potential who destroyed, not God. It seems to me a sacrilege to assume a God of any kind who would put to death six million individuals, for any purpose, for any reason. No good comes out of death, and surely, a Master God knows that. Death is neither glorious nor saving nor dignified. Death is simply death.

Certainly, this one event has had an impact on human history difficult to duplicate. The Holocaust seems to have marked the dividing point or the beginning of an age. At the very least, it produced a crisis in institutional Christianity that has not been resolved. During the Holocaust the Germans killed millions, but they reserved their mad hatred for the Jews. Christianity must at least face the ugly picture of the burning children. Without that image in mind, it must be silent.

Some have reacted to the Holocaust with ennui; others have refused to bring children into a world that produced such an event. Some have demanded silence. But from my perspective, too many asked for the wrong kind of silence, at the wrong time. It is probably fair to suggest that the majority of people in the West have not undergone a crisis of conscience and of heart because of the Holocaust. Evidently we have been too silent.[57]

The camps were horrible places, awful places, stinking places, programmed as they were, to promote killing. The camp concept, however, has outrun its usefulness. For it is simply no longer necessary to create them. Killing and destruction can be done more easily by other means. One wonders, though, whether man still possesses such a precise and highly tuned interest in delivering pain and destruction to a living body. With the enjoyment of the perpetrators that one observed throughout the Holocaust period, it is still possible to wonder if that ghastly, breathtaking indifference is still among us.

The Germans were cruel, but others have been cruel. They were barbaric, but others have been also. The greatest crime of the Germans was their coldblooded systemic scheme to destroy the humanity of their victims. The calculated dehumanization of human beings is so very difficult to understand, to forget, and possibly to forgive. It was an unnatural kind of evil—a satanic rationality in the midst of the madness, a "scarcely governed ache for savagery." The Germans hated the Jew and intended to eliminate him for all time. They feared the Jew because of his staying power. He had been around for thousands of years. Yet the Germans imitated the Jew and dreamed of, fought for, a Thousand Year Reich. Eichmann told a colleague when he went into hiding that he would leap into his grave laughing if caught. Eichmann's joy grew out of the conviction that he had landed a fatal blow by devastating Jewry's central life. With that laughter and that conviction, "one must beware of easy hope" after Auschwitz.[58]

Lessons the Holocaust Taught Us

Because of the Holocaust, certain assumptions in human thought and life are no longer plausible. Instead of appearing as true, or as reasonable options for thought, they disappear into the realm of myth. We may not know what is true, but we have a clearer idea of what is false. Our realm of thought is more clearly focused. The elimination of a *wide range of falsehoods* cleans out the unusable from the attics of our minds:

1. Most of the Western world had accepted—at least, subconsciously—that God punishes those who sin against Him, and rewards, in some manner, those who believe and do good. Conversely, as with Job, suffering could be a test of faith. Those beliefs, troublesome enough in the past, become in the face of the extermination of men, women, and children patently absurd and entirely unpalatable.

2. If people have faith, i.e., religion or commitment to God, that faith must, we thought, yield good, pay off, be rewarded. Faith for those who have it, must now, like virtue, stand on its own.

3. We once held God responsible for major events, especially when the events, such as war and revolution, spelled trouble. No longer. Tornadoes

may be acts of God, but hardly Holocausts or wars. It is now difficult to ignore the obvious: that people decide to torture and destroy other people. These actions become acts of Humans.

4. We believed, I think, that the worst would never happen. Beginning with the Holocaust, the worst has happened and may happen again. Nazi barbarism confronted us with a new reality.

5. "Every day in every way, man gets better and better" is an adage that fairly reflects a nineteenth- and twentieth-century belief popular with both "commoners" and intellectuals and scholars. We spoke of progress, the evolution of man. The Holocaust, however, has effectively silenced voices proclaiming the steady uplifting of man's soul and his moral spirit. What we have is what we should have known we always had—good and bad men; good men capable of horrible things; bad men capable in a puzzling manner of good things. Or maybe all we have are men capable of anything—except perhaps of helping those they feel are nonhuman or subhuman. That latter capability has yet to be demonstrated.

6. We have identified certain "civilizing" aspects of the modern world— music, art, a sense of family, love, appreciation of beauty, intellect, education. After Auschwitz, we realize that being a killer, and a good family man, and a lover of dogs and flowers, and a scientist, or a professor, and a lover of Beethoven are not contradictions. The killers "did not belong to a gutter society of misfits, nor could they be dismissed as just a collection of rabble." They were scholars, artists, lawyers, theologians, aristocrats.[59]

7. We once seized upon institutions and experts to serve as beacons in this complex world. Our societies have tended to submit to authorities. We should know now that the deification of certain institutions and our assumption of moral and ethical behavior in the majority of individuals in those institutions—medicine and science, for example—is a risky business at best and destructive of humans at the least.

Not only have we eliminated important falsehoods and myths from our minds, but we have also acquired a small but terribly helpful *collection of facts* that we did not know or understand before:

1. Man is deeply vulnerable when faced with overwhelming evil.[60] Instead of consolidating his energy to fight it, he wastes valuable time and effort puzzling over it, insisting it is not, cannot possibly be, what it seems.

2. Human actions, we have discovered, have nothing to do with human reactions. Regardless of anything the Jews did or anyone they became, the Nazis destroyed them. The only action the Jews could have taken from

about 1850 to prevent their extermination would have been to disappear—disappear from everywhere.

3.   All protestations aside, it is certainly clear that whatever else it is, Jewishness is, at the least, disagreeable to Gentiles. Often it is abhorrent, but at the least it is disagreeable.

4.   At critical times we realize that no one—or no more than a very few—will reach out to save or help Jews. During the Holocaust only an minuscule number of Gentiles chose to save Jews; most people chose to remain indifferent; and some selected to destroy Jews.

5.   We know that man is truly the only primate who "kills and tortures members of his own species without any reason, either biological or economical, and who feels satisfaction in doing so." Man's record is one of "extraordinary destructiveness and cruelty," a story of intermittent seizures of lust for blood, or vengeance in more civilized terms. Man or men enjoy, almost in a cyclical fashion, destroying life for no reason other than to destroy.[61]

6.   Churches have no greater propensity for good than the men who join them or the countries in which they are found. They do not stand above or hover with angelic wings; and anticipations to the contrary are likely to result in disturbing disillusionment. Dietrich Bonhoffer finally faced himself with that truth when he wrote, too late, that the Church "has often denied to the outcast and to the despised the compassion which she owes them. She was silent when she should have cried out because the blood of the innocent was crying aloud to heaven."[62]

7.   We should not assume that the majority of Western people have learned positive lessons from World War II, the Final Solution, and the Holocaust. "People seemed to have learned more from the Nazis," reflects a Dachau survivor, "than from their victims. Isn't *that* something to be amazed about?"[63]

What does one do then with the lessons? Elie Wiesel, as one man, a "hopeful worshiper," suggests to his students the following basic constants. Try to save one man. Fight evil right away. Don't wait. It won't pass. Never allow the enemy to ask questions or supply the answers. Be intense, every moment. Ask passionate questions.[64]

If studied with caring, the Holocaust reveals, shares, catalyzes, warns, alarms, raises one's thinking level, and eliminates wishful thinking. We can think more clearly than those who preceded us because our span of thinking has been narrowed. It is easier, with the myths gone, to probe human nature, and, if we wish, the nature of God. We ought not to be so impatient with the slowness of our minds to find answers. We ought not to view our search as futile. For we have had such a brief time. For centuries, mankind has held to the concepts of basic human goodness and continual human progress. We have had only thirty years to ponder the contrary.

It would be easy to leave this story filled with rage and agony over human depravity, convinced of the banality of evil and the evil of banality, with a clear view of how bad men live and what bad men do. But must not one also come away with a puzzled awe and reverence for an often observable indomitable human perseverance to retain dignity, raising questions as to how a good man should live, and what a good man ought to do? Does it not require examining one's own interior life, then moving forward to contend with the difficult problems of those others, and pulling it all together in a complex and tangled knot that will be troublesome and tearing for all of one's life?

And why? Because today we find ourselves living in a culture in which the methodical use of torture is so widely established, and in an age crowded with gas ovens, napalm, mass starvation, and the concept of "limited" nuclear war, that we must work to keep their hideousness in sharp focus. We must not allow a sense of the ordinary to develop about human misery and destruction, nor must we permit any dignity to our new knowledge that anything and everything is possible. We must hold deep within ourselves a sense of scandal so overwhelming that it affects every significant aspect of our lives. We must, as Emily Dickinson said, keep one's soul terribly surprised.[65]

APPENDIX I: CAMP DIRECTIONS

CAMP DIRECTIONS

DACHAU
For the quickest route, in *Munich* take E6, the Autobahn to Nürnberg. Continue for about 10 kilometers. Get off at the Dachau exit and onto the road to Schleissheim/Dachau/Fürstenfeldbruck. From the exit, it is about 10 kilometers to the camp at the outskirts of the town of Dachau.

SACHSENHAUSEN/ORANIENBURG
From *East Berlin*, take E95 north about 30 kilometers to Oranienburg. Look for signs to "Gedenkstätte Sachsenhausen." It is located on the outskirts of Oranienburg.

BUCHENWALD
Right outside *Weimar,* GDR.

MAUTHAUSEN
In *Vienna,* take the Vienna-Linz Autobahn, E5. In Linz look for 123 East. Take 123 East about 20 kilometers to the town of Mauthausen. The camp is a few kilometers up the road.

FLOSSENBURG
At Wohenstrauss (on E12 from *Nürnberg*) go to the center of town and follow the signs to Weiden. Just outside of Wohenstrauss (½ kilometer) on the road to Weiden, is a sign on the right which says, "Floss, 13 km"—follow to Floss. In the center of town turn right to Flossenbürg (sign says, "Flossenbürg, 6 km"). In town, stop at the small memorial park. Then continue past a monument to the outskirts and a sign to "Grab-Gedenstätte Flossenbürg."

RAVENSBRÜCK
From *Berlin* take E6/96 north toward Neustrelitz and Neubrandenburg. Road will pass through Oranienburg, Gransee, and Fürstenberg. The town of Ravensbrück is about 89 kilometers on E6/96 from Berlin.

STUTTHOF/SZTUTOWO

Take E81 out of *Gdansk* toward Elblag. About 5 kilometers out of town, look for signs to the left for Sobeszewo and Krynica Morska. Turn left on road to Sobeszewo. Turn left and go about 8 kilometers to a free, efficient ferry that crosses the Vistula right near the ocean. Stetna is 2 kilometers from Stutthof. Or take E81 to (Nw Dwdr Gd) and turn left. Stutthof is 17 kilometers from there.

GROSS-ROSEN

Out of *Wroclaw* take E38/12 about 9 kilometers to E22. Get on E22 toward Katy Wroclaw and Legnica. Go about 28 kilometers to Kostomioty. Turn off there and take the road about 28 kilometers to Strzegom. At Strzegom take the road to Jawor. The town of Rogozmica is 7 kilometers from Strzegom on the road to Jawor. Gross-Rosen is about 1 kilometer from there.

NEUENGAMME

From *Hamburg*, take the road to Bergedorf. Stay on the main road in the direction of Berlin until Curslacker Heerweg. Turn right at the sign, "Gedenk-stätte Neuengamme." Follow the signs from there.

NATZWEILER

Take D392 southwest 21 kilometers from *Strasbourg* to Altorf, passing through Entzheim. Cross over D422, staying on D392 until reaching Schirmeck (about 25 kilometers). D392 will run into N420. Stay on N420 until just before Rothau (about 5 kilometers). Bear left on D130, which is a winding, country road. Pass through the village of Struthof. Continue to climb the steep road to Natzweiler. It is about 6 kilometers from Road 420.

DORA/NORDHAUSEN

Autoroute from Hannover to Berlin from border (E8) until Magdeburg. In Magdeburg, follow signs to *Halle* (E71). Take 80 to Eislehen, Sangerhausen, Berga, Nordhausen. Drive through the town to outskirts. The signs to the camp are well-marked.

TEREZIN/THERESIENSTADT

From *Prague* take E15/8 toward Dresden. The town of Terezin is about 55 kilometers on E15/8 from Prague.

CHELMNO/KULMHOF

Take E8 out of *Poznan* (to Warsaw). On the outskirts of Kolo, 126 kilometers from Poznan, turn right on the road to Lask. The camp is on the right, about 12 kilometers after the turnoff.

BELZEC
From *Lublin* take T12 (E31) 52 kilometers to Krasnystaw. Then continue on E81 to Zamosc (29 kilometers) and on to Tomaszow Lub (34 kilometers) and from there to Belzec (8 kilometers)—total, 123 kilometers. Or go directly from Sobibor. From Sobibor, go back the 9 kilometers to road, turn left. Go 38 kilometers to Chelm; then follow signs to Krasnycyaw (28 kilometers); from there follow above directions. Go through Belzec. See a huge railroad yard again—go slowly and keep looking on the left. Belzec will be on the left and the sign designating a camp on the right.

SOBIBOR
Take T12 69 kilometers from *Lublin* to Chelm. Just before the entrance to Chelm is a traffic circle. Turn left at the circle on the road to Wlodawa. Go straight, 38 kilometers. Turn right at the sign for Sobibor and go 8 kilometers to the end of the road. Sobibor is on the right.

TREBLINKA
From *Warsaw* get on E12 to Ostrow Maz (98 kilometers). Turn right at the second turn off (across Bug) to the tiny town of Sokotow. Treblinka Camp is about 23 kilometers from Ostrow Maz. Go through the town of Treblinka toward Sokotow Podl, over railroad tracks to Poniatowo to a sign: Oboz Treblinka (1 kilometer). Turn right and go over the tracks again. Drive down cobblestone road to the camp, which is approximately 4 kilometers from the highway. The camp is 4 kilometers from the town of Treblinka, and 5 kilometers from the River Bug. Very hard to find.

MAJDANEK (NEAR) LUBLIN
Take E81 166 kilometers from Warsaw to *Lublin*. In Lublin, follow signs to Chelm. Four kilometers from Lublin, Majdanek will be on right side of Road T12.

AUSCHWITZ/BIRKENAU
From *Cracow* take E22a to Chrzánow (42 kilometers). Then, take the road through Libiaz to Oswiecim (10 kilometers). You will see signs to Oswiecim (Auschwitz) from there. Or, from Cracow, you can take the road to Zator (37 kilometers), and then connect to route 221 to Oswiecim (22 kilometers).

BERGEN-BELSEN
Take the Autoroute from *Hannover* to Hamburg past the Hannover Flug-hafen. Take the second exit off the Autoroute to Millendorf. At the end of that exit, turn left to Fuhrberg (4 kilometers). Continue (6 kilometers) to the road to Winson-Aalle (11 kilometers). The road goes through Ovelgamme-Oldau. In Winson-Aalle, once through the town, there is a sign which says,

"Gedenkstätte-Belsen 10.2 kilometers." Continue through Walla. Bergen-Belsen is about 4 kilometers further.

APPENDIX II: THE CAMPS AND COMMANDANTS

1. **Dachau**—West Germany.
   March 1933—American Army occupation, April 29, 1945.

   Wäckerle, Hilmar
   Eicke, Theodor
   Deubel, Heinrich
   Loritz, Hans
   Piorkowski, Alex
   Weiss, Martin
   Weiter, Wilhem

2. **Sachsenhausen**—East Germany.
   September 1936—Soviet Army Occupation, April 22, 1945.

   Koch, Karl
   Helwig, Hans
   Baranowski, Hermann
   Eisfeld, Walter
   Loritz, Hans
   Kaindl, Anton

3. **Buchenwald**—East Germany.
   July 15, 1937—Liberation, April 11, 1945.

   Koch, Karl
   Pister, Hermann

4. **Mauthausen**—Austria.
   August 1938—American Army occupation, May 8, 1945.

   Sauer, Albert
   Ziereis, Franz

5. **Flossenbürg**—West Germany.
   May 1938—American Army occupation, April 23, 1945.

   Weiseborn, Jakob

Künstler, Karl
Fritzsch, Karl
Zill, Egon
Kögel, Max

6. **Ravensbrück**—East Germany.
   May 15, 1939—Soviet Army occupation, April 30, 1945.

   Kögel, Max
   Suhren, Fritz
   Sauer, Albert

7. **Auschwitz I**—Mother Camp—Poland.
   April 27, 1940—Soviet Army occupation, January 22, 1945.

   Höss, Rudolf
   Liebehenschel, Arthur
   Baer, Richard

   Auschwitz II—Birkenau.
   October 1941—January 22, 1945.

   Hartjenstein, Friedrich
   Kramer, Joseph

   Auschwitz III—Monowice/Buna.
   May/September 1942—Soviet Army occupation, January 27, 1945.

   Schwartz, Heinrich

8. **Neuengamme**—West Germany.
   June 1940—British Army occupation, May 3, 1945.

   Weiss, Martin
   Pauly, Max

9. **Gross-Rosen**—Poland.
   August 1940—Soviet Army occupation, February 1945.

   Rödel, Arthur
   Gideon, Wilhelm
   Hassebroek, Johannes

10. **Natzweiler**—France.
    May 1941—early September 1944 (evacuation completed).

Hüttig, Hans
Zill, Egon
Kramer, Joseph
Hartjenstein, Friedrich

11. **Stutthof**—Poland.
September 2, 1939—Soviet Army occupation, May 9, 1945.

Pauly, Max
Hoppe, Paul-Werner

12. **Majdanek**—Poland.
Summer 1941 (POW Camp)/February 16, 1943—Soviet Army
occupation, July 24, 1944.

Koch, Karl
Kögel, Max
Florstedt, Hermann
Weiss, Martin
Liebehenschel, Arthur

13. **Bergen-Belsen**—West Germany.
April 1943—British Army occupation, April 15, 1945.

Haas, Adolf
Kramer, Joseph

14. **Dora/Nordhausen**—East Germany.
September 1943—April 5, 1945 evacuation.

Förschner, Otto
Baer, Richard

15. **Terezin/Theresienstadt**—Czechoslovakia.
November 24, 1941—Soviet Army occupation, May 8, 1945.

Seidl, Siegfried
Burger, Anton
Rahm, Karl

16. **Chelmno/Kulmhof**—Poland.
Late December 1941/early January 1942–1943; then 1944–January
1945.

Lange, Herbert
Bothmann, Hans

17. **Belzec**—Poland.
    March 17, 1942—November 1942 or June 1943.

    Wirth, Christian
    Hering, Gottlieb

18. **Sobibor**—Poland.
    May 8, 1942—October 1943.

    Thomalla, Richard
    Stangl, Fritz
    Reichleitner, Franz

19. **Treblinka**—Poland.
    July 1942—Fall 1943.

    Eberl, Irmfried
    Stangl, Fritz
    Franz, Kurt

APPENDIX III: THE FATE OF THE COMMANDANTS

Baer, Richard
Auschwitz
Dora
Falsified identity and was not arrested by the West Germans until 1960. Died in jail, 1961.

Baranowski, Hermann
Sachsenhausen
Died, 1939.

Bothmann, Hans
Chelmno
Suicide by hanging, April 1946.

Burger, Anton
Terezin
Fate unknown.

Deubel, Heinrich
Dachau
mustered out of the SS 1936. Headed a local police station during war. No punishment.

Eberl, Irmfried
Treblinka
Suicide, 1948.

Eicke, Theodor
Dachau
Killed when his plane was shot down at the eastern front, February 1943.

Eisfeld, Walter
Sachsenhausen
Died April 3, 1940.

Florstedt, Hermann
Majdanek
Found guilty of fraud and corruption by an SS court. Executed by the SS, April 1945.

Förschner, Otto
Dora
Executed by an American tribunal, May 1946.

Franz, Kurt
Treblinka
Lived in Düsseldorf under his own name until arrest in 1959.
Tried in 1964.
Court sentenced him to life.

Fritzsch, Karl
Flossenbürg
Killed in the battle of Berlin.

Gideon, Wilhelm
Gross-Rosen
Detained in Danish and British jails but released. A retired businessman, he is
still under investigation.

Haas, Adolf
Belsen
Killed, March 1945.

Hartjenstein, Friedrich
Birkenau
Natzweiler
Sentenced to death by British and French tribunals.
Died in jail of a heart attack, October 1954.

Hassebroek, Johannes
Gross-Rosen
Arrested by Czechs, Americans, and then British. British sentenced him to
death but remitted his sentence and released him in 1954. Charged again in
1967 but acquitted by the court on insufficient evidence. Charged again in 1970
and acquitted. In 1975, alive, a retired businessman, partially paralyzed from a
stroke.

Helwig, Hans
Sachsenhausen
Died, August 8, 1952.

Hering, Gottlieb
Belzec
Killed in 1945 near Stuttgart.

Hoppe, Paul-Werner
Stutthof
Escaped British capture and lived in Switzerland under an assumed name,
working as a landscape designer. Returned home in 1952 and rejoined his
family. Arrested in 1953 and sentenced by a West German court, in 1957, to
nine years. Released in 1962 and worked with an insurance company. Died in
1974.

Höss, Rudolf
Auschwitz
Hanged in Auschwitz, 1947.

Hüttig, Hans
Natzweiler
Sentenced to life by a French court. Pardoned and released, March 1956.

Kaindl, Anton
Sachsenhausen
Sentenced by a Soviet tribunal to life.
Died, November 1947, in prison.

Koch, Ilse (wife of Karl)
Buchenwald
Acquitted by SS court. U.S. Army captured her. August 1947 sentenced to life but soon released. U.S. Senate created a special investigation commission which led to a new treaty in Germany. Sentenced to life again.
Committed suicide in jail, September 1967.

Koch, Karl
Sachsenhausen
Buchenwald
Majdanek
Found guilty by SS court of corruption, fraud, murder, alcoholism, sexual offenses, etc.
Shot by SS, April 1945.

Kögel, Max
Ravensbrück
Majdanek
Flossenbürg
Arrested by U.S. Army.
Found dead in cell, 1946.

Kramer, Joseph
Natzweiler
Birkenau
Belsen
Tried in 1945. Hanged, December 1945.

Künstler, Karl
Flossenbürg
Killed in battle, April 1945.

Lange, Herbert
Chelmno
Killed in battle, April 1945

Liebehenschel, Arthur
Auschwitz

Majdanek
Executed by Polish tribunal, January 1948.

Loritz, Hans
Dachau
Sachsenhausen
Committed suicide, 1946.

Pauly, Max
Stutthof
Neuengamme
Sentenced to death and executed by the British, October 1946.

Piorkowski, Alex
Dachau
Condemned to death by an American tribunal.
Executed, October 1948.

Pister, Hermann
Buchenwald
Condemned to death by an American tribunal.
Died, September 1948.

Rahm, Karl
Terezin
Hanged by Allies.

Reichleitner, Franz
Sobibor
Killed in partisan activity in the Trieste region.

Rödel, Arthur
Gross-Rosen
Committed suicide, April 1945.

Sauer, Albert
Mauthausen
Ravensbrück—a few days
Killed May 3, 1945.

Schwartz, Heinrich
Auschwitz
Fate unknown.

Seidl, Siegfried
Terezin
Hanged by Austrian Government.

Stangl, Fritz
Sobibor
Treblinka

Escaped to Brazil in 1948. Extradited, 1967. Sentenced to life.
Died of a heart attack.

Suhren, Fritz
Ravensbrück
Executed by a French court, June 1950.

Thomalla, Richard
Sobibor
Killed during the war.

Wäckerle, Hilmar
Dachau
Shot in battle, July 2, 1941.

Weiseborn, Jakob
Flossenbürg
Died of a heart attack, while at Flossenbürg.

Weiss, Martin
Dachau
Neuengamme
Majdanek
One of forty defendants in the 1945 Dachau trial. Sentenced to death by an
American tribunal.
Executed, May 1946.

Weiter, Wilhelm
Dachau
Probably shot by a zealot SS officer.

Wirth, Christian
Belzec
Killed in Italy in 1944.

Ziereis, Franz
Mauthasen
Shot by American soldiers trying to escape, May 1945.

Zill, Egon
Natzweiler
Flossenbürg
Tried in Munich in 1955. Sentenced to life. Released.
Died in 1974 at his home in Dachau.

NOTES

PREFACE

1. Elie Wiesel in Alvin Rosenfeld and Irving Greenberg, eds., *Confronting the Holocaust* (Bloomington: Indiana University Press, 1978), 12, 21.

2. George Steiner, *In Bluebeard's Castle* (New Haven, Conn.: Yale University Press, 1971), eloquently insists upon confronting "dark places." Quotes from Isaiah Trunk, *Jewish Responses to Nazi Persecution* (New York: Stein and Day, 1979), 111.

3. Elie Wiesel in Rosenfeld and Greenberg, *Confronting the Holocaust*, 200.

4. Elie Wiesel in Harry James Cargas, ed., *Responses to Elie Wiesel* (New York: Persea, 1978), 15.

5. Silvano Arieti, *The Parnas* (New York: Basic Books, 1979), 85.

6. K. Feig, *The Voyage of the Damned: An Essayed Bibliography* (Portland: University of Maine, 1974). One can never express enough thanks for Raul Hilberg's *The Destruction of the European Jews* (Chicago: Quadrangle, 1967); Lucy Dawidowicz's *The War Against the Jews* (New York: Holt, 1975); and Nora Levin's *The Holocaust* (New York: Schocken, 1973).

7. Nellie Sachs, *O The Chimneys* (New York: Farrar, Straus, Giroux, 1967), 59.

PART ONE
THE BEGINNING

1. *'Olokauston* is the Greek translation from the Hebrew Bible of the word for *Olah*. Quote from Terrence Des Pres, *The Survivor* (New York: Oxford, 1976), 49. See also Gerd Korman, *Hunter and Hunted* (New York: Viking, 1973), 250. One must only apply the word *Holocaust* to the mass murder of six million Jews, insists Yehuda Bauer. I agree. In his book, *The Holocaust in Historical Perspective* (Seattle: University of Washington Press, 1978), Bauer warns against using the term for all unfortunate occurrences. The Jews alone were singled out for total destruction. "For the first time in history, a sentence of death had been pronounced on anyone guilty of having been born, and born of certain parents" (p. 32). Hitler intended genocide against the Poles and Russians. But a difference exists between "forcible, even murderous, denationalization, and wholesale, total murder of every one of the members of a community" (p. 35). The Holocaust most closely parallels the Armenian massacre by the Turks. The Turks, however, were neither total nor logical in their approach, and Armenians in the center of the empire were allowed to live (p. 37). Bauer says that since World War II there have been several genocides and some near holocausts, and the victims of both suffer the same (I do not

agree). Genocide has been terrible but not total, and it has dealt with *sub*human people. The Holocaust was total and dealt with *non*humans (p. 36). One might add to Bauer's scheme a more simplistic example. Truman erred in ordering the Hiroshima debacle to ensure quick victory and save American lives, but it was a miscalculation. Hitler did not miscalculate or aim at victory or saving any lives—he intended only to destroy. The Turks killed the Armenians but they did not strip their skin for lamp shades, fertilize their gardens with the Armenians' crushed bones, fill their mattresses with their hair, or melt their bodies down for soap.

Recently, Bauer commented on the intent of President Carter and his Commission on the Holocaust to design a memorial to the six million Jews "and the millions of other victims of Nazism during World War II": "The Holocaust in this view is no longer a unique historical event, the result of a quasi-religious ideology which saw in the Jewish people a demonic force ruling the world and consequently tried to annihilate it, but a hold-all term for 'the inhumanity of man to man,' and similar meaningless generalizations. Not only were the six million Jews murdered by their enemies: they now stand in danger of having their unique martyrdom obliterated by their friends. . . . One does not have to confuse Holocaust with genocide in order to oppose the latter—or any other evil, for that matter" (*Jerusalem Post International,* March 2–8, 1980, p. 14). In *The Jewish Return into History* (New York: Schocken, 1978), Emil Fackenheim argues, on the other hand, that the Holocaust is unique because it is the only example of absolute evil in human history. See also Uriel Tal, "On the Study of the Holocaust and Genocide," *YVS,* XIII, 1979, 7–52.

2. Steiner, *In Bluebeard's Castle,* 2, 48; and *Language and Silence* (New York: Atheneum, 1967), ix.

3. Richard Rubenstein, "Some Perspectives on Religious Faith," in Franklin Littell, *The German Church Struggle and The Holocaust* (Detroit: Wayne State University, 1974), 264. Also see Note 18.

4. William Styron, *Sophie's Choice* (New York: Random House, 1979), 216–217; and Steiner, *Language,* 157. For problems in writing of the Holocaust, see Lawrence Langer, *The Holocaust and the Literary Imagination* (New Haven, Conn.: Yale University Press, 1975); and Harry James Cargas, *Harry James Cargas in Conversation with Elie Wiesel* (New York: Paulist Press, 1976), 87. See also Irving Halperin, *Messengers from the Dead* (Philadelphia: Westminster Press, 1969).

5. Quotes in order from Gunter Grass in Langer, *Holocaust and the Literary Imagination,* 7; and Rosenfeld, *Confronting the Holocaust,* 21. See also George M. Kren and Leon Rappaport, "Victims: The Fallacy of Innocence," *Societas,* 4 (1974), 125. Although little mention is made of poetry in studies of Holocaust literature, superior verse exists, in addition to that by Nellie Sachs. This book emphasizes some striking examples. Murray J. Kohn's recent work on Hebrew poetry adds so much sensitivity, *The Voice of My Blood Cries Out* (New York: Shengold, 1979).

6. Steiner, *Language,* 123. Alvin H. Rosenfeld emphasizes persuasively the Steiner/Wiesel point in "The Holocaust According to William Styron," *Midstream,* December 1979, 43–49, when he assesses Styron's efforts (*Sophie's Choice*) to make Auschwitz "the erotic centerpiece of a New Southern Gothic Novel" (p. 49).

7. Langer, *Holocaust and the Literary Imagination,* 31. Writers deal thoughtfully with Wiesel's concept of silence in Rosenfeld and Greenberg, *Confronting the Holocaust,* 4. See also Michael Berenbaum, *The Vision of the Void* (Middletown, Conn.: Wesleyan University Press, 1979). The controversy continues as described by Paula E. Hyman, "New Debate on the Holocaust," *New York Times Magazine,* September 14, 1980, 65–86.

8. Thomas Mann, "Frederick the Great," in *Three Essays* (New York: Knopf, 1929), 215.

9. Very much like the community in Thomas Tryon's novel, *Harvest Home* (New York: Knopf, 1973).

10. See John Toland, *Hitler: The Pictorial Documentary of His Life* (Garden City, N.Y.: Doubleday, 1978), 179; and James O'Donnell, *The Bunker* (Boston: Houghton Mifflin, 1978).

11. *DN*, 24.

12. J. P. Stern, *Hitler* (Berkeley: University of California Press, 1975), 116.

13. Jan T. Gross, *Polish Society under German Occupation* (Princeton, N.J.: Princeton University Press, 1979), 87–88; and Gilbert Allardyce, "What Fascism Is Not," *AHR*, April 1979, 383; DN, 26–27.

14. Adolf Hitler, *Mein Kampf* (New York: Reynal & Hitchcock, 1940), 413, 81–85. A few scholars insist that Hitler's hatred of the Jews came from his "awful suspicion" that he was Jewish. See Robert G. Waite, *The Psychopathic God* (New York: Basic Books, 1977), and the summary article by Martin Ebon, "Why Did Hitler Hate the Jews?" *Midstream*, October 1979, 19–24. For additional insight into Hitler, see the following recent basic works: Rudolph Binion, *Hitler Among the Germans* (New York: Elsevier, 1976); Joachim Fest, *Hitler* (New York: Harcourt, 1974); Richard A. Koenigsberg, *Hitler's Ideology* (New York: Library of Social Science, 1975); Werner Maser, *Hitler: Legend, Myth, and Reality* (New York: Harper, 1975); Robert Payne, *The Life and Death of Adolf Hitler* (New York: Praeger, 1973); John Toland, *Hitler* (New York: Doubleday, 1976); and older works: Alan Bullock, *Hitler: A Study in Tyranny* (New York: Harper, 1960); William Langer, *The Mind of Adolf Hitler* (New York: Basic Books, 1972); H. Trevor-Roper, *The Last Days of Hitler* (New York: Macmillan, 1947). Three recent works, controversial and revisionist, add to the Hitler synthesis: Norman Stone, *Hitler* (New York: Little, Brown, 1980); Sebastian Haffner, *The Meaning of Hitler* (New York: Macmillan, 1980); Leonard L. Heston, *The Medical Casebook of Adolf Hitler* (New York: Stein and Day, 1980).

15. *DN*, 36; Hitler, *Mein Kampf* (London, 1939), 252–273 and 243–248.

16. *DN*, 85, 469; Airey Neave, *On Trial at Nuremberg* (Boston: Little, Brown, 1978).

17. *DN*, 467, 487, 608.

18. Although troubled by basic misconceptions in the film, I was interested in Hans-Jürgen Syberberg's seven-hour movie, *Our Hitler: A Film From Germany*, shown in San Francisco on July 28, 1979. One of his "big shocks," Syberberg told me, was that "I finally accept the slogan: 'Hitler is Germany and Germany is Hitler.' " He made the film, he said, "to speak about the soul," and the "ending of the Life of Mankind." The film portrays Himmler and Hitler in ways that would be impossible with words alone.

19. Jay Baird, *The Mythical World of Nazi War Propaganda* (Minneapolis: University of Minnesota Press, 1975), 6–7.

20. Peter Hoffman, *The History of the German Resistance 1933–1945* (Cambridge, Mass.: MIT Press, 1977), 189.

21. Sam Simon, *Handbook of the Mail in the Concentration Camps, 1933–1945: A Postal History* (privately printed, 1973).

22. A rich field for further Holocaust research is the analysis of the involvement and contribution of different institutions. Raul Hilberg's forthcoming study of the participation of the German railroad system and its trainmen is one example. An excellent case study of one group, the German Foreign Office, is the book by Christopher Browning, *The Final Solution and the German Foreign Office* (New York: Holmes and Meier,

1978). His examination of just one cog in the Nazi murder mechanism provides another example of the contribution of Arendt's banal bureaucrats.

23. Many references have been made to the lack of unity in the American Jewish community; one of the most interesting is the case study of Vaad Ha-Hatzala by Efraim Zuroff, "Rescue Priority and Fund Raising as Issues during the Holocaust," *American Jewish History*, March 1979, 305–326. Zuroff believes that cooperation between the Joint and the Orthodox rabbis would have resulted in many more rescued Jews. Another study that discusses weak responses by organized Jewry is Frederick A. Lazin, "The Response of the American Jewish Committee to the Crisis of German Jewry," *American Jewish History*, March 1979, 283–304. Lazin explains the weak response as the result of fear of increased anti-Semitism, the Depression and unemployment, Hitler's success, the poor health and old age of committee members, and conflicting demands of families and careers. Bernard Wasserstein, in "The Myth of 'Jewish Silence,' " *Midstream,* August-September, 1980, 10–15, calls the notion of the supposed silence of free-world Jews a "myth." The established Jewish leadership in America, Britain, and Palestine rather than blocking attempts to help the victims, and playing into the hands of British and American governmental leadership by meekly agreeing with Roosevelt and by suppressing information, did speak up, criticize, and cajole the governments. Jewish leadership sent forth a stream of life-saving proposals, called public meetings, lobbied. But the Jewish campaign failed because official Washington had no commitment, refused to alter racist immigration laws, and remained adamant against focusing on one group to help.

24. See Dawidowicz, *War Against the Jews*, xv. The author is indebted to Professor Dawidowicz in many ways, primarily because hers was the first major work to focus on the *Jews* and the Holocaust.

25. Hannah Arendt, *Eichmann in Jerusalem* (New York: Viking, 1963), 276. See also Randolph L. Braham, *The Eichmann Case: A Source Book* (New York: World Federation of Hungarian Jews, 1969); a strong rebuttal to Arendt, Jacob Robinson, *And the Crooked Shall Be Made Straight* (Philadelphia: Jewish Publication Society, 1965); and Robert Shaw, *The Man in the Glass Booth* (New York: Samuel French, 1968). In his novel, *The Wind Chill Factor* (New York: Ballantine, 1976), Thomas Gifford remarks that Hitler's idea of taking over the world was a "perfectly rational idea." Fanatics are fascinating, he thinks. "They were a half-step out of line, they possessed the great flaw, but they were far from crazy. They were strong and daring men, somewhat off course, but in another time there's no doubt of it, they would have ruled the world" (p. 113).

26. Quote from Rückerl, 11.

27. The most recent study of the SS Death's Head Division is Charles Sydnor, Jr., *Soldiers of Destruction* (Princeton, N.J.: Princeton University Press, 1977). Sydnor challenges scholars who attempt to divorce the fighting division from the SS. "The history of the SS Death's Head Division clearly reveals a line of authority from Hitler through Himmler to the Waffen SS that was short, direct, and immediate" (344). For a summary of camp and extermination organization, see Adalbert Rückerl, ed., *NS-Prozesse* (Karlsruhe: Verlag C. F. Müller, 1972), 108–123. A book of photographs, Morris Cargill, ed., *A Gallery of Nazis* (Secaucus, N.J.: Lyle Stuart, 1978), is a good collection of the Nazi leaders in victory and in defeat—if one ignores the text and captions, for they contain several serious errors of fact. For additional information on the SS, see older books: Henry V. Dicks, *Licensed Mass Murder* (New York: Basic Books, 1972); Richard Grunberger, *Hitler's SS* (New York: Delacourt, 1970); Heinz Höhne, *The Order of the Death's Head* (New York: Coward-McCann, 1970); Gerald Reitlinger, *The SS: Alibi of a Nation* (London: Heinemann, 1956); and George H. Stein, *The Waffen SS* (Ithaca, N.Y.: Cornell University Press, 1966).

28. Stern, *Hitler,* 122–23.

29. The most serious need in Holocaust research is for in-depth studies of the Final Solution within each European country. Without these studies, scholars generalize about the Holocaust, ignoring the fact that for every theory, every conclusion, one or more countries proves the exception. We need to build the bricks, country by country, before we come to any further conclusions as to causation, and to do this we will need to make greater use of literature. Some examples of helpful studies follow. *Italy:* Robert Katz, *Black Sabbath* (Toronto: Macmillan, 1969); Giolgio Bassani, *The Garden of the Finzi-Continis* (New York: Atheneum, 1965); Fernande Leboucher, *Incredible Mission* (New York: Doubleday, 1969); and Meir Michaelis, *Mussolini and the Jews* (Oxford: Clarendon, 1978). *Hungary:* Randolph L. Braham, *The Hungarian Labor Service* (New York: Columbia, 1977); Randolph L. Braham, *The Destruction of Hungarian Jewry* (New York: Marsten Press, 1962); Nicholas Kallay, *Hungarian Premier* (Westport, Connecticut: Greenwood Press, 1970); Jenö Levai, *Hungarian Jewry and the Papacy* (London: Sands, 1968); Miklos Lacko, *Arrow Cross Men* (Budapest: Akademiai Kiado, 1969); and Jenö Levai, ed., *Eichmann in Hungary* (Budapest: Pannonia Press, 1961). *Denmark:* Elliott Arnold, *A Night of Watching* (New York: Scribners, 1967), and Harold Flender, *Rescue in Denmark* (New York: Simon and Schuster, 1963). *Holland:* Jacob Presser, *The Destruction of the Dutch Jews* (New York: Dutton, 1969); Werner Warmbrunn, *The Dutch under German Occupation* (Palo Alto, Cal.: Stanford University Press, 1963); Anne Frank, *The Diary of a Young Girl* (New York: Doubleday, 1952); Jacob Presser, *Breaking Point* (New York: World Publishing, 1958); Leesha Rose, *The Tulips Are Red* (New York: A. S. Barnes, 1979); and we await the English translation of Louis DeJong's massive study, *Het Koninkrijk der Nederlanden. France:* Claude Lévy and Paul Tillard, *Betrayal at the Vel d'Hiv* (New York: Hill and Wang, 1967); Robert Beauvais, *Half Jew* (New York: Taplinger, 1979); Beate Klarsfeld, ed., *Le Mémorial de la Deportation des Juifs de France* (Paris: Klarsfeld, 1978); Paula Hyman, *Between Dreyfus and Vichy: The Transformation of French Jewry* (New York: Columbia University Press, 1980); and Arthur Miller, *Incident at Vichy* (New York: Viking, 1965). *Germany:* Valentin Senger, *No. 12 Kaiserhofstrasse* (New York: Dutton, 1979); Walter Laqueur, *The Missing Years* (Boston: Little Brown, 1979); Danielle Steel, *The Ring* (New York: Delacorte, 1980); and John Dickinson, *German and Jew* (Chicago: Quadrangle, 1967). *Rumania:* Jules S. Fisher, *Transnistria* (London: Yoseloff, 1969). *Bulgaria:* Frederick Chary, *The Bulgarian Jews and the Final Solution* (Pittsburgh: University of Pittsburgh Press, 1973); and H. D. Oliver, *We Were Saved* (Sofia: Foreign Languages Press, 1967). *Croatia:* Edmond Paris, *Genocide in Satellite Croatia* (Chicago: American Institute for Balkan Affairs, 1961). *Slovakia:* Livia Rothkirchen, *The Destruction of Slovak Jewry* (Jerusalem: Yad Vashem Archives, Vol. III, 1961). *Switzerland:* Alfred Hasler, *The Lifeboat Is Full* (New York: Funk and Wagnalls, 1967). *Czechoslovakia:* Ladislau Grosman, *The Shop on Main Street* (New York: Doubleday, 1970). *South America:* Judith L. Elkin, *Jews of the Latin American Republics* (Chapel Hill, North Carolina: University of North Carolina Press, 1980). While many memoirs exist written by Jews from Lithuania and Latvia together with brief articles, no major Holocaust histories of those countries are available. Two recent books on two major cities begin to address that deficiency. The work on Vilna is encyclopedic in detail and contains a thoughtful discussion of the Judenrat and of resistance, focusing on the struggle and annihilation of Vilna Jewry: Yitzhak Arad, *Ghetto in Flames* (Jerusalem: Yad Vashem, 1980). The Riga work is part memoir, part raw data: Gertrude Schneider, *Journey Into Terror* (New York: Ark House, 1979).

30. Michael Musmanno, *The Eichmann Kommandos* (London: Peter Davies, 1962), 82. See

also Anatole Goldstein, *Operation Murder* (New York: Institute of Jewish Affairs, 1949).

31. Ohlendorf testimony in Musmanno, *Eichmann Kommandos,* 93–100. For the fate of *Einsatzgruppen* leaders, see Rückerl, *NS-Prozesse,* 102–106.

32. Elie Wiesel, "Talking and Writing and Keeping Silent," in Littell, *The German Church Struggle and the Holocaust,* 270.

33. Barbara Fischmann Traub, *The Matrushka Doll* (New York: Richard Marek, 1980), 91.

34. The basic materials on Jewish Councils, and especially the work by Isaiah Trunk, have provided us with the full structure for an evaluation. Scholars will continue to fill in details; and novelists are enriching the picture, e.g., Leslie Epstein, *King of the Jews* (New York: Coward, McCann and Geoghegan, 1979). A novel, however, is no substitute for the solid scholarship of researchers like Trunk, Leonard Tushnet, Yad Vashem, YIVO, and others. See also Shlomo Katz, "Verdicts: A Play in Three Acts," *Midstream,* November 1977, 3–30. An outstanding novel on ghetto life (Vilna) is Icchokas Meras, *Stalemate* (New York: Lyle Stuart, 1980).

35. The lack of order in creating the specialized system surprised some Nazis. "One day," recalled Rudolf Diels, Gestapo chief, "the camps were simply there." Years after his departure from Berlin, he "heard of the existence of some camps of which I had no knowledge in 1933." *DN,* 181.

36. The only novel dealing with the Gypsy experience is Stefan Kanfer's *The Eighth Sin* (New York: Random House, 1978); and the only published research in English is Donald Kenrick and Grattan Puxon's *The Destiny of Europe's Gypsies* (New York: Basic Books, 1972). See also Miriam Novitch: *L'extermination des Tziganes* (Paris: A.M.I.F., 1969). Jehovah's Witness quote from Barbara Distel and Ruth Jakusch, eds., *Concentration Camp Dachau, 1933–1945* (Munich: Lipp, Comité International de Dachau, 1978), 62.

37. See *ITS;* the Soviet and Polish Commission reports; Reuben Ainzstein, *Jewish Resistance in Nazi-Occupied Eastern Europe* (New York: Barnes and Noble, 1974), 714–15, 906–907.

38. Rückerl, 120–126; oath, 125–126. My translation.

39. See Rückerl, *NS-Prozesse,* 35–42, for the transfer of populations from the General Government to the killing centers: a district-by-district account, death statistics for Treblinka, Sobibor, and Belzec, and descriptions of the gruesome journey in cattle cars. Considerable information is available on Treblinka, but it is scattered and difficult to pull together. Some important sources have not been translated into English. Our best information comes from Polish investigation commissions and from survivors. The Poles investigated the killing centers under the guise of the Central State Commission for the Investigation of German Crimes in Poland. For Treblinka, the Central Jewish Historical Commission did studies, both jointly with the State Commission, and by its own scholars and sources. In November 1945 the Polish Commission with its chair, Polish Judge Z. Lukaszkiewicz, survivors Samuel Rajzman, Tanhum Grinberg, M. Mittelberg, Shimon Friedman, Dr. Joseph Kermish, and Rachel Auerbach of the Jewish Commission and others, made an official inspection. Survivor material is available in English in a number of sources: e.g., Michael Elkins, *Forged in Fury* (New York: Ballantine, 1971); and Howard Roiter, *Voices from the Holocaust* (New York: William Friedrick Press, 1975).

40. Rückerl, 130–131. My translation.

41. Richard Rubenstein, *The Cunning of History* (New York: Harper, 1975), 60. In *Less Than Slaves* (Cambridge, Mass.: Harvard University Press, 1979)., Benjamin B.

Ferencz tells the story of the German industrialists, their decision to use the Jews as slave labor, and their avoidance of prosecution.

42. Rubenstein, *Cunning of History,* 65. No Krupp director ever uttered a word of regret during the trials. See Neave, *On Trial at Nuremberg,* 23–41.

43. For a hard look at Nazi architecture in general, see Robert R. Taylor, *The Word in Stone* (Berkeley: University of California Press, 1974), 11. I also found helpful Dr. Werner Rittich, *New German Architecture* (Berlin: Terramare Office, 1941); and Barbara Miller Lane, *Architecture and Politics in Germany, 1918–1945* (Cambridge, Mass.: Harvard University Press, 1968).

44. This area ought to be of enormous interest (and puzzlement) to historians. But there is no published material examining the essential step in the Final Solution—the train transportation of the Jews to the camps. It is hoped that Raul Hilberg will be successful in his laborious and difficult research on the subject. Until then, we shall have to be content with the summary in Rückerl, 112–117; the description of the research problem in Raul Hilberg, "In Search of the Special Trains," *Midstream,* October 1979, 32–38; and a summary article by Hilberg, "German Railroads/Jewish Souls," *Society,* Nov./Dec. 1976, 60–74. The quote is from the last article, p. 61.

45. Rückerl, 114–116. Translation by E. Scecina.

46. Hilberg, "German Railroads," 70.

47. Ibid.

48. Poet unknown; I apologize for my inability to locate this source—the poetry, though, was too stunning to omit. There was another kind of medical study during the Holocaust— carried on in the Warsaw ghetto by valiant Jewish doctors, renowned medical experts who helped the sick ghetto Jews and organized a clinical research project to break new ground with the study of hunger disease. We need to see starvation as a *disease,* not only affecting the body, but also inducing clinical mental and behavioral changes over which the sufferers had no control. Hunger disease, dying disease, brought physical and psychic changes at every stage. See Myron Winnick, ed., Hunger Disease (New York: Wiley, 1979); Leonard Tuschnet, *The Uses of Adversity* (New York: Citadel Press, 1965).

PART
TWO
THE CAMPS

Dachau

1. Michael Selzer, *Deliverance Day* (Philadelphia: Lippincott, 1978), 249–250.

2. William Heyen, "Riddle," *The Swastika Poems* (New York: Vanguard, 1977), 24–25. Information on Dachau in Johann Neuhäusler, *What Was It Like in the Concentration Camp at Dachau?* (Munich: Manz A. G., 1960); Comité International de Dachau, *Konzentrationslager Dachau* (Munich: R. Eimannsberger, 1974); Comité International de Dachau, *Memorial Site Concentration Camp Dachau* (Munich, 1976); Silvia Tennenbaun, "Return to Germany," *Midstream,* December 1976, 39–44; Barbara Greenberg, "Didn't We Meet at Dachau?" *Moment,* December 1976, 46–50; Craig Whitney, "The People Who Live in Dachau Today," *Martyrdom and Resistance,* June–

July 1976, 3; *EJ,* Vol. 5: 1218–30; Stefan Schwarz, *Die Jüdische Gedenkstätte in Dachau* (Münich: Landesverband d. Israelit. Kulturgemeinden im Bayern, 1972); Paul Neurath, "Social Life in the German Concentration Camps of Dachau and Buchenwald," Ph.D. Dissertation, Columbia University, 1951, university microfilms; and Barbara Distel and Ruth Jakusch, eds.: *Concentration Camp Dachau, 1933–1945* (Munich: Lipp, Comité International de Dachau, 1978).

3. Paul Berben, *Dachau, 1933–1945: The Official History* (London: Latimer Trend, 1975), 212; and *ITS* 1: 8–9, 26–27, 32.

4. Neuhäusler, *What Was it Like in Dachau?* 7.

5. Ibid., 8.

6. Ibid., 13.

7. *TWC* IV: 614–615 for crematorium quotes.

8. Nico Rost, *Koncentration-Camp Dachau* (Brussels: Drukerei Hans Danmerhuber, n.d.), 29.

9. Information on gassing in Reitlinger, 141; Harold P. Schowalter, "Letter to the Editor," *National Jewish Monthly,* January 1967, 2; Berben, *Dachau,* 176; Neuhäusler, *What Was It Like in Dachau?,* 15; and Neave, *On Trial at Nuremberg,* 318.

10. Krausnick, 433.

11. Charles W. Sydnor, "The History of the *SS Totenkopfdivision* and the Postwar Mythology of the *Waffen SS," Central European History,* December 1973, 339–362; and Berben, *Dachau,* 45.

12. Statistics from Berben, *Dachau,* 19. Bruno Bettelheim left Dachau in 1939 before it became a bad camp, having spent one year there. As a prominent in a "moderate" camp, he lived better than the inmates in most camps. Yet he persists in taking time off from his field of expertise—child psychiatry—and obsessively writing books about how survivors survived. In his first one he said survivors took on SS attributes and developed father images. In his latest work, *Surviving* (New York: Knopf, 1979), he insists that those who lived, lived for something wider, a transcendent ideal. He speaks for one viewpoint. See also Bruno Bettelheim, "Returning to Dachau," *Commentary* 21 (January 1956–June 1956), 144–151.

13. From regulations in my possession. Translated by Jonaca Driscoll, professor of German, Modesto, California.

14. Berben, *Dachau,* 233.

15. Grunberger, 330, 339.

16. See the discussions in Neuhäusler, *What Was it Like at Dachau?,* 34–38, and Berben, *Dachau,* 7.

17. Berben, *Dachau,* 89.

18. See *TWC* I: 92–199; II: 175, 336–342.

19. *TWC* II: 840.

20. *TWC* I: 173–174.

21. *TWC* I: 200 for freezing studies. Reports on 223.

22. *TWC* I: 201.

23. *TWC* I: 250–251.

24. *TWC* I: 226–242.

25. *TWC* I: 12, 44, 278–314; II: 175.

26. *TWC* I: 418–494; II: 177; quote from I: 453.

27. For secondary sources on the experiments see Kogon; Reitlinger; Berben, 123–138; Shirer; Meltzer. For the Rascher story, see Marc Hillel and Clarissa Henry, *Of Pure Blood* (New York: McGraw-Hill, 1976), 113–115; and Jacques Delarue, *Histoire de la Gestapo* (Paris: 1963), 364.

28. *Martyrdom and Resistance,* January–February 1975, 1.

29. Ibid., 2.

30. Berben, *Dachau,* 145. For solid discussion of the clergy, see Ch. 11.

31. Ibid., 188; and see Trunk, 232.

32. An interesting description of the liberation is contained in Selzer, *Deliverance Day,* 238. See also the memoirs of Peter Churchill, *The Spirit in the Cage* (London: Hodder and Stoughton, 1954); Nerin E. Gun, *The Day of the Americans* (New York: Fleet, 1966); and Marcus J. Smith, *The Harrowing of Hell* (Albuquerque: New Mexico University Press, 1972). The SS plan is described in Ward Rutherford, *Genocide: The Jews in Europe* (New York: Ballantine, 1973), 153.

33. For the Firecloud story, see Selzer, *Deliverance Day*; and Berben, *Dachau,* 179–184. Quotes from Berben, 182, 184; poison story in Selzer, 238.

34. Schowalter, "This Was Dachau," *National Jewish Monthly,* September 1966, 20, 21; see also Joseph Rothenberg, "Dachau," in Gerd Korman, ed., *Hunter and Hunted* (New York: Viking, 1973), 275–278.

35. Neuhäusler, *What Was It Like at Dachau?,* 70.

36. Ibid., 75–78.

Sachsenhausen

1. Leon Szalet, *Experiment "E"* (New York: Didier, 1945), 245.

2. Ibid., 67.

3. Quote from Eduard Ullmann, *Sachsenhausen* (Berlin: VEB Deutscher Verlag, 1967); information on art in *Sachsenhausen* (Berlin: VEB/Deutscher Verlag der Wissenshaften, 1974), Volker Frank, *Antifaschistische Mahnmale in der DDR: Ihre Kunstlerische und Architektonische Gestaltung* (Leipzig: Veb. E.S. Seeman Verlag, 1970), and Komitee Der Antifaschistischen Widerstandskämpter, *Sachsenhausen* (Berlin: Kongress-Verlag, 1961).

4. For the old camps, see Krausnick, 409. Information on all aspects of the camp in the DDR book *Sachsenhausen* not directly quoted because it is published in German; also, *Dokumente, Aussagen, Forschungsergebnisse und Erlebnisberichte über das ehemalige Konzentrationslager Sachsenhausen* (East Berlin: Deutscher Verlag d. Wiss., 1974). For a recent article on the consolidation and organization of the terror, see E. G. Reiche, "From 'Spontaneous' to Legal Terror: SA, Police, and the Judiciary in Nürnberg, 1933–34," *European Studies Review,* 9 (1979): 237–264.

5. Krausnick, 442; and Edward Crankshaw, *The Gestapo* (New York: Pyramid, 1957), 28–29.

6. Freisler in Hannah Vogt, *The Burden of German Guilt* (New York: Oxford, 1964), 175. A comprehensive view of 1938 is in Emil Fackenheim, "Sachsenhausen 1938: Groundwork for Auschwitz," *Midstream,* April 1975, 27–31.

7. Reports in 1980 have it that Jakov Stalin, Joseph's oldest son, went beserk in Sachsenhausen in 1943, threw himself on an electric fence, and died after a German officer

fired a bullet into his head. The British and Americans kept the story from Stalin prior to his death in 1953.

8. Szalet, *Experiment "E,"* 15–16.

9. Ibid., 247, 138.

10. Ibid., 139.

11. Ibid., 20.

12. Ibid., 25.

13. Ibid., 32.

14. Dr. Leo Stein, "Rabbis in Sachsenhausen," *National Jewish Monthly,* January 1942, 154–155.

15. Ibid., 155.

16. *TWC* I: 13, 47, 631–632; Roger Manvell and Heinrich Fraenkel, *Himmler* (New York: Warner, 1972), 120; *Auschwitz,* Vol. I, Pt. 1, 191.

17. Ullmann, *Sachsenhausen,* 21.

18. *TWC* V: 488; Kogon, 93; and quotes from Szalet, *Experiment "E",* 201, 255.

19. Meltzer, 29.

20. Ibid., 30.

21. Bernhard Kruger, "I Was the World's Greatest Counterfeiter," *The Jewish Digest,* January 1959, 59–63. There is a novel rooted in this episode: Joseph E. Persico's *The Spiderweb* (New York: Crown, 1979).

22. Lucien Steinberg, *Not as a Lamb* (Hants, England: Saxon House, 1974), 52.

23. Ibid., 52–53.

24. Hans Peter Bleuel, *Sex and Society in Nazi Germany* (Philadelphia: Lippincott, 1973), 217.

25. For more details see Grunberger, David Schoenbaum, *Hitler's Social Revolution* (New York: Doubleday, 1966); Bleuel, *Sex in Nazi Germany*; and Hillel and Henry, *Of Pure Blood.*

26. Quotes from James Steakley, *The Homosexual Emancipation Movement in Germany* (New York: Arno, 1975), 114 and 116. See also Wolfgang Harthauser, "Der Massenmord an Homosexuellen im Dritten Reich," in Wilhart Schlegel, ed., *Das Grosse Tabu: Zeugnisse und Documente zum Problem der Homosexualität* (Munich, Rütten and Loenig, 1967); and W. J. Krueckl and Ian Johnson, "The New Right as an Old Trick," *Gay Community News,* May 3, 1980, 8–10. One continues to be disappointed in the research on homosexuals in the camps. Researchers have difficulty separating the treatment of homosexual inmates from that of nonhomosexual inmates; they either claim too much hardship or too little. The most recent research claims too little and does not identify the real difficulties for homosexuals. See R. Lautmann, "Pink Triangle: The Persecution of Male Homosexuality in Concentration Camps in Nazi-Germany," manuscript to be published in forthcoming issue of *Journal of Homosexuality,* 1981.

27. Richard Plant, "The Men with the Pink Triangles," *Christopher Street,* February 1977, 10.

28. This insight came from a San Francisco State University student, Jackie Winnow, in a paper, "The Holocaust We Were Never Told About," unpublished, 1979. 19.

29. Toland, *Hitler,* 33. See also *EJ* 14: 597–598.

30. Green, *Holocaust,* 220; and Joseph Goebbels, *Tagebücher, 1945* (Hamburg: Hoffman and Campe, 1977).

Buchenwald

1. Description in Buchenwald books: *Museum Buchenwald; Buchenwald;* Annadora Miethe, ed., *Buchenwald* (DDR, 1974); and *EJ* 4: 1441–1444.

2. Miethe, *Buchenwald*, no page number for quote.

3. The essay on art was completed with the help of Buchenwald museum specialists.

4. Art analysis in Volker Frank, *Antifaschistische Mahnmale.*

5. See Kogon, 53, and Bullock, *Hitler,* 629.

6. Thomas Geve, *Youth in Chains* (Jerusalem: Rubin Mass, 1958), 198.

7. Kogon, 50–51. In *Without Surrender: Art of the Holocaust* (Philadelphia, Pa.: Running Press, 1978), Nelly Toll provides valuable pictures of Buchenwald scenes: the prisoners are gaunt, grim, emaciated, starving piles of living bones. See also Richard Firster and Nora Levin, eds., *The Living Witness* (Philadelphia: Museum of American Jewish History, 1978).

8. David Rousset, "The Days of Our Death," *Politics,* July–August 1957, 151–152. Historians are fortunate to have several important documents available for Buchenwald. An early book by Dr. Eugen Kogon startled the world. He was an inmate from 1939–1945. Since Buchenwald was the first camp to fall intact into Western Allied hands, military leaders intended it to serve as a key to the understanding of the camp system. A military team selected Dr. Kogon to aid in the preparation of a lengthy report. In addition, East German historians have produced a definitive study, available for purchase only in the DDR, *Buchenwald.*

9. Ibid., 156.

10. Norwegian students in Buchenwald received good treatment. They lived in separate barracks and were allowed to wear long hair and civilian clothes—see Richard Petrow, *The Bitter Years* (New York: Morrow, 1974), 304. For additional memoirs, see Pierre d'Harcourt, *The Real Enemy* (New York: Scribner, 1967); Pierre Julitte, *Block 26: Sabotage at Buchenwald* (New York: Doubleday, 1971); Jacques Lusseyran, *And There was Light* (Boston: Little, Brown, 1963); and Eugene Weinstock, *Beyond the Last Path* (New York: Boni and Goek, 1947).

11. Kogon, 45.

12. See Bruno Apitz, *Naked Among Wolves* (Berlin: Seven Seas, 1966). Quote from Geve, *Youth in Chains,* 203.

13. Amos Elon, *Journey Through a Haunted Land* (New York: Holt, Rinehart, 1967), 147.

14. Elie Wiesel, "Agony at Buchenwald," in Korman, *Hunter and Hunted,* 262.

15. Kogon, 78.

16. Ibid., 123.

17. Ibid., 125, for band.

18. Geve, *Youth in Chains,* 209.

19. See Miethe, *Buchenwald,* 15.

20. Work information in Miethe, *Buchenwald,* 10–11, 14–15, 18; *Museum Buchenwald,* 13–16; *ITS* 2: 195–199.

21. Kogon, 84.

22. Ibid., 84.

23. Ibid., 99.

24. Ibid., 209–210.

25. *TWC* V: 353.

26. Ibid., 354–355.

27. *Museum Buchenwald*, 17.

28. Quote from *TWC* I: 14, 53, 56. See also Miethe, *Buchenwald*, 20–21, Höhne, 639–653; *TWC* I: 14, 51, 631–639, 178, 517–518. Personal account in Walter Poller, *Medical Block, Buchenwald* (New York: Lyle Stuart, 1961).

29. *TWC* I: 684–694.

30. Ibid., 51, 508–555, quote from 511. For all experiments, see *Auschwitz*, Vol. I, Pt. 2, 30–32, 120–130; Kogon, 139–157; Shirer, 979–984.

31. *TWC* V: 1088–1089.

32. See Miethe, *Buchenwald*, 18; Shirer, 983–984; *TWC* V: 1089.

33. Geve, *Youth in Chains*, 200.

34. Grunberger, 105.

35. Kogon, 267. Information on the Morgen case in Höhne, 384–387; Grunberger, 105–107; Shirer, 984; Hilberg, 578–579; Kogon, 258–267; and Kurt R. Grossman, "The Trial of Ilse Koch," *Congress Bi-Weekly*, December 18, 1950, 7–9.

36. Christopher Burney, *The Dungeon Democracy* (New York: Buell, 1946), 19.

37. Ibid., 51–54.

38. Eugene Heimler, *Night of the Mist* (London: Bodley Head, 1962), 161; and *Concentration Camp* (New York: Pyramid, 1959).

39. Burney, *Dungeon Democracy*, 117–139.

40. Elie Wiesel, "Death Against Life," in Korman, *Hunter and Hunted*, 302.

41. Geve, *Youth in Chains*, 224.

42. Elie Wiesel, *Night* (New York: Avon-Discus, 1969), 127; and William Heyen, *The Swastika Poems* (New York: Vanguard, 1977), 39.

43. Grunberger, 463.

44. Geve, *Youth in Chains*, 239–240.

45. Ibid., 243.

46. Interview with Maurice Rubinoff, Portland, Maine, October 1976; and letter, April 23, 1945, M. Rubinoff to L. Rubinoff.

47. S. B. Unsdorfer, "The Yellow Star," in Jacob Glatstein et al., eds., *Anthology of Holocaust Literature* (New York: Atheneum, 1968), 261.

48. Ibid., 261–262.

49. Ibid., 263.

50. Journal of Kibbutz Buchenwald, "Homecoming in Israel," in Schwarz, 315. There is greater depth in the treatment of the rebirth of survivors in Israel in Edward Alexander, "Abba Kovner: Poet of Holocaust and Rebirth," *Midstream*, October 1977, 50–60.

51. Journal of Kibbutz Buchenwald, "Homecoming," 331.

52. My translation. Additional information on survivor activity in "Die Glocke vom Ettersberg," by the Mitteilungsblatt der Lagergemeinschaft Buchenwald-Dora.

Mauthausen

1. Hans Marsálek, *Mauthausen* (Wien: Max Ungar, 1958); and *EJ* 11: 1136–1138.

2. For information on SS companies, see Alan S. Milward, *War Economy and Society*,

1939–1945 (Berkeley, University of California Press, 1977), 227. Grades from Krausnick, 482.

3. Evelyn Le Chéne, *Mauthausen: The History of a Death Camp* (London: Methuen, 1971), 35. See also Olga Wormser-Migot and Henri Michel, eds., *Tragedie de la Deportation 1940–45* (Paris: Hachette, 1955). Confession in Julian Bach Jr., "Death of a Killer," *Commentary,* October 1946, 319.

4. Chêne, *Mauthausen*, 59.

5. See ibid. and *ITS* volumes.

6. See Erich Goldhagen, "Albert Speer, Himmler, and the Secrecy of the Final Solution," *Midstream,* October 1971, 43–50; and Lucy Dawidowicz, "In Hitler's Service," *Commentary,* November 1970.

7. Chêne, *Mauthausen*, 66.

8. Shirer, 955.

9. Reitlinger, 355–356; and Chêne, *Mauthausen*, 64–71.

10. Chêne, *Mauthausen*, 119–120.

11. Ibid., 88.

12. Ibid., 133.

13. Ibid., 81.

14. Germaine Tillion, *Ravensbrück* (Garden City, N.Y.: Anchor Press, 1975), 137–139.

15. Chêne, *Mauthausen*, 142.

16. Zdenka Fantlowa, "Long Live Life," in Schwarz, 220; Eugene Davidson, *The Trial of the Germans* (New York: Macmillan, 1967), 321; Reitlinger, 515. Quote from Chêne, *Mauthausen*, 157.

17. Marye Trench, "Mauthausen," in Korman, *Hunter and Hunted,* 283; George Dyer, *12th Corps* (Baton Rouge: Military Press of Louisiana, 1947), 432.

18. Simon Wiesenthal, "Steps Beyond the Grave," in Korman, *Hunter and Hunted,* 286.

19. Chêne, *Mauthausen*, 178–197.

20. Ibid., 209, 212.

21. Ibid., 207.

22. Ibid., 204 for quote; statistics, 218.

23. Ibid., 223.

24. Ibid., 227.

25. First quote from Max Garcia, *As Long as I Remain Alive.* (Tuscaloosa, Ala.: Portals, 1979), 24; for liberation of Ebensee, see 3–10, 15–19. Second quote from Trunk, 106.

26. Chêne, *Mauthausen*, 243–244.

Flossenbürg

1. Höhne, 459; and *ITS* 1: 210–211, and 2: 191–194. Quote from Arnold Lustig, *Darkness Casts No Shadow* (New York: Avon, 1978), 24.

2. See André Brissaud, *Canaris* (London: Weidenfeld and Nicolson, 1973).

3. Isabella Leitner, *Fragments of Isabella* (New York: Crowell, 1978), preface.

4. *TWC* V: 216, 219, 239–240, 247–288. Quote from Meltzer, 91.

5. *ITS* 2: 191–194.

6. Statistics from "Flossenburg, The Story of One Concentration Camp," *National Jewish Monthly,* October 1945, 46.
7. Ibid., 49; Pictures of liberation day, 46–49. See also Stefan Szwarc, "The March to Freedom," *Jewish Frontier,* May 1948, 11–15.
8. Leitner, *Fragments of Isabella,* 53.

Women and the Third Reich:
Part I: Ravensbrück—For Women Only

1. Wanda Kiedrzynska, *Ravensbrück* (Ravensbrück Archives, Warsaw Academy Historical Institute, 1961), no page numbers, translated by K. Feig. See also Victor Frank, *Antifaschistische Mahnmale.*
2. "Experimental Operations in the Ravensbrück Concentration Camp," in *GCP, II,* 133–150; *Auschwitz,* Vol. I, Pt. 2. Additional information from Christian Bernadac, *Le Camp des Femmes-Ravensbrück* (Paris: Eds. France Empire, 1973); and Eduard Ullmann, *Ravensbrück* (DDR: Ravensbrück Archives, 1964).
3. See Kiedrzynska, *Ravensbrück,* and Tillion, *Ravensbrück,* 16–18.
4. Information on 1944 in Tillion, *Ravensbrück,* 17; chronology, 240–245.
5. For 1945, see Kiedrzynska, *Ravensbrück.*
6. Quote in Reitlinger, 517–518. See also Tillion, *Ravensbrück*, 99–111, 167–178.
7. Tillion, *Ravensbrück*, 68–69.
8. Ibid., 69.
9. For prominents, see German Gluck, *My Story* (New York: McKay, 1961), 50–54. Camp social structure in Tillion, *Ravensbrück*, 28–38.
10. Ibid., 28, and Kiedrzynska.
11. Gluck, *My Story,* 31.
12. Ibid., 79.
13. Denise Dufournier, *Ravensbrück: The Women's Camps of Death* (London: Allen, 1948), 7–8, 48–49, 130–131.
14. From Kiedrzynska, *Ravensbrück.*
15. Gluck, *My Story,* 38, 39.
16. Gemma Gluck, "LaGuardia's Sister—Eichmann's Hostage," *Midstream* 7 (Winter 1961), 6.
17. Kiedrzynska, *Ravensbrück*, for schedule. Labor in Tillion, *Ravensbrück,* 42–46.
18. Gluck, *My Story,* 32–33.
19. Gluck, "La Guardia's Sister," 6.
20. Dr. Wanda Poltawska, " 'Guinea Pigs' in the Ravensbrück Camp," *Auschwitz,* Vol. I., Pt. 2, 140. For details on the rabbit story see Poltawska, "Experimental Operations," in *GCP, I, TWC* I, and Tillion, *Ravensbrück,* 79–89.
21. *TWC* I: 355–356.
22. *TWC* I: 360.
23. Tillion, *Ravensbrück,* 88.
24. Gluck, *My Story,* 12; for technical details, see Poltawska, "Experimental Operations."
25. *TWC* I: 48.
26. Ibid.

27. Ibid., 731.
28. Ibid., 50.
29. Poltawska, "Guinea Pigs," 141.
30. Story in Tillion, *Ravensbrück*, 81–83.
31. Quote in Poltawska, "Guinea Pigs," 145. See also *TWC* I: 396.
32. See Tillion, *Ravensbrück*; and Poltawska, "Guinea Pigs," 131–161.
33. Judith Newman, *In the Hell of Auschwitz* (New York: Exposition: 1963), 78; and Reitlinger, 485, for Couturier quote.
34. Tillion, *Ravensbrück*, 9.
35. Ibid., 24.
36. See Kiedrzynska, *Ravensbrück*; and example, Tillion, *Ravensbrück*, xi, 94–98, 141–159, 211–218.
37. Gluck, "La Guardia's Sister," 115.
38. Tillion, *Ravensbrück*, 102.
39. Kiedrzynska, *Ravensbrück*.
40. Tillion, *Ravensbrück*, 102–103.
41. Ibid., 149–150.
42. Ibid., 110.
43. Ibid., 181.

Part II: Nazi Theory and Practice—A Woman's Future

1. The studies of German women that I found helpful include Clifford Kirkpatrick, *Nazi Germany: Its Women and Family Life* (New York: Bobbs-Merrill, 1938); Jill Stephenson, *Women in Nazi Society* (New York: Barnes and Noble, 1975); Renate Bridenthal, "Beyond *Kinder, Küche, Kirche,*" *Central European History* 6 (June 1973): 148–166; Leila J. Rupp, *Mobilizing Women for War* (Princeton, N.J.: Princeton University Press, 1978); Claudia Koonz, "Nazi Women Before 1933," *Social Science Quarterly* 56 (March 1976): 553–563—I appreciated receiving a copy of her work before it went to print; Claudia Koonz, "The Nazi Women's Dilemma: To Sew or Wear Brown Shirts?", paper read at 1974 AHS convention; Werner Thönnessen, *The Emancipation of Women* (Glasgow: Pluto Press, 1973); Renate Bridenthal and Claudia Koonz, eds., *Becoming Visible: Women in European History* (Boston: Houghton Mifflin, 1977), particularly the Koonz article on the Nazi mother, 445–473; Richard J. Evans, *The Feminist Movement in Germany, 1894–1933* (Beverly Hills, Cal.: Sage, 1976); Marion A. Kaplan, "The Campaign for Women's Suffrage in the Jewish Community in Germany," Max Weinrich Center, *YIVO Institute,* February 1976; Dörte Winkler, *Frauenarbeit im "Dritten Reich"* (Hamburg: Hoffman and Campe Verlag, 1977); Gabrielle Bremme, *Die Politische Rolle Der Frau in Deutschland* (Göttingen, 1956); Judith Grunfeld, "Women Workers in Nazi Germany," *Nation,* March 1937, 13; and Marion A. Kaplan, *The Jewish Feminist Movement in Germany* (Westport, Conn.: Greenwood Press, 1979).
2. Hillel, *Of Pure Blood,* 29.
3. *DN,* 364. Fortunately or unfortunately, the Nazis were unwilling to put their money behind their propaganda to arrest the birth decline and promote large families. The allowances and financial incentives were too small and piecemeal to overcome the conviction by a large percentage of the population that a large family equaled long-term

poverty. See Jill Stephenson, *"Reichsbund der Kinderreichen,"* *European Studies Review* 9 (1979): 351–375.

4. Goebbels in Hillel, *Of Pure Blood*, 34; and David Schoenbaum, 187. We also ought not underestimate the "complex image of women" in Nazi ideology—see Leila J. Rupp, "Mother of the *Volk,"* *Signs* 3 (1977), 362–379; also Rolf Dahrendorf, *Society and Democracy in Germany*; (London, 1967); Bleuel, *Sex and Society in Nazi Germany*; Richard N. Hunt, *German Social Democracy, 1918–1933* (New Haven, Conn.: Yale University Press, 1964); George Mosse, *Nazi Culture* (New York: Grossett and Dunlap, 1966).

5. Hillel, *Of Pure Blood,* 36. I found stimulating for the issue of women's support the essays by Tim Mason, "Women in Nazi Germany," Pts. I and II, *History Workshop,* Spring 1976, 74–113, and Autumn 1976, 5–32.

6. Hillel, 38.

7. Ibid., 39.

8. See Richard Grunberger, *"Lebensborn,"* *Bulletin of the Wiener Library,* July 1952.

9. See Grunberger, *The Twelve-Year Reich,* for background chapters.

10. Dorothy Rabinowitz, *New Lives* (New York: Knopf, 1976), 54. See also Richard Baxter, *Women of the Gestapo* (London: Quality, 1943).

11. Himmler in *TWC* I: 34.

12. Hillel, *Of Pure Blood,* 117.

13. Ibid., 123.

14. Ibid., 150.

15. Ibid., 165.

16. Ibid., 174.

17. *TWC* V: 367–368.

18. Sir David M. Fyfe, gen. ed., *War Crimes Series: The Velpke Baby Home Trial* (London: William Hodge, 1950); quote from *TWC* V: 114–115.

19. *TWC* V: 117.

20. *TWC* V: 234–235; and *TWC* II: 1076–1077.

21. Himmler in *TWC* V: 240.

22. Micheline Maurel, *An Ordinary Camp* (New York: Simon and Schuster, 1958), 63.

23. Newman, *In the Hell of Auschwitz,* 21–22.

24. Seweryna Szmaglewska, *Smoke Over Birkenau* (New York: Holt, 1947), 19.

25. Pelagia Lewinska, *Twenty Months at Auschwitz* (New York: Lyle Stuart, 1968), 74, 79.

26. Irén Darvas, "Women in a Nazi Munitions Factory," *YVB*, November 1967, 28–34.

27. See *ITS* volumes.

28. Szmaglewska, *Smoke Over Birkenau,* 5.

29. Ibid., 7.

30. Olga Lengyel, *Five Chimneys* (Chicago: Ziff Davis, 1947), 24–25.

31. Lewinska, *Twenty Months at Auschwitz,* 36–37.

32. Newman, *In the Hell of Auschwitz,* 19, and Szmaglewska, *Smoke Over Birkenau,* 208–209.

33. Lengyel, *Five Chimneys,* 68–69.

34. Ibid., 22.

35. Lewinska, *Twenty Months at Auschwitz*, 141; and Dr. Ella Lingens-Reiner, *Prisoner of Fear* (London: Victor Gollancz, 1948), 70.

36. Lewinksa, *Twenty Months at Auschwitz*, 42–43.

37. Newman, *In the Hell of Auschwitz*, 20; and Trunk, *Jewish Responses*, 109.

38. Quotes and descriptions from Lengyel, *Five Chimneys*, 19–21.

39. Maurel, *An Ordinary Camp*, 98.

40. Szmaglewska, *Smoke Over Birkenau*, 175.

41. Lewinska, *Twenty Months at Auschwitz*, 111, for quotes. Also Lingens-Reiner, *Prisoner of Fear*, 101–102.

42. Lingens-Reiner, *Prisoner of Fear*, 118.

43. Quote and description from Lengyel, *Five Chimneys*, 45. Descriptions also from Lewinska, *Twenty Months at Auschwitz*, 45.

44. Lewinska, 46.

45. Lingens-Reiner, *Prisoner of Fear*, 28–29; and Kitty Hart, *Return to Auschwitz* (London: British Television, 1980).

46. Lewinska, *Twenty Months at Auschwitz*, 46, and Lengyel, *Five Chimneys*, 117.

47. Lewinska, *Twenty Months at Auschwitz*, 130, and Lingens-Reiner, *Prisoner of Fear*, 43.

48. Quote from Maurel, *An Ordinary Camp*, 24.

49. First quote and story from Newman, *In the Hell of Auschwitz*, 39. Second story from Gloria Goldreich, *Four Days* (New York: Harcourt Brace, 1980) 130, 153–54.

50. Szmaglewska, *Smoke Over Birkenau*, 4.

51. Lewinska, *Twenty Months at Auschwitz*, 90–91.

52. First quote, Lewinska, *Twenty Months at Auschwitz*, 99; description from Lingens-Reiner, *Prisoner of Fear*, 66; and final quote from Newman, *In the Hell of Auschwitz*, 25.

53. Maria Nowakowska, "The 'Women's Hospital' in Birkenau," *Auschwitz*, Vol. II, Pt. 2, 144–160, quote from 152.

54. Stanislawa Leszczynska, "Report of a Midwife from Auschwitz," *Auschwitz*, Vol. II, Pt. 2, 186; and Irene Schwarz, "The Still Small Voice," in Schwarz, 193.

55. Lingens-Reiner, *Prisoner of Fear*, 56.

56. Szmaglewska, *Smoke Over Birkenau*, 33–35. Additional material on medical treatment and experimentation comes from Maria Jezierska, "It Is Not Permitted to Be Sick," *Auschwitz*, Vol. II, Pt. 2, 193–216; Jalian Kivala, "At the End of 1942," *Auschwitz*, Vol. II, Pt. 2, 161–180; Wanda Machlejd, ed., *Experimental Operations on Prisoners of Ravensbrück Concentration Camp* (Warsaw: Zachodnia Agencja Prasowa, 1960); Dr. Otto Wolken, "When I Think of Children," *Auschwitz*, Vol. II, Pt. 3, 13–20; Gisela Perl, *I Was a Doctor in Auschwitz* (New York: International Universities Press, 1948).

57. Maurel, *An Ordinary Camp*, 105.

58. Ibid., 13, for quote.

59. Ibid., 24.

60. See Reska Weiss, *Journey Through Hell* (London: Valentine-Mitchell, 1961).

61. Lengyel, *Five Chimneys*, 210.

62. Newman, *In the Hell of Auschwitz*, 43.

63. Reports on childbirth are from Leszczynska, "Report of a Midwife from Auschwitz," 181–192.

64. Quote from Leszczynksa, 190.

65. Newman, *In the Hell of Auschwitz,* 52; and *TWC* V: 663–664.

66. Janina Koscinszkowa, "Children in the Auschwitz Camp," *Auschwitz*, Vol. II, Pt. 2, 219.

67. Szmaglewska, *Smoke Over Birkenau,* 277.

68. Ibid., 266; and Newman, *In the Hell of Auschwitz*, 57.

69. Fania Fenelon, *Playing for Time* (New York: Atheneum, 1977), ix, 70. Fenelon, the daughter of a Christian mother and a Jewish father, was a well-known café singer in Paris during the early years of World War II and worked with the resistance. After being betrayed, incarcerated, and tortured, she was sent to Auschwitz. Years later, her memoir became the center of national turmoil in the U.S. She had sold the film rights to CBS, which selected Arthur Miller to write the screenplay and Vanessa Redgrave to play Fania Fenelon. Fenelon and Redgrave faced each other on a *60 Minutes* program in August 1979. In a segment that was edited out, Fenelon told Redgrave that she was too old to play a teenage girl, and that Redgrave's politics in support of the PLO prevented her from being able to portray a Jewish woman sensitively and truthfully. In San Fancisco, in November 1979, Fenelon publicly criticized the Miller screenplay charging that Miller had distorted the camp atmosphere, fabricated a love story between her and a male prisoner, pictured the SS as humane, and created an environment in which the SS appeared as victims and the inmates as defendants on trial. The movie played in September 1980 to a large TV audience.

70. Szmaglewska, *Smoke Over Birkenau,* 31. Bertha Ferdberber-Salz in her memoir *And the Sun Kept Shining* (New York: Holocaust Library, 1980), 115, describes the importance of diversions. One woman made SS and inmate puppets from cloth and produced a scenario with the Germans hitting and shooting the prisoners.

71. Lingens-Reiner, *Prisoners of Fear,* 106–7. Last quote from Lengyel, *Five Chimneys,* 181.

72. Naomi Munkacsi, "Jewish Religious Observance in Women's Death Camps in Germany," *YVB* 20 (April 1967), 35–38. Other helpful memoirs and literature include Ilse Aichinger, *Herod's Children* (New York: Atheneum, 1964); Gerda Weissmann Klein, *All But My Life* (New York: Hill and Wang, 1957); Eugenia Kocwa, *Flücht aus Ravensbrück* (East Berlin: Union Verlag, 1973); Jack Kuper, *Child of the Holocaust* (Garden City, New York: Doubleday, 1968); R. J. Minney, *I Shall Fear No Evil* (London: Kimber, 1966); Sala Pawlowicz, *I Will Survive* (New York: Norton, 1962); Irene Schwarz, "The Small Still Voice," in Schwartz, 189–200; Krystna Zywulska, *I Came Back* (New York: Roy, 1951); and Livia E. Bitton Jackson, *Elli* (New York: Times Books, 1980).

73. See Sir David Fyfe, *War Crimes Trials, Vol. II, The Belsen Trial*; and other pertinent trial records.

74. Maurel, *An Ordinary Camp,* 138–141.

Stutthof/Sztutowo

1. Tadeusz Matusiak, "Stutthof" (Gdansk: Museum Stutthof, 1974).

2. Quotes from "Stutthof Concentration Camp," in *GCP* II, 119; *ITS* 1: 266; *EJ* 15: 464–466. For museum background, see Tadeusz Matusiak, *Stutthof* (Gdansk: Zaklady Graficzne, for Museum Stutthof, 1969), 48–54.

3. Matusiak, "Stutthof."

4. Matusiak, *Stutthof,* 12.

5. Ibid., 6, for quote. For background to the Nazi takeover, see Herbert Levine, *Hitler's Free*

City (Chicago: University of Chicago Press, 1973). Statistics in Matusiak, *Stutthof,* 9.

6.   Matusiak, *Stutthof,* 8.

7.   Ibid., 16.

8.   *TWC* V: 499.

9.   Ibid., 500.

10. For complete story and quotes, see *TWC* V: 493–501.

11. Matusiak, *Stutthof*, 16–17.

12. Ibid.

13. Olga Pickholz-Barnitsch, "The Evacuation of the Stutthof Concentration Camp," *YVB*, No. 12, December 1945, 37.

14. "Stutthof Concentration Camp," 115, 117.

15. Ibid., 116, for quote.

16. Matusiak, *Stutthof,* 30, for quote.

17. Ibid., 34.

18. Ibid., 35.

19. The soap stories appear to excite enormous controversy. Early scholars said the stories were untrue, that the Nazis did not make soap from human fat, that those bars of soap marked with an "RJF" were not made from humans (letter in author's possession from Herbert Rosenkranz to Lonny Darwin, September 20, 1979). Most East European camp scholars, however, validate the soap stories, and other kinds of bars made from humans are displayed in Eastern Europe—I have seen many over the years. I accept without further question that the Nazis did use every part of the human body, for the evidence now is irrefutable. The Stutthof soap bars do *not* have "RJF" stamped on them. Testimony from *IMT* 7: 598–601. See also Shirer, 971.

20. "Stutthof Concentration Camp," 127–128.

21. Picknolz-Barnitsch, "Evacuation of Stutthof," 47. The story of one excruciating boat trip is found in Trunk, 322–326.

22. Picknolz-Barnitsch, "Evacuation of Stutthof," 39.

23. The evacuation story is well done in Picknolz-Barnitsch; for Hoppe, see Charles Sydnor Jr., *Soldiers of Destruction*, 329.

Gross-Rosen

1.   Considerable material is available on the Nazi occupation of Poland. I appreciated the analysis of Jan T. Gross, *Polish Society under German Occupation.*

2.   *ITS* 2:210; and *TWC* V: 444.

3.   Geve, *Youth in Chains,* 181; and Paul Heller, "A Concentration Camp Diary," *Midstream,* April 1980, 29–36.

4.   Zdenka Fantlowa, "Long Live Life," in Schwarz, 217.

5.   Geve, *Youth in Chains,* 182.

6.   Ibid., 187; and Fantlowa, "Long Live Life," 272.

7.   Paul Trepman, *Among Men and Beasts* (New York: A. S. Barnes, 1978), 168–169.

8.   *TWC* V: 362. See Green, *Holocaust,* 316, for language.

9.   *TWC* V: 363–364.

10. Ibid., 64, for quote.

11. Ibid., 228.

12. Ibid., 229.
13. Ibid., 859–861, 64–67, 226–229, 794–801.
14. Leonard Doob, *Panorama of Evil* (Westport, Conn.: Greenwood Press, 1978), 9.

Neuengamme

1. *TWC* V: 814.
2. Ibid., 219, 488. Categorization in Krausnik, 476.
3. Dr. Stanislaw Klodzinski, "Criminal Experiments with Tuberculosis Carried Out in Nazi Concentration Camps," in *Auschwitz*, Vol. 1, Pt. 2, 163; and Kogon, 155.
4. For entire report, *Auschwitz*, Vol. 1, Pt. 2, 163–175; quote, 166.
5. Ibid., 168.
6. Ibid., 170.
7. *ITS* 1: 93.
8. Klodzinski, "Criminal Experiments," 165.
9. White Buses story in Richard Petrow, *The Bitter Years,* 316–327; all quotes on subject, 321–324.
10. Bernadotte in Reitlinger, 504, et al. See *ITS* 2: 114, 124–126, for *Arcona* story.

Natzweiler/Struthof

1. Gabriel Gersh, "The Zone of Silence," *Congress Bi-Weekly,* February 6, 1956.
2. Ibid., 7.
3. James J. Weingartner, *Crossroads of Death* (Berkeley: University of California Press, 1979), 10.
4. Phrase from Kogon, 189. Natzweiler specifics from Dr. Leon Boutbien, ed., *Natzweiler-Struthof* (Nancy: A. Humblot, 1976), 23; and *EJ* 12: 891–894.
5. Tillion, *Ravensbrück*, 20.
6. Boutbien, *Natzweiler-Struthof,* 22.
7. *TWC* I: 318–324, for experiment report.
8. *TWC* I: 35, 89. For more information on Ahnenerbe Society, see *TWC* I: 54–55, 88–89, 318, 752–754.
9. *TWC* I: 320.
10. Ibid.
11. Ibid., 12, 44, 315, 318–323.
12. Ibid., 50, 519–520, 528–529.
13. Ibid., 13, 47.
14. Quote from Dr. Jan Sehn, "Some of the Legal Aspects of the So-Called Experiments," *Auschwitz*, Vol. I, Pt. 1, 64–65. See also Hilberg, 608–609; and *TWC* I: 739, 748–749.
15. *TWC* I: 740.
16. Tillion, *Ravensbrück*, 184.
17. Quotes (in order) from *TWC* I: 55; Sehn, "Legal Aspects of Experiments," 65; *TWC* I: 741. Additional information in Fyfe, "The Natzweiler Trial," in *War Crime Trial Series,* Vol. V.

Dora/Nordhausen

1. See Volker Frank, *Antifaschistische Mahnmale.*

2. Kogon, 93.

3. Prosecution Staff, *A Booklet With a Brief History of the "Dora"-Nordhausen Labor Concentration Camps and Information on the Nordhausen War Crimes Case of the USA versus Arthur Kurt Andrae et al.* (Nuremberg, 1947), 8.

4. Ibid.

5. Ibid., 10.

6. Kogon, 95.

7. Prosecution Staff, *History of "Dora"-Nordhausen, 13.*

8. Ibid., 20.

9. Kogon, 95–96.

10. *TWC* V: 413.

11. *Daily Mail, Lest We Forget* (London: Northcliffe House, 1945), 12.

12. Ibid., 15–16. One officer with the Nordhausen liberating forces was Major Hugh Carey, the present governor of New York, who was stunned by the "cruelty and barbarism" he saw. Noted in *Martyrdom and Resistance,* January–February 1980, 9.

13. *ITS* 2: 201.

14. Prosecution Staff, *History of "Dora"-Nordhausen, 14–15.*

15. Alan D. Beyerchen, *Scientists Under Hitler* (New Haven, Conn.: Yale University Press, 1977).

Terezin/Theresienstadt

1. Quote in *Terezin* (Prague: Council of Jewish Communities, 1965), 5. See Miroslav Karny, "Das Konzentrationslager Terezin (Theresienstadt) in den Planen der Nazis," *Ceskoslovensky casopis historicky* 22 (1974), 673–702; and Vaclav Novak, *Terezin* (Pamatnik Terezin: 1974).

2. See Gary B. Cohen, "Jews in German Society: Prague, 1860–1914," *Central European History* 10: 28–54.

3. One of my students, a Jewish man from Prague who had been a tour guide, tells me that Jews makes up a large percentage of the guide group. He also admits that many do not acknowledge their Jewishness because of a continuing fear of being singled out.

4. One story of the Torahs is found in Joan Milman, "Bringing Home the Bride," *Moment,* April 1977, 52–56.

5. *The State Museum in Prague* (Prague: State Museum, 1976); *The State Jewish Museum* (Prague, 1976); Tom L. Freudenheim, "The Jewish Museum (NYC)," *Moment,* November 1976, 27–29; Jiri Dolezal and Evzen Vesely, *Pamatky prazskeno ghetta* (Prague: Olympia, 1969); *EJ* 15: 1112–16; 3: 560–594; 13: 964–978; 12: 539; 5: 274–275.

6. Libuse Krylová, *The Small Fortress of Terezin* (Terezin: 1975), 1–5; *The Little Fortress Terezin* (Litomerice: Vytiskla Severografia, 1967).

7. Krylová, *Small Fortress,* 5.

8. Oliva Pechova et al., *Kunst in Theresienstadt, 1941–1945: Katalog Zur Ausstellung* (Pamatnik Terezin: 1972); Milan Kuna et al., *Kunst in Theresienstadt, 1941–45*

(Terezin: 1972). For scenes by Theresienstadt artists, see Kibbutz Lochamei HaGhettaot, Israel, *Spiritual Resistance: Art from the Concentration Camps, 1940–45* (New York: Union of American Hebrew Confederations, 1978). One notes a significant contrast in the noncontribution to the artistic world of Nazi artists producing in the "freedom" of their society: Berthold Hinz, *Art in the Third Reich* (New York: Pantheon, 1980).

9. The production was reviewed in many magazines; for example, *Time,* May 16, 1977, 113; also Viktor Ullmann, "The Emperor of Atlantis," *Midstream,* April 1975, 38–43.

10. The Small Fortress history in *Terezin; The Little Fortress Terezin;* Krylova, *Small Fortress;* Zdenek Lederer, *Ghetto Theresienstadt* (London: Edward Goldston, 1953); and *Rusky a zidovsky hrbitov terezin* (Prague).

11. Lederer, *Ghetto Theresienstadt,* 2.

12. Ibid., 6. My debt to H. G. Adler for information for this essay is obvious: *Theresienstadt 1941–45* (Tübingen, 1955); and *Die verheimlichte Wahrheit* (Tübingen: J. C. B. Mohr, 1958). Also F. Ehrmann, ed., *Terezin, 1941–45* (London: Collet's, 1965).

13. Levin, 192. For the reaction of Zionists, see "Hehalutz in Theresienstadt," *YVS,* II: 1968, 107–24. See also Livia Rothkirchen, "Czech Attitudes Toward the Jews During the Nazi Regime," *YVS,* XIII, 1979, 287–320. For the attitudes by the Czech Jews, the novel by Hana Demetz is helpful: *The House on Prague Street* (New York: St. Martins, 1980).

14. Alfred Werner, "Madhouse Theresienstadt," *Congress Bi-weekly,* March 26, 1956, 13.

15. Lederer, *Ghetto Theresienstadt,* 16.

16. Ibid., 22.

17. Hilberg for description.

18. Quotes in Levin, 480; and Werner, "Madhouse Theresienstadt," 14.

19. Levin, 477.

20. Deportation and population statistics in Lederer, *Ghetto Theresienstadt;* and *Terezin* (Prague).

21. Lederer, *Ghetto Theresienstadt,* 48–49.

22. For a novelist's description of life in Theresienstadt, see Arnold Lustig, *Diamonds of the Night* (Washington, D.C.: Inscape, 1978); and *Night and Hope* (New York: Dutton, 1962).

23. Zdenka Fantlowa, "Long Live Life!" in Schwarz, 210.

24. Virginia Mazer, "I Never Saw Another Butterfly," Eternal Light Broadcast Script, NBC-TV, December 11, 1966, by Jewish Theological Seminary, 6. For an insight into a child's mind looking at the camps from afar, see Anna Rose, *Refugee* (New York: Dial Press, 1977); also Hana Volavkova, ed., *I Never Saw Another Butterfly* (New York: McGraw-Hill, 1962).

25. Levin, 483.

26. Mazer, "I Never Saw Another Butterfly," 7, 10.

27. Zdena Berger, *Tell Me Another Morning* (New York: Harper, 1959), 29–32.

28. Mazer, "I Never Saw Another Butterfly," 13, 17; and Berger, *Tell Me Another Morning,* 48.

29. *Terezin* (Prague), 104, 106–107, 109–111.

30. Michael Jacot, *The Last Butterfly* (New York: Bobbs-Merrill, 1974), 22, 7.

31. Lederer, *Ghetto Theresienstadt,* 104. See also Levin, 490.

32. Quote from Levin, 481. See also Reitlinger, 179.

33. Richard Petrow, *The Bitter Years,* 306.

34. Lederer, *Ghetto Theresienstadt,* 118.

35. See Joseph Bor, *Terezin Requiem* (New York: Knopf, 1963).

36. Quote from Levin, 490. Description of Danes in Petrow, *Bitter Years,* 313.

37. Levin, 492.

38. For Terezin film, see Levin; Lederer, *Ghetto Theresienstadt*; Adler, *Theresienstadt 1941–45 Terezin* (Prague). The Nazis were prolific film-makers. The worst anti-Semitic films the Nazis made are *Jud Süss* (1940, Harlan Veit); *The Eternal Jew* (1940, Fritz Heppler); and *The Rothchilds* (1940, Erich Waschneck). All can be viewed at the National Archives in Washington D.C. Germans in the Weimar Period (1919–1933) led the world in film making, seeming to identify the destructive, murderous forces undermining society. The most important of those films to the Holocaust are *Das Cabinet des Dr. Caligari* (1920, Hans Janowitz); *Dr. Mabuse, The Gambler* (1922, Fritz Lang); *Nibelungen* (1924, Fritz Lang); *The Joyless Street* (1925, G. W. Pabst); *M—The Murderer Among Us* (1930, Fritz Lang); *The Blue Angel* (1930, Josef Sternberg).

    Since the war, film makers in Europe and the United States have made enormously important statements and created vivid pictures of Nazi Germany and the Holocaust. The two major films on Nazi Germany are *Swastika* (1974, RBC Films); and Leni Riefenstahl's gigantic effort of 1934, *Triumph des Willens* (Triumph of the Will). Films focusing on the Holocaust: *Judgment at Nuremberg* (1961, Roxlom-United Artists, Stanley Kramer); *Voyage of the Damned* (1976); *Marathon Man* (1976); QBVII (CBS TV Film); *Ship of Fools* (1965, CCM); *Diary of Anne Frank* (1959, George Stevens); *Exodus* (1960, Otto Preminger); *The Fifth Horseman Is Fear* (1966, Zbynek Brynch); *The Pawnbroker* (1965, Sidney Lunt); *Les Violon du Bal* (1974, France, Michel Drach); *Naked Among Wolves* (1967, Frank Beyer); *The Garden of the Finzi-Continis* (Italy); *Distant Journey* (1950, Czechoslovakia, A. Radok); *The Shop on Main Street* (1965, Czechoslovakia, Jan Kador); *Lacombe, Lucien* (France); *The Witnesses* (1962, CCM, Thomas Craven); *Night and Fog* (1955, McGraw-Hill); *Transport from Paradise* (1963, Czechoslovakia, Arnost Lustig); *Of Pure Blood* (PBS Video-Tape); *The Investigation* (CBS TV Film, Peter Weiss); *The Holocaust* (TV Film, Gerald Green, 1978); *The Night of the Generals*; *I Never Saw Another Butterfly* (1961, Czechoslovakia, Contemporary Films); *Mein Kampf* (1961, Sweden, Columbia Pictures); *Diamonds of the Night* (1964, Prague, Arnost Lustig, Impact Films); *The 81st Blow* (1975, Israel, American Federation of Jewish Fighters); *The Memory of Justice* (1976, France, Marcel Ophuls); and *The Man in the Glass Booth* (1975, American Film Theatre, Robert Shaw). Gripping films have also been produced by camp museum staffs to be shown at the individual camp, such as Auschwitz, Buchenwald, or Dachau. The two best commentaries on film in the Weimar period and Nazi Germany remain Siegfried Kracauer, *From Caligari to Hitler* (Princeton, N.J.: Princeton University Press, 1955), and David Hull, *Film in the Third Reich* (Berkeley: University of California Press, 1969).

39. See Gerald Green, *The Artists of Terezin* (New York: Hawthorn, 1969). Quotes in Green, *The Artists of Terezin* (New York: Schocken, 1978), 18, 20, 27.

40. Adler, *Theresienstadt 1941–1945.*

41. Lederer, *Ghetto Theresienstadt,* 125.

42. *Terezin* (Prague), 207.

43. Green, *Artists of Terezin* (1978), 32.

44. Ibid., 3.

45. Alfred Kantor, *The Book of Alfred Kantor* (New York: McGraw-Hill, 1971).
46. Fantlowa, "Long Live Life," 209.
47. Lederer, *Ghetto Theresienstadt,* 126.
48. For example, see Levin, 485.
49. Green, *Artists of Terezin* (1978), 79, 143.
50. Lederer, *Ghetto Theresienstadt,* 146, 155.
51. For information, see ibid.; Levin; Reitlinger; Adler, *Theresienstadt 1941–45.*

Chelmno/Kulmhof

1. Tenenbaum, 252.
2. Hilberg, 580. See also *ITS* 1: 321; *EJ* 5: 374–376; Rückerl, 259–286.
3. "The Chelmno Extermination Camp," in *GCP I,* 109–111. The Jews who died came primarily from the Lodz ghetto. Mendel Grossman recaptured vividly that ghetto life in *With a Camera in the Ghetto* (New York: Schocken, 1977). See "Chelmno Extermination Camp," 111, for death statistics; and Reitlinger, 145, on euthanasia.
4. Charlotte Delbo, *None of Us Will Return* (New York: Grove Press, 1968), 5–6.
5. "Chelmno Extermination Camp," 111–113; Tenenbaum, 252–253.
6. S. L. Shneiderman, "Attention: The Bundestag in Bonn," *Congress Bi-Weekly,* February 15, 1965, 7.
7. Capacity of vans in Tenebaum, 253; the lost vans and gas problems quote in Reitlinger, 147.
8. "Chelmno Extermination Camp," 114.
9. Höhne, 374.
10. Hilberg, 628–629.
11. "Chelmno Extermination Camp," 115.
12. Re Greiser at Chelmno, see Hilberg, 609–610; and Rückerl, 334. Greiser denied at his trial that he had ever visited Chelmno. Quote from "Chelmno Extermination Camp," 119.
13. *TWC* V: 475–477 for report; quote, 475.
14. Rückerl, 281–283.
15. "Chelmno Extermination Camp," 120; Rückerl, 283–286.
16. Charles Reznikoff, *Holocaust* (Los Angeles: Black Sparrow Press, 1975), 82.
17. Tenenbaum, 253; and "Chelmno Extermination Camp," 121. Summary of Polish Court Proceedings of Chelmno officials in Rückerl, appendix.

Belzec

1. Rückerl, 143–145.
2. Death figures from "Belzec Extermination Camp," in *GCP, II,* 96; also *EJ* 4: 453–456. Some use the figure 400,000 on the destruction of the camp. See Höhne, 376, 378; Krausnick, 484; Hilberg, 574, 585, 629–630.
3. See Reitlinger, 148, for dates. On the reopening of graves, see Tenebaum, 256. Quote from Jan Karski, "Polish Death Camp," *Colliers,* October 14, 1944, 18.
4. "Belzec Extermination Camp," 89–90. See also Rückerl, 140–145.
5. Tenenbaum, 254–255.

6. Jan Karski, "An Eye-Witness Account from Poland," *Jewish Frontiers,* March 1943, 15–17; and *Story of a Secret State* (Boston: Houghton-Mifflin, 1944). Quote from Karski, "Polish Death Camp," 18.

7. Karski, "Polish Death Camp," 18–19.

8. Ibid., 18. Additional information on the use of Ukrainian guards in most killing centers in Jan T. Gross, *Polish Society under German Occupation.*

9. Karski, "Polish Death Camp," 19.

10. Tenenbaum, 255. Description of process in Hilberg, 625; Reitlinger, 147–148; and Krausnick, 99.

11. Quotes from Karski, *Jewish Frontiers,* 15; and Sereny, 112.

12. Gerstein and his reports can be found in Meltzer, 128; Toland, *Hitler,* 713–714; Sereny, 111; Saul Friedlander, *Kurt Gerstein* (New York: Knopf, 1969); and Pierre Joffroy, *A Spy for God* (New York: Harcourt Brace, 1971). See also Gerstein's (and others') report in Rückerl, 61–66, 132–145. Gerstein's report was seen by the International Military Tribunal as the machinations of a sick mind. Because he committed suicide, they could not question him, but his report has been substantiated.

13. All quotes from report in Gerhard Schoenberner, *The Yellow Star* (New York: Bantam, 1973), 171–174. Summary of Belzec gas chambers in Serge Klarsfeld, *The Holocaust and the Neo-Nazi Mythomania* (New York: Beate Klarsfeld Foundation, 1978), 120–138.

14. Sereny, 112.

15. Karski, "Polish Death Camp," 21.

16. *EJ* 4: 455.

17. Elie Wiesel, *Trial of God* (New York: Random House, 1979). Quotes from 15, 32, 54, 125, 157.

Sobibor

1. See Lucien Steinberg, *Not as a Lamb,* 271, for revolt. Estimates in "Sobibor Extermination Camp," *GCP, II,* 102–103; *ITS* 1: 331; and *EJ*: 15; 21–22.

2. "Sobibor Extermination Camp," 99; Hilberg, 573–574; Rückerl, 176; and Miriam Novitch, *Sobibor, Martyre et Révolté* (Paris: Centre du Publication Asie Orientale, 1978).

3. Alexander Pechersky, "Revolt in Sobibor," in Yuri Suhl, ed., *They Fought Back* (New York: Schocken, 1975), 7. Novitch dates the visit as February 1943, and the number of women killed as 200.

4. Quote from "Sobibor Extermination Camp," 100. Gas capacity in Miriam Novitch, *Sobibor: Martyrdom and Revolt* (New York: Holocaust Library, 1980), 12, 26, and *GCP, II,* 100. For camp description, also see Rückerl, 166–175. The various personal accounts in Novitch differ among themselves as to the size and capacity of the five chambers.

5. Rückerl, 167–170.

6. "Sobibor Extermination Camp," 101–102.

7. Hilberg, 629.

8. Pechersky, "Revolt in Sobibor," 18.

9. Trunk, 277.

10. Sereny, 109.

11. Trunk, 19.

12. Sereny, 118.

13. Novitch, *Sobibor* (1980), 55–57, 74–75, 150–151.

14. See Meltzer, 177–178; Novitch, *Sobibor;* Steinberg, *Not as a Lamb,* 271–278; Hilberg, 586; Reitlinger, 153; Tenenbaum, 263–264; Pechersky, "Revolt in Sobibor," 7–50; Tuvia Blatt, "Revolt in the Sobibor Death Camp," *YVB,* No. 5, 36–38; Ada Lichtmann, "I Have Seen with My Own Eyes," *YVB,* No. 5, 38; Reuben Ainsztein, *Jewish Resistance,* 911–913. Additional testimony on the revolt can be found in Trunk, 268–287. See Rückerl for a review of the Sobibor Trial, September 1965–December 1966.

Treblinka

1. J. Gumkowski and A. Rutkowski, *Treblinka* (Warsaw: Council for Protection of Fight and Martyrdom Monuments, 1961); press release, March 29, 1963, Embassy of the Polish People's Republic, WDC: i; *EJ* 15: 1365–72.

2. Polish Embassy press release, March 29, 1963. As with most killing centers, experts differ significantly over the death figures. The one million figure is probably most accurate. One survivor testified that the SS held a gala celebration when they had killed their one millionth victim. The death statistics are staggering for a camp that was in existence for only 400 days.

3. Ibid., 4. The Trial Court information report describes in detail the camp and its processes in Rückerl, 197–242.

4. Höhne, 376.

5. Manvell, *Himmler,* 150; and Meltzer, 109.

6. Levin, 327.

7. Reitlinger, 274.

8. See Reitlinger, 278, for photos. Quote from Sereny, 193.

9. Meltzer, 116.

10. Elon, *Journey Through a Haunted Land,* 204.

11. Sereny, 157, 161.

12. Jean-Francois Steiner, *Treblinka* (New York: Simon and Schuster, 1967), 76. Steiner must be credited with the original concept of the technician. His book created an enormous controversy (his attitudes toward Jewish behavior are so erroneous that I do not even refer to them), but his fictional conceptions of procedures are excellent.

13. Ibid., 94.

14. Ibid., 95.

15. Ibid., 96.

16. Ibid., 110.

17. Samuel Rajzman, "Uprising in Treblinka," in Yuri Suhl, *They Fought Back,* 128. Although several hundred Jews escaped in the uprising, few lived through the war. Most survivors (about fifty) gathered in Poland—briefly—after the war and formed the Circle of Former Treblinka Inmates. A few wrote accounts of Treblinka before the war's end and after, and a few gave formal taped interviews. Available for scholars are materials of several surviving inmates: for example, Samuel Rajzman (the only killing center inmate to testify at Nuremberg); Zygmunt Strawczynski; Tanhum Grinberg, whose Polish testimony is available at Yad Vashem; Jankiel Wiernik; Abraham Krzepicki, whose testimony was recorded in the Warsaw ghetto by Rachel Auerbach, buried with the Ringelblum archives, recovered in 1950, placed in the Jewish Historical Institute in

Warsaw, and first published in *Bleter far Geshikhte,* Vol. XI, Warsaw: 1946. Rachel Auerbach's study, *In the Fields of Treblinka* received its first English publication as a portion of Alexander Donat, ed., *The Death Camp Treblinka* (New York: Walden Press, 1979). Interview with Treblinka survivor Samuel Rajzman, "The Long Road Out of Treblinka," in Howard Roiter, *Voices From the Holocaust* (New York: William-Frederick Press, 1975), 181–213; and interview with survivor Zygmunt Strawczynski, "Treblinka: The Death Factory," 121–141. See also Vassili Grossman, *L'Enfer de Treblinka* (Paris: Arthaud, 1966).

18. Hilberg, 625.

19. Yankel Wiernik, "A Year in Treblinka Horror Camp," in Jacob Glatstein et al., eds., *Anthology of Holocaust Literature* (New York: Atheneum, 1973), 179.

20. Ibid., 179–180.

21. Martin Gray, *For Those Who Loved* (Boston: Little Brown, 1972), 132.

22. Ibid., 136, 139. See also Menachem Z. Rosensaft, "Janusz Korzak," *Midstream,* May 1979, 57.

23. Yankel Wiernik, *A Year in Treblinka* (New York: General Jewish Workers Union, 1945), 8.

24. Gumkowski and Rutkowski, *Treblinka,* 12.

25. Wiernik, *A Year in Treblinka,* 13–15, 18.

26. Steiner, *Treblinka,* 207–209.

27. Ibid., 212.

28. Ibid., 213–214.

29. *DN,* 490.

30. Steiner, *Treblinka,* 286.

31. Sereny, 183.

32. Ibid., 214.

33. First full quote, ibid., 219; Steiner, *Treblinka,* 337, 339 for other quotes.

34. Steiner, *Treblinka,* 340. The Nazis depended on the fact that the killing centers sounded so improbable that no one in the world, including the Jews, would believe they existed. And the victims *were* unable to see the threat clearly. Some writers have insisted, however, that Jews have a special problem: they have a "deep-seated unwillingness . . . to credit the existence of evil." They believed instead, as optimists, in the progress and goodness of man. Treblinka shows that whatever their beliefs, the Jews were faced with one of the most audacious and skilled farces of our time: Edward Alexander, "The Incredibility of the Holocaust," *Midstream,* March 1979, 49. On the orchestra, see Rückerl, 215–216.

35. Wiernik, *A Year in Treblinka,* 28.

36. Steiner, *Treblinka,* 352.

37. Ibid., 346.

38. Tenebaum, 256–257; Sereny, 220.

39. Steiner, *Treblinka,* 354.

40. Wiernik, *A Year in Treblinka,* 29, 30.

41. Quote from Steiner, *Treblinka,* 356.

42. Ibid.

43. Ibid., 357.

44. Ibid., 374.

45. S. Willenberg, "Revolt at Treblinka," *YVB*, No. 7, 40; Sereny, 240. Additional testimony on the revolt in Trunk, 262–268.

46. See Steiner, *Treblinka*, 413–414; Sereny, 239–250; Meltzer, 175–177; Willenberg, "Revolt of Treblinka," 39–40; Steinberg, *Not as a Lamb*, 279–282; Stanislaw Kohn, "The Treblinka Revolt," in Glatstein, *Anthology*, 319–324; Yankel Wiernik, "Uprising in Treblinka," in Schwarz, 115–121; Rajzman, "Uprising in Treblinka," 128–135; Ainsztein, *Jewish Resistance*, 728–739; and Trunk, 352.

47. See Gumkowski and Rutkowski, *Treblinka*.

48. Sereny, 250; and for figures of 700,000–800,000, "The Treblinka Extermination Camp," in *GCP, II*, 104.

49. Wiernik, *A Year in Treblinka*, 5.

50. Information on the Treblinka Trials in Rückerl, *NS Vernichtungslager*.

Majdanek

1. Daniel Siegel and S. Allan Sugarman, *And God Braided Eve's Hair* (New York: United Synagogue of America, 1976), 40.

2. *Przeciw Wojnie* (Majdanku: Panstwowe Museum; Lublin: Pazdziernik, 1969, 1972), Vols. III, IV; for camp today, see Dorothy Rabinowitz, *New Lives* (New York: Knopf, 1976).

3. One Jew who helped build the camp and later escaped to the woods to organize a Jewish partisan movement tells his story in Samuel Gruber, *I Chose Life* (New York: Shengold, 1978).

4. Höhne, 376; Krausnick, 99.

5. Josef Marszalek and Anna Wisniewska, *State Museum Majdanek* (Lublin: Lub. Zakl. Graf., 1971), 8–12.

6. *ITS* 1:331.

7. Quote from Edward Gryn and Zofia Murawska, *Majdanek Concentration Camp* (Lublin: Wydawnictwo Lubelskie, 1966), 26. Alexander Donat, *The Holocaust Kingdom* (New York: Holt, Rinehart, Winston, 1963), has a comprehensive description of life in Majdanek, 167–216.

8. Paul Trepman, *Among Men and Beasts*, 137.

9. See *Auschwitz*, Vol. I, Pt. I., 193.

10. Tuman story in Trepman, *Men and Beasts*, 167–175.

11. Levin, 291.

12. Trepman, *Men and Beasts*, 142; Marszalek and Wisniewska, *State Museum*, 28. A prominent Jewish survivor who lived through the camps disguised as a Gentile, Paul Trepman remembers the killing day as September 3; he also believes the massacre eliminated every known Jew in the camp at the time.

13. Rudolf Vrba and Alan Bestic, *I Cannot Forgive* (New York: Grove, 1964), 71; and Reitlinger, 319.

14. Gryn and Murawska, *Majdanek*, 34–35.

15. Donat, *Holocaust Kingdom*, 297–300, quote from 298. See also *ITS* volumes; and, for a solid memoir of a woman survivor of the camp, Luba Krugman Gurdus, *The Death Train* (New York: Holocaust Library, 1978).

16. Author's summary of material in *TWC* V: 694–697.

17. Ibid., 727–731.

18. Ibid., 1149, 844.

19. Ibid., 703.

20. Ibid., 706–709.

21. Ibid., 710–711. Quote from 713.

22. Ibid., 1148; for the whole story, see 243–249, 673–695, 844–845, 1148–52.

23. Chaim Grade, "At the End of the Days," *Midstream,* April 1978, 34. Translated by Inna Hecker Grade. She read this poem at the White House reception for American Poets in January 1980.

24. Richard Lauterback, "Sunday in Poland," *Life,* September 18, 1944, 17.

25. Ibid., 18.

26. Rabinowitz, *New Lives,* 10–11. For more on the Majdanek episode, see Howard Blum, *Wanted!* (New York: Quadrangle, 1977), 16–17; also *Martyrdom and Resistance,* March–April 1979, 7.

Auschwitz/Birkenau

1. Stunning photographs of Auschwitz in the 1960s are in J. Fracktiewicz, *Oswiecim W Fotografii Artystycznej* (Oswiecim: Panstwowego Museum, 1965); past and present pictures with Polish photography in *GCP-I.*

2. For a literary description of inmates, see Tadeusz Borowski, *This Way for the Gas* (New York: Penguin, 1976), 83; for other literature on Auschwitz by Borowski, see "The People Who Walked," *Commentary,* February 1967, 65–69. See also Tadeusz Konwicki, *A Dreambook for Our Time* (New York: Penguin, 1976).

3. Auschwitz holds significant art collections, primarily by former prisoners. Catalogues: Tom Zbiorowy, *Tworczosci Artystycznej: III, Malarstwo* (Oswiecim: Panstwowego Muzeum, 1962); Tom Zbiorowy, *Tworczosci Artystycznej: IV, Rzezba* (Oswiecim: Pantswowego Muzeum, 1962); and Mieczyslawa Koscielniaka, *Tworczosci Artystycznej: II, Malarstwo* (Oswiecim: Panstwowego, 1961).

4. Borowski, *This Way For the Gas,* 130–131.

5. Impressions of early visitors in S. M. Rosenthal, "There Is No News From Auschwitz," *New York Times Magazine,* April 16, 1961, 26; and Frederick Kuh, "The Curator of Auschwitz, *The New Statesman,* July 3, 1954, 7–8.

6. Menachem Rosensaft, "The Holocaust," *Midstream,* May 1977, 53–55.

7. S. L. Shneiderman, *The River Remembers* (New York: Horizon Press, 1978), 64. Not a single Jew lives there now, 68.

8. See Josef Garlinski, *Fighting Auschwitz* (Greenwich, Conn.: Fawcett, 1975), 28–30.

9. Krausnick, 484.

10. Quote from Bernard Naumann, *Auschwitz* (New York: Praeger, 1966), 172. Additional descriptions of Auschwitz in Philip Friedman, *This Was Oswiecim* (London: United Jewish Relief Appeal, 1946); and Kazimierz Smolen, *Auschwitz* (Oswiecim: Panstwowego Muzeum, 1961).

11. Crematorium description from Filip Müller, *Eyewitness Auschwitz* (New York: Stein and Day, 1979), 14–15; analysis, 14–52. Interesting chapters on Auschwitz in Tenenbaum; Elon, *Journey Through a Haunted Land*; Meltzer; Nathan Shapell, *Witness to the Truth* (New York: McKay, 1974); *EJ* 3: 854–870. Also review Ravensbrück bibliography.

12. Otto Kraus and Erich Kulka, *The Death Factory* (London: Pergamon, 1966), 45; and Isabella Leitner, *Fragments of Isabella*, 2.

13. Smolen, *Auschwitz, 1940–1945*, 69–70.

14. Leitner, *Fragments of Isabella*, 4; and Naumann, *Auschwitz*, 103, 133.

15. Last quote, Smolen, *Auschwitz*, 64; first quote, Naumann, *Auschwitz*, 261.

16. Quote from *GCP, I,* 58. Memoirs with personal descriptions of Auschwitz include Thomas Geve, *Youth in Chains*; Marcel Griner, "Camp Child," in Schwarz, 294–297; Georg Wellers, "Three Portraits in Brown," in Schwarz, 248–257; Primo Levi, *Survival in Auschwitz* (New York: Collier, 1961). Information on special tortures comes from Auschwitz Museum officials. Other helpful literature includes Ka-tzetnik 135633, *House of Dolls* (New York: Pyramid, 1958); Tim Kessel, *Hanged at Auschwitz* (New York: Stein and Day, 1970); Adolf Rudnicki, ed., *Lest We Forget* (Warsaw: Polonia, 1955); I. N. Ben-Yuda, *Too Young to Live* (New York: Vantage, 1964); Suhl, *They Fought Back*; Kitty Hart, *I Am Alive* (London: Abelard-Schumen, 1961); H. G. Adler, et al., *Auschwitz* (Frankfurt, Germany: Europaeische Verlagsanstalt, 1962); and Samuel Pisare, *Of Blood and Hope* (Boston: Little, Brown, 1979).

17. Farben material from *TWC* I: 351; Joseph Borkin, *The Crime and Punishment of I. G. Farben* (New York: Collier Macmillan, 1978); and *TWC* VII: 56–58. Quote is from Borkin, 132. See also Benjamin B. Ferencz: *Less Than Slaves* (Cambridge, Mass.: Harvard University Press, 1979). Medical treatment and experiments at Auschwitz are highlighted in Alexander Mitscherlich and Fred Mielke, *Doctors of Infamy* (New York: Henry Schuman, 1949); Miklos Nyiszli, *Auschwitz* (Greenwich: Fawcett, 1961); Kazimierz Smolen, ed., *From the History of KL Auschwitz*, Vol. II (Oswiecim: Panstwowe Muzeum, 1976); and the seven books of medical anthology taken from the Polish Medical Journal, *Przeglad Lekarski*, and published by the International Auschwitz Commission; and Kraus and Kulka, *Death Factory*, 77. Perhaps even more helpful are the following three books, two of which are fiction. Mavis Hill and Norman Williams, *Auschwitz in England* (New York: Ballantine, 1965); Leon Uris, *QBVII* (New York: Bantam, 1972); Peter Weiss, *The Investigation* (New York: Atheneum, 1966).

18. Donat, *Holocaust Kingdom,* 304, 306.

19. Konnilyn G. Feig, ed., "The Survival Game," transcript of a conversation with Max Garcia, October 22, 1979, 4–5, 12.

20. Garcia, *As Long as I Remain Alive,* 95–96, 98–99; and Feig, "The Survival Game," 3–4.

21. See Kraus and Keuka, *Death Factory.* For additional information, see Müller, *Eyewitness Auschwitz,* 83–89.

22. Arnost Lustig, *A Prayer for Katerina Horovitzova* (New York: Harper, 1973), 53–54, 50, 152, 164. The incident is reported in the deposition of *Sonderkommando* Stanislaw Jankowski, in Jadwiga Bezwinska, ed., *Amidst a Nightmare of Crime: Manuscripts of Members of Sonderkommando* (Oswiecim: State Museum, 1973), 55–56.

23. Borkin, *I. G. Farben,* 45.

24. Ibid., 57.

25. Ibid., 60, 72, 75, 96–100.

26. Ibid., 121.

27. Quote from Kraus and Kulka, *Death Factory,* 20.

28. Vrba and Bestic, *I Cannot Forgive,* 109.

29. Kraus and Kulka, *Death Factory,* 23.

30. For additional information, see Josiah E. Dubois, Jr., *The Devil's Chemists* (Boston: Beacon Press, 1952).

31. Naumann, *Auschwitz*, 134.

32. Kraus and Kulka, *Death Factory*, 127.

33. Vrba and Bestic, *I Cannot Forgive*, 13.

34. Shirer, 971.

35. Vrba and Bestic, *I Cannot Forgive*, 16. In an excellent three-act play, *Patent Pending—Troeltsch and Sons* (Israel, 1979), produced by an off-Broadway group in December 1979, dramatist Wim VanLeer portrays the crematoria building program. Into the offices of a small bakery oven firm, Troeltsch and Sons, strides SS officer Dr. Hamlin. He brings a top-secret assignment—construction of an oven with the capacity of incinerating 24,000 bodies a day. Although faced with enormous technical difficulties, the firm produces the oven on schedule.

36. Vrba and Bestic, *I Cannot Forgive*, 17.

37. Ibid., 18.

38. Dawidowicz, *A Holocaust Reader*, 119.

39. Müller, *Eyewitness Auschwitz*, 60–61. Summary of Auschwitz gas chambers in Serge Klarsfeld, *The Holocaust and Neo-Nazi Mythomania*, 109–119.

40. Müller, *Eyewitness Auschwitz*, 65.

41. Ibid., 99–100.

42. *TWC* V: 624.

43. The Nazis forced prisoners to perform the extermination cleanup work: removing the corpses from the gas chambers, burning the bodies on pyres or stoking the crematoria, grinding the bones to ashes, digging mass graves. The work squads—*Sonderkommandos*—lived isolated from the other prisoners in better conditions. The Nazis murdered the *Sonderkommando* periodically so that extermination details would remain secret. Between 1945 and 1962 Polish offcials found five manuscripts buried at Birkenau by *Sonderkommando* members before their deaths. Additionally, a *Sonderkommando* member, Stanislaw Jankowski, lived to testify and to prepare a written deposition. The published manuscripts and documents relate the specific process of extermination at Birkenau, and provide detailed descriptions of the crematoria and gas chambers—see Jadwiga Brezwinska, *Nightmare of Crime*.

44. *Auschwitz*, Vol. I, Pt. I, 61.

45. Hilberg, 567. Höss spoke of the gas in his memoir, *Commandant of Auschwitz* (London: Weidenfeld and Nicholson, 1959).

46. Naumann, *Auschwitz*, 267; and Müller, *Eyewitness Auschwitz*, 136–137.

47. Müller, *Eyewitness Auschwitz*, 138–139.

48. Kraus and Kulka, *Death Factory*, 210.

49. Wiesel, *Night*, 44.

50. Yuri Suhl, "Rosa Robata," in Yuri Suhl, ed., *They Fought Back*, 221. For *Sonderkommando* plans and the revolts, see Müller, *Eyewitness Auschwitz*, 144–148; 154–162; and Kraus and Kulka, *Death Factory*.

51. Kraus and Kulka, *Death Factory*, 261; for *Sonderkommando*, see also Bezwinska, *Nightmare of Crime*; Ainszstein, *Jewish Resistance*, 915–918, 770–816; and an excellent story, Garlinski, *Fighting Auschwitz*.

52. For more information on the Auschwitz Trials, read Ainsztein, "The Auschwitz Trial"; *EJ* 3: 873–874; and, of course, Naumann, *Auschwitz*.

53. Alexander Zvielli, "Israelis Return to Auschwitz," *Hadassah Magazine*, June-July 1978, 19, 32–33.

54. For examples of the renewed debate, see "A Question of Priorities," *Jerusalem Post,* April 29, 1979, 15; David S. Wyman, "Why Auschwitz Was Never Bombed," *Commentary,* May 1978, 37–46; Roger M. Williams, "Why Wasn't Auschwitz Bombed?" *Commonweal,* November 24, 1978, 746–751; and Bernard Wasserstein, *Britain and the Jews of Europe, 1939–1945* (Oxford, Eng.: Clarendon Press, 1979), 309–320.

Bergen-Belsen

1. *Daily Mail, Lest We Forget* (London: Northcliffe House, 1945). Additional liberation scenes in Dorothy Rabinowitz, *New Lives* (New York: Knopf, 1976), 53–59; and *ITS* 1:112, 2:115.

2. Leslie Mittleman, "T. S. Eliot at Bergen-Belsen," *Reconstructionist,* November 11, 1966, 20 (published by the Jewish Reconstruction Foundation, 432 Park Avenue South, N.Y.).

3. Leslie Hardman, *The Survivors* (London: Vallentine Mitchell, 1958), 2; see also *Belsen* (Israel: Igrun Sheerit Hapleita Me' Haezor Habriti), 110–111.

4. Dutch in Reitlinger, 364. Information on exchange Jews in "Rescue Efforts with the Assistance of International Organizations," *YVS* VIII: 1970, 69–79, 484–485, 276.

5. Ibid., 265–367.

6. Ibid., 497.

7. Marietta Moskin, *I Am Rosemarie* (New York: John Day, 1972), 127.

8. Fantlowa, "Long Live Life," in Schwarz, 223–224; and Grunberger, 362.

9. Robert Collis, *Straight On* (London: Metheun, 1947), 66.

10. Reitlinger, 507.

11. Fantlowa, "Long Live Life," 224–26. See also Uri Orlev, *The Lead Soldiers* (New York: Taplinger, 1980).

12. Reitlinger, 504.

13. Quote from Derrick Sington, *Belsen Uncovered* (London: Burleigh, 1949).

14. Reitlinger, 506.

15. Ibid., 507.

16. Fantlowa, "Long Live Life," 227.

17. See account in memoir by Sara Berkowitz, *Where Are My Brothers?* (New York: Helios, 1965). For additional literature, see Paul E. Napora, *Death at Belsen* (San Antonio, Tex.: Naylor Co., 1967), 4–20; Donia Rosen, *The Forest My Friend* (New York: Bergen-Belsen Press, 1971); Manes Sperber, *Than a Tear in the Sea* (New York: Bergen-Belsen Press, 1967); and Zdena Berger, *Tell Me Another Morning.*

18. Derrick Sington, *The Offenders* (London: Secker and Warburg, 1957), 151–152. See also Trepman, *Men and Beasts,* 224–228.

19. Fyfe, *War Crimes Trials,* Vol. II (London: William Hodge, 1949), xxix, xxxix, xl.

20. Sington, *Offenders,* 159.

21. Leitner, *Fragments of Isabella,* 41.

22. See Martin Gilbert, *Exile and Return* (Philadelphia, Lippincott, 1978).

23. *Daily Mail*; and Sam E. Bloch, *Holocaust and Rebirth* (New York: Bergen-Belsen Press, 1965). In contrast to the sick scenes caused by the Nazis and captured in the photos, the famed artist John Hearffield pictured the contrasting sickness of the Nazis in *Photomontages of the Nazi Period* (New York: Universe, 1977).

24. Quotes from Bloch, *Holocaust and Rebirth*, xlvi, xlviii.

25. First quote from Sholome Gelber, "Wherein Is This Night Different?" *Menorah,* Winter 1947, 25. Rosensaft in Lucy Dawidowicz, "Belsen Remembered," *Commentary,* March 1966, 84.

26. Gelber, "Wherein Is This Night Different?", 29.

27. Bloch, *Holocaust and Rebirth,* li.

28. Ibid., liii.

29. Dawidowicz, "Belsen Remembered," 84.

30. Bloch, *Holocaust and Rebirth,* 209. Additional information on postwar years in *Bergen-Belsen 1945–1975* (Hannover, 1976).

31. Dawidowicz, "Belsen Remembered," 85. Overview in *EJ* 4: 610–612.

Poland

1. Photographers have provided us with the most vivid images for our minds—pictures—of the Eastern European culture that the Nazis destroyed. The photographic collections picture also the communities in the new world where remnants of that culture have survived: Earl Vinecour and Chuck Fishman, *Polish Jews: The Final Chapter* (New York: McGraw Hill, 1977); Mal Warshaw, *Tradition: Orthodox Jewish Life in America* (New York: Schocken, 1976); Abraham Shulman, *The Old Country: The Lost World of East European Jews* (New York: Scribner, 1974); Abraham Shulman, *The New Country* (New York: Scribner, 1976); Roman Vishniac, *Polish Jews* (New York: Schocken, 1972); Lucjan Dobroszycki and Barbara Kirshenblatt-Gimblett, *Image Before My Eyes* (New York: Schocken, 1977); Richard Humble, *The Warsaw Ghetto No Longer Exists* (London: Orbis, 1973). One cannot stand in the Warsaw ghetto without remembering the vivid descriptions written by the man who destroyed that ghetto—Jurgen Stroop, *The Stroop Report* (New York: Pantheon, 1980). One novelist has also painted a stunning portrait: Susan Fromberg Schaeffer, *Anya* (New York: Macmillan, 1975). The literature on prewar Poland and on the Polish Jews is vast, but for the most part the treatment is inadequate, misleading, inaccurate—and often glosses over the Jewish problem. I have found Celia Heller's study to be a groundbreaking effort: *On the Edge of Destruction* (New York: Columbia, 1977). Less satisfying is Richard M. Watt, *Poland and Its Fate 1918–1939* (New York: Simon and Schuster, 1979).

PART
THREE
THE INDIFFERENT, THE SLAUGHTERS,
THE STRUGGLERS

1. David Kranzler, *Japanese, Nazis and Jews* (New York: Yeshiva University Press, 1978), 19. For an excellent map outlining the Jewish search for a country of refuge in 1933–34, see Martin Gilbert, *The Holocaust* (New York: Hill and Wang, 1979), 27–28.

2. Indispensable for this subject are: Saul Friedman, *No Haven for the Oppressed* (Detroit: Wayne State University Press, 1973); Sheldon Spear, "The U.S. and the Persecution of the Jews in Germany, 1933–1939," *Jewish Social Studies,* 30 (1968), 215–243; Arthur Morse, *While Six Million Died* (New York: Random House, 1967); Henry Feingold,

The Politics of Rescue (New Brunswick: Rutgers University Press, 1970); and David S. Wyman: *Paper Walls and the Refugee Crisis, 1938–1941* (Amherst: University of Massachusetts, 1968).

3. Bernard Wasserstein, *Britain and the Jews of Europe, 1939–1945* (Oxford, Eng.: Clarendon Press, 1979), 9. See also Andrew Sharf, *The British Press and Jews under Nazi Rule* (Oxford: Oxford University Press, 1964); and Alan J. Sherman, *Island Refuge* (Berkeley: University of California Press, 1973); Martin Gilbert, "British Government Policy Towards Jewish Refugees," *YVS*, XIII, 1979, 127–167; Meier Sompolinsky, "Anglo-Jewish Leadership and the British Government," *YVS*, XIII, 1979, 211–247; and Gisela Lebzeltek, *Political Anti-Semitism in England, 1918–1939* (New York: Holmes & Meier, 1978).

4. Wasserstein, *Britain and the Jews,* 11, 14, 17. Werner Braatz analyses the Palestine issue in the context of German/Jewish relations in "German Commercial Interests in Palestine," *European Studies Review,* 9 (1979): 481–513.

5. Wasserstein, *Britain and the Jews,* 184. Britain also panicked over a possible "fifth column" in England and interned her refugees. After France fell, the British decided to deport all interned aliens. They sent 2,500 Jewish internees on the *Dunera* to Australia. At sea, the British guards subjected the prisoners to brutal treatment, stole their valuables, and destroyed their documents and papers. Story in Benzion Patkin, *The Dunera Internees* (Melbourne: Cassel Australia, 1979).

6. Wasserstein, *Britain and the Jews,* 34.

7. See Michel Mashberg, "American Diplomacy and the Jewish Refugee, 1938–1939," *YIVO Annual of Jewish Social Science,* 15 (1974): 339–365; and Hans Habe, *The Mission* (New York: Coward-McCann, 1966). A six-volume series uncovers the history of Jewish immigration to the United States during the Nazi years, their adaptation, and their impact: Herbert Strauss, ed., *Jewish Immigrants of the Nazi Period in the U.S.A.* (New York: Saur, 1979), 3 vols. published and 3 vols. forthcoming.

8. Roosevelt and his administration were involved in dozens of grandiose resettlement schemes including the Philippines and Alaska. If the schemes had been implemented energetically, perhaps a million Jews could have been saved—not an inconsiderable number. Resettlement schemes, however, had strong elements of futility, naïveté, and impracticality. No one cared to build a colony in one's own country. See Henry Feingold, "Roosevelt and the Resettlement Question," in *Rescue Attempts during the Holocaust* (Jerusalem: Yad Vashem, 1977), 123–180.

9. Eliezer Berkovitz, *Faith after the Holocaust* (New York: Ktav, 1973), 12.

10. *New York Times,* May 28, 1939, 15:2; May 31, 1939, 8:4; June 1, 1939, 16:5; June 3, 1939, 1:6; June 5, 1939, 1:4; June 10, 1939, 9:2; Berkovitz, *Faith after the Holocaust,* 9; Gordon Thomas, *Voyage of the Damned* (New York: Stein and Day, 1974); James Yaffe, *The Voyage of the Franz Joseph* (New York: Putnam, 1970); and for two letters written from the St. Louis by passengers, see *Sh'ma,* April 18, 1980, 90–93.

11. Berkovitz, *Faith after the Holocaust,* 11.

12. Michael J. Cohen, "American Influence on British Policy in the Middle East during World War Two," *American Jewish Quarterly,* 59. For British policy on Palestine and on the rescue of Hungarian Jewry, and Soviet policy on the rescue of Jews, see Yisrael Gutman and Efraim Zuroff, eds., *Rescue Attempts during the Holocaust* (Jerusalem: Yad Vashem, 1977), 183–246. For the seeds of U.S. policies in the Middle East, and official policies toward refugees, nationalism, and oil, see Kenneth R. Bain, *The March to Zion* (College Station: Texas A & M University Press, 1979).

13. Herbert Barzen, "The Roosevelt Palestine Policy," *American Jewish Archives,* April 1974, 40.

14. Arthur Morse, "The Nazi Murder Plot," *Look* magazine, November 14, 1967, 51. Aaron Berman and Allan Kage make a solid contribution to the study of the American Jewish community's response to the Holocaust and their emphasis on statehood rather than rescue in "Abba Hillel Silver, Zionism and the Rescue of the European Jews," in Paula Hyman, ed., *Working Papers* Vol. II (New York: Columbia University Press, 1979), and "The American Jewish Community's Attitude towards Anti-Semitism, 1919–1921," in the same volume. Kage notes that American Jewish leaders saw anti-Semitism as an "aberration in the steam of American history," a "detour," an "epiphenomenon" (p. 41). They needed to think of Jews as solely a religious group striving to combat an anti-Semitism brought to America by a recent group of European refugees. That America in the twentieth century was irritated by Jews, they refused to see.

   Berman makes it clear that American Zionist leaders "found it impossible to distinguish between the need of world Jewry for a state and the need of European Jewry to survive" (p. 3). Thus the Jewish community argued about the political goal of Jewish nationalism while neglecting the humanitarian goal of rescue. I would point out that Hitler's drive for a Final Solution, his extreme plan to destroy all Jews forever, seemed to catalyze an opposing pole of equal fervor—the drive to save all Jews forever and permanently, putting a final end to anti-Semitism by creating a Jewish state. Jews who disagreed formed the Emergency Committee to attempt to change the focus from statehood to saving large numbers of Jews, and to convincing the Allies to make rescue a major war aim. They were unsuccessful. "American Zionists failed to realize that the war might end with few Jews left in Europe to populate their future Jewish state" (p. 27).

15. Morse, "Nazi Murder Plot," 75. Using generally inaccessible material, Walter Laqueur has managed to quite precisely answer the question: "How and through what channels did news about the 'final solution' first filter out despite the fact that it was intended to be kept secret for as long as possible?" In *The First News of the Holocaust* (New York: Leo Baeck Institute, 1979), Laqueur finds that "the news was received from many more sources and at an earlier date than was commonly believed. But the news did not fully register and in some cases it was altogether disbelieved" (p. 3). Also Ronald Brownstein, "The New York Times on Nazism (1933–39)," *Midstream,* April, 1980.

16. Friedman, *No Haven for the Oppressed,* 228–229.

17. Kranzler, *Japanese, Nazis and Jews,* 8.

18. Ibid., 211 and 195.

19. Marvin Tokayer and Mary Swartz, *The Fuga Plan* (New York: Paddington Press, 1979), 9. Also see Efraim Zuroff, "Attempts to Obtain Shanghai Permits in 1941," *YVS,* XIII, 1979, 321–351.

20. Kranzler, *Japanese, Nazis and Jews,* 152, 268–269.

21. Stern, *Hitler,* 215.

22. The most recent article on knowledge of the Holocaust by Alex Groleman, "What Did They Know: The American Jewish Press and the Holocaust," *American Jewish History,* March 1979, 327–353, concludes that average American Jews had access to enough information to know. Their so-called weak response was not due to ignorance of the facts. Zosa Szajkowski, *An Illustrated Sourcebook on the Holocaust* Vols., I–III (New York: Ktav, 1977, 78, 79), examines the knowledge of the German people by presenting a collection of visual materials easily available to the public in Germany and in occupied and neutral nations. They show an unrelenting outpouring about Jews, a deluge. The

Germans had access to the broad outlines of the Final Solution. They knew as much or as little as they wished. The Poles "remained neutral observers of the horrors of life in the Jewish ghettos and of the German atrocities perpetrated against the Jewish population," Gross, *Polish Society under German Occupation*, 184. In Styron's *Sophie's Choice*, Sophie—a Gentile Polish survivor of Auschwitz—confessed: "So long as the Germans were draining off so much power destroying the Jews, I felt safer for myself," and my children. (467) Many German authors treat the theme; see Heinrich Böll, *Billiards at Half Past Nine* (New York: Signet, 1962); Gunter Grass, *The Tin Drum* (New York: Fawcett, 1961); Hans Kirst, *The Night of the Generals* (New York: Pyramid, 1963). See also David H. Weinberg, *A Community on Trial* (Chicago: University of Chicago Press, 1977), 47; and Hyman, *Between Dreyfus and Vichy*.

For the attitudes of Eastern European Jews, see Erich Goldhagen, "The Mind and Spirit of East European Jews," *Midstream*, March 1980, 10–14; and Joachim Nroschel, ed., *The Shtetl* (New York: Richard Marek, 1980).

23. *New York Times*, June 12, 1972; Cohen, "American Influence on British Policy," 67.

24. Ephraim Dekel, *B'rika* (New York: Herzel, 1974), 23. See also Judah Nadich, *Eisenhower and the Jews* (New York: Twayne, 1953); Leonard Dinnerstein, "The U.S. Army and the Jews," *American Jewish History*, March 1979; Malcolm J. Proudfoot, *European Refugees* (Evanston, Ill.: Northwestern University Press, 1965); and Nathan Shapell, *Witness to the Truth*. Although her book is brief, Dorothy Rabinovitz breaks new ground in *New Lives* (New York: Knopf, 1976). An outstanding survival epic is Jan de Hartog, *The Lamb's War* (New York: Harper and Row, 1980). For the continuing thread between the Holocaust, the survivors, and their children, Helen Epstein's study is a helpful beginning: *Children of the Holocaust* (New York: Putnam, 1979). For a brief psychiatric and medical summary of survivors based on his prior book, see L. Eitinger, "On Being a Psychiatrist and a Survivor," in Alvin Rosenfeld and Irving Greenberg eds., *Confronting the Holocaust*, 186–199.

During a customary nightly drinking session after liberation, a character in Barbara Traub's novel about post–concentration days, Drifter, explains to his fellow survivors that they have lost everything: "To go on living, we now must relearn everything from the beginning. We must learn to feel and ache and love and trust and judge and think in a new way. We must create anew an entire system of thought and feeling and discover new ways of expression. When we'll have learned all that, perhaps we'll also be ready to mourn." *The Matruska Doll* (New York: Richard Marek, 1979), p. 192.

25. For a recent list of the final disposition of camp commandants and officials, see Rückerl, *NS-Prozesse*, 125–129. The authors focus on what they see as the difficulties and problems associated with the clarification, investigation, and prosecution of War Crimes initially, in the 1950s and 1960s, and at the present time. Lately new materials obtained from Eastern block countries, more information, and different methods of questioning have led to revelations of more complex facts concerning mass murders and criminal deeds. For a full reading of war crimes evidence, see the indispensable guide by Jacob Robinson and Henry Sachs, *The Holocaust: The Nuremberg Evidence* (Jerusalem: Yad Vashem, 1976); and John R. Lewis, *Uncertain Judgement* (Santa Barbara, Cal.: ABC-Cleo, 1979). See also Beate Klarsfeld, *Wherever They May Be!* (New York: Vanguard, 1975); Simon Wiesenthal, *The Murderers Among Us* (New York: McGraw-Hill, 1967); Howard Blum: *Wanted: The Search for Nazis in America*.

One of the most interesting sagas of unpunished Nazi war criminals came to an end recently. In their 1978 book, *The Holocaust and the Neo-Nazi Mythomania*, the internationally famous Nazi hunters Serge and Beate Klarsfeld identified the two men primarily responsible for the final solution of the French Jews: Kurt Lischke of Cologne, Germany, and Herbert Hagen of Warstein, Germany. Never punished, these men were openly living out their lives; as was Ernst Heinrichsohn, the mayor of Buergstadt. Suddenly in 1979, in an unprecedented action, a West German court brought all three to trial for the deportation of the French Jews. And after a brief trial the three were convicted in 1980. Lischke, age seventy, received ten years, Hagen, age sixty-six, received twelve years, and the only remorseful defendant, Heinrichsohn, fifty-nine, received six years. Beate Klarsfeld also located the infamous "Butcher of Lyon," Klaus Barbie, who lives securely today in Bolivia. He has never been extradicted.

26. Quotes in order from Arnost Lustig, *Dita Saxova* (New York: Harper, 1979), 47, 118; Bertha Ferderber-Salz, *And the Sun Kept Shining,* 9; Goldreich, *Four Days,* 238; Ferderber-Salz, 232; Goldreich, 249; Jack Eisner, *The Survivor* (New York: William Morrow, 1980), 9; and Elie Wiesel, *The Town Beyond the Wall* (New York: Avon, 1964), 158–159. See also Reeve Brenner, *The Faith and Doubt of Holocaust Survivors* (New York: Free Press, 1980).

27. Elie Wiesel, "Two Images, One Destiny," *United Jewish Appeal,* 1974, 4.

28. Ismar Schorsch, "German Antisemitism," *Yearbook XIX,* Leo Baeck Institute, 1974, 257; and Robert Willis, "Church Theology after Auschwitz," *Journal of Ecumenical Studies,* Fall 1975, 493–515.

29. Malcolm Hay, *Thy Brother's Blood* (New York: Hart, 1975), 26.

30. Ibid., 87.

31. Ibid., 166.

32. *EJ* 3: 106.

33. Hay, *Thy Brother's Blood,* 168. Anti-Semitism has always had a smutty side to it. Anti-Semitic literature from the Middle Ages to the present teems with sexual, scatalogical, and pornographic themes. I wondered if that aspect had changed much when I saw the movies *The Night Porter, Seven Beauties,* and *Ilse, the Bitch of Buchenwald.*

34. *EJ* 3: 120.

35. *The International Jew* (Dearborn, Mich.: Dearborn Publishing House, 1920–22; 4 vols.); and *The Protocols of the Learned Elders of Zion* (Chicago: Patriotic Publishing Co., 1935). See also Franklin H. Littell, *The Crucifixion of the Jews* (New York: Harper and Row, 1975).

36. In the twentieth century, prior to Hitler, it would appear that the German Gentiles fell into two groups: a minority who attacked the Jews, and a majority who remained silent. Most dangerously, no group, no non-Jew (and few Jews) defended vigorously and publicly the Jewish right to ethnic separateness and pride. The changes for Jews in Germany and America rested on what the liberals would allow. When the liberals stopped allowing, positive changes ended and negative changes began. The Jews could have little impact on their own fate. See Michael Marrus, "European Jewry and the Politics of Assimilation," *Journal of Modern History,* March 1977, 89–109; Peter Gay, "Encounter with Modernism," *Midstream,* February 1975, 23–65. The theses and information contained in the excellent older basic works on anti-Semitism in nineteenth- and twentieth-century Germany, taken as a whole, have not changed significantly. Some of the newer material, not cited in this essay, however, is helpful in sharpening perception. For example, Marjorie Lamberti, *Jewish Activism in Imperial Germany* (New Haven, Conn.: Yale University Press, 1978); James and Suzanne Pool, *Who Financed Hitler?* (New York: Dial, 1978)—to be read with care, but the information on Henry Ford reminds us of wider implications; Felix Gilbert, *Bismarkian Society's Image of the Jew* (New York: Leo Baeck Institute, 1978, Memorial Lecture No. 22), for the relationship between the decline of liberalism and the growth of political anti-Semitism; Werner E. Braatz, "The 'Völkish' Ideology and Anti-Semitism in German," *YIVO Annual of Jewish Social*

Science 15 (1974): 166–187. Frederic V. Grunfeld, "The Jews in the Weimar Republic," *Midstream,* October 1979, 29–31, sees the essential function of the German Jews as "the irritating grain of sand in the oyster." Hyman in *Between Dreyfus and Vichy* illustrates the full insecurity of Jewish existence even in the French democracy. The French right saw the Jew as alien and unpatriotic, while the French left identified him as capitalist and unassimilable. The left assumed a stance of strong indifference, while the right actively collaborated with Hitler's Final Solution.

37. Also helpful in this context is the Leo Baeck Institute's *Yearbook XX* (London: Secker and Warburg, 1975); *Yearbook XVIII,* 1973; and *Yearbook XIX,* 1974. It should be clarified here that I am not ignoring the scholarly debates over the discontinuity of medieval and modern anti-Semitism, and over the different types. Nor am I avoiding the whole range of complex relationships between Jew and Gentile. I understand the fatal role played by Darwin and the eugenics movement. I appreciate, however, the virulence in Christian anti-Semitism and the myth of deicide, in softening up the entire Western world, enabling it to respond by killing or by vigorous indifference to killing. We wish to ignore, as Gentiles, the impact of our own Christian rituals and myths. That is all.

Richard Levy's challenge to the assumed link between the political anti-Semitic movement and Nazism is particularly helpful in addressing the roots of Nazi appeal and the history of anti-Semitism. He also indicates that although political anti-Semitism declined, it meant merely a change in the form of German anti-Semitism. Political anti-Semitism, says Levy, failed through bureaucratic and parliamentary means. The failure cleared the way for those who insisted on succeeding by more productive means. Richard S. Levy, *The Downfall of the Anti-Semitic Political Parties in Imperial Germany* (New Haven, Conn.: Yale University Press, 1975); Peter Gay, *Freud, Jews and Other Germans* (New York: Oxford University Press, 1979); Uriel Tal, *Christians and Jews in Germany* (Ithaca, N.Y.: Cornell University Press, 1975). See also Wasserstein's summary of anti-Semitism as a concept gaining an "irresistible momentum as a force in European politics," after 1933 (p. 4–5).

Of course, the intellectual historians have dominated the history of anti-Semitism and racism. The contributions of George Mosse, Norman Cohn, Peter Gay, Bernard Glassman, Paul Massing, Donald Niewyk, Leon Poliakov, and Peter Pulzer, to name a few, serve as important windows to the minds of the intellectuals and leaders of society. One of the most coherent summaries is George Mosse's 1978 publication, *Toward the Final Solution* (New York: Howard Fertig), which deals with anti-Semitism in the context of racism.

38. Irving Greenberg, "Judaism and Christianity after the Holocaust," *Jewish Ecumenical Studies,* Fall 1975, 525.

39. Saul Friedländer, *Pius XII and the Third Reich* (New York: Knopf, 1966), 97; Greenberg, "Judaism and Christianity," 527; Marlis Steinert, *Hitler's War and the Germans* (Athens: Ohio State University Press, 1977), 36. The negative and indifferent behavior of the Protestant churches in Germany toward the Jews and their role as active supporters of Nazism are well documented; for example, Richard Gutteridge, *Open Thy Mouth for the Dumb* (Southampton, England: Camelot Press, 1976). Klaus Scholder, *Die Kirchen und das Dritte Reich, Vol. I, Vorgeschichte und Zeit der Illusionen, 1918–1934* (Frankfurt am Main: Propyläen, 1977), claims the churches' silence came not from cowardice but from preoccupation with their own survival struggle. Also helpful on this subject are Charles Delzell, ed., *The Papacy and Totalitarianism* (New York: John Wiley, 1974); Carlos Falconi, *The Silence of Pius XII* (Boston: Little, Brown, 1965); Anthony Rhodes, *The Vatican in the Age of The Dictators* (New York: Holt, Rinehart, 1973); Sam Waagenaar, *The Pope's Jews* (LaSalle, Ill.: Opencourt, 1974); and Rolf

Hochhuth, *The Deputy* (New York: Grove Press, 1964). A long-awaited study on the role and attitudes of the Vatican based on an analysis of Vatican diplomatic papers by a distinguished Catholic priest and professor, John F. Morley is found in *Vatican Diplomacy and the Jews During the Holocaust, 1939–43* (New York: Ktav, 1980). The Vatican, Morley insists, must be judged not on how many Jews were saved, but rather on the application of its moral voice regardless of how effective a full effort would be. "By its own avowal," Vatican diplomacy was a "model and ideal for all states," and "the injustices committed against the Jews, to say nothing of the atrocities, should have been a major source of effort." (p. 17) And the judgement? The efforts of the nuncios for the Jews were "tangential at best, and minimal at worst." (p. 200) They failed to live up to their calling and missed an unusual opportunity to give witness. The Secretary of State gave little attention to the Final Solution. His feelings toward the Jews at best were "indifferent, at worst they were hostile." (p. 206) Of overriding and short-sighted importance, was the need to preserve diplomatic relations with Germany and keep a diplomatic "presence" in the capitals of Europe. The Pope failed the Jews and his own suffering Catholics. He made a mockery of Vatican diplomacy. Thus the Vatican failed the Jews, failed itself, and betrayed its own ideals.

40. George Steiner, *In Bluebeard's Castle.*

41. Stanley Milgram, *Obedience to Authority* (New York: Harper, 1974). Although his book falls short on scholarship, Hans Askenasy, a clinical psychologist, embellishes the Milgram theme in *Are We All Nazis?* (Secaucus, N.J.: Lyle Stuart, 1978).

42. See Stanford Experiment Slides from Stanford University.

43. Eric Fromm, *The Anatomy of Human Destructiveness* (New York: Holt, Rinehart, 1973), 181–186.

44. Florence Miale, *The Nuremberg Mind* (New York: Quadrangle, 1975).

45. I have not set aside a chapter to discuss Jewish resistance because I think the entire book focuses on that story. So much has been written on resistance that is of value, although much of it has been focused on the tragic and unnecessary question: Did the Jews resist? In addition to Ainsztein's encyclopedia, the following are strong works: Yehuda Bauer, *They Chose Life* (New York: American Jewish Committee, 1973); Ruth Kluger and Peggy Mann, *The Last Escape* (New York: Doubleday, 1973); Moshe Kohn, *Jewish Resistance during the Holocaust* (Jerusalem: Yad Vashem, 1971); and K. Shabbetai, *As Sheep to the Slaughter* (New York: Bergen-Belsen Survivors Assoc., 1963).

46. Arieti, *The Parnas,* 5.

47. Elie Wiesel, *The Oath* (New York: Avon, 1973), 20.

48. Terrence Des Pres, *The Survivor* (New York: Oxford, 1976), 6.

49. Hannah Arendt, "Social Science Techniques and the Study of Concentration Camps," *Jewish Social Studies* II (1949): 49–64. Older studies offer bits of insight that can be helpful in any analysis: Martin Broszut, "The Concentration Camps, 1933–45," in Helmut Krausnick, *Anatomy of the SS State,* 397–505; G. M. Gilbert, "The Mentality of the Murderous Robots," *YVS* 5 (1963): 35–42; W. Glicksman, "Social Differentiation in the German Concentration Camps," *YIVO Annual* 8 (1953): 123–150; Jan F. Triska, "Work Redeems," *Journal of Central European Affairs* 19 (1959): 3–22; Elie Cohen, *Human Behavior in the Concentration Camps* (New York: Norton, 1953); L. Eitinger, *Concentration Camp Survivors in Norway and Israel* (The Hague: Martinus Nijhoff, 1972); and Paul Matussek, *Internment in Concentration Camps* (Berlin: Springer-Verlag, 1975).

50. Feig, "The Survival Game,," 3; and Garcia, *As Long as I Remain Alive,* 100, 120. For a

remarkable fictional/memory description, see Uri Orlev, *The Lead Soldiers* (New York: Taplinger, 1980).

51. Feig, "The Survival Game," 13; and Garcia, *As Long as I Remain Alive,* 83. That the strugglers had an unusual attitude is seen in Edwin Shneidman, *Voices of Death* (New York: Harper and Row, 1980).

52. *Belsen,* 51. The religious or authentic Jew went like a lion to his death, explain the religious scholars. For examples of religious observance, religious courage and the resistance of authentic Jews displaying a "moral grandeur that defies belief," see Gertrude Hirschler, ed., *The Unconquerable Spirit* (New York: Zachor Institute, 1980); Irvine J. Rosenbaum, *The Holocaust and Halaknah* (Jerusalem: Ktav, 1976); and Eliezer Berkovitz, *With God in Hell* (New York: Sanhedrin, 1980). The Berkovitz book is critical for understanding the widespread religious life of Jews as "the most neglected subject of the entire Holocaust literature." (p. 49). It seems to this author that just as Jews have difficulty understanding the power of deicide in the subconscious of Christianity, Gentiles and non-religious Jews have great difficulty understanding the concept of faith to the so-called authentic Jew. It is a triumph of faith when a courageous believer refuses to respond with anger to Nazi indignity and degradation because of the old talmudic principle that "the severity of the insult is relative to the human dignity of the one who administers it . . . A pest does not insult you." (p. 59). The "supreme act of personal autonomy" is to be "unconcerned with what others may do to you, even when your life is at stake, because your are committed to the truth of your own life" (p. 74). With "radical indifference," the authentic Jews risked their lives to be authentic far beyond formal requirements (p. 79).

53. Irving Halperin, "Saul Bellow and the Moral Imagination," *NER* I (1979): 479.

54. Virginia Mishnun-Hardman, *Bright Winter* (New York: New York University Press, 1977), 38–40.

55. Elie Wiesel, *A Jew Today* (New York: Random House, 1978), preface.

56. For twenty years I have been studying the concept of survival in the camps, perusing, categorizing, and labeling the camp record in the form of hundreds of memoirs and diaries. I am indebted to those writers, and also to the many survivors who allowed me to spend time with them over the past two decades—and who shared with me. Obviously, I have been influenced in this essay on struggling—in both the positive and negative—by the older writers: Albert Camus, *The Plague* (New York: Random House, 1948); Bruno Bettelheim, *The Informed Heart* (Glencoe, Ill.: Free Press, 1960); Robert Jay Lifton, *Death in Life* (New York: Random House, 1967); Stanley Elkin, *Slavery* (Chicago: University of Chicago Press, 1959); Elie Cohen, *Human Behavior in the Concentration Camps* (New York: Norton, 1953); particularly Eliezer Berkovitz, *Faith after the Holocaust* (New York: Ktav, 1973); Victor Frankl, *Man's Search for Meaning* (Boston: Beacon Press, 1967); Alexander Solzhenitsyn, *One Day in the Life of Ivan Denisovich* (New York: Dutton, 1963); Hilde O. Bluhm, "How Did They Survive?" *American Journal of Psychotherapy* II (1948): 3–32; Klaus Hoppe, "The Psychodynamics of Concentration Camp Victims," *The Psychoanalytic Forum* 1 (1966): 76–85; Henry Krystal, ed., *Massive Psychic Trauma* (New York: International Universities Press, 1968).

When I completed my research and wrote about survival (see "A Holocaust Commemoration," Holocaust Series Lecture; Temple Beth-El, Portland, University of Maine, Multilith, April 28, 1974), I was still trapped, as so many, defending why the Jews did not resist. "It is true that a great majority of Jews went quietly to their deaths without open defiance or resistance—but not because of a historically conditioned response. Most important, prior to the peak killing period, the victims had undergone thirty months of unimaginable suffering that had almost annihilated their powers of physical and mental resistance" (p. 54). By 1975 I had finally seen the critical importance of the theme of struggling and surviving as a positive, strong, and unique element running through the Holocaust. The survivor, the struggler, I believed then and do now, is the most important story of the Holocaust, one of the most astonishing, strongest, and unusual human actions in modern times. See Feig, "The Voyage of the Damned: A Literary Journey Through the Holocaust," *The Phi Kappa Phi Lecture* (Portland: University of Maine, Multilith, 1975).

57. For particularly creative thinking, see Richard L. Rubenstein, *The Cunning of History*; Eliezer Berkovitz, *Faith after the Holocaust*; George Steiner, *In Bluebeard's Castle*; Irving Greenberg, "Judaism and Christianity after the Holocaust," *Jewish Ecumenical Studies,* Fall 1975, 521–550; Harry James Cargas, *Harry James Cargas in Conversation with Elie Wiesel.*

58. Eichmann in *Nazi Conspiracy and Aggression* (Washington, D.C., Government Printing Office, 1946), Vol. 8, 610; and quotes from Steiner, *Bluebeard's Castle,* 14, 22. Dalton Trumbo, well-known author of *Johnny Got His Gun,* outlined a remarkable novel on the Holocaust before he died. His notes have been published in *Night of the Aurochs* (New York: Viking, 1979). He calls the destruction of the Jews a "God-like act," unique, "a completely new event" in history, far beyond war and evil—"a spiritual, mystical event," an act of God—"the ultimate madness, the final insanity, the apocalypse" (pp. 158–159). The SS killer, devoted to his holy cause, committed his deeds as a *hero* of a Satanic morality (p. 161). Trumbo saw no way to explain the Holocaust but in the context of mysticism. Human beings are cruel, he says, because cruelty is fun. "It gives pleasure" (p. 164). Trumbo judged most Nazi leaders as "perfectly sane." They were "giving vent to passions that are felt by all kinds of men all over the world" (p. 211).

59. Elie Wiesel, *One Generation After* (New York: Avon, 1972), 9–10.

60. Elie Wiesel, "Art and Culture after the Holocaust," in Eva Fleischner, ed., *Auschwitz* (New York: Ktav, 1977), 403.

61. Fromm, *Anatomy of Human Destructiveness,* 5, 181, 211.

62. Eberhard Bethge, ed., *Ethics* (New York: Macmillan, 1961), 49.

63. Selzer, *Deliverance Day,* 237.

64. Elie Wiesel, "Art and Culture," 146; and Arthur Kurzweil, "Encounter with Elie Wiesel," *Hadassah*, December 1978, 16–18.

65. Steiner, *In Bluebeard's Castle,* 48.

SOURCES

A. ARCHIVES, INSTITUTES, MAJOR LIBRARIES

Background and Guides

The materials available are *vast,* often uncatalogued or in crates, and in a wide variety of languages. The major archives also have complex cataloguing systems and printed guides. The National Archives and various government branches publish many guides and indexes, which I have used; they can best be utilized by going directly to the depository. The most useful one-volume sources of primarily English materials are by Jacob Robinson, *The Holocaust and After: Sources and Literature.* Jerusalem: Israel University Press, 1973; Robinson, *The Holocaust: The Nuremberg Evidence.* Jerusalem: Alpha Press, 1976; and Konnilyn Feig, *Hell on Earth: A Holocaust Bibliography.* San Francisco: Multilith, copyright applied for, 1981.

Archives, Institutes, Library Collections

The European countries contain valuable archives, particularly for students of Nazi Germany and the Holocaust such as the Bundesarchiv-Koblenz, and branches at Freiburg, Sachen, West Germany; the International Tracing Service, Arolsen, West Germany; the East German Government Archives at Potsdam; the Central Historical Commission, Munich; the Centre de Documentation Juive Contemporaine, Paris; the Wiener Library, London; and the Jewish Historical Institute, Warsaw (no longer operable). Yad Vashem in Israel as well as the major Holocaust Libraries and Research Centers in major United States cities are becoming vital depositories. Important archives and collections in the United States include the National Archives, Washington, D.C.; the Berlin Document Center, State Department; the Jewish Museum, the Leo Baeck Institute, the Institute of Jewish Affairs, and the Yiddish Scientific Institute in New York; and the libraries at Brandeis and Yeshiva Universities. The most important archives and museums for this study of the camps, however, I found to be devoted to individual camps:

Stutthof Archives. Sztutow, Poland.
Buchenwald Archives. Weimar, East Germany.
Sachsenhausen Archives. Oranienburg, East Germany.
Ravensbrück Archives. Fürstenberg, East Germany.
Majdanek Archives. Lublin, Poland.

Dachau Archives. Dachau, West Germany.

Theresienstadt Archives. Prague and Terezin, Czechoslovakia.

State Jewish Museum. Prague, Czechoslovakia.
>   Contains the entire remaining archives of the strong Prague Jewish community.
>   Holds the Theresienstadt Art Collection.

B. COLLECTIONS AND SECONDARY SOURCES FREQUENTLY CITED IN THE NOTES

Bogusz, Josef. *Auschwitz, an Anthology on Inhuman Medicine.* Warsaw: 1970–
    1974. Several volumes selected from the medical review *Przegladhekarski.*
    Cited as *Auschwitz.*

Encyclopedia Judaica. Jerusalem: Keter, 1972. Cited as *EJ.*

German Crimes in Poland, I and II. Warsaw: Central Commission for the Investi-
    gation of German Crimes, 1947. Cited as *GCP, I, GCP, II.*

Grunberger, Richard. *The Twelve Year Reich.* New York: Ballantine, 1972. Cited as
    Grunberger.

Hilberg, Raul. *The Destruction of the European Jews.* Chicago: Quadrangle, 1967.
    Cited as Hilberg.

Höhne, Heinz. *The Order of the Death's Head.* New York: Coward-McCann, 1970.
    Cited as Höhne.

International Tracing Services. *Catalogue of Camps and Prisons in Germany and
    German-Occupied Territories, September 1930–May 1945. Vols. 1–3.* Arol-
    sen, West Germany: 1945, 1950, 1951. Cited as *ITS–1, ITS–2, ITS–3.*

Kogon, Eugen. *The Theory and Practice of Hell.* New York: Berkeley, 1950. Cited
    as Kogan.

Krausnick, Helmut, et al. *Anatomy of an SS State.* New York: Walker, 1968. Cited
    as Krausnick.

Levin, Nora. *The Holocaust.* New York: Schocken, 1973. Cited as Levin.

Meltzer, Milton. *Never to Forget.* New York: Harper, 1976. Cited as Meltzer.

Noakes, Jeremy, and Pridham, Geoffrey, eds. *Documents on Nazism, 1919–1945.*
    New York: Viking, 1975. Cited as *DN.*

Reitlinger, Gerald. *The Final Solution.* New York: Yoseloff, 1968. Cited as
    Reitlinger.

Rückerl, Adalbert, ed. *NS-Vernichtungslager.* Munich: DTV, 1979. Cited as
    Rückerl.

Schwarz, Leo, ed. *Root and Bough.* New York: Rinehart, 1949. Cited as Schwarz.

Sereny, Gitta. *Into That Darkness.* New York: McGraw-Hill, 1974. Cited as Sereny.

Shirer, William. *The Rise and Fall of the Third Reich.* New York: Simon and
    Schuster, 1960. Cited as Shirer.

Tenenbaum, Joseph. *Underground.* New York: Philosophical Library, 1952. Cited
    as Tenebaum.

Trial of Major War Criminals before the International Military Tribunal. 42 vols.
    Nuremberg: 1947–1949. Cited as *IMT.*

Trials of War Criminals before the Nuremberg Military Tribunals. 15 vols.
    Washington, D.C.: U.S. Government Printing Office, 1951–1952. Cited as
    TWC.

Trunk, Isaiah. *Jewish Responses to Nazi Persecution.* New York: Stein and Day, 1979. Cited as Trunk.

Yad Vashem Bulletin. Cited as *YVS.*

Yad Vashem Studies. Cited as *YVS.*

BIBLIOGRAPHY

This bibliography lists only sources cited in the text. It focuses on the camps. The material on the Holocaust, the Final Solution, Nazi German, Weimar Germany, and Hitler, to which the author is indebted, is too massive to list here.

PREFACE AND PARTS I AND III

Ainzstein, Reuben. *Jewish Resistance in Nazi-Occupied Eastern Europe.* New York: Barnes and Noble, 1974.

Allardyce, Gilbert. "What Fascism is Not." *AHR,* April 1979, 367–393.

Arad, Yitzhak. *Ghetto in Flames.* Jerusalem: Yad Vashem, 1980. On Lithuania.

Arendt, Hannah. *Eichmann in Jerusalem.* New York: Viking, 1963.

———. "Social Science Techniques and the Study of Concentration Camps." *Jewish Social Studies* II (January 1949): 49–64.

Arieti, Silvano. *The Parnas.* New York: Basic Books, 1979. Literature.

Arnold, Elliot: *A Night of Watching.* New York: Scribners, 1967. On Denmark.

Askenasy, Hans. *Are We All Nazis?* New York: Lyle Stuart, 1978.

Bain, Kenneth R. *The March to Zion: United States Policy and the Founding of Israel.* College Station: Texas A&M University Press, 1979.

Baird, Jay. *The Mythical World of Nazi War Propaganda.* Minneapolis: University of Minnesota Press, 1975.

Barzen, Herbert. "The Roosevelt Palestine Policy." *American Jewish Archives,* April 1974.

Bassani, Giolgio. *The Garden of the Finzi-Continis.* New York: Atheneum, 1965. Literature.

Bauer, Yehuda. *They Chose Life: Jewish Resistance in the Holocaust.* New York: American Jewish Committee, 1973.

———. *The Holocaust in Historical Perspective.* Seattle: University of Washington Press, 1978.

———. "Holocaust Questions." *Jerusalem Post International,* March 2–8, 1980, 14.

Beauvais, Robert. *Half Jew.* New York: Taplinger, 1979. On France. Literature.

Becker, George. *The Mad Genius Controversy.* Beverly Hills, Cal.: Sage, 1978.

Berenbaum, Michael. *The Vision of the Void.* Middletown, Conn.: Wesleyan University Press, 1979.

Berkovitz, Eliezer: *Faith after the Holocaust.* New York: Ktav, 1973.

———. *With God in Hell: Judaism in the Ghettos and Death Camps.* New York: Sanhedrin, 1980.

Berman, Aaron. "Abba Hillel Silver, Zionism and the Rescue of the European Jews." In *Working Papers,* Vol. II, edited by Paula Hyman. New York: Columbia University Center for Israel and Jewish Studies, 1979.

Bethge, Eberhard, ed. *Ethics.* New York: Macmillan, 1951.

Bettelheim, Bruno. *The Informed Heart.* Glencoe, Ill.: Free Press, 1960.

Binion, Rudolph. *Hitler Among the Germans.* New York: Elsevier, 1976.

Bluhm, Hilde O. "How Did They Survive?" *American Journal of Psychotherapy* II (1948): 3–32.

Blum, Howard, *Wanted: The Search for Nazis in America.* New York: Quadrangle, 1977.

Böll, Heinrich. *Billards at Half Past Nine.* New York: Signet, 1962. Literature.

Braatz, Werner E. "The 'Volkish' Ideology and Anti-Semitism in Germany." *YIVO Annual of Jewish Social Science* 15 (1974): 166–87.

———. "German Commercial Interests in Palestine." *European Studies Review* 9 (1979): 481–513.

Braham, Randolph L. *The Destruction of Hungarian Jewry, A Documentary Account.* 2 vols. New York: Marsten Press, 1962.

———. *The Eichmann Case: A Source Book.* New York: World Federation of Hungarian Jews, 1969.

———. *The Hungarian Labor Service.* New York: Columbia, 1977. On Hungary.

Brenner, Reeve. *The Faith and Doubt of Holocaust Survivors.* New York: Free Press, 1980.

Broszat, Martin. "The Concentration Camps, 1933–1945." In *Anatomy of the SS State,* edited by Helmut Krausnick et al. New York: Walker and Co., 1965, 397–505.

Browning, Christopher. *The Final Solution and the German Foreign Office.* New York: Holmes and Meier, 1978.

Brownstein, Ronald. "The *New York Times* on Nazism (1933–39)." *Midstream,* April 1980, 14–19.

Bullock, Alan. *Hitler: A Study in Tyranny.* 2nd ed. New York: Harper, 1960.

Camus, Albert. *The Plague.* New York: Random House, 1948. Literature.

Cargas, Harry James. *Harry James Cargas in Conversation with Elie Wiesel.* New York: Paulist Press, 1976.

Cargas, Harry James, ed. *Responses to Elie Wiesel.* New York: Persea, 1978.

Cargill, Morris. *A Gallery of Nazis.* Secaucus, N.J.: Lyle Stuart, 1978. Photos.

Chary, Frederick. *The Bulgarian Jews and the Final Solution, 1940–1944.* Pittsburgh: University of Pittsburgh Press, 1973.

Cohen, Elie. *Human Behavior in the Concentration Camps.* New York: Norton, 1953.

Cohen, Michael J. "American Influence on British Policy in the Middle East during World War Two." *American Jewish Quarterly,* September 1977, 50–70.

Cohn, Norman. *Warrant for Genocide.* New York: Harper, 1967.

Dawidowicz, Lucy. *The War Against the Jews.* New York: Holt, 1975.

Dekel, Ephraim. *B'rika.* New York: Herzel, 1974.

Delzell, Charles F., ed. *The Papacy and Totalitarianism between the Two World Wars.* New York: John Wiley, 1974.

Des Pres, Terrence. *The Survivor.* New York: Oxford, 1976.

Dickinson, John. *German and Jew: The Life and Death of Sigmund Stein.* Chicago: Quadrangle, 1967.

Dicks, Henry V. *Licensed Mass Murder: A Sociopsychological Study of Some SS Killers.* New York: Basic Books, 1972.

Dinnerstein, Leonard. "The U.S. Army and the Jews." *American Jewish History,* March 1979, 353–367.

Distel, Barbara, and Jakusch, Ruth, eds. *Concentration Camp Dachau, 1933–1945.* Munich: Lipp, Comité International de Dachau, 1978.

Ebon, Martin. "Why Did Hitler Hate the Jews?" *Midstream,* October 1979, 19–24.

Eisner, Jack. *The Survivor.* New York: William Morrow, 1980. Memoir.

Eitinger, L. *Concentration Camp Survivors in Norway and Israel.* The Hague: Martinus Nijhoff, 1972.

Elkin, Judith L. *Jews of the Latin American Republics.* Chapel Hill: University of North Carolina Press, 1980.

Elkins, Michael. *Forged in Fury.* New York: Ballantine, 1971.

Elkins, Stanley. *Slavery.* Chicago: University of Chicago Press, 1959.

Epstein, Helen. *Children of the Holocaust.* New York: Putnam, 1979.

Epstein, Leslie. *King of the Jews.* New York: Coward, McCann and Geoghegan, 1979. Literature.

Fackenheim, Emil. *The Jewish Return into History.* New York: Schocken, 1978.

Falconi, Carlos. *The Silence of Pius XII.* Boston: Little, Brown, 1970.

Feig, Konnilyn. "A Holocaust Commemoration." Holocaust Series Lecture; Temple Beth-El. Portland: University of Maine, April 28, 1974.

———. *The Voyage of the Damned: An Essayed Bibliography of the Holocaust.* Portland: University of Maine, 1974.

———. "The Voyage of the Damned: A Literary Journey Through the Holocaust." Phi Kappa Phi Lecture, University of Maine, 1975.

Feig, Konnilyn, ed. "The Survival Game." Transcript of a conversation with Max Garcia, October 22, 1979, San Francisco.

Feingold, Henry. "Roosevelt and the Resettlement Question." In *Rescue Attempts during the Holocaust,* edited by Yisrael Gutman. Jerusalem: Yad Vashem, 1977, 123–180.

Feingold, Henry L. *The Politics of Rescue.* New Brunswick, N.J.: Rutgers University Press, 1970.

Ferderber-Salz, Bertha. *And the Sun Kept Shining.* New York: Holocaust Library, 1980. Memoir.

Ferencz, Benjamin B. *Less Than Slaves.* Cambridge, Mass.: Harvard University Press, 1979.

Fest, Joachim. *Hitler.* New York: Harcourt, 1974.

Fisher, Jules S. *Transnistria: The Forgotten Cemetery.* London: Yoseloff, 1969. On Rumania.

Fleischner, Eva, ed. *Auschwitz: Beginning of a New Era?* New York: Ktav, 1977.

Flender, Harold. *Rescue in Denmark.* New York: Simon and Schuster, 1963.

Frank, Anne. *The Diary of a Young Girl.* New York: Doubleday, 1952.

Frankl, Victor. *Man's Search for Meaning.* Boston: Beacon Press, 1967.

Friedländer, Saul. *Pius XII and the Third Reich.* New York: Knopf, 1966.

Friedman, Saul. *No Haven for the Oppressed.* Detroit: Wayne State University Press, 1973.

Fromm, Eric. *The Anatomy of Human Destructiveness.* New York: Holt, Rinehart, 1973.

Garcia, Max. *As Long as I Remain Alive.* Tuscaloosa, Ala.: Portals Press, 1979. Memoir.

Gay, Peter. "Encounter with Modernism." *Midstream,* February 1975, 23–65.

———. *Freud, Jews and Other Germans.* New York: Oxford University Press, 1979.

Gershon, Karen, ed. *We Came as Children.* London: Victor Gollancz, 1966.

Gifford, Thomas. *The Wind Chill Factor.* New York: Ballantine, 1976. Literature.

Gilbert, Felix. *Bismarkian Society's Image of the Jew.* New York: Leo Baeck Institute, 1978.

Gilbert, G. M. "The Mentality of the SS Murderous Robots." *Yad Vashem Studies* 5 (1963): 35–42.

Gilbert, Martin. *The Holocaust.* New York: Hill and Wang, 1979. Photos.

———. "British Government Policy Towards Jewish Refugees." *YVS,* XIII, 1979, 127–67.

Glassman, Bernard. *Anti-Semitic Stereotypes without Jews.* Detroit: Wayne State University Press, 1975).

Glicksman, W. "Social Differentiation in the German Concentration Camps." *YIVO Annual* 8 (1953): 123–150.

Goldhagen, Erich. "The Mind and Spirit of East European Jewry." *Midstream,* March 1980, 10–14.

Goldreich, Gloria. *Four Days.* New York: Harcourt Brace, 1980. Literature.

Goldstein, Anatole. *Operation Murder.* New York: Institute of Jewish Affairs, 1949.

Grass, Gunther. *The Tin Drum.* New York: Fawcett, 1961. Literature.

Greenberg, Irving. "Judaism and Christianity after the Holocaust." *Jewish Ecumenical Studies,* Fall 1975.

Groleman, Alex. "What Did They Know: The American Jewish Press and the Holocaust." *American Jewish History,* March 1979, 327–353.

Grosman, Ladislau. *The Shop on Main Street.* New York: Doubleday, 1970. Literature.

Gross, Jan T. *Polish Society under German Occupation: The Generalgouvernment.* Princeton, N.J.: Princeton University Press, 1979.

Grunberger, Richard. *Hitler's SS.* New York: Delacourt, 1970.

Grunfeld, Frederic V. "The Jews in the Weimar Republic." *Midstream,* October 1979, 29–31.

Gutman, Yisrael, and Zuraff, Efraim, eds. *Rescue Attempts during the Holocaust.* Jerusalem: Yad Vashem, 1977.

Gutteridge, Richard. *Open Thy Mouth for the Dumb: The German Evangelical Church and the Jews, 1879–1950.* Southampton, England: Camelot Press, 1976.

Habe, Hans. *The Mission.* New York: Coward-McCann, 1966. Literature.

Haffner, Sebastian. *The Meaning of Hitler.* New York: Macmillan, 1980.

Halperin, Irving. *Messengers from the Dead.* Philadelphia: Westminster Press, 1969.

De Hartog, Jan. *The Lamb's War.* New York: Harper and Row, 1980. Literature.

Hasler, Alfred A. *The Lifeboat Is Full: Switzerland and the Refugees, 1933–45.* New York: Funk and Wagnalls, 1967.

Hay, Malcolm: *Thy Brother's Blood.* New York: Hart, 1975.

Heston, Leonard L. *The Medical Casebook of Adolf Hitler.* New York: Stein and Day, 1980.

Hilberg, Raul. "German Railroads/Jewish Souls." *Society,* November/December 1976, 60–74.

———. "In Search of the Special Trains." *Midstream,* October 1979, 32–38.

Hirschler, Gertrude, ed. *The Unconquerable Spirit.* New York: Zachor Institute, 1980.

Hitler, Adolf: *Mein Kampf.* London: 1939, New York: Reynal and Hitchcock, 1940.

Hochhuth, Rolf. *The Deputy.* New York: Grove Press, 1964. Drama.

Hoffman, Peter. *The History of the German Resistance 1933–1945.* Cambridge, Mass.: MIT Press, 1977.

Hoppe, Klaus. "The Psychodynamics of Concentration Camp Victims." *The Psychoanalytic Forum* (1966): 76–85.

Hyman, Paula. *Between Dreyfus and Vichy: The Transformation of French Jewry.* New York: Columbia University Press, 1980.

——. "New Debate on the Holocaust," *New York Times Magazine,* September 14, 1980, 65–86.

The International Jew: The World's Foremost Problem. Dearborn, Mich.: Dearborn Publishing House, 4 vols. 1920–1922.

Kage, Allen. "The American Jewish Committee's Attitude toward Anti-Semitism, 1919–1921." *Working Papers,* Vol. II, edited by Paula Hyman. New York: Columbia University Center for Israel and Jewish Studies, 1979.

Kallay, Nicholas. *Hungarian Premier.* Westport, Conn.: Greenwood Press, 1970. Memoir.

Kanfer, Stefan. *The Eighth Sin.* New York: Random House, 1978. Literature.

Katz, Robert. *Black Sabbath: A Journey Through a Crime Against Humanity.* Toronto: Macmillan, 1969. On Italy.

Katz, Shlomo. "Verdicts: A Play in Three Acts." *Midstream,* November 1977, 3–30. Literature.

Kenrick, Donald, and Puxon, Grattan. *The Destiny of Europe's Gypsies.* New York: Basic Books, 1972.

Kirst, Hans Hellmut. *The Night of the Generals.* New York: Pyramid, 1963. Literature.

Klarsfeld, Beate, ed. *Le Mémorial de la Deportation des Juifs de France.* Paris: Klarsfeld, 1978.

Klarsfeld, Beate. *Wherever They May Be!* New York: Vanguard, 1975.

Klarsfeld, Serge. *The Holocaust and the Neo-Nazi Mythomania.* New York: Beate Klarsfeld Foundation, 1978.

Kluger, Ruth, and Mann, Peggy. *The Last Escape: The Launching of the Largest Secret Rescue Movement of All Time.* New York: Doubleday, 1973.

Koenigsberg, Richard A. *Hitler's Ideology: A Study in Psychoanalytic Sociology.* New York: Library of Social Science, 1975.

Kohn, Moshe. *Jewish Resistance during the Holocaust—Proceedings of the Conference on Manifestations of Jewish Resistance.* Jerusalem: Yad Vashem, 1971.

Kohn, Murray J. *The Voice of My Blood Cries Out.* New York: Shengold, 1979. Poetry.

Korman, Gerd. *Hunter and Hunted.* New York: Viking, 1973.

Kranzler, David. *Japanese, Nazis and Jews.* New York: Yeshiva University Press, 1978.

Kren, George M., and Rappaport, Leon. "Victims: The Fallacy of Innocence." *Societas,* 4 (1974), 111–129.

Krystal, Henry, ed. *Massive Psychic Trauma.* New York: International Universities Press, 1968.

Kurzweil, Arthur. "Encounter with Elie Wiesel." *Hadassah,* December 1978, 16–18. Literature.

Lacko, Miklos. *Arrow Cross Men, National Socialists, 1933–44.* Budapest: Akademiai Kiado, 1969. On Hungary.

Lamberti, Marjorie. *Jewish Activism in Imperial Germany.* New Haven: Yale University Press, 1978.

Lane, Barbara Miller. *Architecture and Politics in Germany, 1918–1945.* Cambridge, Mass.: Harvard University Press, 1968.

Langer, Lawrence. *The Holocaust and the Literary Imagination.* New Haven: Yale University Press, 1975.

Langer, William. *The Mind of Adolf Hitler.* New York: Basic Books, 1972.

Laqueur, Walter. *The First News of the Holocaust.* New York: Leo Baeck Institute, 1979.

———. *The Missing Years.* Boston: Little, Brown, 1979. On Germany. Literature.

Lazin, Frederick A. "The Response of the American Jewish Committee to the Crisis of German Jewry 1933–1939." *American Jewish History,* March 1979, 283–305.

Leboucher, Fernande. *Incredible Mission.* New York: Doubleday, 1969. On Italy.

Lebzelter, Gisela. *Political Anti-Semitism in England, 1918–1939.* New York: Holmes and Meier, 1978.

Leftwich, Joseph. *The Golden Peacock.* New York: Yoseloff, 1961. Literature.

Leo Baeck Institute. *Yearbook.* Vols. XVIII–XX. London: Secker and Warburg, 1973, 1974, 1975.

Levai, Jenö. *Hungarian Jewry and the Papacy: Pope Pius XII Did Not Remain Silent.* London: Sands, 1968.

Levai, Jenö, ed. *Eichmann in Hungary: Documents.* Budapest: Pannonia Press, 1961.

Lévy, Claude, and Tillard, Paul. *Betrayal at the Vel d'Hiv.* New York: Hill and Wang, 1967. On France.

Levy, Richard S. *The Downfall of the Anti-Semitic Political Parties in Imperial Germany.* New Haven: Yale University Press, 1975.

Lewis, John R. *Uncertain Judgement: A Bibliography of War Crimes Trials.* Santa Barbara, Cal.: ABC-Cleo, 1979.

Lifton, Robert Jay. *Death in Life.* New York: Random House, 1967.

Littell, Franklin H. *The German Church Struggle and the Holocaust.* Detroit: Wayne State University, 1974.

———. *The Crucifixion of the Jews: The Failure of Christians to Understand the Jewish Experience.* New York: Harper and Row, 1975.

Lustig, Arnost. *Dita Saxova.* New York: Harper, 1979. Literature.

Mann, Thomas. "Frederick the Great." In *Three Essays.* New York: Knopf, 1929.

Marrus, Michael. "European Jewry and the Politics of Assimilation." *Journal of Modern History,* March 1977, 89–109.

Maser, Werner. *Hitler: Legend, Myth and Reality.* New York: Harper, 1975.

Mashberg, Michael. "American Diplomacy and the Jewish Refugee, 1933–1939." *YIVO Annual of Jewish Social Science,* Vol. 15, 1974.

Massing, Paul. *Rehearsal for Destruction.* New York: Harper, 1949.

Matussek, Paul. *Internment in Concentration Camps and Its Consequences.* Berlin: Springer-Verlag, 1975.

Meras, Icchokas. *Stalemate.* Secaucus, N. J.: Lyle Stuart, 1980. Literature.

Miale, Florence. *The Nuremberg Mind.* New York: Quadrangle, 1975.

Michaelis, Meir. *Mussolini and the Jews.* (Oxford, Eng.: Clarendon Press, 1978. On Italy.

Milgram, Stanley. *Obedience to Authority.* New York: Harper, 1974.

Miller, Arthur. *Incident at Vichy.* New York: Viking, 1965. Drama.

Mishnum-Hardman, Virginia. *Bright Winter.* New York: New York University Press, 1977. Literature.

Morley, John F. *Vatican Diplomacy and the Jews During the Holocaust, 1939–43.* New York: Ktav, 1980.

Morse, Arthur. "The Nazi Murder Plot." *Look,* November 14, 1967.

———. *While Six Million Died.* New York: Random House, 1967.

Mosse, George. *Germans and Jews.* New York: Fertig, 1970.

———. *Toward a Final Solution.* New York: Fertig, 1978.

Musmanno, Michael. *The Eichmann Kommandos.* London: Peter Davies, 1962.

Nadich, Judah. *Eisenhower and the Jews.* New York: Twayne, 1953.

Nazi Conspiracy and Aggression. Washington, D.C.: Government Printing Office, 1946.

Neave, Airey. *On Trial at Nuremberg.* Boston: Little, Brown, 1978.

Neugroschel, Joachim, ed. *The Shtetl.* New York: Richard Marek, 1980.

Niewyk, Donald. *Socialist, Anti-Semite and Jew.* Baton Rouge: Louisiana State University Press, 1971.

Novitch, Miriam. *L'extermination des Tzigenes.* Paris: A.M.I.F., 1969.

O'Donnell, James. *The Bunker.* Boston: Houghton Mifflin, 1978.

Oliver, H.D. *We Were Saved: How the Jews of Bulgaria Were Kept from the Death Camps.* Sofia: Foreign Languages Press, 1967.

Orlev, Uri: *The Lead Soldiers.* New York: Taplinger, 1980. Literature.

Paris, Edmond: *Genocide in Satellite Croatia, 1941–1945: A Record of Racial and Religious Persecutions and Massacres.* Chicago: American Institute for Balkan Affairs, 1961.

Patkin, Benzoin. *The Dunera Internees.* Melbourne: Cassel Australia, 1979. On Britain.

Payne, Robert. *The Life and Death of Adolf Hitler.* New York: Praeger, 1973.

Pinkus, Oskar. *A Choice of Masks.* Englewood Cliffs, N.J.: Prentice-Hall, 1969.

Poliakov, Leon. *The Aryan Myth.* New York: Basic Books, 1974.

Poole, James, and Poole, Suzanne. *Who Financed Hitler?* New York: Dial, 1978.

Presser, Jacob. *Breaking Point.* New York: World Publishing, 1958. On Holland. Literature.

———. *The Destruction of the Dutch Jews.* New York: Dutton 1969.

The Protocols of the Learned Elders of Zion. Chicago: Patriotic Publishing Company, Right Cause Publishing Company, 1935; London: Britons Publishing Society, 1936.

Proudfoot, Malcolm J. *European Refugees: A Study in Forced Population Movement, 1939–1952.* Evanston, Ill.: Northwestern University Press, 1965.

Pulzer, Peter. *The Rise of Political Antisemitism in Germany and Austria.* New York: Wiley, 1964.

Rabinowitz, Dorothy. *New Lives.* New York: Knopf, 1976.

Rhodes, Anthony. *The Vatican in the Age of the Dictators (1922–1945).* New York: Holt, Rinehart, 1973.

Rittich, Werner. *New German Architecture.* Berlin: Terramare Office, 1941.

Robinson, Jacob. *And the Crooked Shall Be Made Straight.* Philadelphia: Jewish Publication Society, 1965.

Robinson, Jacob, and Sachs, Henry. *The Holocaust: The Nuremberg Evidence.* Jerusalem: Yad Vashem, 1976.

Roiter, Howard. *Voices from the Holocaust.* New York: William Friedrick Press, 1975.

Rose, Leesha. *The Tulips Are Red.* New York: A. S. Barnes, 1979. On Holland. Memoir.

Rosenbaum, Irving J. *The Holocaust and Halakhah.* Jerusalem: Ktav, 1976.

Rosenfeld, Alvin H. "The Holocaust According to William Styron." *Midstream,* December 1979, 43–49.

Rosenfeld, Alvin, and Greenberg, Irving, eds. *Confronting the Holocaust: The Impact of Elie Wiesel*. Bloomington: Indiana University Press, 1978.

Rothkirchen, Livia. *The Destruction of Slovak Jewry: A Documentary History*. Yad Vashem Archives, Vol. III. Jerusalem: Yad Vashem Martyr's and Heroes Memorial Authority, 1961.

Rubenstein, Richard L. *The Cunning of History*. New York: Harper, 1975.

Rückerl, Adalbert, hrsq.: *NS-Prozesse*. Karlsruhe: Verlag C. F. Müller, 1972.

Sachs, Nellie. *O The Chimneys*. New York: Farrar, Straus, Giroux, 1967. Poetry.

Schneider, Gertrude. *Journey Into Terror*. New York: Ark House, 1979. On Latvia.

Scholder, Klaus. *Die Kirchen und das Dritte Reich*. Vol. I. *Vorgeschichte und Zeit der Illusionen, 1918–1934*. Frankfurt am Main: Propyläen, 1977.

Schorsch, Ismar. "German Antisemitism." In *Yearbook XIX*, Leo Baeck Institute, 1974.

Selzer, Michael. *Deliverance Day*. Philadelphia: Lippincott, 1978. Memoir.

Senger, Valentin. *No. 12 Kaiserhofstrasse*. New York: Dutton, 1979. On Holland. Memoir.

Shabbatai, K. *As Sheep to the Slaughter: The Myth of Cowardice*. New York: Bergen-Belsen Survivors Association, 1963.

Shapell, Nathan. *Witness to the Truth*. New York: David McKay, 1974.

Sharf, Andrew: *The British Press and Jews under Nazi Rule*. Oxford, Eng.: Oxford University Press, 1964.

Shaw, Robert. *The Man in the Glass Booth: A Drama in Two Acts*. New York: Samuel French, 1968. Drama.

Sherman, Alan J. *Island Refuge*. Berkeley: University of California Press, 1973. On Britain.

Sh'ma. April 18, 1980, 90–93.

Shneidman, Edwin. *Voices of Death*. New York: Harper and Row, 1980.

Simon, Sam. *Handbook of the Mail in the Concentration Camps, 1933–1945, and Related Material: A Postal History*. Privately printed, 1973.

Solzhenitsyn, Alexander. *One Day in the Life of Ivan Denisovich*. New York: Dutton, 1963. Literature.

Sompolinsky, Meier. "Anglo-Jewish Leadership and the British Government." *YVS*, XIII, 1979, 211–247.

Spear, Sheldon. "The U.S. and the Persecution of the Jews in Germany, 1933–1939." *Jewish Social Studies* 30 (October 1968).

Steel, Danielle. *The Ring*. New York: Delacorte, 1980. On Germany. Literature.

Stein, George H. *The Waffen SS*. Ithaca, N.Y.: Cornell University Press, 1966.

Steiner, George. *In Bluebeard's Castle*. New Haven: Yale University Press, 1971.

——. *Language and Silence*. New York: Atheneum, 1967.

Steinert, Marlis. *Hitler's War and the Germans*. Athens: Ohio State University Press, 1977.

Stern, J. P. *Hitler*. Berkeley: University of California Press, 1975.

Stone, Norman. *Hitler*. New York: Little, Brown, 1980.

Strauss, Herbert A. *Jewish Immigrants of the Nazi Period in the U.S.A.* Vol. 1 *(Archival Resources)*, 2 *(Annotated Bibliography*), 3 *(Oral History)*, and forthcoming Vols. 4–6. New York: K. G. Saur, 1979.

Styron, William. *Sophie's Choice*. New York: Random House, 1979. Literature.

Syberberg, Hans-Jürgen. *Our Hitler: A Film from Germany*. Germany: 1977. Film.

Sydnor, Charles Jr. *Soldiers of Destruction*. Princeton, N.J.: Princeton University Press, 1977.

Szajkowski, Zosa. *An Illustrated Sourcebook on the Holocaust,* Vols. I–III. New York: Ktav, 1977, 1978, 1979.

Tal, Uriel, "On the Study of the Holocaust and Genocide." *YVS,* XIII, 1979, 7–52.

———. *Christians and Jews in Germany.* Ithaca, N.Y.: Cornell University Press, 1975.

Taylor, Robert R. *The Word in Stone.* Berkeley: University of California Press, 1974. On architecture.

Thomas, Gordon. *Voyage of the Damned.* New York: Stein and Day, 1974.

Tokayer, Marvin, and Swartz, Mary. *The Fuga Plan: The Untold Story of the Japanese and the Jews during World War II.* New York: Paddington Press, 1979.

Toland, John. *Adolf Hitler.* New York: Doubleday, 1976.

———. *Hitler: The Pictorial Documentary of His Life.* Garden City, N.Y.: Doubleday, 1978. Photos.

Traub, Barbara Fischman. *The Matrushka Doll.* New York: Richard Marek, 1979. Literature.

Trevor-Roper, H. *The Last Days of Hitler.* New York: Macmillan, 1947.

Triska, Jan F. "Work Redeems: Concentration Camp Labor and Nazi German Economy." *Journal of Central European Affairs* 19 (1959): 3–22.

Trumbo, Dalton. *Night of the Aurochs.* New York: Viking, 1979. Literature.

Trunk, Isaiah. *Judenrat.* New York: Macmillan, 1972.

Tryon, Thomas. *Harvest Home.* New York: Knopf, 1973. Literature.

Tushnet, Leonard. *The Uses of Adversity.* New York: Yoseloff, 1966.

———. *The Pavement of Hell.* New York: St. Martin's Press, 1974.

Waagenaar, Sam. *The Pope's Jews.* LaSalle, Ill.: Opencourt, 1974.

Waite, Robert G. *The Psychopathic God.* New York: Basic Books, 1977.

Warmbrunn, Werner. *The Dutch under German Occupation.* Palo Alto, Cal.: Stanford University Press, 1963.

Wasserstein, Bernard. *Britain and the Jews of Europe, 1939–1945.* Oxford, Eng.: Clarendon Press, 1979.

———. "The Myth of Jewish Silence." *Midstream,* August–September, 1980, 10–15.

Weinberg, David H. *A Community on Trial: The Jews of Paris in the 1930's.* Chicago: University of Chicago Press, 1977.

Wiesel, Elie. *The Town Beyond the Wall.* New York: Avon Books, 1964. Literature.

———. *One Generation After.* New York: Avon, 1972.

———. *The Oath.* New York: Avon, 1973. Literature.

———. "Two Images, One Destiny." *United Jewish Appeal,* 1974.

———. "Art and Culture after the Holocaust." In *Auschwitz,* edited by Eva Fleischner. New York: Ktav, 1977.

———. *A Jew Today.* New York: Random House, 1978.

Wiesenthal, Simon. *The Murderers Among Us.* New York: McGraw-Hill, 1967.

Willis, Robert. "Church Theology after Auschwitz." *Journal of Ecumenical Studies,* Fall 1975, 493–515.

Winnick, Myron, ed. *Hunger Disease.* New York: Wiley, 1979.

Wyman, David S. *Paper Walls and the Refugee Crisis, 1939–1941.* Amherst: University of Mass., 1968.

Yaffe, James. *The Voyage of the Franz Joseph.* New York: Putnam, 1970. Literature.

Zuroff, Efraim. "Rescue Priority and Fund Raising as Issues during the Holocaust." *American Jewish History,* March 1979, 305–327.

———. "Attempts to Obtain Shanghai Permits in 1941." *YVS* XIII, 1979, 321–351.

THE CAMPS

1. Dachau

Berben, Paul. *Dachau, 1933–1945: The Official History.* London: Latimer Trend, 1975.

Bettelheim, Bruno. "Returning to to Dachau: The Living and the Dead." *Commentary* 21 (January 1956–June 1956): 144–151.

———. *Surviving.* New York: Knopf, 1979.

Cahnman, Werner. "In the Dachau Concentration Camp." *Chicago Jewish Forum,* Fall 1964, 18–23.

Churchill, Peter. *The Spirit in the Cage.* London: Hodder and Stoughton, 1954. Memoir.

Comité International de Dachau. *Konzenstrationslager Dachau.* Munich: R. Eimannsberger, 1974.

———. *Memorial Site Concentration Camp Dachau.* Munich: 1976.

Delarue, Jacques. *Histoire de la Gestapo.* Paris: 1963.

Distel, Barbara, and Jakusch, Ruth, eds. *Concentration Camp Dachau, 1933–1945.* Munich: Lipp, Comité International de Dachau, 1978.

EJ. Vol. 5, pp. 1219–20.

Greenberg, Barbara. Didn't We Meet at Dachau?" *Moment,* December 1976, 46–50.

Gun, Nerin. *The Day of the Americans.* New York: Fleet, 1966.

Heyen, William. "Riddle." In *The Swastika Poems.* New York: Vanguard, 1977, 24–25. Literature.

Hillel, Marc, and Henry, Clarissa. *Of Pure Blood.* New York: McGraw-Hill, 1976, 113–115.

ITS. Vol. 1, pp. 8–9, 26–27, 32; Vol. 2, pp. 186–190.

Kogon, Eugene. *The Theory and Practice of Hell.*

Litten, Irmgard. *A Mother Fights Hitler.* Part III. London: Allen and Unwin, 1942.

Martyrdom and Resistance, January–February 1975, 1.

Meltzer, Milton. *Never to Forget.*

Neave, Airey. *On Trial at Nuremberg.* Boston: Little, Brown, 1976.

Neuhäusler, Johann. *What Was It Like in the Concentration Camp at Dachau?* Munich: Dachau Museum, 1954.

Neurath, Paul. "Social Life in the German Concentration Camps of Dachau and Buchenwald." Ph.D. dissertation, Columbia University, 1951. On microfilm.

Rost, Nico. *Koncentration-Camp Dachau.* Brussels: Druckerei Hans Danmerhuber, n.d.

Rothenberg, Joseph. "Dachau." In *Hunter and Hunted,* edited by Gerd Korman. New York: Viking, 1973, 275–278.

Rutherford, Ward. *Genocide: The Jews in Europe.* New York: Ballantine, 1973.

Schowalter, Herbert P. "This Was Dachau." *National Jewish Monthly,* September 1966, 20–21.

———. "Letter to the Editor." *National Jewish Monthly,* January 1967, 2.

Schwarz, Stefan. *Die Jüdische Gedenkstätte in Dachau.* Munich: Landesverband d. Israelit. Kultusgemeinden im Bayern, 1972.

Selzer, Michael. *Deliverance Day.* Philadelphia: Lippincott, 1978.

Smith, Marcus J. *The Harrowing of Hell.* Albuquerque: New Mexico University Press, 1972.

Sydnor, Charles W. "The History of the SS *Totenkopfdivision* and the Postwar

Mythology of the Waffen SS." *Central European History,* December 1973, 339–362.

Tennenbaun, Silvia. "Return to Germany." *Midstream,* December 1976, 39–44.

TWC. Vol. I, pp. 12, 44, 92–199, 200, 201, 223, 226–242, 250–314, 418–494; Vol. II, pp. 175, 177, 336–342, 840; Vol. IV, pp. 614–615.

Trunk, Isaiah. *Jewish Responses to Nazi Persecution.*

United Nations War Crimes Commission. *Law Reports of Trials of War Criminals.* Vol. XI. London: Her Majesty's Printing Office, 1949.

Whitney, Craig. "The People Who Live in Dachau Today." *Martyrdom and Resistance,* June–July 1976, 3.

2. Sachsenhausen

a. General

Auschwitz, Vol. I, Pt. 1, p. 191.

Crankshaw, Edward. *The Gestapo.* New York: Pyramid, 1957.

Dokumente, Aussagen, Forschungsergebnisse und Erlebnisberichte über das ehemalige Konzentrationslager Sachsenhausen. East Berlin: Deutscher Verlag d. Wiss., 1974.

EJ. Vol. 14, pp. 597–598.

Fackenheim, Emil. "Sachsenhausen 1938: Groundwork for Auschwitz." *Midstream,* April 1975, 27–31.

Frank, Hans. *Nationalsozialistische Strafrechtpolitik.* Munich: 1938.

Frank, Volker. *Antifaschistische Mahnmale in der DDR: Ihre Kunstlerische und Architektonische Gestalung.* Leipzig: Veb E.S. Seeman Verlag, 1970. Art.

Goebbels, Joseph. *Tagebücher, 1945.* Hamburg: Hoffman and Campe, 1977. Diary.

Green, Gerald. *Holocaust.* New York: Bantam, 1978. Literature.

ITS. Vol. 1, pp. 102, 260, 273, 365–367; Vol. 2, p. 208.

Kogon, Eugene. *The Theory and Practice of Hell.*

Komitee Der Antifachistischen Widerstandskämpter: *Sachsenhausen.* Berlin: Kongress-Verlag, 1961.

Kruger, Bernhard. "I Was the Worlds's Greatest Counterfeiter." *The Jewish Digest,* January 1959, 59–63. Memoir.

Manvel, Roger, and Fraenkl, Heinrich. *Himmler.* New York: Warner, 1972.

Persico, Joseph E. *The Spiderweb.* New York: Crown, 1979. Literature.

Reiche, E. G. "From 'Spontaneous' to Legal Terror: SA, Police, and the Judiciary in Nürnberg, 1933–34." *European Studies Review* 9 (1979): 237–264.

Sachsenhausen. Berlin: VEB Deutscher Verlag der Wissenshaften, 1974. Art.

Stein, Leo. "Rabbis in Sachsenhausen." *National Jewish Monthly,* January 1942, 154–155.

Steinberg, Lucien. *Not as a Lamb.* London: Saxon House, 1974.

Szalet, Leon. *Experiment "E."* New York: Didier, 1945. Memoir.

Toland, John. *Hitler.* New York: Doubleday, 1976.

Ullmann, Eduard, ed. *Sachsenhausen.* Berlin: VEB Deutscher Verlag, 1974.

Vogt, Hannah. *The Burden of German Guilt.* New York: Oxford, 1964.

b. Special Topic: Homosexuals

Bleuel, Hans. *Sex and Society in Nazi Germany.* Philadelphia: Lippincott, 1973.

Grunberger, Richard. *The Twelve-Year Reich.*

Harthauser, Wolfgang. "Der Massenmord an Homosexuellen im Dritten Reich." In *Das Grosse Tabu: Zeugnisse und Dokumente zum Problem der Homosexualität,* edited by Wilhart Schlezel. Munich: Rütten und Loening, 1967.

Hillel, Marc, and Henry, Clarissa. *Of Pure Blood.* New York: McGraw Hill, 1976.

Krueckl, W. J., and Johnson, Ian. "The New Right as an Old Trick." *Gay Community News,* May 3, 1980, 8–10.

Lautmann, R. "Pink Triangle: The Persecution of Male Homosexuality in Concentration Camps in Nazi-Germany." To be published in forthcoming issue of *Journal of Homosexuality,* 1981.

Plant, Richard. "The Men with the Pink Triangles." *Christopher Street,* February 1977, 10.

Schoenbaum, David. *Hitler's Social Revolution.* New York: Doubleday, 1966.

Steakley, James D. *The Homosexual Emancipation Movement in Germany.* New York: Arno Press, 1975.

Winnow, Jackie. "The Holocaust We Were Never Told About." Unpublished Mss, San Francisco State University, 1979.

3. Buchenwald

Alexander, Edward. "Abba Kovner: Poet of Holocaust and Rebirth." *Midstream,* October 1977, 50–60. Literature.

Apitz, Bruno. *Naked Among Wolves.* Berlin: Seven Seas, 1960. Literature.

Auschwitz. Vol. I, Pt. 2, pp. 30–32, 120–25.

Buchenwald: Mahnung und Verpflichten. Berlin: Kongress, Verlag Berlin, 1976.

Buchenwald, Ravensbrück, Sachsenhausen. Fürstenberg/Hovel: 1964.

Bullock, Alan. *Hitler: A Study in Tyranny.* New York: Harper, 1960.

Burney, Christopher. *The Dungeon Democracy.* New York: Buell, 1946. Memoir.

Daily Mail. Lest We Forget. London: Northcliff House, 1945.

Elon, Amos. *Journey Through a Haunted Land: The New Germany.* New York: Holt, Rinehart, 1967.

EJ. Vol. 4, pp. 1441–44.

Firster, Richard, and Levin, Nora. *The Living Witness.* Philadelphia: Museum of American Jewish History, 1978. Art.

Frank, Volker. *Antifaschistische Mahnmale in der DDR.* Leipzig: Veb E. A. Seemann Verlag, 1970. Art.

Geve, Thomas. *Youth in Chains.* Jerusalem: Rubin Mass, 1958. Memoir.

"Die Glocke vom Ettersberg." By the Mitteilungsblatt Der Lagergemeinschaft Buchenwald–Dora.

Grossman, Kurt R. "The Trial of Ilse Koch." *Congress Bi-Weekly,* Decem18, 1950, 7–9.

d'Harcourt, Pierre. *The Real Enemy.* New York: Scribner, 1967. Memoir.

Heimler, Eugene. *Concentration Camp.* New York: Pyramid, 1959. Memoir.

———. *Night of the Mist.* London: Bodley Head, 1962. Memoir.

Heyen, William. *The Swastika Poems.* New York: Vanguard, 1977. Literature.

ITS. Vol. 1, pp. 135, 159, 223–229, 365–366; Vol. 2, pp. 195–199.

Journal of Kibbutz Buchenwald. "Homecoming in Israel." In *Root and Bough,* edited by Leo Schwarz, pp. 308–345.

Julitte, Pierre. *Block 26: Sabotage at Buchenwald.* New York: Doubleday, 1971. Memoir.

Kogon, Eugen. *The Theory and Practice of Hell.*

Lusseyran, Jacques. *And There Was Light.* Boston: Little, Brown, 1963. Memoir.

Miethe, Annadora, ed. *Buchenwald.* DDR: 1974.

Museum Buchenwald. Drukerei Fortschritt, Erfurt, Betriebsteil III, 1975.

Neumann, Robert. *The Pictorial History of the Third Reich.* New York: Bantam, 1962. Photos.

Petrow, Richard. *The Bitter Years: The Invasion and Occupation of Denmark and Norway.* New York: William Morrow, 1974.

Poller, Walter. *Medical Block, Buchenwald: The Personal Testimony of Inmate 996, Block 36.* New York: Lyle Stuart, 1961. Memoir.

Rousset, David. "The Days of Our Death." *Politics,* July–August 1947, 151–157.

Rubinoff, Maurice, interview, Portland, October 1976; and letter, April 23, 1945, M. Rubinoff to L. Rubinoff.

Toll, Nelly. *Without Surrender: Art of the Holocaust.* Philadelphia: Running Press, 1978. Art.

TWC. Vol. I, pp. 14, 51, 53, 56, 178, 517–518, 631–639, 684–694; Vol. V, pp. 353, 1088–89.

Unsdorfer, S. B. :"The Yellow Star." In *An Anthology of Holocaust Literature,* edited by Jacob Glatstein et al. New York: Atheneum, 1968, 259–263. Memoir.

Wartz, Robert. "Experimental Typhus in the Buchenwald Camp." *Auschwitz.* Vol. I, Pt. 2, pp. 120–130.

Weinstock, Eugene. *Beyond the Last Path.* New York: Boni and Goer, 1947. Memoir.

Wiesel, Elie. *Night.* New York: Avon-Discus, 1969. Literature.

———. "Agony at Buchenwald." In *Hunter and Hunted,* edited by Gerd Korman. New York: Viking, 1973. Pp. 257–263. Memoir.

———. "Death Against Life." In *Hunter and Hunted,* edited by Gerd Korman. New York: Viking, 1973. Pp. 301–303. Memoir.

4. Mauthausen

Bach, Julian, Jr. "Death of a Killer: Case History of the Nazi Mind." *Commentary,* October 1946, 316–319.

Camp de Concentration: Natzweiler, Struthof. Natzweiler: Comité National, 1976.

Davidson, Eugene. *The Trial of the Germans.* New York: Macmillan, 1967.

Dawidowicz, Lucy. "In Hitler's Service." *Commentary,* November 1970.

Dyer, George. *12th Corps, Spearhead of Patton's Third Army.* Baton Rouge: Military Press of Louisiana, 1947.

EJ. Vol. 11, pp. 1136–38.

Fantlowa, Zdenka. "Long Live Life." In *Root and Bough,* edited by Leo Schwarz.

Garcia, Max. *As Long as I Remain Alive.* Tuscaloosa, Ala.: Portals, 1979. Memoir.

Goldhagen, Erich. "Albert Speer, Himmler, and the Secrecy of the Final Solution." *Midstream,* October 1972, 43–50.

ITS. Vol. 1, p. 26; Vol. 2, pp. 7–9.

Le Chêne, Evelyn. *Mauthausen: The History of a Death Camp.* London: Methuen, 1971.

Marsálek, Hans. *Mauthausen.* Wien: Max Ungar, 1958.

Milward, Alan S. *War, Economy and Society, 1939–45.* Berkeley: University of California Press, 1977.

Tillion, Germaine. *Ravensbrück.* Garden City, N.Y.: Anchor Press, 1975. Memoir.

Trench, Marye. "Mauthausen." In *Hunter and Hunted,* edited by Gerd Korman. New York: Viking, 1973. Pp. 279–285. Memoir.

Trunk, Isaiah. *Jewish Responses to Nazi Persecution.*
Wiesenthal, Simon: "Steps Beyond the Grave." In *Hunter and Hunted,* edited by Gerd Korman. New York: Viking: 1973. Pp. 286–295. Memoir.
Wormser-Migot, Olga, and Michel, Henri, eds. *Tragedie de la Deportation 1940–1945.* Paris: Hachette, 1955.

5. Flossenbürg

Brissaud, André. *Canaris.* London: Weidenfeld and Nicolson, 1973.
"Flossenberg, The Story of One Concentration Camp." *National Jewish Monthly,* October 1945, 46–49.
ITS. Vol. 1, pp. 210–211; Vol. 2, pp. 191–194.
Leitner, Isabella. *Fragments of Isabella: A Memoir of Auschwitz.* New York: Crowell, 1978. Memoir.
Lustig, Arnost. *Darkness Casts No Shadow.* New York: Avon, 1978. Literature.
Meltzer, Milton. *Never to Forget.*
Szwarc, Stefan. "The March to Freedom." *Jewish Frontier,* May 1948, 11–15.
TWC. Vol. V, pp. 216, 218, 239–240, 247–288.

6. Women and the Third Reich

a. Ravensbrück: For Women Only

ADIR/Ravensbrück Amicale. *Les Françaises à Ravensbrück.* Paris: Gallimard, 1965.
Bernadac, Christian. *Le Camp des Femmes-Ravensbrück.* Paris: Editions France Empire, 1972.
———. *Kommandos de Femmes-Ravensbrück.* Paris: Editions France Empire, 1973.
Dufournier, Denise. *Ravensbrück: The Women's Camp of Death.* London: Allen, 1948. Memoir.
EJ. Vol. 13, p. 1583.
"Experimental Operations in the the Ravensbrück Concentration Camp." In *German Crimes in Poland.* Vol. II, pp. 133–150.
Frank, Victor. *Antifaschistische Mahnmale in der DDR.* Leipzig: Veb E. A. Seemann Verlag, 1970. Art.
Gluck, Gemma La Guardia. *My Story.* New York: David McKay, 1961. Memoir.
———. "La Guardia's Sister—Eichmann's Hostage." *Midstream* 7 (1961): 3–19. Memoir.
ITS. Vol. 1, pp. 204, 264; Vol. 2, p. 209; Vol. 3, p. 31.
Kiedrzynska, Wanda. *Ravensbrück.* In Ravensbrück Archives, Warsaw Academy Historical Institute, 1961.
Kocwa, Eugenia. *Flücht aus Ravensbrück.* East Berlin: Union Verlag, 1973.
Lingens-Reiner, Ella. *Prisoner of Fear.* London: Victor Gollancz, 1948. Memoir.
Machlejd, Wanda, ed. *Experimental Operations on Prisoners of Ravensbrück Concentration Camp.* Warsaw: Zachodnia Agencja Prasowa, 1960.
Playfair, Giles, and Sington, Derrick. *The Offenders.* London: Secker and Warburg, 1957.
Poltawska, Dr. Wanda. " 'Guinea Pigs' in the Ravensbrück Concentration Camp." *Auschwitz.* Vol. 1, Pt. 2, pp. 131–161.

Tillion, Germaine. *Ravensbrück.* New York: Anchor Press, 1975. Memoir.
Ullmann, Eduard. *Ravensbrück.* DDR: Ravensbrück Archives, 1964.

b. Nazi Theory and Practice: A Woman's Future

Baxter, Richard. *Women of the Gestapo.* London: Quality, 1943.
Bleuel, Hans. *Sex and Society in Nazi Germany.* Philadelphia: Lippincott, 1973.
Bremme, Gabrielle. *Die Politische Rolle Der Frau im Deutschland.* Göttingen: 1956.
Bridenthal, Renate. "Beyond *Kinder, Küche, Kirche*: Weimar Women at Work." *Central European History* 6 (June 1973): 148–166.
Bridenthal, Renate, and Koonz, Claudia, eds. *Becoming Visible: Women and European History.* Boston: Houghton Mifflin, 1977.
Dahrendorf, Ralf. *Society and Democracy in Germany.* London: 1967.
Evans, Richard, J. *The Feminist Movement in Germany 1894–1933.* Beverly Hills, Cal.: Sage, 1976.
Grunberger, Richard. *"Lebensborn." Bulletin of the Wiener Library,* July 1952.
Grunfeld, Judith. "Women Workers in Nazi Germany." *The Nation,* March 1937.
Hillel, Marc, and Henry, Clarissa. *Of Pure Blood.* New York: McGraw Hill, 1976.
Hunt, Richard N. *German Social Democracy, 1918–1933.* New Haven, Conn.: Yale University Press, 1964.
Kaplan, Marion A. *The Jewish Feminist Movement in Germany.* Westport, Conn.: Greenwood Press, 1979.
————. "The Campaign for Women's Suffrage in the Jewish Community in Germany." *YIVO Institute,* February 1976.
Kirkpatrick, Clifford. *Nazi Germany: Its Women and Family Life.* Indianapolis: Bobbs Merrill, 1938.
Knodel, John: "Malthus Amiss: Marriage Restrictions in 19th Century Germany." *Social Science,* Winter 1972, 40–45.
Koonz, Claudia. "The Nazi Women's Dilemma: To Sew or Wear Brown Shirts?" Paper delivered at American Historical Association Convention, 1974.
————. "Nazi Women before 1933." *Social Science Quarterly,* March 1979, 56.
Law Reports of Trials of War Criminals. Vol. II. *The Belsen Trial.* London: His Majesty's Stationery Office, 1947.
Law Reports of Trials of War Criminals. Vol. XII. *German High Command Trial.* London: Her Majesty's Stationery Office, 1949.
Mason, Tim. "Women in Nazi Germany," Parts I and II. *History Workshop,* Spring 1976, 74–113; and Autumn 1976, 5–32.
Mosse, George. *Nazi Culture.* New York: Grosset and Dunlap, 1966.
Noakes, Jeremy, and Pridham, Geoffrey. *Documents on Nazism, 1919–1945.*
Phillips, Raymond, ed. *The Belsen Trial.* Vol. II. *Trial of Josef Kramer and Forty-four Others.* London: William Hodge, 1949.
Rabinowitz, Dorothy. *New Lives: Survivors of the Holocaust Living in America.* New York: Knopf, 1976.
Rupp, Leila J. "Mother of the *Volk." Signs* 3 (1977): 362–379.
————. *Mobilizing Women for War.* Princeton, N.J.: Princeton University Press, 1978.
Schoenbaum, David. *Hitler's Social Revolution.* New York: Doubleday, 1966.
Stepheson, Jill. *"Reichsbund der Kinderreichen:* The League of Large Families in the Population Policy of Nazi Germany." *European Studies Review* 9 (1979): 351–375.
————. *Women in Nazi Society.* New York: Barnes and Noble, 1975.

Thönnessen, Werner. *The Emancipation of Women: The Women's Movement in German Social Democracy, 1863–1933.* Glasgow: Pluto Press, 1973.
TWC. Vol. I, pp. 48, 355–356, 360, 396; Vol. II, pp. 1076–77; Vol. V, pp. 114–115, 117, 234–235, 240, 367–368.
Winkler, Dörte. *Frauenarbeit im "Dritten Reich."* Hamburg: Hoffman und Campe Verlag, 1977.

c. Memoirs, Literature, Children

Aichinger, Ilse. *Herod's Children.* New York: Atheneum Press, 1964. Literature.
Darvas, Irén. "Women in a Nazi Munitions Factory." *YVB,* November 1967, 28–34. Memoir.
Fenelon, Fania. *Playing for Time.* New York: Atheneum, 1977. Memoir.
Ferderber-Salz, Bertha. *And the Sun Kept Shining.* New York: Holocaust Library, 1980. Memoir.
Fyfe, Sir David M., gen. ed. *War Crimes Trials Series.* Vol. VII. *The Velpke Baby Home Trial.* London: William Hodge, 1950.
Goldreich, Gloria. *Four Days.* New York: Harcourt Brace, 1980. Literature.
Hart, Kitty. *Return to Auschwitz.* London: British Television, 1980. Film.
Jackson, Livia E. Bitton. *Elli.* New York: Times Books, 1980. Literature.
Jezierska, Maria. "It Is Not Permitted to Be Sick." In *Auschwitz,* Vol. II, Pt. 2, pp. 193–216. Memoir.
Kivala, Jalian. "At the End of 1942." In *Auschwitz,* Vol. II, Pt. 2, pp. 161–180. Memoir.
Klein, Gerda Weissmann. *All But My Life.* New York: Hill and Wang, 1957. Memoir.
Kosciuszkowa, Janina. "Children in the Auschwitz Concentration Camp." In *Auschwitz,* Vol. II, Pt. 2, pp. 217–225.
Kuper, Jack. *Child of the Holocaust.* Garden City, N.Y.: Doubleday, 1968. Memoir.
Lengyel, Olga. *Five Chimneys: The Story of Auschwitz.* Chicago: Ziff Davis, 1947. Memoir.
Leszczynska, Stanislawa. "Report of a Midwife from Auschwitz." In *Auschwitz,* Vol. II., Pt. 2, pp. 181–192. Memoir.
Lewinska, Pelagia. *Twenty Months at Auschwitz.* New York: Lyle Stuart, 198. Memoir.
Maurel, Micheline. *An Ordinary Camp.* New York: Simon and Schuster, 1958. Memoir.
Minney, R. J. *I Shall Fear No Evil: The Story of Dr. Alina Brewda.* London: Kimber, 1966. Memoir.
Munkacsi, Naomi W. "Jewish Religious Observance in Women's Death Camps in Germany." *YVB* 20 (1967): 35–38.
Newman, Judith. *In the Hell of Auschwitz: The Wartime Memoirs of Judith Sternberg Newman.* New York: Exposition, 1963. Memoir.
Nowakowska, Maria. "The Women's Hospital in Birkenau." In *Auschwitz,* Vol. II, Pt. 2, pp. 144–160. Memoir.
Pawlowicz, Sala. *I Will Survive.* New York: Norton, 1962. Memoir.
Perl, Gisella. *I Was a Doctor in Auschwitz.* New York: International Universities Press, 1948. Memoir.
Poltawska, Dr. Wanda. "On Examinations of 'Auschwitz Children.' " In *Auschwitz,* Vol. II, Pt. 3, pp. 21–37.
Poltawska, Wanda, et al. "Results of Psychiatric Examinations of People Born in

Nazi Concentration Camps or Imprisoned There during Their Childhood." In *Auschwitz,* Vol. II, Pt. 3, pp. 37–132.

Schwarz, Irene. "The Small Still Voice." In *Root and Bough,* edited by Leo W. Schwarz, pp. 189–200.

Szmaglewska, Seweryna. *Smoke over Birkenau.* New York: Holt, 1947. Memoir.

Trunk Isaiah. *Jewish Responses to Nazi Persecution.*

Weiss, Reska. *Journey Through Hell: A Woman's Account of the Experiences in the Hands of the Nazis.* London: Valentine-Mitchell, 1961. Memoir.

Wolken, Dr. Otto. "When I Think of Children." In *Auschwitz,* Vol. II, Pt. 3, pp. 13–20.

Zywulska, Krystyna. *I Came Back.* New York: Roy, 1951. Memoir.

7. Stutthof/Sztutowo

EJ. Vol. 15, pp. 464–466.

IMT. Vol. 7, pp. 598–601.

ITS. Vol. 1, p. 266.

Levine, Herbert S. *Hitler's Free City.* Chicago: University of Chicago Press, 1973.

Matusiak, Tadeusz. *Stutthof.* Gdansk: Zaklody Graficzne, for Museum Stutthof, 1969.

Matusiak, Tadeusz. "Stutthof." Gdansk: Muzeum Stutthof, 1974.

Pickholz-Barnitsch, Olga. "The Evacuation of the Stutthof Concentration Camp." *YBV,* No. 12, December 1945, 31–49. Memoir.

"Stutthof Concentration Camp." *In German Crimes in Poland.* Vol. II, pp. 107–126.

Sydnor, Charles Jr.: *Soldiers of Destruction.* Princeton, N.J.: Princeton University Press, 1977.

TWC. Vol. V, pp. 493–501.

Trunk, Isaiah. *Jewish Responses to Nazi Persecution.*

8. Gross-Rosen

Doob, Leonard. *Panorama of Evil.* Westport, Conn.: Greenwood Press, 1978.

Fantlowa, Zdenka. "Long Live Life." In *Root and Bough,* edited by Leo Schwarz, pp. 201–211.

Geve, Thomas. *Youth in Chains.* Jerusalem: Rubin Mass, 1958. Memoir.

Green, Gerald. *Holocaust.* New York: Bantam, 1978. Literature.

Gross, Jan T. *Polish Society under German Occupation: The Generalgouvernment.* Princeton, N.J.: Princeton University Press, 1979.

Heller, Paul. "A Concentration Camp Diary." *Midstream,* April 1980, 29–36. Memoir.

ITS. Vol. 1, p. 273; Vol. 2, p. 210; Vol. 3, pp. 11–13, 34, 38–39, 42–44.

Trepman, Paul. *Among Men and Beasts.* New York: A. S. Barnes, 1978. Memoir.

TWC. Vol. V, pp. 64–67, 226–229, 362, 363–364, 444, 794–801, 859–861.

9. Neuengamme

Auschwitz. Vol. I, Pt. 2, pp. 163–175.

ITS. Vol. 1, pp. 90–93; Vol. 2, pp. 114, 124–126.

Klodzenski, Dr. Stanislaw. "Criminal Experiments with Tuberculosis Carried Out in Nazi Concentration Camps." *Auschwitz.* Vol. I, Pt. 2, pp. 163–175.

Kogon, Eugen: *The Theory and Practice of Hell.*
Petrow, Richard. *The Bitter Years.* New York: William Morrow, 1974.
TWC. Vol. V, pp. 219, 488, 814.

10. Natzweiler/Struthof

Boutbien, Dr. Leon, ed. *Natzweiler-Struthof.* Nancy: A. Humblot, 1976.
EJ. Vol. 12, pp. 891–894.
Fyfe, Sir David Maxwell, gen. ed. *War Crimes Trial Series.* Vol. V. *"The Natzweiler Trial."* London: William Hodge, 1949.
Gersh, Gabriel. "The Zone of Silence." *Congress Bi-Weekly,* February 6, 1956, 6–7.
ITS. Vol. 1, p. 65.
Kogon, Eugen. *The Theory and Practice of Hell.*
Sehn, Jan. "Some of the Legal Aspects of the So-Called Experiments Carried Out by SS Physicians in Concentration Camps." *Auschwitz.* Vol. I, Pt. 1, pp. 43–84; and "The Case of the Auschwitz SS Physician, J. P. Kremer," *Auschwitz.* Vol. I, Pt. 1, pp. 206–258.
Tillion, Germaine. *Ravensbrück.* New York: Anchor Press, 1975. Memoir.
TWC. Vol. I, pp. 35, 54–55, 88–89, 318, 320, 739, 740, 741, 748–749, 752–754.
United Nations War Crimes Commission. *Law Reports of Trials of War Criminals.* Vol. XIV. London: Her Majesty's Stationery Office, 1949.
Weingartner, James J. *Crossroads of Death.* Berkeley: University of California Press, 1979.

11. Dora/Nordhausen

Beyerchen, Alan D. *Scientists under Hitler.* New Haven, Conn. Yale University Press, 1977.
Daily Mail. Lest We Forget. London: Northcliff House, 1945.
Frank, Volker. *Antifaschistische Mahnmale in der DDR.* Leipzig: Veb. E. S. Seemen Verlag, 1970. Art.
ITS. Vol. 2, p. 201.
Kogon, Eugen. *The Theory and Practice of Hell.*
Martyrdom and Resistance, January–February 1980.
Prosecution Staff. *A Booklet with a Brief History of the "Dora"-Nordhausen Labor Concentration Camps and Information on the Nordhausen War Crimes Case of the USA versus Arthur Kurt Andrae et al.* Nuremburg, 1947.

12. Terezin/Theresienstadt

Adler, H. G.: *Theresienstadt 1941–45.* Tübingen: 1955.
Adler, H. G., ed. *Die verheimlichte Wahrheit. Theresienstaedter Dokumente.* Tübingen: J. C. B. Mohr, 1958.
Berger, Zdena. *Tell Me Another Morning.* New York: Harper, 1959. Memoir.
Bor, Josef. *Terezin Requiem.* New York: Knopf, 1963. Literature.
Cohen, Gary B. "Jews in German Society: Prague, 1860–1914." *Central European History* 10: 28–54.
Demetz, Hana. *The House on Prague Street.* New York: St. Martins, 1980. Literature.

Dolezal, Jiri, and Visely, Evzen. *Pamatky prazskeho ghetta.* Prague: Olympia, 1969. Art.

Ehrmann, F., ed. *Terezin, 1941–45.* London: Collet's, 1965.

EJ. Vol. 15, pp. 1112–16; Vol. 3, pp. 560–594; Vol. 13, pp. 964–978; Vol. 12, p. 539; Vol. 5, pp. 274–276.

Fantlowa, Zdenka. "Long Live Life." In *Root and Bough,* edited by Leo Schwarz, pp. 201–211.

Freudenheim, Tom L. "The Jewish Museum (NYC)." *Moment,* November 1976, 27–29. Art.

Friedlander, Albert H. *Leo Baeck: Teacher of Theresienstadt.* New York: Holt, Rinehart, 1968.

Green, Gerald. *The Artists of Terezin.* New York: Hawthorn, 1969. Art.

———. *The Artists of Terezin.* New York: Schocken, 1978. Art.

"Hehalutz in Theresienstadt." *YVS* VII (1968): 107–125.

Hinz, Berthold. *Art in the Third Reich.* New York: Pantheon, 1980. Art.

Hull, David. *Film in the Third Reich.* Berkeley: University of California Press, 1969. Film.

Jacot, Michael. *The Last Butterfly.* New York: Bobbs-Merrill, 1974. Literature.

Kantor, Alfred. *The Book of Alfred Kantor.* New York: McGraw-Hill, 1971. Art.

Karny, Miroslav. "Das Konzentrationslager Terezin (Theresienstadt) in den Planen der Nazis." *Ceskoslovensky casopis historicky* 22 (1974): 673–702.

Kerr, Judith. "KZ Theresienstadt als Schaufenster." *Welt am Sonntag,* August 1, 1976, 36.

Kibbutz Lochamei HaGhettaot, Israel. *Spiritual Resistance: Art from the Concentration Camps, 1940–45.* New York: Union of American Hebrew Congregations, 1978. Art.

Kracauer, Siegfried. *From Caligari to Hitler.* Princeton, N.J.: Princeton University Press, 1955. Film.

Krylová, Libuse. *The Small Fortress of Terezin.* Terezin: 1975.

Kuna, Milan, et al. *Kunst in Theresienstadt, 1941–1945.* Terezin: 1972. Art.

Lederer, Zdenek. *Ghetto Theresienstadt.* London: Edward Goldston, 1953. Memoir.

The Little Fortress Terezin. Litomerice: Vytiskla Severografia, 1967.

Lustig, Arnost. *Night and Hope.* New York: Dutton, 1962. Literature.

———. *Diamonds of the Night.* Washington, D.C.: Inscape, 1978. Literature.

Mazer, Virginia. "I Never Saw Another Butterfly." Eternal Light Broadcast, December 11, 1966, by Jewish Theological Seminary. Radio drama.

Milman, Joan. "Bringing Home the Bride." *Moment.* April 1977, 52.

Novak, Vaclav. *Terezin.* Pamatnik Terezin: 1974.

Pechova, Oliva, et al. *Kunst in Theresienstadt, 1941–1945: Katalog Zur Ausstellung.* Pamatnik Terezin: 1972. Art.

Petrow, Richard. *The Bitter Years.* New York: William Morrow, 1974.

Rose, Anna. *Refugee.* New York: Dial Press, 1977. Memoir.

Rothkirchen, Livia. "Czech Attitudes Toward the Jews During the Nazi Regime." *YVS,* XIII, 1979, 287–320.

Rusky a zidovsky hrbitov terezin. Prague, n.d..

The State Jewish Museum. Prague: 1976. Art.

The State Museum in Prague. Prague: State Museum, 1974. Art.

Terezin. Prague: Council of Jewish Communities, 1965.

Time, May 16, 1977, 113.

Tsur, Muki, and Yanai, Nathan, eds. *The Holocaust.* New York: American Zionist Youth Foundation, n.d.

Ullmann, Viktor. "The Emperor of Atlantis." *Midstream,* April 1975, 38–43. Drama.

Volavkova, Hana, ed. *I Never Saw Another Butterfly: Children's Drawings and Poems from Terezin Concentration Camp, 1942–44.* New York: McGraw-Hill, 1962. Literature.

Werner, Alfred. "Madhouse Theresienstadt." *Congress Bi-Weekly,* March 26, 1956, 13–15.

13. Chelmno/Kulmhof

Delbo, Charlotte. *None of Us Will Return.* New York: Grove Press, 1968. Memoir.

EJ. Vol. 5, pp. 374–375.

Grossman, Mendel. *With a Camera in the Ghetto.* New York: Schocken, 1977. Art.

ITS. Vol. 1, p. 321.

Reznikoff, Charles. *Holocaust.* Los Angeles: Black Sparrow Press, 1975. Literature.

Rückerl, Adalbert. *NS-Vernichtungslager.*

Shneiderman, S. L. "Attention: The Bundestag in Bonn." *Congress Bi-Weekly,* February 15, 1965, 7–9.

Tenebaum, Joseph. *Underground: The Story of a People.*

"The Chelmno Extermination Camp." In *German Crimes in Poland.* Vol. I, pp. 109–121.

TWC. Vol. V, pp. 475–477.

14. Belzec

"Belzec Extermination Camp." In *German Crimes in Poland.* Vol. II.

EJ. Vol. 4, pp. 453–456.

Friedlander, Saul. *Kurt Gerstein.* New York: Knopf, 1969.

Gross, Jan. T. *Polish Society under German Occupation: The Generalgouvernment.* Princeton, N.J.: Princeton University Press, 1979.

ITS. Vol. 1, pp. 332.

Joffroy, Pierre. *A Spy for God: The Ordeal of Kurt Gerstein.* New York: Harcourt Brace, 1971.

Karski, Jan. "An Eye-Witness Account from Poland." *Jewish Frontier,* March 1943, 15–17. Memoir.

———. "Polish Death Camp." *Colliers,* October 14, 1944, 12. Memoir.

———. *Story of a Secret State.* Boston: Houghton-Mifflin, 1944. Memoir.

Klarsfeld, Serge. *The Holocaust and the Neo-Nazi Mythomania.* New York: Beate Klarsfeld Foundation, 1978.

Meltzer, Milton. *Never to Forget.*

Rückerl, Adalbert. *NS Vernichtungslager.*

Schoenberner, Gerhard. *The Yellow Star.* New York: Bantam, 1973.

Sereny, Gitta. *Into That Darkness: From Mercy Killing to Mass Murder.*

Tenebaum, Joseph. *Underground.*

Toland, John. *Hitler.* New York: Doubleday, 1976.

Wiesel, Elie. *The Trial of God.* New York: Random, 1979. Drama.

15. Sobibor

Ainsztein, Reuben. *Jewish Resistance in Nazi-Occupied Eastern Europe.* New York: Barnes and Noble, 1974.

Blatt, Tuvia. "Revolt in the Sobibor Death Camp." *YVB,* No. 5, 36–38. Memoir.
EJ. Vol. 15, pp. 21–22.
ITS. Vol. 1, p. 331.
Lichtmann, Ada. "I Have Seen with My Own Eyes." *YVB,* No. 5, 38. Memoir.
Meltzer, Milton. *Never to Forget.*
Novitch, Miriam. *Sobibor: Martyrdom and Revolt.* New York: Holocaust Library, 1980.
———. *Sobibor, Martyre et Révolte.* Paris: Centre de Publication Asie Orientale, 1978.
Pechersky, Alexander. "Revolt in Sobibor." In *They Fought Back,* edited by Yuri Suhl. New York: Schocken, 1975. Pp. 7–50. Memoir.
Rückerl, Adalbert. *NS-Vernichtungslager.*
Sereny, Gitta. *Into That Darkness.*
"Sobibor Extermination Camp." *In German Crimes in Poland.* Vol. II, pp. 99–106.
Steinberg, Lucien. *Not as a Lamb.* London: Saxon House, 1974.
Tenenbaum, Joseph. *Underground.*
Trunk, Isaiah. *Jewish Responses to Nazi Persecution.*

16. Treblinka

Ainsztein, Reuben. *Jewish Resistance.* New York: Barnes and Noble, 1974.
Alexander, Edward. "The Incredibility of the Holocaust." *Midstream,* March 1979, 49–59.
Auerbach, Rachel. "In the Fields of Treblinka." In *The Death Camp Treblinka,* edited by Alexander Donat. New York: Walden Press, 1979.
Crankshaw, Edward. *Gestapo.* New York: Pyramid, 1957.
Elon, Amos. *Journey Through a Haunted Land.* New York: Holt, Rinehart, 1967. Memoir.
Embassy of the Polish People's Republic, press release, Washington, D.C., March 29, 1963.
EJ. Vol. 15, pp. 1365–72.
Gray, Martin: *For Those Who Loved.* Boston: Little, Brown, 1972. Memoir.
Grossman, Vassili. *L'Enfer de Treblinka.* Paris: Arthaud, 1966.
Gumkowski, J., and Rutkowski, A. *Treblinka.* Warsaw: Council for Protection of Fight and Martyrdom Monuments, 1961.
ITS. Vol. 1, p. 329.
Kohn, Stanislaw. "The Treblinka Revolt." In *Anthology of Holocaust Literature,* edited by Jacob Glatstein et al. New York: Atheneum, 1973. Pp. 319–324. Memoir.
Meltzer, Milton. *Never to Forget.*
Noakes, Jeremy, and Pridham, Geoffrey. *Documents on Nazism, 1919–1945.*
Rajzman, Samuel. "Uprising in Treblinka." In *They Fought Back,* edited by Yuri Suhl. New York: Schocken, 1975. Pp. 128–135. Memoir.
Roiter, Howard. *Voices from the Holocaust.* New York: William Frederick Press, 1975.
Rosensaft, Menachem Z. "Janusz Korzak." *Midstream,* May 1979, 53–57.
Rückerl, Adalbert. *NS-Vernichtungslager.*
Sereny, Gitta. *Into That Darkness.*
Shulstein, Moses. "The Mountain." In *The Golden Peacock,* edited by Joseph Leftwich. New York: Yoseloff, 1961. Pp. 639–640. Literature.
Steinberg, Lucien. *Not as a Lamb.* London: Saxon House, 1974.

Steiner, Jean-François. *Treblinka.* New York: Simon and Schuster, 1967.
Tenenbaum, Joseph. *Underground.*
"The Treblinka Extermination Camp." In *German Crimes in Poland.* Vol. I, pp. 95–106.
Trunk, Isaiah. *Jewish Responses to Nazi Persecution.*
Wiernik, Yankel. *A Year in Treblinka.* New York: General Jewish Workers' Union, 1945. Memoir.
——. "A Year in Treblinka Horror Camp." In *Anthology of Holocaust Literature,* edited by Jacob Glatstein et al. New York: Atheneum, 1973. Pp. 178–185. Memoir.
——. "Uprising in Treblinka." In *Root and Bough,* edited by Leo Schwarz. Pp. 115–121.
Willenberg, S. "Revolt at Treblinka." *YVB,* No. 7, 39–40, 51. Memoir.

17. Majdanek

Blum, Howard. *Wanted: The Search for Nazis in America.* New York: Quadrangle, 1977.
Donat, Alexander. *The Holocaust Kingdom.* New York: Holt, Rinehart, Winston, 1963.
EJ. Vol. 11, pp. 794–796.
Grade, Chaim. "At the End of the Days." *Midstream,* April 1978, 34. Literature.
Gruber, Samuel. *I Chose Life.* New York: Shengold, 1978. Memoir.
Gryn, Edward, and Murawska, Zofia. *Majdanek Concentration Camp.* Lublin: Wydawnictwo Lubelskie, 1966.
Gurdus, Luba Krugman. *The Death Train.* New York: Holocaust Library, 1978. Memoir.
ITS. Vol. 1, p. 331; Vol. 3, p. 79.
Lauterbach, Richard. "Sunday in Poland." *Life,* September 18, 1944, 17–18.
"Lublin Funeral." *Life,* August 28, 1944, 34.
Marszalek, Josef, and Wisniewska, Anna. *State Museum Majdanek.* Lublin: Lub. Zakl. Graf., 1971. Art.
Martyrdom and Resistance, March–April 1979, 7.
Przeciw Wojnie Vols. III and IV. Majdanku: Panstwowe Muzeum; Lublin: Pazdziernik, 1969, 1972. Art.
Rabinowitz, Dorothy. *New Lives.* New York: Knopf, 1976.
Siegel, Daniel, and Sugarman, S. Allan. *And God Braided Eve's Hair.* New York: United Synagogue, 1976. Literature.
Snow, Edgar. "Here the Nazi Butchers Wasted Nothing." *Saturday Evening Post,* October 28, 1944, 18–21.
Trepman, Paul. *Among Men and Beasts.* New York: A. S. Barnes, 1978. Memoir.
TWC. Vol. V, pp. 694–697, 706–709, 710, 711, 713, 727–731, 844, 1148, 1149.
Vrba, Rudolf, and Bestic, Alan. *I Cannot Forgive.* New York: Grove, 1964. Memoir.

18. Auschwitz/Birkenau

Adler, H. G., Langbein, Hermann, and Lingens-Reiner, Ella, eds. *Auschwitz, Zeugnisse und Berichte.* Frankfurt am Main: Europaeische Verlagsanstalt, 1962.
Ainsztein, Reuben. "The Auschwitz Trial." *Midstream,* March 1965, 3–22.

Bedford, Sybil. "Auschwitz: The Worst Crime That Ever Happened." *SEP,* October 22, 1966, 29.

Ben-Yuda, I. N. *Too Young to Live.* New York: Vantage, 1964. Memoir.

Berger, Zdena. *Tell Me Another Morning.* New York: Harper, 1959. Literature.

Bezwinska, Jadwiga, ed. *Amidst a Nightmare of Crime: Notes of Prisoners of Sonderkommando Found at Auschwitz.* Oswiecim: Panstwowe Muzeum, 1973.

Bonhoeffer, Emmi. *Auschwitz Trials: Letters from an Eyewitness.* Richmond, Va.: John Knox Press, 1965.

Borkin, Joseph. *The Crime and Punishment of I. G. Farben.* New York: Collier Macmillan, 1978.

Borowski, Tadeusz. "The People Who Walked." *Commentary,* February 1967, 65–69. Literature.

———. *This Way for the Gas.* New York: Penguin, 1976. Literature.

Central Commission for Investigation of German Crimes in Poland. *German Crimes in Poland.* Vol. I, pp. 27–94.

Dawidowicz, Lucy, ed. *A Holocaust Reader.* New York: Behrman, 1976.

DeJong, Louis. "The Netherlands and Auschwitz." *YVS* VII: 39–55.

Donat, Alexander. *The Holocaust Kingdom.* New York: Holt, Rinehart, Winston, 1963.

Dubois, Josiah E. Jr. *The Devil's Chemists.* Boston: Beacon, 1952.

Elon, Amos. *Journey Through a Haunted Land.* New York: Holt, 1967. Memoir.

EJ. Vol. 3, pp. 854–874.

Feig, Konnilyn, ed. "The Survival Game." Transcript of conversation with Max Garcia, October 22, 1979, San Francisco.

Ferencz, Benjamin B. *Less Than Slaves.* Cambridge, Mass.: Harvard University Press, 1979.

Frackiewicz, J. *Oswiecim W Fotografii Artystycznej.* Oswiecim: Panstwowego Muzeum, 1965. Art.

Friedman, Philip. *This Was Oswiecim.* London: United Jewish Relief Appeal, 1946.

Garcia, Max R. *As Long as I Remain Alive.* Tuscaloosa, Ala.: Portals, 1979. Memoir.

Garlinski, Jozef. *Fighting Auschwitz.* Greenwich, Conn.: Fawcett, 1975.

Geve, Thomas. *Youth in Chains.* Jerusalem: Rubin, Mass., 1958. Memoir.

Griner, Marcel. "Camp Child." In *Root and Bough,* edited by Leo Schwarz, pp. 294–297.

Hart, Kitty. *I Am Alive.* London: Abelard-Schumen, 1961. Memoir.

Hill, Mavis, and Williams, Norman. *Auschwitz in England.* New York: Ballantine, 1965.

Höss, Rudolf. *Commandant of Auschwitz.* London: Weidenfeld and Nicholson, 1959. Memoir.

International Auschwitz Commission: *Przeglad Lekarski, Auschwitz: Inhuman Medicine, Anthology.* Warsaw: 1970, 1971. Vol. I, Pts. I and II.

———. *Przeglad Lekarski, Auschwitz: In Hell They Preserved Human Dignity, Anthology.* Warsaw: 1971. Vol. II, Pts. I and III.

———. *Przeglad Lekarski, Auschwitz: It Did Not End in Forty-Five, Anthology.* Warsaw: 1971. Vol. III, Pts. I and II.

Ka-tzetnik 135633. *House of Dolls.* New York: Pyramid Books, 1958. Literature.

Kessel, Tim. *Hanged at Auschwitz.* New York: Stein and Day, 1970. Memoir.

Klarsfeld, Serge. *The Holocaust and the Neo-Nazi Mythomania.* New York: Beate Klarsfeld Foundation, 1978.

Konwicki, Tadeusz. *A Dreambook for Our Time.* New York: Penguin, 1976. Literature.

Koscielniaka, Mieczyslawa. *Tworczosci Artystycznej: II, Malarstwo.* Oswiecim: Panstwowego, 1961. Art.

Kraus, Otto, and Kulka, Erich. *The Death Factory. Document on Auschwitz.* London: Pergamon, 1966.

Kuh, Frederick. "The Curator of Auschwitz." *The New Statesman,* July 3, 1954, 7–8.

Levi, Primo. *Survival in Auschwitz.* New York: Collier, 1961. Memoir.

Leitner, Isabella. *Fragments of Isabella.* New York: Crowell, 1978. Memoir.

Lustig, Arnost. *A Prayer for Katerina Horovitzova.* New York: Harper, 1973. Literature.

Meltzer, Milton. *Never to Forget.*

Mikes, George. *Prison: A Symposium.* London: Routledge, 1963.

Mitscherlich, Alexander, and Mielke, Fred. *Doctors of Infamy: The Story of the Nazi Medical Crimes.* New York: Henry Schuman, 1949.

Müller, Filip. *Eyewitness Auschwitz. Three Years in the Gas Chambers.* New York: Stein and Day, 1979. Memoir.

Naumann, Bernard. *Auschwitz.* New York: Praeger, 1966.

Nyiszli, Miklos. *Auschwitz: A Doctor's Eyewitness Account.* New York: Fell, 1960; Greenwich: Fawcett, 1961. Memoir.

Pisar, Samuel. *Of Blood and Hope,* Boston: Little, Brown, 1979. Memoir.

"A Question of Priorities." *Jerusalem Post,* April 29, 1979, 15.

Rosensaft, Menachem. "The Holocaust." *Midstream,* May 1977, 53–55.

Rosenthal, S. M. "There Is No News from Auschwitz." *New York Times Magazine,* April 16, 1961, 26.

Rudnicki, Adolf, ed. *Lest We Forget.* Warsaw: Polonia, 1955.

Shapell, Nathan. *Witness to the Truth.* New York: McKay, 1974. Memoir.

Shneiderman, S. L. *The River Remembers.* New York: Horizon Press, 1978.

Smolen, Kazimierz. *Auschwitz, 1940–1945.* Oswiecim: Panstwowe Muzeum, 3rd ed., 1969.

Smolen, Kazimierz, ed. *From the History of KL Auschwitz.* Vol. II. Oswiecim: Panstwowe Muzeum, 1976.

Suhl, Yuri, ed. *They Fought Back.* New York: Crown, 1967.

Tenenbaum, Joseph. "Auschwitz in Retrospect." *Jewish Social Studies* 15 (1953): 203–236.

Tenenbaum, Joseph. *Underground.*

Uris, Leon. *QBVII.* New York: Bantam, 1972. Literature.

Van Leer, Wim. *Patent Pending—Troeltsch and Sons.* Israel: 1979. 3-act play produced December 1979 in New York by Shelter West at Vandane Theatre.

Vrba, Rudolf, and Bestic, Alan. *I Cannot Forgive.* New York: Grove, 1964.

Wasserstein, Bernard. *Britain and the Jews of Europe.* Oxford, Eng.: Clarendon, 1979.

Wiesel, Elie. *Night.* New York: Avon, 1960. Literature.

Weiss, Peter. *The Investigation.* New York: Atheneum, 1966. Literature.

Wellers, George. "Three Portraits in Brown." In *Root and Bough,* edited by Leo Schwarz, pp. 248–257.

Williams, Roger M. "Why Wasn't Auschwitz Bombed?" *Commonweal,* November 24, 1978, 746–751.

Wyman, David S. "Why Auschwitz Was Never Bombed." *Commentary,* May 1978, 37–46.

Zbiorowy, Tom. *Tworczosci Artystycznej.* Vol. III. *Malarstwo.* Oswiecim: Panst-wowego Muzeum, 1962. Art.

———. *Tworczosci Artystycznej.* Vol. IV. *Rzezba.* Oswiecim: Panstwowego Muzeum, 1962. Art.

Zvielli, Alexander. "Israelis Return to Auschwitz." *Hadassah Magazine,* June–July 1978, 19, 32–33.

19. Bergen-Belsen

Belsen. Israel: Igrun Sheerit Hapleita Me' Haezor Habriti.

Bergen-Belsen 1945–1975. Hannover: 1976.

Berger, Zdena. *Tell Me Another Morning.* New York: Harper, 1959. Literature.

Berkowitz, Sara. *Where Are My Brothers?* New York: Helios, 1965. Memoir.

Bloch, Sam E. *Holocaust and Rebirth: Bergen Belsen, 1945–1965.* New York: Bergen-Belsen Press, 1965.

Collis, Robert. *Straight On: Journey to Belsen and the Road Home.* London: Metheun, 1947.

Daily Mail. Lest We Forget. London: Northcliffe House, 1945.

Dawidowicz, Lucy. "Belsen Remembered." *Commentary,* March 1966, 82–85.

EJ. Vol. 4, pp. 610–612.

Fantlowa, Zdenka. "Long Live Life." In *Root and Bough,* edited by Leo Schwartz, pp. 201–211. Memoir.

Fyfe, Sir David M., gen. ed. *War Crimes Trials.* Vol. II. *Trial of Josef Kramer and Forty-Four Others (The Belsen Trial),* edited by Raymond Phillips. London: William Hodge, 1949.

Gelber, Sholome. "Wherein Is This Night Different?" *Menorah,* Winter 1947, 21–30.

Gilbert, Martin. *Exile and Return.* Philadelphia: Lippincott, 1978.

Hardman, Leslie. *The Survivors: The Story of the Belsen Remnant.* London: Valentine-Mitchell, 1958.

Hearffield, John. *Photomontages of the Nazi Period.* New York: Universe, 1977. Art.

ITS. Vol. 1, p. 112; Vol. 2, p. 115.

Leitner, Isabella. *Fragments of Isabella.* New York: Crowell, 1978. Memoir.

Mittleman, Leslie. "T. S. Eliot at Bergen-Belsen." *Reconstructionist,* November 11, 1966, 20. Literature.

Moskin, Marietta. *I Am Rosemarie.* New York: John Day, 1972. Memoir.

Napora, Paul Edward. *Death at Belsen.* San Antonio, Tex.: Naylor, 1967. Literature.

Orlev, Uri. *The Lead Soldiers.* New York: Taplinger, 1980. Literature.

Rabinowitz, Dorothy. *New Lives.* New York: Knopf, 1976.

"Rescue Efforts with the Assistance of International Organizations." *YVS* VIII (1970): 69–79.

Rosen, Donia. *The Forest My Friend.* New York: Bergen-Belsen Memorial Press, 1971. Literature.

Sington, Derrick. *Belsen Uncovered.* London: Burleigh, 1949.

———. *The Offenders.* London: Secker and Warburg, 1957.

Sperber, Manes. *Than a Tear in the Sea.* New York: Bergen-Belsen Memorial Press, 1967. Literature.

Trepman, Paul. *Among Men and Beasts.* New York: A. S. Barnes, 1978. Memoir.

20. Poland

Dobroszycki, Lucjan, and Kirshenblatt-Gimblett, Barbara. *Image Before My Eyes.* New York: Schocken, 1977. Photos.

Heller, Celia. *On the Edge of Destruction.* New York: Columbia, 1977.

Humble, Richard. *The Warsaw Ghetto No Longer Exists.* London: Orbis, 1973. Photos.

Schaeffer, Susan Fromberg. *Anya.* New York: Macmillan, 1975. Literature.

Shulman, Abraham. *The Old Country: The Lost World of East European Jews.* New York: Scribner, 1974. Photos

Shulman, Abraham. *The New Country.* New York: Scribner, 1976. Photos.

Stroop, Jurgen. *The Stroop Report.* New York: Pantheon, 1980.

Vinecour, Earl, and Fishman, Chuck. *Polish Jews: The Final Chapter.* New York: McGraw-Hill, 1977. Photos.

Vishniac, Roman. *Polish Jews: A Pictorial Record.* New York: Schocken, 1972. Photos.

Warshaw, Mal. *Tradition: Orthodox Jewish Life in America.* New York: Schocken, 1976. Art.

Watt, Richard M. *Poland and Its Fate 1918–39.* New York: Simon and Schuster, 1979.

INDEX

Each concentration camp has a separate listing. Individual artists are listed only under "Artists." Individual camp commandants are listed only under "Commandants."

Action Reinhardt (Operation Reinhardt), 29–30, 329
Aftermath (of Holocaust), 13–14, 365, 419–20, 436
  and the Auschwitz Complex, 333, 365
  and Belsen, 386–93
  and Belzec, 275
  and Buchenwald, 110–14
  and Dachau, 62–64
  and Theresienstadt, 238–39
  and Treblinka, 311
Ahnenerbe Society, 221–25
Allies
  and Auschwitz, 363, 365–68
  and bombing of Auschwitz, 366–68, 407, 411, 416
  and children, 412–13
  and the Evian Conference, 407, 412
  and the Final Solution, 418, 487 *n*34, 495–96 *n*15 and *n*22
  and Jews: immigration of, 409–10, 412–13; indifference to, xx, 12–13, 16–17, 23, 365–68, 407, 409, 422, 434–35, 445
  and knowledge of the Final Solution, 418, 487 *n*34, 495–96 *n*15, *n*22
  postwar policy of, 365, 407, 419–20
  prewar attitudes of, 407, 409, 412, 417, 421
  and War Crimes, 419–20
  wartime policy of, 407, 410–11, 413–16
Anti-Semitism, xxi, 419, 421–31
  and churches, 421–30
  and deicide, 423–29

  and Lutheranism, 425
  modern, 428–30, 497 *n*36, 498 *n*37
  myths about the Jews, 426–29
  theological, 421–30
  and the Vatican, 425, 427, 436, 499 *n*39
  See also Jews
Architecture, 34–35
Arendt, Hannah, 14–15, 433
Art
  by inmates: *see* Theresienstadt and Majdanek
  in Belsen, 373
  in Belzec, 276
  in Buchenwald, 88–91
  in Chelmno, 267
  in Dachau, 45
  in Dora/Nordhausen, 227–28
  in Majdanek, 314–17
  in Mauthausen, 117
  in Natzweiler, 217
  in Neuengamme, 209
  in Prague, 234–37
  in Ravensbrück, 134–36
  in Sachsenhausen, 69–71
  in Sobibor, 284
  in Stutthof, 193–95
  in Theresienstadt, 239–40, 259–62
  in Treblinka, 295
  in Warsaw, 397–99
Artists
  of monuments: Buskievicz, 267; Cremer, Fritz, 89–91, 117–18, 135–36; Dieters, Ludwig, 69, 89; Duszenko, Franciszek, 295; Falke, 372; Fennaux, L., 216–17; Fiwejski, Fjodor, 69; Graetz, René, 69–70, 91; Grotewohl, Hans, 89; Grzimek, W., 69, 91; Haupt, Adam, 295; Kies, Hans, 91, 136; Kollwitz, Käthe, 136; Kutzat, Horst, 69, 89; Lammert, Will, 135–36;

533